Collector's Guide to

DIECAST TOYS

& SCALE MODELS

Identification & Values

Second Edition

COLLECTOR BOOKS
A Division of Schroeder Publishing Co., Inc.

Dana Johnson

The current values in this book should be used only as a guide. They are not intended to set prices, which vary from one section of the country to another. Auction prices as well as dealer prices vary greatly and are affected by condition as well as demand. Neither the Author nor the Publisher assumes responsibility for any losses that might be incurred as a result of consulting this guide.

Searching For A Publisher?

We are always looking for knowledgeable people considered to be experts within their fields. If you feel that there is a real need for a book on your collectible subject and have a large comprehensive collection, contact Collector Books.

Front cover:

Tootsietoy (193), $4 – 5; Racing Champions Mint Editions "Hot Rods" #4, 1964 Chevy Impala, $4 – 5; Mira 1954 Corvette, 1:18 scale, $15 – 20.

Back cover:

Racing Champions Mint Editions #72, 1955 Bel Air Convertible, $4 – 5; Brooklin 1949 Buick Roadmaster Coupe, 1:43 scale, $75 – 200.

Page 1:

Viceroy 37 Bus, 1972, $25; 1950 Chrysler Town & Country, $55 – 70; James Bond Aston Martin, $60.

Book and cover design by Terri Stalions

COLLECTOR BOOKS
P.O. Box 3009
Paducah, Kentucky 42002-3009

Dana Johnson Enterprises
P.O. Box 1824
Bend, OR 97709-1824
email: toynutz@teleport.com
website: http://www.teleport.com/~toynutz

Copyright © 1998 by Dana Johnson

Printed in the U.S.A. by Image Graphics, Paducah, KY

Preface

The idea of this book is to showcase diecast and related toys and scale model vehicles that otherwise would go undocumented in any published source. As I researched the various brands, I found many from all around the world of which I had never heard. In the process, a vast number of invaluable sources were discovered for a majority of the models represented herein.

Particularly, such sources as Diecast Miniatures, EWA & Miniature Cars USA, and Toys for Collectors have been so valuable that I could not have written this book without them.

In this second edition, I've added to the 416 brands represented in the first edition, resulting in a listing of some 575 brands found for the second edition.

Dedication

This second edition is dedicated to all those collectors and dealers who have contributed to the success of the first edition. Thanks to all who support this continuing project.

Acknowledgments

The list of people to whom I am in debt is growing constantly. Thanks to all those whose books, lists, letters, catalogs, and samples contributed to the completeness of this book. Special thanks to Jim Bray of Diecast Miniatures for access to his list of 200+ brands of toys and models; to Liz, Gerhard, and Tina Klarwasser of Toys for Collectors for granting permission to replicate pages from their exquisite Auto Miniatures catalog; to Alger Podewil, Joe Altieri, and Ivan Fedorkew for their extensive lists of Majorette and other variations; to Bob Blum for his invaluable information on Tomicas; to Boyd Dunson for his extensive information and photos on Russian diecast toys; to Dr. Craig S. Campbell, Harvey Goranson, Russell Alameda, Aaron Robinson, and Bill Cross for filling in details on various lesser known brands; to Jeff Koch for his photos of models otherwise missing from this book; and to many others for providing price lists, variation lists, and mounds of other information used in this book. Special thanks to Claudia Valiquet for encouraging me to collaborate with Collector Books in the first place.

Thanks especially to Lisa Stroup, editor at Collector Books, and Billy Schroeder, publisher, for their continuing enthusiastic support of all my book projects, and to Sharon and Bob Huxford for their book *Schroeder's Collectible Toys*.

Appreciation also goes to Richard O'Brien for information provided from his book *Collecting Toy Cars & Trucks,* and to Markus R. Karalash for his contributions on the various brands of DeTomaso Pantera models.

Photos are taken with a Canon EOS Rebel X 35mm SLR camera with standard zoom lens and a set of Tiffen (+1, +2, +4) macro attachment lenses. For the most part, the film used was Kodak Gold ASA 100 & ASA 200.

Introduction

The Purpose of this Book

There are just a few books on the market that cover the most popular brands of diecast and related toys and scale models: Corgi, Dinky, Hot Wheels, Lledo, Matchbox, Solido, Tootsietoys. Many lesser known brands meanwhile have been essentially ignored: Bburago, Dugu, Joal, Maisto, Majorette, Oto, Pocher, Siku, Tomica, Yatming, Zylmex, just to name a few. While the original intent of this book was to present the most comprehensive guide to diecast toy vehicles, as I researched this book, I found that what I thought at first were diecast models were actually white metal castings. The difference is in the process used to make the castings and the material used in the alloy, with larger amounts of aluminum, tin, or metals other than zinc.

The main reasons for producing this book are to encourage more people to collect diecast toys; to show collectors how affordable diecast toy collecting can be as a hobby; to demonstrate the value of collecting new models well as old ones; to showcase current and obsolete models; and to demonstrate to collectors everywhere that they are not alone in their fascination for these diminutive cars and trucks.

Arrangement of this Book

This book is arranged alphabetically by brand name. Whenever applicable, manufacturer model numbers are included, along with description, scale, color, distinguishing marks, and value. The author has attempted to provide a brief profile of each brand represented when any background information is available.

Values

Regardless of the values indicated in this or any price guide, you can often purchase items for far below book value, and I encourage you to seek the lowest price for a particular acquisition. You will most often need to sell for far less than book value as well, especially when you intend to sell an entire collection. So what good are values if not for buying and selling? Stated book values establish a basis for personal evaluation of your collection, for insurance purposes, speculation, auctions and estate sales, and for your own future purchases, because occasionally you may agree to pay full book value for an item if you feel it is desirable and worth the asking price. Consider the values indicated in this book to be the "highest average" value of a given model.

In order to establish a standard for grading diecast toys, the following is offered as a generally accepted grading system. Note the popular word *mint* has been replaced by the word *new*, since it has been argued that *mint condition* indicates something in perfect, unflawed and untouched condition. *New condition,* on the other hand, represents a more fair classification of toys that could show wear even within the sealed package, whether from friction with the package itself, or whether from flaws and defects overlooked at the factory. Condition is abbreviated "C" or "c" in most books, with a C10 being the best, and C1 being the worst. All grading systems are arbitrary and somewhat flexible, but are relatively similar for grading most toys. In addition, some collectors base a part of the condition rating on the condition of the package. So here is a guide to help determine the condition of a particular model.

Condition Rating Chart:

C10: 100%. New condition with original container

C9: 90 – 95%. New condition without container

C8: 80 – 85%. Near new condition, close inspection reveals minor wear

C7: 70 – 75%. Excellent condition, visible minor wear

C6: 25 – 35%. Very good condition, visible wear, all parts intact

C5: 7 – 10%. Good condition, excessive wear, paint chipped or heavily worn

C4: 4 – 5%. Fair condition, parts broken or missing

C1 – 3: 2 – 3%. Poor condition, worn paint, parts broken or missing

C0: .5 – 1%. Salvage for parts only

Brands Represented

While this book attempts to represent every brand and manufacturer of toys that fits the definition of diecast, it is impossible to represent every model and variation ever produced by each manufacturer. A separate book could be written for each of the 575 brands represented in this book. But the small market for such books would be understandably cost-prohibitive to the consumer as well as the publisher. So, as with most things in life, a compromise is reached by presenting a sampling of each brand of toys produced over nearly a century.

Of course, for every rule, there is an exception. Several brands, such as Tomica, Majorette, Siku, and a few others, are a major force in the diecast toy collector market. Many requests have come to me for a book on Tomica Pocket Cars and Majorettes in particular. So, I have made a special effort to present these brands as comprehensively as possible.

I wish I could find more information on Ertl toys, both the collector limited edition series and the standard issues. It seems that the information on models, variations, and values is something Ertl collectors don't easily share. There have been a few books published in small quantities, but they are now out of print.

Origin of Diecast Toys

The process of diecasting was first introduced to the world at the Columbian Exposition of 1893, when Charles Dowst observed a new machine known as the Line-O-Type. Mr. Dowst applied the process to the manufacture of various items, eventually producing the first diecast toys in 1910. These first diecast toys soon after became known as Tootsie Toys. (Later the name was changed to Tootsietoys.)

The Diecasting Process
(and a short spelling lesson)

Diecasting is an injection mold process using a zinc alloy commonly known as "zamak" (96% zinc, 4% aluminum, trace magnesium) to produce accurately formed metal components. Early diecasting used a lead alloy process known as "slushmold," but was eventually replaced by comparatively non-toxic zamak. The manufacturing of a die for diecasting is very expensive, so production of large numbers of items from one die is necessary to offset the initial cost.

White metal casting is a much less expensive process, using a rubber die, instead of metal, into which is poured a softer alloy. The problem with white metal casting, even though the die is cheaper, is that the die won't hold up to producing a high number of copies. So white metal models are invariably produced in much lower numbers, usually in the hundreds rather than in tens or hundreds of thousands.

On the matter of spelling, "die cast" is most commonly two separate words without a hyphen. The *Software Toolworks Multimedia Encyclopedia* places a hyphen between the two words. While the Die Cast Car Collectors Club separates the two words as well, the Diecast Toy Collectors Association and this author chooses, for brevity and convenience, to merge the two words together to form a single word. While all forms are acceptable, the combined form "diecast" is used in this book for standardization.

Plastic, Resin, and Cast-Iron Toys

Although this book is devoted mostly to diecast toys, some plastic, resin, and cast-iron toys are included due to their historical significance or because of their scale, detail, or other distinguishing characteristics. Since plastic is now used in addition to metal alloys in most modern diecast toys, the result is a blurring of the line between diecast and non-diecast toys.

A few early toys were made of flour-base paste. These toys are rare and valuable if found in mint or near-mint condition, because of their tendency to crumble or discolor with age and handling.

Safety Factor

Cast-iron toys, while popular at the turn of the century, were heavy and would occasionally become destructive weapons when wielded by a rambunctious child bent on rendering them airborne.

Later, the manufacture of lead alloy toys in the thirties and forties, especially toy soldiers, was eventually stopped when was it was discovered that small children were suffering from lead poisoning after putting such things in their mouths.

Safety, therefore, has been a major factor in the growth and popularity of diecast toys made of zamak.

Diecast Toys and Scale Model Miniatures

Many diecast toys demonstrate such precise detail that they can no longer be called toys, but qualify as precision scale models. References to precision models as toys is for simplicity and not for condescension. Whether a toy or a model, they are all represented in this book with apologies to collectors of the latter.

Scale: O, HO, N, Z Gauge, and Other Scales

The purpose of all this "scale talk" is to acquaint you with the relative size of a model based on its scale, and to expose collectors to the many different sizes of models available on the market.

With the rising popularity of model railroads, it was important to establish a standard track size so that various manufacturers could make model railroad cars that fit on each others tracks. O gauge was arbitrarily established as the standard, with rails approximately 1¼" apart. This results in a scale of 1:43. It seemed a convenient size at the time for economically producing the electrical systems inside the locomotive that drove the whole system. 1:43 scale automobile models typically measure about 4" to 4½" long.

Later on, HO, or half O, gauge was introduced with rails about ⅝" apart. HO translates to 1:87 scale, allowing for a more elaborate layout in less space. Miniature automobiles of this scale are generally about 1½" long and many are made of plastic rather than diecast metal.

The more recent introduction of N gauge model railroads is due to the advance in technology that allowed smaller and smaller electric motors and mechanical parts to be produced, giving rise to what was until recently the smallest gauge railway system produced, with rails just 9 mm apart. This scale is so small that few if any diecast car models are made for this scale, opting instead for diminutive plastic models.

Even smaller than N gauge is Z gauge. The fact that electric motors and tracks can be manufactured to fit such a small scale is incredible on its own. Accompanying vehicles are obviously extremely small and almost invariably one piece plastic models, measuring barely ½" long. Recently, L gauge has been established for what are referred to as lawn trains, a scale of about 1:24.

In addition, double O, or OO, gauge was developed for smaller models of around 1:76 scale, Dinky Dublo models having set the precedent. Why the designation "double O" when size is closer to "HO" remains a mystery to this author unless it means "twice as small as O gauge."

While O scale (1:43) and HO scale (1:87) have been adopted for manufacturers of diecast model vehicles intended for model railroads, other scales were established for diecast models that were popular enough on their own. Siku of Germany established the popular 1:55 scale, in which most of their diecast toys are produced, and which many other manufacturers have adopted.

Manufacturers of heavy equipment miniatures meanwhile lean toward producing 1:50 scale models. Conrad in particular has concentrated on this scale, though they have produced a few models in other scales.

1:64 scale is another popular scale for miniatures, and is the scale to which Matchbox, Hot Wheels, and others are referred, even though their actual scale varies from one model to the next. In fact, most current diecast miniature cars of the 3" long variety hover around 1:55 to 1:60 scale, while trucks of the same length tend to fall closer to the 1:87 scale down to 1:100 or smaller scale. Ertl is the only company that produces a line of specifically 1:64 scale models. 1:72 scale is a common scale worldwide as well.

Becoming more popular recently are 1:24 and 1:18 scale models, with a few 1:12 scale models reaching the market as well. Very expensive models, such as Pochers, are even made to 1:8 scale, but their price begins at $500 each for new model of such scale.

Racing Collectibles

Some collectors specialize in racing collectibles. Racing Champions and Quartzo are primary examples of a company that specializes in producing diecast models specifically for these collectors, but it is hardly the only one. While an entire book could be written on racing diecast, this book will necessarily present just a survey. Resources at the end of this book provide information on dealers in this specialty.

Livery

Livery, as it relates to diecast toys, refers to the various products and companies represented on various toys. Many diecast toys are produced specifically with licensed trademarks, logos, promotion, and advertising on them, such as Coca-Cola, Frito-Lay, and so on. Livery is often the primary attraction for collectors, hence its significance.

Details, Details...

A process many manufacturers use in applying printing to diecast toys is called "tampo" or "tempa." This has been the most common technique of applying logos, trim colors, and accents since the early seventies. Before that time, decals, labels, and hand painting were the main methods of applying detail to models. The tampo process is now the prevalent form of applying details, particularly on inexpensive toys. Occasionally, other types of detailing are mentioned in this book to illustrate a variation to the tampo version of a particular model.

Customizing

Much debate continues between "purists" — those people who feel that any altering, such as repainting or detailing, of production models renders a model worthless — and "hobbyists" — those who believe they can make a model better by customizing it. Depending on the original value of a model and the degree of skill involved in making such alterations, a model can in fact be rendered worthless or more valuable. One man, Dan Coviello, a retired New York City policeman now living in North Carolina, makes a living customizing production model police cars and others to suit whatever state, county, or municipality the buyer wishes to have represented.

Second Market

Retail chains such as K-Mart, Shopko, Target, Toys R Us, Wal-Mart, and others provide the primary sources for many currently available models. But much of the collector market is supported by what is known as the "second market," consisting of individuals and dealers who buy selected models in smaller quantities, often from wholesale and retail sources, but perhaps just as often from private individuals and estate auctions. Because they purchase whole private collections, they usually try to buy at well below book value. They then resell to individual collectors, usually through mail-order price lists.

Bibliography/Resources

Many of the toys listed in this book are still available from various second-market dealers around the country. At the end of this book is a list of some sources for purchasing such toys.

The Diecast Toy Collectors Association

Their are many collector clubs devoted to one brand or another of diecast toys, such as Corgi, Ertl, Hot Wheels, and Matchbox, but there is a relatively new club that represents a broader appeal, the Diecast Toy Collectors Association (DTCA). Through its monthly newsletter, Diecast Toy Collector, members receive information on new models and old favorites representing many of the manufacturers listed in this book. DTCA membership rates are as indicated below:

1 year — $15 to USA, $18 to Canada, $24 to rest of the world
2 years — $26 to USA, $32 to Canada, $44 to rest of the world
3 years — $37 to USA, $46 to Canada, $64 to rest of the world
(U.S. funds, please)
To join, send check or money order payable to:
Dana Johnson Enterprises
P O Box 1824
Bend OR 97709-1824

A-LINE

Most of A-Line's product line is devoted to freight cars, motors, and parts for HO gauge train sets. Their Fruehauf "Z" Van series features a miniature version of the prototype 40 foot Fruehauf "Z" van commonly seen on piggyback trains and highways. These Fruehauf semi trailer kits are molded in aluminum and black styrene with separate tires, spoked wheel hubs, mudflaps, doorbars, and other details. Each kit includes two undecorated trailers with complete instructions and a list of correct decals. Kits sell for $11 – 12.

AARDVARK

Aardvark of St. Paul, Minnesota, is a small manufacturer of precision handcrafted models, of which only one model is known.

241B 1961 Maserati Type 61, 1:24 scale . . . . $330 – 350

A.B.C. BRIANZA (SEE BRIANZA)

A. C. WILLIAMS (CAST IRON)

It is historically interesting to note that the popularity of cast-iron toys declined around the same time that diecast toys, which offered lighter weight, more detailed alternatives to the heavy iron models, established their initial dominance in the world toy market.

Adam Clark Williams purchased the J. W. Williams Company from his father in 1886, thus beginning of one of the more successful toy companies of the era. The Ravenna, Ohio, company specialized in cast-iron toys until 1938 when the company changed direction away from toys. Few A. C. Williams toys are marked, so most often the only clues to their heritage are turned steel hubs and starred axle peens. Most A. C. Williams toys were "so crude as to barely qualify as doorstops," according to Ken Hutchison and Greg Johnson in their book *The Golden Age of Automotive Toys 1925 – 1941*. But A. C. Williams did produce a few exceptional toys. In fact, some are considered the best examples of cast-iron toys. A. C. Williams toys are steadily gaining in value, up to $1,100 for the rarest mint condition specimen, an 11¾" 1917 touring car with two passengers, and an average $400 – 600 for most other examples.

Chrysler Airflow, 4¾"	$100 – 160
Chrysler Airflow, 6½"	$500 – 600
Dodge Woodie Pickup, 5"	$150
Ford, 1935, 4½"	$350 – 450
Graham Sedan, 5"	$120
Graham Coupe, 5"	$120
Packard 900 Light Eight Sedan, 1932, 8"	$550 – 900
Packard 900 Light Eight Sedan, 1932, 7"	$300 – 500
Packard 900 Light Eight Stake Truck, 1932, 8"	$300 – 500
Packard Coupe, 4½"	$125
Packard Roadster, 4½"	$125
Packard Sedan, 4½"	$125
Packard Stake Truck, 4½"	$125
Plymouth Coupe, 1933, 5¼"	$150
Plymouth Sedan, 5¼"	$150
REO Sidemount Sedan, 5"	$120
Rolls Royce, 3½"	$75 – 90
Stake Truck, 4¼"	$175 – 275
Studebaker Coupe, 4¼"	$125
Studebaker Truck, 4½"	$125

ACCUCAST

Around the fifties or early sixties, a company called Accucast reproduced some early Tootsietoy models of the twenties, some from original dies, others from new dies. Thanks to Dave Weber of Warrington, Pennsylvania, for the information. No model list available.

ACTION/RACING COLLECTIBLES

The alleged largest competitor to Racing Champions is Action/Racing Collectibles. Here is a small sampling.

ACTION RACING COLLECTIBLES, 1:24 SCALE

Larry Dixon/Miller/Black Splash	$75
Larry Dixon/Miller/Silver Splash	$75
Cory McClenathan/McDonalds Olympic	$55
Mike Dunn/Mopar	$55
Kenji Okszaki/Mooneyes	$55
John Force/Castrol	$75

ACTION RACING COLLECTIBLES BRICKYARD 400 SET, 1:64 SCALE

Limited edition of 25,000, with collector cards, set includes: Dale Earnhardt #3, Jeff Gordon #24 . . . . $30

Dale Earnhardt Monte Carlo, 1:64, $12 – 15.

Photo by Jeff Koch.

ADJ

ADJ is an obscure brand with just one known model, as listed in *Schroeder's Collectible Toys Antique to Modern*.

Citroen CX Fire Chief Station Wagon . . . . $30 – 35

AGAT (ALSO SEE RADON)

Agat is a new brand of diecast models that has recently emerged from the reformation of the Radon company of Russia. Plans are in the works to produce a series of GAZ replicas based on the noted Russian brand of cars and trucks.

AGM

AGM is a British firm that produced kits made of white metal.

AHC (ALSO SEE AUTO PILEN, PILEN)

Many AHC models are made from dies obtained from the defunct Escuderia Pilen company of Spain, producers of 1:43 scale models known as Pilen or Auto Pilen. While based in the Netherlands, many of AHC's models are made in Spain and later China. AHC is also known as the manufacturer of Hess Oil collectibles.

Volvo 480ES, 1:43. . . . . $25 – 45

AHI

Ahi toys are 1:80 to 1:90 scale diecast toys produced in Japan in the late fifties and early sixties. The line offers an assortment of mostly American cars, but also includes some British and other European cars as well as 1:120 scale Dodge military trucks and some antique autos.

Alfa Romeo Giuletta Sprint, 1:90. . . . . $16
Austin A105, 1:90. . . . . $16
Austin Healey, 1:90 . . . . $16
Buick, 1:90 . . . . $16
Cadillac, 1:90. . . . . $16
Chevrolet Impala, 1:90. . . . . $16
Chrysler, 1:90. . . . . $16
Citroen DS 19, 1:90 . . . . $16
Daimler, 1:90. . . . . $16
DeSoto Diplomat, 1:90. . . . . $16
Dodge, 1:90. . . . . $16
Ferrari 375 Coupe, 1:90 . . . . $24
Ferrari 500 Formula 2, 1:90. . . . . $24
Fiat 1800, 1:90. . . . . $16
Ford, 1:90 . . . . $16
Imperial, 1:90. . . . . $16
International Harvester, 1:90. . . . . $16
Jaguar Mk IX, 1:90 . . . . $16
Jaguar XK150 Roadster, 1:90. . . . . $16
Maserati Racer, 1:90 . . . . $16
Mercedes-Benz 220SE, 1:90 . . . . $16
Mercedes-Benz 300SL Roadster, 1:90. . . . . $16
Mercedes-Benz W 25 Racer, 1:90 . . . . $16
Mercedes-Benz W 196 Racer, 1:90 . . . . $16
Mercedes-Benz RW 196 Racer, 1:90 . . . . $16
MG TF Roadster, 1:90. . . . . $16
MGA 1600, 1:90 . . . . $16
Midget Racer, 1:90 . . . . $16
Oldsmobile, 1:90 . . . . $16
Opel Kapitan, 1:90. . . . . $16
Plymouth, 1:90. . . . . $16
Pontiac, 1:90 . . . . $16
Porsche 356A, 1:90. . . . . $16
Rambler, 1:90 . . . . $16
Renault Floride, 1:90 . . . . $16
Rolls-Royce Silver Wraith, 1:90 . . . . $20
Simca Aronde P 60, 1:90 . . . . $16
Volkswagen 1200, 1:90. . . . . $20
Volvo Amazon 122 S, 1:90 . . . . $16
Volvo PV 544, 1:90. . . . . $16

AHI ANTIQUE CARS

1902 Ali Coold Frankline, 1:80 . . . . $12
1903 Cadillac, 1:80 . . . . $12
1903 Rambler, 1:80 . . . . $12
1904 Darracq, 1:80. . . . . $12
1904 Oldsmobile, 1:80. . . . . $12
1904 Oldsmobile Truck, 1:80. . . . . $12
1907 Vauxhall, 1:80 . . . . $12
1909 Stanley Steamer, 1:80 . . . . $12
1911 Buick, 1:80 . . . . $12
1914 Stutz Bearcat, 1:80 . . . . $12
1915 Ford Model T, 1:80 . . . . $12

DODGE MILITARY TRUCKS

Ambulance, 1:120 . . . . $12
Barrel Truck, 1:120 . . . . $12
Cement Mixer, 1:120. . . . . $12
Covered Truck, 1:120. . . . . $12
Crane Truck, 1:120. . . . . $12
Lumber Truck, 1:120 . . . . $12
Missile Carrier, 1:120 . . . . $12
Radar Truck, 1:120 . . . . $12
Rocket Launcher, 1:120 . . . . $12
Searchlight Truck, 1:120 . . . . $12
Tank Carrier, 1:120 . . . . $12
Truck with Machine Gun, 1:120 . . . . $12

AHL (SEE AMERICAN HIGHWAY LEGENDS)

ALEZAN

Alezan of France is another obscure brand with just one known model, as listed in *Schroeder's Collectible Toys Antique to Modern*. In addition, a white metal kit exists of a Pantera, according to Markus R. Karalash.

Alfa Romeo Evoluzion, dark red . . . . $75 – 85
DeTomaso Pantera, white metal kit. . . . . $45 – 60

ALJ

ALJ models are 1:43 scale vehicles.

Late 1950s Ford 2-door convertible with top down, white/red . $11
Delahaye 2-door roadster, metallic green. . . . . $11 – 14
Early 1950s Buick 2-door roadster, cream $11
Late 1950s Ford 2-door convertible with top up, red/gray $11
Early 1950s Buick 2-door convertible with top up, pink. $11

ALL-AMERICAN

All-American of Los Angeles, California, is known to have produced just one model, in 1949.

All-American Hot-Rod, 9" long $400

ALL AMERICAN TOY COMPANY

Clay Steinke, founder of the All American Toy Company of Salem, Oregon, produced a total of 26,000 1:12 scale cast metal toy trucks from its beginnings in 1948 to 1955. Its assortment of large scale toy trucks distinctive for their "air horn steering" includes the popular Timber Toter log truck, popular with children whose families worked in the Pacific Northwest logging industry. They originally sold for around $20, considered high-priced for toys back in the 1950s. Today's values are in the hundreds, even thousands of dollars. Model numbers appeared on the box only, not on the model.

ALL AMERICAN ORIGINALS

Play-Dozer, 9" long	$1,000 – 1,500
C-5 Cattle Liner, 38" long	$1,500 – 2,000
CL-8 Cargo Liner, 38" long	$1,200 – 1,700
D-3 Dyna-Dump, 20" long, early sandcast cab	$800 – 1,500
D-3 Dyna-Dump, 20" long, diecast cab	$500 – 700
HD-6 Play-Loader, 11" long	$400 – 600
HH-9 Heavy Hauler, 38" long	$800 – 1,200
L-2 Timber Toter, 38" long, early sandcast cab	$800 – 1,000
L-2 Timber Toter, 38" long, diecast cab	$400 – 650
LJ-4 Timber Toter Jr. with Trailer, 20" long	$600 – 1,000
MS Midget Skagit Log Loader, 18" long	$300 – 500
S-1 Scoop-A-Veyor, 16" long	$450 – 600
Hay-Grain-Feed-Seed with Trailer	$1,000 – 1,500
Hay-Grain-Feed-Seed without Trailer	$500 – 800

ALL AMERICAN NEW MODELS

After a false restart in 1990, the All American Toy Company is back in business in its home town of Salem, Oregon, purchased lock, stock, and barrel in 1992 by Patrick Russell, with all the original tooling intact. The company is now reproducing some of those classic models. Here is a list of available new models and prices. As you will note, current second market values are already on the rise. For more information, contact the company at All American Toy Company, Patrick Russell, president, 540 Lancaster SE, Salem OR 97301, 503-399-8609, Mon – Fri 9 – 6 Pacific.

Founder's Edition Timber Toter, 1992 replica	$900 – 1,000
(original retail $595)	
"Rocky" Galion Dump Truck, 1995 Dyna-Dump replica, maroon cab, silver box (113 made)	$700 – 1,000
($595 retail)	
"Rocky" Galion Dump Truck, 1995 Dyna-Dump replica, white cab, blue box (limited to 112)	$700 – 900
($595 retail)	
The Heavy Hauler II, double axle "lowboy" trailer	$700 – 900
($595 retail)	
The Heavy Hauler II, triple axle "lowboy" trailer	$700 – 900
($695 retail)	
Motorcycle Hauler, only 100 made	$600 – 750
($449 retail)	
Custom Classic Motorcycle for Motorcycle Hauler	$60
1948 Indian Chief, maroon or yellow	$60

ALLOY FORMS, INC.

Alloy Forms models are 1:87 scale kits intended for use with HO gauge train sets. Kits consist of unpainted white metal detail parts. Truck kits also include styrene, brass, and rubber parts.

ALLOY FORMS AUTOMOBILES

1953 Buick Skylark Convertible with Continental Package	$7
1949 Buick Roadmaster	$7
1959 Cadillac Eldorado Convertible	$7
1955 Cadillac Fleetwood	$7
1950 Chevrolet 4-Door Fastback	$7
1953 Chevrolet Bel-Air	$7
1955 Chevrolet Bel-Air 2-Door	$7
1957 Chevrolet Bel-Air Sport Coupe	$8
1953 Chevrolet Corvette	$7
1959 Chevrolet El Camino	$7
1959 Chevrolet Impala Convertible	$7
1955 Chevrolet Nomad Wagon	$7
1949 Desoto 4-Door	$7
1949 Ford Club Coupe with Engine	$8
1948 Ford Convertible	$8
1956 Ford Thunderbird	$7
1949 Hudson 4-Door	$7
1949 Mercury 2-Door	$7
1948 Studebaker Starline	$7
Plymouth Coupe	$8
Plymouth Coupe without Engine	$8

ALLOY FORMS TRUCKS

Autocar Block Truck	$20
1955 Chevrolet 2-Ton Stake Truck	$10
Ford Lts Block Truck	$20
1951 Ford Panel Delivery Truck	$8
1956 Ford Pickup	$8
1956 Ford Pickup with Camper	$10
1956 Ford Pickup with Rack	$10
1954 Mack B-42 Flatbed Truck	$18
Mack B-42 3-Axle Block Truck	$20
Mack B-61 2-Axle Refrigerated Box Truck	$20
Mack BQ 3-Axle Box Truck	$20
Mack BQ 3-Axle Stake Truck	$18
Mack CJ COE 3-Axle Stake Truck	$18

ALLOY FORMS DUMP TRUCKS/TRAILERS

Length indicated refers to the original length of the trailer on which the miniature replica is based.

Autocar with 12' Dump Box	$20
Autocar with 22' Dump Trailer	$25
Autocar with Large Dumper	$25
Autocar Special Dump Truck	$35
Diamond REO with 7' Dump Bed	$20
Diamond REO with 11' Dump Bed	$20
Diamond REO with 22' Dump Trailer	$20
Ford LNT 2-Axle with 7' Dump Trailer	$20
Ford LNT 3-Axle with 7' Heil Dump Body	$20
Ford LNT 3-Axle with 30' 3-Axle Dump Trailer	$35
Ford LNT Coal/Gravel with Tandem Axle Dump Trailer	$23
Ford LTS with 12' Heil Dump Bed	$20
Ford LTS with Dump Body	$23
Ford LTS with 22' Dump Trailer	$25
GMC Astro with 22' Dump Trailer	$25
Mack B-61 Dump Truck	$25
Mack B-61 2-Axle Dump Truck	$20
Mack B-61 3-Axle Dump Truck	$20
Mack B-71 with 30' 3-Axle Dump Trailer	$35
Mack B-71 20' Coal/Gravel with Tandem Axle Dump Trailer	$23
Mack Universal Chassis Dump Truck	$20
22' 2-Axle Dump Trailer	$18
30' 3-Axle Dump Trailer	$25

ALLOY FORMS SEMI-TRACTORS/TRAILERS

Length indicated refers to the original length of the trailer on which the miniature replica is based.

Autocar Chassis	$15
Autocar with Log Trailer	$20
Autocar with 45' "Lowboy" Flatbed Trailer	$30

Diamond REO BBC Refrigerated. $20
Diamond REO Delivery $20
Diamond REO Universal Chassis. $15
Diamond REO with 40' Flatbed Trailer $18
Ford LNT Cab with Universal Chassis $15
Ford LNT 2-Axle with Refrigerated Body. $20
Ford LNT 3-Axle $18
Ford LTS with Universal Chassis $15
GMC Astro 2-Axle $15
GMC Astro 2-Axle with 40' "Lowboy" 16-Wheel Flatbed Trailer. $30
GMC Astro 3-Axle with Rectangular Gas Tanks $15
GMC Astro Short Cab 2-Axle $15
GMC Astro Short Cab 3-Axle $15
GMC Astro Short Cab with 16' body $20
GMC Astro Sleeper. $15
Mack B-61 Tank 2-Axle $20
Mack B-61 Universal Chassis $15
Mack B-61 with 16' Body $20
Mack B-61 with Logging Trailer $30
Mack B-70 with Universal Chassis. $15
Mack B-71 with Heavy Duty Flatbed Trailer $18
Mack CF/Pierce $30
Mack CF with Universal Chassis $20
Mack CF 4-Door $20
Mack DM-800 Offset Cab with Universal Chassis $15
30' Logging Trailer. $20
37' Depressed Center Flatbed Trailer. $20
45' 16-Wheel "Lowboy" Trailer $20

Alloy Forms Emergency Equipment
Diamond REO Pierce Tanker $27
Ford LNT Fire Pumper $27
Ford LS Fire Pumper $27
Mack B-61 2-Axle Fire Pumper $30
Mack B-61 Fire Tanker. $20
Mack B-61 Open Fire Truck $27
Mack CF NYC Fire Pumper. $30
Pierce Ford LN Pumper $27
Pierce Ford LS Pumper. $27

Alloy Forms Miscellaneous
1947 Clark Fork Lift. $4

American Highway Legends (also see Hartoy)
Hartoy produces a series of 1:64 scale trucks of forties and fifties vintage called American Highway Legends that have become very popular with collectors. Models retail for $10 to $30 each, and sometimes bring higher prices at toy shows and from specialty dealers.

"Breyer's" Box Truck $18
"Coca-Cola" Box Van $18
"Coca-Cola" Mack City Delivery Truck $18
"Coca-Cola" Mack Stake Truck $18
"Coca-Cola" Ford Tractor Trailer $18
"Evinrude" Box Truck $18
"Ford Parts" Ford Tractor Trailer $18
"Fram Filters" Mack Covered Truck. $18
"Kelly Springfield" GMC Box Truck $18
"Mobil" GMC Tanker Truck $18
"Pennzoil" Peterbilt Tanker Truck. $18

"Ray-O-Vac" Mack Stake Truck $18
"Scott Paper" Mack Tandem Trailer. $18
"Shell Fuel Oil" Tractor Trailer $18
"Timken" Mack Covered Stake Truck $18
Wrigley's Mack Box Truck $18

The Great American Brewery Collection from American Highway Legends

"Dixie Beer," Dixie Brewing Co., Peterbilt 260 Tandem Trailer Truck, **$30**

"Hamm's Beer, Pabst Brewing Co., Ford F-7 Freight Truck, **$30**

"Jax Beer," Jackson Brewing Co. (Pearl Brewing Co.), GMC T-70 Stake Truck, **$12**

"Olympia Beer," Olympia Brewing Co. (Pabst Brewing Co.), GMC T-70 Covered Truck, **$12**

"Pearl Lager Beer," Pearl Brewing Co., Ford F-5 Box Truck, $12

"Point Special Beer," Stevens Point Beverage Co., Ford F-5 Truck, $12

AMERICAN PRECISION MODELS (APM)

A company heretofore unknown, APM offers a 1:87 scale plastic models of notable quality.

1951 Visicoach American Bus, 1:87 scale

v.1 blue	$16
v.2 green	$16
v.3 orange	$16
v.4 red	$16
AM001 Flexible Visicoach, unpainted kit	$17
AM002 Flexible Visicoach, five colors, built	$22
AM007 GM 4509 Old look coach, kit	$17
AM007 GM 4509 Old look coach, four colors, built	$22

AMPERSAND

The release of a 1:43 scale model of Arie Luyendyk's 1990 Indy winning Lola T-90 punctuates the 1997 return of Ampersand resin cast kits. Previous issues of Indy racers were marketed a few years ago by Ampersand. The Lola with Domino's Pizza livery is available in kit or factory-built form from Motorsports Miniatures, 82 Wall Street, New York NY, phone 212-509-2612.

AMR - CENTURY

AMR models are hand-built white metal kits reportedly produced by Andre M Ruff, a notable maker of hand-built models from France. The first AMR-produced replica was a Renault R8 Gordini.

Fiat Abarth 1300, limited edition, red	$375
Mercedes-Benz 500 SCL, off white	$95
Morgan 2+2, white	$495

Renault Alpine, limited edition, red	$250
Renault R8 Gordini	$600

Century models are a less expensive assortment of models from AMR. A considerable assortment of these 1:43 scale Century white metal models is currently available.

3 1949 Volkswagen Split Window	$77
4 1986 Chevy Corvette Convertible, top down	$77
5 1986 Volvo 480 ES	$77
6 1966 Ford Mustang	$97
8 1987 Mercedes-Benz 300CE	$77 – 95
9 1950 Volkswagen Beetle Hebmueller Convertible	$77
10 1988 Porsche 911 Speedster	$97
12 1959 Volkswagen Karmann Ghia Coupe	$77
13 1959 Volkswagen Karmann Ghia Convertible	$77 – 97
14 1965 Lincoln Continental Convertible	$97
15 1951 Volkswagen Beetle Convertible	$77
16 1966 Ford Mustang Convertible	$77 – 97
18 1989 Porsche Carrera 4	$97
19 1989 Ferrari 348 GTB	$117
22 1989 Mazda MX5 Miata	$97
24 Volvo 480 Cabriolet	$97
30 1948 Lincoln Loewy	$97
901/902 1950 Volkswagen Beetle Hebmueller Convertible	$97
3004 1959 Volkswagen Karmann Ghia Coupe, chrome	$117
3005 1959 Volkswagen Karmann Ghia Convertible, chrome	$117
3010 1988 Porsche 911 Speedster Racer	$97
3013 1948 Lincoln Mk 1 Loewy/Derham	$117
3014 1949 Volkswagen Beetle 1200 Convertible	$117
S3001 1950 Volkswagen Beetle Krankenwagen, white	$97
S3002 1949 Volkswagen Beetle (only 250 made), chrome	$97
S3003 1950 Volkswagen Beetle Hebmueller (only 250 made), chrome	$97

AMT

AMT is best known for its plastic model kits. But for a short time around 1968, they produced an inexpensive series of diecast toys called "Pups," 1:64 scale boxed toy cars made in Hong Kong. No model list available.

ANGUPLAS MINI CARS

Made in Spain, Anguplas Mini Cars are small scale plastic replicas of popular cars of the sixties. They were likely produced in the same era. Mostly produced in 1:86 scale, a few were produced in 1:43. They feature relatively accurate plastic bodies on a diecast chassis with separate plastic tires on metal hubs. Typical of plastic models, fatigue tends to deform the bodies of the vehicles over the years, making mint specimens rare. Original prices for models listed are in parentheses.

7 Ford Edsel Convertible, 1:86 ($.39)	$10
38 VW Beetle, 1:86 ($.25)	$10
47 1960 Studebaker Lark, 1:86 ($.29)	$10
51 Mercedes Benz Microbus, 1:86 ($.49)	$10
56 Ford Falcon, 1:86 ($.29)	$10
61 Jeep Wagon, 1:86 ($.39)	$10
76 Jaguar Mark Nine, 1:86 ($.39)	$10
83 Karmann Ghia, 1:86 ($.25)	$10
86 Cadillac Fleetwood, 1:86 ($.49)	$10

89 Ford Comet, 1:86 ($.39) $10
92 Studebaker Hawk, 1:86 ($.39) $10
99 Volvo Sport, 1:86 ($.29) $10

ANKER

A few Anker 1:25 scale models from Germany are offered by Diecast Miniatures for $18 each.

Alfa Romeo 1300 . . . . $18
Audi 100 . . . . $18
Barkas 153 Van $18
Jaguar XJS $18
Renault Rodeo Jeep $18

ANSO (SEE ANSON)

ANSON

Anson began in the late 1980s, according to best information. Because of the Anson logo with a displaced "N," some collectors have misread the name as "Anso." Ansons are larger scale limited edition diecast models made in China, manufactured and exported by Ontrade Industrial Ltd., 702-5 New East Ocean Centre, 9 Science Museum Road, T.S.T. East, Hong Kong, China.

1992 Bugatti EB-110, red, blue, or metallic silver . . . . . . $25 – 40
30301 Ferrari Dino 246 GT, 1:18, scale . . . . $20 – 35
30302 1969 Lamborghini Miura Coupe, 1:18 scale, silver, red, yel-
　low, metallic blue, orange, or lime green . . . . $25 – 40
30305 1992 Porsche 911 Carrera 2 Targa, 1:18 scale, red, purple, or
　green . . . . $25 – 40
30308 Ferrari 328 GTS, 1:18 scale . . . . $25 – 40

30309 1992 Porsche 911 Carrera 4 Cabriolet, 1:18 scale, red yellow, mint, or black, $25 – 40

30313 Porsche Carrera 4 Cabriolet with top down, 1:14 scale. . $95

ANTEX

Only a single model has so far been found to represent this brand.
Porsche 944, 1:43 . . . . $5

APM (SEE AMERICAN PRECISION MODELS)

AQULI

Argentina is home to the Aquli brand, makers of Matchbox-like knockoffs, poorly cast but retaining some of the charm and accuracy of their legitimate counterparts.
Alfa Carabo $1

A.R.

A.R. is among the earliest of French manufacturers of miniature vehicles, dating back to the 1920s. A.R. produced toys in a variety of media, including tin plate, cast iron, lead, and zinc alloy. Its cars, mostly Peugeots, are valued at $100 and up. A series of Peugeot 301 trucks is listed as well, with models valued at $75 to $100 each. Below is a sampling of models and values.

Bluebird Record Car, 5" $100
Peugeot Andreau Coupe. $100
Peugeot Andreau Limousine $100
Peugeot 301 Mail Truck, 3⅜" $100
Renault Paris Bus, 3⅞" $100

ARBUR

Among the many more prominent British toy companies was this obscure one, known as Arbur Products. The products they manufactured in the late forties and early fifties were toys based on Dinky Toys and others.

Fire Truck, 1:50 . . . . $50
MG Record Car, 1:43 . . . . $40
Scammell Tractor Trailer, 1:50 . . . . $35
Sunbeam Coupe, 1:43 . . . . $50
Tractor Trailer Flatbed Truck, 1:50 . . . . $35
Tractor Trailer Open Bed Truck, 1:50 . . . . $35
Tractor Trailer Van, 1:50. . . . . $35

ARCADE

The most prominent name in cast-iron and zinc alloy toys, Arcade began in 1868 as the Novelty Iron Works in Freeport, Illinois. Arcade reached prominence in 1921 with the introduction of a series of Yellow Cab replicas. The company continued producing toys until the Second World War. Arcade's classic style and detailing creates a bridge between cast-iron toys of the day and diecast zinc alloy toys of the future. Here is just a sampling of the over 260 models offered.

A.C.F. Bus, 1927, 11½". $3,500
Ambulance, 1932, 7¾". $750
Car Carrier with cars, 1931, 24½" $2,000
Double Decker Bus, 1929, 8½". $900
Double Decker Bus, Chicago Motor Coach, 1936, 8¼". $900
Greyhound Cruiser Coach Bus, 1941, 9⅛". $500
Greyhound Cruiser Coach Bus, 1937, 7¾". $400
Red Baby Truck, 1923, 10¾" $1,250
Yellow Coach Double Decker Bus, 1925, 14" $4,000

ARPRA

Kits and ready-built models of plastic or metal are available under the Arpra brand.

1 Mercedes-Benz 1513 Refrigerated Cargo Truck, 1:50 . . . . . . $20
2 Mercedes-Benz 1513 Refrigerator Van, blue/white $24
3 Mercedes-Benz 1513 Van, blue/white $24
4 Mercedes-Benz 608 . . . . $24
8 Scania LKS-141 Semi-Tractor with Tandem Axles, 1:50 . . . . . $20
9 Scania LK-141 Semi-Cab, orange $24
10 Scania LKS-141 Cab, orange. $24
11 Scania LK-111 Semi-Cab, orange $24
12 Scania T-112 Semi-Cab, orange $24
13 Scania R-142 Semi-Cab, orange $24
16 Trailer Refrigerator, white $24
19 Trailer Oil, white. $24
20 Trailer LP Gas, white $24
29 Dynapac CA25PD $24
30 Dynapac CA25D Roller, yellow $24
37 Scania T112 Semi Gas Truck, orange $45
39 Mercedes-Benz 1932 Semi-Cab, white $24
136 Scania T112 Semi-Cab, green $24
302 Mercedes-Benz O 371 2-Axle Highway Bus, silver/orange/
red. $65
304 Scania Fire Tanker. $65
310 Scania L111 Semi Gas Truck, orange, 1:50 . . . . $65

ARS

ARS of Italy produces high quality 1:43 scale versions of Alfa Romeo automobiles.

101 Alfa Romeo Spider, top up, red, green, silver, yellow $24
103 Alfa Romeo 33 Boxer 16V, red, black $24
104 Alfa Romeo 33 Sedan 1.5L 1E, dark green. $24
105 Alfa Romeo 33 Sedan Permanente, orange $24

ART MODEL

Art Model miniatures are licensed 1:43 scale versions of various Ferrari models, manufactured in Pesaro, Italy. Incidentally, *stradale* is Italian for street (as in Fiat Strada), as compared to *prova,* which indicates a racing, proving grounds, or prototype version.

001 Ferrari 166 MM Coupe, "Prova," red $34
002 Ferrari 166 MM Coupe, "Stradale," cream $34
003 Ferrari 166 MM Coupe, "Stradale," black $34
004 Ferrari 195 S Coupe "Mille Miglia 1950," blue $34
005 Ferrari 166 MM Spyder, "Prova," red $34
006 Ferrari 166 MM Spyder, "Stradale," white $34
007 Ferrari 166 MM Spyder, "Stradale," black $34
008 Ferrari 166 MM Spyder, "Mille Miglia 1949," red $34
009 Ferrari 195 S Coupe, "Le Mans 1950," blue $34
010 Ferrari 166 MM Coupe, "Mille Miglia 1951," red. $34
011 Ferrari 166 MM Spyder, "Le Mans 1949," red. $34
012 Ferrari 166 MM Spyder, "12 Ore di Parigi," yellow. $34
014 Ferrari 500 TRC 1956, "Prova," red $34
015 Ferrari 500 TRC, "Clienti," yellow $34
016 Ferrari 166 MM Coupe, "Le Mans 1950," yellow $34
017 Ferrari 166 MM Spyder, "Mille Miglia 1950," silver $34
Ferrari 410 S, 1955 . . . . $34
Ferrari 340 Mexico, 1952 . . . . $34

ASAHI MODEL PET

Asahi models are made in Japan. Asahi Toy Company first made tin-plate toy cars in the late forties and early fifties. It wasn't till 1960 or so that the company produced diecast toys under the "Model Pet" brand. While production reportedly ended in the early seventies, the 1:43 scale Rolls Royce Camargue has been produced later, as recently as 1980 or so, and is the only recent offering known of the brand.

1 Toyota Crown, 1:43 . . . . $125
1A Toyota Crown, gold plated, 1:43 . . . . $150
2 Toyota Masterline Station Wagon, 1:43 . . . . $125
2A Toyota Masterline Ambulance, white, 1:43 . . . . $225
3 Subaru 360, 1:40 . . . . $125
4 Toyota Land Cruiser, green, 1:43 . . . . $150
5 Datsun Bluebird, 1:43 . . . . $125
6 Prince Skyline, 1:43 . . . . $125
7 Toyota Corona Station Wagon, 1:43 . . . . $100
8 Austin A50 Cambridge, 1:43 . . . . $150
9 Hillman Minx, 1:43 . . . . $150
10 Nissan Cedric, 1:43 . . . . $125
10A Nissan Cedric Taxi, 1:43. . . . . $150
11 Toyota Crown Station Wagon, 1:43. . . . . $100
12 Toyota Crown, 1:43 . . . . $125
12A Toyota Crown Police, 1:43 . . . . $175
13 Mazda R360 Coupe, 1:43 . . . . $125
14 Toyota Publica, 1:43 . . . . $100
15 Prince Skyline Sports Convertible, 1:43. . . . . $125
16 Prince Skyline Sports Coupe, 1:43 . . . . $125
17 Datsun Bluebird, 1:43 . . . . $100
18 Isuzu Bellett, 1:43 . . . . $125
19 Toyota Sports Coupe, 1:43 . . . . $100
20 Toyota Crown, 1:43 . . . . $100
20A Toyota Crown, gold plated, 1:43 . . . . $125
20B Toyota Crown Police, black and white, 1:43. . . . . $150
21 Toyota Masterline Station Wagon, 1:43 . . . . $100
21A Toyota Masterline Ambulance, white, 1:43 . . . . $150
22 Prince Gloria, 1:43 . . . . $100
22A Prince Gloria Taxi, 1:43 . . . . $150
23 Toyota Land Cruiser, green, 1:43 . . . . $150
24 Mitsubishi Colt 1000, 1:43 . . . . $75
25 Datsun Bluebird, 1:43 . . . . $75
26 Hino Contessa 1300, 1:43. . . . . $75
27 Toyota Corona, 1:43 . . . . $100
29 Hino Contessa 1300 Coupe, 1:43 . . . . $75
30 Mazda Familia, 1:43 . . . . $75
31 Toyota Sports 800, 1:43 . . . . $75
32 Nissan Silvia Coupe, 1:43 . . . . $75
33 Nissan Cedric, 1:43 . . . . $75
34 Honda S800 Roadster, 1:43 . . . . $100
35 Honda S800 Coupe, 1:43 . . . . $100
36 Toyota 2000GT Coupe, 1:43 . . . . $75
37 Honda N360, 1:43 . . . . $75
38 Toyota Crown Super, 1:43 . . . . $50
39 Toyota Crown Coupe, 1:43 . . . . $50
40 Mitsubishi Galant GTO, 1:43 . . . . $50
41 Toyota Crown Police, black and white, 1:43. . . . . $50
43 Honda RC162 Motorcycle, 1:35 . . . . $30
44 Suzuki 750GT Motorcycle, 1:35 . . . . $30

45 Nissan Skyline 2000GT Coupe, 1:35 . . . . $30
46 Yamaha 650XS Motorcycle, 1:35 . . . . $30
47 Datsun Sunny Coupe 1400, 1:43 . . . . $50
48 Honda 750 Motorcycle, 1:35 . . . . $30
50 Honda 750 Police Motorcycle, 1:50 . . . . $30
51 Toyota Corona Mk. II 2000G SS, 1:43 . . . . $50
52 Datsun Bluebird UHT, 1:43 . . . . $50
54 Nissan Cedric 2600 GX, 1:43 . . . . $50
55 Toyota Crown Taxi, yellow, 1:43 . . . . $50
56 Toyota Crown Firecar, red, 1:43 . . . . $50
57 Toyota Crown Ambulance, white, 1:43 . . . . $50
58 Mitsubishi Galant GTO Rally, 1:43 . . . . $50
59 Nissan Skyline 2000GT Rally, 1:43 . . . . $50
60 Yamaha Police Motorcycle with Sidecar, 1:35 . . . . $30
61 Yamaha Police Motorcycle, 1:35 . . . . $30
62 Yamaha Motorcycle with Sidecar, 1:35 . . . . $30
101 Toyota Toyoace Truck, 1:48 . . . . $150
102 Toyota Toyoace Covered Truck, 1:48 . . . . $150
103 Honda Motorcycle, 1:40 . . . . $75
Rolls Royce Camargue, yellow, orange, or gray, 1:43 . . . . . . $20

ASHTON

Ashton Models of New England are finely detailed hand-built 1:43 scale fire fighting equipment. The most popular model is the Ahrens-Fox Fire Engine.
20A 1951 Mack Pumper Type 95 "Chicago" $109
22A 1927 Ahrens-Fox Chemical Truck "Bristol" Engine No. 3 . $135
25 1951 FWD Model F50T Pumper "Cedarburg" . . . . . $140 – 155
27 1921 Ahrens-Fox Piston Pumper "Cincinnati" $109

27 1921 Ahrens-Fox Piston Pumper "New Orleans," $109

30 1953 Mack Pumper "Centerport" $109
33 1923 Ahrens-Fox City Service "Cincinnati" $165
35 1921 Ahrens-Fox Piston Pumper "Harrisburg" $109
38 1952 Mack 750 GPM Pumper "Hanover" $109
39 1925 Ahrens-Fox NS4 Pumper "Vandergrift" $135
40 Ahrens-Fox Aerial Ladder Truck "Clifton" $179
44 1948 Mack L Type Rescue Truck No. 1 "FDNY" $139
46 1923 Ahrens-Fox Ladder Truck "Nashua" $189
52 1941 Mack Tanker "FDNY" $120
ASHTON "GOLD COLLECTION"
31G Mack Tow Truck "Detroit" $175
34G FWD Open Cab Truck "Cody" $175
36G Ahrens-Fox Aerial Ladder Truck "Newark" $229
37G Mack Quad "Whitehall" $229

41G Ahrens-Fox Pumper "Newark" $169
42G Mack Pumper "Ellensburg" $175
43G Mack Pumper "Glendale" $189
45G Mack Rescue "Silver Springs" $169
48G FWD Foam "Chicago" $189

AURORA CIGAR BOX

Aurora is best known for HO gauge slot cars. Their Cigar Box line of cars of the mid to late sixties were models with plastic bodies, with diecast metal bases held on with two screws so that the chassis could be easily removed and replaced with slot car chassis and motor. Popularity of these little cars has increased in just the last couple of years. Prices below were recently listed for new condition specimens in original box.
6103 Mako Shark, blue $35
6104 Ford J Car, yellow $35
6105 Ford GT, metallic lavender/pink $35
6107 Ford XL-500, white $35
6110 Thunderbird, yellow $35
6110 Thunderbird, white $35
6111 Dino Ferrari, yellow $35
6112 Porsche 904, red $35
6114 Chaparral, white $35
6116 Mercury Cougar $35

AUTHENTICAST (SEE COMET)

AUTO BUFF

This series of 1:43 scale vintage Ford models were hand-built in California by Le Buff Stuff and produced in very small quantities. The series has long since been discontinued and models are now quite scarce. Auto Buff dies were sold to Oakland Models of Michigan in 1982.
Ford Model A Roadster, top down, blue/black $115
Ford Model A Convertible, top down, medium green $115
1930 Ford Model A Pickup $115
1930 Ford Model A Roadster $115
1940 Ford Pickup, red $115
1940 Ford Convertible, top down, brown $115
1940 Ford Convertible, top up, maroon/tan $115
1948 Ford Coupe, black $115
1948 Ford Coupe, red $345
1948 Ford Coupe, maroon $115
1948 Ford Convertible, top up, black $115
1948 Ford Convertible, top down, dark green $115
1953 Ford Pickup, black $115
1953 Ford "Coke" Panel Van, red $345
1953 Ford Stake Truck, white/black $115

AUTOHOBBY

Autohobby models are limited edition resin hand-builts. Resin models are generally sold unfinished with rough, unfinished edges, for hobbyists to finish, assemble, and customize.
610 1938 Citroen 11B Coca-Cola Van $58

AUTO PILEN (ALSO SEE PILEN)

Escuderia Pilen of Spain produces these toy cars under

the brand names Pilen, Auto Pilen, and Escuderia Pilen. Dr. Craig S. Campbell, assistant professor of geography at Youngstown State University, reports that the predominant scale for these toys is 1:43. Many, but not all, of Pilen's superior line were recastings of French Dinkys, such as the Citroën DS Pallas and the Matra Simca Bagheera. After Pilen's demise in the eighties, some Pilen dies were used by AHC of the Netherlands. Pilens are comparable to Solido in detail, though their colors are brighter, comparable to SpectraFlame colors on the earliest Hot Wheels.

AUTO PILEN 1:43 SCALE

Adams Brothers Probe $40
Buggy Playero $40
Chevrolet Astro I $45
Chevrolet Corvette Stingray Split-Window, 1967 . . . . $50
Citroën 2 CV $40
DeTomaso Mangusta $40
Ferrari 512 . . . . $40
Ferrari P5 . . . . $40
Ford Mark II $45
Ghibli Maserati $45
Javelin $60
Mercedes 250 Coupe $45
Mercedes Ambulance $45
Mercedes C-111 . . . . $40
Mercedes Taxi $45
Mini Cooper $40
Modulo Pininfarina $40
Monteverdi Hai 450 SS, yellow with black trunk and hood, #347 . $45
Monza Spider $40
Oldsmobile Police $60
Oldsmobile Toronado $55
Porsche 917 . . . . $40
Porsche Carrera 6, shocking pink with clear windows, #303 . . $45
Renault R-12 S $40
Renault R-12 G. C. Trafico $40
Seat 124 Sport $45
Seat 127 . . . . $45
Seat 600 . . . . $45
Seat 850 Spyder $45
Stratos Bertone, #509 . . . . $35
Vauxhall SRV $40

AUTO PILEN 1:64 SCALE

Fiat 131 Wagon, 1:64 . . . . $4

Photo by Jeff Koch.

Peugeot 504, 1:64, $6

AUTO REPLICAS

Great Britain is where Auto Replicas are produced. The company, owned by foremost model maker Barry Lester, manufactures white metal kits.

AUTOREPLICA

Diecast Miniatures of Amston, Connecticut, last offered a selection of these obscure 1:43 scale miniatures believed to be Italian made. In addition, *Schroeder's Collectible Toys Antique to Modern Price Guide* lists a couple more.

1 1934 ERA GP Racer "Romulus," light blue and yellow $59
4 1921 Bugatti Brescia Racer, #3, blue $59
16 1937 Packard 12 Roadster, top down, blue $59
24 1937 Packard Formal Sedan $59
24 1937 Packard Tourer/Town Car $59
28 1954 Sunbeam Alpine Roadster, top down $59
29 1932 Alfa 8C Roadster, top down, red $59
33 1955 Chevrolet Bel Air Convertible, top down, sea green . . $39
38 1939 Morgan Plus 4 Tourer $59
42 1936-37 Tatra 77-77A, blue $59
44 1936 Morgan 2 Seater, green and black $59
101 1925 Austin Van, "Lucas," dark green $59
Kit 1 1950 Fiat Panel Van $19
Kit 21 1925-26 Renault Record $19
Amilcar Italiana $45

AVIVA (ALSO SEE HASBRO)

Hasbro has been a powerful force in the toy industry since the 1960s. Toys such as Mr. Machine, the see-through gear-driven walking, animated robot with a top hat, was possibly one of the best known toys of the period, at least if you watched Saturday morning cartoons. The most popular and sustaining line of toys for Hasbro has been G.I. Joe. They have since also purchased the Kenner brand. Hasbro has continued through to the present, but it has been overshadowed by the giant called Mattel. In the late seventies and on, Hasbro has produced Aviva character toys usually sold at Hallmark shops. Predominantly Peanuts characters from the comic strip of the same name, Aviva at last word continues to market such items in diecast and plastic. Here is a brief sampling.

#72039/1 - Snoopy drives a red hook and ladder fire truck, wearing a red helmet. Woodstock sits in the rear . . . . $5 – 8
#72039/2 - Snoopy drives a yellow convertible with red and green accents. Woodstock sits on the back . . . . $5 – 8
#72039/3 - Snoopy as the flying ace pilots yellow biplane with red wings, "Snoopy." Woodstock's face is on the tail of the plane . . . . $5 – 8

AVIVA/HASBRO MINI DIECAST

#72044-2 - Snoopy wearing a black tuxedo and top hat, yellow open car . . . . $3 – 5
#72044-5 - Snoopy wearing a red hat drives a truck called "Cat Catcher" . . . . $3 – 5
#72044-6 - Snoopy as the flying ace drives a red racer . . . . . $3 – 5

BANDAI

Bandai is best known for high-quality, accurately scaled, lithographed tin battery-operated models from Japan. Values

are high for their tin-plate models, but only a few diecast models are known to exist of this brand.

BMW 320i, No. 3, orange-red with cross and deer head in a circle, "Fagermeister" on roof and hood . . . . $8 – 12

BANDI

Another one of those obscure brands listed in *Schroeder's Collectible Toys Antique to Modern Price Guide,* possibly a misspelling of Bandii. Only one model is listed.

1962 Volkswagen Sedan #742 . . . . $195

BANDII

Although possibly related, Bandii is not the same Japanese company as Bandai, a brand famous for their tin friction and battery-operated toy cars and trucks of great detail and quality. Bandii is a comparatively obscure company that did however produce an interesting assortment of diecast toys.

Hato Bus, blue/white, 4½" $16
Hino Gas Tanker "JAL," 1:87 scale $5
Lancia Stratos "Alitalia," 1:87 scale $5
Mazda RX7 252i, 1:64 scale $5
Mitsubishi Galant, 1:64 scale $5
Nissan "JAL" Vacuum Car, 1:87 scale $5
Nissan "KLM" Vacuum Car, 1:87 scale $5
Nissan "Nippon" Vacuum Car, 1:87 scale $5
Nissan Ambulance, 1:87 scale $5
Porsche 928, blue, 1:43 scale $16
Porsche 930, silver, 1:43 scale $16
Porsche 935, 1:64 scale $5
Tank Lorry "JAL," 1:87 scale $5
Tank Lorry "KLM," 1:87 scale $5
Tank Lorry "Nippon," 1:87 scale $5

BANG

When Box Model of Pesaro, Italy, reorganized in 1991, the result was several new companies, Art Model, Bang, and Best of Italy. All Bang models are manufactured to exacting 1:43 scale.

401 Ferrari 250 GTO Prova 1962-63, red $25
402 Ferrari 250 GTO Le Mans 1962, white $25
405 Ferrari 250 GT 1956-57 Prova, red $25
406 Ferrari 250 GT 1956-57 Stradale, silver $25
407 Ferrari 250 GTO 3 Ore di Pau, red $25
409 Ferrari 250 GTO Tourist Trophy 1963, red $25
410 Ford AC Cobra Spyder Stradale, red $25
411 Ford AC Cobra Spyder Stradale, black $25
412 Ford AC Cobra Spyder, with top up, turquoise, black/white . $22
414 Ford AC Cobra Sebring 1963 . . . . $25
415 Ferrari 250 GT, Mille Miglia 1957 . . . . $25
420 Ford AC Cobra Le Mans 1963 . . . . $25
421 Ford AC Cobra Laguna Seca, white $25
422 Ford AC Cobra Spyder, Riverside 1962 . . . . $22
423 Ford AC Cobra, Targa Florio 1964, lavender $22
424 Ferrari 250 Tour de France Prova, red $22
425 Ferrari 250 Tour de France Stradale, silver $25
426 Ferrari 250 Tour de France, Gran Prix de Paris 1960, red . . $25
427 Ferrari 250 Tour de France 1959, white $25
431 Ferrari 250 Tour de France 1958, gray $25

432 Ferrari 250 GTO Sebring 1962, light blue $25
433 Ferrari 250 GTO Laguna Seca 1963 . . . . $25
438 Ford AC Cobra 289 LeMans 1963, green $22
441 Ferrari 250 Tour de France 1958, light blue $25
444 Ferrari 250 GTO Spa 1965, yellow $25
453 Ford GT40 LeMans 1966, white $22
455 Ford GT40 Mallory Park 1968, red $22
456 Ford GT40 Le Mans 1966, white $25
458 Ferrari 250 GTO Tour de France 1964, gray $25
464 Ferrari 250 GTO Le Mans 1962, red $25
504 Ferrari 250SWB Coupe Tour De France 1961 . . . . $22
1007 Ford GT40 LeMans 68 Race 1968, light blue $22
1008 Ferrari 250SWB Coupe SportItalia #7, red $22
1009 Ford GT40 Coupe SportItalia Limited, yellow $22
1010 Ferrari 250GT Tour De France 1957, red $24
1011 Mercedes-Benz 300SL Mille Miglia 1989, red $22
1012 Ferrari 250 SWB Montlhery 1991, silver $24
1013 Ferrari 250 GTO Thirty Years, chrome $35
1014 Ferrari 250 Tour de France Mille Miglia 1958, red . . . $25
7071 Ford GT40 Stradale 1966, gold $22
7072 Ford GT40 LeMans 1968, "11" blue $22
7073 Ford GT40 LeMans 1968, "10" blue $22
7074 Ford GT40 LeMans 1969, "6" blue $22
7075 Ferrari 250 GT SWB Prova 1961, red $22
7076 Ferrari 250 GT SWB Stradale 1961, silver $22
7077 Ferrari 250 GT SWB Stradale 1961, yellow $22
7078 Ferrari 250 GT SWB Le Mans 1961, red $22
7079 Ford Mk II Le Mans Stradale 1966, black $22
7080 Ford Mk II Le Mans 1966, blue $22
7081 Ford Mk II Le Mans 1966, black $22
7082 Ford Mk II Le Mans 1966, red $22
7083 Ferrari 250 GT SWB Le Mans 1961, blue $26
7084 Ferrari 250 GT SWB Tour De France 1961, red $26
7085 Ferrari 250 GT SWB LeMans 1961, white $22
7086 Ferrari 250 GT SWB LeMans 1961, silver $26
7087 Mercedes-Benz 300 SL Gullwing 1954, cream $22
7088 Mercedes-Benz 300 SL Gullwing 1954, red $22
7089 Mercedes-Benz 300 SL Gullwing Coupe 1955, silver $24
7090 Mercedes-Benz 300 SL Gullwing Coupe 1955, black $24
7091 Ford Mk II Sebring 1966, metallic blue $22
7092 Ford Mk II LeMans 1966, gold $22
7093 Ford Mk II LeMans 1966, yellow $22
7094 Ford Mk II Roadster Sebring 1966 . . . . $22
7095 1962 Ferrari 250 GTO De Montlhery, red $22
7096 1958 Ferrari 250 Tour De France 3 Ore di Pau 2D #59, blue $22
7097 Ferrari 330 P.4 Prova, red $25
7098 Ferrari 330 P.4 1967 24 Ore Le Mans, red $25
7099 Mercedes-Benz 300SL Gullwing Mille Miglia 1989 "224" mint blue $22
7100 Mercedes-Benz 300 SL Gullwing Tour de France 1956 "81," red $25
7101 Mercedes-Benz 300 SL Gullwing Le Mans 1956 "7," silver . $25
7102 Mercedes-Benz 300 SL Gullwing Tour de France 1956 "149," silver $25
8001 Ferrari 348ts Stradale TD 1991, red $22
8002 Ferrari 348ts Stradale TD 1991, yellow $24
8003 Ferrari 348ts Stradale TD 1991, black $22

8004 Ferrari 348tb Stradale, blue $24
8005 Ferrari 348tb Stradale, red $24
8006 Ferrari 348tb Stradale, white $24
8007 1990 Ferrari 348tb Challenge #48, red $22
8013 1993 Ferrari 456GT Prova, red $27
9301 1993 Ferrari 348tb Challenge Cutrera #1, white $24
9302 1993 Ferrari 348tb Challenge Giudici, white $24
9303 1993 Ferrari 348tb Challenge Ragazzi #2, white $24
9305 1993 Ferrari 348tb Challenge Rossi #5, yellow $24
9306 1993 Ferrari 348tb Challenge Peitra #6, red $24
9308 1993 Ferrari 348tb Challenge Benaduce #8, red $24

BAM (BOUTIQUE AUTO MOTO)

Aaron Robinson reports that BAM was a small shop in Paris, France, that at one time produced their own line of white metal models, most notably a line of IMSA Lolas and in particular a "Red Lobster" car from around 1981.

BANTHRICO

Banthrico Inc., of Chicago, Illinois, proclaims itself as "The Coin Bank People." Models are generally antiqued brass-like 1:25 scale vehicles, generally with a slot in the bottom for coins, often with printing on them for the various banks that gave them away to customers when they opened an account. The Nash in particular was a dealer promo model. The company began in the mid-1950s and continued until the mid-70s. Here is a list of models offered in a recent series. Last known address for Banthrico is Banthrico Inc., 4615 W. Roosevelt Rd., Chicago IL 60650, 312-242-0963 or 312-656-7815.

1908 Buick . . . . $20 – 25
1900 Buick Pillowbox coupe . . . . $20 – 25
1954 Buick Skylark convertible . . . . $20 – 25
1930 Cadillac Roadster . . . . $20 – 25
1954 Cadillac Sedan . . . . $20 – 25
1915 Chevrolet . . . . $20 – 25
1953 Chevrolet Corvette coupe . . . . $20 – 25
1963 Chevrolet Corvette coupe . . . . $20 – 25
1954 Chevrolet 4-door sedan . . . . $20 – 25
1928 Chevrolet Pick Up Truck . . . . $20 – 25
1946 Chrysler Town & Country . . . . $20 – 25
1929 Ford Model "A" . . . . $20 – 25
1926 Ford Model "T" . . . . $20 – 25
1934 Ford Panel Truck . . . . $20 – 25
1955 Ford Thunderbird . . . . $20 – 25
1955 Jaguar . . . . $20 – 25
1927 Lincoln Brougham . . . . $20 – 25
1941 Lincoln Continental . . . . $20 – 25
1906 Mack Truck . . . . $20 – 25
1954 Mercury 2-door hardtop . . . . $20 – 25
1949 Nash Airflyte . . . . $25 – 30
1956 Oldsmobile 98 convertible . . . . $20 – 25
1954 Packard 4-door sedan . . . . $20 – 25
1937 Rolls Royce . . . . $20 – 25
1910 Stanley Steamer . . . . $20 – 25
1977 Volkswagen Beetle . . . . $20 – 25

BARCLAY

From 1924 to 1971, Barclay produced a large assortment of toys from various headquarters in West Hoboken, Union City, and North Bergen, New Jersey, beginning with lead alloy models in the thirties and forties and later changing to zamak (zinc alloy). Most models are fairly common in appearance, but a few represent sleek, streamlined "futuristic" styling that reflects the Art Deco influence of the period. Below is just a sampling of models.

Ambulance, #194, 3½" $40
Ambulance, #50, 5" $50
Anti-Aircraft Gun Truck, #198, 4" $35
Armored Army Truck, #152, 2⅞" $25
Army Car with two soldiers lying down, gunner on right, driver on left $25
Army Car with two silver bullhorns, 2½" $40
Army Tractor (Minneapolis-Moline), 2¾" $25
Army Truck with Gun, #151, 2¾" $30
Army Truck with Anti-Aircraft Gun, #151, 2½" $25
Army Tank Truck, #197, 3⅛" $30
Auburn Speedster, #58, ... $30
Austin Coupe, 2" $30
Auto Transport Set, truck with small trailer, 4½" and 2 cars . . . $60
Beer Truck, with barrels $50
Bus, Futuristic, 3" $25
Bus, "Coast to Coast," "Barclay Toy," two-piece, #405, 2⅞" . . . $75
Cannon Car, battery powered light (1935), 3½" $200
Chrysler Airflow, 4" $85
Chrysler Imperial Coupe, #39 . . . . $25
Cord Front Drive Coupe, #40, 3⅝" $35
Double Decker Bus, 4" $60
1937 Federal Truck $25
1940 Anti Aircraft $25
Mack Pick Up Truck, 3½" $25
"Milk & Cream" Truck, 3⅝", #377, white rubber tires $60
Milk Truck, 3⅝", #377, black rubber tires $40
Milk Truck shaped like a milk bottle, #567 . . . . $250
"Parcel Delivery," #45, 3⅝" $100
Renault Tank, #47, 4" $35
Searchlight Truck, 4¹⁄₁₆" $150
Silver Arrow Race Car, 5½" $35
Station Wagon, 2-piece "Barclay Toy," #404, 2¹⁵⁄₁₆" $60
Steam-Roller, 3¼", slush lead with tin roof $50
Streamline Car, #302, 3⅛" $35
Taxi, #318, 3¼" $20
Wrecker, two-piece diecast , #403, 2⅞" $70

BARLUX

The Italian firm of Barlux started producing diecast toys around 1970 and continued until about 1983. Barlux toys failed to gain popularity due to their comparatively crude design. They weren't widely distributed, at least not outside of Italy, and are hard to find.

100 Fiat Wrecker, 1:24 . . . . $30
101 Fiat Ambulance, 1:24 . . . . $30
102 Fiat Carabinieri, 1:24 . . . . $30
705 Fiat 697 Fire Truck, 1:43 . . . . $16
739 Fiat 697 Flat Truck & Fork Lift, 1:43 . . . . $16
747 Fiat 697 Flat Truck & Trailer, 1:43 . . . . $16
762 Fiat 697 Dump Truck & Loader, 1:43 . . . . $16

73001 Matra MS-120, 1:66	$10
73002 Lotus-Ford 72, 1:66	$10
73003 BRM, 1:66	$10
73004 Tyrrell-Ford, 1:66	$10
73005 Ferrari B2, 1:66	$10
73006 March-Ford, 1:66	$10
73007 McLaren-Ford, 1:66	$10
73008 Brabham-Ford, 1:66	$10
73009 Surtees-Ford, 1:66	$10
73010 Lotus Turbine, 1:66	$10
73062 Land Rover and Caravan, 1:43	$16
73081 MTS-20 Shovel Loader, 1:43	$16
73082 MTS-10 Fork Lift, 1:43	$16
73083 MTS-30 Trencher, 1:43	$16
73084 MTS-20 Snowplow-Sander, 1:43	$16
73085 Garbage Truck, 1:43	$16
73086 Road Roller, 1:43	$16
73810 Public Works Vehicle With Snowplow, 1:50	$16

BASTELTIP

Diecast Miniatures of Amston, Massachusetts, listed one model from this otherwise unknown brand.

Raba Fire Crane, 24"	$28

BBR

EWA & Model Miniatures says it best in one of their recent catalogs: "BBR models are outstanding for their superb hand-built quality and detailing. The company was started just over ten years ago in a small town midway between Lake Como and Milan and not far from Monza, in the north of Italy. It quickly achieved world fame for its finely detailed 1/43rd scale models with the super paint finish. The cars modeled, as befits an Italian company, are mostly race cars and mostly Ferraris, with some Alfa Romeos and Lancias. Other subjects have been covered too, including Porsche, McLaren, Benetton, Williams (and other F1 cars), and Nissan, plus some Lincolns as raced in the Carrera Pan Americana in the early '50s. Many of the cars modeled are also available as kits."

1938 Alfa Romeo 2900B 8C, maroon, "19"	$194
1938 Alfa Romeo 2900B 8C, maroon, "8"	$194
1939 Alfa Romeo 6c 2500 "Duxia"	$159
1939 Alfa Romeo 2900 Berlinetta Touring Long	$149
1949 Alfa Romeo 2500SS "Villa d'Este Coupe"	$139
1949 Alfa Romeo Villa D'Este Coupe, silver	$168
1950 Alfa Romeo 6C 2500	$159
1952 Alfa Romeo Villa D'Este, convertible top down	$154
1952 Alfa Romeo 2500SS Coupe Monte Carlo, burgundy	$188
1956 Alfa Romeo 6C 2500 Street, maroon	$184
1956 Alfa Romeo 6C 2500 MM Fangio, maroon, "730"	$184
1993 Alfa Romeo 155 V6 DTM Nannini	$229
1947 Ferrari 125S Street, red	$178
1950 Ferrari 212 International Nurbr.-TD, blue	$178
1951 Ferrari 212 Carrera Panamerican "No. 9 Ascari"	$159
1952 Ferrari 212 "Interpininfarina"	$139
1952 Ferrari 212 International Pininfarina Bordeaux, black	$154 – 178
1951 Ferrari 212 Carrera Panamerican "No. 3"	$175
1954 Ferrari 250 Europa Street, red	$154

1954 Ferrari 250 Europa "Cabriolet Pininfarina"	$149
1954 Ferrari 250 Europa NY Show, maroon/gray	$194
1956 Ferrari 250 Europa "Boano"	$159
1957 Ferrari 250GT PR Bernhard, black	$184
1959 Ferrari 250 GTE	$159
1959 Ferrari 250 "Enzo Ferrari"	$159
1962 Ferrari 250 GTO	$159
1965 Ferrari 275 GTB	$169
1984 Ferrari 288 GTO	$159
1984 Ferrari 288GTO 2-door coupe, red	$178
1982 Ferrari 308GTB coupe, red	$178
1982 Ferrari 308GTB coupe, silver	$178
1982 Ferrari 308GTB coupe, blue	$178
1982 Ferrari 308GTB coupe, yellow	$178
1965 Ferrari 330 GT 2+2, available in red, blue, metallic green, or dark gray	$199
1967 Ferrari 330GTC Liliana Di R, blue	$178
1967 Ferrari 330 P4 LeMans #24	$198
1993 Ferrari 348 Cabriolet	$159
1954 Ferrari 375 Am Vign- Turin, yellow	$184
1954 Ferrari 375 MM Pan Am Chinetti, red	$129 – 144
1955 Ferrari 375 AM "Giovanni Agnelli"	$159
1955 Ferrari 375 Am Agnl-Torino, green	$178
1956 Ferrari 410SA di Parigi, beige	$168
1985 Ferrari 412T 2+2, available in red, silver, blue, or metallic green	$199
1994 Ferrari 412 T1 Berger F1 Racer	$219
1976 Ferrari 512BB coupe, yellow	$184
1997 Ferrari 550 Maranello, available in red or yellow	$199
1991 Ferrari F40 Koenig Coupe, red	$174
1991 Ferrari F40 Koenig Coupe, yellow	$174
1996 Ferrari F50 Coupe, red	$199
1996 Ferrari F50 Spyder, red	$199
1987 Ferrari Testarossa "Giovanni Agnelli" Convertible, silver	$138
1987 Ferrari Testarossa Straman Convertible, red	$164
1988 Ferrari Testarossa "Koenig"	$139
1953 Porsche 356A	$188
1993 Porsche 911 Carrera	$188

BBURAGO (ALSO SEE MARTOYS)

Bburago (spelled with two B's) is seemingly a recent entry into the diecast miniature market, and their predominance on the US market has risen steadily. Producing precision scale models as well as toys since 1974, Bburago models are among the few diecast collectibles still manufactured in

Europe instead of Asia... Milan, Italy, to be specific. Bburagos were previously sold as Martoys. Bburago models mostly replicate Italian sports cars such as Ferrari, Lamborghini, Alfa Romeo, and Bugatti. But also represented are Mercedes-Benz, Jaguar, Porsche, and even a couple of Dodge Vipers, with an ever-expanding assortment. Many models are available both as pre-assembled models and unassembled kits, as listed below. In addition, one collector claims that Bburago made at least one 1:12 scale model, listed below.

1937 Jaguar SS100, 1/12th scale . . . . $80 – 110

Bburago Super 1:24 Scale (0100 series models)

0102 Porsche 911S	$15 – 20
0104 Ferrari Testarossa	$15 – 20
0105 Mercedes-Benz 190 E	$15 – 20
0111 Mercedes-Benz 500 SEC	$15 – 20
0112 Range Rover Safari	$15 – 20
0115 Lancia Delta S4	$15 – 20
0116 Peugeot 205 Safari	$15 – 20
0119 Alfa Romeo 75 Gr.A	$15 – 20
0121 Porsche 959	$15 – 20
0125 Fiat Tipo	$15 – 20
0129 Ferrari 348 tb Evoluzione	$15 – 20
0130 Mercedes-Benz 300 SL	$15 – 20
0131 Peugeot 405 Raid	$15 – 20
0133 Ferrari 512 BB	$15 – 20
0137 Lamborghini Countach 5000 Quattrovalvole	$15 – 20
0148 Ferrari 308 GTB	$15 – 20
0188 Alfa Romeo 75 Polizia	$15 – 20
0189 Alfa Romeo 75 Carabinieri	$15 – 20
0190 Alfa Romeo 75 Guardia Di Finanza	$15 – 20
0192 Ferrari GTO Rally	$15 – 20
0194 Fiat Cinquecento	$15 – 20
0198 Renegade Jeep CJ-7	$15 – 20
0199 Porsche 924 Turbo Gr.2	$15 – 20

Bburago VIP 1:24 scale models (0500 series models)

0503 Bugatti Atlantic (1936)	$15 – 20
0504 Ferrari Testarossa (1984)	$15 – 20
0506 Ferrari 250 Le Mans (1965)	$15 – 20
0510 Ferrari 250 GTO (1962)	$15 – 20
0511 Ferrari 275 GTB 4 (1966)	$15 – 20
0513 Ford AC Cobra 427 (1965)	$15 – 20
0522 Mercedes-Benz 300 SL (1954)	$15 – 20
0532 Ferrari F40 (1987)	$15 – 20
0535 Bugatti EB 110 (1991)	$15 – 20
0537 Lamborghini Countach (1988)	$15 – 20
0538 Bugatti "Type 55" (1932)	$15 – 20
0541 Lamborghini Diablo (1990)	$15 – 20
0542 Ferrari F40 Evoluzione (1992)	$15 – 20
0563 Porsche 959 Turbo (1986)	$15 – 20
0572 Ferrari GTO (1984)	$15 – 20

Bburago Early 1500 Series

From 1974 to 1980, the 1500 series was represented by 1:43 scale Fiat 50 NC Trucks.12 These truck models were discontinued in favor of the newer Bijoux series.

1501 Covered Dump Truck	$25
1502 Crane Truck	$25
1503 Quarry Dump Truck	$25
1504 Lumber Truck	$25
1505 Dump Truck	$25
1506 Cement Mixer	$25
1507 Lumber Truck	$25
1508 Tank Truck	$25
1509 Fire Ladder Truck	$25
1510 Milk Tank Truck	$25
1511 Fire Crane Truck	$25
1512 Flatbed with Boat	$25

Bburago 1:14 scale Formula One models (issued from 1976 until 1981)

2101 Ferrari 312T2 (1976)	$50
2102 Tyrell P34/2 (1976)	$40
2103 Brabham BT46 (1976)	$40
2105 Lotus 79/JPS MK4 (1978)	$40
2106 Lotus Essex MK3 (1981)	$40
2107 Tyrell 009 (1979)	$40
2108 Ferrari 312T5 (1980)	$50
2109 Renault RE20 (1980)	$40

Bburago Bijoux 1:24 scale models (1500 series models)

1501 Citroen 15 CV TA (1938)	$15 – 20
1502 Jaguar XK 120 Roadster (1948)	$15 – 20
1503 Bugatti Atlantic (1936)	$15 – 20
1506 Ferrari 250 LM "Monza" (1966)	$15 – 20
1507 Ferrari Testa Rossa (1957)	$15 – 20
1508 Jaguar XK 120 Coupe (1948)	$15 – 20
1509 Mercedes-Benz SSK (1928)	$15 – 20
1510 Ferrari 250 GTO (1962)	$15 – 20
1511 Ferrari 275 GTB 4 (1966)	$15 – 20
1524 Chevrolet Corvette (1957)	$15 – 20
1532 Ferrari 456 GT (1992)	$15 – 20
1535 Bugatti EB 110 (1991)	$15 – 20
1536 Ferrari 456 GT (1992)	$15 – 20
1539 Ferrari 348 tb (1989)	$15 – 20

Bburago Diamonds 1:18 scale models (3000 series models)

3001 Rolls Royce Camargue, 1:22, $20 – 30

3002 Mercedes-Benz SSKL "Caracciola" (1931)	$20 – 30
3004 Ferrari Testarossa (1984)	$20 – 30
3005 Bugatti "Type 59" (1934)	$20 – 30
3006 Jaguar SS 100 (1937)	$20 – 30
3007 Ferrari 250 Testa Rossa (1957)	$20 – 30
3008 Alfa Romeo 2300 Spider (1932)	$20 – 30
3009 Mercedes-Benz SSK (1928)	$20 – 30
3010 Lancia Aurelia B24 Spider (1955)	$20 – 30
3011 Ferrari 250 GTO (1962)	$20 – 30
3013 Mercedes-Benz 300 SL (1954)	$20 – 30
3014 Alfa Romeo 8C 2300 Monza (1931)	$20 – 30

3015 Mercedes-Benz 300 SL (1954) . . . . $20 – 30

3016 Jaguar "E" Cabriolet (1961) . . . . $20 – 30

3018 Jaguar "E" Coupe (1961) . . . . $20 – 30

3019 Ferrari Testarossa (1984) . . . . $20 – 30

3020 Mercedes-Benz 500 K Roadster (1936) . . . . $20 – 30

3021 Porsche 356 B Coupe (1961) . . . . $20 – 30

3022 Ferrari F40 (1987) . . . . $20 – 30

3024 Chevrolet Corvette (1957), $20 – 30

3025 Dodge Viper RT/10 (1992) . . . . $20 – 30

3026 Jaguar "E" Cabriolet (1961) . . . . $20 – 30

3027 Ferrari GTO (1984) . . . . $20 – 30

3028 Lamborghini Diablo (1990) . . . . $20 – 30

3029 Ferrari 348 tb Evoluzione (1992) . . . . $20 – 30

3031 Porsche 356 B Cabriolet (1961) . . . . $20 – 30

3032 Ferrari F40 (1987) . . . . $20 – 30

3034 Chevrolet Corvette (1957) . . . . $20 – 30

3035 Bugatti EB 110 (1991) . . . . $20 – 30

3036 Ferrari 456 GT (1992) . . . . $20 – 30

3037 Lamborghini Countach (1988) . . . . $20 – 30

3038 Jaguar "E" Coupe (1961) . . . . $20 – 30

3039 Ferrari 348 tb (1989) . . . . $20 – 30

3041 Lamborghini Diablo (1990) . . . . $20 – 30

3042 Ferrari F40 Evoluzione (1992) . . . . $20 – 30

3045 Bugatti EB 110 (1991) . . . . $20 – 30

3047 Lamborghini Countach (1988) . . . . $20 – 30

3051 Porsche 356 B Cabriolet (1961) . . . . $20 – 30

3055 Bugatti EB 110 (1991) . . . . $20 – 30

3057 Ferrari GTO Rally (1986) . . . . $20 – 30

3065 Dodge Viper RT/10 (1992) . . . . $20 – 30

Bburago Deluxe 1:18 scale kits (3500 series kits)

3505 Bugatti "Type 59" (1934) . . . . $25 – 30

3507 Ferrari 250 Testa Rossa (1957) . . . . $25 – 30

3509 Mercedes-Benz SSK (1928) . . . . $25 – 30

3511 Ferrari 250 GTO (1962) . . . . $25 – 30

3513 Mercedes-Benz 300 SL (1954) . . . . $25 – 30

3514 Alfa Romeo 8C 2300 Monza (1931) . . . . $25 – 30

3516 Jaguar "E" Cabriolet (1961) . . . . $25 – 30

3519 Ferrari Testarossa (1984) . . . . $25 – 30

3520 Mercedes-Benz 500K Roadster (1936) . . . . $25 – 30

3521 Porsche 356 B Coupe (1961) . . . . $25 – 30

3525 Dodge Viper RT/10 (1992) . . . . $25 – 30

3527 Ferrari GTO (1984) . . . . $25 – 30

3528 Lamborghini Diablo (1990) . . . . $25 – 30

3529 Ferrari 348 tb Evoluzoine (1991) . . . . $25 – 30

3534 Chevrolet Corvette (1957) . . . . $25 – 30

Bburago Executive 1:18 scale kits (3700 series kits)

3702 Mercedes-Benz SSKL "Caracciola" (1931) . . . . $25 – 30

3718 Jaguar "E" Coupe (1961) . . . . $25 – 30

3721 Porsche 356 B Coupe 1961) . . . . $25 – 30

3724 Chevrolet Corvette (1957) . . . . $25 – 30

3725 Dodge Viper RT/10 (1992) . . . . $25 – 30

3731 Porsche 356 B Cabriolet (1961) . . . . $25 – 30

3732 Ferrari F40 (1987) . . . . $25 – 30

3735 Bugatti EB 110 (1991) . . . . $25 – 30

3737 Lamborghini Countach (1988) . . . . $25 – 30

3739 Ferrari 348 tb (1989) . . . . $25 – 30

3741 Lamborghini Diablo (1990) . . . . $25 – 30

3746 Ferrari 456 GT (1992) . . . . $25 – 30

Bburago 4000 Series 1:43 scale models issued in 1988

4001 Lancia Stratos . . . . $5 – 7

4002 Peugeot 205 . . . . $5 – 7

4003 Audi Quattro . . . . $5 – 7

4004 Ferrari 512 BB . . . . $5 – 7

4005 Fiat Panda . . . . $5 – 7

4006 Jeep Renegade . . . . $5 – 7

4007 BMW M1 . . . . $5 – 7

4008 Alfa Romeo 33 . . . . $5 – 7

4009 Saab 900 Turbo . . . . $5 – 7

4010 Ferrari 308 . . . . $5 – 7

4011 Range Rover . . . . $5 – 7

4012 Porsche 935 . . . . $5 – 7

4021 Lancia Stratos . . . . $5 – 7

4022 Peugeot 205 . . . . $5 – 7

4023 Audi Quattro . . . . $5 – 7

4024 Ferrari 512 BB . . . . $5 – 7

4025 Fiat Panda . . . . $5 – 7

4026 Jeep Renegade . . . . $5 – 7

4027 BMW M1 . . . . $5 – 7

4028 Alfa Romeo 33 . . . . $5 – 7

4029 Saab 900 Turbo . . . . $5 – 7

4030 Ferrari 308 . . . . $5 – 7

4031 Range Rover . . . . $5 – 7

4032 Porsche 935 . . . . $5 – 7

Bburago Pocket 1:43 scale models
(Box 4100 series, Blister 4800 series)

4101 Saab 900 Turbo, $3 – 5

4102 Mercedes-Benz 190 E . . . . $3 – 5

4103 Porsche 924 Turbo . . . . $3 – 5

4104 Ferrari Testarossa, red with white interior . . . . $3 – 5

4105 BMW M1 IMSA . . . . $3 – 5

4105 Dodge Viper RT/10, black with silver racing stripes. . . $3 – 5

4106 Ferrari 512 BB Daytona, $3 – 5

4107 Ferrari GTO Rally, red with rally accents, white interior. $3 – 5
4108 Lancia Stratos VSD . . . . $3 – 5

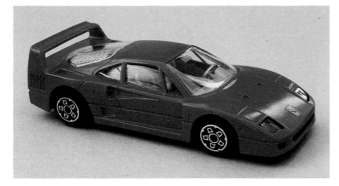

4108 Ferrari F40, red with silver gray interior, $3 – 5

4109 Renault 9 . . . . $3 – 5
4109 Mercedes-Benz 300 SL convertible, top down, metallic blue,
    cream interior . . . . $3 – 5
4110 Alfa Romeo Giulietta Alpilatte. . . . . $3 – 5
4110 Porsche 928 Grand Am . . . . $3 – 5
4111 Porsche 924 Turbo Gr. 2 . . . . $3 – 5
4112 Renault R9 Rally. . . . . $3 – 5
4112 Suzuki Vitara Raid . . . . $3 – 5
4113 Fiat Panda Rally . . . . $3 – 5
4114 Porsche 911. . . . . $3 – 5
4115 Renault R5 Turbo. . . . . $3 – 5

4115 Dodge Viper GTS, metallic blue with white racing stripes, $3 – 5

4116 Fiat Ritmo Totip. . . . . $3 – 5
4116 Peugeot 205 Safari . . . . $3 – 5

4117 Ferrari 308 GTB, $3 – 5

4118 Mazda RX7 . . . . $3 – 5
4119 Fiat Uno . . . . $3 – 5
4120 Fiat Uno Rally . . . . $3 – 5
4121 Fiat Regata. . . . . $3 – 5

4122 Renegade Jeep, $3 – 5

4123 Peugeot 205 Turbo 16 . . . . $3 – 5
4124 Alfa Romeo 33 Rally. . . . . $3 – 5
4125 Peugeot 205 GTI . . . . $3 – 5

4125 Dodge Viper RT/10, red, $3 – 5

4126 Porsche 959 Rally. . . . . $3 – 5
4127 Lamborghini Countach 5000 . . . . $3 – 5
4128 Ferrari F40. . . . . $3 – 5
4129 Ferrari 348 tb Evoluzione, red with rally decals, cream interi-
    or . . . . $3 – 5
4130 Renault Clio RT . . . . $3 – 5
4131 Land Rover 109 Aziza . . . . $3 – 5
4132 Jeep CJ5 Renegade. . . . . $3 – 5
4133 Ferrari 512 BB . . . . $3 – 5

4134 Fiat Regata Rally . . . . $3 – 5
4134 Fiat Tipo Rally . . . . $3 – 5
4135 Lancia Delta S4 . . . . $3 – 5
4136 Ferrari 456 GT, red . . . . $3 – 5

4137 Lamborghini Countach 400S, $3 – 5

4138 Fiat Cinquecento Rally . . . . $3 – 5
4139 Ferrari 348 tb, red with cream interior. . . . . $3 – 5
4140 MCA Centenaire, metallic silver blue. . . . . $3 – 5
4141 Lamborghini Diablo, yellow . . . . $3 – 5
4142 Porsche 935 Vaillant. . . . . $3 – 5
4143 Ford Sierra Group A. . . . . $3 – 5
4144 Fiat Punto . . . . $3 – 5
4146 Ferrari 456 GT, metallic dark blue with pale beige interior . $3 – 5
4147 Porsche 911 Turbo. . . . . $3 – 5

4148 Ferrari 308 GTB Rally, red "PIONEER" rally accents, black interior, light gray steering wheel and rally lights on nose, $3 – 5

4149 Mercedes-Benz 190 E. . . . . $3 – 5
4150 Peugeot 405 Raid. $3 – 5
4151 Lamborghini Diablo, red with cream interior . . . . . $3 – 5
4152 Chevrolet Corvette . . . . $3 – 5
4153 Porsche 911 Carrera Super Cup, yellow with rally accents, light gray interior . . . . $3 – 5
4155 Citroen Xantia . . . . $3 – 5
4156 Range Rover T Castrol . . . . $3 – 5
4157 Ferrari Testarossa, yellow with cream interior . . . . $3 – 5
4158 BMW 535i, metallic dark champagne red with light gray interior. . . . . $3 – 5
4159 Audi Quattro GT Sanyo . . . . $3 – 5
4160 Renault R5 Turbo Monte Carlo . . . . $3 – 5
4160 Renault Clio 16V . . . . $3 – 5
4161 Porsche 959. . . . . $3 – 5

4164 Alfa Romeo Giulietta Group 2 . . . . $3 – 5
4165 Mercedes-Benz 450 SC Mampe. . . . . $3 – 5
4165 Citroen Xantia . . . . $3 – 5
4165 Dodge Viper RT/10, yellow . . . . $3 – 5
4166 Lancia Stratos Pirelli . . . . $3 – 5
4167 BMW M3 G.T. Cup, green with "tic tac" rally accents, gray interior . . . . $3 – 5
4168 Fiat Ritmo Abarth. $3 – 5
4168 Ferrari F40 Evoluzione, red with rally accents, silver gray interior . . . . $3 – 5
4169 BMW M1. . . . . $3 – 5
4170 Lancia Beta Martini . . . . $3 – 5
4170 MIG Georgia Centenaire. . . . . $3 – 5
4171 Land Rover Raid . . . . $3 – 5
4172 Lancia Beta Alitalia. . . . . $3 – 5
4174 Mazda RX7 Group 2. . . . . $3 – 5

4175 Ferrari GTO, yellow with cream interior, $3 – 5

4176 Alfa Romeo Giulietta Polizia . . . . $3 – 5
4177 Alfa Romeo Giulietta Carabinieri. . . . . $3 – 5
4178 BMW 535i . . . . $3 – 5
4179 Fiat Tipo . . . . $3 – 5
4180 Lancia Delta Rally . . . . $3 – 5
4181 Mercedes-Benz 300 SL . . . . $3 – 5
4183 Ford Sierra Group A Rally . . . . $3 – 5
4184 Porsche 935 Momo . . . . $3 – 5
4185 Porsche 911 Carrera '93, red with light gray interior. . . $3 – 5
4186 Alfa Romeo 33 Polizia . . . . $3 – 5
4187 Alfa Romeo 33 Carabinieri . . . . $3 – 5
4189 Ferrari 348tb . . . . $3 – 5
4190 Peugeot 405 Safari . . . . $3 – 5
4191 Porsche 928, red with light gray interior . . . . $3 – 5

4192 Chevrolet Corvette, $3 – 5

4193 Alfa Romeo 33. . . . . $3 – 5

4193 Fiat Cinquecento . . . . $3 – 5
4194 Suzuki Vitara . . . . $3 – 5

Bburago Portachiavi 1:87 scale (4500 series models)

4513 Mercedes-Benz 300 SL . . . . $2 – 5
4519 Ferrari Testarossa. . . . . $2 – 5
4532 Ferrari F40. . . . . $2 – 5
4563 Porsche 959. . . . . $2 – 5

Bburago Kit Super 1:24 scale (5100 series kits)

5102 Kit Porsche 911 Armel . . . . $15 – 20
5105 Kit Mercedes-Benz 190 E . . . . $15 – 20
5106 Kit Peugeot 205 Turbo 16 . . . . $15 – 20
5115 Kit Lancia Delta S4 . . . . $15 – 20
5119 Kit Alfa Romeo 75 . . . . $15 – 20
5121 Kit Porsche 959 Raid. . . . . $15 – 20
5129 Kit Ferrari 348 tb Monteshell . . . . $15 – 20
5131 Kit Peugeot 405 Raid . . . . $15 – 20
5133 Kit Ferrari 512 BB Daytona . . . . $15 – 20
5142 Kit Kremer Porsche 935 Turbo . . . . $15 – 20
5148 Kit Ferrari 308 GTB . . . . $15 – 20
5172 Kit Ferrari GTO Pioneer . . . . $15 – 20
5173 Kit BMW 635 CSi . . . . $15 – 20
5194 Kit Fiat Cinquecento Rally. . . . . $15 – 20
5199 Kit Porsche 924 Turbo . . . . $15 – 20

Bburago Kit Bijoux 1:24 scale (5500 series kits)

5501 Kit Citroen 15 cv TA (1938). . . . . $15 – 20
5502 Kit Jaguar XK 120 Roadster (1948). . . . . $15 – 20
5504 Kit Ferrari Testarossa (1984) . . . . $15 – 20
5506 Kit Ferrari 250 LM Daytona (1966). . . . . $15 – 20
5507 Kit Ferrari Testa Rossa (1957) . . . . $15 – 20
5509 Kit Mercedes-Benz 300 SL (1954) . . . . $15 – 20
5510 Kit Ferrari 250 GTO (1962) . . . . $15 – 20
5513 Kit Ford AC Cobra 427 (1965) . . . . $15 – 20
5524 Kit Chevrolet Corvette (1957) . . . . $15 – 20
5532 Kit Mercedes-Benz 300 SL (1954) . . . . $15 – 20
5537 Kit Lamborghini Countach (1988) . . . . $15 – 20
5539 Kit Ferrari 348 tb (1989) . . . . $15 – 20
5540 Kit Ferrari F40 (1987) . . . . $15 – 20

Bburago Grand Prix 1:24 Scale Formula One Racers
(6100 series models)

6101 Ferrari 641/2, "27" . . . . $15 – 20
6102 Benetton Ford . . . . $15 – 20
6103 Grand Prix F.1 . . . . $15 – 20
6104 Race Champion . . . . $15 – 20
6108 Williams FW14 . . . . $15 – 20
6109 Bburago Team . . . . $15 – 20
6110 Formula USA . . . . $15 – 20
6121 Formula 3000 . . . . $15 – 20
6122 Indy Team . . . . $15 – 20
6128 Ferrari 641/2, "28" . . . . $15 – 20

Bburago Kit Diamonds 1:18 scale (7000 series kits)

7002 Kit Mercedes SSKL Mille Miglia (1931) . . . . $25 – 30
7005 Kit Bugatti "Type 59" Grand Prix (1934) . . . . $25 – 30
7006 Kit Jaguar SS 100 Targa Florio (1937). . . . . $25 – 30
7007 Kit Ferrari Testa Rossa Le Mans (1957) . . . . $25 – 30
7008 Kit Alfa Romeo 2300 Touring (1932) . . . . $25 – 30
7009 Kit Mercedes SSK Montecarlo (1928) . . . . $25 – 30
7010 Kit Lancia Aurelia B24 Spider (1955) . . . . $25 – 30
7011 Kit Ferrari 250 GTO Nurburgring (1962) . . . . $25 – 30

7013 Kit Mercedes-Benz 300 SL (1954) . . . . $25 – 30
7014 Kit Alfa Romeo 8C G. P. Mon. (1931) . . . . $25 – 30
7016 Kit Jaguar "E" Cabriolet T. d. Fr. (1961) . . . . $25 – 30
7018 Kit Jaguar "E" Coupe (1961) . . . . $25 – 30
7019 Kit Ferrari Testarossa (1984) . . . . $25 – 30
7020 Kit Mercedes-Benz 500K Roadster (1936). . . . . . . $25 – 30
7021 Kit Porsche 356 B Coupe (1961) . . . . $25 – 30
7024 Kit Chevrolet Corvette (1957) . . . . $25 – 30
7025 Kit Dodge Viper RT/10 (1992). . . . . $25 – 30
7027 Kit Ferrari GTO (1984) . . . . $25 – 30
7032 Kit Ferrari F40 (1987) . . . . $25 – 30
7035 Kit Bugatti EB110 (1991) . . . . $25 – 30
7039 Kit Ferrari 348 tb (1989) . . . . $25 – 30
7041 Kit Lamborghini Diablo (1990) . . . . $25 – 30

Beaut

Beaut Manufacturing Company was based in northern New Jersey and produced just a few simple castings of pre-World War II models from 1946 until 1950. The cars were made of a single casting like Tootsietoys, with large tires.

Fire Chief Car. . . . . $20 – 30
Police Car . . . . $20 – 30
Sedan . . . . $20 – 30
Taxi . . . . $20 – 30
Van . . . . $20 – 30

Beckman Collection

Beckman Jr./Sr. High School takes advantage of its location in Dyersville, Iowa, home of the world-renowned Ertl company, to offer an assortment of customized Ertl Scale Models and First Gear models to raise funds, with all proceeds benefitting the educational enrichment of its students. If you have questions about any of the items listed below, or if you would like to order any of the items, call or write Beckman Jr/Sr High School, 1325 9th St. SE, Dyersville IA 52040, 319-875-7188.

Tractor Trailers, 1:64 Scale

Ertl International Harvester with "Chrysler" logos . $192 per case (12) or $20 each
Ertl International Harvester COE with "Chrysler" logos. . . . . $192 per case (12) or $20 each
Ertl GMC with "GMC Motorsports" logos. . . . . $192 per case (12) or $20 each
Spec Cast, "Goodyear". . . . . $192 per case (12) or $20 each
Spec Cast, "Beckman Collection" . . $192 per case (12) or $20 each
Ertl, "Cadillac" logos . . . . $264 per case (12) or $27 each
Ertl, "Pontiac" logos. . . . . $264 per case (12) or $27 each

Other Toys Available

Ertl "Beckman 2nd Edition" 1913 Bank, 1:25. . . . $72 per case (12) or $8 each
Ertl "Beckman 3rd Edition" 1950 Bank, 1:25 . . . $132 per case (12) or $15 each
Scale Models "Beckman 4th Edition" 1931 Bank, 1:25 . . . . . . $132 per case (12) or $15 each
Scale Models "Co-Op" Tanker Bank (Sampler), 1:25 . . . . $132 per case (12) or $15 each
Scale Models "Co-Op" Tanker Bank (Production), 1:25 . . . . . $132 per case (12) or $16 each

Ertl "Mountain Dew" Delivery Truck, 1:64 . . . . . $180 per case (12)
or $10 each
Ertl "Diet Pepsi" Delivery Truck, 1:64 . . . . $180 per case (12)
or $12 each
Ertl "7-Up" Beverage Delivery Truck, 1:64 . . . . $228 per case (12)
or $20 each
First Gear "Dyersville" Grain Truck, 1:34 . . . . . $192 per case (12)
or $20 each
First Gear 1951 Ford Dry Goods Van, 1:34 . . . . $192 per case (12)
or $22 each
Ertl International Harvester 90s School Bus Bank, 1:50 . . . . . . $204
per case (12) or $26 each
Ertl "University of Notre Dame" 1938 Panel Truck Bank $252
per case (12) or $26 each
Ertl Premier Edition 1955 Ward LaFrance Firetruck Bank,
"Dyersville, Iowa" . . . . $242 for 12 or 26 each
Scale Models 1:16 Scale Tractor Series: John Deere A, Allis-
Chalmers Series IV, D17 . . . . $37.50 (6 or more)

BELGIUM TRUCKS

Diecast Miniatures lists two versions of a Ford T-Bird under the Belgium Trucks brand. No other information is available as of this writing.

1960 Ford Thunderbird Convertible, green/yellow/beige $268
1960 Ford Thunderbird Convertible, pink/blue/black $268

BENBROS

Benbros of Great Britain, originally known as Benson Brothers, was actually started by Nathan and Jack Benenson. The Benbros name was adopted in 1951. They produced diecast models around the same time as Lesney Products Co. introduced Matchbox toys and were similar in quality. A few models have even been confused with their Matchbox counterparts, especially the Coronation Coach.

BENBROS NUMBERED MODELS

1 Horse Drawn Hay Cart $25
2 Horse Drawn Log Cart $25
3 Military Motorcycle and Sidecar, "AA" $30
4 Stage Coach with Four Horses $25
5 Horse Drawn Gypsy Caravan $15
6 Horse Drawn Milk Cart $25
7 Three-Wheeled Electric Milk Trolley $25
8 Foden Tractor and Log Trailer $25
9 Dennis Five Engine with Escape Ladder $25
10 Crawler Bulldozer $15
11 Crawler Tractor with Hay Rake $15
12 Army Scout Car $15
13 Austin Champ $15
14 Centurion Tank $15
15 Vespa Scooter with Rider $25
16 Streamlined Express Locomotive (TV Series only) $25
16 Chevrolet Nomad Station Wagon (Mighty Midget only) $15
17 Crawler Tractor with Dise Harrow $15
18 Hudson Tourer $15
19 Crawler Tractor and Trailer $15
20 Foden 8-wheel Flat Lorry $15
21 Foden 8-wheel Open Truck $15
22 ERF Petrol Tanker $25

23 AEC Box Van $15
23 AEC Box Van $25
24 Field Gun $10
25 Spyker $10
26 1904 Vauxhall 5 HP $10
27 1906 Rolls-Royce $10
28 Foden 8-wheel Flatbed Truck with Chains $25
29 RAC Motorcycle and Sidecar $40
30 AEC Army Box Van $30
30 Bedford Army Box Van $25
31 AEC Lovry with Tilt $15
31 Bedford Lorry with Tilt $25
32 AEC Compressor Lorry $15
32 Bedford Compressor Truck $25
33 AEC Crane Lorry $15
33 Bedford Crane Lorry $25
34 Land Rover, "AA" $25
35 Army Land Rover $25
36 Royal Mail Land Rover $25
37 Wolseley Six-Eighty Police Car $15
38 Daimler Ambulance $30
39 Bedford Milk Float $15
40 American Ford Convertible $15
41 Army Hudson Tourer $25
42 Army Motorcycle and Sidecar $40
43 Bedford Articulated Box Van $25
44 Bedford Articulated Lowside Truck $25
45 Bedford Articulated Low Loader $25
46 Bedford Articulated Petrol Tanker $40
47 Bedford Articulated Crane Truck $15
48 Bedford Articulated Flatbed Truck with Chains $25
49 Karrier Bantam "Coca-Cola" Bottle Truck $55
50* RAC Land Rover (*Number not confirmed) $40

BENBROS UNNUMBERED MODELS

AA Land Rover, 1:38 . . . . $80
AEC Flat Truck with Chains 1:45 . . . . $75
AEC Truck, 1:45 . . . . $75
AEC Covered Truck, 1:45 . . . . $75
AEC Army Covered Truck, 1:45 . . . . $75
AEC Excavator Truck, 1:45 . . . . $85
AEC Truck-Mounted Crane, 1:45 . . . . $85
Bulldozer, 1:43 . . . . $40
Coronation Coach, Souvenir of the Coronation of Queen Elizabeth
II, 4½", 1953 . . . . $150
Daimler Ambulance, 1:43 . . . . $75
Dodge Army Radar Truck, 1:50 . . . . $85
Euclid Dump Truck, 1:50 . . . . $50
Excavator, 1:43 . . . . $35
Ferguson Tractor, 1:43 . . . . $65
Ferguson Hydraulic Shovel, 1:43 . . . . $45
Tanker, "Esso Motor Oil," 1:45 . . . . $75
Tanker, "Petrol Goes a Long Way," 1:45 . . . . $25

BEST

There are actually four toy manufacturers named Best, all unrelated. One started in the 1930s in Kansas by John M. Best, Sr., another in just the past decade in Pesaro, Italy, by Marco Grassini. A third company called Best-Box is an obscure brand of miniature vehicles made in Holland. Their resemblance to Efsi toys of Holland may not be coincidental. A fourth company is based in Taiwan.

Best Toys of Kansas

It was in the midst of the hard economic times of the 1930s that John M. Best, Sr., started Best Toy & Novelty Factory. His main business as a printer who worked with metal alloys lent itself to a sideline in lead alloy toys. The company started as a family hobby and continued until 1939 when Best was purchased by Ralstoy of Ralston, Kansas. In the meantime, Best maintained a close association with the Kansas Toy Company in John Best's home town of Clifton, Kansas, occasionally swapping dies. Many early Best models are actually Ralstoy or Kansas Toy models. Unlike recent reproductions, Best originals are distinguished by white rubber wheels or embossing of the words "Made in USA." Several models used the metal wheels common to Kansas Toy originals, while others possessed wooden hubs with rubber tires. The familiar oversized white tires made of soft rubber eventually became a standard on Best models. The original line of Best toys were an assortment of generic sedans, coupes, and racers typically 3½ to 4" long, along with an oil transport measuring 6¾".

Racer #76, 4¼" long. $30
Racer #81, 4½". $30
Racer #85, record car with large square fin and driver, 4" $30
Sedan #86, 2-door fastback, slant grille with grid pattern, possibly a Lincoln, 4" $30
Sedan #87, possibly a Brewster. $30
Sedan #90, 2-door airflow, hood reaches front bumper with no grille, 3½". $30
Sedan #91, 2-door airflow, high style vee grille, faired front fenders, possibly a Cadillac, 3½" $30
Coupe #92, chopped top, heart-shaped grille, possibly a Dodge, 3¾" $30
Coupe #93, streamlined with hood similar to #91, grid pattern grille, possibly a Cadillac, 3⅝". $30
Large Sedan Taxi #94, 2-door airflow, similar to #90, 4½" $30
Sedan #95, 2-door, similar to #94, with 3 headlamps, similar to a Chrysler-Briggs show car, 3½". $30
Sedan #95, same as #94 with "Police Dept." shield on doors, 3½". $30
Coupe #96, same as #93, 3⅝". $30
Large Bluebird Racer #97, record car with driver, large fin, 12 exhaust ports, 4½" $30
Coupe #98. . . . . $30
Coupe #99, similar to a Pontiac, 4" $30
Sedan #100 Pontiac, 4". $30
Oil Transport Cab Unit #101, sleeper cab, slanted grille, similar to an International, 3¼". $25
Oil Transport Trailer #102, streamlined "GASOLINE," attaches to #101 Cab Unit, 6¾". $30
Sedan, 2-door airflow, similar to a DeSoto, 3⅞". $30

Best Model of Italy

New 1:43 scale precision models are currently being produced from Pesaro, Italy, by Marco Grassini under the Best brand name. They represent models of Porsches, Alfa Romeos, Jaguars, and Ferraris. While it would seem their product line is extensive, it is actually based on issuing many variations of just a few models. An interesting observation is that Bang, Best Model, and Art Model replicas are all 1:43 scale, all three brands are based at 61100 Pesaro, Italy, Via Toscana, 85, and their catalogs are similar, as well as their models. Box Model seems to have a similar relationship.

Alfa Romeo TZ1 Clienti, red, #9059. . . . . $22
Alfa Romeo TZ1 Monza, 1963, white, #9060 . . . . $22
Alfa Romeo TZ1 Targa Florio, 1965, yellow, "60," #9061 . . . . . $22
Alfa Romeo TZ1 Targa Florio, 1965, red, "70," #9062. . . . . . . $22
Alfa Romeo TZ1 Targa Florio, 1964, red, "58," #9067. . . . . . . $18
Alfa Romeo TZ1 Le Mans, 1964, blue, "40," #9068. . . . . $18
Alfa Romeo TZ2, 1965 . . . . $25
Ferrari P2 Prova, red, #9019 . . . . $25
Ferrari 250 GT Lusso, 1964. . . . . $23
Ferrari 250 LM, 1964 Prova, red, #9008 . . . . $25
Ferrari 250 LM Nurburgring, 1964, red, #9009 . . . . $25
Ferrari 250 LM Le Mans, 1965, yellow, #9010. . . . . $25
Ferrari 250 LM Le Mans, 1965, red, #9025 . . . . $25
Ferrari 250 LM Le Mans Nurburgring, 1965, green, "8," #9054. . $25
Ferrari 250 LM Monza, 1966, white, #9011. . . . . $25
Ferrari 250 LM Bridgehampton, 1965, silver, #9017 . . . . $25
Ferrari 250 LM Kyalami, 1966, yellow, #9018. . . . . $25
Ferrari 250 LM Tour de France, 1969, red, #9023 . . . . $25
Ferrari 275 GTB/4 Stradale (Street) Hardtop, red, #9001. . . . . $25
Ferrari 275 GTB/4 Stradale Hardtop, yellow, #9002 . . . . $25
Ferrari 275 GTB/4 Convertible Spyder, top down, yellow, #9003R1 . . . . $25
Ferrari 275 GTB/4 Convertible Spyder, top down, red, #9003G2 . $25
Ferrari 275 GTB/4 Convertible Spyder, top up, white, #9004 . . $25
Ferrari 275 GTB/4 Convertible Spyder, top down, black, #9005 . $25
Ferrari 275 GTB/4 Rally Montecarlo, 1966, hardtop, yellow, #9006. . . . . $25
Ferrari 275 GTB/4 Targa Florio, 1966, hardtop, red, #9007. . . $25
Ferrari 275 GTB/4 Tour de France, 1969, silver, 9015 . . . . . . $25
Ferrari 275 GTB/4 Le Mans, 1967, red, #9024 . . . . $25
Ferrari 290 MM Prova, 1957, red, #9063 . . . . $22
Ferrari 290 MM Buenos Aires, 1957, red, "10," #9064. . . . . . . $22
Ferrari 290 MM Mille Miglia, 1956, red, "600," #9069 . . . . . . $25
Ferrari 290 MM Mille Miglia, 1956, red, "548," #9070 . . . . . . $25
Ferrari 330 GTC, 1966 . . . . $25
Ferrari 330 P2 Nurburgring, 1965, red, #9020. . . . . $25
Ferrari 330 P2 Limited Edition, silver plated $44
Ferrari 330 P2 Limited Edition, gold plated $44
Ferrari 365 P2 Le Mans, 1965, "17," red, #9026. . . . . $25
Ferrari 365 P2 Le Mans, 1965, "18," red, #9021 . . . . $25
Ferrari 750 Monza Prova, red, #9044. . . . . $25
Ferrari 750 Monza Daytona, 1955, white, #9055. . . . . $25
Ferrari 750 Monza Carrera Panamericana, 1954, black, "2," #9058 . . . . $25
Ferrari 750 Monza Goodwood, 1955, red, #9045. . . . . $22
Ferrari 750 Monza Spa, 1955, yellow, "34," #9046 . . . . $25
Ferrari 750 Monza Spa, 1955, yellow, "33," #9049 . . . . $25
Ferrari 750 Monza Targa Florio, 1955, red, #9047 . . . . $25
Ferrari 750 Monza Tourist Trophy, 1955, red, #9048 . . . . $25
Ferrari 750 Monza MM #254 Alesi, 1992 . . . . $28
Ferrari 750 Monza Limited Edition, 1992, silver plated $44
Ferrari 750 Monza Limited Edition, 1992, gold plated. $44

Ferrari 860 Monza Prova, red, #9051 . . . . $24
Ferrari 860 Monza Sebring, 1956, red, "17," #9052 . . . . . $24
Ferrari 860 Monza Mille Miglia, 1956, red, "556," #9053 . . . . . $24
Ferrari 860 Monza MM "328," 1992 . . . . $28
Jaguar E Coupe Guida Sinistra, red, #9012R1 . . . . $25
Jaguar E Coupe Guida Sinistra, black, #9012N3 . . . . $25
Jaguar E Coupe Inglese Guida Destra, black, #9014V4 . . . . . . $25
Jaguar E Coupe Inglese guida Destra, white, #9014B5 . . . . . . $25
Jaguar E Coupe Tourist Trophy, 1962, blue, #9016 . . . . . $25
Jaguar E Coupe Le Mans, 1962, white, #9022 . . . . $25
Jaguar E Spyder, top down, black, red, or silver, #9027 . . . . $25
Jaguar E Spyder, top down, amaranth or green, #9028 . . . . . . $25
Jaguar E Spyder, top up, white with black top, #9029 . . . . $25
Jaguar E Spyder, hard top, red, #9030 . . . . $25
Jaguar E Spyder Tourist Trophy, 1962, white, #9038 . . . . $25
Jaguar E Spyder Oulton Park, 1961, blue, #9036 . . . . . . $25
Jaguar E Spyder Nurburgring, 1963, silver, #9037 . . . . $25
Jaguar E Spyder Brands Hatch, 1965, white, #9038 . . . . $25
Jaguar E Spyder, 1961 . . . . $22
Jaguar E Spyder, 1962 . . . . $22
Jaguar E Spyder, 1963 . . . . $24
Jaguar E Spyder, 1965 . . . . $24
Porsche 908/2 Prova, white, #9040 . . . . $25
Porsche 980/2 Brands Hatch, 1969, "54," #9041 . . . . $25
Porsche 980/2 Brands Hatch, 1969, "53," #9042 . . . . $25
Porsche 980/2 Brands Hatch, 1969, "55," #9043 . . . . $25
Porsche 980/2 Watkins Glen, 1972, yellow, #9065 . . . . $25
Porsche 980/2 Zeltweg, 1970, white, #9066 . . . . $25
Porsche 908/3 Prova, red, #9033 . . . . $25
Porsche 908/3 Nurburgring, 1970, white $25
Porsche 908/3 Targa Florio, 1970, light blue, "40," #9034 . . . . . $25
Porsche 908/3 Targa Florio, 1970, light blue, "36," #9034 . . . . . $25
Porsche 908/3 Targa Florio, 1970, light blue, "12," #9039 . . . . . $25
Porsche 908/3, 1969 . . . . $24
Porsche 908/3 Targa Florio 1970, white with red "20," #9050 . . $22

BEST MODEL OF ITALY - GOLD AND SILVER SERIES

1001 Ferrari 275 GTB/4 Coupe, silver $60
1002 Ferrari 275 GTB/4 Spyder, silver $60
1003 Ferrari 330 P2, silver $60
1004 Ferrari 750 Monza, silver $60
2001 Ferrari 275 GTB/4 Coupe, gold $75
2002 Ferrari 275 GTB/4 Spyder, gold $75
2003 Ferrari 330 P2, gold $75
2004 Ferrari 750 Monza, gold $75

BEST-BOX OF HOLLAND

Best-Box toys were made in Holland in the 60s. Even the crudest of these hard-to-find toys have features that make them distinctive. The Ford Model T's are simple castings. But the plastic spoked wheels and black plastic tires add to their realism. The Porsche 911S features opening doors and represents a fairly accurate representative of the actual car after which the toy is styled.

501 DAF 600 Saloon $25
502 DAF 1400 Refuse Truck $20
503 DAF 1400 Fire Engine $25
504 DAF Torpedo Dump Truck $25
505 DAF Torpedo Open Truck $20
506 DAF Torpedo Closed Truck $20

2501 Ford Model T Pickup $20
2502 Ford Model T Tanker $20

2502A Porsche 911S, $25

2503 Ford Model T Breakdown Truck $20
2504 Ford Model T Delivery Van $20
2505 Ford Model T Coupe $20
2506 Ford Model T Sedan $20
2507 Ford Model T Advertisement $20
2507A BMW 2000 CS $25
2508 Volkswagen 1600 TL $30
2509 Mercedes-Benz 220 SE Coupe $20
2509A BRM Formula 1 . . . . $20
2510 Citroën ID19 Station Wagon $20
2511 Ford Taurus 17 M Super $20
2512 Opel Rekord $20
2512A Honda Formula 1 . . . . $20
2513 Jaguar E-Type Convertible $20
2514 Mercedes-Benz 280 SL Convertible $20
2515 Opel Rekord 1900 . . . . $20
2516 Mercedes-Benz 250 SE Coupe $20
2517 1966 Ferrari 312 Formula 1 . . . . $15
2518 Brabham Formula 1 . . . . $15
2519 Cooper-Maserati Formula 1 . . . . $15
2520 Lotus Formula 1 . . . . $15
2521 Citroën Dyane $20
2522 Ford Transit Van $20

BEST TOY CO., LTD.

No.9, Lane 410, Niu Pu Rd., Hsinchu, Taiwan, R.O.C. Not much is known about this company. It is believed that it is not in any way connected with any of the other companies and does not produce any diecast toys.

BIJOU (SEE MODELAUTO)

BISON

Bison models are made in Germany.
Tatra Dump Truck, 1:43 . . . . $5

BITSI-TOYS (SEE LEHIGH)

BLUE BOX

Car Toys magazine editor Jeff Koch discovered an unusual Porsche Targa with retractable roof made by an obscure company known only as Blue Box. He paid less than a dollar for it in 1996. More information is needed.
Porsche Targa with retractable roof, 3" . . . . $1 – 2

BOLEY (ALSO SEE HIGH SPEED)

A seemingly new company, Boley of Los Angeles, California, is a marketing company for essentially generic toys, specifically formula racers. Packaged as "Formular Die Cast," three sets of two cars each, upon removal from the package, reveal themselves as High Speed brand toys. Each body style of the six cars is different, not only in color, but in actual casting. Two-car sets sell for 99¢ each at popular retail chains.

BONUX (ALSO SEE CLE)

Bonux is a brand of ready-made and kit models marketed by the Cle firm of France in the 1960s. Several models have been produced under this brand. While Cle primarily produced plastic models, their Bonux brand was devoted to diecast miniatures.

Fiat Torpedo 1901 . . . . $15
Ford 1903 . . . . $15
Isotta-Fraschini 1902 . . . . $6
Leyland Double Deck Bus 1920 . . . . $12
Packard 1912 Town Sedan $15
Peugeot 1898 Brougham $7
Peugeot 203 . . . . $12
Regal 1914 Sedan. $15
Renault 1910 Truck $15
Road Roller $7
Rolls-Royce 1911 Silver Ghost Landau. $15
Sizaire-Naudin 1906 Racing Car $15

BOSS

1970 AMC Javelin, gold $154
1970 Dodge Challenger TransAm HT, pink $134
1970 Dodge Challenger TransAm, "Posey #77," green $134

BOSSAT DERMOV

Just when I thought I'd seen the ultimate in diecast in the name of Pocher 1:8 scale models (retail $499 and up), along comes Bossat Dermov! These French masterpieces are outrageously detailed and even more outrageously priced, as you will see from these 1:8 scale models listed in the January-March 1995 Exoto, Inc., quarterly publication called *Exoto Tifosi*. For your copy of this unusual magazine/catalog, contact Exoto Inc., 1040-F Hamilton Road, Duarte, CA, 91010, 818-305-1358. Prices listed below are not typographical errors. They are actual prices as listed in the publication.

Bugatti Type 13 Brescia $5,800
Bugatti Type 59/50B $16,400
Bugatti Type 55 . . . . $16,400
Bugatti Type 50 Coupe $19,900
Bugatti Atalante $26,900
Facel Vega III $26,900
Aston Martin DB4 Zagato $26,900
Mercedes-Benz 540K $22,900
1929 Bentley "Le Mans" $19,900
BMW 328 . . . . $19,900
Ferrari 512M $22,900
Ferrari Daytona Group IV $26,900
1957 Ferrari 250 TR "Pontoon" $9,950

BOURBON

Two models of this obscure French toy manufacturer are known.

Peugeot D4A Van $25
Berliet Tanker Semi $30

BOX MODEL

Ferraris and Jaguars dominate the Box Model assortment, made in Italy, all 1:43 scale. Box Model precedes Best and Bang, which are two companies that resulted from the reorganization of the company in 1991.

Ferrari 250 GTO, silver plated, #101 . . . . $28
Ferrari 250 GT, silver plated, #102 . . . . $28
Ferrari 250 GTO, gold plated, #201 . . . . $38
Ferrari 250 GT, gold plated, #202 . . . . $38
1962 Ferrari GTO Coupe Street, red, #8401 . . . . $22
1962 Ferrari GTO Coupe LeMans '62, light green, #8402 . . . . . $22
1963 Ferrari GTO Coupe TT '63, green, #8403. . . . . $22
1956 Ferrari 250 GT Prova Street, red, #8405 . . . . $22
1956 Ferrari 250 GT Prova, silver, #8406 . . . . $22
1957 Ferrari 250 GT Pau 3 Hours, red, #8407 . . . . $22
1962 Ferrari GTO Targa Florio O/P, white/brown, #8408. . . . . $18
1963 Ferrari GTO Coupe TT '63, red, #8409 . . . . $22
AC Cobra 289 Open, wire wheels, red, #8410 . . . . $18
AC Cobra 289 Open, alloy wheels, black, #8411 . . . . $18
Ferrari 250 GT Long, Mille Miglia, #8415 . . . . $22
1966 Ferrari 275 GTB Spyder, top down, red, #8418R $18
Ferrari 275 GTB Spyder, top up, white, #8419 . . . . $22
1960 Ferrari 250 GT Tour de France Street, blue, #8425. . . . . $8
1960 Ferrari 250 GT Tour de France, red, #8426 . . . . $8
1959 Ferrari 250 GT Tour de France, white, #8427 . . . . . . $22
1966 Ferrari 275 GTB Spyder, wire wheels, black, #8428 . . . . $18
1966 Ferrari 275 GTB Monte Carlo, #8429 . . . . $22
1966 Ferrari 275 GTB4 Targa Florio, red, #8430 . . . . $22
1958 Ferrari 250 Tour de France, silver, #8431 . . . . $22
1962 Ferrari 250 GTO Sebring, #8432 . . . . $22
1963 Ferrari 250 GTO Laguna Seca, #8433 . . . . $18
Ferrari 250 LM Street, red, #8434. . . . . $18
1964 Ferrari 250 LM Nurburgring Rindt, red, #8435 . . . . . . $22
1965 Ferrari 250 LM LeMans Dumay, yellow, #8436 . . . . . $22
1966 Ferrari 250 LM Monza, white with stripe, #8437 . . . . $22
1962 Jaguar E Coupe O/P, black, #8439N $22
1962 Jaguar E Coupe left hand drive, red, #8439R $22
1962 Jaguar E Coupe right hand drive, green/white, #8440 . . . $22
1958 Ferrari 250 Tour de France Shell/Peron, #8441 . . . . . . $22
1969 Ferrari 275 GTB4 Tour de France, "142," silver, #8442 . . . $22
1962 Jaguar E Coupe TT, "14," blue, #8443 . . . . $22

BRADSCARS

Brighton, England, was home to Bradshaws Model Products, producer of a hard-to-find series of crude one-piece casted toy cars. Produced from around 1952 to 1954 to roughly 1:75 scale, or double O, they were priced higher than the better-made Matchbox toys of the same period, which was likely the reason for their quick demise.

Austin A30 (Austin A7 on base), black, red, or green. $50
Morris 6, black, red, tan, blue, or light green. $50
Riley 1.5, red, black, gray, or green $50

BRAND S

Brand S models are from Hong Kong.

2 Audi 100, white $5
3 Ford Sierra, yellow $5
9 Lancia Stratos, white $5
15 1911 Renault Truck, green $5

BRESLIN

Breslin toys are lead alloy, mostly copies of Barclay and Manoil, manufactured in Toronto, Canada, and are distinguished from the originals by the words "Made in Canada" or "Canada" on them.

Brinks Armored Car, 9" $500
Brinks Truck Bank, aluminum, 8" $70
Motorized Machine Gunner $40
Tank $40
Truck with Cannon Wagon $40

BRIANZA (ALSO ABC BRIANZA)

Diecast Miniatures offers an assortment of 1:43 scale Brianza models of Italy, while Exoto Tifosi offers an assortment of 1:14 scale models. According to Exoto Tifosi January-March 1995 catalog, "A Brianza is more than a model, it's a work of art, an investment. Each 1:14 scale replica is a limited and numbered edition, all hand formed and assembled using genuine Ferrari paint for the finish, leatherette, and carpeting for the interior." Suggested retail for the 1:14 scale models is $2,450. A.B. Carlo Brianza is the founder of the company, hence the "ABC" commonly associated with the brand name.

1:14 SCALE

1961 Ferrari 250 GT SWB $1,600
1962 Ferrari 250 GT SWB California Spyder $1,600
1965 Ferrari 250 LM Le Mans $1,900
1965 Ferrari 275 GTB Short Nose $1,600
1967 Ferrari 275 GTB4 . . . . $1,600
1967 Ferrari 275 GTB4 Spyder N.A.R.T. $1,600
1967 Ferrari 330 P4 "Monza" $1,650
1974 Ferrari 246 GTB Dino $1,600
1974 Ferrari 246 GTS Dino $1,600
1974 Ferrari 365 GTB4 Daytona $1,600
1974 Ferrari 365 GTB4 Daytona Spyder $1,600
1980 Ferrari 365 GT4 BB $1,650
1984 Ferrari 288 GTO $1,850
1984 Ferrari 512 BB $1,650

1:43 SCALE

1928 Alfa Romeo 1500 Campari Mille Miglia Winner, #13C . . . $240
1930 Alfa Romeo 1750 Mille Miglia-Nuvolari/Guidotti, top down, #16 . . . . $240
1948 Ferrari 166 All Mille Miglia Winner, #12 . . . . . $240
1949 Ferrari 166 Mille Miglia, red, #14 . . . . $240
Maserati Grand Prix Transporter $900
Maserati Grand Prix Transporter with 3 Maserati 250 F cars . $1,650
1927 Om Superba-Minoja/Morandi, Mille Miglia Winner, red #15 . . . . $240
1954 Pontiac Chieftain Custom Catalina, tan, #22 . . . . $300
Scuderia Ferrari Transporter $900
Scuderia Ferrari Transporter with 3 Ferrari 801 F1 cars $1,650

1936 Scuderia Ferrari Classic Transporter $300
1971 Scuderia Ferrari Transporter O.M. 107 Rolfo $700
Scuderia Lancia Support Van Carrera Panamericana $650
1951 Team Alfa Romeo Transporter $300

BRIMTOY POCKETOYS

The pre-World War I English company of Wells-Brimtoy Distributors, Ltd., better known for tin and plastic toys, produced a series of toys from the late forties to early fifties called "Pocketoys."

Bedford LWB Truck $50
Buick, blue, red, green, or cream $50
Sunbeam Talbot, cream, green, or blue $50
Vauxhall Coupe, blue, yellow, red, or green $50
Vauxhall Saloon, red or blue $50
Wolseley Sedan $50

BRITAINS

William Britain introduced a line of hollow-cast toy soldiers in 1893. The company is still in business, still producing diecast soldiers, as well as a number of vehicles, mostly farm machinery and military vehicles.

Armored Car #274 . . . . $75
Armored Car #1321 . . . . $400
Army Ambulance #1512, wounded man and stretcher, doors open, 6" $200
Army Lorry, caterpillar type, #1333 . . . . $250
Army Lorry, 4-wheel type, #1334 . . . . $200
Army Lorry with driver, #1335 . . . . $225
Army Staff Car with officer and driver, #1448 . . . . $350
    v.1 smooth white tires, black fenders $350
    v.2 white tires, khaki colored body and fenders $350
    v.3 rubber tires, 1948-1950 version, rectangular windshield . $300
    v.4 lead tires, 1951-1957, gray colored $325
    v.5 black plastic tires, 1958-1959 . . . . $275
Army Tender, caterpillar type, covered, #1433 . . . . $175
Army Tender, 10-wheel covered, #1432 . . . . $175
Balloon Barrage Unit with lorry, winch, and balloon, #1757 . . . . $1,500
Bren Gun Carrier #876 . . . . $75
Corporation Motor Ambulance with driver, wounded patient, and stretcher, #1514 . . . . $800
Covered Lorry with gun and drivers, #1462 . . . . $425
Dispatch Rider #200 . . . . $40
Dispatch Rider #1791 . . . . $175
Heavy-Duty Lorry with driver, searchlight, battery and lamp, #1642 . . . . $700
Heavy-Duty Lorry, underslung, #1641 . . . . $500
Heavy-Duty Lorry, underslung with driver, #1643 . . . . . $1,000
Howitzer 4.5", #1725 . . . . $30
Mobile Searchlight #1718 . . . . $60
Mobile Unit, 2-Pounder, #1717 . . . . $60
Motorcycle Machine Gun #199 . . . . $100
Police Car with two officers, #1413 . . . . $750
Range Rover Discovery, 1:32, 1996 . . . . $20
Regular Limber #1726 . . . . $25
Speed Record Car, "The Bluebird," #1400 . . . . $350
Tank #1203 . . . . $200

Range Rover, 1:32, 1996, $20

BRITISH MOTORING CLASSICS

British Motoring Classics are 1:43 scale models. The Austin/Morris/Cooper legacy is similar to other car companies that manufacture several different brands of automobiles. British Motoring Classics presents high-quality replicas of Mini Coopers, Morris Minis, and Austin Minis with various liveries and colors. Models are currently offered at $88 each.

BROOKFIELD COLLECTORS GUILD

"Exquisite" is a word that best describes diecast models produced by Brookfield Collectors Guild, Inc., 16312 West Glendale Drive, New Berlin, Wisconsin 53151-9917. Brookfield Collectors Guild, Inc., has existed since 1992. Meanwhile, back in 1980, even before Brookfield had a name, company president Kenneth Dahlke established a reputation for excellence when he produced lavish models of the 1908 Model T for the Henry Ford Museum in Dearborn, Michigan. Around the same time, his company released a replica of Louis Chevrolet's first car for the company that bears his name. These two early models were clad in silver plate and fitted with diamond headlights and ruby taillights, and manufactured in very limited edition. Since then, an assortment of diecast banks have been produced. The first ones, Chevy Suburbans, had the coin slot in the top. Later versions put the slot on the bottom so as not to ruin the integrity of the model. Presented below is a complete Brookfield product history, including part number, description, quantity produced, issue price, and current value. The reason some models list no price is that they were offered as incentive bonuses for dealers purchasing a certain quantity of the regular production models.

EARLY BROOKFIELD MODELS

1908 Model T Ford, issued in 1980, produced for the Henry Ford Museum (no pricing information available), author's best guess at current value . . . . $10,000 – 25,000

First Chevrolet, issued in 1980 as a commemorative for corporate executives of General Motors. (no pricing information available), author's best guess at current value . . . . . $750 – 1,500

THE UNABRIDGED BROOKFIELD COLLECTION

The April 1997 issue of *Brookfield Forecast,* published by Brookfield Collectors Guild, provides the most comprehensive list to date on Brookfield issues. Dale Earnhardt/GM Goodwrench products are available through GM Goodwrench dealers first exclusively.

* These models are banks with a hidden coin slot in chassis.

** Only available to dealers when they purchase a case.

CHEVROLET SUBURBANS*

'92 Dale Earnhardt #3, 25,000, Goodwrench, sold out $125
525 '93 Indy 500 Suburban Bank, 25,000, $29.95, sold out. . . . $40
532 '93 Indy 500 Emergency Truck, 1,000, dealers**. $250
'93 Jeff Gordon Rookie of the Year, 25,000, sold out. $40
563 '94 Brickyard 400, 25,000, $29.95, sold out $35
563A '94 Brickyard 400, white box 158, pre-production sold out . $200
564 '94 Brickyard 400, yellow truck, 1,041, dealers** $200
'94 Chevrolet Racing Thunder, 5,000, sold out. $45
572 '95 #3 Goodwrench, white truck, 600, dealers**. $400
'95 John Force, 5,000, $39.95, sold out $45
577 '95 Dale Earnhardt, 7 Time Champion, 30,000, Goodwrench, available. $45
577S '95 Dale Earnhardt, silver, 1,500, dealers, sold out. $90
517 '95 teal Chevrolet Suburban, 5,000, $29.95, sold out $45
646 '95 Indy 500, 10,000, $34.95, available $35
644 '95 Brickyard 400, 5,000, $39.95, available $40

GMC SUBURBANS*

'94 Don Prudhomme 5,000, $39.95, sold out. $40
617 '95 #30 Pennzoil, M. Waltrip, 5,000, $34.95, available $35
'95 #30 Pennzoil Brickyard 400, 280, sold out $200
'95 #30 Pennzoil, silver, 600, dealers**. $275
600 '95 #42 Mello Yello, Kyle Petty 5,000, $34.95, available . . . $35
605 '95 #42 Mello Yello, Thanks Fans, 5,000, $34.95, available . $35
602 '95 #42 Mello Yello, silver, 400, dealers** $90
518 '95 teal GMC Suburban, 5,000, $29.95, sold out. $45
643 '95 7&7 Split Petty/Earnhardt 25,000, $39.95, sold out $40
643R '95 7&7 Split, reverse colors, 1,000, dealer $80

GMC & CHEVROLET*

633 '95 7&7 Twin Pack, Petty/Earnhardt, 15,000, $59.95, available . $75
656 '95 7&7 Twin Pack, reverse colors, 1,250, dealers** $125

CHEVROLET DUALLY* & TRAILER

(DIECAST CREW CAB TRUCK/BANK WITH OPENING REAR TRAILER DOOR)
528 '94 Dale Earnhardt Combination, 25,000, $69.95, sold out. $150
632 '94 Dale Earnhardt Combo, silver, 1,000, dealers**. $200
561 '94 Brickyard 400 15,000, $59.95, sold out $75
565 '94 Brickyard 400, yellow, 1,250, dealers** $90
670 '95 Racing Thunder, 5,000, $75.00, available. $75
638 '95 Indy 500 Hauler 5,000, $59.95, sold out. $65
'95 Indy 500, silver special, 1,000, dealers**. $120

CHEVROLET DUALLY*

636 '95 Brickyard 400 Pace Truck, 15,000, $39.95, available. . . $40

GMC DUALLY & TRAILER

(DIECAST CREW CAB TRUCK/BANK WITH OPENING REAR TRAILER DOOR)
599 '95 #42 Kyle Petty Mello Yello, 1,750, $59.95, sold out . . . $65
601 '95 #42 Kyle Petty, silver, 300, dealers** $200
635 '95 7&7 Portrait: Earnhardt/Petty, 6,000, $59.95, sold out . . $65
N/A '95 7&7 Portrait, reverse colors, 1,000, dealers** $85
616 '95 #30 M. Waltrip Pennzoil, 2,500, $59.95, sold out $60
618 '95 #30 M.Waltrip, silver, 400, dealers**. $175

CHRYSLER DIECAST (OPENING HOOD, DOORS, TRUNK)

538 '94 Dodge Intrepid, Ram blue, 10,000, $34.95, sold out . . . $45
537 '94 Chrysler Concorde, green, 10,000, $34.95, available . . . $35
515 '94 Chrysler New Yorker, black, 10,000, $34.95, sold out. . . $40
519 '94 Chrysler LHS, Char, gold, 10,000, $34.95, sold out. . . . $40
642 '95 Dodge Intrepid, black, 10,000, $34.95, available $35
649 '95 Chrysler Concorde, red, 10,000, $34.95, available. $35
650 '95 Chrysler New Yorker, wild berry, 10,000, $34.95, sold out . $40

508 '93 Dodge Intrepid, cherry, 10,000, $34.95, sold out, $40

506 '93 Chrysler Concorde, CharGold, 10,000, $34.95, sold out, $40

651 '95 Chrysler LHS, spruce pearl, 10,000, $34.95, available . . $35

682 '96 Chrysler LHS, Drama gold, 2,500, $34.95, available . . . $35

680 '96 Chrysler Concorde, spruce, 2,500, $34.95, available . . . $35

679 '96 Dodge Intrepid, candy apple red, 2,500, $34.95, available . . $35

642R '95 Dodge Intrepid, rosewood, 1,000, dealers** $75

649R '95 Chrysler Concorde, rosewood, 1,000, dealers** $75

650R '95 Chrysler New Yorker, rosewood, 1,000, dealers** $75

651R '95 Chrysler LHS, rosewood, 1,000, dealers** $75

CHRYSLER DIECAST BANKS

540 '93 Plymouth Minivan, gold wheels, 7,500, $24.95, sold out . $30

539B '93 Jeep Grand Cherokee, black, 10,000, $24.95, available . $25

539R '94 Jeep Grand Cherokee, red, 10,000, $24.95, sold out . . $30

539W '94 Jeep Grand Cherokee, white, 10,000, $24.95, sold out . $30

539LD '94 Jeep Grand Cherokee, orchid, 1,000, dealers** $55

540 '94 Plymouth Minivan, silver wheels (4 mil.), 7,500, $24.95, sold out $30

540RE '95 Plymouth Minivan, red graphics, 1,041, dealers** . . . $55

539C '95 Jeep Grand Cherokee, Camp Jeep, 2,500, $24.95, available $25

539G '95 Jeep Grand Cherokee, Orvis, 2,500, $24.95, available $25

PLASTIC PROMOTIONAL MODELS

558 '94 Brickyard 400 Monte Carlo, tan interior, 25,000, $26.95, sold out $30

558A '94 Brickyard 400 Monte Carlo, black interior, 1,000, dealers**. $60

566 '94 Brickyard 400 Monte Carlo, T. George, 7,500, $27.95, sold out $35

568 '94 Dodge Neon Sedan, emerald green, 10,000, $19.95, available $20

544 '94 Plymouth Neon Sedan, emerald green, 10,000, $19.95, available $20

542 '94 Dodge Neon Sedan, nitro green, 10,000, $19.95, sold out $25

567 '94 Plymouth Neon Sedan, nitro green, 10,000, $19.95, sold out $25

534 '94 Neon Sedan, white racer, 10,000, $19.95, available . . . $20

545 '95 Neon Sedan, special black, 1,000, dealers** $60

661B '95 Chevrolet Monte Carlo, black, 3,500, $24.95, available . $25

661R '95 Chevrolet Monte Carlo, red, 3,000, $24.95, sold out . . $30

661S '95 Chevrolet Monte Carlo, silver, 500, dealers. $60

552 '95 Chrysler Cirrus, med. fern, 2,500, $24.95, available. . . . $20

552R '95 Chrysler Cirrus, rosewood, 1,000, dealers** $60

551 '95 Dodge Stratus, light fern, 2,500, $24.95, available. $25

551R '95 Dodge Stratus, rosewood, 500, dealers** $150

694 '96 Plymouth Neon Coupe, white, 2,500, $24.95, sold out . $30

640 '96 Earnhardt Street Monte Carlo, 2,500, $24.95, available . $25

SPECIAL RACING PROMOTIONAL MODELS (TWIN PACKS)

573 '95 Jeff Gordon Brickyard 400 Twin Pack: Monte Carlo Pace Car & Lumina Race Car, 10,000, $49.95, sold out $60

662 '95 Earnhardt Racer & Custom Monte Carlo 10,000, $49.95, available. $50

662S '95 Earnhardt Racer & Silver Monte Carlo, 500, dealers** . $90

RECENT HITS & UPCOMING MODELS

PREMIERE EDITION MODELS EDITION ISSUE ESTIMATED

726 Dodge Viper GTS Coupe, blue w/white stripe, $99.00, available $100

504 Dodge Viper RT/10 Convertible, red, $99.00 . . . . $100

DIECAST MODELS (1:25 SCALE) EDITION ISSUE ESTIMATED

767R Chrysler Sebring Convertible, red, 5,000, $34.95 . . . . $35

767N Chrysler Sebring Convertible, green, 5,000, $34.95 . . . . . $35

767G Chrysler Sebring Convertible, gold, 5,000, $34.95 . . . . . . $35

758 Oldsmobile Bravada, $39.95. . . . . $40

672W Chevrolet Express, white, 10,000, $39.95, available $40

672B Chevrolet Express, Adriatic blue, 2,500, $39.95, available . $40

717 Chevrolet Tahoe, Truck of the Year, 8,000, $39.95, available . $40

682 Chrysler LHS, drama gold, 2,500, $34.95, available $35

680 Chrysler Concorde, spruce blue, 2,500, $34.95, available . . $35

679 Dodge Intrepid, candy apple red, 2,500, $34.95, available . . $35

672BF 1996 Brickyard 400 Chevy Express Van, 500, $39.95, sold out $45

PLASTIC PROMOTIONAL MODELS (1:25 SCALE) EDITION ISSUE ESTIMATED

743 Dodge Stratus, candy apple red, 2,500, $24.95 . . . . $25

742 Chrysler Cirrus, black, 2,500, $24.95 . . . . $25

736B Chevrolet Monte Carlo, Adriatic blue, 2,500, $24.95. . . . . $25

736P Chevrolet Monte Carlo, purple pearl metallic, 2,500, $24.95. . . . . $25

648T Oldsmobile Aurora, dark teal metallic, 2,500, $24.95, sold out $30

648W Oldsmobile Aurora, white, 2,500, $24.95, available $25

648C Oldsmobile Aurora, champagne, 2,500, $24.95, sold out . $30

648R Oldsmobile Aurora, garnet red, 2,500, $24.95, sold out . . $30

648S Oldsmobile Aurora, silver teal, 600, dealer $60

648P Indy Racing League Aurora Pace Car, 2,500, $24.95, sold out . $30

718 Neon Celebrity Challenge Racer, yellow, 2,500, $24.95, sold out $30

696 Neon Celebrity Challenge Racer, black, 2,500, $24.95, available $25

678 Dodge Neon Coupe, magenta, 2,500, $24.95, available . . . $25

695 Dodge Neon Sedan, light iris, 2,500, $24.95, available . . . $25

693 Plymouth Neon Expresso Coupe, lapis, 2,500, $24.95, available $25

669 Dodge Neon SCCA Club Racer, black, 2,500, $24.95, available . $25

WINSTON CUP RACING COLLECTIBLES (1:25 SCALE DIECAST)

EDITION ISSUE ESTIMATED

764 Jeff Gordon/DuPont Trackside Crew Cab Truck, Trailer, & Race Car, 10,000, $75.00 . . . . $75

765 Budweiser Trackside Crew Cab Truck, Trailer & Race Car, 5,000, $75.00, available $75

766 Terry Labonte Kellogg's Trackside Crew Cab Truck, Trailer, & Race Car, 5,000, $75.00 . . . . $75

754 Jeff Gordon/DuPont Chevrolet Tahoe, 5,000, $39.95 . . . . . $40

752 Ricky Craven/Budweiser Chevrolet Tahoe, 5,000, $39.95. . $40

753 Terry Labonte/Kellogg's Chevrolet Tahoe, 5,000, $39.95 . . $40

575 Dale Earnhardt Goodwrench Chevrolet Tahoe, 10,000, $39.95, sold out $45

722 Dale Earnhardt Stars & Stripes 3-Car Set, 10,000, $125.00, sold out $135

723 Dale Earnhardt Olympic Trackside Tahoe, 7,000, $39.95, sold out $45

724 Dale Earnhardt Olympic Combination Set, 10,000, $75.00, sold out $85

757 Jeff Gordon DuPont Chevy Express Van, 5,000, $39.95, available $40

756 Terry Labonte Kellogg's Chevy Express Van, 5,000, $39.95, available. $40

761 Dale Earnhardt #3 Goodwrench Van, 10,000, $39.95, available . $40

755 Ken Schrader Budweiser Chevy Express Van, 5,000, $39.95, available $40

579C Jeff Gordon DuPont Crew Cab Truck (CCT), 5,000, $69.95, sold out $75

607C Ken Schrader Budweiser Crew Cab (CCT), 3,000, $69.95, sold out. $75

589C Terry Labonte Kellogg's Crew Cab (CCT), 3,000, $69.95, sold out $75

763 Dale Earnhardt Trackside Crew Cab Truck, Trailer, & Race Car (CCC), 10,000, $75.00, available. $75

708 Dale Earnhardt Show Car Trailer (CCT), 10,000, $69.95 . . . $70

580C Jeff Gordon/DuPont Chevrolet Suburban, 6,000, $39.95, available. $40

607C Ken Schrader/Budweiser Chevrolet Suburban, 3,500, $39.95, available. $40

590C Terry Labonte/Kellogg's Chevrolet Suburban, 3,500, $39.95, available. $40

700 Dale Earnhardt Victory Suburban, 5,000, $39.95, sold out . $45

701 Dale Earnhardt Victory Crew Cab, 5,000, $39.95, available. $40

777 Johnny Benson, Jr./Pennzoil GMC Transporter, 2,500, $69.95. $70

776 Johnny Benson, Jr./Pennzoil GMC Suburban, 1,250, $39.95 . $40

584C Bobby Labonte/Interstate Crew Cab (CCT), 5,000, $69.95. $70

585C Bobby Labonte/Interstate Chevy Suburban, 5,000, $39.95 $40

594C Sterling Marlin/Kodak Crew Cab CCT, 5,000, $69.95 . . . . $70

595C Sterling Marlin/Kodak Chevy Suburban, 5,000, $39.95. . . $40

611C Darrell Waltrip/Parts America Crew Cab (CCT), 5,000, $69.95. $70

612C Darrell Waltrip/Parts America, Chevy Suburban, 5,000, $39.95. $40

636 Brickyard 400 Pace Truck, 10,000, $39.95, available $40

644 Brickyard 400 Chevy Suburban, 5,000, $39.95, available . . $40

600 Kyle Petty GMC Suburban, 5,000, $39.95, available $40

646 Indy 500 Trackside Chevy Suburban, 10,000, $39.95, available . $40

670 Earnhardt Chevrolet Racing Thunder (CCT), 3,333, $75.00, available $75

744 Earnhardt AC Delco Replica (GM Dealer), 15,000, $49.95, sold out $55

788 Earnhardt AC Delco Replica (Distributor), 15,000, $49.95, sold out $55

785 Earnhardt AC Delco Trackside Combo. Set, 10,000, $99.95, available $100

789 AC Delco Distribution Version, 7,500, $99.95, available . . $100

790 Earnhardt AC Delco Suburban, 5,000, $44.95, sold out . . . $50

784 Earnhardt AC Delco/Goodwrench Twinpack, 10,000, $89.95, sold out $95

BROOKLINS

Brooklin, Lansdowne & Robeddie are all brands of Brooklin Models Limited of Brooklin, Ontario, Canada. Started in 1974 by John Hall in his basement, the company has since become the world's leading manufacturer of hand-built 1:43 scale collectible model automobiles. Brooklins are now manufactured in a 10,000 square foot factory in Bath, England. While their replication of fifties and sixties vintage US cars makes them popular with collectors, Brooklins sometimes lack the fine detailing of comparable models, opting instead for heavy, solid construction and exacting scale. Some enthusiasts prefer to add chrome foil for finish trim, applying thin metallic film in a fashion similar to gold leaf. This preference leads back to the argument of the purist versus the hobbyist, as mentioned in the introduction to this book. While Brooklins focus on American cars, Lansdowne models are replicas of British cars. The series was introduced in 1993 to present a completely new line of models for collectors. Robeddie models meanwhile concentrate on Swedish vehicles — Volvos mostly, with a 1969 Saab 99 thrown in for variety.

THE BROOKLIN COLLECTION

Current regular issues $55 each; current special issues $75 – 115 each; obsolete issues $200 – 350 each. Richard O'Brien's book *Collecting Toy Cars & Trucks* presents a comprehensive listing of Brooklins, both the original Canadian issues and the newer British issues. Presented below is a survey of those issues.

BROOKLIN CANADIAN ISSUES

1 1933 Pierce Arrow Silver Arrow . . . . $350 – 500

2 1948 Tucker Torpedo $200

3 1930 Ford Victoria 2-Door . . . . $100 – 250

4 1937 Chevrolet Coupe. $325

5 1930 Ford Model A 2-Door Coupe $500

6 1932 Packard $325

7 1934 Chrysler Airflow $200

8 1940 Chrysler Newport 4-Door. $200

8A 1941 Chrysler Newport Pace Car $475

9 1940 Ford Van . . . . $500 – 600

BROOKLIN BRITISH ISSUES

1 1933 Pierce Arrow . . . . $65 – 350

2 1948 Tucker Torpedo. . . . . $65 – 200

3 1930 Ford Victoria 2-Door . . . . $150 – 175

4 1937 Chevrolet Coupe. . . . . $160 – 400

5 1930 Ford Model A 2-Door Coupe . . . . $100 – 300

6 1932 Packard Standard 8 . . . . $125 – 200

7 1934 Chrysler Airflow . . . . $65 – 125

8 1940 Chrysler Newport	. . . .	$125
8A 1941 Chrysler Newport Indy Pace Car.	. . . .	$65 – 300
9 1940 Ford Delivery	. . . .	$75 – 550

10 1949 Buick Roadmaster Coupe, $75 – 200

11 1956 Lincoln Continental Mark II	. . . .	$75 – 200
12 1931 Hudson Greater 8 Boattail	. . . .	$75 – 550
13 1957 Ford Thunderbird.	. . . .	$80 – 350
14 1940 Cadillac V16.	. . . .	$65 – 375
15 1950 Mercury Convertible	. . . .	$65 – 200
16 1935 Dodge Van	. . . .	$65 – 500
16 1935 Dodge Pickup	. . . .	$75 – 400
17 1950 Studebaker Starlight	. . . .	$65 – 110
18 1941 Packard Clipper	. . . .	$65 – 400
19 1955 Chrysler C300	. . . .	$65 – 75
20 1953 Buick Skylark	. . . .	$350
21 1963 Chevrolet Corvette	. . . .	$65 – 400
22 1958 Edsel Citation.	. . . .	$65 – 150
23 1956 Ford Fairlane Victoria.	. . . .	$65 – 90
24 1968 Shelby Mustang	. . . .	$200
24 1968 Ford Mustang	. . . .	$200
25 1958 Pontiac Bonneville Convertible	. . . .	$65 – 250
26 1955 Chevrolet Nomad.	. . . .	$65 – 275
27 1957 Cadillac Eldorado Brougham	. . . .	$200
28 1957 Mercury Turnpike Cruiser.	. . . .	$65 – 300
29 1953 Kaiser Manhattan	. . . .	$65 – 275
30 1954 Dodge Royal 500 Convertible.	. . . .	$65
31 1953 Pontiac Van	. . . .	$65
32 1953 Studebaker Starliner	. . . .	$65
33 1938 Phantom Corsair	. . . .	$65
34 1954 Nash Ambassador	. . . .	$65
35 1957 Ford Sunliner	. . . .	$65
36 1952 Hudson Hornet	. . . .	$65
37 1960 Ford Sunliner	. . . .	$65
38 1939 Graham "Sharknose"	. . . .	$65
39 1953 Oldsmobile Fiesta	. . . .	$65
40 1948 Cadillac Sedanet	. . . .	$65
41 1959 Chrysler 300E	. . . .	$65
42 1952 Ford F1 Ambulance	. . . .	$65
43 1948 Packard Station Sedan	. . . .	$65
44 1961 Chevrolet Impala	. . . .	$65
45 1948 Buick Roadmaster	. . . .	$65
46 1959 Chevrolet El Camino	. . . .	$65
47 1965 Ford Thunderbird	. . . .	$65
48 1958 Chevrolet Impala.	. . . .	$65
49 1954 Hudson Italia	. . . .	$65
50 1948 Chevrolet Aero Sedan	. . . .	$65

51 1951 Ford Victoria.	. . . .	$65
52 1941 Hupmobile Skylark	. . . .	$65
53 1955 Chevrolet Cameo Pick-Up Truck	. . . .	$65
54 1953 Airstream Wanderer Travel Trailer	. . . .	$65
55 1951 Packard Mayfair	. . . .	$65

LANSDOWNE MODELS

1 1958 Austin Healey Sprite Mk I	. . . .	$65
2 1957 Vauxhall Cresta.	. . . .	$65
3 1956 MG Magnette 2A	. . . .	$65
4 1962 Morris Mini Van Mk I	. . . .	$65
5 1957 Rover 90 P4	. . . .	$65
6 1961 Wolseley 6-110	. . . .	$65
7 1954 Ford Zephyr Zodiac	. . . .	$65
8 1954 Triumph Renown	. . . .	$65
9 1953 Austin Somerset	. . . .	$65
10 1956 Hillman Minx	. . . .	$65
11 1963 Sunbeam Alpine	. . . .	$65

ROBEDDIE MODELS

1 1969 Volvo P1800S	. . . .	$65
2 1973 Volvo 144GL.	. . . .	$65
3 1969 Saab 99	. . . .	$65
4 1950 Volvo PV831.	. . . .	$65
5 1946-50 Volvo PV60	. . . .	$65
6 1964 Volvo PV544.	. . . .	$65
7 1953 Volvo PV445 Duett	. . . .	$65
8 1953 Volvo PV445 Van	. . . .	$65
9 1957 Volvo Amazon 120	. . . .	$65

BRUDER

Bruder produces a large variety of plastic items, but their assortment of 1:87 scale hard plastic toy cars are especially realistic scale. Pictured are an assortment called "Bruder Mini" that includes, from front to back, Porsche 924 (red), Citroen CX (blue), Citroen 2CV (light green), Volkswagen Van (light orange), Volkswagen Golf (red), Mercedes-Benz convertible (yellow), Porsche 924 (light green), and Mercedes-Benz 280 GE (red). Each one sells for 50¢.

Bruder also offers larger scale models in plastic. Diecast Miniatures lists the following models in various colors.

Porsche 911 Coupe, 1:25	. . . .	$11
Volkswagen Golf, 1:43.	. . . .	$6

BRUMM

Brumista was the name given towards the end of the nine-

teenth century to the hackney-coach drivers of Milan, those grandfathers of today's taxi drivers, and it is from this word, el Brumm, that the trademark Brumm, miniature styling for collectors of models scale 1:43, was derived. The Brumm Company of Oltrona S. Mamette (a small village near Como, Italy) was the creation of three friends who began their activities with the production of models of period horse-drawn carriages, with and without horses in the Brumm and Historical series. Then in 1976, they expanded ranges to include steam-powered vehicles (Old Fire) and the first motor cars in the now famous Revival series, of which the three wheeler Morgan was the first. Today the company manufacturers some 250 different models, all faithfully reproduced in 1:43 scale. The car models produced by Brumm have been mainly dedicated to those of a more historical nature, the exception being one or two contemporary racing cars. Since 1986, the company has also produced a yearly series of limited edition models of 5,000 pieces each, all now eagerly sought after. Likewise, in 1987, production ceased on the first ten models in the Revival car series which immediately became coveted collectors items. Brumm will continue its policy of bringing to the collectors releases of interesting and well made models, all of which may take pride and place in any collection the world over.

Brumm Revival (classic cars)

R001 Morgan sport (Aperta) 1923	$20
R002 Morgan sport (Chiusa) 1923	$20
R003 Darmont sport (Aperta) 1929	$20
R004 Darmont sport (Chiusa) 1929	$20
R005 Bedelia sport (Aperta) 1913	$20
R006 Bedelia sport (Chiusa) 1913	$20
R007 Sanford sport (Aperta) 1922	$20
R008 Sanford sport (Chiusa) 1922	$20
R009 Fiat 75 HP corsa 1904	$20
R010 Fiat 110 HP corsa 1905	$20
R011 Fiat S 74 Corsa 1911	$20
R012 Fiat 500 C 1949 – 55 (Aperta)	$20
R013 Fiat 500 C 1949 – 55 (Chiusa)	$20
R014 Fiat Mefistofele 1923	$20
R015 Ford 999 1902	$20
R016 Fiat F2 1907	$20
R017 Fiat S 61 1903	$20
R018 Renault G.P. 3B 1906	$20
R019 Benz-Blitzen 1909	$20
R020 Locomobile 'Old 16' 1906	$20
R021 Fiat 500 I Serie 1936 (Aperta)	$20
R022 Fiat 500 I Serie 1936 (Chiusa)	$20
R023 Fiat 500 I Serie Metano	$20
R024 Fiat 500 I Serie Vigili Del Fuoco	$20
R025 Ford 999 Record 1905	$20
R026 Alfa Corsa 1911	$20
R027 Renault (Parigi-Madrid) 1903	$20
R028 Fiat 500 C Belvedere (Aperta)	$20
R029 Fiat 500 C Belvedere (Chiusa)	$20
R030 Fiat 1100 Monocolore 1937 – 39	$20
R031 Fiat 1100 Bicolore 1937 – 39	$20
R032 Fiat 1100 Metano	$20
R033 Fiat 1100 (508C) Gasogeno 1937 – 39	$20

R034 Fiat 1100 (508C) Forze Armate 1937 – 39	$20
R035 Ferrari 500 F2 1952	$20
R036 Alfa Romeo 158 1950	$20
R037 Mercedes W154 1939	$20
R038 Auto Union 12 Cil. 1936	$20
R039 Bugatti 'Brescia' (GB) 1921	$20
R040 Bugatti 'Brescia' (F) 1921	$20
R041 Bugatti 'Type 59' 1933	$20
R042 Bugatti 'Type 59' Biposto 1933	$20
R043 Alfa Romeo 159 1952	$20
R044 Ferrari 500/F2 1952	$20
R045 Fiat 500B Furgoncino PT 1946 – 49	$20
R046 Fiat 500 B Furgoncino Stipel	$20
R047 Fiat 500 A Mille Miglia 1937	$20
R048 Fiat 500 C Giardinetta (Aperta)	$20
R049 Fiat 500 C Giardinetta (Chiusa)	$20
R050 Fiat 500 A Furgoncino	$20
R051 Fiat 500 C Furgoncino	$20
R052 Fiat 500 A Ramazotti	$20
R053 Fiat 500 C Ramazotti	$20
R054 Fiat 500 A Campari	$20
R055 Fiat 500 C Campari	$20
R056 Fiat 500 A Isobella	$20
R057 Fiat 500 C Isobella	$20

R058 Lancia Aprilia 1936 – 48, $20

R059 Lancia Aprilia Metano 1939 – 48	$20
R060 Lancia Aprilia Gasogeno 1939 – 44	$20
R061 Lancia Aprilia Mille Miglia 1947	$20
R062 Fiat 1100 (508 C.) Taxi 1937 – 39	$20
R063 Fiat 1100 (508 C.) Vigili Del Fuoco	$20
R064 Fiat 1100 B 1948 – 49	$20
R065 Fiat 1100 E 1949 – 53	$20
R066 Ferrari 815 Sport 1940	$20
R067 Ferrari 815 Mille Miglia 1940	$20
R068 Ferrari D 246 1958	$20
R069 Ferrari D 246 G.P. Italia 1958	$20
R070 Mercedes W 125 1937	$20
R071 Mercedes W 125 1938	$20
R072 Mercedes W 196 1954 – 60	$20
R073 Blitzen Benz 1911	$20
R074 Talbot Lago F1 1948	$20
R075 Maserati 8 Cil. 1939	$20
R076 Ferrari-Lancia D 50 1956	$20
R077 Alfa Romeo 2300 1931	$20
R078 Alfa Romeo 2300 Mille Miglia 1932	$20
R079 Fiat 500 B Gilette	$20

R080 Fiat 500 C Vigili Del Fuoco $20	R124 Ferrari 156 G.P. Monza 1961 . . . . $20
R081 Blitzen Benz Indy 1911 . . . . $20	R125 Ferrari 375 F1 1951 . . . . $20
R082 Bugatti 'Brescia' 1921 . . . . $20	R126 Ferrari 375 Indianapolis 1952 . . . . $20
R083 Fiat 1100 (508C) Spider 1937 – 39 . . . . $20	R127 Lancia Ferrari D50 Montecarlo 1956 . . . . $20
R084 Fiat 1100 (508C) Chiuso 1937 – 1939 . . . . $20	R128 Lancia Ferrari D50 Belgio 1956 . . . . $20
R085 Fiat 1100 (508C) Coloniale $20	R129 Jaguar D Type 1954 . . . . $20
R086 Fiat 1100 (508C) Corpo Diplomatico $20	R130 Jaguar D Type Le Mans Cunningham 1954 . . . . $20
R087 Bugatti 57-S Blu $20	R131 Lancia B24 (Aperta) 1955 . . . . $20
R088 Bugatti 57-S Nera $20	R132 Lancia B24 (Chiusa) 1955 . . . . $20
R089 Alfa Romeo 1900 . . . . $20	R133 Lancia B24 America (Aperta) 1956 . . . . $20
R090 Alfa Romeo 1900 Mille Miglia $20	R134 Lancia B24 America (Chiusa) 1956 . . . . $20
R091 Alfa Romeo 1900 Polizia $20	R135 Maserati 250F Muso Corto Montecarlo 1957 . . . . $20
R092 Maserati 250 F 1957 . . . . $20	R136 Maserati 250F Muso Corto 1957 . . . . $20
R093 Ferrari Testa Rossa Le Mans 1957 . . . . $20	R137 Maserati 250F Iniezione 1957 . . . . $20
R094 Ferrari Testa Rossa $20	R138 Alfa Romeo 2300 Bicolore 1931 . . . . $20
R095 Lancia Aurelia B20 1951 . . . . $20	R139 Alfa Romeo 8C 2900 B 1938 . . . . $20
R096 Lancia Aurelia B20 Mille Miglia $20	R140 Alfa Romeo 8C 2900 B 1938 . . . . $20
R097 Lancia Aurelia B20 Carrera Mexico $20	R141 Alfa Romeo 8C 2900 B Mille Miglia 1938 . . . . $20
R098 Vanwal 1957 . . . . $20	R142 Ferrari 126 C4 Alboreto Agosto 1984 . . . . $20
R099 Bentley (Aperta) 1930 . . . . $20	R143 Ferrari 126 C4 Arnoux Gennaio 1984 . . . . $20
R100 Bentley (Chiusa) 1930 . . . . $20	R144 Porsche 356 Coupe Targa Florio 1952 . . . . $20
R101 Jaguar XK 120 Roadster (Aperta) 1948 . . . . $20	R145 Alfa Romeo 1900 Carrera Mexico 1954 . . . . $20
R102 Jaguar XK 120 Roadster (Chiusa) 1948 . . . . $20	R146 Jaguar D Type Mille Miglia 1957 . . . . $20
R103 Jaguar XK 120 Roadster Mille Miglia $20	R147 Jaguar D Type 1∞ Le Mans 1955 . . . . $20
R104 Jaguar XK 120 Roadster Le Mans $20	R148 Jaguar D Type Prototipo 1954 . . . . $20
R105 Jaguar XK 120 Coupe 1948 . . . . $20	R149 Jaguar D Type 1∞ Le Mans SC. Ecosse 1956 . . . . . . $20
R106 Jaguar XK 120 Linas-Montlhlery $20	R150 Jaguar D Type Le Mans Biposto 1956 . . . . $20
R107 Auto Union Rekordwagen 1935 . . . . $20	R151 Jaguar D Type SC. Belga 1956 . . . . $20
R108 Auto Union Rekordwagen Carenata 1937 . . . . $20	R152 Jaguar D Type Silverston SC. Ecosse 1956 . . . . $20
R109 Auto Union Tipo D 1938 . . . . $20	R153 Jaguar D Type Le Mans Francia 1957 . . . . $20
R110 Auto Union 12 Cil. Ruote Gemellate 1936 . . . . $20	R154 Jaguar D Type Record 1960 . . . . $20
R111 Maserati 8 Cil. Indianapolis 1940 . . . . $20	R155 Ferrari Testa Rossa Mexico $20
R112 Maserati 8 Cil. G.P. Tripoli 1938 . . . . $20	R156 Ferrari Testa Rossa P. Rodriguez $20
R113 Talbot LAGO F.1. Belgio 1951 . . . . $20	R157 Ferrari 330 P3 1∞ 1000km Spa 1966 . . . . $20
R114 Bentley Compressore 1932 . . . . $20	R158 Ferrari 330 P3 Spider Le Mans 1966 . . . . $20
R115 Darracq V8 1905 . . . . $20	R159 Ferrari 330 P4 1∞ 1000km Monza 1967 . . . . $20
R116 Napier 6 1905 . . . . $20	R160 Ferrari 330 P4 Spider Le Mans 1967 . . . . $20
	R161 Ferrari 330 P4 Le Mans Filipinetti 1967 . . . . $20
	R162 Lancia Aurelia B20 Le Mans 1951 . . . . $20
	R163 Jaguar XK 120 Coupe Rally Alpi 1953 . . . . $20
	R164 Jaguar XK 120 Roadster Rally Alpi 1953 . . . . $20
	R165 Fiat 1400 B 1956 – 58 . . . . $20
	R166 Fiat 1400 B Bicolore 1956 – 58 . . . . $20
	R167 Ferrari 500 F.2 SC.EPADON 1953 . . . . $20
	R168 Ferrari 375 Indianapolis 1952 . . . . $20
	R169 Bugatti 57S 8 Cil. 3900 C.C. 1936 . . . . $20
	R170 Bugatti 57S (Chiusa) 1936 . . . . $20
	R171 Ferrari 312 F.1 Jacky Ickx 1968 . . . . $20
	R172 Ferrari 312 F.1 Chris Amon 1968 . . . . $20
	R173 Bugatti Type 59 Ruote Gemellate 1933 . . . . $20
	R174 Bugatti Type 59 1933 . . . . $20
	R175 Mercedes W 154 Indianapolis 1947 . . . . $20
	R176 Simca 5 1956 . . . . $20
	R177 Fiat 1100 E Furgone 1947 – 48 . . . . $20
	R178 Fiat 1100 E Furgone Vigili Fuoco 1947 – 48 . . . . $20
	R179 Fiat 1100 E Furgone Croce Rossa 1947 – 48 . . . . $20
	R180 Fiat 1100 E Furgone Croce Rossa Militare $20
	R181 Fiat 1100 E Vigili Fuoco $20

R117 Porsche 356 Speedster 1952, $20

R117S Porsche 356 Speedster 1952 . . . . $20	
R118 Porsche 356 Speedster (Chiusa) 1952 . . . . $20	
R119 Porsche 356 Coupe 1952 . . . . $20	
R120 Porsche 356 Coupe Mille Miglia 1952 . . . . $20	
R121 Porsche 356 Coupe Tetto Aperto 1952 . . . . $20	
R122 Ferrari 801 1957 . . . . $20	
R123 Ferrari 156 1961 . . . . $20	

R182 Ferrari 125 Mille Miglia 1947 . . . . $20
R183 Ferrari 125 Circuito Di Pescara 1947 . . . . $20

R184 Bentley Speed Six "Barnato" 1928, $20

R185 Bentley Speed Six Bleu-Train Match 1928 . . . . $20
R186 Lancia B24 Mille Miglia 1955 . . . . $20
R187 Mercedes 300 SLR Coupe 1955 . . . . $20
R188 Mercedes 300 SLR Le Mans 1955 . . . . $20
R189 Mercedes 300 SLR Targa Florio 1955 . . . . $20
R190 Mercedes 300 SLR Mille Miglia 1955 . . . . $20
R191 Ferrari 375 G.P. Monza 1951 . . . . $20
R192 Ferrari 375 Thin Wall Special 1951 . . . . $20
R193 Porsche 550 Coupe Le Mans 1956 . . . . $20
R194 Porsche 550 Spyder Le Mans 1955 . . . . $20
R195 Porsche 550 Spyder Mille Miglia 1954 . . . . $20
R196 Ferrari Squalo 1953 . . . . $20
R197 Ferrari Squalo G.P. Italia 1953 . . . . $20
R198A Porsche 356 Polizia Tedesca 1952 . . . . $20
R198B Porsche 356 Polizia Olandese 1952 . . . . $20
R198C Porsche 356 Polizia Portoghese 1952 . . . . $20
R198D Porsche 356 Polizia Svizzera 1952 . . . . $20
R199 Vanwall F.1 G.P. Belgio 1957 . . . . $20
R200 Ferrari 512 S Daytona 1970 . . . . $20
R201 Ferrari 512 S SC. Francorchamps 1970 . . . . $20
R202 Ferrari 512 S Spa 1970 . . . . $20
R203 Ferrari 512 S Buenos Aires 1970 . . . . $20
R204 Lancia D24 Ascari Mille Miglia 1954 . . . . $20
R205 Lancia D24 Fangio Carrera Mexico 1953 . . . . $20
R206 Porsche 356 Carrera Mexico 1952 . . . . $20
R207 Porsche 356 Spider Mille Miglia 1952 . . . . $20
R208 Porsche 356 Coupe Carrera 1952 . . . . $20
R209 Lancia D24 Taruffi Targa Florio 1954 . . . . $20
R210 Ferrari 512 BB LM Prototipo 1980 . . . . $20
R211 Ferrari 512 BB LM Le Mans Sc. Rosso 1980 . . . . $20
R212 Ferrari 512 BB LM SC. Emka 1980 . . . . $20
R213 Ferrari 512 BB LM Le Mans Ch. Pozzi 1980 . . . . $20
R214 Ferrari 512 BB LM Le Mans 1980 . . . . $20
R215 Fiat 1100 E Taxi 1949 – 53 . . . . $20
R216 Fiat 1400 B Taxi 1956 – 58 . . . . $20
R217 Porsche 917 Prototipo 1970 . . . . $20
R218 Porsche 917 Le Mans Porsche-Salzburg $20
R219 Porsche 917 Monza Wyer/Gulf 1970 . . . . $20
R220 Porsche 917 Le Mans Martini Racing 1971 . . . . $20
R221 Porsche 917 Monza Wyer/Gulf 1971 . . . . $20
R222 Ferrari 156 Baghetti G.P. Francia 1961 . . . . $20

R223 Maserati 250/12 cil. Prova 1957 . . . . $20
R224 Porsche 356 C Spyder 1963/65 . . . . $20
R225 Porsche 356 C Spyder Chiusa 1963/65 . . . . $20
R226 Porsche 356 C Coupe 1963/65 . . . . $20
R227 Ferrari 512 M Prototipo 1970 . . . . $20
R228 Ferrari 512 M 1000km Austria 1970 . . . . $20
R229 Ferrari 512 M Daytona 1971 . . . . $20
R230 Ferrari 512 M Le Mans 1971 . . . . $20
R231 Ferrari 512 M Watkins Glen 1971 . . . . $20
R232 Porsche 550 RS Stradale 1954 . . . . $20
R233 Porsche 550 RS Stradale Bicolore 1954 . . . . $20
R234 Porsche 550 RS America $20
R235 Porsche 550 RS Carresa Mexico 1953 . . . . $20
R236 Porsche 550 RS 1000km Nurburgring 1956 . . . . $20
R237 Alfa Romeo 33TT12 Prototipo 1974 . . . . $20
R238 Alfa Romeo 33TT12 1000Km Monza 1975 . . . . $20
R239 Alfa Romeo 33TT12 1000Km Monza 1975 . . . . $20
R240 Alfa Romeo 33TT12 1000Km Spa 1975 . . . . $20
R241 Alfa Romeo 33TT12 1000Km Spa 1975 . . . . $20
R242 Fiat 1100 E.I.A.R. 1948 . . . . $20
R243 Simca 5 Militare D-Day 1944 . . . . $20
R244 Simca 5 Furgoncino 1936 . . . . $20
R245 Fiat 1100 Furgone Campari 1952 . . . . $20
R246 Fiat 500B Furgone Vigili Del Fuoco 1946/49 . . . . $20
R255 Ferrari 312 F1 G.P. Italia (1967) Chris Amon $20
R256 Ferrari 312 F.1 G.P. Italia (1969) Pedro Rodriguez $20

BRUMM LIMITED EDITION

1986

S001 Porsche 365 - Circuito Avus $35
S002 Fiat F1 - Corsa $35
S003 Ferrari 815 - Circuito Di Pescara $35
S004 Porsche 365 - Rally Delle Alpi $35

1987

S005 Vanwall F1 '58 . . . . $35
S006 Mercedes W196 '54 . . . . $35
S007 Jaguar XK120 - '48 . . . . $35
S008 Ferrari D246 - G.P. Belgio '48 . . . . $35

1988

S009 Ferrari 156 - G.P. Belgio '61 . . . . $35
S010 Alfa Romeo 2900 - G.P. Bremgarten $35
S011 Benz Blitzen - Berlino-Avus '11 . . . . $35
S012 Bugatti 57-S - Tourist Trophy '35 . . . . $35

1989

S013 Ferrari 330 - Piper-Atwood '66 . . . . $35
S014 Ferrari 330 P4 - NART '67 . . . . $35
S015 Ferrari 330 P4 - Francorchamps '67 . . . . $35
S016 Ferrari 330 P4 - Scud. Maranello $35

1990

S017 Porsche 356 Rally Delle Alpi '52 . . . . $35
S018 Porsche 356 Targa Florio '52 . . . . $35
S019 Porsche 356 Carrera Mexico '52 . . . . $35
S020 Porsche 356 Rally Montecarlo '52 . . . . $35

1992

S072/92 Ferrari 512 BB LM 1980, prodotta per il 20∞ anno di attivit‡ della ditta $35

1993

FANGIO WORLD CHAMPION F.1

S021 Alfa Romeo 159 (1951) $35

S022 Mercedes W196 (1954) $35
S023 Mercedes W196 (1955) $35
S024 Ferrari D50 (1956) $35
S025 Maserati 250F '57 . . . . $35

1994
DAYTONA 1967

S026 Ferrari 330 P4 Spider 1967 Daytona $35
S027 Ferrari 330 P4 Coupe 1967 Daytona $35
S028 Ferrari 330 P3 Coupe 1967 Daytona $35

LE MANS 1967

S029 Ferrari 330 P4 Coupe 1967 Le Mans $35
S030 Ferrari 330 P4 Coupe 1967 Le Mans $35
S031 Ferrari 330 P4 Coupe 1967 Le Mans $35

1995
79A TARGA FLORIO

S032 Fiat 500C Copmmissari Di Gara 1954 . . . . $35
S033 Lancia D24 1954 . . . . $35
S034 Mercedes 300SLR 1955 . . . . $35
S035 Ferrari TR59 1959 . . . . $35
S036 Ferrari 330P3 1966 . . . . $35
S037 Ferrari 330P4 1967 . . . . $35

TARGA FLORIO 1995 5000 PIECES LIMITED EDITION

S032 Fiat 500C Belvedere, Commissari Di Gara, 38a Targa Florio
    1954 . . . . $45
S033 Lancia D24, Commissari Di Gara, 38a Targa Florio 1954 . $45
S034 Mercedes 300SLR, 1∞ Piero Taruffi, 38a Targa Florio 1954 . $45
S035 Ferrari TR59, Behra-Brooks, 43a Targa Florio 1959 . . . . . $45
S036 Ferrari 330P3, Bandini-Vaccarella, 50a Targa Florio 1966 . $45
S037 Ferrari 330P4, Vaccarella-Scafiotti, 51a Targa Florio 1957 . $45

BRUMM BIS (REVIVAL MODEL VARIANTS)
1989 OUT OF PRODUCTION

R22 bis Fiat 500A Stato Del Vaticano (1936) $50
R33 bis Fiat 1100 508c Versione Gasogeno (1937) $50
R47 bis Fiat 500A Mille Miglia (1947) $50
R67 bis Ferrari 815 Mille Miglia (1940) $50
R76 bis Ferrari D50 G.P. Italia - Monza (1956) $50
R77 bis Alfa Romeo 2300 Allestimento Speciale (1931) $50
R90 bis Alfa Romeo 1900 Mille Miglia (1954) $50
R120 bis Porsche 356 Mille Miglia (1952) $50
R145 bis Alfa Romeo 1900 Carrera Mexico (1954) $50

BRUMM BIS 1992

R36 bis Alfa Romeo 159 Farina - G.P. Spagna (1951) $40
R37 bis Mercedes W154 S.Lang - G.P. Tripoli (193) $40
R58 bis Lancia Aprilia Prima Serie (1958) $40
R131 bis Lancia B24 Allestimento Speciale (1955) $40
R171 bis Ferrari 312/F.1 C.Amon-G.P. USA (1968) $40

BRUMM BIS 1993

R13 bis Fiat 500C Mille Miglia (1937) $40
R21 bis Fiat 500A Targa Florio (1948) $40
R117 bis Porsche 356 Speedster James Dean (1954) $40
R156 bis Ferrari Testa Rossa Governors Trophy Race (1960) . . $40
R183 bis Ferrari 125S- Circuito Di Piacenza (1947) $40

BRUMM BIS 1994

R101 bis Jaguar XK120 Stirling Moss Silverstone (1951) $40
R114 bis Speed Six Birkin-Chaasagne Le Mans (1930) $40
R162 bis Lancia Aurelia B20 Bonetto-Anselmi Le Mans (1952) . $40
R173 bis Bugatti Type 59 G.P. Italia (1931) $40
R188 bis Mercedes 300SLR Levegh-Fich Le Mans (1955) $40

BRUMM CLASSIC CARRIAGES

B01 Landaulet $65
B02 Landaulet (Aperto) $65
B03 Coupe $65
B04 Coupe Dormeuse $65
B05 Landau $65
B06 Landau (Aperto) $65
B07 Spyder $65
B08 Spyder (Aperto) $65
B09 Phaeton $65
B11 Dog Cart $65
B12 Vis-A-Vis $65
B13 Vis-A-Vis (Aperto) $65
B14 Milord $65
B15 Milord (Aperto) $65
B16 Coupe A Huit Ressorts $65
B17 Mail-Coach $65
B18 Duc A Huit Ressorts $65
B19 Brumm De Milan $65
B20 Berlina Papale Da Viaggio $65
B21 Cab $65
B22 Dress Chariot $65
B23 Post - Caise $65
B24 Royal Mail-Coach $65
B25 Tilbury $65
B26 Carrozza Napoleonica $65

BRUMM HISTORICAL (CARRIAGES WITH HORSES)

H00 Cavallo Con Finimenti Ed Attacchi $65
H01 Pariglia Eques. Con Finimenti Ed Attacchi $65
H02 Doppia Pariglia Con Finimenti Ed Attacchi $65
H03 Brumm De Milan Con Cavallo $65
H04 Berlina Da Viaggio Pio X $65
H05 Duc A Huit Ressorts of Napoleon III $65
H06 Mail Coach Vettura Da Posta Inglese $65
H07 Cab Dell'attrice Rejane $65
H08 Coupe Dormeuse of Paolina Bonaparte $65
H09 Phaeton of Emile Loubet $65
H10 Vis-A-Vis Gran Gala Nuziale $65
H11 Dog Cart of Guglielmo II of Germany $65
H12 Botticella De Roma $65
H13 Dress Chariot of Count of Caledonia $65
H14 Milord of Eugenia Montijo $65
H15 Spyder of George Sand $65
H16 Poste Chaise Vettura Da Noleggio Inglese $65
H17 Landau Bavarese $65
H18 Royal Mail-Coach $65
H19 Tilbury $65
H20 Portantina Spagnolesca $65
H21 Carrozza Napoleonica Da Campo $65

BRUMM OLD FIRE (STEAM POWERED VEHICLES)

X01 Fardier Par Cugnot 1769 . . . . $65
X02 Carro Di Newton 1680 . . . . $65
X03 Diligenza Di Gurney 1825 . . . . $65
X04 Carro Di Trevithick 1803 . . . . $65
X05 Carro Di Bordino 1854 . . . . $65
X06 Turbina Di Verbiest 1681 . . . . $65
X07 Vettura Di Pecquer 1828 . . . . $65
X08 Anfibio Di Evans 1801 . . . . $65

BRUMM 1996 TOY FAIRS

S96/01 Fiat 600 1a serie (1955), Milan Toy Fair, qty. 1,000 pieces for the Italian market. . . . . $75 – 90

S96/02 Fiat 600 1st serie (1955), Nourimberg Toy Fair, qty. 100 pieces numbered items. . . . . $500 – 750

BRUMM LIMITED EDITION FOR REPLICARS, THE NETHERLANDS

S96/03 Ferrari 357 (1951), First Ferrari victory in F.1, Silverstone, 1951 with Gonzales, qty. 600 pieces. $125

S96/04 Fiat 500A (1936), Roman Holiday, qty. 600 pieces . . . $125

BRUMM LIMITED EDITION FOR FEDERICO MOTTA EDITORE, MILAN, ITALY

S96/05 Fiat 600 Multipla (1956), Advertisment vehicol, qty. 1,000 pieces. . . . . $75 – 90

BRUMM LIMITED EDITION FOR LA MINI MINIERA, CUNEO, ITALY

S96/06 Ferrari 156 F1 G.P. Siracusa (1961), 1∞ classified Baghetti, qty. 1,000 pieces . . . . $75 – 90

S96/07 Fiat 500B Furgoncino, Expo Model Fossano 4-12/5/1996, qty. 1,000 pieces . . . . $75 – 90

BUBY (ALSO SEE COLLECTOR'S CLASSICS)

Reasonably priced but hard to find, Buby models were made in Argentina, and are nice models for the price. Many models are from old Solido dies, but some are original.

BUBY 1:64 SCALE MODELS

10 Mercedes-Benz 1112 Dump Truck	$5
20 Fiat 1500 Rally	$5
25 Fiat 128 Rally	$5
27 Renault 12 Rally	$5
1030 Maserati Indy	$5
1030 Peugeot 504	$5
1040 Mercedes-Benz 350SL	$5
1041 Mercedes-Benz 350SL Rally	$5
1050 Ford Mustang II	$5
1051 Ford Mustang, "Dukes of Hazzard"	$5
1052 Ford Mustang II Cobra	$5
1060 Citroen 3CV	$5
1070 Ford Sierra	$5
1081 Chevrolet Nova	$5
1090 Maserati Bora	$5
1091 Maserati Bora Rally	$5
1120 Volkswagen Facel (Fox)	$5
1140 Renault 12	$5
1141 Renault 12 Rally	$5
1142 Renault 12, "Polizia"	$5

Photo by Jeff Koch.

1160 Renault 18, $5

1161 Renault 18, "Polizia"	$5
1162 Renault 18, "Marlboro"	$5
1170 Renault 12 Station Wagon	$5
1171 Renault 12 Station Wagon, "Rescue"	$5
1180 1964 Opel Kapitan Ambulance	$5
1190 Ford F100 Tow Truck	$5
1212 VW Buggy	$5
1220 Ford Bronco	$5
1221 Ford Bronco with roll bar	$5
1224 Ford Bronco, "NASA"	$5
1227 Ford Bronco Wagon	$5
1230 Ford Van, "Marlboro"	$5
1231 Ford Van, "Coca Cola"	$5
1233 Ford Van, "John Player"	$5
1234 Ford Van, "Las Lenas"	$5
1235 Ford Van, "Peugeot"	$5
1240 Renault Fuego	$5
1241 Renault Fuego, "Cazalis"	$5
1250 Ford Sierra XR4	$5
1251 Ford Sierra XR4, "Bardahl"	$5
1260 Renault Kombi	$5
1261 Renault Kombi, "Aerolineas"	$5
1262 Renault Kombi Ambulance	$5
1263 Renault Kombi School Bus	$5
1264 Renault Kombi, "World Tour"	$5
1265 Renault Kombi, "Lufthansa"	$5
1270 Jeep CJ5	$5
2020 Chevrolet C60, "Esso"	$5
2030 Chevrolet C60 Fire Pumper	$5
2040 Chevrolet Semi Refrigerator	$5
2050 Chevrolet Semi Cattle	$5
2060 Fiat Cement Mixer	$5
3010 Ford Van 4x4, "Thunder"	$5
3020 Ford Van 4x4, "Cracker"	$5
3030 Jeep CJ5 4x4, "Mad Mex"	$5
3040 Jeep CJ5 4x4, "Vagabond"	$5
3050 Ford Bronco 4x4, "Old Iron"	$5
3060 Ford Bronco 4x4, "Outlaw"	$5

BUBY 1:43 SCALE MODELS

1000 Buick Century Ambulance, white	$100
1000A Buick Century Army Ambulance, green	$100
1001 Buick Century Station Wagon, blue and white	$100
1002 Ford Fairlane 500, blue and white	$100
1002A Ford Fairlane 500 Rally, red	$100
1003 Ford Fairlane 500 Policia, blue and white	$100
1004 Ford F100 Pickup, red	$60
1004A Army Pickup, green	$60
1004B Covered Pickup, blue and black, or green and black	$60
1023 Ika Torino Rally	$45
1033 1968 Chevrolet Nova Rally	$45
1036 Fiat 128	$18
1037 Fiat 128 Rally	$18
1046 1967 Chevrolet Camaro	$45
1047 1967 Chevrolet Camaro Rally	$45

BUCCANEER

Until collector Steve Mason provided photos of a toy 1937 Packard with the brand name "Buccaneer"

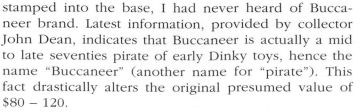
stamped into the base, I had never heard of Buccaneer brand. Latest information, provided by collector John Dean, indicates that Buccaneer is actually a mid to late seventies pirate of early Dinky toys, hence the name "Buccaneer" (another name for "pirate"). This fact drastically alters the original presumed value of $80 – 120.

1937 Packard, green	$15 – 20
1939 Chrysler	$15 – 20

BUDGIE (ALSO SEE MORESTONE)

Like Corgi, Dinky, Impy, and other diecast toys of the fifties and sixties, Budgies are a product of Great Britain. While Corgi is named after the Welsh corgi, a popular dog in Wales, Budgie is named after a budgerigar (parakeet), another popular pet for many Brits as well as bird lovers around the world. Budgie was originally owned by Morris and Stone (Morestone), who introduced the first castings as Esso promotional models before changing their name to Budgie The brand was later purchased by Guitermans. Budgie toys were popular in England and the US in the sixties, but were eclipsed by Corgi, Dinky, and especially Matchbox, eventually going out of business. Latest news indicates dies and castings have been purchased by a new company in England called "Autocraft" that is reproducing Budgie models in small quantities.

Twin Pack with Standard London Taxi, black, and London Bus, red	$45 – 60
Crane Truck, red with blue crane, 4"	$20
1 1960 Volkswagen Pickup, "Coca-Cola," 1:43	$115
12 1960 Volkswagen Micro Van, 4"	$25
18 Dump Truck, 1:64	$20
30 Rover Squad Car	$12
57 "REA Express" Parcel Delivery Van	$30 – 40
102 Rolls-Royce Silver Cloud	$30 – 40
224 Railway Engine	$25 – 30
236 Routemaster Double Decker Bus, 4"	$25 – 30

BUGATTIANA (SEE MODELAUTO)

BURAGO (SEE BBURAGO WITH TWO B'S)

BUSCH PRALINE (SEE PRALINE)

CAM-CAST

Cam-Cast produced just a few toy trucks from Edgerton, Ohio, in the 50s. They appear to be one fairly thick, crude lump of metal with details painted on or applied with decals. They carry a high value for such simple toys, mostly due to rarity.

Van, "Western Auto"	$40 – 75
Van, "North American Van Lines"	$40 – 75
Van, "Pillsbury's Best"	$40 – 75
Van, "Evan Motor Freight	$40 – 75
Oil Tanker, "Gulf"	$40 – 75
Oil Tanker, "Marathon Oil"	$40 – 75
Oil Tanker, "Sunoco"	$40 – 75

CARMANIA

Currently available is an assortment of Carmania models of France in 1:64 scale, and one 1:43 scale model.

CARMANIA 1:64 SCALE

10 1976 Chevrolet Camaro Z28, pink	$5
11 1981 Chevrolet Camaro, yellow	$5
12 Chevrolet Corvette Convertible, silver	$5
13 Chevrolet Corvette Coupe, maroon	$5
14 1974 Ferrari 308 Coupe, blue	$5
15 1974 Ferrari 308 Coupe, maroon	$5
16 1974 Ferrari 308 Roadster, red	$5
17 Ferrari 365 GT, yellow or pink	$5
18 Ferrari Testarossa, red	$5
19 1989 Ford Thunderbird Rally, orange	$5
21 Ford F250 4WD Pickup, white	$5
22 Honda CRX Coupe, red	$5
23 Lamborghini Countach, blue	$5
26 Mercedes 307 Van, yellow/white	$5
27 Morgan Plus 4 Roadster, green	$5
28 Nissan Mid 4 Coupe, black	$5
32 1969 Pontiac GTO Hardtop	$5
33 1981 Pontiac Firebird Convertible	$5
34 1976 Pontiac Firebird T-Top	$5
36 Porsche 928, blue	$5
37 Porsche 928, "Pennzoil"	$5
39 Suzuki Samurai	$5
40 Toyota Extended Cab Pickup	$5
42 1920 Vauxhall	$5
43 1980 Camaro Z28, purple	$5
44 Volkswagen Beetle Baja Bug, yellow	$5

CARMANIA 1:43 SCALE

100 Schnauzer Team P7 "Esso," white	$15

C. A. W. NOVELTY COMPANY

C.A.W. Novelty Company was started in 1925 in Kansas by Charles A. Wood. His fine examples of "slushmold" (lead alloy) toys were not fully appreciated by collectors until as late as 1990 when one collector named Chic Gast described a group of unidentified toys as "orphans." The toys were also marketed by the name of Mid-West Metal Novelty Manufacturing Company in 1929. World War II brought lead casting to a halt in 1940 and C.A.W. went with it. The last employee of the company, Rod Hemphill, and newfound partner Howard Clevenger purchased the company assets and started C&H Manufacturing Company. C.A.W. toys originally sold for 10¢ to $1.

Air Drive Coach, #25, 3⅞"	$30 – 40
Desoto Sedan, #32, 3⅞"	$30 – 40
Dump Truck, 3⅛"	$30 – 40
Fuel Tanker, 3¾"	$30 – 40
Marvel Racer, #31, 3⅜"	$30 – 40
New Design Racer, #38, 3⅜"	$30 – 40
Overland Bus, 3¾"	$30 – 40
Sport Roadster, 3½"	$30 – 40
Streamline Coupe, #30, 3"	$30 – 40
Tank Truck, 3³⁄₁₆"	$30 – 40
Transparent Windshield Racer, #39, 3"	$30 – 40
Wonder Special, #33, 3⅜"	$30 – 40

C.B.Car

From Milan, Italy, Esci produces a series of 1:24 scale cars called "Real Cars" under the "C.B.CAR" brand.

#105 Porsche 959, opening doors and engine compartment, wheels steer, $16

CCC

Collector Bill Cross reports that these are resin models, handmade in France. The range now includes "unusual" European cars like Ford Vedettes, Peugeot 203, and the tiny Rovin microcar.

1936 Ford Roadster	$125
1955 Ford Crown Victoria	$125
Ford Vedette	$130
Delahaye Fire T-140	$135
Peugeot 203	$130
Rovin Microcar	$130

C.D.

One of the most obscure French toy companies, C.D. produced a small assortment of cast toy vehicles in the 1920s that are now valued around $100 each.

Bugatti Sports Car	$100
Chenard & Walcker Ambulance	$100
Chenard & Walcker Limousine	$100
Chenard & Walcker "Ricard" Van	$100
Chenard & Walcker Wrecker, 3⅜"	$100
Delage Limousine	$100
Delahaye Ambulance	$100
Delahaye Fire Truck	$100
Delahaye Limousine	$100
Delahaye Torpedo	$100
Delahaye Van	$100
Ford Model T	$100
Hotchkiss Limousine	$100
Latil Farm Truck	$100
Latil Van, 3¾"	$100
MG Record Car	$100
Panhard Tractor	$100
Peugeot Sans Soupape	$100
Renault 40CV Berline	$100
Renault 40CV Coupe	$100
Renault 40CV Limousine	$100
Renault 40CV Torpedo	$100
Renault 40CV Ambulance	$100
Renault 40CV Truck	$100

Renault Vivaquatre Coupe	$100
Rosengart Super Traction Fastback	$100
Rosengart Super Traction Roadster	$100

CDC (see Detail Cars)

Century (see AMR)

Chad Valley

Chad Valley, as the name implies, is a brand of scale model cars made by a British firm based in South Africa. Models were produced starting in the late forties. Some models were especially made for "the Rootes Group" as promotionals at dealerships. Diecasting continued until 1956.

220 Rolls-Royce Razor Edge Saloon, 1:43	$165
221 Rolls-Royce Razor Edge Traffic Control, 1:43	$165
222 Rolls-Royce Razor Edge Police Car, 1:43	$165
223 Record Car, 1:43	$175
224 Double Decker Bus, 1:76	$250
225 Commer Open Truck	$150
226 Commer Flat Truck	$150
227 Commer Timber Wagon	$150
228 Commer Cable Layer	$165
229 Commer Breakdown Truck	$165
230 Commer Milk Truck with eight milk cans	$175
231 Commer Fire Engine	$175
232 Commer Tower Repair Wagon	$150
233 Commer Milk Tanker	$175
234 Commer Petrol Tanker	$150
235 Tractor, 1:43	$150
236 Hillman Minx, 1:43	$140
237 Humber Super Snipe, 1:43	$125
238 Sunbeam-Talbot, 1:43	$150
239 Dust Cart	$150
240 Commer Avenger Coach, 1:76	$200
241 Karrier Public Health Vehicle	$150
242 Commer Truck	$175
243 Bulldozer	$150
244 Farm Trailer	$40
245 Manure Spreader	$75
247 Stacutrac	$175
500 Guy Van, "Chad Valley"	$225
500 Guy Van, "Guy Motors"	$225
503 Fordson Tractor, 1:43	$175
504 Guy Ice Cream Truck, 1:43	$250
507 Humber Hawk, 1:43	$200
509 Hay Rake	$60
550 Saloon, 1:70	$35
551 Single Decker Coach, 1:70	$35
552 Van, 1:70	$35
553 Post Office Van	$35
554 Ambulance	$35

Charbens

Leslie and John Barker of Guelph, Ontario, Canada, report that Charbens were made in England probably in the fifties and early sixties. The accuracy of scale is average, quality of casting is good. Some cars are cast in two pieces.

While casting detail is low, fenders are attached separately. Detailing was likely by hand. Wheels are painted on outside only. Lights and grill, if present, are painted.

CHARBENS OLD CROCK SERIES

OC1 1894 Darracq Genevieve, red, orange, or blue $20

OC2 1904 Spyker, yellow & black $20

OC3 1914 "Old Bill" Double Decker Bus

    v.1 cast in two halves $20

    v.2 single cast. $30

OC4 1907 Ford Model T, blue $20

OC5 1907 Vauxhall, green $20

OC6 1906 De Dion Bouton $20

OC7 1898 Panhard, blue, light green & silver, or brown & silver . $20

OC8 1906 Rolls-Royce Silver Ghost, silver $20

OC9 1903 Standard 6 HP $15

OC10 1902 Wolseley, turquoise $20

OC11 1908 Packard Runabout, light green $20

OC12 1905 Packard Runabout $20

OC13 1900 Straker Steam Lorry $20

OC14 Stephenson's Rocket Locomotive $20

OC15 Rocket Tender $20

OC16 1909 Albion Pickup $20

OC17 1912 Rover Roadster $20

OC18 1911 Mercedes-Benz $20

M19 Bedford Horse Transport $25

OC20 1910 Lanchester $20

OC21 1922 Morris Cowley Roadster $20

OC22 1900 Daimler $20

OC23 1904 Autocar $20

OC24 1870 Grenville Steam Carriage $20

OC25 1905 Napier Record Car $20

OC26 Fire Engine $25

OC27 Articulated Breakdown Truck $20

OC28 1913 Mercer Runabout $20

M30 Mobile Searchlight $20

M31 Mobile Twin Bofor Gun $20

M32 Mobile Radar $20

M33 Mobile Field Gun $20

M34 Mobile Rocket Gun $20

M35 Armoured Car $20

OTHER CHARBENS

6 Farm Tractor $65

8 Tipping Truck $50

9 Motor Coach $75

10 Royal Mail Van $65

11 Ambulance $65

12 Van, "Carter Paterson" $60

13 Police Van $65

14 Post Office Van $65

15 Dennis Fire Engine $75

17 Tractor and Three Trailers $75

18 Tractor and Grass Cutter $75

19 Tractor and Harvester $75

20 Mobile Crane $45

21 Muir Hill Dumper $50

26 Armoured Car $50

28 Steam Roller $45

31 Cable Truck $65

32 Alfa Romeo Racinge Car $100

33 Cooper-Bristol Racing Car $100

34 Ferrari Racing Car $100

36 Horse Transport Box $75

37 Rocket Gun on Truck and Trailer $70

Javelin Saloon $100

Morris Fire Engine $75

Morris Station Wagon $75

Morris Van, "Esso" $65

Pedestrian Electric Vehicle, "Dairy Milk" $100

Pedestrian Electric Vehicle, "Hovis" $100

Scammell GWR Mechanical Horse $65

Tanker $65

Van $50

CHARMERZ (ALSO SEE PLAYART)

According to Dave Weber of Warrington, Pennsylvania, Playart at one time produced a series of models called Charmerz for New York distributor Charles Merzbach. No other information is currently available as of this writing.

CHERRYCA PHENIX

Taiseiya of Japan originally marketed these exceptional 1:43 scale diecast models, some with battery-operated lights, under the "Micropet" brand in the early sixties. Taiseiya was later purchased by Yonezawa, known for Diapet diecast models.

1 Hino Contessa $250

2 Nissan Cedric Station Wagon $250

3 Mercedes-Benz 300 SL Roadster $275

4 Datsun $100

5 Chevrolet Impala $275

6 Buick Electra $275

7 Ford Falcon $275

8 Volkswagen 1200 . . . . $275

9 Volkswagen Karmann Ghia Roadster $325

10 Dodge Polara $235

11 Mercedes-Benz 300 SL Hardtop $275

12 Datsun 1200 Station Wagon $250

13 Datsun 1200 Pickup $250

14 Isuzu Bellel 2000 De Luxe $275

15 Ford Thunderbird $275

16 Datsun Fairlady Roadster $275

17 Lincoln Continental $300

18 Mercedes-Bent 220 SE $275

19 Citroen DS 19 Convertible $325

20 Cadillac 62 Special $300

21 Chevrolet $125

22 Datsun Bluebird $425

23 Jaguar Type E Roadster $250

24 Prince Gloria $250

25 Nissan Cedric $250

26 Toyota Crown $250

27 Toyota Crown Station Wagon $250

28 Toyota Corona $250

29 Mercedes-Benz 300 SL Roadster $275

30 Isuzu Bellet $250

31 Prince Skyline 1500 . . . . $250

32 Datsun Bluebird $225

33 Mitsubishi Colt 1000	$225
34 Hino Contessa	$225
35 Nissan Cedric Taxi	$275
36 Toyota Crown Police Car	$275
37 Toyota Crown Taxi	$275
38 Honda S 600 Roadster	$225
39 Prince Sprint Coupe	$225
40 Toyota Corona Coupe	$225
41 Daihatsu Compagno	$200
42 Mitsubishi Debonair	$200
43 Nissan Cedric Police Car	$250
44 Mazda Luce	$225
45 Mitsubishi Colt 1000 Rally	$250
46 Datsun Bluebird Rally	$250
47 Nissan Skyline Rally	$250
48 Prince Gloria Rally	$250
50 Isuzu Bellet GT	$250
001 Fordson Major Tractor and Trailer	$225
0T1 1892 Peugeot	$75
0T2 1896 Peugeot	$75
0T3 1898 Peugeot Victoria	$75
0T4 1899 Peugeot Victoria	$75
0T5 1901 Decauville Vis-a-Vis	$75
0T6 1901 Delahaye Vis-a-Vis	$75
FL-1 Buick Electra	$275
FL-2 Ford Falcon	$275

CHICO (SEE TEKNO)

CIBA

1:43 scale Mercedes-Benz cars appear to be the only models issued by Ciba.

Mercedes-Benz 300E, blue, green, red, or yellow $11

CIGAR BOX (SEE AURORA)

C.I.J.

Compagnie Industrielle du Jouet, better known as C.I.J. of France, first produced 1:43 scale models in 1933 out of plaster and flour. Other materials used in producing models included tin plate, lead cast, and, from 1938 to 1964, diecast. The firm of J.R.D. was purchased in 1963, and a few C.I.J. models were reissued unchanged as J.R.D. models and vice versa. Here is an assortment of known models. Introduction year and current value follows the description.

Berliet GLR 19 Tank Truck, #3/23, 1959	$75
Berliet GLR 19 "Shell" Tanker, #3/24, 1959	$75
Berliet Semi-Trailer Truck, #3/77, 1965	$110
Berliet Weitz Mobile Crane, #3/84, 1964 – 65	$90
Caravan Trailer, #3/27, 1959	$55
Cattle Trailer, #3/28, 1962	$55
Chrysler Windsor Sedan, #3/15, 1956	$140
Citroen AMI 6, #3/6, 1964	$55
Citroen ID19 Ambulance, #3/41, 1964	$85
Citroen ID19 Estate Car, #3/4, 1958 – 59	$85
Citroen 11CV, #3/11, 1964-65 (reissued as J.R.D. #112)	$55
Citroen 1200KG Van, #3/89, 1965	$90
Citroen 1200KG Police Van, #3/89, 1964 – 65	$90
Citroen 2CV Mail Van, #3/76, 1965	$80
Crane Truck, #3/81, 1956	$90
De Rovin Open Two-Seater, #3/1, 1954	$85
Facel Vega Facellia, #3/3, 1958 – 60	$90
Fire Engine, #3/30, 1959	$110
Mercedes-Benz 220 Sedan, #3/12, 1959	$55
Panhard "BP" Tank Truck, #3/20, 1951	$60
Panhard Dyna 130, #3/47, 1950	$70
Panhard Dyna 54, #3/54, 1955	$70
Panhard Dyna Junior, #3/5, 1954	$85
Peugeot 403 Break, #3/46, 1955	$60
Peugeot 403 Ambulance, #3/46, 1962	$75
Peugeot 403 Police Car, #3/46, 1960	$55
Peugeot 404 Sedan, #3/13, 1965 (reissued as J.R.D. #151)	$55
Plymouth Belvedere Sedan, #3/16, 1957	$140
Renault 1000KG Van, #3/60, 1955	$55
Renault 1000KG Astra Van, #3/60, 1957	$90
Renault 1000KG Boucherie Van, #3/60, 1960	$90
Renault 1000KG Mail Van, #3/60, 1957	$90
Renault 1000KG Belgian Mail Van, #3/60, 1957	$125
Renault 1000KG "Shell" Van, #3/60, 1956	$90
Renault 1000KG Van and Trailer, #3/60, 1957	$115
Renault 1000KG Ambulance, #3/61, 1955	$110
Renault 1000KG Army Ambulance, #3/61, 1959	$110
Renault 1000KG Bus, #3/62, 1955	$90
Renault 1000KG Police Van, #3/63, 1955	$80
Renault 2.5 Ton Bottle Truck, #3/94, 1963	$95
Renault 2.5 Ton Fire Engine, #3/95, 1963	$120
Renault 2.5 Ton Gun Truck, #3/99, 1964	$100
Renault 2.5 Ton Radar Truck, #3/98, 1964	$100
Renault 300KG Van, #3/67, 1957	$55
Renault 300KG Mail Van, #3/68, 1957	$70
Renault 4CV, #3/48, 1950	$70
Renault 4CV Police Car, #3/49, 1950	$70
Renault 7-Ton Covered Truck, #3/25, 1953	$40
Renault Alpine Coupe, #3/50, 1958-59	$55
Renault Atomic Pile Transporter, #3/75, 1957	$180
Renault Bus, #3/40, 1954	$80
Renault Colorale Ambulance, #3/55, 1956	$80
Renault Colorale, #3/44, 1953	$55
Renault Covered Trailer, #3/26, 1953	$40
Renault Domane Break, #3/53, 1958	$60
Renault Domane Ambulance, #3/53, 1960	$75
Renault Dauphine, #3/56, 1956	$60
Renault Dauphine Taxi, #3/56, 1958	$60
Renault Dauphine Police, #3/57, 1958	$60
Renault Dauphinoise Break, #3/66, 1956 – 57	$55
Renault Dauphinoise Police Car, #3/69, 1955	$80
Renault Dump Truck, #3/80, 1955	$80
Renault E-30 Farm Tractor, #3/33, 1959	$110
Renault E-30 Tractor and Trailer, #3/34, 1959	$165
Renault Estafette Bus, #3/92, 1961	$70
Renault Estafette Van, #3/90, 1963	$75
Renault Estafette Police Bus, #3/93, 1962	$75
Renault Estafette Police Van, #3/91, 1963	$75
Renault Etoile Filante Record Car, #3/2, 1957	$90
Renault Excavator, #3/88, 1964 – 65	$75
Renault Floride, #3/58, 1960	$55

Renault Fregate, #3/51, 1951. . . . . $60
Renault Fregate Grand Pavois, #3/52, 1958 . . . . $60
Renault Police Pickup and Trailer, #3/65, 1962 . . . . $100
Renault Prairie, #3/42, 1953 . . . . $55
Renault Prairie Taxi, #3/45, 1955 . . . . $55
Renault Savane, #3/43, 1953. . . . . $55
Renault Searchlight Truck and Trailer, #3/96, 1963. . . . . $100
Renault Semi-Trailer Truck, #3/70, 1955 . . . . $80
Renault Semi-Trailer Tank Truck, #3/72, 1958 . . . . $100
Renault Semi-Trailer Log Truck, #3/73, 1956 . . . . $80
Renault "Shell" Tank Truck, #3/21, 1952 . . . . $60
Renault Tractor and Sling Cart Trailer, #3/39, 1959. . . . . $160
Renault Tractor and Trailer, #3/38, 1959 . . . . $160
Renault Wrecker, #3/83, 1964. $90
Sailboat on Trailer, #3/76, 1964 . . . . $55
Saviem Bottle Truck, #3/79, 1965 . . . . $100
Saviem Missile Launcher, #3/97, 1964 . . . . $100
Seed Trailer, #3/32, 1959 . . . . $55
Shovel Truck, #3/82, 1958 . . . . $90
Simca 1000 Coupe Bertone, #3/9, 1964. . . . . $55
Simca 1000 Sedan, #3/7, 1962-63 . . . . $55
Simca 1000 Police Car, #3/8, 1963. . . . . $55
Sling Cart Trailer, #3/36, 1959. . . . . $60
Sugar Beet Trailer, #3/31, 1959 . . . . $60
Tipping Farm Trailer, #3/37, 1959. . . . . $60
Unic Cab and Trailer with railroad Car, #3/78 . . . . $140
Volkswagen, #3/10, 1954 . . . . $65
Water Tank Trailer, #3/35, 1959 . . . . $55

CKO

The trademark logo on the bottom of CKO models is all that identifies these models. The C forms an arc around the K, and the O encircles both. Models are made in Germany and are quite rare for their vintage, being produced sometime between the mid-60s and mid-70s. *Schroeder's Collectible Toys Antique to Modern* lists just three models. At a recent toy show, Chris Quimby of Vancouver, Washington, offered one more specimen, a yellow Volkswagen Beetle.

Ferrari Formula 1, red $125
Mercedes-Benz Taxi, cream $125
Volkswagen Pickup, blue. $145
Volkswagen Beetle, #425, yellow $45

CLASSIC CONSTRUCTION MODELS

Brass construction comprises these scale model construction vehicles from Classic Construction Models made in Beaverton, Oregon. The series represents 12 models issued in limited edition of 1,000 each. Classic Construction Models, 6590 SW Fallbrook Place, Beaverton OR 97008. Phone 503-626-6395, fax 503-646-1996. Worldwide website: http://www.teleport.com/~ccmodels.

#1 Caterpillar 325 L, 1:87. . . . . $40 – 60
#2 Caterpillar D8R, 1:87 . . . . $40 – 60

CLASSY CHASSIES (SEE MEGAMOVERS)

CLAU-MAR

One of the many obscure brands currently available is a series of 1:43 scale Clau-Mar models from Argentina, all are variations of a particular bus with various liveries.

Camello 3-Deck Bus
   v.1 silver, "Chevallier". $15
   v.2 white, "El Condor" $15
   v.3 white, Expreso Rojas" $15
   v.4 white, "Expreso Singer". $15
   v.5 silver, "International". $15
   v.6 white, "La Estrella" $15
   v.7 white, "Rio Del Plata" $15
   v.8 white, "Sierra Cordoba". $15

CLE (ALSO SEE BONUX)

Clement Gaget founded the Cle firm of France, manufacturer of plastic toy vintage cars since 1958. The company also produced a series of diecast models under the Bonux brand. For a listing of models and values, see the Bonux section of this book.

CLOVER (ALSO SEE NEW CLOVER)

Clover models are manufactured in Korea, China, and other Asian manufacturing centers.

Bobcat X225 Skid Loader, 1:25 . . . . $35
Bobcat 743B Skid Loader, 1:19 . . . . $25
Bobcat 753 Skid Loader, 1:50 . . . . $10
Bobcat 753 Skid Loader, 1:25 . . . . $25
Bobcat 7753 Skid Loader, 1:25 . . . . $25

1959 – 1962 Melroe (Bobcat) M-200 Loader, 1:25 (replica of first machine built by Melroe Company), $18

Semi Flatbed with three Bobcat 753 Skid Loaders, 1:50 . . . . . . $55
Kiamaster Ambulance, 1:43 . . . . $18
Kiamaster Kombi, 1:43. . . . . $18
Pontiac Firebird Coupe, 1:59 . . . . $5

CMA

CMA is reputed to make a number of top-quality 1:24 scale diecast. They are more expensive than the Mints — Franklin and Danbury — in the $600 to $2,000 range. Marshall Buck is the reported owner of the company. Attention to exact detail is apparently what sets CMA models apart from the rest. No listing available as of this writing.

CMC

CMC of Germany is one of the more recent arrivals on the diecast scale model scene. Their 1:24 scale models are offered by just a few dealers. The price is already rising on these exceptionally fine models. Exoticar and TfC (see Resource Directory in back of book) both offer a 1:24 scale model of The Black Prince. Created and built from a 1930 Mercedes SSK chassis as a one-of-a-kind sports car by Count Trossi, The Black Prince survived 60 years and many different owners. Now owned by Ralph Lauren, it won the Concours d'Elegance at Pebble Beach. The 1:24 scale model offers amazing detail that includes a beautiful black lacquer finish, photo etched metal wire wheels, brakes, grille and exhaust, hand-painted engine detail with exposed metal exhaust headers, complete with leather bonnet strap, and photo etched metal buckle. The interior is leather and fully carpeted with accurately detailed gauges and steering wheel, and an opening trunk with spare tire. In addition, TfC offers another 1:24 scale CMC model of a 1936 Mercedes Benz 500 K Spezialroadster of which only 25 of the real car were ever made. Only five of the original cars exist, but the miniature model is just as beautiful. Hand assembled from over 200 parts, it has exquisite engine and chassis detail and real leather seats. The red body is offset with 30 chrome moldings and chrome wire wheels with whitewall tires.

1 "The Black Prince" 1930 Mercedes Benz SSK . . . . . . $135 – 140
2 1936 Mercedes Benz 500 K Spezialroadster, available in blue or
     red . . . . $140 – 155
CMC 1:43 hand built in China for Germany
CM001 Jiefang fire tanker, Beijing. $62

CODE 3 COLLECTIBLES

One of the newest emerging diecast model companies is Code 3 Collectibles of Woodland Hills, California. The first model to appear on the market, in the summer of 1997, was a 1:64 scale Seagrave fire engine. It is beautifully packaged in an elegant clear display package and sold for around $20. The following listings are variations of that fire engine, with month and number issued. Code 3 Collectibles, 6115 Variel Avenue, Woodland Hills CA 91367-3727. Worldwide website: http://www.code3.net.

v.1 City of Los Angeles, April, 25,000 (archived) . . . . . . $25 – 30
v.2 Houston Fire Department, July, 25,000 . . . . $20
v.3 Philadelphia Fire Department, September, 25,000 . . . . $20
v.4 Fire Department of New York, November, 25,000 . . . . $20
v.5 Honolulu Fire Department, November, 15,000 . . . . . $25 – 30
v.6 Louisville Fire Department, November, 15,000 . . . . . $25 – 30

COFRADIS

Two Cofradis models are currently known. They are listed as 1:43 scale models for $24 each. Most Cofradis issues are modified Solido models.

100 Shelter Euro Missile $24
117 Mack "Danone" Van $24

COLLECTOR CASE

Most unpainted models such as Collector Case resemble pewter, but are likely made of cast aluminum or the more common "zamak," the zinc alloy common to diecast models. If these didn't cost so much, I would think the intent would be for the collector to paint them. But I would be very hesitant to alter a model that costs $60 to $80. Unless expertly done, it would likely render the model worthless. Diehard hobbyists, however, would likely consider it a challenge to do a good job of customizing. Collector Case models are available in unpainted base metal, except where noted.

COLLECTOR CASE 1:43 SCALE

602 1963 Chevrolet Corvette Coupe $65
604 1974 Chevrolet Corvette Convertible, top down $65
606 1974 Chevrolet Corvette T-Top. $55
607 1936 Ford Phaeton 4-door, top up, black & tan. $47
608 1936 Ford Convertible 4-door, top down $47
609 Shelby Cobra 427 . . . . $60
612 1937 Mercedes-Benz 540 K $47
614 1948 Ford Convertible 2-door, top down $65
615 1936 Ford Roadster $65
616 1956 Ford Thunderbird Coupe $47
617 1966 Ford Mustang GT Coupe $60
618 1948 MG TC $55
619 1986 Chevrolet Corvette Coupe $47
620 1986 Chevrolet Corvette, top down $47
621 1953 Austin Healy 3000 RDS, top down $65
622 Porsche 928. . . . . $47
624 1932 Ford Coupe. $47
625 1936 Auburn Speedster $47
628 1956 Ford Thunderbird Convertible, top down $60
629 1933 Duesenberg SJ. $47
631 1961 Chevrolet Stingray Racer $65
633 1957 Porsche 356 Speedster, top down. $60
701 1956 Chevrolet Corvette, red $47

COLLECTOR CASE 1:72 SCALE AIRPLANES

901 F4U-1 Corsair $65
902 P-51 Mustang $65
903 F4F Wildcat. $65
904 P-40 Warhawk $65
905 Douglas DC-3 . . . . $65
907 F-15 "Desert Storm" $65

COLLECTOR CASE 1:76 SCALE

A series of Chevrolet Corvette coupes and convertibles from 1963 to 1982 are currently offered for $18 each, with the exception of a 1964 Corvette on a pewter-like base for $30.

COLLECTOR'S CLASSICS (ALSO SEE BUBY)

These fabulous 1:43 scale models of American cars from the 40s, 50s, and 60s are made in Argentina by Buby.

1h 1955 Chevrolet Bel Air hard top. $55
1o 1955 Chevrolet Bel Air convertible, top down $55
2c 1953 Ford Sunliner convertible, top up. $55
2h 1953 Ford Sunliner hard top $55
2o 1953 Ford Sunliner convertible, top down $55
2p 1953 Ford Indy Pace Car, limited $55
3c 1954 Mercury Monterey, top up $55
3h 1954 Mercury Sun Valley Coupe $55
3o 1954 Mercury Monterey, top down $55
4c 1956 Packard Carribean convertible, top up $55

4h 1956 Packard Carribean hard top $55
4o 1956 Packard Carribean convertible, top down $55
5h 1956 De Soto Fireflite hard top $55
5c 1956 De Soto Fireflite convertible, top up $55
5o 1956 De Soto Fireflite convertible, top down $55
5p 1956 De Soto Indy Pace Car $55
6c 1946 Lincoln Continental convertible, top up $55
6o 1946 Lincoln Continental convertible, top down $55
6p 1946 Lincoln Continental Indy Pace Car $55
7 1956 De Soto Adventurer, white & gold $55
8 1956 De Soto Adventurer, black & gold $55
A 1964 Studebaker Avanti Sports Coupe, #21 . . . . $55
BU2 1969 Chevrolet Camaro RS convertible, top down $55

COLLECTORS MINT

These are pewter models in 1:43 scale made by Richardi
Auto Models of New Jersey.

COMET-AUTHENTICAST

Comet-Authenticast was started in Queens, New York, by
the Slonim family around 1940. Starting with toy soldiers,
Comet switched to producing identification models of military vehicles for the government on the verge of World War
II. They continued selling them as toys after the war until
the early 1960s. Reissues have recently been produced by
Quality Castings of Alexandria, Virginia, using the original
molds. Original models are currently valued at $10. Reissues
are worth around $5.

CON-COR

Con-Cor vehicles are 1:87 scale prepainted plastic models
that feature full-color lettering on sides and ends. All vehicles are preassembled. Included in the series are semis with
trailers, separate semi trailers, rail containers, cars, and
buses, all designed for use with HO gauge railroad layouts.

CON-COR SEMI WITH TRAILER

Atchinson, Topeka & Santa Fe Freight Truck $8
Brillion Freight Truck. $8
Chiquita Freight Truck $9
Evergreen Freight Truck. $8
Hi-Way Dispatch Freight Truck $8
Mayflower Moving Van $12
Miller Truck Log Truck $8
Pacific Fruit Express. $8
Palumbo Open Back Truck $8
Pepsi Freight Truck $8
Registered Texas Longhorns. $8
Riteway Double Freighter. $11
Rollins Freight Truck $8
Safety Kleen Tanker. $10
Texaco Tanker. $10
Texas Oil Tanker. $8
Transcon Double Freight Truck $11
Union Tanker $8
US Mail Freight Truck $9

CON-COR "AMERICA 500 YEARS" SEMI W/TRAILER, SPECIAL EDITION

Columbus $17
Monuments $17

New York Skyline $17
Space $17
US Capital $17
Wild West $17

CON-COR BLUEBIRD SCHOOL BUSSES

Camp Woebegon. $11
County #4 . . . . $11
Good Shepherd $11
Helping Hand Temporary Labor $11
Maintenance-of-Way $11
Unified School Dist. #2. . . . . $11
US Army $11
Washington HS $11

CON-COR AUTOS & OTHERS

'57 Chevy $8
'69 Mustang. $8
Ferrari Testarossa. $8
Fire Chief 4x4 . . . . $3.50
Ford Mustang $8
Lamborghini $8
Mercedes-Benz 300E $3

CONQUEST

Conquest models are exquisite 1:43 scale cars hand built
in England. Toys for Collectors offers a beautiful assortment
of these models.

1 1954 Oldsmobile Starfire 98 convertible, top down, two-tone. $189
1a 1954 Oldsmobile Starfire 98 convertible, top down, one-tone. $169
2 1960 Chevrolet Impala convertible, top down. $189
2a 1960 Chevrolet Impala convertible, top up $189
3 1955 Buick Super hard top, three-tone $210
4 1963 Ford Galaxie 500 XL convertible, top down $189
4a 1963 Ford Galaxie 500 XL hard top, limited $210
5 1954 Oldsmobile 98 Holiday hard top $198
6 1957 Imperial Crown Southhampton 4-door hard top $198
7 1957 Buick Roadmaster 75 Riviera 4-door hard top $198
8 1954 Pontiac Star Chief convertible, top down $198
9 1963 Ford Country Squire station wagon $198
10 1950 Lincoln Cosmopolitan 4-door sedan $198
11 1955 Buick Super convertible, top down $198
11a 1955 Buick Super convertible, top up $198
11D 1955 Buick Super convertible, top down, continental kit. $279
12 1960 Cadillac Fleetwood Sixty Special 4-door hard top . . . $198
13 1956 Plymouth Savoy 4-door sedan $179
14 1948 Pontiac Torpedo Eight Deluxe convertible, top down . $189
14a 1948 Pontiac Torpedo Eight Deluxe convertible, top up . $189
15 1956 Buick Special convertible, top down $198
16 1957 Ford Thunderbird hard top $189
17 1954 Pontiac Star Chief Custom Catalina hard top $189
18 1958 Cadillac Fleetwood $235
19 1955 Oldsmobile 98 Holiday 4-door hard top $235
20 1960 Plymouth Fury. $210

CONRAD (ALSO SEE GESCHA)

Conrad of Germany is a brandname applied in the 1970s
to a line of heavy equipment models originally introduced
under the Gescha brand in the 1960s. Conrad models are
currently available. Gescha models meanwhile are no

longer made, rare and highly valued.

1000 Mercedes-Benz 230 C-280 CE, 1:35	$18
1001 Mercedes-Benz 200-280 T Wagon, 1:35	$18
1002 Mercedes-Benz 280-450 Sedan, 1:35	$18
1010 Volkswagen Passat GLS, 1:43	$18
1011 Volkswagen Passat Variant, 1:43	$18
1012 Audi 80 Coupe, 1:43	$9

Photo by Jeff Koch.

1013 Volkswagen Scirocco GLI, 1:43, $9

1014 Volkswagen Polo C, 1:43 . . . . $9
1015 Volkswagen Santana GL, 1:43 . . . . $18
1016 Volkswagen Kombi, 1:43 . . . . $24
1017 Volkswagen Kombi with Glass Rack, 1:43 . . . . $24
1018 1917 Graf & Stift Fire Truck, 1:43 . . . . $60
1018 OAF Fire Truck, 1:43 . . . . $52
1019 American LaFrance Fire Truck, 1:43 . . . . $60
1020 Audi Quattro Coupe, 1:43 . . . . $18
1021 Volkswagen Polo Coupe, 1:43 . . . . $18
1022 Audi 100, 1:43 . . . . $9
1023 American LaFrance Fire Truck, 1:43 . . . . $78
1024 American LaFrance Fire Truck, 1:43 . . . . $94
1025 1910 Dennis Fire Truck, 1:43 . . . . $52
1026 1928 Volvo Flat Truck, 1:43 . . . . $60
1027 1921 MAN Old Timer Fire Engine, 1:43 . . . . $55
1028 1947 Volvo LV153 Stake Truck, 1:43 . . . . $46
1029 1949 Volvo LV293 C2LF Stake Truck, 1:43 . . . . . . $49
1030 1928 Volvo Old Timer Fire Engine, 1:43 . . . . $49
1031 1902 White Old Timer Pie Wagon, 1:43 . . . . $32
1032 MAN KVB "Messer Griesheim" Gas Van, 1:50 . . . . . $35
1033 1958 Magirus Stetter Old Timer Concrete Mixer, 1:43 . . . . $54
1034 1955 Mercedes-Benz Racing Transporter, 1:43 . . . . $45
1035 1920 MAN Gas Tanker "Messer Griesham," 1:43 . . . . . . $44
1035 Mercedes-Benz Liquid Truck, 1:43 . . . . $38
1036 1950 Magirus Low Side Dump Truck, 1:43 . . . . $42
1037 Volvo Titan L395 Flatbed Truck, 1:43 . . . . $48
1076 Mercedes-Benz 280-450, 1:35 . . . . $18
1501 Mercedes-Benz 230 C-280 CE $18
1502 Mercedes-Benz 200-280 T Wagon, 1:35 . . . . $18
1503 Mercedes-Benz 200 TD-300 TD Wagon, 1:35 . . . . $34
1504 Mercedes-Benz 300CE Coupe, 1:35 . . . . $34
1601 Mercedes-Benz 230 C-300 CE, 1:35 . . . . $18
1602 Mercedes-Benz 207 D Bus, 1:50 . . . . $18
1603 Mercedes-Benz 207 D Van, 1:50 . . . . $18
1604 Mercedes-Benz Van, 1:50 . . . . $18
1605 Mercedes-Benz 100/130/150 Bus, 1:50 . . . . $60
1606 Mercedes-Benz 170 Van, 1:50 . . . . $34

1607 Mercedes-Benz 206 Van, 1:50 . . . . $34
1608 Mercedes Van Type 208, 1:50 . . . . $34
1620 Mercedes-Benz 507D Van, 1:43 . . . . $18
2000 Condecta Mobile Crane, 1:87 . . . . $85
2010 Peiner Tower Crane, 1:87 . . . . $85
2011 Potain Truck Crane, 1:87 . . . . $79 – 88
2012 Zeppelin ZBK 100 Truck Crane, 1:87 . . . . . . $79 – 88
2013 BPR Cadillon GT2210 Truck Crane, 1:87 . . . . $79 – 88
2014 Potain GMR Crane, 1:50 . . . . $79 – 88
2020 Liebherr HC120 Tower Crane, 1:87 . . . . $69 – 78
2021 Liebherr 21K Tower Crane, 1:50 . . . . $75
2022 Liebherr 112 HC-K Tower Crane, 1:87 . . . . $104
2023 Liebherr 28K Mobile Tower Crane, 1:50 . . . . . $87 – 94
2030 MAN-Wolff Tower Crane, 1:87 . . . . $85
2040 Putzmeister Cement Pump, 1:50 . . . . $100
2070 Krupp 80T Crane Truck, 1:50 . . . . $85
2071 P & H T-1300 Crane Truck, 1:50 . . . . $85
2072 Liebherr Crane Truck, 1:50 . . . . $85
2073 Clark 720 Crane Truck, 1:50 . . . . $85
2074 Gottwald Hydraulic Crane, 1:50 . . . . $85
2075 P & H Omega Crane, 1:50 . . . . $85
2076 Liebherr LTM 1030 Crane, 1:50 . . . . $85
2077 Krupp 250 GMT Crane, 1:50 . . . . $85
2078 Wirth Rotary Drill Truck, 1:50 . . . . $95
2079 Liebherr LT 1060 Crane, 1:50 . . . . $95
2080 Krupp 70 GMT Crane, 1:50 . . . . $95
2081 Demag AC435 Superlift Crane, 1:50 . . . . . . $109 – 118
2082 Liebherr 1160 Truck Crane $109
2083 Liebherr LTM1025 Truck Crane, 1:50 . . . . $69-78
2084 Faun Mobile Crane, 1:50 . . . . $89 – 98
2085 Liebherr 1090 Crane, 1:50 . . . . $99-108
2086 Demag AC155 Truck Crane, 1:50 . . . . $79 – 88
2110 Peiner Container Lift, 1:87 . . . . $75
2410 Terex 72/71 Wheel Loader, 1:43 . . . . $85
2411 Terex TS-14B Scraper, 1:43 . . . . $85
2420 Dresser Wheel Loader, 1:50 . . . . $65
2421 Furukawa 345 Wheel Loader, 1:50 . . . . $64
2422 O&K L55 Wheel Loader, 1:50 . . . . $58 – 65
2425 Hanomag 70E Wheel Loader, 1:50 . . . . $60
2426 Case 621 Wheel Loader with attachments, 1:35 . . . $60
2427 Hanomag 15F Wheel Loader, 1:50 . . . . $38 – 42
2428 Hanomag CL310 Compactor/Bucket . . . . . . $65 – 70
2430 GHH LF12 Wheel Loader, 1:50 . . . . $65
2501 Tamrock Tunnel Drill $50
2502 Grove AMZ66 Manlift, 1:50 . . . . $35 – 64
2701 Voest-Alpine Road Roller, 1:35 . . . . $60
2702 Losenhausen Vibromax Roller, 1:35 . . . . $60
2703 Case Vibromax 1102 Roller, 1:35 . . . . $58
2704 Case Vibromax 854K Roller, 1:35 . . . . $45-58
2705 Case W102 Roller $32
2710 Bomag BW213D Roller, 1:50 . . . . $48
2711 Bomag BW120 AD-2 Roller, 1:50 . . . . $34 – 55
2721 Dresser 830E 200 Ton Dumper, 1:50 . . . . . . $109 – 118
2722 Dresser 210M 55 Ton Mining Dump Truck, 1:50 . . . $69 – 78
2741 Caterpillar PS500 Compactor $49
2762 Terex Articulated Dump Truck $52
2771 O&K RH120C Shovel, 1:50 . . . . $124
2772 Demag H135S Hydraulic Shovel, 1:50 . . . . $108

2801 Liebherr 731 Dozer-Ripper, 1:50 . . . . $55	2934 Case 580 Super K with serial number, gold, 1:35 . . . . . . $88
2802 Liebherr Track Loader, 1:50 . . . . $60	2935 Case 580 K Tractor Loader, 1:50 . . . . $65
2803 Liebherr 722 Dozer, 1:50 . . . . $54	2936 Case 590X Tractor Backhoe Load, 1:35 . . . . $78
2804 Liebherr RL422 Pipelayer, 1:50 . . . . $58	2951 Massey Ferguson 50B Loader, 1:35 . . . . $75
2810 Sennebogen Mobile Crane, 1:50 . . . . $60	2952 Massey Ferguson 50D Loader, 1:35 . . . . $75
2812 Sennebogen Backhoe, 1:50 . . . . $60	2954 Massey Ferguson 60HX Loader/Backhoe, 1:35 . . . . $92
2814 Sennebogen 526 Excavator, 1:50. . . . . $60	2960 Case Drott 50 Track Backhoe, 1:35 . . . . $75
2815 Zeppelin ZR28 ABI Pile Driver Excavator, 1:50 . . . . $79 – 88	2961 Case Drott 980B Track Backhoe, 1:35 . . . . $75
2817 Sennebogen Backhoe with Blade $60	2962 Case 1280 Track Excavator, 1:35 . . . . $75
2817 Zeppelin ZM15 Wheel Excavator, 1:50. . . . . $42 – 54	2963 CaseDH4B Trencher, 1:32 . . . . $75
2817 Hanomag Wheel Loader, 1:50. . . . . $42	2964 Case 1085B Wheel Backhoe, 1:35 . . . . $65
2818 Furukawa W625E Wheel Backhoe, 1:50 . . . . $54	2965 Case 125B Track Backhoe, 1:35 . . . . $65
2818 Dresser Wheel Excavator, 1:50 . . . . $36	2966 Case 760 Trencher, 1:35 . . . . $65
2819 Furukawa 625E Track Backhoe, 1:50 . . . . $54	2970 Clark H500 Forklift, 1:25 . . . . $45
2819 Dresser Track Excavator, 1:50. . . . . $40	2971 Clark ECA Forklift, 1:25 . . . . $45
2821 Liebherr 921 Excavator, 1:50. . . . . $60	2972 Clark Forklift, 1:25 . . . . $29
2822 Liebherr 912 Excavator, 1:50. . . . . $60	2980 Caterpillar Forklift, 1:25 . . . . $35
2823 Liebherr 991 Backhoe, 1:50 . . . . $60	2981 Linde R14 Forklift, 1:25 . . . . $64
2824 Liebherr 991 Excavator, 1:50. . . . . $60	2982 Linde R16 Forklift, 1:25 . . . . $54
2825 Liebherr 922 Hydraulic Excavator, 1:50 . . . . $65	2983 Fenwick T20 Forklift, 1:25 . . . . $32
2826 Liebherr 952 Excavator, 1:50. . . . . $60	2983 Linde Lift Truck, 1:25 . . . . $25
2827 Liebherr 984 Shovel, 1:50 . . . . $88	2984 Jungheinrich ECE Forklift, 1:25 . . . . $34
2828 Liebherr 984 Backhoe, 1:50 . . . . $88	2985 Linde E25 Forklift, 1:25 . . . . $58
2829 Liebherr R912 Track Hoe, 1:50 . . . . $58	2990 Yale Forklift, 1:25 . . . . $65
2830 Liebherr A912 Lit. Wheel Clam, 1:50 . . . . $64	2991 Kalmar LMV 22 Forklift, 1:50 . . . . $65
2831 Liebherr HS881 Hydraulic Cable Excavator, 1:50 . . . . . $109	2992 Yale Forklift, 1:25 . . . . $65
2831 Liebherr HS882 Track Lat Crane, 1:50 . . . . $118	2993 Case 586E Forklift, 1:35 . . . . $65
2832 Liebherr A932 Scrap Grapple Excavator, 1:50 . . . . $65	2994 Jungheinrich Forklift, 1:25 . . . . $64
2833 Liebherr A310 Wheel Backhoe, 1:50 . . . . $58	2995 Jungheinrich Forklift, 1:25 . . . . $64
2834 Liebherr 954 Backhoe, 1:50 . . . . $65	2996 Lansing Forklift, 1:25 . . . . $42
2835 Liebherr 932 Track Scrap Hand, 1:50 . . . . $65	2997 Jungheinrich EJC 12.5 Forklift, 1:25. . . . . $48
2840 Caterpillar 950 Loader, 1:25 . . . . $90	2998 Yale Forklift, 1:25. . . . . $42 – 58
2841 Caterpillar 950 Loader-Ripper, 1:50 . . . . $65	2999 Kalmar Forklift 40' Container, 1:50 . . . . $88
2842 Fuchs Excavator with Magnet Lift, 1:50 . . . . $64	3009 Mercedes-Benz Titan Truck Tractor, 1:50 . . . . $90
2850 Caterpillar D10 Dozer-Ripper, 1:50 . . . . $65	3010 Mercedes-Benz Low Loader Semi, 1:50 . . . . $90
2851 Caterpillar D6H Bulldozer, 1:50 . . . . $65	3011 Mercedes-Benz Truck & Trailer "BayWa," 1:50 . . . . $90
2852 Caterpillar D11N Dozer-Ripper, 1:50. . . . . $65	3012 Mercedes-Benz Truck & Trailer, 1:50 . . . . $90
2853 Hanomag Dozer, 1:50 . . . . $42	3013 Mercedes-Benz TRuck & Trailer "Spedition Lueg," 1:50 . . $90
2854 Caterpillar D11 Dozer, 1:50 . . . . $99	3014 Mercedes-Benz Spitzer Silo Semi, 1:50 . . . . $90
2862 Caterpillar D400 Dump Truck, 1:50. . . . . $62	3015 Mercedes Semi Bulker L Hoist, 1:50 . . . . $84
2873 1931 Caterpillar 60 Diesel, limited numbered edition, 1:25 . $75	3016 Mercedes-Benz Truck & Trailer "Mobelspedition" or "Pfen-
2882 Liebherr L522 Wheel Loader, 1:50. . . . . $44	ning" logo, 1:50 . . . . $90
2883 Liebherr L507 Wheel Loader, 1:50. . . . . $40	3019 Mercedes-Benz Gas Cylinder Semi "Air Products," 1:50 . . $90
2886 Caterpillar 936 Wheel Loader, 1:50 . . . . $42	3020 Mercedes-Benz Container Semi, 1:50 . . . . $90
2887 Liebherr 531 Wheel Loader, 1:50 . . . . $64	3021 Mercedes-Benz Pipe Carrier, 1:50 . . . . $90
2889 Caterpillar CS653 Roller, 1:50 . . . . $44	3022 Mercedes-Benz Tanker Semi, 1:50 . . . . $90
2892 Case-Poclain 1088 Maxi Backhoe, 1:50 . . . . $48	3023 Mercedes-Benz Gas Tanker Semi "L'Air Liquide" or Fedgas," . $90
2893 Case-Poclain 81P Excavator, 1:50 . . . . $52	3024 Mercedes-Benz Gas Cylinder Semi "Messer Griesheim," 1:50 . $90
2894 Case 2188 Track Excavator, 1:50. . . . . $54	3025 Mercedes-Benz Low Loader Semi, 1:50 . . . . $90
2901 Atlas Wheel Backhoe with Blade, 1:50 . . . . $60	3026 Mercedes-Meiller Dump Truck, 1:50 . . . . $90
2902 Atlas 1704 Track Excavator, 1:50. . . . . $60	3027 Mercedes-Benz Semi Tanker "Linde," 1:50. . . . . $78
2903 Atlas 1704 Track Backhoe, 1:50 . . . . $48	3029 Mercedes-Benz Semi Trailer Truck, 1:50 . . . . $90
2904 Atlas 1304 Wheel Excavator/Clam, 1:50. . . . . $54	3030 Mercedes-Benz Open Semi, 1:50 . . . . $90
2910 Fiat-Allis Dozer-Ripper, 1:50 . . . . $65	3030 Mercedes-Benz Covered Semi, 1:50 . . . . $90
2920 Scheid PV 60 Roller, 1:50 . . . . $75	3031 Mercedes-Benz Covered Truck & Trailer, 1:50 . . . . $90
2931 Case 580 D Tractor Loader, 1:35 . . . . $80	3032 Mercedes-Benz Covered Truck, 1:50 . . . . $90
2932 Case 580 G Tractor Loader, 1:35 . . . . $80	3033 Mercedes-Kuka Garbage Truck, 1:50. . . . . $90
2933 Case 580 E Tractor Loader, 1:35 . . . . $80	3034 Mercedes-Hegla Glass Truck, 1:50 . . . . $90

3037 MAN Small Truck, 1:43. . . . . $18

3038 Mercedes-Benz Refrigerator Truck, 1:50 . . . . $90

3039 Mercedes-Haller Garbage Truck, 1:50 . . . . $90

3040 Mercedes-Benz Dump Truck, 1:50 . . . . $90

3041 Mercedes-Leach Garbage Truck, 1:50 . . . . $90

3042 Mercedes-Schorling Sweeper, 1:50 . . . . $90

3043 Mercedes-Benz 1300 Tractor, 1:50. . . . . $60

3044 Mercedes-Benz Cement Mixer, 1:50 . . . . $90

3045 Mercedes-Benz Cement Mixer, 1:50 . . . . $90

3046 Mercedes-Benz Open Semi, 1:50 . . . . $90

3047 Schorling Street Sweeper, 1:50 . . . . $90

3048 Mercedes-Benz Container Truck, 1:50. . . . . $90

3049 Mercedes-Faun Garbage Truck, 1:50 . . . . $90

3050 Mercedes-Liebherr Cement Mixer, 1:50 . . . . $90

3052 Mercedes-Benz Putzmeister Mixer/Pumper, 1:50 . . . . . . $94

3053 Mercedes-Benz Tank Truck, 1:50 . . . . $90

3054 Mercedes-Benz Single Car Transporter, 1:50 . . . . $90

3060 Mercedes-Benz Semi Suction Unit, 1:50. . . . . . . $94

3064 Mercedes-Benz Mixer "Blank Betonova," 1:50 . . . . $72

3066 Mercedes-Benz Suction Vehicle Vacuum TA, 1:50 . . . . . $64

3069 Mercedes-Benz Schorling P17 Snow Sweeper, 1:50 . . . $98

3079 Mercedes-Benz Faun Drain Cleaner Vacuum, 1:50. . . . . $68

3085 Ericsson Radar, 1:50. $39

3086 Mercedes-Benz Putzmeister 52/5 5-Axle Concrete Pump, 1:50 . . . . $94

3088 Liebherr LTF1030 Crane, 1:50 . . . . $94

3093 Mercedes-Benz Schwing 32XL Pump, 1:50 . . . . . . $84

3095 Putzmeister 3-Axle Concrete Pump, 1:50 . . . . . . $78

3245 Magirus Liebherr Mixer, 1:50 . . . . $46

3264 Iveco Stetter 4-Axle Mixer, 1:50 . . . . $78

3274 Iveco 4-Axle Dump, 1:50 . . . . $68

3274 Magirus 4-Axle Dump, 1:50 . . . . $39

3330 Bedford Semi Flatbed, 1:50. . . . . $72

3464 Steyer/Stetter 4-Axle Mixer, 1:50 . . . . $72

3519 Freightliner with "Air Products" Trailer, 1:50 . . . . . . $59

3520 Freightliner T/T Container, 1:50 . . . . $92

3523 Mercedes-Benz "Messer Griesheim" Bulk Gas Semi, 1:50 . $78

3640 Mack Dump Truck, 1:50. . . . . $65

3641 Mack Refuse Truck, 1:50 . . . . $55

3669 Mack Airport Plow and Sweeper, 1:50. . . . . $109

3744 Volvo NL12 Concrete Mixer, 1:50 . . . . $78

3755 Volvo NL12 Atlas Gondola Truck, 1:50 . . . . $72

3775 Volvo NL12 Conventional Dump Truck, 1:50. . . . : . $72

3776 Volvo Low Sideboard Truck, 1:50 . . . . $49

3777 Volvo NL10 Water Truck, 1:50 . . . . $72

3812 Freightliner Conventional "Talbert," 1:50 . . . . . . $78

3819 Freightliner Conventional "Air Products," 1:50 . . . . . . $92

3820 Freightliner Truck with Box Trailer, 1:50. . . . . . $59

3826 Freightliner Conventional Dump Trailer, 1:50 . . . . . . $65

3912 Volvo Semi with Talbert Lowboy, 1:50 . . . . $78

3928 Volvo NL12 Semi with Refrigerator Trailer, 1:50. . . . $92

4111 MAN Schmitz Heavy Haulage Trailer, 1:50 . . . . . . $94

4127 MAN Semi Linde TVTS30 Tanker, 1:50 . . . . $72

4150 MAN Semi Concrete Mix Stetter, 1:50 . . . . $72

4165 MAN 4-Axle Mixer "Liebherr," 1:50 . . . . $64

4166 MAN Haller Suction Truck, 1:50 . . . . $78

4167 MAN 4-Axle Roll-Off, 1:50 . . . . $58

4178 Huffermeister Roll-Off, 1:50 . . . . $75

4179 MAN Drain Cleaner, 1:50 . . . . $55

4196 Mercedes-Benz Silo Transporter, 1:50 . . . . $72

4199 MAN Atlas 130.1 Crane Truck, 1:50. . . . . $64

4220 Iveco Transporter, 1:50 . . . . $39

4236 Iveco Euro Cargo Truck, 1:50 . . . . $48

4298 Iveco Eurotech Truck, 1:50. . . . . $58

4315 Volvo F12 Semi Bulk Carrier, 1:50 . . . . . . $69 – 92

4317 Volvo F16 Logging Truck/Trailer, 1:50. . . . . . $69 – 94

4327 Volvo Double Trailer truck, 1:50. . . . . $55

4372 Volvo Euro Trotter, 1:50. . . . . $59

4392 Volvo F12 Air Crash Tender, 1:50 . . . . $78

4564 Volvo FL10 3X Concrete Mixer, 1:50 . . . . $64

4589 Volvo FL6 Container Tailgate Lift, 1:50 . . . . $65

4594 Volvo Schwing KVM52 Concrete Pump, 1:50. . . . . . $118

4608 Volvo FH12 with Refrigerator Trailer, 1:50. . . . . $88

4609 Volvo FH16 with 4-Axle Trailer, 1:50 . . . . $94

4840 Iveco Euro Trekker Dump Truck, 1:50 . . . . $44

4961 Iveco Eurostar with Tank Trailer, 1:50. . . . . $72

4898 Iveco Euro Truck, 1:50. . . . . $45

5016 Mercedes Farm Tractor, 1:43. . . . . $25

5017 Mercedes-Benz 800 Tractor, 1:43. . . . . $18

5018 Steyer Farm Tractor, 1:43 . . . . $25

5066 Elgin Pelican Street Sweeper, 1:50 . . . . $68

5068 Multicar Utility, 1:50. . . . . $42

5201 Kassbohrer Pisten Bully Snow, 1:43 . . . . $92

5401 Case 1845C Uniloader, 1:50 . . . . $42

5402 Putzmeister Worm Pump, 1:50 . . . . $35

5403 Rosenbauer Fox Fire Pump, 1:50 . . . . $38

5404 Mercedes-Benz Messer Griesheim Acetylene Cutte, 1:50 . $98

5405 Putzmeister Concrete Mixer Trailer, 1:35 . . . . . . $54

5406 Demag SC40DS-2 Compressor, 1:24 . . . . $42

5421 Mercedes-Benz Highway Bus, 1:50. . . . . $55

5422 Mercedes-Benz Articulated Bus, 1:50 . . . . $98

5423 MAN Luxury Coach Bus, 1:50 . . . . $78

5505 E-1 Hush 95' Ladder Fire Truck, 1:50 . . . . $84

5506 E-1 Hush 80' Ladder Fire Truck, 1:50 . . . . $84

5507 E-1 Titan III, 1:50. . . . . $75

5510 E-1 Hush Pumper Fire Truck, 1:50 . . . . $84

5512 Falcon Fire Truck, 1:50. . . . . $75

6036 MAN Type L2000 Truck, 1:50 . . . . $44

6107 MAN F2000 Semi Container Truck, 1:50 . . . . . . $84

6165 MAN F2000 Liebherr 904 Mixer, 1:50 . . . . $62

9996 Liebherr Boom Extensions, 1:50 . . . . $14

9997 Lattice Tower Extensions for 2011 Potain Tower Crane, 1:87 . . . . $14

9998 Lattice Tower Extensions for 2012 Zeppelin ZBK100 Tower Crane, 19:50 1:87 . . . . $14

9999 Lattice Tower Extensions for 2013 BPR Cadillon GT2210 Tower Crane, 1:87. . . . . $14

COPy Cars

Jeff Mantyak reports that COPy Cars are similar to Road Champs police cars (likely customized off Road Champs chassies), but are produced by a Canadian model company. The models are Chevrolet Caprices representing an assortment of Canadian police vehicles, with opening doors and trunks, and pullback action. Order from Coppers Collectibles, 2514-23 Avenue South, Lethbridge, Alberta T1K

1K9 Canada, phone: 403-329-8378, fax: 403-329-4055, email: coppers@telusplanet.net.

Ontario Provincial Police . . . . $15 – 20
Peel Regional Police . . . . $15 – 20

CORGI

The Corgi legacy is a rich one, beginning in 1934 with parent company Mettoy of Swansea, South Wales. In 1956 Mettoy merged with Playcraft Ltd. to form Mettoy Playcraft Ltd. In 1993, Mattel bought the Corgi brand and is maintaining the tradition of producing memorable toys, with the emphasis on collectability. Several books have been written about Corgis, and the multitude of models produced certainly could fill a book or more. So instead we present a survey of the models produced over the years, along with current collector values. Popular Corgi models such as the Beatles' Yellow Submarine are now being reproduced to give new collectors a second chance at getting the good ones at a reasonable price.

AEC Bus, $18

AEC Routemaster London Transport Bus. $20
Aston Martin DB4 . . . . $40
Austin Healey 3000 Mk 1, D735 . . . . $20
Batman and Robin Batboat, 1967 . . . . $350
Beatles Yellow Submarine, 1969 . . . . $600
Bedford O Series Pantechnicon Van $40
Bedford type OB Coach, C949/1. . . . . $30
1954 Bentley R Type, 815. . . . . $20
BMW 325i Saloon, 353 . . . . $12
'57 Chevrolet Bel Air, C825/1 . . . . $20

Chevrolet Camaro SS 350, 338, $100

Chipperfield's Circus Crane $95
Chitty Chitty Bang Bang Car $150

Citroen Ski Team, $45

Film Service Van $50

1957 Ford Thunderbird, 810, $20

Jaguar XJS, 318/1, $15

Jaguar XK120, 870 . . . . $20
James Bond Gold Aston Martin, 1965 . . . . $525
James Bond Moon Buggy, 1972 . . . . $600
James Bond Toyota 2000 GT, 1967 . . . . $625

1956 Mercedes-Benz 300S, C805/1 . . . . $20
1953 MG TF, 812 . . . . $20
1955 MG TF, 813 . . . . $15

James Bond Aston Martin, $60

MGC GT, 345, $30

James Bond Lotus Esprit, $60

MGA 1600 Mk. 1, D730, $20

Mack Truck, C906/1, $22

MGA 1600 Mk. 1, D731, $20

The Monkees Monkeemobile, 1968 . . . . $525

Man from U.N.C.L.E. Blue Oldsmobile, 1966 . . . . $450
1956 Mercedes-Benz 300S, 806 . . . . $20

Morris Minor Saloon, D702, $20

Metrobus, $15

Morris Minor 1000, D702/4 . . . . $20

Morris Minor Van, C957/7, $20

Popeye's Paddle Wagon, 1969 . . . . $650

Renault Tour de France, $40

Rolls-Royce Corniche, C279/1, $30

The Saint's Volvo, P1800, 1965 . . . . $275

Triumph TR3A, D736, $20

1919 Thornycroft Bus, "National Motor Museum, $20

1919 Thornycroft Bus, "Charlie Chaplin's," $20

Triumph TR3A, D737, $20

Triumph TR3A, D738, $20

VW Bus, $20

Ford "Duckham's" Tanker, $3 – 4

CORGI TRUCKERS

In the early 80s, Corgi issued a series of 1:64 scale contemporary trucks marketed as Corgi Truckers that have since been incorporated into Mattel's Corgi Auto-City line. New models as of 1997 are called Hot Wheels Haulers.

Kenworth "7UP," $3 – 4

M.A.N. "Raleigh" Truck, $3 – 4

Ford "Pepsi" Cargo Truck, $3 – 4

Ford "Kraft Dairylea Cheese Spread" Cargo Truck . . . . $3 – 4

M.A.N. Dump Truck, $3 – 4

M.A.N. "BP" Tanker, $3 – 4

Ford Dump Truck, $3 – 4

NEW CORGI MODELS

Listed below are new and recent models currently offered. Many are reproductions of favorite Corgi models from the past, offering collectors a second chance at building a great collection of classics.

'57 Chevy Fire Chief "Chicago" $18
'57 Chevy "Highway Patrol" Car $20
AEC Reliance Oxford Omnibus. $17

A.L.F. Pumper "Vero Beach" $30
Birmingham Daimler Fleetline Bus $41
Chipperfield Circus Bedford Articulated Truck $29
Chipperfield Circus Booking Van $18
Chipperfield Circus Living Van $31
Chipperfield Circus Pantechnicon $29
Crosville Omnibus $34
Ladder Truck "Centerville" $60
Ladder Truck "Orlando" $60
Ladder Truck "Denver" $60
Leyland Leopard Ribble Omnibus $17
London Taxi $3
Manchester Daimler Fleetline Bus $41
Morris Minor Traveller, dark green $10
Prototype MCI Tour Bus $35
Thames Valley Omnibus $34
Beatles' Yellow Submarine $50

CORGI GREYHOUND BUSSES

Greyhound's "Dog and Target" design was first used to demonstrate solidarity with Great Britain during the attack on London by the Germans in 1939. Below are listed several variations of one bus style. All of these models were currently available as of this writing.

v.1 "Philadelphia," $35

v.2 "New York Central RR" $30
v.3 "Pennsylvania RR" $30
v.4 "Trailways," teardrop design $30
v.5 "Trailways," pinstripe design $30
v.6 "Champlain," with billboard $30
v.7 "Los Angeles" $35
v.8 "New York" Public Service Coach $35
v.9 "WACS" $30
v.10 "WAVES" $30
v.11 New York/Albany/Montreal Coach with billboard $30

CORGI MACK FIRE TRUCKS

Mack Pumper, "Chicago," 1994 . . . . $25
Mack "B" Pumper, "Paxtonia," 1995 . . . . $35

CORGI RACE IMAGE COLLECTIBLES

"The Corgi brand has been the hallmark of high-quality diecast models for over 40 years and, as a result, has worldwide following for both old and new production. All products are designed in Britain to the highest standards and traditions which guarantee the authenticity of every model. Corgi now brings this considerable experience to the US racing collectibles market and offers the following features

on exciting models at an affordable price: super detailed 1:64 scale semi's, strictly limited editions, numbered certificates of authenticity, chromed stack and wheels, diecast cabs, chrome mirrors, soft tires, twin wheels, Ford Aeromax and Kenworth T800 cabs." — Specialty Diecast, Medford, NJ

CORGI RACE IMAGE TRANSPORTER & CAR 1/64 SCALE

The Family Channel Racing Team . . . . $15 – 20
Kellogg's Corn Flakes Racing . . . . $15 – 20
Kodak Racing . . . . $15 – 20
La Victoria/Winnebago with rail dragster . . . . $20 – 25
Maxwell House/Bobby Labonte . . . . $15 – 20
Mopar Xpress/Tommy Johnson Jr. Top Fuel with rail dragster . . . . $20 – 25
Quaker State/Brett Bodine . . . . $15 – 20
Slick 50/Ricky Smith . . . . $15 – 20
Slick 50/Western Auto . . . . $15 – 20
Slick 50/Winston Drag Racing . . . . $15 – 20
Syntec with rail dragster . . . . $20 – 25
Texaco Havoline/Davey Allison . . . . $15 – 20
Valvoline/Mark Martin . . . . $15 – 20
Winn Dixie Racing . . . . $15 – 20
LaVictoria/Mike Dunn $40
Pennzoil/Eddie Hill $40
Castrol Syntec/Pat Austin $40
Valvoline/Joe Amato $40
Western Auto/Al Hofmann $40
Mooneyes/Kenji Okszaki $40
Kendall/Chuck Etchells $40

CORGI RACE IMAGE CARS ONLY 1/64 SCALE

John Force, 2 Car Set $45
Don Prudhomme/Skoal Bandit $45
NHRA 40th U.S. Nationals Drags $45

HUSKY MODELS

Corgi produced a series of small, inexpensive models in the sixties called Husky, later changed to Corgi Jrs. Here are just a few examples of Husky models. Typical current values are around $15 – 20 each, with a few notable exceptions.

Batmobile, Husky Extra, 1966 . . . . $350

Bedford TK 7-Ton Skip Truck, #27, $25

Chitty Chitty Bang Bang, 1967 . . . . $400
James Bond Silver Aston Martin, 1966 . . . . $400
Man from U.N.C.L.E., 1966 . . . . $375

Jeep, #5, with #19 Boat and Trailer, $30

Garbage Truck, $3

Monkeemobile, 1967 . . . . $400

CORGI JRS.

Corgi Jrs., successors to the Husky line, are still being produced today. Current models are available for about $2 – 4 each. Here is a sampling of current and past models. While the prices on a few models may seem extremely high, they are nevertheless what at least one dealer is asking for these apparently hard-to-find items. When Mattel purchased Corgi, Corgi Jrs. became Corgi Auto-City models.

Batmobile, 1967 . . . . $325
Batboat, 1967 . . . . $325

Helicopter, $3

BMW, $3

Ironside Police Van, 1970 . . . . $325

BP Van $3

Jaguar Racer, $3

Buick Regal Police, $3

James Bond Silver Aston Martin, 1966 . . . . $400
Mercedes Convertible $3

Chitty-Chitty Bang-Bang, 1968 . . . . $275

Corvette, $3

Mercedes-Benz Ambulance, $3

Military Jeep, $3

Monkeemobile, 1968 . . . . $275
Popeye's Paddle Wagon, 1971 . . . . $275

Porsche Targa, $3

Shell Tanker $3
Stagecoach $12

Stern Wheeler, $12

Team Racing Van, $3

Mercedes Taxi $3
Tipping Lorry $3

KIKO TOYS FROM CORGI

Kiko is the Mexican division of Corgi Jrs. Here is a small sampling of models from this series.

Austin Metro, #55, white . . . . $4 – 5
Caravan, #61, red . . . . $4 – 5
Caravan Fire, #806, red . . . . $4 – 5
Caravan Police, #821 . . . . $4 – 5
Chevy Van "Monica" . . . . $4 – 5
Renault 4 Van, #M5, red . . . . $4 – 5
Rover 3500 Fire Chief, #805 . . . . $4 – 5
Scania Van "Cascao" . . . . $4 – 5
Simca 1308, #M9 . . . . $4 – 5
Volkswagen Golf, #51, red . . . . $4 – 5
Volkswagen Golf Fire Chief, #809, red . . . . $4 – 5
Volkswagen Van "Correios," #M6 . . . . $4 – 5

CORGI 1:18 SCALE

With the rise in popularity of 1:18 scale models, this is Corgi's first entry into this genre.
95102 1996 MGF Convertible, green, introduced in 1996 . . . . . $39

CPM

1:43 scale models presumably made in England comprise this series of vehicles.

Austin Healey 100-6 Roadster $39
1939 Buick 4-Door Sedan $39
Daimler SP250 Roadster $39
Guy "Eveready" Van $125
Jensen 541 Coupe $39
Morris 1000 4-Door Sedan, gray $39
Morris 1000 Convertible, white $39
1939 Studebaker Commander 2-Door Sedan, navy blue $39
Sunbeam Alpine Roadster, red/white/green $39
Sunbeam Tiger Roadster $39
Triumph Spitfire Roadster, red $39

CRAFTOYS

Omaha, Nebraska, was the home of Craftoys, an assortment of slush mold (lead alloy) toys similar to the early Best, Ralstoy, and Kansas Toy models. A short-lived company, it lasted just a few years before World War II set in, and the lead was needed for the war.

Cement Mixer, #78, 3¾" $16
Fire Truck, #101, 4½" $30
Fordson Tractor, #17, 2½" $16
Freight Train, #3600, 16½", includes:
   Locomotive 0-6-4 "KT&N RR," 4½" $12
   Railroad Cars, 3¼" . . . . $12 each
   Caboose, 2¾" $12
Miller FWD Indy Racer, #81, 4½" $20
Oil Truck, #104, 3¾" $30
Racer, #100, 4¼" $30
Speed Car, #103, 4¼" $30
Station Wagon, #105, 3¾" $30
Streamlined 2-Door Sedan, #92, 4" $30
Tanker, #102, 6¾" $30

CRAGSTAN

Cragstan is most known for battery operated robots, of which Cragstans' Mr. Atomic is the most highly valued. In the late 60s to early 70s, Cragstan dabbled in diecast and produced some noteworthy 1:43 scale models. Dr. Craig S. Campbell, professor in the Department of Geography at Youngstown State University collects diecast toys and finds that it relates well to his field of teaching. He reports that his Cragstan "Detroit Senior" is a 1:43 scale 1966 Chevrolet Impala sedan police car with an opening trunk. It is just a tad lighter in shade than a Navy blue, with a chrome plastic base. The kicker is that it was made in Israel. On both sides are red shields with blue stars within the shields. I don't know if all Cragstans were made in Israel, but this one was and I believe that they may have been made under contract by the Israeli diecast company Gambda-Sabra, whose name I've seen in several places. The model has good detail and proportion and looks like an old Corgi or Dinky. Perhaps it is a casting borrowed from another diecast company. Does anyone know of a 1966 Chevy Impala sedan that was made by Dinky or Solido or some other company?" Further research may reveal the facts.

1966 Chevrolet Impala Detroit Senior Police Car, 1:43, blue. $30 – 45
1967 Corvair Coupe . . . . $30 – 45
1968 Chevrolet Impala Coupe . . . . $30 – 45

Photo by Jeff Koch.

1968 Chevrolet Corvette Coupe, $30 – 45

CREATIVE MASTERS (ALSO SEE REVELL)

In December 1995, Revell introduced a 1:20 scale diecast replica of the original 1989 Dodge Viper R/T 10 Roadster. The manufacturer of this model is so serious about faithfully reproducing this model in miniature that included on the model is a miniature price sheet on the windshield.

1989 Dodge Viper R/T 10, 1:20 . . . . $135

CRESCENT TOYS (ALSO SEE D.C.M.T.)

The Crescent Toy Company was born in a 30 square foot backyard workshop in London, England, in 1922. Through the twenties and thirties, Henry Eagles and Arthur Schneider manufactured lead alloy toy soldiers, cowboys, kitchen sets, and other items. After World War II, Crescent resumed making their toys, adding "DCMT" into the casting, evidence of their marketing of toys from the firm of Die Casting Machine Tools Ltd. The DCMT mark was removed from

models made in 1948 and later. DCMT meanwhile went on to make Lone Star models. Crescent continued making toys until 1981.

155 Artillery Gun	$32
223 Forties Race Car	$48
235 Cannon, operable	$75
422 Forties Nash Roadster	$45
423 Forties Petrol Tanker	$25
424 Forties Flat Truck.	$25
425 Forties LaSalle Sedan	$40
650 Military Set, includes two 696 British Tanks, 698 Scout Car, 699 Russian Tank	$225
695 Howitzer, unpainted, with spring and plunger	$15
696 British Tank	$50
698 Scout Car	$40
800 Forties Jaguar	$40
804 Forties Jaguar Police Car	$36
1221 Forties Fire Engine with Extending Ladder	$64
1268 Mobile Space Rocket	$120
1269 Mobile Crane.	$68
1272 Scammell Scarab Articulated Truck	$116
1274 Scammell Scarab and Low Loader Trailer . .	$116
1276 Scammell Scarab and Oil Tanker, Shell or Esso	$150
1284 Mercedes-Benz W196 Racing Car	$100
1285 B.R.M. Mk ll Racing Car	$100
1286 Ferrari 625 Racing Car	$100
1287 Connaught A Series Racing Car.	$100
1288 Cooper Bristol Racing Car.	$100
1289 Gordini 2.5 Litre Racing Car	$100
1290 Maserati 25OF Racing Car.	$100
1291 Aston Martin DB3S Racing Car	$80
1292 Jaguar D-Type Racing Car	$85
1293 Vanwall Racing Car	$150
1350 Seventies Container Truck	$32
1351 Seventies Petrol Tanker	$32
1352 Seventies Girder Truck.	$32
1353 Seventies Platform Truck	$32
1360 Seventies Cement Mixer.	$16
1361 Seventies Covered Truck	$10
1362 Seventies Tipper Truck	$16
1363 Seventies Recovery Vehicle	$16
1364 Seventies Super Karner	$10
1813 Horse Drawn Timber Wagon	$136
1814 Plough Trailer	$24
1815 Hayloader	$20
1816 Roller Harrow	$16
1817 Timber Trailer	$16
1818 Tipping Farm Wagon	$16
1819 Large Farm Wagon.	$36
1822 Bulldozer	$30
2700 Western Stage Coach	$110
2705 Scammell Scarab Set.	$350
6300 Set 1, includes 1284 through 1289.	$600
6300 Set 2, includes 1285 through 1290.	$600

CRISTIAN

The Cristian brand represents inexpensive 1:43 scale models made in Argentina.

Renault Dauphine $4
Ifa Torino Coupe $4
1960 Mercedes 220 . . . . $4
Fiat 1500 Ramco Coupe $4
1960 Fiat Car Transporter $4
DAF Car Transporter $4

CROSSWAY MODELS

Jemini models, a white metal model car manufacturer in England, at one time produced some unusual British car models. Now Jemini has merged with Crossway Models of England. Issues are limited from 10 to 500 of each model. Every Crossway Model is hand finished and exquisitely detailed. Crossway Models, 2 Salem St., Gosberton, Spalding, Lincs, PE11 4NQ England, phone 011-44-1775-841-171.

CROSSWAYS CK SERIES
CK 01 Austin/Morris 11/1300 . . . . $90

CROSSWAYS CM SERIES
CM 01 Rover 75 Saloon
   v.1 black $96
   v.2 connaught green $90
   v.3 ivory $90

CROSSWAYS CMM SERIES, 25 PRODUCED OF EACH MODEL
CMM 1 Austin A70 Saloon, black $90
CMM 2 Austin 1100 MK2, flame red $90
CMM 3 MG TD, red with wire wheels $90

CROSSWAYS CP SERIES
CP 10 Sunbeam Rapier, velvet/sage green $90

CROSSWAYS JMR SERIES, 500 OF EACH MODEL IN EACH COLOR, EXCEPT JMR 002 OF WHICH 150 ARE TO BE ISSUED
JMR 002 Wolseley Six, Black $96
JMR 003 Wolseley 1300 MK2, teal, harvest gold, green mallard or
   black tulip $90
JMR 006 Austin 1300 GT, flame red $90
JMR 007 MG 1300 GT MK2, Bermuda blue or snowberry
   white $90

CROSSWAYS JSE SERIES
JSE 002 Standard Vanguard Estate, black, 50 issued $100
JSE 002 Standard Vanguard Van, black, 100 issued $90
JSE 003 Morris 100 Traveler, green and red, 100 issued $90
JSE 004 Sunbeam Tiger, open, white, (Metropolitan Police) . . . $90
JSE 004 Sunbeam Tiger, closed, white, (Metropolitan Police) $90
JSE 007 MGB, black $90
JSE 008 Austin A70, black $90
JSE 009 Austin 1100 MK3, Bermuda blue and white (Metropolitan
   Police) $90

CROWN PREMIUM

Perhaps the newest diecast model company is Crown Premium, started in 1996, and specializing in 1:6 scale pedal car replicas. Each issue is limited to 5,000 units. For more information, contact Brian O'Hara at 941-495-6964 or Mark Hoeger at 319-875-2694.
1947 BMC Racer . . . . $120 – 130

C-SCALE

C-Scale represents 1:43 scale white metal kits made in Great Britain.

CURSOR

Although the Cursor line consists mainly of plastic models, these models from Germany are practically indistinguishable from diecast models in their precision, scale, and appearance. Newer Cursor models are diecast as well. Cursor models represent a variety of German and other European cars and trucks, including the first Daimler and Benz cars produced in 1886. Cursor models are available from Diecast Miniatures, Toys for Collectors (TfC), and other fine scale model dealers.

VW Bus, light gray, 1:43 . . . . $120
1 1886 Benz First Three-Wheel Car, 1:43 . . . . $15
2 1896 Daimler Fire, red, 1:43 . . . . $18
3 1897 Daimler Taxi, blue, 1:43 . . . . $18
8 1911 Benz Blitzen Racer, silver, 1:43 . . . . $18
14 1904 Bussing Bus, 1:35 . . . . $18
100 Mercedes-Benz Unimog, 1:50 . . . . $18
189 Graft & Stift Kaiser Wagon, 1:40 . . . . $49
266 Matador Van Pickup, blue $70
280 Iveco Dump Truck, 1:50 . . . . $25
311 Panther 6x6 Fire Truck $120
312 Panther 8x8 Fire Truck $129
484 Holder Farm Tractor, 1:35 . . . . $25
569 Hanomag Wheel Loader $30
677 Fendt LS Farm Tractor, green, 1:43 . . . . $18
678 Fendt LB Farm Tractor, green, 1:43 . . . . $18
780 Magirus Oil Truck $20
880 Holder Culitrac Farm Tractor, 1:35 . . . . $25
982 Double Decker Bus, 1:35 . . . . $39
982T 1903 MAN Truck $39
986 Kaessborer Setra S8 Bus, 1:60 . . . . $49
1084 Mercedes-Benz 300E $19
1182 Mercedes-Benz 190E, 1:35 . . . . $19
1300 Mercedes-Benz L408D, silver, 1:43 . . . . $18
2911 Mercedes-Benz 500 with closed sunroof, 1:43 . . . . $27
2912 Mercedes-Benz 500 with open sunroof, 1:43 . . . . $27
12932 MAN Truck, 1:35, new model for 1995 . . . . $27
12935 MAN Wood Transporter, 1:35, new model for 1995 . . . . $27

CUSTOM MINIATURES

One limited edition model is available from this brand, of which only 500 were made.
1957 Chevrolet Bel Air 2-Door Hardtop, 5-spoke mag wheels,
   maroon/white/silver, 1:43 . . . . $119

DALIA (ALSO SEE TEKNO)

Dalia of Spain was begun in the 1920s. By World War II, Dalia had produced a number of diecast toys. By the late 1950s, Dalia produced a series of 1:38 scale Vespa and Lambretta scooters. Around the same time, the company became the licensed distributor for Solido in Spain. About a decade later, Dalia established a working relationship with Tekno of Denmark to produce a group of 1:43 scale models made in Spain. While the original box says "Dalia-Tekno," the models only say Tekno on the base.

1 Vespa Scooter, green $75
2 Lambretta A Scooter, blue and orange $75
3 Lambretta B Scooter, gray and pink $75

4 Lambretta Motor Tricycle, beige and green. $75
5 Vespa Scooter with Sidecar, light blue $75
6 Lambretta A Scooter with Sidecar, silver. $75
7 Lambretta B Scooter with Sidecar, orange and black. $75
8 Lambretta Motor Tricycle"Butano," orange $75
9 Vespa Scooter Red Cross, white and gray. $75
10 Vespa Scooter with Sidecar Red Cross, white and gray $75
11 Lambretta A Scooter, orange and black $75
12 Lambretta A Scooter with Sidecar, orange and black. $75
13 Lambretta Motor Tricycle with Buckets, orange and beige. . $75
14 Lambretta Motor Tricycle with Drums, orange and beige. . . $75
15 Lambretta Motor Tricycle Milk Delivery, white and beige . . $75
16 Lambretta Motor Tricycle Wine Delivery, light blue and
beige $75
17 Lambretta Motor Tricycle Water Delivery, silver and beige . $75
18 Vespa S Scooter, white and green $75
19 Vespa S Scooter with Sidecar, green and yellow. $75
20 Lambretta A Army Scooter, olive $75
21 Lambretta A Army Scooter with Sidecar, olive. $75
22 Vespa S Army Scooter, olive $75
23 Vespa S Army Scooter with Sidecar, olive. $75
24 Vespa Scooter "Policia," black $75
25 Vespa Scooter "Policia" with sidecar, black. $75
26 Go-kart, red and blue $90
27 Lambretta Army Motor Tricycle, olive. $75
28 Vespa Scooter "Telegrafos," beige $75
29 Vespa Scooter with Sidecar, "Telegrafos," beige $75
30 Lambretta Motor Tricycle with Cases, white and beige $75
31 Vespa Scooter, "Iberia," silver $75
32 Vespa Scooter with Sidecar, "Iberia," silver. $75
33 Lambretta Motor Tricycle "Coca-Cola," white and orange . . $75
34 Vespa Scooter Rally, blue $75
35 Vespa Scooter with Sidecar, Rally, blue $75
36 Lambretta Motor Tricycle, Red Cross, gray and white $75
37 Lambretta A Scooter, "Coca-Cola," white and orange $75
38 Lambretta A Scooter with Sidecar, "Coca-Cola," white and
orange $75
39 Vespa Scooter, "Mop," yellow and beige $75
40 Vespa Scooter with Sidecar, "Mop," yellow and beige. $75
41 Lambretta Scooter, "Butano," orange $75
42 Lambretta Scooter with Sidecar, "Butano," orange. $75

Dalia 1:66 Scale Cars

501 Porsche Carrera 6 . . . . $40
502 Ford GT Le Mans. $40
503 Chaparral 2F $40
504 Seat 850 Coupe $40
505 De Tomaso Mangusta $40
506 Renault Alpine. $40

Dalia–Solido models

1 Jaguar D Le Mans, red, green, or blue $100
2 Maserati 250F, red, yellow, or green. $100
3 Vanwall Racing Car, light blue or green $100
4 Ferrari Testa Rossa, red, white, cream $150
5 Porsche 550/1500 RS, red and black, yellow and black, or silver
and green $125
6 Cooper 1500 F.Z, tan, white, and blue, or yellow and white. $100
7 Porsche F.2, silver and red, yellow and black, or orange and silver $125

8 Seat 1400-C, black and green, black and silver, red, or green and
yellow $150
9 Renault Floride Convertible, copper, red, or blue $100
10 Mercedes-Benz 190SL Roadster, copper, silver, or white . . $100
11 Lotus F.1, yellow or black $75
12 Lancia Flaminia Coupe Pinin Farina, red, silver, blue, or
green. $100
13 Fiat Abarth Record, orange, red, or white $100
14 Seat 1400-C Taxi, Barcelona, black and yellow $150
15 Seat 1400-C Taxi, Madrid, black and red. $150
16 Alfa Romeo Giulietta Roadster, red, orange, light blue, or
green. $75
17 Ferrari 250 GT 2+2, red, green, or yellow $125
18 Aston Martin DB4, blue, yellow, red, silver, copper. $100
19 Citroen Ami 6, white and green or white and blue $100
20 Ferrari 156 F.1, light blue or red. $100
21 Fiat Abarth 1000, orange, silver, or tan $100
22 Mercedes-Benz 220 SE Coupe
v.1 "Autopistas," orange. $150
v.2 "Falck," white $150
v.3 "Policia," black $150
v.4 "PTT," white $150
v.5 blue or red $100
v.6 Red Cross, white $150
23 Alfa Romeo 2600 Coupe Bertone, cream, dark red, blue, green,
or silver $100
24 Seat1400-C"Policia," black. $150
25 Panhard DB Le Mans, blue, silver, or white $75
26-1 Aston Martin DB 5 Vantage, white, cream, blue, green, or
copper $100
26-2 Aston Martin DB 5 Vantage, "The Saint," white $175
27 Seat 1400-C, "Iberia," silver. $150
28 NSU Prinz, red, blue, green, or orange and black $75
29 Porsche GT Le Mans, green, blue, silver $125
30 Fiat 2300 S Ghia Convertible
v.1 "Autopistas," orange. $150
v.2 green, red, blue, or white $100
31 Ford Thunderbird, red, blue, tan, metallic green $100
32 Ferrari 2.5 L, red $100
33 Seat 1500
v.1 "Policia," black $150
v.2 Taxi Barcelona, black and yellow. $150
v.3 Taxi Madrid, black and red $150
v.4 white, green, or metallic blue $125
34 Harvey Indianapolis, dark green or yellow. $75
35 Simca Oceare Convertible, green or metallic blue $100
36-1 Maserati 3.5 L Mistral
v.1 copper, beige, yellow, or metallic blue. $100
v.2 "NASA," orange. $150
37 Ford Mustang, red, white, metallic light blue $100
38 B.R.M. F.1, yellow or metallic green. $75
39 Alpine F.3, dark green . . . . $ 75
40 Lola Climax V8 F.1, tan and red. $70
41 Porsche Carrera 6, yellow and red $75
42 Ford GT 40 Le Mans, yellow and blue $70
43 Ferrari 330 P3, light blue $100
44 Alfa Romeo Giulia TZ, blue or orange $90
45 Oldsmobile Toronado, orange or green $65

46 Panhard 24 BT

   v.1 "Urgencias," white $125

   v.2 silver $60

47 Chaparral Z D, red $50

48 BMW 2000 CS, white $65

49 Simca 1100, yellow $75

50 De Tomaso Mangusta, tan $60

51 Chaparral 2F, blue and red, blue and black, or white and red $60

52 Citroen Ami 6 S.W.

   v.1 "Butano," orange $150

   v.2 "Falck," white $150

   v.3 Ambulance, white $150

   v.4 blue, green $75

54 Opel GT 1900, metallic blue, metallic green $75

55 Ford Thunderbird Taxi, black and yellow $125

56 Ford Thunderbird, "Policia," black $150

57 Ford Mustang Rally, red $75

58 Ford Mustang "Policia," black $125

59 Ford Mustang Taxi Barcelona, black and yellow $125

60 Ford Mustang Taxi Madrid, black and red $125

61 Oldsmobile Toronado Rally, orange $75

62 Simca 1100 Red Cross, white $150

63 Simca 1100 Taxi, black and yellow $125

64 Alfa Romeo 2600 Coupe "Iberia," silver $120

65 Alfa Romeo Carabo Bertone, orange $75

66 Alpine Renault, yellow $75

67 Maserati 3.5 L Mistral Rally, yellow and black $75

68 Lola T70 MK 3B, red $50

69 McLaren M8 B Can Am, orange $65

70 Matra 650, blue $65

71 Porsche 914/6, yellow $60

72 Ferran 365 GTB4, red $75

73 Buggy Bertone, metallic green $50

DALIA-TEKNO

415 Ford Taunus Van

   v.1 "Autopistas," orange $250

   v.2 "Butano" $250

   v.3 "Iberia," black $250

   v.4 "Mop Projectos," yellow and tan $250

   v.5 "Policia," black $250

   v.6 "Tekno" $250

   v.7 "Telegrafos" $250

   v.8 Ambulance (white) $250

829 Lincoln Continental $65

832 M.G. 1100 . . . . $50

833 Ford Mustang Hardtop $50

834 Ford Mustang Convertible $50

914 Ford D 800 Truck $50

915 Ford D 800 Stake Truck $50

928 Mercedes-Benz 230SL Hardtop $50

929 Mercedes-Benz 230SL Roadster $50

930 Monza GT Coupe $50

931 Monza GT Roadster $50

933 Oldsmobile Toronado $50

DANBURY MINT

Between Danbury Mint and Franklin Mint, some of the most popular and collectible precision models have been produced. Jay Olins, editor of the monthly Precision Die Cast Car Collectors Club newsletter, is perhaps the most avid collector of both. Every three months, he publishes a complete up-to-date list of models produced by each company. Collectors are very critical of authenticity and detail, so they often write to the manufacturer and to Mr. Olins regarding any discrepancies discovered. Olins apparently has the inside track with both companies, and he relays all such comments to the manufacturer. All Danbury Mint models are currently available. This list represents all known models as of March 10, 1995. Danbury Mint, 47 Richards Avenue, Norwalk CT 06857.

1:24 SCALE

1953 Buick Skylark Convertible, blue/blue-gray . . . . . . $85 – 125

1959 Cadillac Series 62 Convertible, red/red . . . . $85 – 125

1932 Cadillac V-16 Sport Phaeton, green/beige . . . . . . $85 – 125

1953 Chevrolet 3100 Pickup, green . . . . $85 – 125

1957 Chevrolet Bel Air Convertible, blue/light and dark blue . . . . $85 – 125

1958 Chevrolet Impala Convertible, turquoise/blue . . . . $85 – 125

1969 Chevrolet SS/RS Camaro Convertible, blue/white . . $85 – 125

1969 Chevrolet SS/RS Camaro Convertible, orange-white/orange-maroon . . . . $85 – 125

1948 Chrysler Town & Country Convertible, maroon-wood/maroon . . . . $85 – 125

1935 Duesenberg SSJ Speedster, gray-red/beige . . . . . . $85 – 125

1958 Ferrari 250 Testa Rossa, red/red . . . . $85 – 125

1931 Ford Model A Deluxe Roadster, black-brown/tan . . $85 – 125

1940 Ford Deluxe Coupe, red/beige . . . . $85 – 125

1955 Ford Fairlane Crown Victoria, cream-black/cream-black . $85 – 125

1956 Ford F-100 Pickup, red . . . . $85 – 125

1956 Ford Thunderbird, red/red-white . . . . $85 – 125

1966 Ford Mustang Convertible, cream/blue-cream . . . . $85 – 125

1934 Hispano Suiza J-12, blue . . . . $85 – 125

1949 Jaguar XK120, sand/red . . . . $85 – 125

1931 Mercedes-Benz SSKL, white/black . . . . $85 – 125

1949 Mercury Club Coupe, black/beige . . . . $85 – 125

1950 Mercury Custom, plum/magenta . . . . $85 – 125

1965 Pontiac GTO, lavender/white . . . . $85 – 125

1934 Packard V12 LeBaron Speedster, red/black . . . . . . $85 – 125

1933 Pierce Silver Arrow, silver/silver . . . . $85 – 125

1938 Rolls Royce Phantom III, maroon/black . . . . $85 – 125

1927 Stutz Custom Series Black Hawk, black/red . . . . . $85 – 125

DANHAUSEN

As reported by Aaron Robinson, Danhausen models and kits come from Danhausen, Germany, near the Belgium/Lichtenstein border. They produced a glossy, colorful catalog issued yearly. Besides the proprietary Danhausen line, the company offered models from Pocher, ABC Brianza, and some Russian-made diecast.

1931 Mercedes SSK L, 1:43 kit $17

Ferrari BB Spyder, red, 1:43 . . . . $65

DARDA

Dardas of Germany are mostly plastic-body toy cars with a distinction. Pullback action and the wildest track this side of Hot Wheels helps Dardas fly around loops and curves at a scale speed of over 600 miles per hour! A huge assortment of Darda models are available, along with a large assortment of track sets. Models sell for about $5 each.

Days Gone (see Lledo)

D.C.M.T. (also see Crescent, Impy, Lincoln, Lone Star, River and Roadmaster)

Die Casting Machine Tools Ltd. of Great Britain started producing toys as a sideline in the 1940s in North London in order to demonstrate the potential of their equipment. While most of their toys were produced under the Crescent brand, a few were simply marked "D.C.M.T." Some had friction motors in them. The Crescent Toy Company originated from England in 1922. Through the twenties and thirties, Henry Eagles and Arthur Schneider manufactured lead alloy toy soldiers, cowboys, kitchen sets, and other items. After World War II, Crescent resumed making their toys, adding "DCMT" into the casting, evidence of their marketing of toys from the firm of Die Casting Machine Tools Ltd. Crescent became the marketing firm for these models as well as their own Crescent brand. One brand of which there is some dispute is a series of toys issued under the "River" brand. Neither the model or the box had any mention of Lone Star, Crescent, or D.C.M.T., and the castings were inferior to the other lines produced, which led to metal fatigue with which D.C.M.T. models were not so plagued. Regardless of such controversy of whether D.C.M.T. produced them or not, the author lists them below. The D.C.M.T. mark was removed from models made in 1948 and later. D.C.M.T. meanwhile went on to make Lone Star models. Crescent continued making toys until 1981. Here are a few models made under the D.C.M.T. mark, followed by the "River" series. Lincoln Industries of Auckland, New Zealand, reportedly produced remakes from old D.C.M.T. tooling.

D.C.M.T. Models

Low Loader Tractor Trailer	$45 – 60
Military Truck	$45 – 60
Tanker Truck	$45 – 60
Timber Truck with real "log"	$60 – 75

River Models

Austin A40 Somerset	$60 – 75
Buick Roadmaster	$75 – 90
Daimler Conquest	$60 – 75
Ford Prefect	$60 – 75
Standard Vanguard Saloon	$60 – 75
Standard Vanguard Station Wagon	$60 – 75

DDR

With a predominance of Deutz models, it may be assumed that these 1:87 scale DDRs are made in Germany, although I may be wrong.

1950 Deutz Dump Truck	$5
1950 Deutz Fire Ladder	$5
1950 Deutz Lumber Truck	$5
1950 Deutz-Fahr Farm Tractor	$5
1980 Zetor Tractor	$5

1985 IFA Semi Fish Van	$5
1985 IFA Van "Fernverkehr"	$3
Deutz Fire Trailer	$5

Dehanes

Dehanes brand models are 1:55 scale models, mostly of freight trucks, with a few exceptions.

001 1939 Dodge Airflow	$155
101 Mack B "Heinz 57"	$69
103 White 3000 "Threemor"	$69
103 White 3000 "Mason Dixon"	$69
104 Ford C600 "Johnny Walker"	$69
105 Ford C600 "UPS"	$69
106 Mack COE "Johnny Walker"	$69
205 Mack B80 Dump Truck	$69
801 Mack L Oil Truck "Hooker"	$69
914 1955 Mack H63T "Hennis"	$145
915 International Conventional "PIE"	$145
916 White 3000 Semi "Mason Dixon"	$135
956 Mack "Coca Cola" Van	$69
957 Mack Semi "Navajo"	$115
SPC 1946 Chevrolet "Western Pacific"	$155
WISE 1955 White Semi "Wise"	$115

Deles

Discovered in a drug store recently is an assortment of inexpensive toy cars in roughly 1:43 scale with the name Deles on the bottom and made in China. A couple of late model Mercedes-Benz coupes, a Porsche 356 convertible, and a few other models sell for $1.25 each. Typically models have very lightweight bodies, plastic chasses, and rubber tires on crude wheel hubs. The Porsche 356 Convertible is arguably the most charming and attractive of the bunch.

Dent Hardware Company

Since 1895, Dent Hardware Company operated out of Fullerton, Pennsylvania. Dent toys are historically significant for their contribution to the toy market of the early twentieth century. Their first cast-iron vehicles emerged in 1898. In the 1920s, Dent attempted to market aluminum toys, but they failed to catch buyers' attention and were quickly phased out. Even though the company survived till 1973, toy production ceased during the Great Depression of the 1930s. Very few, if any, of Dent's toys were marked. Experts recognize them because of extensive experience in buying, selling, and trading. Richard O'Brien's book *Collecting Toy Cars and Trucks* provides a list of known Dent models. If identifiable as Dent cast-iron models, values start at $110 and go up to $10,000 for the rarest models.

Mack American Oil Co. Tanker, 10½"	$1,600
Mack American Oil Co. Tanker, 15"	$2,700
Bus, 6¼"	$750
Coast to Coast Bus, 7½"	$250
Coast to Coast Bus, 15"	$1,500
Coupe, 5"	$250
Mack Junior Supply Company, New York — Philadelphia, 16"	$10,000
Public Service Bus, 13½"	$4,500

DEOMA MICROMODELS (OR MICROTOYS) OF ITALY

A series of military models were sold under the Deoma Micromodels name during the late 1950s and early 1960s. Some models are crude copies of Dinky models of that era.

1 T-34 Tank, 2½"		$20 – 30
2 Daimler Armored Car, 1⅝"		$20 – 30
3 Austin 1-Ton Open Truck, 1¾"		$20 – 30
4 Bedford Open Truck, 2¼"		$20 – 30
5 Bedford Covered Truck, 2¼"		$20 – 30
6 Austin 1-Ton Covered Truck, 1¾"		$20 – 30
7 General Patton Tank, 2⅝"		$20 – 30
8 Combat Car, 2"		$20 – 30
9 Jeep, 1⅝"		$20 – 30
10 High Speed Tractor, 2¼"		$20 – 30
11 Three-Axle Open Truck, 2⅜"		$20 – 30
12 Three-Axle Civilian Truck, 2⅜"		$20 – 30
14 Tank Transporter, 2¾"		$20 – 30
15 Three-Axle Covered Truck, 2⅜"		$20 – 30
16 "Long Tom" 155mm Cannon, 3¾"		$20 – 30
23 Austin 1-Ton Covered Truck, 1¾"		$20 – 30

DESIGN STUDIO (ALSO SEE MOTOR CITY & U.S.A. MODELS)

Design Studio 1:43 scale models are made in the United States by partners Alan Novak and Gene Parrill since 1986. Their USA Models collection are less detailed and less expensive models than their Motor City and Design Studio counterparts.

3 1949 Hudson Commodore	$149
4 1958 Oldsmobile Convertible	$125
5 1948 Buick Coupe	$125
6 1956 Chevrolet Convertible 2-Door, top down	$179
7 1956 Chevrolet Convertible	$145
9 1940 Ford Convertible, top up	$219
10 1956 Airstream Trailer	$125

DESORMEAUX

Two 1:43 scale lead alloy vehicles are known to have been produced by Desormeaux of France. Description, production year, and value are indicated below.

1923 Citroen 5CV, 1957	$125
1910 Le Zebre, 1958	$125

DETAIL CARS - CDC

Collector Bill Cross reports that these are not hand built, as previously described, but are mass produced in China, often looking as if they come from the same source as Minichamps. They are marketed by CDC in Italy and by Corgi in Great Britain. As of January 1997, the US distributor for CDC is Dual Connection, P O Box 569, Gibsonia, PA 15044. Phone 412-381-1143 or 1-800-351-1141. Fax 412-381-1006.

110 1990 Lamborghini Diablo, yellow		$25
111 1994 Lamborghini Diablo S, red		$25
112 1992 Lamborghini Diablo Roadster, yellow		$25
113 1990 Lamborghini Diablo Roadster, blue		$25
114 1993 Lamborghini Diablo Coupe, black		$25
131 1992 Jaguar XJS Convertible, top down, blue		$25
132 1992 Jaguar XJS Convertible, top up, silver		$25
133 1992 Jaguar XJS Coupe, red		$25

140 1993 Ferrari 512 TR Coupe, red		$25
142 1993 Ferrari 512 TR, top down, yellow		$25
144 1993 Ferrari 512 TR, top up, yellow		$25
150 1987 Ferrari F-40, red		$25
151 1987 Ferrari F-40 LeMans, red		$25
153 1991 Ferrari F-40, Italian Racing Club, red		$25
154 1993 Ferrari F-40 Monte Shell, multicolor		$25
155 1994 Ferrari F-40 Totip, multicolor		$25
160 1991 Nissan 300ZX Coupe, black		$25
161 1991 Nissan 300ZX Convertible, red		$25
162 1991 Nissan 300 ZX Softtop, blue		$25
163 1991 Nissan 300 ZX Convertible, red		$25
164 1991 Nissan 300ZX Coupe, silver		$25
165 1991 Nissan 300 ZX Monza, multicolor		$25
170 1993 Jaguar XJ220 Coupe, silver		$25
171 1993 Jaguar XJ220 Coupe, green		$25
172 1993 Jaguar XJ220 GT LeMans		$25
174 1993 Jaguar XJ220 GT Martini		$25
190 1993 Ferrari 456GT, metallic blue		$25
191 1993 Ferrari 456GT, metallic red		$25
193 1993 Ferrari 456GT, red		$25
200 1958 Alfa Romeo Giulietta Spyder, red		$25
201 1958 Alfa Romeo Giulietta Spyder, white		$25
202 1958 Alfa Romeo Giulietta Spyder, blue		$25
203 1958 Alfa Romeo Giulietta Spyder Hardtop, red		$25
204 1958 Alfa Romeo Giulietta Spyder Hardtop, white		$25
205 1958 Alfa Romeo Giulietta Spyder Softtop, gray		$25
206 1958 Alfa Romeo Giulietta Monoposto Mille Miglia, red		$25
210 1993 Chevrolet Corvette ZR1 Coupe, white		$25
211 1993 Chevrolet Corvette ZR1 Convertible, top down, red		$25
212 1993 Chevrolet Corvette ZR1 Convertible, top up, yellow		$25
213 1993 Chevrolet Corvette ZR1, metallic blue		$25
214 1993 Chevrolet Corvette ZR1 Convertible, top down, green		$25
215 1993 Chevrolet Corvette ZR1 Coupe 40th Anniversary, red		$25
220 1959 Porsche 356A Coupe, red		$25
221 1959 Porsche 356A Coupe, silver		$25
222 1959 Porsche 356A Convertible, top up, red		
223 1959 Porsche 356A Convertible, top down, silver		$25
224 1959 Porsche 356A Convertible, top up, blue		$25
225 1959 Porsche 356A Convertible, top down, metallic yellow		$25
226 1959 Porsche 356A Coupe Mille Miglia, silver		$25
227 1959 Porsche 356A Coupe Carrera Panamerica #200, white		$25
228 1959 Porsche 356A Coupe Carrera Panamerica #153, silver		$25
229 1959 Porsche 356A Convertible, silver		$25
230 1994 Mercedes-Benz 320 SL Convertible, metallic silver		$25
231 1994 Mercedes-Benz 320 SL Convertible, red		$25
233 1994 Mercedes-Benz 320 SL Coupe, metallic blue		$25
234 1994 Mercedes-Benz 320 SL Coupe, blue		$25
235 1994 Mercedes-Benz 320 SL Coupe, gray		$25
240 1952 BMW 502 Coupe, black		$25
241 1952 BMW 502 Coupe, red		$25
242 1952 BMW 502 Convertible, top down, blue		$25
243 1952 BMW 502 Convertible, top up, silver		$25
244 1952 BMW 502 Convertible, top down, red		$25
245 1952 BMW 502 Coupe, two-tone gray		$25
246 1952 BMW 502 Convertible, cream		$25
250 1959 BMW 503 Coupe, red		$25
251 1959 BMW 503 Coupe, silver		$25

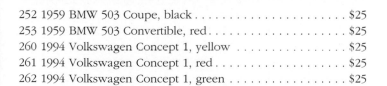

252 1959 BMW 503 Coupe, black $25
253 1959 BMW 503 Convertible, red $25
260 1994 Volkswagen Concept 1, yellow $25
261 1994 Volkswagen Concept 1, red $25
262 1994 Volkswagen Concept 1, green $25

263 1994 Volkswagen Concept 1 Convertible, yellow, $25

264 1994 Volkswagen Concept 1 Convertible, red $25
265 1994 Volkswagen Concept 1 Convertible, green $25
266 1994 Volkswagen Concept 1 Convertible, silver $25
270 Volkswagen Golf, red $25
271 Volkswagen Golf, silver $25
272 Volkswagen Golf, white $25
273 Volkswagen Golf Cabriolet, red $25
274 Volkswagen Golf Cabriolet, silver $25
275 Volkswagen Golf Cabriolet, yellow $25
277 Volkswagen Golf Silverstone, multicolor $25
280 1994 Ford Mustang GT, red $25
281 1994 Ford Mustang GT Coupe, yellow $25
282 1994 Ford Mustang GT, blue $25
285 1994 Ford Mustang GT Convertible, bright blue $25
287 1994 Ford Mustang Indy Pace Car, red $25
290 1994 Ferrari F355 Berlinetta Coupe, red $25
291 1994 Ferrari F355 Berlinetta Coupe, yellow $25
292 1994 Ferrari F355 Berlinetta Coupe, blue $25
293 1994 Ferrari F355 Berlinetta Spyder, red $25
294 1994 Ferrari F355 Berlinetta Convertible, yellow $25
295 1994 Ferrari F355 Berlinetta Convertible, blue $25
296 1994 Ferrari F355 Berlinetta TS, top up, gray $25
305 1973 Ford Capri 2600 GT, metallic red with black roof . . . $25
311 1964 Fiat 600 D, white $25

DG

DG stands for Dave Gilbert, the producer of white metal hand builts and kits from Great Britain. Two series, one regular and one "Dinky style" were produced, although numbers may be intermingled. DG was started in 1973. The Dinky series are models Dinky could have made in the thirties and forties but didn't. Thanks to Harv and Kay Goranson for updates and information.

2 1944 Dodge 4x4 Army Ambulance $35
3 1934 Morris "Chivers" $35
4 1930 Bentley Speed 6 . . . . $35
5 1936 Cord $35
1938 MG Tickford (kit) $50
MG Y Saloon (kit) $50

1921 Murphy Duesenberg (kit) . . . . : $50

DIAMOND
Russell Alameda provides the following information on this otherwise unknown brand.
1964 Shelby Cobra 427 SC, white, 1:18, limited edition of 2,100 . $75

DIAPET
Diapet is a popular Japanese brand of quality toys produced by Yonezawa Toys.
Airport Bus, B32 . . . . $18
Bus "Hishi Nippon," 231 . . . . $18
Cordia XG1600 Turbo, G13 . . . . $18
Corvette, G76 . . . . $75
Datsun 280Z, G3, G116 . . . . $18
Datsun 280Z Police, P53 . . . . $18
Datsun F2 Coupe, G15 . . . . $18
Datsun Leopard 4-Door Sedan, G2 . . . . $18
Datsun Mail Van, 271 . . . . $18
Datsun Silvia 200SX, G39/G125 . . . . $18
Datsun Tow Truck, 272 . . . . $18
1930 Deusenberg, G124, 1:27 . . . . $34
DP2 Backhoe, K23 . . . . $18
DP2 Backhoe/Loader, K24 . . . . $18
Fuso Bus, B36 . . . . $18
Fuso Truck Crane, K30 . . . . $18
Hato Bus, B40 . . . . $24
Hato Double Decker Bus, B47, 1:75 . . . . $24
Honda Acura NSX, SV26, 1:40 . . . . $25 – 32
Honda Beat, SV33, 1:35 . . . . $19
Honda Prelude, SV34, 1:40 . . . . $21
Honda Prelude 2.0 SI, G55, 1:40 . . . . $18
Ihi 1600 Clamshell Bucket Crane, K21, 1:40 . . . . $34
Ihi IS-110 Power Shovel, K3, 1:50 . . . . $18
Ihi IS-110 Clamshell (Bucket), K5, 1:50 . . . . $22
Ihi IS-110 Track Backhoe, K4, 1:50 . . . . $22
Ihi IS-220 Track Backhoe, K17, 1:40 . . . . $34
Infiniti Q45, SV18, 1:40 . . . . $24 – 34
Isuzu "Shell," 107 . . . . $18
Isuzu Shovel, K53 . . . . $18
Isuzu Mixer, 109 . . . . $18
Isuzu Semi TV, B47 . . . . $18
Jr. Highway Bus, B5, 1:60 . . . . $24
Kawasaki 88 ZII Wheel Loader, K31, 1:28 . . . . $28
Komatsu D20QF Track Loader, K31, 1:28 . . . . $22
Lexus Coupe, SV22 . . . . $30
Mack Car Carrier, T54, 1:40 . . . . $37
Mazda Cosmo 2-Door Hardtop, G10 . . . . $18
Mazda Miata MX 5, SV14, 1:40 . . . . $21
Mazda RX7, SV35, 1:40 . . . . $24
Mazda RX7 Police, P57 . . . . $18
Mercedes-Benz 560SEL, G8, 1:40 . . . . $24
Mini Cooper 1000, SV3 . . . . $24
Mitsubishi Crawler Crane, K39, 1:60 . . . . $22
Mitsubishi GTO, SV27, 1:40 . . . . $21
Mitsubishi MS280 Track Backhoe, K42, 1:60 . . . . $22
Mitsubishi School Bus, B35 . . . . $18
Mitsubishi Starion 2000 GSR Coupe, silver, G17 . . . . $38

Neoplan Skyliner Bus, B41, 1:60 . . . . $28
Nissan Ambulance, P13, 1:35 . . . . $22
Nissan Cedric Ambulance, 283 . . . . $18
Nissan Cedric Police, P64 . . . . $18
Nissan Cedric Taxi, P65 . . . . $18
Nissan Cedric Ultima Station Taxi, P29 . . . . $35
Nissan Cherry Camper, T8 . . . . $18
Nissan Kombi "1008," T4 . . . . $18
Nissan Kombi Police, P3 . . . . $18
Nissan Fairlady 300 ZX, red, SV15 . . . . $27
Nissan Infiniti, SV18, 1:40 . . . . $25
Nissan Prairie, G22 . . . . $18
Nissan S&B 30 Mini Backhoe, K16, 1:26 . . . . $32
Nissan Safari, T1 . . . . $18
Nissan Silvia Coupe, G37 . . . . $18
Nissan Skyline Police Car, P43, 1:30 . . . . $18
Nissan Taxi, P16/P65, 1:40 . . . . $18
1980 Pontiac Firebird, G67 . . . . $18
Rolls-Royce Silver Shadow, G71, 1:40 . . . . $25
Sakai Roller, K8 . . . . $18
Sakai TS150 Tire Roller, K12, 1:40 . . . . $22
School Bus, B4 . . . . $18
Seibu Tour Bus, B1, 1:75 . . . . $18
Sightseeing Bus, B39 . . . . $18
Subaru Leon 2-Door Hardtop, G128 . . . . $18
Subaru Mail Van, 462 . . . . $18
Sumitomo-FMC LS3400 Track H, K37, 1:42 . . . . $34
Suzuki Fronte Police, 296 . . . . $18
Toyota Carib (Tercel) 4x4 Wagon, G23 . . . . $18
Toyota Carib (Tercel) Radio Car, P5 . . . . $18
Toyota Celica 2800 GT/G5 . . . . $18
Toyota Corolla 1500SR 3-Door Sedan, G21 . . . . $18
Toyota Corolla Levin Coupe, G29 . . . . $18
Toyota Crown Police, 613/P62 . . . . $18
Toyota Crown Taxi, P63 . . . . $18
Toyota Fire Chief's Car, P17, 1:40 . . . . $22
Toyota Hiace Ambulance, P43/P55, 1:36 . . . . $12 – 18
Toyota Hiace Camper, T6 . . . . $18
Toyota Jobsun 7 Skid Loader, K11, 1:22 . . . . $24
Toyota Landcruiser, T-100, 1:30 . . . . $30
Toyota Landcruiser Army, T2, 1:30 . . . . $18
Toyota Lexus SC, SV22, 1:40 . . . . $25
Toyota Mini School Bus, B37 . . . . $18
Toyota Pickup 4x4, T3 . . . . $18
Toyota Police Van, P42 . . . . $18
Toyota Previa Van, T-70, 1:40 . . . . $25
Toyota Soarer (Lexus) Coupe, G1/G27 . . . . $18
Toyota Supra 3.0GT Turbo, G50, 1:40 . . . . $18
Yamaha Snowmobile, 287 . . . . $18

DINKUM

It was previously assumed that Dinkum toys of Australia were given their name to capitalize on the similar-sounding Dinky brand name of England. But as collector Bill Cross reports, Dinkum is Australian vernacular which, roughly translated, means "good," or "true," as in "fair dinkum, mate!"

Ford Falcon GT, red & black $95
1969 Ford Mustang Boss, red, 1:43 . . . . $68

1985 Holden Commodore, white, 1:43 . . . . $35
Holden FJ Panel Van, dark blue $85

DINKY

Excellent collector reference books have already been written on these great little gems from Great Britain, as indicated in this book's bibliography section. So, instead of trying to duplicate those works, this book will present a short history and highlight only a few of the numerous models produced.

Dinky Toys started out in 1933 as Modelled Miniatures, produced and marketed under the Frank Hornby name, the original manufacturer. Hornby also produced electric trains, and the first models produced were intended as accessories to these train sets. Simultaneously in Liverpool, England, and Bobigny, France, the British and French Dinky Toys were put into production in 1934. French-made Dinky Toys, particularly the post-war models, are more highly valued in the U.S., and perhaps Europe, because the French models focused on American cars of the era, and serve as accurate models of the era.

The advent of Hot Wheels by Mattel in 1968 posed a major threat to companies such as Dinky Toys, contributing to the close of the French facility in 1972, although Pilen of Spain continued to produce some French Dinky models later in the seventies, while Solido of France attempted a similar feat in 1981.

The British firm, meanwhile, attempted to stay in business by farming out production of some models to Polistil of Italy and to Universal of Hong Kong. Universal eventually purchased the rights, and incorporated the brand into the Matchbox line, which Universal had purchased in 1982. Several other firms staked a claim on the Dinky brand from time to time, including Tri-Ang of England in 1963, Mercury of Italy, Mercury Industries based in the US and Canada, Gibbs of Ohio, Best-Box/Efsi of the Netherlands, and most notably Meccano of England. The Dinky brand vanished with the purchase of Matchbox in 1992 by Tyco. All that is now left of Dinky models are there frequent appearance as Matchbox Collectibles out of Beaverton, Oregon, a division of Tyco that markets models through mail-order advertising in such publications as *Parade,* and in specialty magazines such as *Collecting Toys, Diecast Digest,* and others.

For a more complete detail of the line, Dr. Edward Force's book on Dinky Toys is available in bookstores or by special order. *Dinky Toys and Modelled Miniatures* is an older book, retailing for around $75, that first documented the full line of Dinky toys from their beginnings through the late 70s. The Dinky Collection from Matchbox is featured in *Matchbox Toys 1947 – 1996* by Dana Johnson from Collector Books ($18.95 retail), as well as in the third book in a four-volume set on Matchbox toys, *Universal's Matchbox Toys,* by Charles Mack.

MODELLED MINIATURES — THE FIRST DINKY TOYS, 1933

Sports Roadster $350
Sports Coupe $250
Motor Truck $175

Delivery Van $300
Farm Tractor $200

DINKY TOYS THROUGH THE YEARS

Meccano Delivery Van, 1934. . . . . $250

Speed of the Wind, 1936, $125

Mercury Seaplane, 1939 . . . . $100
Packard Super 8, 1939 . . . . $250
Riley Saloon, 1947 . . . . $85
Studebaker Commander, 1949 . . . . $425
Talbot Lago, 1953 . . . . $75
Buick Roadmaster, 1954 . . . . $225

Jaguar XK120, 1954, $125

Plymouth Belvedere, 1957 . . . . $150

Austin A105, 1958, $20

Hudson Hornet, 1958 . . . . $150
Maserati 2000, 1958 . . . . $90
Studebaker Golden Hawk, 1958 . . . . $150
Rolls-Royce Silver Wraith, 1959. . . . . $90
Bristol Canadian Pacific Airline, 1959 . . . . $95
Rambler Cross Country, 1961 . . . . $95
Buick Riviera, 1965 . . . . $90
Corvair Monza, 1965 . . . . $90
Oldsmobile 88, 1965 . . . . $90

Berliet Dump Truck, 1961, $125

Rambler Classic, 1965. . . . . $90
Ford GT, 1966 . . . . $50
Johnson Street Sweeper, 1977. . . . . $45
Pontiac Police Car, 1971 . . . . $75

Viceroy 37 Bus, 1972, $25

Cadillac Superior Ambulance, 1974, $75

Rover 3500 Police, 1979. . . . . $50
USS Enterprise, #371, 1980 . . . . $25
Klingon Cruiser, #372, 1980 . . . . $25

DMP STUDIOS

DMP is a Canadian company that specializes in custom hand built or "studio" models and factory-approved conversions of Brooklins. DMP models are distributed in the US by Brasilia Press, P O Box 2023, Elkhart IN 46515.

1961 Chevrolet Impala Convertible (converted Brooklin Impala
      Sports Coupe), Honduras maroon $125

DOEPKE

The Charles Wm. Doepke Mfg. Co., Inc. of Rossmoyne, Ohio, began manufacturing sturdy large scale toys called Doep-

ke (pronounced DEP-key) "Model Toys" at the end of World War II. The full story of Doepke Model Toys can be found in Richard O'Brien's book *Collecting Toy Cars and Trucks,* from Books Americana. Doepke toys are cast metal toys with heavy rubber tires, accurate scale, and solid construction.

#2000 Wooldridge Heavy Duty Earth Hauler, 25" long $275
#2001 Barber-Greene High Capacity Bucket Loader, 13" high. $350
#2002 Jaeger Concrete Mixer, 15" long $350
#2006 Adams Diesel Road Grader, 26" long. $200
#2007 Unit Mobile Crane, 11½". $250
#2008 American LaFrance Aerial Ladder Truck. $475
#2009 Euclid Earth HAuler Truck, 27" long $325
#2010 American LaFrance Pumper Fire Truck, 18" long $350
#2011 Heiliner Earth Scraper, 29" long $300
#2012 Caterpillar D6 Tractor and Bulldozer, 15" long. $500
#2013 Barber-Greene Mobile High-Capacity Backet Loader, 22" long $450
#2014 American LaFrance Aerial Ladder Fire Truck, 23" long . $500
#2015 Clark Airport Tractor and Baggage Trailers $450
#2017 MG, 1954 , 15" long $450
#2018 Jaguar, 1955. . . . . $650
#2023 Searchlight Truck, 1955. . . . . $1200

DOORKEY

Doorkey models are mostly 1:43 scale diecast made in various worldwide factories for the Holland-based company. Note that besides being marketed under the Doorkey brand, they are also produced for AHC.

DOORKEY MODELS MADE IN CHINA

DO150 Toyota Celica, 1:43. . . . . $21
DO151 Toyota Landcruiser, 1:43. $21
DO152 Toyota MR-2, 1:43. . . . . $21
DO153 Toyota Supra, 1:43 . . . . $21
DO154 BMW 2000 saloon, 1:43 . . . . $21
DO155 BMW 507 sports, 1:43. . . . . $21
DO401 1994 BMW 325i, 1:43 . . . . $8
DO402 1994 Mercedes 500SEL, 1:43 . . . . $8
DO403 1994 Lexus SC 400, 1:43 . . . . $8

DOORKEY MODELS MADE IN SPAIN

DO101T Mercedes 100 van plain colors, 1:50 . . . . $24
DO101T Mercedes 100 van Spanish Telephones, 1:50 . . . . . . $24
DO101C Mercedes 100 van Spanish Post, 1:50 . . . . $24
DO104 Suzuki Samurai 4 x 4 . . . . $24
DO106 Opel Kadett Combo van lhd. $24
DO108Q Vauxhall Astramax van Q8 Lubricants. $30
DO108Q Vauxhall Astramax van rhd $24
DO110 Ford Escort van 1993 various colors $24
DO114 Nissan Maxima + spoiler. $24
DO115 Nissan Maxima. $24
DO116 Nissan Serena 'people carrier'. $24
DO117 Nissan Micra three door RHD or LHD $24
DO118 Nissan Micra five door RHD or LHD $24
DO125 SEAT Ibiza hatchback. $24
DO126 SEAT Toledo various colors $24
DO130 Volvo 440 GL 1994 restyle $24
DO131 Volvo 440 Turbo 1994 restyle $24
DO133 Volvo 480 Turbo 1994 restyle $24
DO135 Volvo 850 GLT (10 colors) $24

DO136 Volvo 850 Estate car 1996. . . . . $27
DO139 Volvo 850 T-5 (10 colors) stock $24
DO1xx Volvo 460 saloon 1996 ($27 US)

DOORKEY MADE FOR AHC OF SPAIN, 1:43 MADE IN SPAIN, REFINISHED IN HOLLAND

D130DP Volvo 440 Politie, Dutch police. $45
D135SP Volvo 850 GLT Polis, Swedish police $38
D135D Volvo 850 GLT Douane (Customs) $38
D135DP Volvo 850 GLT Politie, Dutch police $38
D200SM Volvo B10M bus Maastricht (300 made) $61
D200LP DAF MB230 bus Lila Pause (300 made) $61
D200DP Daf-den Oudsten bus Politie (300 made). $61

DUGU

One of the premier miniature model companies of Italy was known as Dugu, a company that produced some beautiful models in 1:43 to 1:50 scale. The company started in 1963 by marketing Miniautotoys and Museo models. They represented real cars from the Automotive Museum of Torino, Italy. Miniautotoys are high-quality 1:43 scale models similar to Rio, while Museo models are 1:50 scale simplified, less expensive models. A third series called Sispla was also produced in 1974.

DUGU MINIAUTOTOYS, 1:43

1 1911 Fiat 4 Closed Tourer, 1962. . . . . $50
2 1925 Lancia Lambda Sedan, 1962. . . . . $50
3 1911 Fiat 4 Open Tourer, 1963 . . . . $50
4 1907 Fiat Grand Prix, 1964 . . . . $55
5 1925 Lancia Lambda Torpedo, 1964. . . . . $50
6 1907 Itala Palombella, 1966 . . . . $50
7 1912 Itala 25/35HP Closed Tourer, 1965. . . . . $50
8 Itala 25/35HP Open Tourer, 1965 . . . . $50
9 1896 Bernardi 3.5HP, top up, 1967 . . . . $50
10 1896 Bernardi 3.5HP, top down, 1966 . . . . $50
11 1899 Fiat 3.5HP, top down, 1966 . . . . $45
12 1899 Fiat 3.5HP, top up, 1966 . . . . $45
13 1967 Duesenberg SJ Town Car, 1967 . . . . $140
14 1925 Fiat 509 2-Door Sedan, 1967 . . . . $50
15 1925 Fiat 509 Open Tourer, 1967 . . . . $50
16 1909 Itala 35/45HP Limousine, 1968. . . . . $50
17 1934 Fiat Balilla Coppa D'Oro, 1968. . . . . $55
18 1936 Cord Phaeton, top up, 1968 . . . . $180
19 1931 Duesenberg SJ, 1968 . . . . $135
20 1936 Cord Phaeton, top down, 1968. . . . . $180
21 1934 Rolls-Royce Silver Ghost, top up, 1969 . . . . $120
22 1934 Rolls-Royce Silver Ghost, top down, 1969. . . . . $120
23 Fiat-Eldridge Grand Prix, 1975 . . . . $80
24 1911 Fiat S-76 Record Car, 1971. . . . . $80

DUGU MUSEO, 1:50

M1 1893 Benz Victoria, 1964 . . . . $40
M2 1894 Peugeot Vis-a-Vis, 1964 . . . . $40
M3 1899 Benz Estate Car, 1964. $40
M4 1902 Darracq Tourer, 1964 . . . . $40
M5 1903 De Dion-Bouton Populaire, 1964. . . . . $40
M6 1908 Legnano 6/8HP Spider, top up, 1965. . . . . $40
M7 1908 Legnano 6/8HP Spider, top down, 1965 . . . . $60
M8 1936 Fiat 500A Coupe, 1966 . . . . $60
M9 1908 Brixia Zust Phaeton, 1967 . . . . $40

M10 1948 Cisitalia 202 Coupe, 1968 . . . . $55
M11 1914 Lancia Theta, 1968 . . . . $40
M12 1923 Ansaldo 4C Open Tourer, 1970 . . . . $40
M13 1936 Fiat 500A Convertible Coupe, 1969 . . . . $60
M14 1923 Fiat 519S Tourer, 1971 . . . . $40

DUGU SISPLA, 1:43, 1974

1 Same Centauro Farm Tractor $260
2 Fiat 56 550HP Farm Tractor $260
3 Fiat 697N Dump Truck $90
4a Fiat 90NC Dump Truck $90
4b OM Dump Truck $90
5 Fiat Tank Truck $90

DURAVIT

Duravit models are made in Argentina. Not much else is known as of this writing.

Mercedes Semi Oil Truck, 23". $18

DURHAM CLASSICS

A small assortment of Durham Classics of Canada are currently available. These American classic cars are exquisitely represented in 1:43 scale. These are some of the best-detailed and most accurate 1:43 scale models on the market.

1F 1934 Chrysler Airflow Two-Door 30th Anniversary $119
1G 1934 Chrysler Airflow "California Highway Patrol" $119
2 1953 Ford Pick-Up, blue $99
2H 1953 Ford Pick-Up, red with "Wurlitzer" juke box $119
3S 1939 Ford Panel Delivery "Sacramento Bee" $119
4 1938 Lincoln Zephyr Coupe, black . . . . $95 – 99
5 1941 Chevrolet Coupe, blue . . . . $95 – 99
5D 1941 Chevrolet "Michigan State Police" $99
5E 1941 Chevrolet Coupe "Idaho State Police" $99
6A 1953 Ford Telephone Repair Truck "General" $109
7 1954 Ford Panel Wagon "Canadian Colonial Airways" $99
7A 1954 Ford Panel Wagon "Prairie Airways" $99
9 1938 Lincoln Zephyr Convertible, top down . . . . $95 – 99
9D 1938 Lincoln Zephyr Convertible, top up $95
10A 1941 Chevrolet Convertible, top down $99
12 1941 Chevrolet Panel Delivery Van $99
12B 1941 Chevrolet Panel Delivery Van "Labatts" $99
13A 1939 Ford Panel Delivery "The Sacramento Bee" $99
14A 1951 Ford Monarch 2-Door Coupe $99
15A 1941 Ford Coupe $99
17 1941 Chevrolet Suburban "Niagara Tours" $109

DUST & GLORY (SEE GREAT AMERICAN DREAMCARS)

DUX

An otherwise unknown company, Dux at one time produced a large-scale Studebaker model.

DYNA-MO (SEE DYNA-MODEL PRODUCTS COMPANY)

DYNA-MODEL PRODUCTS COMPANY

Dyna-Mo brand models, 1:87 scale, are manufactured on Long Island, New York, specifically for use with HO gauge railroad layouts. They feature cast metal bodies with separate tires and wheels. (Some assembly required.) Models are available prepainted or unpainted.

Airport Platform Tractor & Two Baggage Wagons - painted $8, unpainted. $6
1908 Buick - painted $7, unpainted $4
Caterpillar Bulldozer - painted $10, unpainted $6
Caterpillar Crawler - painted $8, unpainted $5
Coal Conveyor - painted $4, unpainted $4
1947 Ford Pickup Truck - painted $7, unpainted $4
Fork Lift (2-pack) - painted $10, unpainted $6
1911 Maxwell - painted $7, unpainted $4
1916 Packard Twin Six - painted $7, unpainted $4
1909 Stanley Steamer - painted $7, unpainted $4
1914 Stutz Bearcat - painted $7, unpainted $4

EDIL

Edil Toys of Italy are detailed 1:43 scale models produced from 1965 to 1970. Models reproduced afterwards in Turkey by Meboto still hold the Edil brand name but are comparably inferior castings with crude finishes that give them away as later models.

1 Alfa Romeo Giulia GT, 1965 . . . . $45 – 75
2 Fiat 850, 1966 . . . . $45 – 75
3 Lancia Flavia Coupe, 1966 . . . . $45 – 75
4 Alfa Romeo Giulia TI, 1966 . . . . $45 – 75
5 Alfa Romeo Giulia Police Car, 1966 . . . . $45 – 75
6 Fiat 1500 Sedan, 1966 . . . . $45 – 75
7 Fiat 124 Sedan, 1967 . . . . $45 – 75
8 Fiat 850 Coupe, 1967 . . . . $45 – 75
9 Ferrari 275 GTB, 1967 . . . . $45 – 75
10 Lamborghini Miura, 1968 . . . . $45 – 75
11 Mercedes-Benz 250SE . . . . $45 – 75
12 Iso Grifo, 1968 . . . . $45 – 75
13 Lamborghini Bertone Marzal, 1968 . . . . $45 – 75

EDOCAR (ALSO SEE ZEE TOYS/ZYLMEX)

Edocars is believed to be a Netherlands-based company. As with many toy companies, Edocar was at one time or another connected with other toy companies. Intex Recreation and Zyll Enterprises are two companies that provided U.S. marketing and packaging for selected Edocar toys, at least for a brief time. On its own, Edocar remains obscure in the vast toy market. One recent model was discovered of this otherwise unknown brand. Most likely, Edocar markets others toys as their own, much like Model Power repackages Playart and Eidai models and Megatoys remarkets Maistos. A set of Coca-Cola race cars from Edocar were definitely castings from Action/Racing Collectibles, according to David Weber of Warrington, Pennsylvania. He indicates that these were unauthorized alterations of the latter suspected to be illegally obtained from the Action/Racing Collectibles factory in China. Listed below is one Zee Toy issued as an Edocar.

Mercedes-Benz 500 SL, #13, marked as a Zee Toy on the base . $1

EFE (SEE EXCLUSIVE FIRST EDITIONS)

EFSI

Efsi are well-made 1:64 scale toys from Holland. They are

durable, authentic replicas representing mostly European vehicles.

1010 Ford Model T Truck	$10
1020 Ford Model T Tanker	$10
1030 Ford Model T Crane Truck	$10
1040 Ford Model T Van	$10
1050 Ford Model T Two Seater	$10
1060 Ford Model T Sedan	$10
1070 Ford Model T Ambulance	$10
1100 Ford Model T Fire Van	$10
2010 B.R.M. Formula I	$10
2020 Honda Formula l	$10
2030 Ferrari Formula I	$15
2040 Brabham Formula 1	$10
2050 Mclaren Formula I	$10
2060 Lotus 49 C Formula I	$10

3020 Commer Van, $15

3021 Commer Ambulance	$15
3022 Commer Service Van	$15
3023 Commer Fire Van	$15
3024 Commer Army Ambulance	$15
3021 Commer U.S.A. Army Van	$15
3030 Mercedes-Benz Open Truck	$10
3040 Mercedes-Benz Covered Truck	$10
3041 Mercedes-Benz Red Cross Truck	$10
3042 Mercedes-Benz Army Truck	$10
3050 Mercedes-Benz Dump Truck	$10
3051 Mercedes-Benz Army Dump Truck	$10
3060 Trailer	$10
3061 Red Cross Trailer	$10
3062 Army Trailer	$10
3080 Mercedes-Benz Fire Engine	$10
3090 Mercedes-Benz Tanker "SHELL"	$15
3091 Mercedes-Benz Tanker "ELF"	$15
3092 Mercedes-Benz Tanker "ARAL"	$15
3093 Mercedes-Benz Army Tanker	$15
4010 Ford Taunus l7 M	$15
4011 Ford Taunus Stock Car	$15
4020 Porsche 911 S	$15
4021 Porsche 911 S Dutch Police Car	$15
4022 Porsche 911 S Rally	$15
4030 Jaguar E Type	$15
4040 Mercedes-Benz 280SL	$15

4050 Opel Rekord 1900	$15
4060 Mercedes-Benz 250 SE Coupe	$15
4061 Mercedes-Benz 250 SE Coupe Rally	$15
4070 BMW 2000 CS	$15
4071 BMW 2000 CS Rally	$15
4080 Volkswagen 1600 TL	$20
4090 Citroën ID 19	$15
4091 Citroën ID 19 Ambulance	$15
4100 Citroën Dyane 6	$15
4110 Ford Transit Van	$15
4111 Ford Transit Ambulance	$15
4112 Ford Transit Police Van	$15

E.G.M.

E.G.M. toys were manufactured in Italy in 1959.

Alfa Romeo Giulietta Spyder (if ever actually produced)	$175 – 250
Dean Van Lines Special	$125
Tarf Speed Record Car	$125

Eidai (also see Grip Zechin)

Made in Japan, these scale models are occasionally sold under the Model Power brand. The two examples pictured, provided by Anderson's Hobby Center, Redmond, Oregon, are excellent representations of the detailing offered in these delightful little models. The Grip Zechin brand is a line of toys produced by Eidai and listed in their own section.

Airport Bus, 1:100 . . . . $14 – 17

Boom Truck, 1:87, $12 – 15

DeTomaso Pantera GT-35, 1:28 (Technica series) . . . . $25 – 30

Ladder Truck, 1:87, $12 – 15

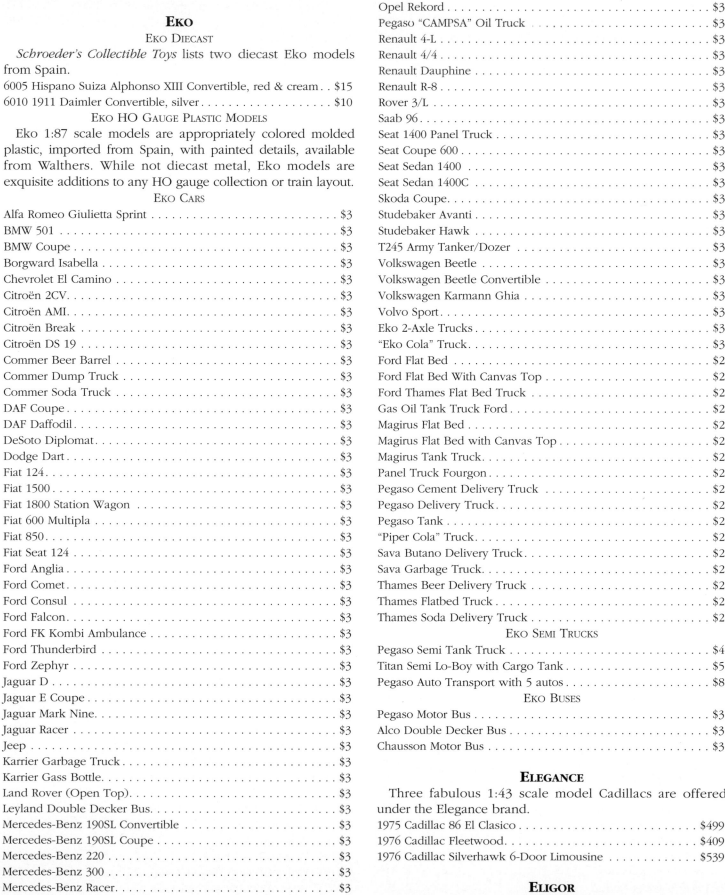

March 761B "Rothmans" #10 Ian, 1:43 . . . . $18 – 24

EKO

EKO DIECAST

Schroeder's Collectible Toys lists two diecast Eko models from Spain.

6005 Hispano Suiza Alphonso XIII Convertible, red & cream. . $15
6010 1911 Daimler Convertible, silver $10

EKO HO GAUGE PLASTIC MODELS

Eko 1:87 scale models are appropriately colored molded plastic, imported from Spain, with painted details, available from Walthers. While not diecast metal, Eko models are exquisite additions to any HO gauge collection or train layout.

EKO CARS

Alfa Romeo Giulietta Sprint	$3
BMW 501	$3
BMW Coupe	$3
Borgward Isabella	$3
Chevrolet El Camino	$3
Citroën 2CV	$3
Citroën AMI	$3
Citroën Break	$3
Citroën DS 19	$3
Commer Beer Barrel	$3
Commer Dump Truck	$3
Commer Soda Truck	$3
DAF Coupe	$3
DAF Daffodil	$3
DeSoto Diplomat	$3
Dodge Dart	$3
Fiat 124	$3
Fiat 1500	$3
Fiat 1800 Station Wagon	$3
Fiat 600 Multipla	$3
Fiat 850	$3
Fiat Seat 124	$3
Ford Anglia	$3
Ford Comet	$3
Ford Consul	$3
Ford Falcon	$3
Ford FK Kombi Ambulance	$3
Ford Thunderbird	$3
Ford Zephyr	$3
Jaguar D	$3
Jaguar E Coupe	$3
Jaguar Mark Nine	$3
Jaguar Racer	$3
Jeep	$3
Karrier Garbage Truck	$3
Karrier Gass Bottle	$3
Land Rover (Open Top)	$3
Leyland Double Decker Bus	$3
Mercedes-Benz 190SL Convertible	$3
Mercedes-Benz 190SL Coupe	$3
Mercedes-Benz 220	$3
Mercedes-Benz 300	$3
Mercedes-Benz Racer	$3
MG 1600	$3

Morris Mini	$3
Opel Rekord	$3
Pegaso "CAMPSA" Oil Truck	$3
Renault 4-L	$3
Renault 4/4	$3
Renault Dauphine	$3
Renault R-8	$3
Rover 3/L	$3
Saab 96	$3
Seat 1400 Panel Truck	$3
Seat Coupe 600	$3
Seat Sedan 1400	$3
Seat Sedan 1400C	$3
Skoda Coupe	$3
Studebaker Avanti	$3
Studebaker Hawk	$3
T245 Army Tanker/Dozer	$3
Volkswagen Beetle	$3
Volkswagen Beetle Convertible	$3
Volkswagen Karmann Ghia	$3
Volvo Sport	$3
Eko 2-Axle Trucks	$3
"Eko Cola" Truck	$3
Ford Flat Bed	$2
Ford Flat Bed With Canvas Top	$2
Ford Thames Flat Bed Truck	$2
Gas Oil Tank Truck Ford	$2
Magirus Flat Bed	$2
Magirus Flat Bed with Canvas Top	$2
Magirus Tank Truck	$2
Panel Truck Fourgon	$2
Pegaso Cement Delivery Truck	$2
Pegaso Delivery Truck	$2
Pegaso Tank	$2
"Piper Cola" Truck	$2
Sava Butano Delivery Truck	$2
Sava Garbage Truck	$2
Thames Beer Delivery Truck	$2
Thames Flatbed Truck	$2
Thames Soda Delivery Truck	$2

EKO SEMI TRUCKS

Pegaso Semi Tank Truck	$4
Titan Semi Lo-Boy with Cargo Tank	$5
Pegaso Auto Transport with 5 autos	$8

EKO BUSES

Pegaso Motor Bus	$3
Alco Double Decker Bus	$3
Chausson Motor Bus	$3

ELEGANCE

Three fabulous 1:43 scale model Cadillacs are offered under the Elegance brand.

1975 Cadillac 86 El Clasico $499
1976 Cadillac Fleetwood $409
1976 Cadillac Silverhawk 6-Door Limousine $539

ELIGOR

Eligor is the name of popular vintage models manufactured by Jacques Greilsamer in Martignat, France, in 1976, and available from finer hobby shops and mail-order houses for around $20 – 35 each. The company used many of Norev's original tooling. In 1986, Greilsamer sold the brand to Louis Surber, who had been producing Eligor models for Greilsamer. Eligor lbs., 445 rte Talour, 01810 Martignat, France, phone 33-74 81 1281, Fax 33-74-81-1194.

ELIGOR 1:43 SCALE

'32 Ford Roadster Fire Chief	$25
'32 Ford Roadster, baby blue	$25
'32 Ford Roadster Police	$25
'32 Ford Sedan, green	$25
'32 Ford Sedan Police	$25
'32 Ford Van Police	$25
'33 Ford Pickup, "Texaco"	$35
'33 Ford Pickup "Goodrich"	$25
'33 Ford Pickup V-8, black	$25
'34 Ford Panel Truck "Air Show"	$25
'34 Ford Panel Truck "Castrol"	$25
'34 Ford Panel Truck "Firestone"	$25
'34 Ford Panel Truck "RCA"	$25
'34 Ford Panel Fire Truck	$25
'34 Ford Pickup Fire Truck	$25
'34 Ford Sedan, green	$25
'34 Ford Tanker	$25
'34 Ford Fire Dept. Wrecker	$25
'58 Chrysler New Yorker Convertible	$25
'60 Jaguar Mk 1	$25
'60 Jaguar E-Type	$25
'68 Triumph TR5	$25

ELIGOR 1:25 SCALE

Citroën Fire	$55

ELYSEE

Likely made in France, more information is needed on this brand, although one model is known.

1940 Dodge Coupe, 1:43	$55

ENCHANTED

The Enchanted brand is typified by 1:43 scale models of exacting detail. Little else is known.

3 1953 Kaiser Manhattan	$85
4 1947 Desoto Convertible	$85
5 1950 Meteor Convertible	$85
6 1941 Lincoln Mark 1 Two-Door Hardtop	$115
7 1951 Allstate Sedan	$115
9 1960 Ford Thunderbird	$85
10 1949 Buick Riviera	$115
11 1947 Chrysler Convertible	$85
12 1956 Lincoln Mark 2 Convertible	$115
13 1968 Pontiac Convertible	$85
14 1947 Chrysler Durham	$115
17 1947 Chrysler Town Car	$85
18 1948 Ford Convertible	$85
19 1955 Chrysler Convertible	$115
20 1953 Buick, top down	$115
21 1957 Chevrolet Nomad	$85
22 1958 Ford Edsel Convertible	$115
23 1956 Ford Convertible	$115

ENCHANTED 1937 PACKARD COLLECTION

P1 Packard Phaeton	$85
P3 Packard Wagon	$85
P4 Packard Convertible Sedan	$85
P5 Packard Landaulet	$85
P6 Packard Club Coupe	$85
P7 Packard Pickup	$85
P9 Packard Panel Truck	$85
P13 Packard Victoria	$85
P15 Packard 12 Passenger	$115
P16 Packard Club Sedan	$85
P19 Packard Coupe Police	$85

ENCHANTMENT LAND COACH BUILDERS

Specializing in 1:43 scale limousines and hearses, these custom hand-built cars are created both on and off major model manufacturers' chassies. The home base for the company is believed to be in New Mexico (Land of Enchantment).

B5 1947 Buick Flexible Landau Hearse, black	$139
B6 1947 Buick Flexible Limousine Hearse, black	$139
B7 1947 Buick Flexible Limousine Ambulance, white	$139
C1 1947 Chrysler Durham Continental Hardtop	$109
C2 1947 Chrysler Town & Country Coupe	$99
C3 1947 Chrysler Windsor Convertible	$99
C4 1978 Cadillac Seville	$99
C6 1947 Chrysler Stretch Limousine, maroon	$119
C7 1947 Chrysler Hearse, maroon	$119
C8 1947 Chrysler Flower Car, maroon	$119
C10 1931 Cadillac Indy 500 Pace Car, white	$139
C11 1957 Chevrolet Nomad Wagon	$109
C12 1947 Cadillac Meteor Hearse Limousine, black	$139
C13 1947 Cadillac Series 75 Ambulance, white	$139
C14 1947 Cadillac Series 75 Limousine, black	$139
C16 1966 Cadillac Superior Hearse, black	$139
D1 1947 DeSoto Convertible	$99
D2 1940 Dodge Station Wagon, tan	$119
F2 1951 Ford Victoria Hardtop	$99
F3 1935 Ford Siebert Hearse Limousine, gray	$129
F4 1935 Ford Siebert Ambulance, white	$139
G1 1940 Graham Hollywood Sedan, maroon	$139
K1 1954 Kaiser Darrin Roadster, top down, yellow	$119
K2 1951 Kaiser Henry J Sedan	$99
K3 1953 Kaiser Manhattan	$89
K5 1953 Kaiser Manhattan	$89
L1 1941 Lincoln Mark 1 Two-Door Hardtop	$109
L4 1938 LaSalle Carved Panel Hearse, black	$139
L5 1938 LaSalle Limousine Hearse, black	$139
L6 1938 LaSalle Limousine Ambulance, white	$139
M2 1988 Ford Mustang GT Convertible	$99
M4 1986 Mustang Convertible, top down	$99
M5 1982 Ford Mustang Notchback Coupe	$99
P1 1937 Packard Dual Cowl Phaeton	$89
P1 1968 Pontiac Convertible	$99
P2 1937 Packard Town Car	$99
P3 1937 Packard Station Wagon, beige	$99
P4 1937 Packard Continental Sedan	$79
P5 1937 Packard Landaulet	$89

P6 1937 Packard Club Coupe $89
P7 1937 Packard Pickup. $89
P8 1937 Packard Stretch Limousine, black $119
P9 1937 Packard Panel Delivery $89
P10 1937 Packard Victoria $79
P11 1937 Packard Hollywood Darrin Convertible $99
P13 1937 Packard Victoria, top down $89
P14 1937 Packard 4-Door Taxi $109
P15 1937 Packard 12-Passenger Coach bus $119
P16 1937 Packard Club Sedan $99
P17 1937 Packard Coupe Fire Service $129
P18 1937 Packard Pickup Fire Service. $129
P19 1937 Packard Coupe Police Service $99
P20 1937 Packard Art-Carved Hearse, black. $119
P21 1937 Packard Art-Carved Flower Car, black. $119
P22 1937 Packard Van Police Service $129
P23 1937 Packard Van Fire Service $129
P24 1937 Packard Van Funeral Service, black $119
T1 1960 Ford Thunderbird 2-Door Hardtop. $99
T2 1965 Ford Thunderbird Convertible, top down. $99
W1 1937 Willys Coupe. $99
W21 1950 Meteor Convertible. $99
W22 1948 Ford Convertible $79
W23 1957 Chevrolet Nomad $109
Z10 1949 Buick Riviera. $139
Z11 1956 Lincoln Mark 2 Convertible $139
Z19 1955 Chrysler Convertible $119
Z20 1953 Buick, top down $119
Z22 1958 Ford Edsel Convertible $119
Z23 1956 Ford Convertible $139

EPI Sports Collectibles

Chris Reynolds is president of EPI Group Limited, 250 Pequot Ave., Southport, CT 06490, phone 203-255-1112. The EPI Sports Collectibles division is known to have produced at least one very accurate Shell oil tanker in approximately 1:43 scale. As with most diecast models in recent years, EPI models are manufactured in China.

1995 Shell Oil Company's Die-Cast Collectible Tanker Truck, short
    tanker truck with tandem tanker, yellow and chrome, 1:43,
    10,000 produced . . . . $25 – 30

Equipe Gallois

Bryan Garfield-Jones of Great Britain produced a number of white metal kits under the Equipe Gallois brand.

Eria

Eria of France produced ten 1:46 scale models between 1957 and 1961.

31 Peugeot 403, 1957. . . . . $25
32 Renault Dauphine, 1958 . . . . $25
33 Simca P60 Aronde, 1959 . . . . $25
34 Panhard PL17, 1960. . . . . $25
35 Renault Estafette Van, 1960 . . . . $30
36 Jaguar D Type, 1960 . . . . $25
37 Peugeot 404, 1961. . . . . $25
38 Citroën ID19 Ambulance, 1961. . . . . $25
39 Citroën ID19 Break, 1961. . . . . $25

Erie

Parker White Metal Company of Erie, Pennsylvania, is the source of Erie toys, manufactured prior to World War II.

Cabover Truck, 1937, 3¼" $30
Ford Ice Truck, 1935, 5". $70
Ford Pickup Truck, 1935, 5". $60
Ford Tow Truck, 5" $70
Futuristic Sedan, 1939, 4¼". $40
Lincoln Zephyr Sedan, 1936, 5½" $60
Lincoln Zephyr Sedan, 1936, 3½" $35
Packard Roadster, 1936, 6" $60
Packard Roadster, 1936, 3½" $35
Tow Truck, 1939, 4¼" $40

Ertl (also see Peachstate Muscle Car)

Fred J. Ertl Sr. started The Ertl Company in 1945 from his Dubuque, Iowa, home. He applied the diecasting techniques he had learned in his homeland Germany to manufacture licensed farm toys from John Deere and International Harvester's original blueprints. Soon after, he moved operations to Dyersville, Iowa, where the company remains today. From diecast farm toys, Ertl has expanded to the manufacture of pressed steel and diecast toy trucks, diecast scale model cars, and an assortment of other toys. Their large assortment of diecast vehicle banks has been extremely popular for decades. Ertl's immense product line represents thousands of models, all designed after real vehicles. As you might guess, an entire book is needed to present the broad range of models produced. Ertl collectors are an elite group, many of whom only collect special issue limited edition models. Others specialize in just Ertl tractors or Ertl banks.

Several collectors' clubs exist for Ertl models. While the official Ertl collectors' club no longer exists, Ertl still published *The Replica* newsletter. *The Replica* is a full-color publication featuring product previews from their farm toy and collectibles lines. It is a bi-monthly magazine that also includes subscriber exclusives, feature articles related to the industry, as well as a classified ad/show listing section. Circulation is around 30,000 worldwide and current subscription rates are U.S. – $12.00 for 1 year (6 issues); outside the U.S. – $16.00 for 1 year (6 issues). The address for subscriptions is Ertl A/R Replica Subscriptions, P.O. Box 500, Dyersville, IA 52040. Also of note, The Ertl Company is now owned by USI in New Jersey.

Ertl previously was a subsidiary of Kidde, Inc., makers of fire extinguishers, smoke detectors, and a broad range of other products. Other brands such as Spec-Cast, Liberty Classics, First Gear, and a few others have sprung up in Iowa, inspired by Ertl's success. Spec-Cast, in fact, is a direct offspring of the Ertl Company.

While Ertls were originally made in Iowa, most are now manufactured in China, Korea, or other Asian manufacturing centers. A confusing numbering system on the package is rarely reflected on the model, so an alphabetical listing is therefore presented by description, followed by model number, scale, introduction year, where made, and current value. Many models are reissued year after year, so information is often incomplete. Here is just a sampling.

ERTL 1:18 SCALE AMERICAN MUSCLE COLLECTION

Corvette Stingray, $30

7001E 1993 Pontiac Grand Prix Miller Genuine Draft #2, Rusty
Wallace $75
7190 1970 Chevelle SS 454 LS6, yellow with black accents. . . . $30
7208 1996 Pontiac TransAm Coupe, metallic red or burgundy . $25
7210 1995 Monte Carlo Goodwrench #3, Dale Earnhardt $75
7223 1996 Ford F-150 Pickup, red or green. $25
7231 1996 Camaro Z28 Convertible, green or red $25
7280 1970 Ford Mustang Boss 429, Grabber green. $40
7297 1967 Corvette L-71 Roadster, Sunfire yellow $40
7321 1963 Corvette coupe, dark blue $30
7323 1970 Chevelle SS 454 LS6, metallic blue with white accents . $30
7326 1970 Boss 302 Mustang, yellow with black accents $30
7328 1969 Pontiac GTO "The Judge," green/yellow/white $30
7332 1995 Dodge Ram Truck, red or black $25
7348 Pontiac GP, Pennzoil, M. Waltrip $30
7355 Chevy Lumina, Western Auto, D. Waltrip $30
7356 Chevy Lumina, Goodwrench, Earnhardt $30
7358 Ford T-Bird, Budweiser, Elliott $30
7368 1969 Plymouth Hemi Roadrunner, yellow $30
7368L 1969 Plymouth Hemi Roadrunner, limited edition Scorch
Red $30
7369 Shelby Cobra 427 S/C, red/white $30
7379 1970 Plymouth AAR 'Cuda, lime green $30
7383 1978 Dodge Warlock pickup truck $30
7385 1978 Dodge Li'l Red Truck $30
7447 Chevy Lumina, Interstate, Jarrett $30
7448 Pontiac GP, Mello Yello, K. Petty $30
7455 1969 Camaro Z-28, red/white $30
7456 1969 Camaro SS 396, orange/white $30
7457 Ford T-Bird, Valvoline, Martin $30
7461 Pontiac GP, STP, R. Petty $30
7466 1969 Pontiac GTO, metallic light blue. $30
7576 1995 Ford Smokin' Joes #23, Jimmy Spencer $75
7597 1990 Pontiac Grand Prix Miller Genuine Draft #27, Rusty
Wallace $75
7598 1992 Ford Thunderbird #1 Baby Ruth, Jeff Gordon $75
7599 1994 Chevrolet Lumina #24 Dupont, Jeff Gordon $75
7603 1970 Buick GSX, yellow/red/black $30
7604 1971 Buick GSX, black/gold $30
7483 Ferrari 275 GTB4, red $30

ERTL AIR & SPACE

Army Helicopter $3
Coast Guard Helicopter, #1509, AIR & SPACE series $3

Space Shuttle with Booster Rockets & Launch Pad, #1515, 1:500,
Hong Kong $5

ERTL FARM MACHINES 1:64

Allis-Chalmers 8070 Tractor, #1703-1819, China. $6
Case 2594 Tractor, #1704, 1986, Korea $6
Ford TW-20 Tractor with Cab, #1703-1621, China $6
Ford TW-35 Tractor with Cab, #1703-832, Korea. $6
International Harvester 5088 Tractor with Cab, #1703-1797, Korea . $6

John Deere Tractor with Cab, #1703-1619, Hong Kong, $6

Massey-Ferguson 2775 Tractor, #1703-1622, China $6
Anhydrous Ammonia Tank, #1589-1550, Hong Kong. $3
International Harvester Farm Wagon, #1589-1755, Korea $3
International Harvester Mixer Mill, #1589-1551, Korea. $3
International Harvester Round Baler, #1589-1758, Korea $3
John Deere Forage Wagon. $3

New Holland Forage Wagon, #1589AO, 1986, Korea, $3

International COE Grain Hauler, #1518-1238, China $8

ERTL JOHN DEERE TRACTOR COLLECTION

1892 Froelich. . . . . $6 – 8
1914 Waterloo Boy . . . . $6 – 8
1923 John Deere Model D . . . . $6 – 8
1939 John Deere Model A Row Crop . . . . $6 – 8
1952 John Deere Model 60. . . . . $6 – 8
1958 John Deere 730 Row Crop . . . . $6 – 8

1960 John Deere 4010 Row Crop . . . . $6 – 8

ERTL MIGHTY MOVERS 1:64

Case 1845C Uni-Loader $8
Caterpillar Road Grader, #1848, China $8

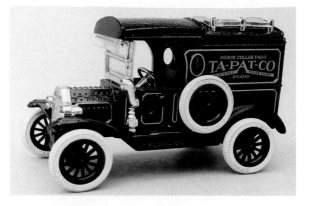

#2 1913 Ford Model T Van "TaPatCo," #2502, China, $15

International Excavator 640, #1854, $8

International Hauler 350 Dump Truck, #1852, China $8
International Scraper 412B, #1855 Earth Mover, China $8

International TD20 Series E Crawler, #1851, China, $8

#3 1930 Chevrolet Stake Truck, #2503, China, $15

#4 1932 Ford Panel Truck "Perfection Stoves," #2504, $15

International Wheel Loader 560, #1850, China, $8

ERTL VINTAGE VEHICLES 1:43

#1 1932 Ford Roadster, #2501, China $15

#5 1912 Buick, #2516, 1985, China, $15

#6 1940 Ford Woody Station Wagon, #2517, China $15

#7 1930 Chevrolet 1/2-Ton Delivery Truck, #2518, $15

#8 1923 Ford Fordor, #2519, China, $15

#10 1930 Packard Boat Tail Speedster, #2542 . . . . $15

#11 1957 Chevrolet BelAir 2-Door Hardtop, #2540, China, $15

#12 1952 Cadillac Coupe DeVille Model 62 4-Door, #2541, China, $15

72

#14 1960 Corvette, #2588 . . . . $15
#16 1959 Checker Cab, #2587 . . . . $15
#17 1957 Ford Thunderbird, #2802 . . . . $15
F-2 1936 Massey-Harris Challenger, #2511 . . . . $15
F-4 International Harvester Farmall 300, #2513 . . . . $15

ERTL *BATMAN, THE MOVIE* COLLECTIBLES

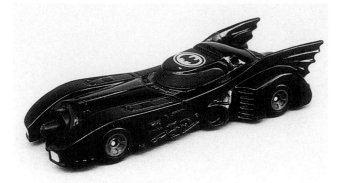

Batmobile, 1:64, $5

Batmobile, 1:43, $15

Joker Van, 1:43 . . . . $12

ERTL *BATMAN, THE ANIMATED SERIES* COLLECTIBLES, 1:64

Batmobile, $6

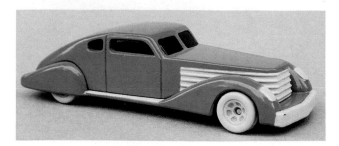

Bruce Wayne's Car, $6

Police Helicopter $6

ERTL *DICK TRACY* MOVIE REPLICAS 1989, 1:64

Dick Tracy's 1936 Ford Fordor Police Car, #2676 . . . . $6

Itchy and Flattop's 1939 Chevrolet, 1990, #2677, $6

Tess's 1937 Plymouth, 1990, #2678 . . . . $6
Dick Tracy's 1936 Ford, #2679 . . . . $6

ERTL *DUKES OF HAZZARD* TV SERIES REPLICAS 1:64

Dukes' Dixie Challenger $15
Cooder's Pickup Truck $10
Hazzard County Sheriff's Car $10
Boss Hogg's Cadillac $10

ERTL *THE CANNONBALL RUN* MOVIE REPLICAS 1:64

Ferrari Dino 246 GT $8

ERTL MADE IN AMERICA SERIES

Corvette, Made In USA $1
Charger, Made In USA $1
Fiero, Made In USA $1
Firebird, Made In USA $1

OTHER ERTL MODELS

1951 Chevrolet, 1:64, $6

Lamb Chops Train, 1994, $5

Chevy Stepside Pickup "Bell System," 1:64 . . . . $15
Horse-Drawn Van "Telephones 5¢ Per Day" and "New Nickel Service" . . . . $60 – 75
Land Rover, 1:64 . . . . $3
Mack 1926 Bull Dog "Let Your Fingers Do The Walking" Yellow Pages delivery truck . . . . $60 – 75

Pontiac GTO, 1:43, $8

ERTL NASA COMMEMORATIVES

"Columbia" Command Module-Apollo 11 . . . . $10 – 12
"Friendship 7" Mercury Capsule . . . . $10 – 12

Lunar Rover-Apollo 15, $10 – 12

"Eagle" Lunar Module-Apollo 11 . . . . $10 – 12

ESCI (SEE C.B.CAR)

ESDO

Only a representative model is known of this brand. No information has so far been found.

Oldsmobile Omega Sedan, gold $65

ESPEWE

Espewe of Germany makes these models of various scales.

1911 Horch 4-Door Car, 1:43 . . . . $18
1913 Audi Convertible, top down, 1:43 . . . . $18
Ifa Truck, 1:120 . . . . $5

ESTETYKA

Estetyka is a manufacturer from Poland that produces an assortment of 1:43 scale models of mostly Italian vehicles.

1 1926 Bugatti 35 Roadster $8
2 1926 Isotta Fraschini $8

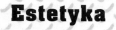

4 1904 Wanderer Roadster $8
5 Ferrari P4 . . . . $11
6 Ferrari Dino $11
7 Fiat 126 2-Door Sedan. $8
8 Polonez 4-Door Sedan $8
9 Ursus C385 Tractor $18

EXCEL

1950 Jeep CJ2, 5" $20

EXCLUSIVE FIRST EDITIONS (EFE)

Bill Cross reports that Exclusive First Editions are 1:76 scale, in tune with the scale of British "00" gauge model trains. They now produce a very extensive range of vintage and modern British buses, and trucks. The brand was started in 1989 in Milton Keyes, England. Models are produced in Asia.

AUTOMOBILES

401 Triumph Roadster . . . . $10 – 12
403 Triumph Roadster . . . . $10 – 12
501 MGB . . . . $10 – 12
503 MGB . . . . $10 – 12
601 Triumph Vitesse. . . . . $10 – 12
603 Triumph Vitesse. . . . . $10 – 12
701 Austin-Healey Sprite. . . . . $10 – 12
703 Austin-Healey Sprite. . . . . $10 – 12

COMMERCIAL SERVICE VEHICLES

10101 AEC RT London Transport Bus "Duracell" . . . . $12 – 15
10102 AEC RT Greenline Bus "Buxted" . . . . $12 – 15
10103 AEC RT London Country Bus "Birds Eye". . . . . . $12 – 15
10104 AEC RT London Transport Bus "Schweppes" . . . . . $12 – 15
10107 AEC RT London Transport Bus "Dulux". . . . . . . $12 – 15
10109 AEC RT London Transport Bus "Bird's Custard" . . . $12 – 15
10111 AEC RT London Transport Bus "Barclays" . . . . . $12 – 15
10112 AEC RT London Transport Bus "Vernons" . . . . . . $12 – 15
10113 AEC RT Dundee Bus "Courier" . . . . $12 – 15
10114 AEC RT Bradford Bus . . . . $12 – 15
10201 AEC RT Open Top Bus "Beachy Head" . . . . $12 – 15
10202 AEC RT Open Top Bus "Colemans". . . . . $12 – 15
10203 AEC RT Open Top Bus "Caronation" . . . . $12 – 15
10204 AEC RT Open Top Bus "TyphooTea". . . . . $12 – 15
10301 AEC Mammoth Major 6 Wheel Dropside "Fenland" . $12 – 15
10302 AEC Mammoth Major 6 Wheel Dropside "Cyril Ridgeon & Son" . . . . $12 – 15
10303 AEC Mammoth Major 6 Wheel Dropside "J. D. Lown" . $12 – 15
10401 AEC Mammoth Major 8 Wheel Flatbed "Bath & Portland" . . . . $12 – 15
10402 AEC Mammoth Major 8 Wheel Flatbed "London Brick". $12 – 15
10501 AEC Mammoth Major Box Van "London Carriers". . $12 – 15
10502 AEC Mammoth Major Box Van "Startrite" . . . . $12 – 15
10503 AEC Mammoth Major Box Van "BRS" . . . . $12 – 15
10504 AEC Mammoth Major Box Van "PEK" . . . . $12 – 15
10505 AEC Mammoth Major Box Van "Oxydol" . . . . $12 – 15
10601 AEC Mammoth Major 8 Wheel Tanker "Century Oils". $12 – 15
10602 AEC Mammoth Major 8 Wheel Tanker "J. & H. Bunn" . $12 – 15
10604 AEC Mammoth Major 8 Wheel Tanker "Mobilgas" . $12 – 15
10605 AEC Mammoth Major 8 Wheel Tanker "Regent" . . . $12 – 15
10701 AEC Mammoth Major 6 Wheel Flatbed "Furlong Bros.". $12 – 15
10702 AEC Mammoth Major 6 Wheel Flatbed "Blue Circle". $12 – 15

10703 AEC Mammoth Major 6 Wheel Flatbed "Wimpey". . $12 – 15
10703R AEC Mammoth Major 6 Wheel Flatbed "Wimpey". $12 – 15
10801 AEC Mammoth Major 8 Wheel Dropside "British Steel". $12 – 15
10802 AEC Mammoth Major 8 Wheel Dropside "Whitbread". $12 – 15
10803 AEC Mammoth Major 8 Wheel Dropside "Marley" . $12 – 15
10804 AEC Mammoth Major 8 Wheel Dropside "Macready's". $12 – 15
10901 AEC Mammoth Major 6 Wheel Tanker "Haygates" . $12 – 15
10902 AEC Mammoth Major 6 Wheel Tanker "Lord Rayleighs Farms" . . . . $12 – 15
10903 AEC Mammoth Major 6 Wheel Tanker "LPG Transport" . $12 – 15
10908 AEC Mammoth Major 6 Wheel Tanker "Welch's" . . $12 – 15
11001 AEC Mammoth Major Box Van "Croft" . . . . $12 – 15
11002 AEC Mammoth Major Box Van "Pickfords". . . . . . $12 – 15
11005 AEC Mammoth Major Box Van "Lacons" . . . . $12 – 15
11106 AEC Mammoth Major Box Van "Rose's" . . . . $12 – 15
11104 RTL Double Decker Bus "Lockey's" . . . . $12 – 15
11105 RTL Double Decker Bus "Brylcreem" . . . . $12 – 15
11901 Harrington Cavalier Coach . . . . $12 – 15
11903 Harrington Cavalier Coach "Gray Green" . . . . . . $12 – 15
12001 AEC Mammoth Major 8 Wheel Tipper "Wimpey" . . $12 – 15
12002 AEC Mammoth Major 8 Wheel Tipper "Tarmac". . . $12 – 15
12101 Harrington Cavalier Coach . . . . $12 – 15
12102 Harrington Cavalier Coach "East Yorkshire" . . . . . $12 – 15
12103 Harrington Cavalier Coach "Hebble" . . . . $12 – 15
12201 Harrington Grenadier Coach . . . . $12 – 15
12202 Harrington Grenadier Coach "Premier Travel" . . . . $12 – 15
12301 Harrington Grenadier Coach . . . . $12 – 15
12302 Harrington Grenadier Coach "Gray Cars" . . . . $12 – 15
12501 Atkinson 6 Wheel Box Van "Wells" . . . . $12 – 15
12601 Atkinson 6 Wheel Dropside "McNicholas" . . . . . . $12 – 15
12701 Atkinson 8 Wheel Tanker "Charringtons" . . . . $12 – 15
12801 Atkinson 8 Wheel Flatbed "McPhees" . . . . $12 – 15
12901 Atkinson 8 Wheel Box Van "Fyffes". . . . . $12 – 15
13001 Atkinson Car Transporter . . . . $12 – 15
13002 Atkinson Car Transporter "Swift's" . . . . $12 – 15
13303 Atkinson Car Transporter "Midlands" . . . . $12 – 15
13301 Atkinson 8 Wheel Tipper "St. Albans" . . . . $12 – 15
13402 Leeds Horsefield Tramcar "CWS/Tizer" . . . . $12 – 15
13403 Leeds Horsefield Tramcar "Jacob's" . . . . $12 – 15
19901 Tate & Lyle 3-Piece Gift Set. . . . . $12 – 15
19902 Rank Hovis 3-Piece Gift Set. . . . . $12 – 15
19904 Taylor Woodrow Gift Set . . . . $12 – 15
19003 RTL 3-Piece Gift Set . . . . $12 – 15
19006 Fisherman's Friend 3-Piece Gift Set . . . . $12 – 15
99903 Deluxe Road Transport Set . . . . $12 – 15

ENSTONE EMERGENCY MODELS

British hand-built white metal models and kits in 1:48 scale are produced under the Enstone brand.

Daimler DC27 Ambulance . . . . price unknown

EXEM

This unusual brand from Portugal offers this assortment of 1:43 scale Austin Healey Sprites.

\# 7004 Austin-Healey "Bugeye" Sprite, 1:43, red, open top . . . $30
\# 7005 Austin-Healey "Bugeye" Sprite, 1:43, British racing green, open top $30
\# 7006 Austin-Healey "Bugeye" Sprite, 1:43, black, top up. . . . $30

EXEMPLERS

No information is available except for a single model produced under this brand name.

DeTomaso Pantera, silver, 1:45 . . . . $15 – 20

FAIE

It is unknown who is the US distributor for Faie models of Hong Kong. It is common for such "generic" models to be widely sold in drugstores and supermarkets, among other places. You'll likely notice that once removed from the package, these models have no identifying marks. The maximum value these toys will likely reach is about a buck, owing mostly to being cheaply made, having no discernable markings and being mass produced in quantities nearing a million of each. Note the misspelling of McLaren on the package back (Mc Larem). Such mistakes indicate they were produced and marketed for the English-speaking market by non-English-speaking manufacturers, a common trait of cheaply made Asian knockoffs, whether of diecast toys or other products.

Ferrari 412 M. $1
Fox Bat FW 1 . . . . $1
Heskith B 52 . . . . $1
Lotus TPS76, yellow with Goodyear #9. . . . . $1
McLaren M32, red with Dunlop/Goodyear F1 #2. . . . . $1
Porsche Audi. $1
Porsche Turbo 936 . . . . $1
Simca Matra 670 . . . . $1
Tiager Jawg 18, orange with Agip/Lucas #4 . . . . $1

FAIRFIELD MINT

A new entry to the diecast model market is Fairfield Mint of Norwalk, Connecticut. The company has contracted with several companies to produce models for them, including Solido, Yat Ming, and others. The difference is in color variations issued exclusively under the Fairfield Mint brand name.

The first in the series of 1:12 scale models is a white '58 Chevy Corvette produced for Fairfield by Solido of France, now a division of Majorette. It sells for $94, according to the December 1995 Die Cast Car Collectors Club newsletter. Other models include a 1959 Chevy Impala convertible in 1:18 scale and a 1955 Ford Fairlane Crown Victoria in 1:18 scale, both produced for Fairfield by Yat Ming. Variations of these models are also packaged as Road Legends. They sell for $20 – 35 each.

Also available is a 1953 Chevrolet Pickup in 1:18 scale that appears to be one produced by Mira of Spain.

For more information, write to The Fairfield Mint, 1004 Hope Street, Box 4185, Stamford CT 06907-0185.

1958 Chevrolet Corvette, 1:12, white with silver side
    scoops. . . . . $50 – 94
1959 Chevrolet Impala Convertible, 1:12, top down, metallic cornflower blue with white interior. . . . . $25 – 40
1955 Ford Crown Victoria, 1:12, bright pink and white. . . $25 – 40
1953 Chevrolet Pickup, 1:12, red. . . . . $30 – 45

FALLER

These beautifully rendered 1:18 scale Mercedes-Benz models from Germany are currently available.

4310 Mercedes-Benz 220 SE cabriolet, top down, white. $39
4311 Mercedes-Benz 220 SE cabriolet, top down, burgundy. . . $39
4312 Mercedes-Benz 220 SE cabriolet, top up, limited edition . $42
4315 Mercedes-Benz 220 SE coupe, blue or white. $39
4321 Mercedes-Benz 220 S, 1956, black or gray. $39
4322 Mercedes-Benz 220 S Taxi $42
4325 Mercedes-Benz 220 S, two-tone, open sun roof. $39
4326 Mercedes-Benz 220 S, two-tone, closed roof $39

Other Faller models, available from WalthersG, are motorized plastic vehicles designed to travel on special roadways as part of an HO gauge railroad layout.

FARACAR

Faracar was made in France for a Chicago company. They produced only one car, an Indy 500 STP turbine car in 1:43 scale similar to Hot Wheels Shelby turbine. Nicely detailed, it was one of two models planned. The second car, reportedly a Novi Special, was planned but something went wrong and it never happened. Thanks to Greg Ford for the information.

Indy 500 STP Turbine Car, 1:43 . . . . $20

FASTWHEEL (SEE YAT MING)

FEIL

Richard Feil, reportedly of Germany, has produced mostly pewter replicas in 1:43 scale.

1934 Auto Union Racer, 1:43 . . . . $45

FIDART

Any clue to the background of this brand would be appreciated.

1 Volkswagen Dune Buggy, 1:64 . . . . $3
2 Lola GT Coupe, 1:64 . . . . $3
3 Super Turbo, 1:64 . . . . $3

FIMCAR

Fimcar models are from Australia. Only a few other notable brands hail from there, Fun Ho!, Top Gear Trax, Micro Models, and probably one or two others. Where Fimcar fits into the picture, I don't know. But based on the price, they must be fairly nice representations of the real thing.

1948 Holden Pickup, light blue, 1:43 . . . . $35
1953 Holden Pickup, 1:43 . . . . $35

FIRST CHOICE

Since about 1987, First Choice has produced plastic toys with electronic lights and sounds. In 1997, the Canadian company produced their first diecast vehicle, a Seagrave Fire Pumper in two current Windsor, Ontario, liveries. A limited production of 1,000 of the first color and 2,500 of the second will assure a high resale value for collectors and dealers.

FIRST GEAR

First Gear models are 1:34 scale trucks made of heavy diecast metal that are often customized to the buyers

requirements. Various clubs and companies contract First Gear to produce a limited edition model or series of models that feature their company logo or advertising (known as livery). Just a few base models are used, but the variations are numerous. Winross uses similar marketing in producing models of various livery.

FIRST GEAR TOY COLLECTOR CLUB OF AMERICA 1994 REMINGTON ARMS COMPANY COMMEMORATIVE SERIES

1st in the series: "Mallard" #10-1082 '52 GMC $40
2nd in the series: "Dove" #10-1098 '51 Ford $40

3rd in the series: "Pheasant" #10-1139 '51 Ford, $40

4th in the series: "Quail" #10-1094 '51 Ford. $40
5th in the series: "Goose" #10-1134 '52 GMC. $40
6th in the series: "Turkey" #10-1133 '51 Ford. $40

OTHER FIRST GEAR MODELS

1949 Chevrolet variations:
"Genuine Chevrolet". $29
"Mercy Hospital" Ambulance. $31
"Pepsi Big Shot" $38
"Rock Solid Chevrolet" $29

1951 Ford variations:

"GlasUrit Autolack System" Box Van, $45

"1995 Hershey" Stake Bed. $44
"Auto Value" Box Van $59
"Barq's Root Beer" $40
"Navajo" Box Van. $31
"Red Star" Box Van. $49
"Royal Crown Cola" Beverage Truck $40

1952 GMC variations:
"Burlington" Box Van $32
"Carstar" Wrecker $40
Chicago Fire Wrecker $99

"Falstaff Beer" $39
"FDNY Oxygen" Stake Bed $37
"Harley Custom Chrome" $49
"McLean Trucking" $99
Montgomery County Wrecker $43
"Morton Salt" Stake Bed $31
"O'Doul's Oasis Beer". $33
Philadelphia Rescue $49
"Railway Express" Stake Truck $39
"Stroh's Beer" $39
U. S. Mail Stake Truck. $39
"Whitney Volunteer" Tanker $39

1953 Ford C600 variations:
"Roadway" Box Van $32

1957 International Harvester variations:
"AAA of Sacramento" Wrecker $42
"Atlas Van Lines" $69
Boston Engine #54 Fire Truck $69
"Campbell Soup" Box Van $39
"Dart Towing of the Bronx" $39
"Esso" Tanker. $34
"FDNY Garage" Tow Truck. $44
"Gulf Oil Refinery" Fire Truck $39
"Gulf Oil" Wrecker $49
"Hershey Chocolate" Van $54
"Mobil Oil Refinery" Fire Truck $43
"Paul Arpin" Double Freighter Moving Van $49
Philadelphia Tow Truck $59
"Shell" Aviation Tanker $33
"SOCAL" Tanker. $44
"Tow Times" Wrecker $59
US Army Wrecker. $45
"Von Der Ahe" Double Freighter Moving Van $49
Zephyr Lubes" Box Van $29

1960 Mack variations:
"Adley Express" $89
"Campbell Soup" $69
"Columbian" Moving Van $79
"Eagle Snacks" $55
"Eastern Express" $52
"Great Northern" $89.0
"Hershey Anniversary" $64
"Humble Oil" $89
"Mack Trucks" $139
"New York Central" $54
"Pepsi Cola" $89
"Red Star". $129
"Smith & Wesson" $89
"St. Johnsbury". $57

FORMA

Forma of Italy became Yaxon after 1977. Prior to that time though, an assortment of 1:43 scale models were marketed under the Forma name.

300 Fiat 130 Semi-Trailer Truck $30
301 Fiat 170 Overhead Service Truck $30
302 Fiat 170 Garbage Truck $30
303 Fiat 170 Lumber Semi-Trailer Truck $30

304 Fiat 170 Open Semi-Trailer Truck $30
305 Fiat 170 Covered Semi-Trailer Truck $30
306 Fiat 170 Container Semi-Trailer Truck $30
311 Mercedes-Benz 2232 Truck and Trailer $30
317 Mercedes-Benz 2232 Container Truck $30
355 Fiat 780 Farm Tractor $30
356 Fiat 880 Farm Tractor $30
370 Two-Wheel Open Farm Trailer $30
371 Manure Spreader $30
372 Tank Trailer $30
381 Four-Wheel Open Farm Trailer $30
382 Hay Loader Trailer $30
385 Same 130 Farm Tractor $30
386 Lamborghini Farm Tractor $30

43RD AVENUE/GEMS 'N' COBWEBS

Sinclair's Auto Miniatures is one of the few sources for this eclectic British brand of hand-built white metal replicas of US cars. 43rd Avenue's assortment of English replicas called Gems & Cobwebs features a 1997 release of a 1938 prototype Jaguar SS-100 Coupe in 1:43 scale which was showcased in an article in the February 1997 issue of *Mobilia* magazine. The fact that this model even exists celebrates the rarity of the real car which was never put into production.

43RD AVENUE

1959 Cadillac Flattop 4-Door Sedan, 1:43 . . . . $89
1951 Studebaker Business Coupe 2-Door, 1:43 . . . . $89
1951 Studebaker Coupe 2-Door, 1:43 . . . . $89

43RD AVENUE GEMS 'N' COBWEBS

1938 Jaguar SS-100 Prototype Coupe, 1:43 . . . . $100

FOURNIER ENTERPRISES

Fournier produces hand-built 1:8 scale models of Kurtis Indy Roadsters. These all-metal models represent momentous times in Indianapolis history and feature hand-fabricated aluminum bodies, leather seats, and treaded rubber tires. Models measure approximately 21 inches long and are limited editions of 500 each. Fournier Enterprises, 1884 Thunderbird St., Troy MI, 48084. Tel: 1-800-501-3722. Fax: 1-810-362-2866.

Trio Brass Special, Johnnie Parsons . . . . no price provided
Fuel Injection Special, Bill Vukovich . . . . no price provided

FRANCE JOUETS

Marseilles, France, was the home of France Jouets, founded in 1959. When production was discontinued in 1969, the dies were sold to Safir, also of France. Just six basic chassis provided the basis for a variety of models.

FRANCE JOUETS 100 SERIES BERLIET GAK TRUCKS

101 Tank Truck, 1962 . . . . $75
102 Lumber Truck, 1962 . . . . $75
103 Covered Truck, 1962 . . . . $75
104 Dump Truck, 1962 . . . . $75
105 Grocery Truck, 1962 . . . . $75
106 Street Sweeper, 1962 . . . . $75
107 Cement Mixer, 1962 . . . . $75
108 Crane Truck, 1964 . . . . $75
109 Garbage Truck, 1964 . . . . $75

110 Overhead Service truck, 1964 . . . . $75
111 Farm Truck, 1964 . . . . $75
112 Pipe Truck, 1964 . . . . $75
113 Glass Truck, 1964 . . . . $75
114 Crane Truck, 1964 . . . . $75
115 Tow Truck, 1964/65 . . . . $75
116 Bucket Truck, 1965 . . . . $75

FRANCE JOUETS 200 SERIES PACIFIC HEAVY TRUCKS

201 Crane Truck, 1967 . . . . $125
202 Pipe Carrier Truck, 1959 . . . . $125
203 Rocket Launcher Truck, 1959 . . . . $125
204 Transformer Carrier, 1965 . . . . $125
205 Cement Truck, 1966 . . . . $125
206 Atomic Cannon Truck, 1966/67 . . . . $125
207 Atomic Cannon, not mounted on a truck, 1967 . . . . $125
208 Atomic Cannon Truck, 1967 . . . . $125

FRANCE JOUETS 300 SERIES GMC TRUCKS

301 Ambulance Truck, 1959 . . . . $75
302 Covered Truck, 1961 . . . . $75
303 Anti-Aircraft Gun Truck, 1959 . . . . $75
304 Lance-Rocket Truck, 1959 . . . . $75
305 Rocket Carrier Truck, 1965 . . . . $75
306 Dump Truck with Shovel, 1961 . . . . $75
Crane Truck, 1961 . . . . $75
Dump Truck, 1961 . . . . $75
Dump Truck and Trailer, 1961 . . . . $75
Fire Truck, 1961 . . . . $75
Lumber Truck, 1959 . . . . $75
Quarry Dump Truck, 1961 . . . . $75
Radar Truck, 1959 . . . . $75
Road Repair Truck, 1961 . . . . $75
Searchlight Truck, 1959 . . . . $75
Sweet Sweeper, 1961 . . . . $75
Tank Truck, 1961 . . . . $75
Troop Carrier, 1959 . . . . $75

FRANCE JOUETS 400 SERIES DODGE TRUCKS

401 Open Army Truck, 1960 . . . . $75
402 Army Troop Carrier, 1964 . . . . $75
403 Covered Army Truck, 1960 . . . . $75
404 Anti-Aircraft Truck, 1960 . . . . $75
405 Radar Truck, 1960 . . . . $75
406 Searchlight Truck, 1960 . . . . $75
407 Fire Truck, 1966 . . . . $75
408 Lance-Rocket Truck, 1966 . . . . $75
409 Ambulance Truck, 1966 . . . . $75

FRANCE JOUETS 500/600 SERIES JEEPS

501 Open Army Jeep, 1961 . . . . $65
502 Covered Army Jeep, 1964 . . . . $65
503 Army Jeep with Anti-Aircraft Guns, 1961 . . . . $65
504 Army Jeep with Lance-Rockets, 1961 . . . . $65
505 Army Radar Jeep, 1961 . . . . $65
506 Army Jeep with Searchlight, 1961 . . . . $65
507 Fire Jeep, 1961 . . . . $65
508 Police Jeep, 1965 . . . . $65
601 Jeep and Anti-Tank Gun, 1961 . . . . $65
602 Jeep and Generator Trailer, 1961 . . . . $65
603 Jeep and Open Trailer, 1961 . . . . $65
605 Anti-Tank Gun without Jeep, 1961 . . . . $65

Anti-Aircraft Gun Trailer, 1960 . . . . $65
Lance-Rocket Trailer, 1960 . . . . $65
Radar Trailer, 1960. . . . . $65
Searchlight Trailer, 1960 . . . . $65

FRANCE JOUETS 700 SERIES BERLIET STRADAIR TRUCKS

701 Dump Truck, 1967. . . . . $75
702 Grocery Truck, 1967 . . . . $75
703 Tow Truck, 1967 . . . . $75
704 Glass Truck, 1967 . . . . $75
706 Street Sweeper, 1967 . . . . $75
707 Garbage Truck, 1967 . . . . $75
708 Coca-Cola Truck, 1967. . . . . $75

FRANKLIN MINT

Between Danbury Mint and Franklin Mint, some of the most popular and collectible precision models have been produced. Jay Olins, editor of Precision Die Cast Car Collectors Club newsletter, is perhaps the most avid collector of both. Every three months, he publishes a complete up-to-date list of models produced by each company. Collectors are very critical of authenticity and detail, so they often write to the manufacturer and to Mr. Olins regarding any discrepancies discovered. Olins apparently has the inside track with both companies, and he relays all such comments to the manufacturer.

Below are listed Franklin Mint models currently available as of March 10, 1995, except where noted by italics. Because of their lack of availability and resulting rarity, some models may be considerably more valuable than indicated herein. Prices listed indicate approximate retail value. Ruth Gessner, Franklin Mint Precision Models, Mail Drop 185, Franklin Center, PA 19091.

1:8 SCALE

1886 Benz Patent Motorwagen. . . . . $125 – 145
1957 Corvette 283HP Engine . . . . $125 – 145

1:10 SCALE

1942 Indian 442 Motorcycle. $120 – 140
1957 Harley-Davidson XL Sportster Motorcycle. . . $120 – 140
1985 Harley-Davidson Heritage Softail Classic Motorcycle . $120 – 140

1:16 SCALE

1931 Bugatti Royale Coupe De Ville. . . . . $115 – 135
1930 Ford Model A . . . . $115 – 135
1913 Ford Model T . . . . $115 – 135
1905 Rolls Royce 10HP . . . . $115 – 135
1911 Stanley Steamer 62 Runabout. . . . . $115 – 135

1:24 SCALE

1938 Alvis Speedster 4.3 Litre, green-silver/beige . . . . . $85 – 125
1935 Auburn 851 Speedster, white/red . . . . $85 – 125
1949 Buick Skylark Convertible, pale yellow/red . . . . . $85 – 125
1949 Buick Riviera, light blue-gray/gray. . . . . $85 – 125
1936 Bugatti Atalante Type 57 SC, red-black/beige. . . . $85 – 125
1930 Bugatti Royale Coupe Napoleon 2, black-blue . . . . $85 – 125
1953 Cadillac Eldorado, white/red. . . . . $85 – 125
1959 Cadillac Eldorado Biarritz, light blue/white . . . . . $85 – 125
1957 Cadillac Eldorado Brougham, black-stainless/blue-white . $85 – 125
1910 Cadillac Thirty Roadster, black/beige. . . . . $85 – 125
1932 Cadillac V-16, blue 2-tone, canvas top/brown . . . . $85 – 125
1955 Chevrolet Bel Air Hardtop, red-white/red-white . . . $85 – 125
1955 Chevrolet Bel Air Hardtop, blue-white/blue-white . $85 – 125

1955 Chevrolet Bel Air Convertible, gypsy red-white/red-white . . . . $85 – 125
1955 Chevrolet Bel Air Fire Chief #12, red/red & white . $85 – 125
1955 Chevrolet Bel Air Police Chief #67, black & white . $85 – 125
1956 Chevrolet Bel Air Convertible, green-white/green-white. $85 – 125
1957 Chevrolet Bel Air Hot Rod, black-flames/black. . . . $85 – 125
1957 Chevrolet Bel Air Hardtop, red-white/red . . . . . . $85 – 125
1957 Chevrolet Bel Air Convertible, black/red-silver - issued March 1995 . . . . $85 – 125
1957 Chevrolet Bel Air Convertible, red/red-silver . . . . $85 – 125
1953 Chevrolet Corvette, cream/red. . . . . $85 – 125
1955 Chevrolet Corvette, metallic blue/beige . . . . $85 – 125
1956 Chevrolet Corvette, turquoise-white/white. . . . . . $85 – 125
1957 Chevrolet Corvette, red/white . . . . $85 – 125
1957 Chevrolet Corvette Fuel Injected, black-silver/red. . $85 – 125
1959 Chevrolet Corvette, red/red - issued March 1995 . . $85 – 125
1963 Chevrolet Corvette Sting Ray, black-blue/black . . . $85 – 125
1967 Chevrolet Corvette Sting Ray, black-blue/black . . . $85 – 125
1967 Chevrolet Corvette L-88 Sting Ray, blue/blue . . . . . $85 – 125
1978 Chevrolet Corvette Silver Anniversary Edition, silver/silver . . . . $85 – 125
1986 Chevrolet Corvette, yellow/black. . . . . $85 – 125
1986 Chevrolet Corvette, white/white-black . . . . $85 – 125
1960 Chevrolet Impala, white/white . . . . $85 – 125
1960 Chevrolet Impala, red . . . . $85 – 125
1912 Christie Front Drive Steamer Fire Engine . . . . $85 – 125
1948 Chrysler Town & Country Convertible, dark green-wood/red-beige. . . . . $85 – 125
1937 Cord 812 Phaeton Coupe, light yellow/black . . . . . $85 – 125
1933 Duesenberg Twenty Grand SJ, silver-beige/green. . $85 – 125
1930 Duesenberg J Derham Tourist, maroon-beige/gray. $85 – 125
1930 Duesenberg J Derham Tourist (Gary Cooper), silver-black/black . . . . $85 – 125
1933 Duesenberg J Victoria (Greta Garbo), blue-black/blue. $85 – 125
1935 Duesenberg Model J550 Convertible, maroon/white. $85 – 125
1958 Edsel Citation, pink/pink. . . . . $85 – 125
1989 Ferrari F40, red/red. . . . . $85 – 125
1932 Ford Deuce Coupe, black/beige . . . . $85 – 125
1955 Ford Fairlane Crown Victoria, pink-white/pink-white . $85 – 125
1957 Ford Fairlane 500 Skyliner, white-red/white/red. . . $85 – 125
1956 Ford Thunderbird, turquoise/turquoise . . . . $85 – 125
1949 Ford "Woody" Wagon, maroon/beige . . . . $85 – 125
1924 Hispano Suiza Tulipwood Speedster, wood/copper. $85 – 125
1925 Hispano Suiza Kellner H6B, maroon/white . . . . . . $85 – 125
1938 Jaguar SS-100, cream/brown . . . . $85 – 125
1961 Jaguar XKE, gray/beige. $85 – 125
1985 Lamborghini Countach 5000S, red/beige . . . . $85 – 125
1985 Lamborghini Fraternal Order of Police, black-white. $85 – 125
1941 Lincoln Continental Mark I, maroon/red . . . . $85 – 125
1939 Maybach Zeppelin, black/gray . . . . $85 – 125
1904 Mercedes Simplex, white/brown . . . . $85 – 125
1935 Mercedes-Benz 500K Roadster, red-beige/red-black . $85 – 125
1935 Mercedes-Benz 770K Pullman Limousine, red-black . $85 – 125
1954 Mercedes-Benz Gullwing 300SL, silver/plaid . . . . . $85 – 125
1954 Mercedes-Benz Gullwing 300SL, red/plaid . . . . . . $85 – 125
1926 Mercedes-Benz Model K, midnight blue/burgundy & paisley . . . . $85 – 125
1954 Mercedes-Benz W196 Racer, silver/red . . . . $85 – 125

1957 Mercedes-Benz 300 SC Roadster, burgundy/tan & black . $85 – 125
1948 MG TC Roadster, red/beige . . . . $85 – 125
1956 Nash Metropolitan, aqua-white/aqua/white . . $85 – 125
1977 Oldsmobile Petty NASCAR, blue-red "43" . . . . $85 – 125
1912 Packard I-48 Victoria, white/black . . . . $85 – 125
1970 Plymouth Superbird Petty NASCAR, blue "43" . . . . $85 – 125
1988 Porsche 911 Carrera targa, red/black . . . . $85 – 125
1988 Porsche 911 Carrera targa, black . . . . $85 – 125
1929 Rolls Royce Phantom I Cabriolet De Ville, black-
    blue/black . . . . $85 – 125
1907 Rolls Royce Silver Ghost, silver/black . . . . $85 – 125
1925 Rolls Royce Silver Ghost Tourer, silver-black/black . $85 – 125
1911 Rolls Royce Tourer, cream/brown . . . . $85 – 125
1992 Rolls Royce Corniche IV, white/beige . . . . $85 – 125
1992 Rolls Royce Corniche IV, blue/tan . . . . $85 – 125
1915 Stutz Bearcat, yellow. . . . . $85 – 125
1928 Stutz Black Hawk, red/black . . . . $85 – 125
1948 Tucker, light blue/gray . . . . $85 – 125
1962 Volkswagen Microbus, salmon & cream/cream . . . $85 – 125
1967 Volkswagen Cabriolet, red/black. . . . . $85 – 125
1967 Volkswagen Beetle, yellow/white . . . . $85 – 125
1967 Volkswagen Beetle, white . . . . $85 – 125

1:32 Scale

1922 Ahrens Fox R-K-4 Pumper Fire Engine. . . . . $70 – 115
1954 American LaFrance Fire Engine . . . . $70 – 115
1988 Peterbilt Truck Model 739 - Cab & Trailer . . . . . . $70 – 115

1:43 Scale Classic Cars Of The 50s

1953 Buick Skylark. . . . . $55 – 70
1959 Cadillac Eldorado. . . . . $55 – 70
1955 Chevrolet Bel Air . . . . $55 – 70
1957 Chevrolet Bel Air Convertible . . . . $55 – 70
1953 Chevrolet Corvette . . . . $55 – 70
1957 Chevrolet Corvette . . . . $55 – 70
1956 Chevrolet Nomad . . . . $55 – 70

1950 Chrysler Town & Country, $55 – 70

1952 DeSoto. . . . . $55 – 70
1958 Edsel Citation . . . . $55 – 70
1955 Ford Crown Victoria . . . . $55 – 70
1959 Ford Skyliner . . . . $55 – 70
1950 Ford Station Wagon . . . . $55 – 70
1956 Ford Thunderbird. . . . . $55 – 70
1958 Ford Thunderbird. . . . . $55 – 70
1951 Hudson Hornet . . . . $55 – 70
1956 Lincoln Continental Mark II. . . . . $55 – 70
1951 Mercury Monterey . . . . $55 – 70
1950 Nash . . . . $55 – 70

1956 Oldsmobile Starfire. . . . . $55 – 70
1955 Packard . . . . $55 – 70
1953 Packard Caribbean . . . . $55 – 70
1957 Plymouth Fury . . . . $55 – 70
1953 Studebaker Starliner . . . . $55 – 70

1:43 Scale Classic Cars Of The 60s

1963 Buick Riviera . . . . $55 – 70
1963 Cadillac Eldorado . . . . $55 – 70
1967 Chevrolet Camaro. . . . . $55 – 70
1960 Chevrolet Corvair . . . . $55 – 70

1963 Corvette Sting Ray, $55 – 70

1968 Dodge Charger. . . . . $55 – 70
1964 Ford Mustang. . . . . $55 – 70
1962 Ford Thunderbird. . . . . $55 – 70
1961 Lincoln Continental . . . . $55 – 70
1964 Pontiac LeMans GTO . . . . $55 – 70
1963 Rambler Classic 660 . . . . $55 – 70
1963 Studebaker Avanti . . . . $55 – 70

1:43 Scale Luxury Car Series

1931 Bugatti Royale Berline DeVoyage . . . . $55 – 70
1930 Cadillac V-16 . . . . $55 – 70
1931 Cord L-29 . . . . $55 – 70
1929 Duesenberg J . . . . $55 – 70
1928 Hispano Suiza H6B. . . . . $55 – 70
1928 Isotta Fraschini . . . . $55 – 70
1946 Jaguar Mark IV . . . . $55 – 70
1927 Lincoln Sport Touring . . . . $55 – 70
1939 Mercedes-Benz 770K Grosser Cabriolet . . . . $55 – 70
1934 Packard . . . . $55 – 70
1933 Pierce Silver Arrow . . . . $55 – 70
1922 Rolls Royce Silver Ghost . . . . $55 – 70

FROBLY

According to collector Bill Cross, "Frobly models are hand-built resin/white metal models made in France. The proprietor has recently discontinued the range — he is associated with a French collector's model shop, the name of which escapes me at present. The first model in the Frobly range was an incredibly ugly Packard Hawk."

Citroën DS19 4-Door Sedan $65
Citroën DS19 Convertible $65
Citroën ID19 4-Door Sedan $65
1961 Ford Econoline Van $79
1961 Ford Econoline Pickup. $79
1951 Mercury Convertible. $89
Packard Hawk $100

FREEWHEELS

Mercedes 190E, silver. $10

FUN HO!

Collector David Weber reports that Fun Ho! castings were made about 20 years ago by the Underwood Engineering Company of New Zealand, and that some 40 different castings were produced. Collector Bill Cross adds that the remaining castings of the now defunct company were purchased and assembled by Message Models in Australia. They are finished somewhat better than the originals, having better paint, and translucent windows. In Australia and New Zealand, pickup trucks are referred to as utility trucks, or "utes." There are only five models available from Message Models: Jaguar MK X, Ford Thames Ute, Holden HR Ute, Holden HR Sedan, and Chevrolet Bel Air, each offered for around $30.

ORIGINAL CASTINGS

Chevrolet BelAir $30
Ford Thames Ute $30
Holden HR Ute $30
Holden HR Sedan $30
Jaguar MK X $30
MG 1100 4-Door Sedan, pale green, 1:87 . . . . $15
Rolls Royce Phantom V $30

RECASTS FROM MESSAGE MODELS

Chevrolet Bel Air $20
Ford Thames Ute $20
Holden HR Ute $20
Holden HR Sedan $20
Jaguar MK X $20

FYP

Harvey Goranson reports that Yves Pebernet produced this range of resin models from 1986 until 1995.

Rolls Royce Phantom V Landaulet, white & black $450
Rolls Royce Silver Wraith "Gulbenkian," dark green. $385

GAD (SEE GREAT AMERICAN DREAMCARS)

GAIA

Model Power, Inc., has repackaged Gaia brand American LaFrance fire trucks as models for 1:87 (HO scale) railroad sets. Other models from Model Power are made by Playart, another manufacturer famous for repackaging their models under a different brand.

American LaFrance Fire Pumper, 1:87 . . . . $13
American LaFrance Ladder Truck, 1:87 . . . . $15
American LaFrance Snorkel Truck, 1:87 . . . . $15

GALGO

An interesting assortment of these inexpensive models are available in 1:43 and 1:64 scale, most likely from Spain.

1:64 SCALE

Dodge Challenger "A-Team," white & red. $3
Fiat Dump Truck $3
Fiat Snorkel Fire Truck. $3
Fiat Semi "BJ Bear" $3

Lancia Stratos $3
Scania Oil Tanker "Aeronafta" $3
Scania Oil Tanker "Agip" $3
Scania Oil Tanker "Esso" $3
Scania Oil Tanker "Shell" $3
Scania Semi "Camel Cigarettes" $3
Scania Semi "Cazalis". $3
Scania Semi "Coca Cola" $5
Scania Semi "Fargo". $3
Scania Semi "Frigor" $3
Scania Semi "Lee" $3

1:43 SCALE

1 BMW 3.5 "1st National" $14
2 Cametal Luxury Bus $14
26 Mercedes School Bus. $14
27 Peugeot 505 4-Door Sedan $14
29 Porsche 935 "Canon". $14
30 Porsche 935 "Rothmans" $14
31 Porsche 935 "Jagermist" $14
32 Renault Alpine "Elf". $14
33 Renault 18 4-Door Sedan $14
34 Renault 18 Fire Chief $14
35 Scania Semi "Adidas". $8
36 Scania Semi Van $8
37 Scania Semi "Cheese" $8
38 Scania Semi "A-Team" $8
39 Scania Semi "Coca Cola" $8
40 Scania Semi "Paint" $8
42 Scania Semi "Wine". $8
43 Scania Semi "VW Parts" $8
44 Ford Falcon 4-Door Sedan Rally $8
45 Dodge Dart 2-Door Hardtop Rally, orange $8
46 Volkswagen Van "Bagley" $8

GAMA

Gama models are manufactured in Furth, Bavaria, by the Georg Adam Mangold company. Begun in 1882, Gama only started producing diecast models in 1959. New Gama models are still being produced in Germany today, and remain some of the more distinctive models of our time. These models are detailed in other books. To list them all here would be too huge an undertaking. So, as with Corgi, Dinky, and others, herein is presented just a survey. Prices represent top book value. Gama models have been issued under the Schuco brand starting in 1994.

BMW 600, #907, 1959. . . . . $48
Demag Excavator, #9251, 1969 . . . . $54
Faun Cement Truck, #919, 1962 . . . . $54
Ford Taunus 17M, #901, 1959. . . . . $48
Henschel Wrecker, #31, 1969 . . . . $24
NSU Ro-80, #5, 1:63, 1968 . . . . $24
Opel Astra GSi, 1013, 1:43 . . . . $30
Opel Kadett, #890, 1:43, 1979 . . . . $30
Opel Rekord, #893, 1:43, 1978 . . . . $30
Porsche Carrera Six, #1, 1:63, 1968 . . . . $24
Volkswagen 1302, #13, 1:63, 1969. . . . . $24
1011 BMW 525i Touring Wagon, 1:43. . . . . $15
1021 BMW 325i Coupe, 1:43. . . . . $15

1173 Audi 80, 1:43	$15
1020 Ford Mondeo, 1:43	$15
1168 Mercedes-Benz 300CE, 1:43	$15
1003 Opel Frontera, 1:43	$15
1026 Opel Astra Cabriolet, 1:43	$15
1009 Messerschmitt Tiger, silver, closed, 1:43	$24
1150 BMW Isetta, 1:43	$35
1007 Messerschmitt Tiger, red, closed, 1:43	$21
1013 Opel Astra GSi, 1:43	$30
1005 Opel Corsa, 1:43	$15
1008 Messerschmitt Tiger, yellow, open, 1:43	$21
1010 Messerschmitt Tiger, black, open, 1:43	$24
2103 BMW 325i, 1:24	$42
2105 BMW M3, 1:24	$42

GAMA FOR AHC

1:43 diecast in Germany, refinished in Holland.

GA001R Opel Kadett, boot, Rijkspolitie (Dutch police)	$28
GA001R Opel Kadett hatch, Marechausee (Dutch customs police)	$28

GAMDA
(ALSO SEE CRESCENT, D.C.M.T., IMPY, LONE STAR, SABRA)

An Internet bulletin board posting on America OnLine was from a collector seeking Gamda diecast cars and trucks made in Israel in the early to mid-1960s, alternately known as Gamda-Sabra and Gamda-Koor. Collector Bill Cross reports, "There was an article in a recent issue of *Model Collector* on this range. If memory serves, the range had its beginnings in the Lone Star products of the D.C.M.T. company in Great Britain. There were few models in the range and were, I think, mostly post-WW2 British vehicles." If my latest research is any indication, it seems a lot of brands originated from D.C.M.T., including Crescent and Lone Star. Some Gamda models are in fact enhanced versions of D.C.M.T. models, with windows added and better paint jobs applied. Reissues of Dinky toys also made it into the Gamda line-up. In addition, the brand name Gamda-Sabra can be found on the bases of several models. Cragstan is yet another associated brand.

25-Pounder Gun, tan	$30
Armored Car, tan	$50
Articulated Flat Truck, blue and red	$75
Articulated Tanker, "DELEK"	$100
Articulated Tanker, "PAZ"	$100
Articulated Tanker, "SONOL"	$100
Articulated Tanker, "TNUVA"	$100
Articulated Tanker, UN, white	$100
Articulated Timber Truck, blue and red	$75
Bedford "Driving School" Truck	$90
Centurion Tank, 1:45, tan	$60
Centurion Tank, 1:90, tan	$45
Centurion Tank, 1:120, tan	$30
Covered Dairy Truck, "TNUVA," blue and cream	$75
Covered Mail Truck	$75
Covered Truck, "AMCOR"	$60
Daimler Conquest Saloon, gray	$100
Dump Truck	$50

Ford Prefect, cream or green	$65
Leyland "Egged" Bus, blue and gray	$150
Massey Ferguson Tractor, red	$60
Military Covered Truck, tan	$75
Military Truck, tan	$50
Mobile Canteen Truck	$75
Roadmaster Coupe, white and red	$80
Tank Transporter, tan	$85
Tipping Truck	$65
Truck	$65
Truck with Gas Cylinders	$75
Quicklime Spreader	$30
Vanguard Ambulance, white	$90
Vanguard Military Ambulance, tan	$75
Willys Jeep, white or red	$45
Willys Jeep, UN, white	$55
Willys Military Ambulance, tan	$60
Willys Military Jeep, tan	$45
Willys Military Police Jeep, green	$45
Willys Station Wagon Ambulance, white	$100
Willys Station Wagon Army Van, tan	$100
Willys Station Wagon Police Van, green	$100
Willys Station Wagon Van, orange	$100

GASQUI (OR GASQUY)

Belgium is the source for these quality toys, first produced around 1947. The company only lasted a few years before going out of business in the early 50s.

Army Bus, green	$150
Buick Coupe, green, blue, or red	$125
Buick Coupe with clockwork motor, red	$175
Bus, red, yellow, green, or gray	$150
Chevrolet Sedan, red, blue, or gray	$325
FN Breakdown Truck, gray or green	$100
FN Covered Military Truck, green	$100
FN Military Breakdown Truck, green	$100
FN Open Truck, green, red or gray	$100
FN Stake Truck, red or green	$100
FN Tanker, green, red, gray and green, gray and red, gray and yellow	$100
Ford Tudor, blue, gray, red, or green	$325
Maserati Race Car, green, red, or cream	$75
Mercury Ambulance, white, cream, and red	$150
Mercury Army Ambulance, green	$125
Mercury Mail Van, yellow	$225
Mercury Van, red	$150
Mercury Van with clockwork motor, red	$150
Plymouth Sedan, red, brown, green, gray, or chrome-plated	$125
Plymouth Staff Car, green	$200
Studebaker Champion, blue, brown, gray, or green	$450
Tatra, blue, red, brown, green, or gray	$450
Willys Army Jeep, green	$75
Willys Jeep, red	$100
Willys Jeep Station Wagon, red and yellow	$325
Willys Red Cross Jeep, white	$75

GEGE

Plastic bodies and diecast chassis typify these 1:20 and

1:43 scale Gege toys from France. Just a few 1:43 scale models exist, all produced in 1956.

Citroën DS19 . . . . $72
Ford Vendome $72
Ford Vedette $72
Peugeot 203 . . . . $72
Peugeot 403 . . . . $72
Renault Fregate Amiral $72
Simca Aronde $72
Simca Versailles $72

GEMS 'N' COBWEBS (SEE 43RD AVENUE)

GENERIC

So-called "generic" diecast toys are those that, while the package in which they were originally sold may be marked with one brand or another, the model itself is basically unmarked, other than "made in Hong Kong" or "made in China." A few, such as Zee Toys and M C Toys, may have just a logo and perhaps a model number on the base. Often, these generic models are unlicensed copies, or "knockoffs," of established brands such as Matchbox or Tomica, matching size and sometimes even markings. Brands such as Imperial Diecast, Rhino, Superior Racers, Sunshine (usually designated only with an "SS" number), and MegaMovers are only identified by the package they come in. Once removed from the package, they become unbranded generic toys, some nicely produced, others made cheaply.

Listed below and pictured is a sampling of generic models with no markings to indicate brand or manufacturer. Because it is difficult to determine brand or manufacturer, their value is not due to rise, but some are especially good copies of name-brand models.

Ambulance, based on Mercedes 280G, pull-back action 1:43 . . . $4

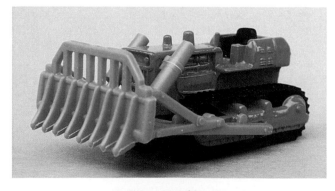

Bulldozer, 1:64, 50¢

Cadillac Stretch Limousine (identical to Majorette 300 Series models except for raised plastic chassis to accommodate pull-back mechanism) $2
Crane, 1:100, made in China $1
Double Decker Buses, pull-back action $2
Esso Tanker, made in Hong Kong . . . . 50¢
Mini Cooper Rally, made in China, pull-back action $1
Mini Loader, 1:64, made in China . . . . 50¢

GESCHA (ALSO SEE CONRAD)

Since 1923, Gescha has manufactured a variety of toys, but they didn't start producing diecast models until the 1960s. In the seventies, the line of Gescha diecast toys was renamed Conrad, while the Gescha name continued with its mechanical tinplate and other toys. Because the Gescha name is not included on diecast models produced after 1977, it becomes easier to recognize these earlier models, now considered quite valuable.

Fiat-Allis 41-B Dozer, $100 – 125

Caterpillar 769B Quarry Truck, $75 – 90

GINGELL

Gingell Diecasting Manufacturing Ltd. produces a line of inexpensive generic diecast toys manufactured in China and packaged in 25-car sets for $5. As with typical budget toys, they are cheaply produced, lack much detail, and are lightweight metal with plain plastic chassis. Value of these will not likely rise, and identification of individual models is difficult or impossible, which also detracts from any future collector value. Gingell toys are best considered as a novelty rather than a serious addition to a collection.

GIODI

Giodi is a relatively obscure Italian manufacturer of mostly Fiat models. Below is a list of models and current prices.
73030 Fiat "Jumbo" Farm Tractor, yellow/black, 1:28 . . . . $17

73035 Fiat Turbo DT 180-90 Farm Tractor, brown/white/black, 1:28 . . . . $17

73038 Fiat Farm Tractor/Loader, 1:28 . . . . $17

73039 Fiat Farm Tractor/Backhoe, 1:28 . . . . $17

73051 Fiat Jeep "Grand Canyon," blue/white, 1:25. . . . . $15

73053 Fiat Jeep "Algiers-Cape Town," orange/white, 1:25 . . . . $15

73056 Fiat Jeep "Police," blue/white, 1:25. . . . . $17

73062 Fiat Jeep/Camper "Expedition," orange/white, 1:25 . . . . $17

73064 Fiat Jeep "Safari," tan, brown, camouflage, 1:25. . . . . . $17

73070 Fiat Snorkel Fire Engine, 1:35 . . . . $22

73073 Fiat Flatbed Truck with Load, orange/black/silver, 1:35. $17

73074 Fiat Flatbed with Trailer & 2 Loads, orange/black/silver, 1:35 . . . . $22

73076 Fiat Dump Truck with Tractor, yellow/black/red, 1:35. . $17

73077 Kenworth Conventional Semi-Cab & Load, 1:35. . . . . . $15

73082 Fiat MTS-10 Forklift with Pallet, yellow/silver/orange, 1:43. $17

73084 Fiat 4WD Tractor with Snowplow, orange, 1:43. . . . . . $17

73085 Fiat MTS-40 Road Roller, orange/black, 1:43 . . . . $17

73091 Fiat Jeep "SOS" Road Service Tow, orange/yellow, 1:25. $17

73092 Fiat Jeep "Ambulance," white, 1:25 . . . . $17

73093 Fiat Jeep/Camper "Grand Canyon," blue/white, 1:25 . . . $17

73104 Kenworth Semi Milk Truck, orange/blue/gray, 1:35. . . . $22

73106 Kenworth Cement Truck, orange, 1:35 . . . . $17

73107 Kenworth Flatbed Semi with F. Dump, red/black/yellow, 1:35 . . . . $17

73109 Fiat Crane Truck, 1:35 . . . . $17

GLOOR

The improbable and otherwise unknown Gloor brand is represented by one model.

1960 Chevrolet Stepvan "UPS," 1:43 . . . . $35

GOLDEN CLASSICS (SEE GOLDEN WHEEL)

GOLDEN WHEEL (ALSO SEE JA-RU)

Ja-Ru toys represent small, inexpensive toy cars and trucks made by Golden Wheel Die Casting. The new Golden Classics Mord Model T gift banks from the same company are so similar to Ertl banks that they can be easily mistaken for them at first glance. Closer inspection shows a few differences, most notably a plastic roof secured to the windshield by a crudely melted post, and the distinctive phrase "Coins Bank" in script on each model. These models are such a blatant attempt to capitalize on the popularity of Pepsi-Cola collectibles and coin banks that they even say gift bank on the box, and the tanker even declares "Collectable Models" right on the tank. Still, considering the $12 price tag, they are comparably nice models to the more expensive $20 – 35 Ertl versions, and they do make attractive, affordable gifts.

Ford Model T Delivery Van, white with blue roof and fenders "Drink Pepsi-Cola". . . . . $12 – 15

Ford Model T Tanker, white with red roof and fenders, "Pepsi-Cola". . . . . $12 – 15

Ford Model T Tanker, "Mountain Dew". . . . . $12 – 15

Tractor Trailer, 1:87, "Pepsi" . . . . $4 – 5

Tractor Trailer, 1:87, "Mountain Dew" . . . . $4 – 5

Tractor Trailer, 1:64, "Pepsi" . . . . $9 – 12

Tractor Trailer, 1:64, "Mountain Dew" . . . . $9 – 12

GOLDVARG

The Goldvarg Collection is a series of 1:43 scale classic American cars offered by Mariana and Sergio Goldvarg of Buenos Aires, Argentina. The uniqueness of Goldvarg models is that the company offers a free lifetime guarantee for replacement of any broken or damaged parts. The Goldvarg Collection, Mendoza 1059, 1er piso A (1428), Buenos Aires, Argentina. 541-788-4790 (telephone/fax), 541-466-1044 (telephone).

0001 1957 Oldsmobile Starfire 98 hardtop, blue. $89

0002 1946 Chevrolet Stylemaster 4-door $62

0003 1951 Chrysler Crown Imperial limousine LWB, blue, $62 – 89

0004 1956 Lincoln Premiere hardtop coupe. $89

0005 1955 Pontiac Star Chief convertible, red. . . . . $62 – 89

0006 1950 Packard Woodie wagon, green . . . . $62 – 89

0007 1956 Mercury Montclair coupe . . . . $62 – 89

0008 1954 Chevrolet Bel Air 4-door sedan. $89

0009 1952 Nash Golden Airflyte Ambassador Sedan Pininfarina . $89

0010 1959 Pontiac Bonneville 2-door hardtop $89

0011 1959 Mercury Park Lane 2-door hardtop $89

0012 1951 Kaiser Henry J 2-door sedan, dark gray . . . . . $62 – 89

0013 1949 Plymouth Commercial Utility Station Wagon . . $62 – 89

0014 1958 Oldsmobile sedan. $62 – 89

0015 1949 Cadillac Series 62 4-door sedan. . . . . $62 – 89

0016 1946 Ford Deluxe sedan. $62 – 89

GONIO

These 1:24 scale tin-plate military models from Czechoslovakia are made to the highest degree of authenticity. Though they do not exactly fit the definition of "diecast," they represent an important contribution to the area of highly collectible authentic scale models. Examples below are provided by Toys for Collectors and Diecast Miniatures. Features include steerable wheels and other working parts.

Dodge WC-51 with foldable side guards, #1007. . . . . $65

Dodge WC-51 Powerwagon Weapons Carrier, #08657, USA, olive drab. $88

Jeep Kommando with trailer and supplies, #1010 (sold out). . $125

M3 Halftrack Armoured Personnel Carrier, #1011. . . . . $125

VW T-82 Porsche Ambulance Kubelwagen East, #1002, top down . $59

VW T-82 Porsche Kubelwagen, #086XX, sand $82

VW T-82 Porsche Kubelwagen, #1001, top down, Africa Corps, sand. $54

VW T-82 Porsche Kubelwagen, #1001L, top up, camouflage, limited edition. $69

VW T-82 Porsche Kubelwagen East, #1004, top down $54
VW 166 Porsche Schwimmwagen (Amphibious Vehicle),# 08655,
   olive drab $88
VW 166 Porsche Schwimmwagen West (Amphibious Vehicle),
   #1006 . . . . $59
White 160AX Powered M-3 Halftrack, #08661, USA, olive drab. $128
Willys Jeep, foldable windshield, #1008, opening hood $79

GOODEE

Goodee models are very similar to Tootsietoys, in that they generally are single-cast bodies with no chassis or windows. Goodee diecast vehicles were manufactured by Excel Products Company of New Jersey. Six-inch and three-inch models were made, some of the larger models with windup motors.

6" MODELS

1953 GMC Pickup Truck $25
1953 Ford Police Cruiser $25
1954 DeSoto Station Wagon $25
1955 Ford Fuel Truck $25
American LaFrance Fire Pumper $25
Military Jeep $25

3" MODELS

1953 Ford Police, 2-door sedan $28
1953 GMC Pickup Truck $15
1953 Studebaker Coupe $20
1953 Lincoln Capri Hardtop $15
1953 Cadillac Convertible $15
1954 DeSoto Station Wagon $15
1954 Ford C600 Oil Truck $28
1955 Ford Fuel Truck $15
American LaFrance Fire Pumper $15

Military Jeep, $15

Moving Van, $15

Step Van $15
Land Speed Racer $15

GOVROSKI (ALSO SEE RUSSIAN MODELS)

Quality diecast toys from Russia, Govroski is represented in *Schroeder's Collectible Toys* by just one model.

Volga Sedan, metallic blue $35

GRAND PRIX

Grand Prix models are available in 1:43 scale.

Austin Seven Twin Cam (kit) $18
Ford Escort "Castrol" (kit) $18
Lotus Elan Roadster (built) $45
1983 Ferrari "Martini" (kit) $18

GREAT AMERICAN DREAMCAR/DUST & GLORY/ QUARTER MILE

Great American Dreamcars, occasionally also known as Great American Dream Machines or simply "Gad," are 1:43 scale white metal models marketed by Phil Alderman's Autofare of New Jersey. He also offers Dust & Glory, a line of vintage American racers, and Quarter Mile dragster replicas. Original models are casts of SMTS, MCM, and possibly a few others.

1M Don Garlits Swamp Rat 1 Dragster $179
2 1954 Chevrolet Corvette Nomad, blue $179
3 1939 Buick Y Job Show Car, black $179
3MC 1939 Buick Y Job - Exc 4 Minicar, gray $179
4 1955 Lincoln Futura Show Car, green $179
5 1954 Cadillac La Espada Show Car, yellow $179
6 1965 Chevrolet Corvette Mako Shark II, dark blue $179
7 1954 Cadillac El Camino 2-door coupe, silver $179
8 1951 Chrysler K-310 Show Car, 2-tone blue $179
9 1956 Packard Predictor Show Car, pearl white $179
12 1956 Buick Centurian 2-door Show Car, red/white/clear . . $179
14 1952 Chrysler C-200 Convertible Show Car, black/green . . $179

GRIP ZECHIN (ALSO SEE EIDAI)

Grip Zechin is a hard-to-find brand of unusual toys believed to be made in Japan by Eidai. Only a few examples have been found and documented for this book. One is a Yamaha motorcycle and sidecar from Chris Quimby, Vancouver, Washington. Another is a DeTomaso Pantera also listed under the Eidai brand, which has been associated with Grip models. More recently, Jeff Kopis of Clallam Bay, Washington, reports a few more models found in 1977 in a Seattle, Washington, Bon Marche department store, where he recalls that the store had a complete line of Grip Zechin models. Unfortunately, he only purchased three at the time, all Caterpillar models. Nevertheless, his additional information is invaluable.

47 Yamaha Policeman Side Car, 1:43 . . . . $45
DeTomaso Pantera GT-35, Eidai/Grip Technica series, 1:28. $25 – 30
5 Caterpillar D5 Bulldozer . . . . $25 – 30
8 Caterpillar D5 Rakedozer . . . . $25 – 30
23 Caterpillar 14E Snowplow Motor Grader . . . . $30 – 35

GUILOY

Guiloy is a brand of models made in Spain. They are best

known for their great miniature renditions of motorcycles. But they also produced a truck series called Mini Camiones and a few car models.

MINI CAMIONES, CIRCA 1970S

Guiloy Mini Camiones are a series of trucks in 1:66 scale, all based on the same truck tractor with various backs or trailers attached to create a variety of models. Based on photocopied catalogs from Dr. Craig Campbell, assistant professor of geography at Youngstown State University, I was able to translate the Spanish descriptions of most models by the pictures. Some however remain a mystery, such as #50 "Bombero." The Spanish descriptions are in italics. The 50-66 series represents the same truck with different backs. The 1000 series represents the same truck with various trailers attached.

50 *Bombero* - Ladder Fire Truck (?) . . . . $10 – 15
51 *Gria* - Crane Truck. . . . . $10 – 15
52 *Gasolina* - Texaco Tanker . . . . $10 – 15
53 *Misil* - Missile Launcher . . . . $10 – 15
54 *Ametralladora* - Military Anti-Aircraft Gun Truck. . . . . $10 – 15
55 *Catæn* - Military Cannon Truck . . . . $10 – 15
56 Dumper. . . . . $10 – 15
57 *Toldo* - Covered Lorry . . . . $10 – 15
58 *Toldo Militar* - Military Covered Lorry. . . . . $10 – 15
59 *Contenedor Mudanzas* - Container Truck . . . . $10 – 15
60 *Contenedor Frigorifico* - Refrigerator Truck. . . . . . . $10 – 15
61 *Contenedor Militar* - Military Container Truck . . . . . . $10 – 15
62 *Cajun Militar* - Military Open Lorry . . . . $10 – 15
63 *Cajun Normal* - Open Lorry. . . . . $10 – 15
64 *Vigas* - Flatbed Truck with I-Beams . . . . $10 – 15
65 *Tubos* - Pipe Truck. $10 – 15
66 *Troncos* - Log Truck. . . . . $10 – 15

1:66 SCALE TRACTOR/TRAILERS

1000 *Campsa* Gasoline Tanker . . . . $15 – 20
1001 *Toldo* - Covered Lorry. . . . . $15 – 20
1004 *Cajun* - Open Lorry . . . . $15 – 20
1005 *Tubos* - Pipe Truck. . . . . $15 – 20
1008 *Tanques Militar* - Military Tank Transporter with two armored tanks . . . . $25 – 30
1009 *Planeador Militar* - Military Glider Transporter with glider. $15 – 20
1013 *Cemento* - Pressurized Tanker. . . . . $15 – 20
1014 *Amoniaco* - Pressurized Tanker. . . . . $15 – 20
101? Esso Gasoline Tanker . . . . $15 – 20
1018 Elf Gasoline Tanker . . . . $15 – 20
10?? Crane Truck . . . . $15 – 20

MOTORCYCLES

G15 1948 Indian Motorcycle Anniversary Edition, burgundy or yellow $50
GY17227 1948 Indian Chief, 1/10 scale. $30
GY2802 Honda "Repsol," 1:18 . . . . $16
GY2803 Honda "Campsa," 1:18 . . . . $16
GY2804 Kawasaki "Metzeler," 1:18 . . . . $16
GY2807 Suzuki "Pepsi" racer, 1:18 . . . . $16
GY2815 Harley Davidson Custom Classic, 1:18 . . . . $18
GY2872 Harley Davidson Custom Sport, 1:18 . . . . $18
GY2896 BMW R1000RS street bike, 1:18 . . . . $16
GY3106 Honda racing motorcycle, 1:10 . . . . $45
GY3147 BMW R 100RT street bike, 1:10 . . . . $45

GY3163 BMC Ecureuil motocross bike, 1:10 . . . . $45
GY3166 Honda "Castrol," 1:10 . . . . $45
GY3187 Suzuki "Pepsi," 1:10 . . . . $45
GY3118 BMW R-80 motocross bike, 1:10 . . . . $45
GY3146 Yamaha "Garriga" racer, 1:10. . . . . $45
GY3801 Harley Davidson Custom Classic, 1:10 . . . . $50
GY6244 Yamaha, 1:6 . . . . $100
GY6247 Yamaha, 1:6 . . . . $100

1:18 SCALE MODELS

G1 1995 Aston Martin DB-7, wine, green, black or blue. . $35 – 40
G2 1993 McLaren F-1, red, blue, silver or metallic burgundy. $35 – 40
G16 1969 Mercedes C111, metallic orange or silver . . . . . $35 – 40

1:25 SCALE MODELS

50 Mercedes-Benz 350SL Coupe. $24
51 Porsche 911 Coupe $24
524 Porsche 911 Rally, "Rothmans," white/blue/red/green. . . . $24
525 Porsche 911 Rally, Martini," yellow. $24

1:64 SCALE MODELS

1 Land Rover Range Rover wagon $3
2 Fiat Ritmo 4-door sedan $3
3 Talbot 150 4-door sedan $3
4 Renault 4 Van. $3
5 Ford Fiesta 2-door sedan $3
6 Peugeot 504 4-door sedan. $3
7 Fiat (Seat) 131 wagon $3
8 1976 Ford Torino $3

GUISVAL

Besides the unusual 1:30 scale models, Guisval of Spain offers an assortment of vehicles in the more conventional 1:43 and 1:64 scale. Some are said to be direct knockoffs of Matchbox Models of Yesteryear, such as the Mercedes 540K. Guisval started in 1967 and survives to this day.

1:30 SCALE

Ferrari Testarossa. $24
Porsche 959. . . . . $24

1:43 SCALE

1 Goofy Train $15
2 Daffy Duck Plane $15
105 Renault 17 Coupe $15
108 1979 Chevrolet Camaro $15
115 Renault 17 Coupe $15
117 Mercedes 406 Kombi $15
128 Chevrolet Van "Moto Club" $15
139 Chevrolet Van "Paris Dakar". $15
144 Renault 17 Coupe $15
331 Lancia 037 "Marlboro" $15
332 Lancia 037 "Mobil". $15
333 Lancia 037 "Bridgestone" $15
337 Toyota Celica "Esso" $15
338 Toyota Celica "Avis" $15
339 Toyota Celica "Avis" $15
402 Ford Sierra 4-door Sedan $15
403 Citroën BX 4-door Sedan $15
404 Peugeot 505 4-door Sedan $15
406 Ford Sierra "Esso" $15
441 Citroën BX "Autoveri" $15
442 Ford Sierra "Esso" $15

444 Citroën BX "Shell" $15
446 Ford Escort "Goodyear" $15
447 Audi Quattro Coupe $15
449 Ford Sierra "Gitnes" $15
453 Peugeot 505 "Esso" $15
457 Ford Sierra Police $15
461 Renault 9 "Road Services" $15
462 Ford Sierra "NASA" $15
463 Peugeot 505 Ambulance $15
467 Ford Escort Ski $15
516 Chevrolet Fire Van. $15
523 Caravan Ski $15
529 Chevrolet Van "Polar" $15
752 Bugatti T50 Coupe. $15
754 Mercedes 540K $15
755 1928 Lincoln 4-door Sedan. $15
901 Nissan Jeep Tow Truck $15
903 Nissan Jeep with Plow. $15
904 Renault Espace School Bus $15
905 Nissan Fire Jeep $15
906 Renault Espace Police $15
917 Porsche 959. . . . . $15
918 Ferrari Testarossa. $15
922 Mercedes Unimog Fire. $15
923 Mercedes Unimog Safari $15

1:64 Scale

72 Kenworth Fire Ladder . . . . $3 – 5
95 1926 Hispano Suiza Convertible, top down . . . . $3 – 5
96 1926 Hispano Suiza Convertible, top up. . . . . $3 – 5
97 1931 Cadillac Roadster. . . . . $3 – 5
98 Caravan Ambulance. $3 – 5
99 Audi Quattro Ambulance. . . . . $3 – 5
665 Peterbilt Semi Cow Transporter . . . . $3 – 5
707 Datsun Pickup with Cage. . . . . $3 – 5
802 Renault 5 2-door Sedan . . . . $3 – 5
803 Fiat Ritmo/Strada 4-door Sedan . . . . $3 – 5
805 Plymouth Horizon 4-door Sedan . . . . $3 – 5

GULLIVER

Four models were produced by Gulliver of France, three in the late 1930s, one in 1950.

Berliet Bus, 6" $130
Berliet Covered Truck, 5¼" $90
Renault Celtaquatre, 4" $130
Renault 4CV, 1950 . . . . $145

HALLMARK (ALSO SEE KIDDIE CAR COLLECTIBLES)

Hallmark produces numerous promotional and novelty items for their stationery stores. Among the offerings are a few whimsical diecast toys, not much more than a heavy lump of zamak, in simplified shapes for toddlers.

Banana Flash. . . . . $5 – 8
Fuzzmobile . . . . $5 – 8

HARTOY
(ALSO SEE AMERICAN HIGHWAY LEGENDS, LLEDO)

Hartoy is an American promotional company that, besides producing its own American Highway Legends series of

1:64 scale trucks in various liveries, takes basic models from Lledo and others and, through a licensing agreement with numerous companies, customizes them with advertising and logos. A series of Coca-Cola vehicles and Chevron gas station promotionals are some of the better-known models from Hartoy.

American Highway Legends is now the most prominent series from Hartoy, and is dealt with in its own section. (See American Highway Legends.) Lledo and Days Gone models marketed by Hartoy are likewise listed with the rest of the Lledo models. (See Lledo.)

HASBRO (ALSO SEE AVIVA)

Hasbro has been a powerful force in the toy industry since the 1960s. Toys such as Mr. Machine, the see-through gear-driven walking, animated robot with a top hat, was possibly one of the best known toys of the period, at least if you watched Saturday morning cartoons. But Hasbro's solid claim to fame is G.I. Joe action figures and accessories, a perennial favorite for some 30 years.

Hasbro has continued through to the present, but it has been overshadowed by the giant called Mattel. In fact, Mattel failed in an attempt to purchase Hasbro in 1995.

G.I. Joe aside, Hasbro's product line at one time included a line of Aviva character toys usually sold at Hallmark shops. Predominantly Peanuts characters from the comic strip of the same name, Aviva at last word continues to market such items in diecast and plastic. More research is in progress. See Aviva for a sampling of a few of the diecast items issued.

HERPA

Among the wide assortment of models available under the Herpa brand name is a series of 1:87 scale cars and trucks with plastic bodies. The accuracy and detail of these diminutive vehicles is remarkable, and are listed in this book because of their value as scale model miniatures. In the larger 1:43 scale, Herpa produces an assortment of diecast models that are especially nice, although they feature no working parts such as opening doors, hood, or trunk.

1:43 Scale Models

BMW 740i, arctic white $18
BMW 740i, bright red. $18
BMW 740i, metallic blue $18
BMW 740i, Oxford green $18
Ferrari 288 GTO, red $18
Ferrari 288 GTO, yellow. $18
Mercedes-Benz E320 sedan, metallic blue $18
Mercedes-Benz E320 sedan, metallic gray $18
Mercedes-Benz E320 sedan, red $18
Mercedes-Benz E320T, black $18
Mercedes-Benz E320T, blue $18
Mercedes-Benz E320T convertible, blue $18
Mercedes-Benz E320T convertible, white $18
Mercedes-Benz 320 convertible $20
Mercedes-Benz 320 coupe $20
Mercedes-Benz 320 sedan $20
Mercedes-Benz 320 wagon. $20
Mercedes-Benz 600 SEL, green $18

Mercedes-Benz 600 SEL, gray, $18

Mercedes-Benz 600 SEL, purple	$18
Mercedes-Benz 600 SEL, red	$18
Volkswagen Polo 4-door	$20
Volkswagen Polo 2-door	$20

HITECH 1:43 SCALE MODELS

Ferrari F40, black	$45
Ferrari F40, red	$45
Ferrari F40, yellow	$45
Ferrari Testarossa, red	$45
Ferrari Testarossa Convertible, red	$45
Ferrari Testarossa Coupe, yellow	$45
Ferrari Testarossa Spyder, yellow	$45
Ferrari Testarossa Spyder, silver	$45
Ferrari 348tb, black	$45
Ferrari 348tb, metallic blue	$45
Ferrari 348tb, red	$45
Ferrari 348tb, red	$45
Ferrari 348tb, yellow	$45
Ferrari 348ts, metallic green	$45
Mercedes-Benz 600AMG	$40
Mercedes-Benz 600SEL	$40

HERPA JR. 1:66 SCALE MODELS

BMW 528 Fire Chief Car (plastic), red	$5
BMW 325i, blue	$5
BMW 325i, green	$5
BMW 325i, red	$5
BMW 325i, yellow	$5

HESS

While Hess trucks are plastic, they represent a large portion of the scale model truck collector market, and are mentioned here due to their popularity. Hess trucks are issued by the Hess Oil Company. Information provided below is from the *1996 Hess Price Guide* by Thomas G. Nefos, publisher and editor of The National Toy Connection, reprinted by permission.

HESS PROMOTIONAL TOYS
[ORIGINAL SELLING PRICES IN BRACKETS]

1964 B-Model Mack Tanker Truck, made in Hong Kong (same tanker was used by Service, Wilco, Gant, Billups, Etna & Travelers) [$1.39]. $1,900

1965 same as 1964

1966 "Hess Voyager" Tanker Ship, made in the U.S.A. by Marx Toys [$1.89] $2,300

1967 Split Window Tanker Truck with "Red Velvet" base on box, no rivets on battery switch, made in the U.S.A. [$2.89] . $2,400

1968 same as 1967 except no velvet box was used, no rivets on battery switch, made in Hong Kong [$1.49] $675

1969, same as 1968

1969, Split Window Tanker "Amerada Hess," Made in Hong Kong, rare, not sold to public $2,500

1970, Red Pumper Fire Truck, made in Hong Kong by Marx Toys [$1.69]. $695

1971, same as 1970 except box was labeled "Season's Greetings" [$1.69] $3,000

1972, Split Window Tanker Truck, Same as 1968 except has "rivets" on battery switch [$1.79] $375

1973, no promotion offered

1974, same as 1972 [$1.89] $375

1975, Semi Box Truck, 3 oil drums, no Hess labels on drums, 1pc. cab on tractor, made in both U.S.A. & Hong Kong [$1.99] $395

1976, same as 1975 except oil drums have Hess labels & tractor cab is made in 2 pieces [$2.29] $395

1977, Semi Tanker Truck, large rear label 1.5" x 1", made in Hong Kong [$2.39] $175

1978, same as 1977 except, small rear label 1" x ⅞" [$2.49] . . $185

1979, no promotion offered

1980, GMC Training Van, dated 1978 sold but sold in 1980, Made in Hong Kong [$3.29] $395

1981, no promotion offered

1982, '33 Chevy "Home Delivery" Tanker Truck, box marked "First Hess Truck," not a bank, made in Hong Kong [$4.69]. . . . $95

1983, same as 1982 (reissued), not a bank, made in Hong Kong [$5.29] $95

1984, similar to 1977 – 78 Semi Tanker Truck except made into a bank, made in Hong Kong [$4.99] $95

1985, '33 Chevy "Home Delivery" Tanker bank, distributed in the North $125

1985, reissued 1984 Tanker, distributed in the south $95

1986, White Semi Box Truck with 3 Hess labeled oil drums, made in both Hong Kong & China [$5.49] $100

1987, same as 1986 [$5.99] $75

1988, White "Toy Truck & Racer," made in both Hong Kong & China [$6] $70

1989, White Aerial Ladder Fire Truck with dual siren sounds, made in China ($8.99] $65

1990, White Semi Tanker Truck, back up and air horn sounds, made in China [$9.99] $45

1991, same as 1988 except different style race car, larger truck cab, made in China [$10.99] $35

1992, White "18 Wheeler" Box Truck with racer, made in China [$11.99]. $40

1993, Hess Patrol Car, white and green, sirens & lights, larger scale toy [$11.99] $28

1993, Hess Premium Diesel Tanker given as a gift to Hess bulk diesel dealers, reissue of the 1990 semi tanker with new graphics, special box wrapped in green paper, and special gift card from the Hess company, not sold to public . . $1,000

1994, same as 1993, not sold to public $1,000

1994, Hess Rescue Truck, white and green with red ladder, larger scale toy [$14.99]. $25

1995, Hess Toy Truck & Helicopter, white, green, flatbed semi with detachable helicopter [$15.99] $20

National Toy Connection offers a full color photo album of all of the previously described toys and their boxes. This album can be updated each year with the purchase of only one photo — it's never out of date! To get yours send $26 + $3 shipping and handling U.S.A. (foreign orders please send International Postal Money Order in U.S. $34) to: National Toy Connection, Suite 2346, 779 E. Merritt Island Causeway, Merritt Island, FL 32952. 1-800-704-1232 nationwide toll-free order line (sorry, phone number only available in the U.S.A.).

HIGH SPEED

Whether High Speed brand toys can be considered diecast is debatable. These inexpensive generic toys are mostly plastic. On the samples found, only the truck cab and upper chassis are diecast. Nevertheless, they possess the charm of a well-designed toy, while lacking the identity of a scale model. While suggested retail of $2.49 seems high to me, the $.99 paid at Toy Liquidators makes them reasonably priced. Values will not likely rise on such toys in the near future, let's say the next 20 years, but they are "cute" additions to a well-rounded diecast toy collection.

CONSTRUCTION MASTER SERIES

Box Truck . . . . $1 – 2

Dump Truck, $1 – 2

Cement Truck . . . . $1 – 2
Utility Truck . . . . $1 – 2

HIGHWAY TRAVELERS

Highway Travelers are white-metal models whose "finish, craftsmanship, and attention to detail are as good as you'll find." The specimen referred to is a 1962 Studebaker Lark convertible in Indy Pace Car trim. Price and other model listings were not provided. For more information, write to Highway Travelers, PO Box 187, Oakdale, NY 11769-0187.

HOT WHEELS

The author of this book purposely makes no attempt to present the full Hot Wheels line in this book. To do justice to the entire line of toys, it would take an entire book, of which there are several. For more information on these and other books on diecast toys, send two first class stamps to Dana Johnson, P O Box 1824, Bend, OR 97709-1824 USA.

Since 1968, Mattel's Hot Wheels line has maintained a

solid lock on the diecast toy car market. While many other toy manufacturers, even Matchbox, suffered the humiliation of lost market share, near bankruptcy, and repeated buyout, Hot Wheels have remained market stable.

Prototypes and production models alike from Hot Wheels' first few years are commanding high prices, as are new special issues and even some regular issues. Much speculation — and some would say overspeculation — and debate ensues over the value of new regular production issues.

One such prototype is a 1969 issue #6274 Beach Bomb, a Volkswagen van with two surfboards projecting out the back window. While the production model with side panels added to the cast to hold the surfboards is fairly common and priced at $40 to $80, only some 14 – 20 specimens of the prototype are believed to exist. The latest edition of *Tomart's Price Guide to Hot Wheels* (Second Edition, 1997) lists the value of this rarest Hot Wheels model at $3,500, but one such specimen sold at Christy's auction house in February 1995 for $4,025.

In late 1996, Mattel made the announcement that the company was working on purchasing Tyco Toys, the current owner of Matchbox, Dinky, and several other toy brands. By mid-1997, the sale was complete. A few years earlier, Mattel purchased the Corgi brand and incorporated many of the Corgi Jrs. into the Hot Wheels line. Eventually, though, the original employees of Corgi in Swansea, South Wales, bought back the larger scale Corgi Collectibles series from Mattel. Will the same thing happen to Matchbox? Will some Hot Wheels take on the look of Matchbox models? Or will the Matchbox series be kept distinct from the Hot Wheels offerings? As 1998 closes in, Matchbox toys reportedly have already been seen in Hot Wheels five-packs, and retail advertising has had Matchbox five-packs shown with the Hot Wheels logo on them.

HOT WHEELS "FREAKS"

Rather than attempting to represent the entire Hot Wheels line, presented here instead is a showcase of a few lesser known and relatively undocumented series offered since the beginning in 1968, sort of a Hot Wheels "freak show."

HOT WHEELS GRAN TOROS

One of the lesser known offerings from the Hot Wheels line are Gran Toros models, introduced in 1970, 1:43 scale beauties rarely seen and highly valued.

6601 Ferrari Can Am	$175 – 225
6602 Chevrolet Astro II	$175 – 225
6603 T'rantula	$175 – 225
6604 Torpedo	$175 – 225
6605 Lamborghini Miura	$175 – 225
6606 Chapparal 2G	$175 – 225
6607 Ford Mk II	$175 – 225
6608 Abarth 695 SS	$175 – 225
6611 Mustang Boss Hoss	$175 – 225
6612 Alpha Romeo 33/3	$175 – 225
6613 Porsche Carrera	$175 – 225
6614 Ferrari P4	$175 – 225
6615 Twinmill	$175 – 225
6616 Silhouette	$175 – 225
6617 Toyota 2000 GT	$175 – 225
6618 Lotus Europa	$175 – 225
6621 Ferrari 512 S	$175 – 225
6622 Mercedes C-111	$175 – 225
6623 Porsche 917	$175 – 225
6624 Abarth 3000	$175 – 225
6625 Mantis	$175 – 225
6626 McLaren M8D Can Am	$175 – 225
6627 De Tomaso Pantera	$175 – 225
6628 Chapparal 2J Can Am	$175 – 225
6629 Lola T212 Can Am	$175 – 225

Hot Wheels Farbs

Another series relatively undocumented is Farbs, introduced in 1972, four particularly odd models that are not much more than a cartoon-like man lying on his back with a motor on his stomach and wheels underneath. Initially proving unpopular, Farbs died a deserving death in their first year. Now a few collectors who still have one or more are wondering what they're worth. So presented below is the four-car line-up with gift sets as well.

#5850 HyGear	$3 – 4
#5851 Myles Ahead	$3 – 4
#5853 Red Catchup	$3 – 4
#5854 Hot Rodney	$3 – 4
#5864 Head-Over-Heels Set	$12 – 16
#5865 Human Race Set	$12 – 16

Hot Wheels Pro Racing Superspeedway - First Edition 1997

A new series from Mattel is the Hot Wheels Pro Racing series that deserves mention here because of its distinctive packaging and double-angled approach. Pro Racing models are packaged both with and without a collectors card and priced accordingly. Models with collector card retail for about $3 – 4 each, while models without card (BP) sell for around $2 – 3.

17407-#5 Kellogg's, Terry Labonte
17408-#4 Kodak, Sterling Martin
17409-#43 STP, Bobby Hamilton
17410-#7 QVC, Geoff Bodine
17411-#6 Valvoline, Mark Martin
17412-#37 K-Mart, Jeremy Mayfield
17413-#16 Primestar/Family Channel, Ted Musgrave
17414-#99 Exide, Jeff Burton
17416-#5 Kellogg's, Terry Labonte
17417-#4 Kodak, Sterling Marlin

17422-#16 Primestar/Family Channel, Ted Musgrave
17423-#99 Exide, Jeff Burton
17580-#44 Hot Wheels, Kyle Petty (1997 Collector 1st edition)
17581-#28 Havoline, Ernie Irvan
17582-#96 Caterpillar, David Green
17583-#94 McDonald's, Bill Elliott
17584-#44 Hot Wheels, Kyle Petty
17585-#28 Texaco, Ernie Irvan
17587-#94 McDonald's, Bill Elliott
17808-#98 RCA, John Andretti
17812-#10 Tide, Ricky Rudd
17813-#30 Pennzoil, Johnny Benson
17816-#10 Tide, Ricky Rudd
17817-#30 Pennzoil, Johnny Benson
18084-#8 Circuit City, Hut Stricklin
18087-#8 Circuit City, Hut Stricklin
18088-#21 Citgo, Michael Waltrip
18089-#91 Spam, Mike Wallace

Hot Wheels by Collector Number

For the past several years, Mattel has assigned not only a model number, but also a collector number. Some models have more than one collector number. Some collector numbers represent more than one model. The model number and collector number can only be found on the original package. Because of this, prices listed below are for mint condition models in original blisterpack.

1 Old Number 5 Fire Engine, red with louvers, $10

2 Sol-Aire CX4, black	$12
3 Cat Wheel Loader, yellow	$6
4 XT-3, purple	$8
4 Zender Fact 4, purple	$3
5 Good Humor Truck, white version	$6
5 Good Humor Truck, red version	$8
6 Blazer 4x4, blue	$12
7 Troop Convoy, olive	$100
8 Vampyra, purple	$6
10 Thunder Roller	$4
11 Baja Breaker Van, white "RACING TEAM A.T.V."	$4
11 Baja Breaker Van, metallic orange with Real Rider tires	$10
11 Baja Breaker Van, black with red accent	$5
12 '31 Doozie, maroon	$6
15 Peterbilt Tank Truck, yellow	$20
16 Earth Mover, yellow	$15
18 Mercedes 540K, black	$12
19 Shadow Jet, yellow with maroon accents	$15

20 Rocket Tank, olive $12
21 Mercedes-Benz 540K, red $7
21 Mercedes-Benz 540K, black $7

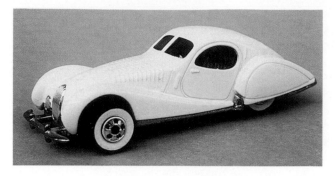

22 Talbot Lago, white, $4

23 '80's Firebird, yellow $10
24 Hiway Hauler, "PEPSI" $6
26 '65 Mustang Convertible, light blue with black interior $18
26 '65 Mustang Convertible, light blue with tan interior $6

27 Talbot Lago Darracq T150C Coupe, burgundy, $6

28 '37 Bugatti, blue with gray $10
29 Hiway Hauler, "NASA SPACE SHUTTLE GROUND SUPPORT" . $7
29 Hiway Hauler, "Goodyear Racing Tires" $5
31 '65 Mustang Convertible, black with tan interior $5
31 Classic Cobra, red $5
32 Sharkruiser, lavender. $3
33 Peterbilt Cement Truck $4
33 Camaro Z28, purple $5
33 Camaro Z28, orange $5
33 Camaro Z28, red. $8
34 '37 Bugatti, yellow with red $10
35 Ferrari Testarossa, red with red interior $8
35 Ferrari Testarossa, red with tan interior $12
35 Ferrari Testarrossa, black. $5
36 '80s Corvette, black. $5
36 '80s Corvette, red $5
36 Baja Bug, white. $20
37 Hot Bird, black $12
37 Hot Bird, white $9
37 Hot Bird, metallic blue $10
38 Cat Dump Truck, yellow $3
38 Classic Cobra, red $5
39 Monster Vette, purple $12

40 Power Plower, black $10
41 Cat Bulldozer, yellow $8
42 Ferrari Testarossa, red $6
42 Oshkosh Snowplow, lime green all metal $6
44 Hot Bird $4
45 Cat Dump Truck, yellow $3
45 Rescue Ranger $6
46 Rig Wrecker, white $10
49 Gulch Stepper, red "Pennzoil" $8
50 Oshkosh Snowplow, orange all metal $10
52 Delivery Truck "Wonder Bread" $6
52 Delivery Truck "Larry's Mobile Tune-Up" $12
52 '35 Classic Caddy, metallic blue. $5
53 Zombot, gold $5
54 Rescue Ranger $6
54 Nissan 300ZX, white $4
55 Rig Wrecker, "Steve's 24 Hour Towing" $4
56 Bronco 4-Wheeler, turquoise with red & white accents, white roof, red motorcycle on back $15
57 3-Window '34, purple with light green $12
58 Blown Camaro, turquoise $20
59 Highway Patrol, black & white "POLICE" $5
59 Fiero 2M4, white with red, black & yellow accents. $6
60 Peterbilt Tank Truck, "California Construction Co." $7
60 Lamborghini Countach LP500S, white with red & blue $8
62 Rolls-Royce Phantom II, metallic blue $6
62 Alien, silver and red $5
63 Radar Ranger, silver $5
65 '40' Woodie. $10
65 VW Bug, red. $5
66 Custom Corvette, red. $12

67 '32 Ford Delivery, yellow, $12

68 Nissan 300ZX, yellow with red/white/blue. $6
68 T-Bucket, yellow. $3
69 Cat Road Roller, yellow. $3
69 Ferrari F40, red. $3
70 Bronco 4-Wheeler $4
71 Ambulance, white $5
72 School Bus, wide single stripe on sides $2
73 Street Roader Suzuki 4x4, white. $3
74 GT Racer, black $5
74 GT Racer, purple $6
75 Sheriff Patrol, metallic blue $5

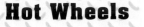

76 Big Rig, black with blue/red/orange accents $5
76 Lamborghini Countach, red $4
77 Flame Stopper, red $5
77 Bywayman, black with blue/yellow/white accents $5
78 Peterbilt Cement Truck, white & red $10
79 Big Bertha, olive $5
80 Porsche 959, red $5
80 Radar Ranger $5
81 Ratmobile, white $2
82 Fire Eater Snorkel Fire Truck, red $5
82 Porsche 959, metallic red $5
83 Tank Gunner, olive $20
84 Probe Funny Car $6
86 Proper Chopper $5
87 Purple Passion $5
88 T-Bird Stocker, white & black, #28 . . . . $10
89 Mini Truck, turquoise $5
92 Mercedes 380 SEL, black $8
94 Auburn 852, red with red fenders $4
95 '55 Chevy, white $8
95 '55 Chevy, yellow $8
98 Nissan Custom "Z," metallic red $5
99 Ford Stake Bed Truck, metallic blue "RAPID DELIVERY" with
    yellow stake bed $4
100 Peterbilt Dump Truck, red $6
102 Surf Patrol, yellow with red interior $3

103 Range Rover, white, $2

104 Turbo Streak F1 Racer, hot pink $3
105 Peugeot 205 Rallye, white $8
106 VW Golf, bright red, "GTi" $5
106 VW Golf, white with pink/green/blue accents $4
108 Ramp Truck, "International Dream Cars" $6
110 Trailbuster, turquoise with hot pink interior $3
111 Street Beast, white upper, turquoise lower body $4
112 Limozeen, white $4
113 Speed Shark, purple with hot pink interior $2
114 Fiero 2M4, black $5
115 Roll Patrol, olive $6
116 Mazda MX-5 Miata, red $5
117 Classic Ferrari Testarossa 250, yellow $5
117 Classic Ferrari Testarossa 250, red $8
118 Ferrari 348, red $5
118 Ferrari 348, yellow $5

122 Toyota MR2 Rally, white with red/yellow/orange accents . . $2
123 Lamborghini Diablo, red $4
125 Zender Fact 4, silver $3

126 Chevy Lumina APV, $5

127 Power Plower, purple with yellow plow $4
129 Suzuki Quadracer, white $5
131 Nissan Hardbody 4x4 Pickup, black with hot pink interior . $5
133 Shadow Jet, purple, "Inter Cooled F-3" $2
134 Mercedes, white $8

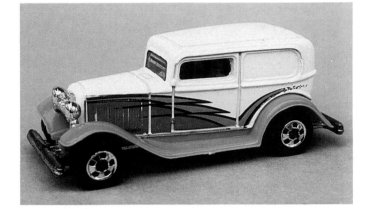

135 '32 Ford Delivery, white with turquoise/pink/blue, $5

136 '56 Flashsider Pickup, turquoise $5
137 Goodyear Blimp $5
140 Flashfire, black with red interior $7
141 Shock Factor, black with bright pink interior $2
142 Hiway Hauler, "Kool-Aid Wacky Warehouse" $5
143 Recycling Truck, orange "Recycler" $2
144 Oshkosh Cement Mixer, white, red & blue $5
145 Tractor, yellow with front loader $3
145 Tractor, red with front loader $3
146 Bulldozer, yellow $5
147 Tank Truck, "Unocal" $3
148 Porsche 930, red $6
149 BMW 850i, blue with white stripes, pink & yellow accents . $6
150 BMW 323 Convertible, black with beige interior $8
151 Ford Aerostar, purple with chrome windows $5
153 Thunderstreak F1 Racer, yellow "Pennzoil" $3
154 '59 Cadillac, white with red interior $5
155 Turboa, yellow $2
156 Rodzilla, purple $3
157 '57 Chevy, yellow with flame accents $10
158 Mercedes-Benz Unimog, "CASTROL RESEARCH TEAM" . . . $5

159 Big Bertha, gray $3
160 Command Tank, white $5
161 Roll Patrol, gray $5
162 '65 Mustang Convertible, red with tan interior $6

163 Talbot Lago, metal flake red, $6

164 Mercedes 540K, metal flake blue $6
165 Suzuki Quad Racer, hot pink $3
166 Vampyra, black $5
167 '80s Firebird T-Top, bright orange $5
168 GT Racer, black $5
169 Sol-Aire CX4, blue $5
170 Chevy Stocker, fluorescent orange with sparkles $5
171 VW Bug, metallic purple $5
172 Mazda MX-5 Miata, yellow $2
174 Limozeen, metal flake blue $4
175 Ferrari 348, white with red interior, pink/red/purple accents . $8
176 Lamborghini Diablo, metal flake blue with red tinted windows $4
177 Zender Fact 4, metal flake purple $5
178 Chevy Stocker, metal flake red $10
178 Hot Bird, metal flake black $4
179 Porsche 959, purple $5
181 Pontiac Fiero 2M4, fluorescent green with sparkles $5
182 Shadow Jet, bright green, "Inter Cooled F-3" $2
183 VW Golf, metal flake hot pink $5
184 Mercedes-Benz 380 SEL, metal flake blue $3
185 Proper Chopper, black & white "Police" $5

186 Ford Aerostar, "Speedie Pizza," $4

187 Ramp Truck, "Hot Wheels 24 Hr. Emergency Towing" $4
188 Hummer, beige camouflage $4
189 Gleamer Patrol, silver $5

190 '57 T-Bird, gold Gleam Team Edition, $3

191 Aeroflash, purple Gleam Team Edition $4
192 Corvette Stingray, lime green $10
192 Corvette Stingray, Gleam Team silver patterned $3
193 Porsche 959, Gleam Team metallic magenta $4
194 Goodyear Blimp $5
195 Troop Convoy, tan $4
196 3-Window '34, white with fuchsia fenders $5
197 Corvette Split Window, bright blue with black wheels $15
197 Corvette Split Window, bright blue with white wall tires . . . $6
198 Path Beater with plow, lime green, "ECOLOGY RECYCLE CENTER" $3
199 Double Demon, lime green $4
200 Custom Corvette convertible, pearl $5
201 Oshkosh Snowplow, orange with plastic back $5
202 1993 Camaro, purple $8
203 Jaguar XJ220, silver $5
203 Jaguar XJ220, metallic dark blue $5

204 Oscar Mayer Weinermobile, $3

205 Treadator, red $2
206 Pipe Jammer, yellow $2
207 Vector "Avtech" WX-3, purple $3
208 Audi Avus Quattro, silver $3
209 Lexus SC400, black $3
210 Dodge Viper, red $4
211 Twin Mill II, lime green $3

212 Silhouette II, purple. $3
213 '57 Chevy, aqua $3
214 Swingfire, metallic blue upper, white lower body (variation of 111 Street Beast). $4
215 Auburn 852, red with brown or black fenders $3
216 Fat Fendered '40, purple $10
217 40's Woodie, turquoise with black fenders $10
218 Street Roader, green $3
219 Gulch Stepper, lime green $3
220 Bywayman, white with pink accents $3
221 Range Rover, black $2
222 Blazer 4x4, metal flake blue with fluorescent yellow interior . $3
223 Baja Bug, metallic red $12
224 Zombot, blue chrome $3
225 Limozeen, metal flake black. $3
226 Ferrari 348, pink, red. $3
227 Lamborghini Diablo, yellow. $4
228 Zender Fact 4, metallic blue. $5
229 Mercedes 380 SEL, pink $3
230 XT-3, white. $3
231 Mini Truck, orange $3
232 Lamborghini Countach, red with white & black stripes $3
233 Toyota, white $3
234 Nissan Custom Z, metallic purple. $4
235 Turbo Streak, lime green $3
236 Ford Aerostar, black "Rollerblade" $5
237 Ford Stake Bed Truck, red "Rapid Delivery" with yellow stake bed $4
238 Hiway Hauler, purple "Hot Wheels Delivery" $12
239 Mercedes-Benz Unimog, tan $3
242 1993 Camaro, metallic blue $3
242 1993 Camaro, enamel blue. $20
244 "No Fear" F1 Racer $5
245 Driven To The Max Dragster, fluorescent orange $4
246 Shadow Jet II $3
247 Rigor Motor, metallic red $4

248 Splittin' Image II, $4

249 Fuji Blimp. $3
250 Talbot Lago, metallic black with whitewall tires $5
   (also 22 & 27)
255 BMW 851, metallic dark blue. $3
258 Blazer 4x4, metallic light blue $3
261 Cyber Cruiser, metallic and chrome purple (variation of 206 Pipe Jammer) $3
262 1993 Camaro. $4
263 Mean Green Passion $3
264 Lexus SC400, metal flake deep red $3

265 Oldsmobile Aurora, metallic mint green $3
266 '59 Caddy, metallic lavender with white interior $4
268 GM Lean Machine, Fluorescent yellow and black $3
273 Tail Gunner, white $5

274 Super Cannon, olive, $3

HOT WHEELS REVEALERS (1993 – 1994)

Of particular interest is the Revealers collection, a series of models marketed in 1993 and 1994, packaged in concealing wrappers numbered one through twelve. Three color variations exist for each model.

Blue or gold tokens could be found in a number of wrappers. The blue token, when mailed away, resulted in winning a ten-car collection of limited edition Revealers models. The gold token granted the holder a Hot Wheels all-terrain bike, and a gold-plated Hot Wheels Ferrari Testarossa currently valued at $100! Listed below is the complete series, including the 10-car blue token winner set and gold Ferrari.

#1 Sol-Aire CX4
   v.1 white with accents $4
   v.2 periwinkle blue with accents. $4
   v.3 fluorescent yellow with accents $4
#2 Ferrari 348
   v.1 white with accents $4
   v.2 black with accents $4
   v.3 metallic bronze with accents $4
#3 Lamborghini Diablo
   v.1 red. $4
   v.2 black $4
   v.3 metallic blue. $4
#4 Zender Fact 4
   v.1 metallic mint green. $4
   v.2 metallic purple $4
   v.3 black $4
#5 Mercedes 380 SEL
   v.1 fluorescent lime green with accents $4
   v.2 metallic silver with accents $4
   v.3 white with accents $4
#6 Ferrari F40
   v.1 red with accents $4
   v.2 metallic burgundy with accents $4
   v.3 yellow with accents $4
#7 Lamborghini Countach
   v.1 white with accents $4

v.2 silver with accents $4
v.3 hot pink with accents $4

#8 Ferrari Testarossa
v.1 lime green with accents $4
v.2 hot pink with accents $4
v.3 fluorescent orange with accents. $4

#9 Porsche 930
v.1 metallic blue. $4
v.2 metallic light green $4
v.3 maroon $4

#10 Nissan 300ZX
v.1 black with accents $4
v.2 yellow with accents $4
v.3 purple with accents $4

#11 Corvette ZR-1 Convertible
v.1 white with accents $4
v.2 metallic blue with accents $4
v.3 metallic gray with accents $4

#12 Jaguar XJ220
v.1 metallic purple $4
v.2 metallic blue. $4
v.3 red. $4

Blue token 10-car prize set . . . . $150 – 200
Sol-Aire CX4, bright blue with chrome trim & accents . . . $15 – 20
1993 Camaro Stock Car, fluorescent lime green . . . . $15 – 20
AC Cobra 427, white with accents . . . . $15 – 20
Porsche 930, fluorescent light orange . . . . $15 – 20
Pontiac Banshee, red with white hood . . . . $15 – 20
'51 Mercury Blue Passion, metallic cobalt blue. . . . . . . $15 – 20
Ferrari Testarossa, metallic purple . . . . $15 – 20
Alien, metallic lower, red upper body, "ALIEN" on hood . $15 – 20
Lamborghini Diablo, fluorescent red with blue spoiler . . . $15 – 20
'65 Mustang Convertible, fluorescent light green . . . . . . $15 – 20
Ferrari Testarossa, gold plated, gold token prize model $100

Hot Wheels 1995 Model Series

Mattel offered 12 models for 1995, as listed below.
Car #1 Speed Blaster, 13609 . . . . $1 – 2

Car #2 Mercedes SL, 13610, $1 – 2

Car #3 '58 Corvette Coupe, 2015. . . . . $1 – 2
Car #4 Speed-a-saurus, 13341 . . . . $1 – 2
Car #5 Power Pistons, 13343. . . . . $1 – 2
Car #6 Hydroplane 13342 . . . . $2 – 4
Car #7 Dodge Ram 1500, 13344 . . . . $1 – 2
Car #8 Camaro Convertible, 13340 . . . . $1 – 2
Car #9 Power Pipes, 13346 . . . . $1 – 2

Car #10 Ferrari 355, 13338 . . . . $1 – 2
Car #11 Power Rocket, 13348 . . . . $1 – 2
Car #12 Big Chill, 13347 . . . . $3 – 5

Hot Wheels 1995 Treasure Hunt Series

Much speculation ensues amongst collectors about the value of these 1995 reissued classics, of which Treasure Hunt versions limited to a production run of 10,000 of each model. Some collectors have seen them offered for as much as $80. Is anybody buying it? Actual value is around $25.

Car #1 Olds 442, 13349 . . . . $25
Car #2 Gold Passion, 13350 . . . . $25
Car #3 '67 Camaro, 13351 . . . . $25
Car #4 '57 T-Bird, 13352. . . . . $25
Car #5 VW Bug, 13353 . . . . $25
Car #6 '63 Split Window, 13354 . . . . $25
Car #7 Stutz Blackhawk, 13355 . . . . $25
Car #8 Rolls-Royce, 13356 . . . . $25
Car #9 Classic Caddy, 13357 . . . . $25
Car #10 Nomad, 13358. $25
Car #11 Cobra, 13359 . . . . $25
Car #12 '31 Doozie, 13360 . . . . $25

Hot Wheels 1995 Pearl Driver Series

Special luster colors make this four-car series an attractive assortment for '95.

Car #1 Talbot Lago, $1 – 2

Car #2 Pearl Passion '51 Mercury . . . . $1 – 2

Car #3 VW Bug, $1 – 2

Car #4 Jaguar XJ220. . . . . $1 – 2

Hot Wheels 1995 Steel Stamp Series

Metallic paint jobs with metalized accents creative a distinctive look for this 1995 four-car assortment.
Car #1 Steel Passion '51 Mercury. . . . . $3 – 5

Car #2 Zender Fact 4 . . . . $3 – 5
Car #3 '56 Flashsider . . . . $3 – 5
Car #4 '57 Chevy . . . . $3 – 5

HOT WHEELS 1995 RACE TEAM SERIES

All four models in this 1995 four-car collection are done in the same attractive metallic blue with Hot Wheels logos and racing accents.

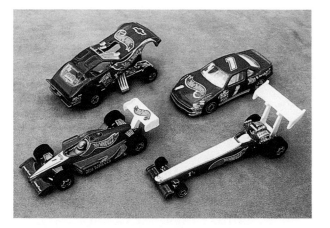

Car #1 Lumina Stocker, Car #2 Hot Wheels 500, Car #3 Side-Splitter, Car #4 Dragster, $3 – 5 each

HOT WHEELS 1995 KRACKLE CAR SERIES

The newest technology in paint application is used for 1995 to create these unusual color variations on familiar cars.

Car #1 Sharkruiser . . . . $3 – 5
Car #2 Turboa . . . . $3 – 5
Car #3 '63 Split Window Corvette . . . . $3 – 5

Car #4 Flashfire, $3 – 5

HOT WHEELS 1995 DARK RIDER SERIES

Black metal flake paint jobs, rakish wheels and low-profile tires typify this line of "Batmobile wannabees."

Car #1 Splittin' Image II . . . . $3 – 5
Car #2 Twin Mill II . . . . $3 – 5
Car #3 Silhouette II . . . . $3 – 5
Car #4 Rigor-Motor. $3 – 5

HOT WHEELS 1995 ROARIN' RODS SERIES

Bright colors and zebra stripes decorate these stock models to set them apart from the herd.

Car #1 Street Roader . . . . $3 – 5
Car #2 Roll Patrol. . . . . $3 – 5
Car #3 Silhouette II . . . . $3 – 5
Car #4 Rigor-Motor. $3 – 5

HOT WHEELS 1995 HOT HUBS SERIES

Brightly colored low profile tires and wheel hubs make these variations of stock models unusual.

Car #1 Cyber Cruiser . . . . $3 – 5
Car #2 Vampyra. . . . . $3 – 5
Car #3 Shadow Jet . . . . $3 – 5
Car #4 Suzuki Quadracer . . . . $3 – 5

HOT WHEELS 1995 SPEED GLEAMER SERIES

Chrome bodies and special wheels make up the Speed Gleamer assortment.

Car #1 3-Window '34 . . . . $3 – 5
Car #2 T-Bucket. . . . . $3 – 5
Car #3 Ratmobile . . . . $3 – 5
Car #4 Limozeen . . . . $3 – 5

HOT WHEELS 1995 SILVER SERIES

These are silver chrome variations.

Car #1 Fire Eater . . . . $3 – 5
Car #2 Rodzilla . . . . $3 – 5
Car #3 Propper Chopper . . . . $3 – 5
Car #4 School Bus . . . . $3 – 5

HOT WHEELS 1995 PHOTO FINISH SERIES

Car #1 . . . . $3 – 5
Car #2 . . . . $3 – 5
Car #3 . . . . $3 – 5
Car #4 . . . . $3 – 5

HOT WHEELS 1995 RACING METALS SERIES

Car #1 . . . . $3 – 5
Car #2 . . . . $3 – 5
Car #3 . . . . $3 – 5
Car #4 . . . . $3 – 5

HOT WHEELS 1996 REAL RIDERS SERIES

Dump Truck . . . . $7 – 9
Mercedes Benz Unimog 13305 . . . . $7 – 9
59 Caddy 13307 . . . . $5 – 7
Corvette Stingray 13308 . . . . $6 – 8

HOT PURSUIT

There seems to be no shortage of new diecast companies. Hot Pursuit Collectibles is one of those. Based in Cherry Hill, New Jersey, Hot Pursuit Collectibles offers these 1:24 scale coin banks through various specialty outlets, particularly Specialty Diecast Company and Joel's Toys (see Appendix). The models, introduced in 1997, are similar to the 1:43 scale Chevrolet Caprice police cars first introduced by Road Champs a few years ago, except that opening the trunk reveals a hidden coin slot. Why a bank? It immediately appeals to more collectors — those that collect diecast models and those that collect diecast banks, as well as those that collect model police cruisers. Hot Pursuit Collectibles, PO Box 3621, Cherry Hill, NJ 08034 USA. Telephone 609-654-8484, fax 609-654-2281.

New York Police Department. $25
California Highway Patrol. $25

Michigan State Police $25
Oklahoma Highway Patrol $25
Ohio State Highway Patrol $25
Arkansas State Trooper $25
New York City Taxi $25
New Jersey $25
Virginia $25
Florida $25
Alabama $25
Georgia $25
New York $25
Maryland Police (2 car set) . . . . $40 – 45
Chicago Fire Department $25
New York Fire Department $25
San Francisco Fire Department $25
Philadelphia Fire Department $25

HP TOYS

The fact that HP Toys were made in Denmark is all the author so far knows about this brand. More information would be greatly appreciated.
1984 Leyland Farm Tractor, 1:25 . . . . $22

HUBLEY

Hubleys were made in Lancaster, Pennsylvania. Hubley is known as the maker of some of the most popular and collectible toys on the collector market. The first Hubley toys were cast iron. The company that made them has been traced back to 1892. By 1940, lighter diecast zinc alloy replaced heavy cast iron, thus cutting the cost of worldwide shipping. Plastic toys make up a significant portion of the Hubley line. O'Brien's book *Collecting Toy Cars and Trucks* provides a detailed history of Hubley toys. Besides the assembled toys, Hubley also produced diecast model kits in the 60s. These kits, unassembled and still in the original box, are gaining renewed popularity with collectors.

Hubley was recently purchased by Ertl, and a few Hubleys have been re-released by Ertl. A good example is the classic Hubley school bus. The original Hubley version featured clear plastic labels and no windows. The earlier Ertl version is windowless while a later issued by Ertl has dark tinted plastic windows. The Hubley version is priced around $45 – 55. The two Ertl versions are currently available for around $12 – 17.
Airflow Car, 5¼" $84
Bell Telephone Truck with telephone pole trailer, 24" $185
Jaguar, 7½" $190
Packard Sedan, 1939 – 1940, 5½" $75
Panama Digger, 3½" $600
Panama Digger, 9½" $1,650

KIDDIETOYS

A popular series of Hubley toys were marketed as Kiddietoys. Here is a sampling.
Dump Truck, #476 . . . . $140
Dump Truck, #510 . . . . $250

MG Sport Car, 9" $190
Racer, #457, 6½" $55
Sedan, #452, 7" $29
Taxi, #5 . . . . $25
1946 Ford Stake Truck, #461 . . . . $170

MODEL KITS

Duesenberg SJ, #4864 . . . . $60 – 75

REAL TOYS (U.S.A.)/REAL TYPES (CANADA), 1:60 SCALE

A few toys representing U.S. cars were issued around 1958 to 1960 in 1:60 scale. They were marketed in the U.S. as Real Toys, and in Canada as Real Types, a series of cars of approximately 3" – 3½" long.
Ford Country Squire, #RT250, two-tone cream and brown . $55 – 70
Chevrolet Corvair, #RT340, turquoise . . . . $55 – 70
Buick, #RT 90, light blue . . . . $55 – 70
Studebaker Hawk, #RT 50, red . . . . $65 – 80
GMC Firebird III, #RT 350, red . . . . $60 – 75
Ford Fairlane, #RT 20, mint green . . . . $55 – 70
RT 80 Chevrolet Corvette, red . . . . $45 – 70

HUSKY (ALSO SEE CORGI)

Husky toys were the first series of smaller toys produced by Corgi. Later the line would be renamed Corgi Juniors. Husky toys were lightweight and inexpensive, but highly accurate renderings of common European vehicles of the mid-sixties, considering their original price of 39¢ – 49¢ each. For a sample listing of Husky models, see Corgi.

ICIBI

The only information found on Icibi models of Greece is listed below.
270 Deutz Fire Ladder Truck, 1:25 . . . . $7
900 McLaren CanAm, 1:25 . . . . $7
1431 Porsche 911 Police, 1:25 . . . . $7
5020 Deutz Fire Engine, 1:25 . . . . $7

IGRA

Igra models are quality 1:38 and 1:43 scale plastic models from the Czech Republic (formerly Czechoslovakia). These rare models are offered by Modelauto and others.
1 1924 Tatra Sedan $15
2 1924 Tatra Phaeton $15
6 1906 Laurin/Klement $15
7 1907 Praga Charon $15
9 1906 Velox Car $15
12 Zetor Crystal Tractor $15
13 Zetor Tractor/Loader $15
14 Zetor Manure Spreader $15
IG463 Skoda 120 LS saloon car $6
IG464 Tatra T613 saloon car $6
IG465 Bugatti T35 (Yesteryear copy) $6

IG999 SELECTION PACK OF VETERAN AND VINTAGE CARS
Laurin & Klement, Tatra, Praga etc, different from above listed
   items, approx 1:43 scale, ea $5
Or pack of 10 different assorted $31

IMPERIAL DIECAST

Imperial Toy Corporation has its US headquarters in Los Angeles, California. Other international headquarters include Imperial Toy Canada Ltd, in Missisauga, Ontario, and Titan Toys International Ltd. in Great Britain. The distinction of these models may lie mostly in their colorful packages and regal logo. The actual models are made better than most generics, and sell for comparably more. Featured are pull-back action motorcycles with tiny "training wheels" to propel them, nicely made commercial jets, a series of helicopters that are also equipped with pull-back action, and various other somewhat attractive toys. While these models possess more charm than most generic toys, as with most generic diecast toys, value will likely remain at retail price of $1 – 2 each, partly due to the fact that the name is only on the package, not on the toy.

IMPY
(ALSO SEE CRESCENT, D.C.M.T., AND LONE STAR)

A British company called Lone Star produced a series of toys known as Impy toys. But the actual name on the base is "Lone Star Road-Master Impy Super Cars." No wonder everyone called them Impy. For more on Impy models, see Lone Star.

IMRA (OR IMRA)

Likely originating in southern California, these white metal models are likely prepainted kits, according to Harvey Goranson. As nearly as Goranson can recall, several Imra molds may have ended up as Precision Miniatures kits.

1975 Indy 500 Winner Jorgenson #48, 1:40	$275
Eagle Dan Gurney/Bobby Unser, 2-tone blue, 1:40	$275

INTERCAR (SEE AUTOPILEN)

INTEX (SEE ZEE TOYS)

IRWIN

Beginning with celluloid baby rattles and pinwheels, Irwin Cohn started the Irwin Company in 1922. Toy cars and trucks produced by Irwin were made of an assortment of materials. In 1973, Irwin was purchased by Miner Industries. New models are sold as Joal brand by Irwin and listed separately in this book under Joal heading as well as below.

Army Bus, plastic	$45
Barney Rubble Car, plastic, circa mid-Sixties	$30
Buick Convertible, plastic, 1948, 5"	$15
Chevrolet Panel Delivery, plastic, 6"	$15
Chevrolet Pickup Truck, plastic, 1952, 5¼"	$15
Dream Car Convertible, metal, 16"	$350
Ford Sunliner, plastic friction, 9"	$75
Ice Cream Truck, plastic	$80
Ives Horseless Carriage Runabout, plastic, 6½"	$4,000
Ives Steamer, cast iron, 19½"	$800
Jaguar Roadster, plastic, 6"	$55

Packard Sedan, plastic friction, 1952, 9"	$30
Pontiac Hardtop Coupe, plastic friction, 1952, 6"	$20
"Skipper" Convertible, plastic, 1962	$250
Steeraway Wonder Car, plastic	$160

JOAL CLASSICS COLLECTION BY IRWIN
(SEE ILLUSTRATIONS UNDER JOAL LISTING.)

50100 Jaguar E Cabriolet, British racing green with beige interior	$6
50107 Mercedes-Benz 300SL Cabriolet, black with red interior	$6
50109 Mercedes-Benz 230SL, white with black roof, red interior	$6
50111 Porsche Carrera 6 Deslizante, white with blue doors and hood	$6
50114 Ferrari 250 LeMans, red	$6
50125 Lamborghini Miura 6 P-400 Deslizante, yellow	$6

ITES

Ites is an obscure brand from Czechoslovakia of which more information would be greatly appreciated.

Mirage Racer, 1:32	$18

JACO

Listed below is a small assortment of 1:43 scale models of construction equipment of which little else is known.

531 Shovel	$11
532 Compactor	$11
534 Bulldozer	$11
535 Loader	$11
544 Road Roller	$11
733 Dozer/Ripper	$11
933 Compactor/Loader	$11

JANE FRANCIS TOYS

Jane Francis started making toys in 1942, during World War II. Her first toys were stuffed handmade gingham dogs, calico cats, and Jumbo the Elephant toys for a Pittsburgh hospital gift shop. When Gimbel's department store requested 12 dozen stuffed toys, Jane Francis Toys was begun. Her husband joined the operation towards the end of the war to introduce a line of crude diecast cars and trucks, among other items. In 1945, the first models reached the market. By 1949, the last diecast toys were produced. The Francis' daughter Jane Francis Vanyo continued her father's business, the A.W. Francis Company, in producing diecast lawn and garden accessories. As of 1993, the company was still in operation from its headquarters in Somerset, Pennsylvania.

This author found one Jane Francis toy buried in a backyard with only a vestige of its original beige paint left on it but with no rust or corrosion, and with axles and wheels missing. It has since been repainted in red. On the underside of this single-cast toy is clearly marked "Jane Francis." Value in this condition is only $1 – 4 at best, but in near mint original condition, wheels, axles, and paint intact, it would be worth around $20. Below is a list of the models produced from 1945 to 1949.

Gulf Box Truck with tin cargo cover, 5" $45
Pickup Truck, 5" $25
Pickup Truck, 5" $25
Pickup Truck, 6½" $45
Sedan, futuristic, 6½" $35
Sedan, futuristic with wind-up motor $45
Tow Truck, 5" $35

JA-RU

Jacksonville, Florida, is home base for Ja-Ru toys made in China. Several lines of toys appear to exist under the Ja-Ru brand. "Golden Wheels" are inexpensive toy cars and trucks made by Golden Wheel Die Casting of China for Ja-Ru. Golden Classics Ford Model T gift banks are so similar to Ertl banks that they can be easily mistaken for them at first glance. But closer inspection shows a few qualitative differences, most notably a plastic roof secured to the windshield by a crudely melted post, and the distinctive phrase "Coins Bank" in script on each model. These models are such a blatant attempt to capitalize on the popularity of Pepsi-Cola collectibles and Ertl coin banks that they even say gift bank on the box. The Model T tanker truck even declares "Collectable Models" right on the tank. Talk about obvious!

Still, considering the $12 price tag, they are comparably nice models to the more expensive $20 – 35 Ertl versions, and they do make attractive, affordable gifts. Ja-Ru has also recently produced some fairly attractive Matchbox-size models called "Real Wheels." Among the assortment are some fairly nice models of military vehicles labeled "Fighting Army" and some notable toy cars sold under the "Collectors" moniker. Removed from the brightly colored package, the models are rendered generic, with no markings on them to distinguish them from other such generic toys, except for some models which feature a number on the base and the words "Made In China." An exception is a stock car that looks like a Toyota Supra. The name on the bottom exposes it as a Yat Ming.

JA-RU GOLDEN WHEELS
Ford Model T Delivery Van, white with blue roof and fenders, "Drink Pepsi-Cola". . . . . $12 – 15
Ford Model T Tanker, white with red roof and fenders, "Pepsi-Cola". . . . . $12 – 15
Ford Model T Tanker, "Mountain Dew". . . . . $12 – 15
Tractor Trailer, 1:87, "Pepsi". . . . . $4 – 5
Tractor Trailer, 1:87, "Mountain Dew". . . . . $4 – 5
Tractor Trailer, 1:64, "Pepsi". . . . . $9 – 12
Tractor Trailer, 1:64, "Mountain Dew". . . . . $9 – 12
Diet Pepsi Tanker, white with red and blue accents, opaque silver-gray windows and base, 2½" . . . . $1 – 2

Pepsi Nissan Pathfinder, white with red and blue accents, opaque silver-gray windows, rally lights, and base, 2¼" . . . . . . $1 – 2

JA-RU REAL WHEELS
Army Jeep, No. 1608, army green with tan and dark green camouflage markings, 2¾" . . . . $1 – 2

Military Covered Truck, #1362, army green with tan and dark green camouflage, $1 – 2

Military Helicopter, army green with tan and dark green camouflage. . . . . $1 – 2

Military Tank, #1102, army green with tan and dark green camouflage, $1 – 2

Cadillac Seville, metallic blue with gold, silver and black stripe accents on sides, $1 – 2

Toyota Supra, white with red accents, "36," "yatming no.1036" on base . . . . $1 – 2
Audi Quattro, white with two-tone blue accents, "35" . . . $1 – 2
BMW, metallic gray to magenta with rally markings, #1029 . $1 – 2
F1 Racer, green, #1312 . . . . $1 – 2
F1 Racer, white, #1308 . . . . $1 – 2
F1 Racer, pale orange, #1311 . . . . $1 – 2

JE TOYS

Like so many inexpensive toys, Je Toys is a manufacturer of an assortment of generic toys that includes cars, motorcycles, airplanes, racers, etc. Quality and scale are not issues with these miniatures. They are strictly low-budget toys built for play. As collectibles, they are an oddity. In terms of collector value, they are worthless. Once removed from the vaguely identifiable packaging, they are rendered anonymous. Regardless of that fact, Je Toys have produced a cute set of miniature antique vehicles in roughly 1:43 scale called Classic Cars that sell for about $2 apiece.

JEMINI

Jemini models are white models made in England. Most recently, Jemini merged with Crossways Models of England. See Crossways for a list of current and recent models.

JEP (SEE JOUETS DE PARIS)

JET

One example from Jet Mechanics of Argentina is listed in *Schroeder's Collectible Toys*. Another Jet model is listed from an earlier Diecast Miniatures catalog.

Lamborghini Countach, red $35
1976 Ford Taunus, 1:64 . . . . $4

JNG

From an otherwise unknown brand comes a replica DeTomaso Pantera in 1:45 scale.

DeTomaso Pantera, lime green, 1:45 . . . . $18 – 30

JOAL

Juguetes Joal S.A. was originally based in Spain. But recently, Irwin Toy Limited of Toronto, Canada, purchased the rights to distribute Joal toys in North America. Models are typically 1:43 scale. Joal models are currently manufactured in Macau and marketed by Irwin. A recent release of a six car series called the Joal Classics Collection harkens back to the 60s when companies such as Matchbox, Corgi, and Dinky flourished. Their models then were detailed, accurate, and realistic, usually with opening doors, hoods, and trunks. Models possessed an ephemeral charm that is not often reproduced these days. But this collection succeeds in mimicking that appealing style. Gaps in numbering indicates there may be other models from which these six were selected.

CLASSICS COLLECTION BY IRWIN

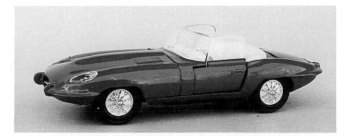

50100 Jaguar E Cabriolet, British racing green with beige interior, $6

50107 Mercedes-Benz 300SL Cabriolet, black w/red interior, $6

50109 Mercedes-Benz 230SL, white w/black roof, red interior, $6

50111 Porsche Carrera 6 Deslizante, white with blue doors and hood, $6

50114 Ferrari 250 LeMans, red, $6

50125 Lamborghini Miura 6 P-400 Deslizante, yellow, $6

HEAVY EQUIPMENT AND OTHER MODELS

100 Jaguar E Type Roadster, 1:43	$30
101 Simca 1000	$25
102 Renault R 8	$25
103 Seat 850 Coupe	$25
104 Renault R 10	$25
105 Alfa Romeo Giulia TZ1 Canguro	$25
106 Seat 124	$25
107 Mercedes-Benz 300SL	$25
108 Chevrolet Monza	$25
109 Mercedes-Benz 230SL Hardtop	$25
110 Mercedes-Benz 230SL Roadster	$25
111 Porsche Carrera 6	$25
112 Alfa Romeo Giulia 55	$25
113 Chaparral 2F	$25
114 Ferrari 250 Le Mans	$25
115 Iso Rivolta Coupe, 1:43	$25
116 Ferrari 612 Can-Am	$25
117 Mercedes Benz C-lll	$25
118 Adams Probe 16	$25
119 Ferrari 512S, 1:43	$35
120 Twin Mill	$25
121 Porsche 917K	$25
122 McLaren M80	$25
123 Fiat (Seat) 132 4-door Sedan, 1:43	$16
124 Mercedes 350SL Coupe, 1:43	$16
125 Lamborghini Miura Coupe, 1:43 (see 50125 above)	$16
126 Citroën SM	$25
127 Citroën CX Pallas	$25
128 Chrysler 150	$25
129 Ford Fiesta	$25
149 Volvo Coach, 240mm, 1:50	$18
151 Mercedes-Benz 230SL and Trailer	$25
152 Citroën CX Pallas and Trailer	$25
153 Citroën SM, Ford Fiesta and Trailer	$25
154 Wrecker and Ford Fiesta	$25
155 Chrysler 150, Ferrari Formula I and Trailer	$25
160 Akerman H-7C Digger, 160mm, 1:50	$16
161 JCB-930 Tough Terrain Forklift, 146mm, 1:35	$16
162 JCB-801 Mini Backhoe Excavator, 146mm, 1:35	$16
163 Volvo L-70 with Pallet Fork, 170mm, 1:50	$16
164 Volvo-70 with Snow Blade, 173mm, 1:50	$16
165 Volvo-70 with Handing Arm, 215mm, 1:50	$16
166 JCB 525-58 with Pallet Fork, 210mm, 1:35	$16
167 Volvo A-35 Cement Mixer, 245mm, 1:50	$19
168 PPM 530 ATT Crane, 1:50	$40
169 PPM Superstacker, 1:50	$34
170 Volvo A-35 Grapple Stacker, 260mm, 1:50	$22
171 Carmix Mixer, 161mm, 1:50	$16
172 Akerman H-25D Excavator, 210mm, 1:50	$22
173 Fire Engine, 215mm, 1:50	$24
174 CAT D5C Tractor, 79mm, 1:50	$14
175 JCB 4CX Sitemaster Backhoe Loader, 345mm, 1:35	$28
176 International Transport, 350mm, 1:50	$16
177 CAT 918F Wheel Loader, 265mm, 1:25	$30
178 Valmet 4-Wheel Tractor, 140mm, 1:35	$14
179 Valmet 8-Wheel Tractor, 140mm, 1:35	$16
180 Akerman EC620ME Digger, 250mm, 1:50	$24

181 Volvo L70CWheel Loader, 1:50	$16
182 Agusta Helicopter, 220mm	$14
183 Komatsu PC400 LC Excavator, 425mm, 1:32	$48
184 CAT IT18F Loader, 280mm, 1:25	$32
185 JCB 4CX Centermount Backhoe Loader, 345mm, 1:35	$30
186 Komatsu PC400 EX, 1:32	$58
187 BT Forklifts and Pallet Lift, 1:25	$24
188 BT RT1350SE Forklift	$16
189 Caterpillar 375 Excavator, 1:50	$24
191 Valmet Pulling Tractor, 1:35	$16
192 Massey Ferguson Skat 516 Load, 1:32	$16
200 Aveling Dump Truck, 1:43	$14
200 Leyland Dumper	$25
200 Leyland Dumper "Construccion"	$25
201 Taylor Crane Truck	$25
201 Taylor Crane Truck "Autopistas"	$25
202 Albion Cement Mixer, 1:43	$14
203 Massey Ferguson Tractor	$25
204 Farm Trailer	$12
205 Farm Pulverisator	$12
206 Massey Ferguson Tractor with Mechanical Shovel	$25
207 Pegaso Truck with Boat Motor	$25
208 Pegaso Tanker, "BUTANO"	$25
209 Pegaso Tanker, "CAMPSA"	$25
210 Bulldozer	$25
211 Pegaso Multibucket	$25
212 Pegaso Articulated Truck	$25
213 Caterpillar 935 Traxcavator	$25
213 CAT-955/L Track-Type Loader, 100mm, 1:50	$18

214 CAT-920 Wheel Loader, 123mm, 1:50, $16

215 CAT-V80F Lift Truck, 113mm, 1:25	$16
216 CAT-225 Hydraulic Excavator, 216mm, 1:43	$18
217 CAT-12-G Leveller/Road Grader, 168, 1:50	$18
218 Cat 825-B Compactor, 147mm, 1:43	$16
219 CAT 631-D Wheel Tractor Scraper, 204mm, 1:70	$18
220 CAT D-10 Chain Tractor, 150mm, 1:70	$18
221 Steam Roller, 114mm, 1:50	$12
222 CAT-631 Tilt Tractor, 173mm, 1:70	$16
223 CAT-773 Truck, 133mm, 1:70	$14
224 CAT-591 Pipelayer, 105mm, 1:50	$22
225 CAT Digging Crane, 260mm, 1:43	$20
226 CAT-518 Grapple Skidder, 193mm, 1:43	$16
227 Volvo BM L-160 Wheel Loader, 160mm, 1:50	$16

228 Euclid R-32 Dump Truck, 160mm, 1:50. . . . . $16
229 CAT "V" Snow Plough with Spreader, 175mm, 1:43. . . . . $16
230 Volvo BM 6300 Excavator Loader, 210mm, 1:50 . . . . $22
231 Volvo BM A-25 Articulated Dump Truck, 195mm, 1:50 . . . $16
232 Akerman EW200 Wheel Backloader/Excavator, 1:50 . . . . . $16
233 CAT Challenger 65 Tractor, 122mm, 1:50 . . . . $16
234 Volvo L-70 Wheel Loader, 148mm, 1:50 . . . . $16
235 Volvo L-70 Skidder, 160mm, 1:50 . . . . $16
236 Akerman Telescopic Crane, 205mm, 1:50 . . . . $18
237 Volvo BM L-160 High Lift, 212mm, 1:50 . . . . $19
238 Volvo BM A-35 Articulated Dumper, 216mm, 1:50. . . . . . $18
239 Michigan L-320 Wheel Loader, 217, 1:50. . . . . $19
240 New Holland TX-34 Combine Harvester, 227mm, 1:42 . . . $22
241 Volvo L-160 Compactor, 160mm, 1:50. . . . . $16
242 Euclid R-858 Dump Truck, 205mm, 1:50. . . . . $24
243 JCB 435 Track-Type Loader, 211mm, 1:35. . . . . $19
244 CAT CB-534 Compactor with Cab, 99mm, 1:50 . . . . $14
245 JCB 525-58 Telescopic Loader, 210mm, 1:35 . . . . $16
246 JCB 712 Dump Truck, 72mm, 1:35 . . . . $16
247 New Holland TX-34 Combine Harvester with Maice (Corn)
 Head, 254mm, 1:42 . . . . $22
248 CAT CB-534 Compactor, 99mm, 1:50 . . . . $14
249 Akerman H7C with Hydraulic Hammer, 160mm, 1:50 . . . . $16
250 Ebro 6100 Tractor, 117mm, 1:38. . . . . $16
251 Ebro 6100 Tractor and Trailer with Hay Bails, 255mm, 1:38. $24
252 Ebro 6100 Tractor with Sprayer, 260mm, 1:50 . . . . $14
253 CAT Challenger 65 with Disc Harrow, 230mm, 1:50 . . . . . $22
254 Valmet Tractor with Grapple Skidder Trailer, 363mm,
 1:35. . . . . $29
320 Heavy Duty Transporter with #216, 363mm $29
321 Heavy Duty Transporter with #220, 363mm $29
322 Heavy Duty Transporter with #229, 363mm $29
323 Heavy Duty Transporter with #225, 363mm $29
324 Heavy Duty Transporter with #227, 363mm $29
325 Heavy Duty Transporter with #237, 363mm $29
326 Heavy Duty Transporter with #182, 363mm $24
387 CAT IT18F Tool Carrier, 1:25 . . . . $39

JOHNNY LIGHTNINGS (ALSO SEE TOPPER TOYS)

Johnny Lightnings were originally produced by Topper Toys, owned by Henry Orenstein, from 1969 to 1971. But charges of business fraud forced Orenstein out of business. Twenty-three years later, Thomas E. Lowe, a businessman who remembers as a kid the toy cars that beat Hot Wheels on their own track, purchased the Johnny Lightnings license to reproduce several of the original designs in a commemorative series under the new company name of Playing Mantis. The series has proven itself so popular with collectors that ten color variations, limited to 10,000 each, have been issued during 1994, and indicated as series A through J.

For 1995, Playing Mantis has made a major departure from its original direction by creating all-new models called Muscle Machines, relying on the popularity of the brand name and the passion for American muscle cars. Each model/color variation is produced in limited quantities of 20,000 or less.

Johnny Lightnings really took off in 1996, with many new issues. Dragsters USA feature popular funny cars from the seventies, eighties, and nineties. Indy Race Cars and Pace Cars consist of a two-pack of one Indy winning race car and the corresponding pace car for that year. Wacky Winners are the brainchild of Tom Daniel, noted automotive designer with a flair for the bizarre.

Aside from all the regular production models, several promotional models were issued as well. By special order, private individuals, groups, and dealers had various models reproduced with special markings to designate them as promotionals for their business or organization. All are listed below following a chronology of the original Topper line.

JOHNNY LIGHTNINGS BY TOPPER, 1969 TO 1971

1969

Prices listed first are for mint condition out of package, then for models in original blister pack.

Custom GTO. $125 − 150; $250
Custom El Camino. . . . . $125 − 150; $250
Custom T-Bird. . . . . $80 − 100; $150
Custom Toronado . . . . $80 − 100; $175
Custom Eldorado. $60 − 80; $125
Custom Mako Shark, doors open . . . . $75 − 100; $125
Custom Mako Shark, doors don't open. . . . . . . $25 − 30; $50
Custom XKE, doors open . . . . $75 − 100; $125
Custom XKE, doors don't open . . . . $25 − 30; $50
Custom Ferrari, doors open . . . . $90 − 110; $135
Custom Ferrari, doors don't open. . . . . $25 − 30; $50
Custom Turbine, painted interior . . . . $75 − 100; $125
Custom Turbine, unpainted interior . . . . $15 − 20; $30
Custom Dragster . . . . $15 − 25; $35
Custom '32 Ford . . . . $25 − 30; $40

1970

Nucleon . . . . $30 − 40; $60
Vicious Vette. . . . . $30 − 35; $45
Frantic Ferrari . . . . $15 − 20; $30
Jumpin Jag . . . . $20 − 25; $35
Sand Stormer . . . . $15 − 20; $30
Vulture . . . . $40 − 50; $70
Sling Shot . . . . $25 − 30; $45
Flame Out. . . . . $35 − 40; $55
TNT . . . . $25 − 30; $40
Al Unser Indy Special . . . . $30 − 35; $65
A.J. Foyt Indy Special . . . . $30 − 35; $65
Parnelli Jones Indy Special. . . . . $30 − 35; $65
Leapin Limo . . . . $35 − 40; $75
Double Trouble. . . . . $35 − 40; $75
Triple Threat . . . . $20 − 30; $40
Bug Bomb . . . . $25 − 35; $45
Condor . . . . $70 − 85; $120
Movin Van . . . . $15 − 25; $35
Mad Maverick . . . . $20 − 30; $45
Wasp . . . . $35 − 45; $65
Baja . . . . $35 − 45; $70
Whistler . . . . $45 − 55; $100
Custom Spoiler . . . . $15 − 25; $35
Smuggler . . . . $20 − 30; $40
Stiletto . . . . $10 − 20; $35

1970 Jet Powered Cars

Flying Needle	$20 – 30; $40
Wedge	$20 – 30; $40
Screamer	$20 – 25; $35
Glasser	$25 – 35; $45
Monster	$15 – 20; $30
Bubble	$20 – 25; $35

1971 Custom Cars

Wild Winner	$40 – 50; $90
Pipe Dream	$40 – 50; $90
Hairy Hauler	$40 – 50; $90
Big Rig	$40 – 50; $90
Twin Blaster	$40 – 50; $90

Prototypes (cars planned but never put into production)

Custom Mustang	$2,000 – 3,000
Custom Camaro	$2,000 – 3,000
Custom Charger	$2,000 – 3,000
Custom Continental	$2,000 – 3,000

Johnny Lightning Commemoratives by Playing Mantis, 1994

Each model has been produced in ten different color variations and designated Series A through J. Polished metal-flake colors include cherry red, emerald green, slate blue, light purple, and chocolate, while high-gloss enamel colors are black, yellow, turquoise, and hot pink. Aside from the regular issues listed below, exclusive sets were issued by FAO Schwarz in red, gold, silver, or blue chrome colors.

103 Custom XKE, 1994, $3 – 5 ($10 – 12 for FAO Schwarz version)

104 '32 Roadster, 1994, $3 – 5 ($10 – 12 for FAO Schwarz version)

101 Custom El Camino, 1994, $3 – 5 ($10 – 12 for FAO Schwarz version)

105 Bug Bomb, 1994, $3 – 5 ($10 – 12 for FAO Schwarz version)

102 Custom GTO, 1994, $3 – 5 ($10 – 12 for FAO Schwarz version)

106 Movin' Van, 1994 . . $3 – 5 ($10 – 12 for FAO Schwarz version)
107 Vicious Vette, 1994. $3 – 5 ($10 – 12 for FAO Schwarz version)

108 The Wasp, 1994 . . $3 – 5 ($10 – 12 for FAO Schwarz version)

Johnny Lightning Commemoratives Round 2 by Playing Mantis, 1995

109 Custom Continental, 1995	$3 – 5
110 Custom Toronado, 1995	$3 – 5
111 Custom Thunderbird, 1995	$3 – 5
112 Custom Mustang, 1995	$5 – 8
113 Custom Spoiler, 1995	$3 – 5
114 Custom Mako Shark, 1995	$3 – 5
115 Custom Turbine, 1995	$3 – 5
116 Triple Threat, 1995	$3 – 5
117 Nucleon, 1995	$3 – 5
118 T.N.T., 1995	$3 – 5

Johnny Lightning Muscle Cars by Playing Mantis, 1995

According to the package, "each car is painted in several of these 16 famous Musclepaint™ colors mixed from GM,

Ford & Chrysler's original paint formulas!" Grabber Blue, Plum Crazy, Daytona Yellow, Sublime, Gold Rush, Vitamin-C Orange, Blue Fire, Starlight Black, Moulin Rouge, Glacier Blue, Rallye Green, Tor-Red, Quicksilver, Aspen Green, Cameo White, Champagne.

'70 Superbird. . . . . $4 – 5
'71 Hemi 'Cuda . . . . $4 – 5
'70 Boss 302 . . . . $4 – 5
'70 Super Bee . . . . $4 – 5
'69 GTO "The Judge" . . . . $4 – 5

'70 Chevelle SS, $4 – 5

'69 Cougar Eliminator, $4 – 5

'69 Olds 442, $4 – 5

'72 Nova SS, $4 – 5

'65 GTO Ragtop. . . . . $4 – 5

JOHNNY LIGHTNING MUSCLE CARS SERIES 2 BY PLAYING MANTIS, 1996 – 97

So popular was this series that Tom Lowe decided to continue it with all new castings and a larger number of colors.

'66 Chevrolet Malibu . . . . $3 – 4
'68 Ford Shelby GT-500 Mustang . . . . $3 – 4
'68 Dodge Charger. . . . . $3 – 4
'69 Pontiac Firebird . . . . $3 – 4
'69 Plymouth Roadrunner. $3 – 4
'70 Dodge Challenger. . . . . $3 – 4
'70 Buick GSX . . . . $3 – 4
'72 AMC Javelin AMX. . . . . $3 – 4

JOHNNY LIGHTNING INDY 500 CHAMPIONS AND PACE CARS BY PLAYING MANTIS, 1996

Two-packs include the winning Indianapolis 500 racer for the selected year, along with the pace car for that race.

1969 Mario Andretti and 1969 Chevy Camaro . . . . $5 – 6
1970 Al Unser and 1970 Olds 442. . . . . $5 – 6
1974 Johnny Rutherford and 1974 Hurst Olds . . . . $5 – 6
1975 Bobby Unser and 1975 Buick Century . . . . $5 – 6
1977 A. J. Foyt and 1977 Olds Delta 88. . . . . $5 – 6
1978 Al Unser and 1978 Chevy Corvette . . . . $5 – 6
1979 Rick Mears and 1979 Ford Mustang. . . . . $5 – 6
1992 Al Unser Jr. and 1992 Cadillac Allante. . . . . $5 – 6

JOHNNY LIGHTNING DRAGSTERS U.S.A. BY PLAYING MANTIS, 1996

Commemorating the wildest funny cars on the dragstrip are these 1:64 scale replicas. Each one is issued in its original color plus several other color combinations.

Shirley Shahan's '69 Drag-On Lady . . . . $3 – 4
Roland Leong's '71 Hawaiian . . . . $3 – 4
Raymond Beadle's '71 Blue Max. . . . . $3 – 4
Roger Lindamood's '72 Color Me Gone . . . . $3 – 4
Al Bergler's '71 Motown Shaker . . . . $3 – 4
Pat Minick's '72 Chi-Town Hustler . . . . $3 – 4
Ed McCulloch's '71 Revellution. . . . . $3 – 4
Richard Earle's '58 Christine . . . . $3 – 4
Tony Foti's '92 LAPD . . . . $3 – 4
Norm Wizner's '55 Jukebox . . . . $3 – 4
Ronnie Sox's '71 Sox & Martin . . . . $3 – 4

JOHNNY LIGHTNING DRAGSTERS U.S.A. ROUND 2 BY PLAYING MANTIS, 1997

Why I've never seen or heard of these models until August 1997 is beyond me. They are modern funny cars offered through Full Grid Racing & Diecast, and possibly nowhere else. 20,000 of each model and color variation are produced.

Pioneer. $5
Rug Doctor $5
Otter Pops. $5
Sentry Gauges $5
Kendall $5
Burnouts. $5
Mooneyes $5
Western Auto $5
Fast Orange. $5

JOHNNY LIGHTNING DRAGSTERS U.S.A. ROUND 3 BY PLAYING MANTIS, 1997

More models commemorating the wildest funny cars on

dragstrip are these 1:64 scale replicas. Each one is issued in its original color plus several other color combinations.

Jungle Jim Liberman. . . . . $3 – 4
Texas Gene Snow's Snowman . . . . $3 – 4
Wild Willy Borsch's Wildman . . . . $3 – 4
Big Daddy Don Garlits. . . . . $3 – 4
Ramchargers . . . . $3 – 4
Barry Setzer. . . . . $3 – 4
Don Schumacher's Wonder Wagon. . . . . $3 – 4
Mr. Norm's Super Charger . . . . $3 – 4
Bob Banning Dodge . . . . $3 – 4
Trojan Horse . . . . $3 – 4
White Lightning Funny Car. $8 – 12

JOHNNY LIGHTNING WACKY WINNERS BY PLAYING MANTIS, 1996
Tom Daniel has designed some crazy cars for Monogram Model Company, but this is his first venture into diecast miniatures. Some of his wackiest creations are captured in these Johnny Lightning replicas from Playing Mantis.

T'rantula, $3 – 4

Cherry Bomb, $3 – 4

Bad Medicine, $3 – 4

Tijuana Taxi, $3 – 4

Bad News, $3 – 4

Root Beer Wagon, $3 – 4

Badman, $3 – 4

Garbage Truck, $3 – 4

Draggin' Dragon, $3 – 4

Trouble Maker, $3 – 4

JOHNNY LIGHTNING CLASSIC CUSTOM CORVETTES
BY PLAYING MANTIS, 1997

This series documents some of the classic prototypes devised by Chevrolet Corvette designers.

Sting Ray III	$6 – 8
Corvette Indy	$6 – 8
Aerovette	$6 – 8
1954 Nomad	$6 – 8
1965 Mako Shark	$6 – 8
1967 Coupe 427	$6 – 8
1962 Roadster	$6 – 8
1957 Roadster	$6 – 8

1995 ZR-1	$6 – 8
1982 T-Top	$6 – 8

JOHNNY LIGHTNING HOLIDAY DRAGSTERS BY PLAYING MANTIS, 1996

Series A:

Nitro Santa, red	$10 – 15
Roarin' Rudolph, silver	$10 – 15

Series B:

Nitro Santa, gold	$10 – 15
Roarin' Rudolph, green	$10 – 15

JOHNNY LIGHTNING DRAGSTERS USA SUMMERFEST BY PLAYING MANTIS, 1997

Special "stars & stripes" decorative accents set these models apart from the usual "Dragsters" line-up. Two models in two color versions are issued as a four-car set for around $25. Only 15,000 sets produced.

JOHNNY LIGHTNING DRAGSTERS USA PLATINUM ISSUE BY PLAYING MANTIS, 1997

Not available at any mass market stores, these dragsters consist of all diecast bodies, Cragar rims, Goodyear rubber tires, and more. Only 10,000 produced.

Pabst Blue Ribbon	$12 – 15
Pure Hell	$12 – 15

JOHNNY LIGHTNING FRIGHTNING LIGHTNING BY PLAYING MANTIS, 1996

Scarier and scarier is the Johnny Lightning Frightning Lightning series featuring some bizarre inventions from some of this planet's most innovative custom car designers. Tom Daniel's influence is seen in this series that includes the famous car from *Ghostbusters* fame and the possessed homicidal Plymouth named Christine from the horror thriller of the same name.

Haulin Hearse	$4 – 6
Elvira Macabre Mobile	$4 – 6
Boothill Express	$4 – 6
Vampire Van	$4 – 6
The Mysterion	$4 – 6
Christine	$4 – 6
Ghostbusters Ecto-1A	$4 – 6

JOHNNY LIGHTNING "SPEED RACER" SERIES BY PLAYING MANTIS, 1997

Commemorating the cult classic cartoon, Playing Mantis will issue several models from the Japanese animated TV series introduced to America in 1967. Four 1:64 scale models will be available in the original colors as sets for $16 or in single packs with various colors for $4 each. Sets will include:

1. The Mach 5 (Speed Racer's car)
2. Racer X's (Speed's long-lost brother, Rex Racer)
3. The "Fastest Car" (the GR-X)
4. The "Assassin Car"

JOHNNY LIGHTNING HOT RODS BY PLAYING MANTIS, 1997

Scheduled for September 1997 are these 1:64 scale diecast replicas of real street rods. Production of 15,000 or less is guaranteed for each model. The list of models below is not complete, as Playing Mantis is still finalizing production as this goes to print. Ten models are planned.

'29 Crew Cab	$4 – 5
Rumblur	$4 – 5
Bumongous	$4 – 5
Frankenstude	$4 – 5
Tom Hammond's '69 Pro Street Chevelle	$4 – 5

Mike Lloyd's '72 Goin' Goat GTO . . . . $4 – 5
Pro Street Camaro . . . . $4 – 5
'62 Bad Bird T-Bird . . . . $4 – 5
Beastmobile. . . . . $4 – 5
Flathead Flyer . . . . $4 – 5

SPEED REBELS BY PLAYING MANTIS, 1997

"Ten great cars in a brand new scale" is how Fred Blood of Full Grid describes these models of classic custom American cars, although just what scale that is he doesn't say.

Vicious Villain . . . . $2 – 3
Street Freak . . . . $2 – 3
Speed King . . . . $2 – 3
Dominator. . . . . $2 – 3
Rat Attack . . . . $2 – 3
Wing Thing . . . . $2 – 3
Big Boss . . . . $2 – 3
Goat Buster . . . . $2 – 3
Alley Cat . . . . $2 – 3
Spoiler. . . . . $2 – 3

JOHNNY LIGHTNING EXCLUSIVE SETS BY PLAYING MANTIS, 1996

Dragsters USA at Service Merchandise and Hills, limited edition of 4800 each packaged in display box . . . . $15 – 20 each
VW Vans at Venture, 4,800 each, two-tone black and red, or two-tone sky blue and antique white . . . . $20 – 25 each
'56 Chevys at Ames, 4,800 each, two-tone Nassau blue & harbour blue, or two-tone India ivory & matador red. . . $20 – 25 each

JOHNNY LIGHTNING "MEMBERS ONLY" CARS BY PLAYING MANTIS

Subscribers to the *NewsFlash* newsletter have an opportunity to purchase exclusive variations of Johnny Lightning models not offered anywhere else. Many are already sold out and only available from second market dealers. Values are rising steadily on these very limited edition models.

1956 Chevrolet BelAir (sold out) . . . . $25 – 30
1965 Dodge A-100 Pickup (sold out). . . . . $25 – 30
1960s Volkswagen Van (sold out) . . . . $25 – 30
1996 White Lightnings (set of 10) (sold out) . . . . $40 – 50
1996 Toy Fair Car, "Ride the Storm" (only 800 made, sold out) . $75 – 100
Plymouth Prowler. . . . . $10 – 12
1965 Dodge A-100 Little Red Wagon . . . . $15 – 20
1998 Volkswagen Concept One . . . . $10 – 12
Volkswagen "Thing" Kubelwagen . . . . $10 – 12
1933 Hot Rod Willy's . . . . $10 – 12

JOHNNY LIGHTNING PROMOTIONAL MODELS BY PLAYING MANTIS

Several businesses and dealers have contracted with Playing Mantis to issue special promotional models especially made for them. Below are listed the models with color variation, production quantity, markings, who the promoter is, and their phone number to reach them.

1956 Chevy BelAir
    v.1 Hot Pink, 5,000 made, "Sweet Little Rock n Roller," Mike Stead, 1-818-558-8099 . . . . $25 – 40
    v.2 Seafoam, 5,000 made, car hop picture, Mike Stead, 1-818-558-8099 . . . . $25 – 40
    v.3 Cherry Red, 5,000 made, "Steadly Quickwheels," Mike Stead, 1-818-558-8099 . . . . $25 – 40
Dodge A-100 Pickup
    v.1 Pearl White, 5,000 made, blue flames with "Pyromaniac," Bob Goforth, 1-510-889-6676 . . . . $25 – 40

    v.2 Purple, 5,000 made, "Purple Hazed Express," Mike Stead, 1-818-558-8099 . . . . $25 – 40
    v.3 Black, 5,000 made, "Bad to the Bone," Mike Stead, 1-818-558-8099 . . . . $25 – 40
    v.4 Red with Astroblades wheels, 10,000 made, Little Red Wagon, Bill "Maverick" Golden . . . . $20 – 30
    v.5 Red with Cragar SS wheels, 10,000 made, Little Red Wagon, Playing Mantis . . . . $20 – 30
1954 Sedan Delivery
    v.1 Cherry Red, 5,000 made, Lane Automotive Logo, Lane Automotive, 1-800-772-2682 . . . . $25 – 40
    v.2 Gold Rush and Purple, 2,500 made, "Johnny Lightning," Eastwood Company, 1-800-343-9353; and
    v.3 Quick Silver and Purple, 2,500 made, "Johnny Lightning," Eastwood Company, 1-800-343-9353, both packaged with Lionel train . . . . $90 – 120
    v.4 Cherry Red, 5,000 made, "Steadly's Toy Fair '96," Steadly Quickwheels, 1-818-558-8099 . . . . $40 – 50
1987 Buick Grand National
    v.1 Black with Astroblades wheels, 5,000 made, no markings, Toy Time, 1-508-827-5261 . . . . $40 – 50
    v.2 Black with Cragar SS wheels, 5,000 made, no markings, Toy Time, 1-508-827-5261 . . . . $40 – 50
Custom XKE
    v.1 Cherry red, 3,500 made, Steadly Quickwheels, 1-818-558-8099 . . . . $40 – 50

JOHNNY LIGHTNING SIZZLERS BY PLAYING MANTIS, 1996 – 97

The original Sizzlers by Mattel represented the first commercial application of nickel cadmium (NiCad) rechargeable batteries. Now, since Mattel has abandoned the Sizzlers name, it is currently owned by the Centuri/Estes model rocket company. Playing Mantis has negotiated a licensing contract with Centuri/Estes for the exclusive right to market toy cars using the their trademark. The first of the new Sizzlers from Playing Mantis showed up in Wal-Mart on December 1, 1996. As with most Johnny Lightnings, Sizzlers are issued in at least eight color variations each.

'68 Racing Camaro. . . . . $8 – 10
Trans Am Firebird . . . . $8 – 10
'71 Hemi 'Cuda . . . . $8 – 10
Camaro Highway Patrol . . . . $8 – 10
Viper GTS . . . . $8 – 10
Sting Ray III . . . . $8 – 10
Whistler Mustang. . . . . $8 – 10
Rain-X Camaro . . . . $8 – 10

For more information on Johnny Lightnings and how to receive the quarterly *NewsFlash* newsletter, contact Playing Mantis, PO Box 3688 3600 McGill Street, Suite 300, South Bend IN 46619-3688. 1-800-MANTIS-8.

JOLLY ROGER

Jolly Roger diecast toys are made in England. The line includes a few Gasquy reissues.

JOUEF (ALSO SEE UNIVERSAL HOBBIES LTD., INC.)

Until recently, the head office for Jouef was in Champagnole, France, with US distribution based in Mequon, Wis-

consin. Since Jouef's bankruptcy in 1996, models are now being produced by Universal Hobbies Ltd., Inc. The primary source for Jouef models is Auto Imagination Inc., 6841 N. Rochester Rd., Suite 200, Rochester Hills MI 48306 USA. Plastic models were once the predominant Jouef product, but recently the company has produced an exceptional assortment of diecast models in 1:18, 1:24, and 1:43 scale. Dubbed Jouef Evolution, named after their flagship model Ferrari, the models represented are high-quality replicas for a reasonable price.

1:18 SCALE
3001 Ferrari GTO Evoluzione $20

3002 Ferrari 250 GTO 64, $20

3005 Ferrari 330 P4 Spyder. $20
3008 Ford GT 40, #6 Le Mans Winner, 1969 . . . . $20
3012 Ferrari 250 GT SWB, Le Mans, 1961 . . . . $20
3016 Ferrari 250 GTO, #27 Le Mans, 1964. . . . . $19
3017 Ferrari 330 P4 Coupe B, #21 Le Mans, 1967. . . . . $19
3018 Ferrari 412 P, #23 Le Mans, 1967 (limited edition) $30
3019 Ford GT 40 Mk II, #21 Le Mans Winner, 1966 . . . . $20
3021 Ford Mk II Street Version $20
3022 Ferrari 250 GT SWB, 1961, red $20
3023 Ferrari 250 GT SWB, 1961, yellow $19
3024 Ferrari 412 P, #25 "N.A.R.T." Le Mans, 1967. . . . . $20
3029 Ferrari 330 P4 Coupe $19
3030 Ferrari 330 P4 Coupe, #24 Le Mans, 1967 . . . . $19
3031 Ferrari 330 P4 Spyder, Targa Florio, 1976 . . . . $19
3101 Ford Mustang 350 GT, 1965 . . . . $20
3108 Ford Mustang Cobra Convertible, 1994 Indy Pace Car, red. $25
3110 Ford Mustang GT Convertible, 1994, red, teal, or yellow . $25
3111 Ford Mustang GT Coupe, 1994, red, teal, or yellow. $25
3119 Ford Mustang Cobra Coupe, 1994, Rio red, white, or black. $25
3201 Porsche 911 RS 2.7 L, 1973, white/red. $19
3203 Porsche 911 RS 2.7 L, 1973, yellow/black $19
3204 Porsche 911 RS 2.7 L, 1973, black/red. $19
3205 Porsche 911 S 2.4, 1973, red. $19
3301 Alfa Romeo Spyder $20
3302 Alfa Romeo Spyder with hard top. $19
3303 Alfa Romeo Spyder with soft top $20
3304 Alfa Romeo Spyder, open top. $19
3501 Nissan 300 ZX, red. $20
3502 Honda NS-X, gray $20
3503 Nissan 300 SX, gray $20
3504 Nissan 300 SX, yellow $20

1:24 SCALE
3003 Ferrari 250 GTO 64 . . . . $15
3007 Ford GT 40 . . . . $15

3027 Ferrari 330 P 4 Spyder $20
3028 Ferrari 250 GTO, #25 Le Mans 1964 . . . . $20

1:43 SCALE
3000 Ferrari GTO Evoluzione $12
3004 Ferrari 250 GTO 64 . . . . $12
3006 Ford GT 40 . . . . $12
3009 Ferrari 330 P4 . . . . $12
3011 Ferrari 250 GT SWB, 1961 . . . . $12
3025 Ferrari 330 P 4, #2 Le Mans Winner, 1966 . . . . $12
3026 Ford GT 40 Mk II, #2 Le Mans Winner, 1966 . . . . $12
3027 3202 Porsche 911 RS 2.7 L 73 . . . . $12

JOUETS DE PARIS (JEP)
The Societe Industrielle de Ferblanterie was founded in 1899. In 1928, the name Jouets de Paris was adopted, then later changed to Jouets en Paris (abbreviated J.E.P.), until 1965 when the company went out of business. A variety of models and materials make up this eclectic collection of toys from France, with a predominance of tinplate models. *The Golden Age of Automotive Toys 1925 – 1941* by Ken Hutchison and Greg Johnson showcases an exquisite assortment of rare tin-plate JEPs in 1:11 and 1:16 scale valued at $1,500 – 10,000.

Delage Limousine, 13½", circa 1929 . . . . $2,000
"Madeline-Bastille" Autobus, 10¼", circa 1928. . . . . $2,000
Peugeot, 1:43, 1958 plastic body, diecast chassis . . . . . $150 – 200
Citroën DS19, 1:43, 1958 plastic body, diecast chassis. . $150 – 200
Simca Versailles, 1:43. 1958 plastic body, diecast chassis. $150 – 200
Panhard Dyna, 1:43, 1958 plastic body, diecast chassis . $150 – 200
Renault Dauphine, 1:43, 1958 plastic body, diecast chassis . $150 – 200
Renault Town Car 40HP President of the Republic, tin plate, 1:11 scale, 17" . . . . $6,000 – 10,000

JOUSTRA
The resemblance of Joustra models of France to early Gama trucks indicates that Joustra may have manufactured these models under license from Gama, since most Joustra toys are tin windups.

Meiller Excavator Truck, 6¼" $40
Meiller Dump Truck, 4⅜". $40

J.R.D
From 1935 to 1962, J.R.D produced toys from Montreuil, France. Beginning in 1958, J.R.D. started marketing diecast models. Prior to that time, they were made of plaster and flour. When J.R.D. failed in 1962, C.I.J. purchased the dies and packaging, and marketed them as their own, sometimes by placing a simple label over the previous brand name on the package. Their diecast assortment is listed below.

106 Citroën 1200 KG Police Van, 1:45, 1962 . . . . $75
107 Citroën 1200 KG Red Cross Van, 1:45, 1958 . . . . $80
108 Citroën 2CV EDF Van, 1:45, 1958 . . . . $75
109 Citroën 2CV Fire Van, 1:45, 1958 . . . . $85
110 Citroën 2CV Sedan, 1:45, 1958 . . . . $75
111 Citroën 2CV Van, 1:45, 1958. $65
112 Citroën 11CV Sedan, 1:45, 1958 . . . . $80
113 Citroën 1200 KG Van "Esso," 1:45, 1958 . . . . $90
114 Citroën P55 Covered Truck, 1:45, 1958 . . . . $65

115 Citroën P55 Army Truck & Trailer, 1:45, 1958 . . . . $80
116 Citroën DS19 Sedan, 1:45, 1958 . . . . $70
117 Citroën 2CV Road Service Van, 1:45, 1958 . . . . $80
118 Citroën 2CV "Air France" Van, 1:45, 1958 . . . . $80
120 Berliet Semi-Trailer "Kronenbourg," 1:45, 1958 . . . . . $160
121 Berliet Semi-Trailer Tanker "Total," 1:45, 1958. . . . . . $150
122 Unic Tank Truck "Antar," 1:45, 1958 . . . . $130
123 Unic Cab, Trailer & Railroad Car, 1:45, 1958 . . . . $180
124 Unic Izoard Circus Train, 1:45, 1958 . . . . $180
125 Berliet Weitz Crane Truck, 1:45, 1959 . . . . $125
126 Unic Van "Hafa," 1:45, 1959 . . . . $160
127 Unic Van "Transports Internationaux," 1:45, 1959 . . . . . $160
128 Unic Milk Tank Truck, 1:45, 1959. . . . . $150
129 Fruehauf Truck Trailer, 1:45, 1959 . . . . $100
130 Unic Liquid Transporter, 1:45, 1960 . . . . $130
131 Berliet Garbage Truck, 1:45, 1960. . . . . $130
132 Berliet Semi-Trailer "Antargaz," 1:45, 1961. . . . . $150
133 Berliet Fire Truck, 1:45, 1961 . . . . $160
134 Berliet Bottle Truck, 1:45, 1962 . . . . $150
151 Peugeot 404 Sedan, 1:45, 1962 . . . . $60
152 Citroën DS19 Cabriolet, 1:45, 1962 . . . . $60
153 Mercedes-Benz 220S Sedan, 1:45, 1962 . . . . $60
154 Citroën Ami 6, 1:45, 1962. . . . . $60
155 Simca 1000 Sedan, 1:45, 1962. . . . . $60

J.R.D. 1980s Reissues from C.I.J.

111 Citroën DS19, previously 116 . . . . $20
112 Citroën DS19 Convertible, previously 152 . . . . $20
211 Citroën 2CV Sedan, previously 110 . . . . $20
221 Citroën 2CV Fire Van, previously 109 . . . . $20
223 Citroën 2CV Van, previously 111 . . . . $20
301 Citroën HY Van, previously 113 . . . . $20
401 Citroën 11CV Sedan, previously 112 . . . . $20

JRI (see Road Champs)

JTE

A single model has been identified from JTE. Harvey Goranson reports that John Day produced an Inaltera, among hundreds of other early crude white metal kits. There may be a connection.

1978 Inaltera Team, blue, 1:43 . . . . $18

Juguinsa

Juguinsa models are made in Venezuela.

Monteverdi Coupe, 1:43 . . . . $18
Fiat 124 Coupe, 1:43 . . . . $18
AMC Javelin 343 Coupe, 1:43 . . . . $18

Jurgens

Jurgens models are hand-built 1:43 scale models.

1937 Packard Wagon $65
1940 Dodge Wagon $65
1948 Chrysler Town & Country Convertible $65
1950 Buick Wagon. $65

K & M

K & M Planning Co., Ltd., of Japan is known to have issued just one model, a 1979 Dome-O RL LeMans entry,

according to Harvey Goranson, who attended LeMans in 1981 and witnessed a single such car sponsored by Amada. ("The team had cool samurai shirts!")

1979 Hayashi Dome-O Exotic Car, white with orange and black stickers, sponsored by Roland, 1:43 . . . . $38

K & R

K & R represents 1:43 scale white metal kits and hand-built models, mostly of British sports cars. Harvey Goranson reports that they have been around since the late seventies to early eighties, and may have been at one time connected with Abington Classics. No representative models are known.

K-Line

Primarily known for their electric trains, K-Line also produces a series of HO gauge (1:87 scale) semi tractor/trailers in various liveries, intended as accessories for HO gauge train sets. Here is an assortment of models offered by K-Line Electric Trains, Inc., Chapel Hill, North Carolina.

K-665603TT Ringling Bros. and Barnum & Bailey Circus Tractor Trailer $30
K-666703TT Diet Coke Tractor Trailer with railroad flat car . . . $30
K-811201TT Hershey's "Take a Bite" $30
K-811202TT Hershey's "The Great American Chocolate Bar" . . $30
K-811203TT Hershey's "Life is Sweet!" $30
K-811204TT Hershey's "First Love" $30
K-813301TT Ferrara Nougat Candy Tractor Trailer. $30
K-8201 K-Line Electric Trains Vintage Delivery Truck Bank . . . $30
K-820202 Special Addition Vintage Truck Bank (Boy) $30
K-820301 Father's Day Bank. $30
K-820302 Valentine's Gift Bank. $30
K-820801 Special Addition Vintage Truck Bank (Girl) $30
K-82601 K-Line Oil Company Vintage Tanker $30
K-826101 Happy Birthday Gift Bank $30

Kado

Three 1:43 scale Kado models of Japan (not to be confused with Kato, also of Japan) are offered.

Hayashi Dome-O Exotic Car. $38
Porsche 930 Coupe $38
1957 Opel Rekord (tin) $38

Kansas Toy & Novelty Company

Kansas Toy & Novelty Company started in 1923 when Arthur Haynes, an auto mechanic, began making toys out of his Clifton, Kansas, shed.

Army Tank #74, 2¼" $50
Austin Bantam Sedanette #58, 2¼" $35

Bearcat Racer #26, 4" $75
Bearcat Racer #33, 3" $50
Buick Roadster with rumble seat #54, 2⅜" $20
Buick Roadster with no trunk #54, 2¼" $35
Case Steam Tractor #25, 3" $70
Chevrolet Sedan, 2⅞" $30
Chevrolet Sedan, 2¼" $40
Chrysler Convertible Coupe #8, rear mount spare, 3⅛" $40
Chrysler Convertible Coupe #8, no rear mount spare, 3⅛" . . . $60
Chrysler Convertible Coupe, 5" $75
Chrysler Roadster #14, 3⅛" $35
Chrysler Roadster, no number, 3⅛" $50
Convertible Coupe, 2⅞" $60
Convertible Coupe #35, 2¼" $50
Coupe, 3⅛" $60
Dump Truck #42, 3½" $70
Fageol Overland Bus #9, 3½" $75
Fageol Overland bus, no number, 3½" $60
Farm Dirt Scraper #65, 3⅝" $50
Farm Dirt Tumble #64, 4" $40
Farm Disc Harrow #62, 4" $70
Farm Planter #61, 4" $70
Farm Plough #63, 4" $60
Farm Tractor #17, 2⅞" $50
Farm Tractor, no number, 2⅝" $60
Fire Engine #70, 2¼" $75
Ford Pickup Truck #51, 2¾" $50
Ford Stake Truck Semi & Trailer #55, 4" $65
Fordson Farm Tractor #57, 1¾" $25
Golden Arrow Record Car Racer #46, 2⅞" $25
Indy Racer #10, 3⅛" $50
John Deere Model D Large Farm Tractor, no number, 4⅞" . . . $75
Large Lady Racer with driver, 6" $60
Midget Racer with no driver, 3" $40
Midget Racer with driver, 3" $80
Midget Racer #31, 2⅛" $20
Midget Racer #67, 1½" $90
Pickwick 1928 COE Nite Coach Tour Bus #49, 2⅜" $60
Pickwick COE Tour Bus #59, 3⅜" $50
Racer, 1" $35
Railroad Box Car #38, 3¼" $40
Railroad Caboose #40, "KT&N RR," 2¾" $60
Railroad Livestock Car #41, "KT&N RR" $60
Railroad Locomotive Tender #36, 4⅜" $15
Railroad Pullman Car #37, 3½" $40
Railroad Tank Car #39, "KT&N RR," 3⅛" $60
Sedan Limousine, 3⅜" $60
Sedan #60, 3½" $45
Separator-Thresher #27, 3" $70
Separator-Thresher #72, 2" $50
Steam Road Roller #43, 3¼" $20
Steam Tractor #71, 2½" $20
Three-Wheel Coupe #66, 3½" $60
Truck #20, 3⅛" $30
Warehouse Tractor #48, 3" $35

KAWADA

Kawada is one of those brands mentioned by collector Henry McFarland inquiring via e-mail in February 1997. This is the first I've heard of this brand from Japan.

KAZAN

Only since the fall of the Iron Curtain have we in the USA discovered such a gold mine of diecast toys from the former Soviet Union. Kazan models are named after the town in which they were produced. Started in 1979, Kazan's main focus was on the many variations of the Kamaz truck introduced in 1978. The following list offers the various versions.

43105 Military Truck 6x6 . . . . $24
5320 Dropside Truck $24
5320 Dropside Truck "1945 – 1985" $24
5320 Dropside Truck "1917 – 1987" $24
5320 Dropside Truck with Tilt $24
5320 Dropside Truck with Tilt "Lada Spares" $24
53212 Long Wheelbase Truck $24
53212 Long Wheelbase Truck with tilt $24
53212 Long Wheelbase Truck with tilt "Sovtransavto" $24
53212 Tanker "Moloko" $24
5325 4x2 Dropside Truck $24
5325 4x2 Dropside Truck with Tilt "Sovtransavto" $24
5410 Tractor Unit $12
5410 Tractor Unit and Trailer $24
5410 Tractor Unit, Trailer and Tilt $32
55105 Dump Truck $24
5511 Dump Truck $24
5511 Dump Truck "Mocctpon" $24
5511 Dump Truck "Moscow 1980" $24

KEMLOWS

Kemlows Diecasting Products Ltd. was one London, England, toy manufacturer that remains relatively unknown. The box is typical of 50s diecast from Great Britain. The distinction is that it is marked "A Wardie Product," likely indicating its distributor B.J. Ward Ltd. "Master Model" and "Wee World Series" are other monikers applied to the model's box. Recognizing such models out of their respective boxes is a bit more difficult. Here is a list of known models.

Armored Car, 1:60 . . . . $50
Articulated Lumber Truck, 1:50 . . . . $50
Caravan, 1:43 . . . . $50
Field Gun, 1:60 . . . . $25
Flat Truck, 1:50 . . . . $50
Ford Zephyr Mark I, 1:43 . . . . $100
Removal Van "Pickford's," 1:60 . . . . $100
Thornycroft Mighty Antar, 1:43 . . . . $75
Thornycroft Mighty Antar, 1:60 . . . . $50
Tractor and Farm Cart $50

KENNA

Pete Kenna makes these beautiful 1:43 scale handbuilts in the United Kingdom.
MG TD, top up, side curtains . . . . no price known
Austin A40 van . . . . no price known

KENNER

Kenner, now owned by Hasbro, is well known for its

huge assortment of toys. It's Girder & Panel and Bridge & Turnpike construction sets were extremely popular in the 60s and 70s. Hasbro in turn is sustained by the popularity of its G.I. Joe action figures. Most familiar of the Kenner diecast line is Kenner Fast 111's, produced around 1980 and styled after the wildest Hot Wheels and Johnny Lightnings. But their popularity (and speed) could never compete much with either of them. Still, Kenner Fast 111's are slowly and steadily gaining popularity as a collectible and can still be purchased very cheaply, around $2 apiece or less.

Kenner has recently produced a five-car set of 1:64 scale vehicles based on the movie "Batman Forever" which is slowly rising in value. The set is currently worth about $8 – 10. Currently, the Kenner brand mostly encompasses Star Wars figures and playsets. In March of 1996, Mattel failed in an attempt to buy out Hasbro, securing the integrity of the Kenner brand as well.

The most recent offering (1997) from Kenner is a line called "Winners Circle." 1997 Stock Car Series Winners Circle cars are 1:64 scale with a trading card depicting the driver. Also produced are a couple of rail dragsters and funny cars.

Dale Earnhardt Stock Car $5
Jeff Gordon Stock Car $5
John Force Castrol GTX Funny Car $5
Pat Austin Red Wing Shoes Funny Car $5

KIBRI

Walthers devotes several pages to their extensive assortment of 1:87 scale plastic Kibri models, worth mentioning for their detail and accuracy. Kibri of Germany at one time produced at least one diecast model as listed below.

Auto-Union Streamlined Racing Car, 4⅛" $50

KIDCO

Somewhere around 1985, Kidco, an American firm based in Illinois, was purchased by Universal while they still owned the Matchbox brand. The Burnin' Key Cars assortment was originally a Kidco product that was incorporated into the Matchbox line-up for a short time in the 80s.

Photo by Jeff Koch.

Firebird Trans Am V8, 1981, Hong Kong, $1

KIDDIE CAR CLASSICS

Hallmark offers these exquisite miniature replicas of vintage pedal toys made of heavy diecast metal and great paint

jobs. They are working models with pedals that turn the wheels and functional steering. Values indicated are Hallmark retail prices.

1935 American Airflow Coaster, limited edition of 29,500 made, 5" long $45
1964½ Ford Mustang, 7" long $55
1940 Garton Aero Flite Wagon, limited edition of 24,500 made, 7" long $48
1959 Garton Deluxe Kidillac, issued 3/95, retired 1/97, 7½" long . $55
1961 Garton Casey Jones Locomotive, issued 3/95, retired 1/97, 6½" long $55
1950 Garton Delivery Cycle, 6¾" long $38
1956 Garton Dragnet Polic Car, limited edition of 24,500 made, 6¼" long $50
1956 Garton Hot Rod Racer, 5½" long $55
1956 Garton Kidillac, issued 7/94, retired 12/94, 7⅜" long $50
1956 Garton Mark V, limited edition of 24,500 made, 6¼" long . $45
1963 Garton Speedster, 5" long $38
1966 Garton Super-Honda, 6¼" long $45
1964 Garton Tin Lizzie, 5¾" long $50
1941 Keystone Locomotive, 5" long $45
1939 Mobo Horse, 3⅞" long $45
Late 1940s Mobo Sulky, limited edition of 29,500 made, 7" long . $48
1941 Murray Airplane, limited edition of 14,500, issued 10/92, retired 10/93, 7¼" long $50
1958 Murray Atomic Missile, limited edition of 24,500 made, 7¾" long $55
1968 Murray Boat Jolly Roger, limited edition of 19,500 made, issued 3/93, retired 2/96, 6⅛" long $50
1955 Murray Champion, limited edition of 14,500, issued 10/92, retired 10/93, 6⅛" long $45
1961 Murray Circus Car, limited edition of 24,500 made, 7" long $48
1953 Murray Dump Truck, yellow, limited edition of 14,500, issued 10/92, retired 10/93, 7½" long $48
1955 Murray Dump Truck, orange/black, limited edition of 19,500, issued 3/94, retired 3/96, 7½" $48
1955 Murray Fire Chief, limited edition, issued 9/93, retired 1/96, 6⅛" long $45

1955 Murray Royal Deluxe, limited edition of 29,500 made, 6¼" long, $55

1955 Murray Fire Truck, red, limited edition of 14,500 made, issued 10/24, retired 10/93, 7" long $50

1955 Murray Fire Truck, red/white, limited edition of 19,500 made, issued 3/94, retired 1/96, 7" long $50

1958 Murray Police Cycle, limited edition of 29,500 made, 5½" long $55

1948 Murray Pontiac, 5⅞" long. $50

1955 Murray Ranch Wagon, limited edition of 19,500 made, issued 1/94, retired 2/96, 6⅛" long. $48

1955 Murray Red Champion, limited edition of 19,500 made, issued 3/94, retired 3/96, 6⅛" long $45

1961 Murray Speedway Pac Car, limited edition of 24,500 made, 6⅛" long $45

1962 Murray Super Deluxe Fire Truck, 7½" long $55

1961 Murray Super Deluxe Tractor with Trailer, 7¼" long tractor, 4¼" long trailer. $55

1950 Murray Torpedo, issued 3/95, retired 1/96, 6¼" long. . . . $50

1955 Murray Tractor and Trailer, limited edition of 14,500, issued 10/92, retired 12/93, 11⅛" long $55

1935 Sky King Velocipede, 5" long $45

1937 Steelcraft Airflow by Murray, luxury edition, 24,500 made, 6⅞" long $55

1935 Steelcraft Airplane by Murray, limited edition of 29,500 made, 7¾" long $50

1937 Steelcraft Auburn, luxury edition, 24,500 made, issued 7/95, retired 4/96, 8½" long $65

1935 Steelcraft by Murray, luxury edition, 24,500 made, 7¼" long . $65

1939 Steelcraft Lincoln Zephyr by Murray, limited edition of 24,500, 6¾" long. $50

1941 Steelcraft Spitfire Airplane by Murray, limited edition, 19,500, issued 3/94, retired 1/96, 7¼" $50

1937 Steelcraft Streamline Scooter by Murray, 6¼" long. $35

1935 Steelcraft Streamline Velocipede by Murray, 4½" long . . . $45

KIDDIETOY (SEE HUBLEY)

KIKO (SEE CORGI)

KILGORE

Westerville, Ohio, was home to Kilgore, a company that produced some of the most elegant toys of the 1930s. These cast-iron cars were accurate representations of vehicles of the period, comparable to the best diecast of any era. Graham models were the specialty for these high quality miniature marvels. Ken Hutchison and Greg Johnson have written a delightful book entitled *The Golden Age of Automotive Toys 1925 – 1941* in which they showcase these and other rare and beautiful toy cars and trucks in spectacular photos, with entertaining and informative text. The hardbound edition from Collector Books is a prize to cherish at just $24.95 suggested retail price.

1932 Graham Blue Streak Coupe, 6½" . . . . $2,200 – 2,500

1932 Graham Blue Streak Roadster, 6½" . . . . $2,200 – 2,500

1932 Graham Blue Streak Sedan, 6½" . . . . $2,200 – 2,500

1932 Graham Blue Streak Coupe, 4" . . . . $175 – 350

1932 Graham Blue Streak Roadster, 4" . . . . $175 – 350

1932 Graham Blue Streak Sedan, 4" . . . . $175 – 350

Graham Stake Truck, 4". . . . . $100 – 150

Graham Wrecker, 4" . . . . $100 – 150

Graham Dump Truck, 4" . . . . $100 – 150

Pierce Arrow-styled Coupe, 4" . . . . $100 – 150

Pierce Arrow-styled Roadster, 4" . . . . $100 – 150

Pierce Arrow-styled Sedan, 4", $100 – 150

Pierce Arrow-styled Coupe, 5" . . . . $125 – 175

Pierce Arrow-styled Roadster, 5" . . . . $125 – 175

KIM CLASSICS

From England come these new 1:43 scale models of which four are so far known, as offered by Toys for Collectors.

2 Cadillac Limousine "Maloney" $198

3Z GMC Sierra Police Suburban $149

6 1992 Jaguar XJ6 Sedan. $115

7 1960 Chrysler Saratoga $129

KING K (ALSO SEE XONEX)

Since 1987, King K has been the business of Ed and Ken Kovach from Frankfort, Illinois, producing some of the most exquisite miniature cars, buses, and flivvers ever made. So when Ken Kovach made his first resin-cast miniature pedal car in 1990, a 1955 Champion, he started the newest trend in collectible toys. His replicas average about 12" long (1:3 scale), bigger than average for such models. (Compare to Kiddie Car Classics at approximately 6".) Limited production runs of 10, 50, or 100 make these rare and highly collectible. Newer models are also produced in a much smaller 1:18 scale. Xonex has since reproduced King K's models in diecast, and in larger production runs of 10,000 for around $60 – 80 each. King K, c/o Ken Kovach, 8300 W. Sauk Trail, Frankfort IL 60423. 815-469-5937.

1955 Champion, 1:3 scale, 1990 original price $165 . . . $250 – 400

1940 Silver Pursuit Plane, 1991 original price $300 . . . . $250 – 450

KINGSBURY

The Kingsbury company dates back to 1886 in Keene, New Hampshire. Around 1910, Harry Kingsbury purchased the Wilkins Toys Company. After World War I, He changed the Wilkins brand name to Kingsbury to produce toys made usually of pressed steel with windup motors. While the firm remains in business, toy production apparently ceased after 1942. Values range from $400 – 2500.

KING STAR

King Star toys of Korea, while lightweight and low priced, are relatively accurate scale models. Here is a sampling of models produced.

Mercedes-Benz 450 SLC 5.0, 1:50 . . . . $5

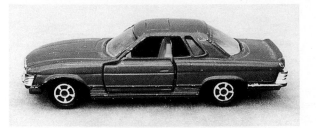

Mercedes-Benz 450 SLC Police Car, $5

Pontiac Firebird $5
Fuso Van $5
Fuso Cement Truck $5

KIRBY

An Atlas Backhoe is the only known model by Kirby.
Atlas 2004LC Track Backhoe, 1:87 . . . . $26

KIRK

The Kirk brand of Denmark is hard to find, since most of the models they marketed were first produced by other companies. The connection is somewhat confusing, but Tekno and H. Lange are two Danish companies whose products ended up in the Kirk product line. Even though Kirk produced models since 1960, it wasn't until 1969 that the company actually put the Kirk name on the base. Here is a list of models issued under the Kirk brand.

Chevrolet Monza GT $60
Chevrolet Monza Spyder $45
Ford D 800 Tipper Truck $45
Ford D 800 Covered Truck $45
Ford D 800 Lumber Truck $45
Ford D 800 Brewery Truck $65
Jaguar E Type $65
Mercedes-Benz 0302 Bus $60
Mercedes-Benz 0302 Bus, "PTT" $75
Mercedes-Benz 280 SL $65
Mercedes-Benz 280 SL Police $45
Oldsmobile Toronado $65
Porsche 911 S $45
Saab 99 . . . . $65
Toyota 2000 GT $60

KOOKABURRA

Kookaburra is the name brand of 1:43 scale white metal models are from Melbourne, Australia, as recently reported by Australian collector Gary Hallett. More research pending.

KYOSHO

These fine quality scale models from Japan are part of a line of toys that include radio-controlled cars, boats, and planes, and detailed plastic model kits. EWA and Exoticar offer some terrific 1:18 scale Kyosho models as listed below.

7001 1991 Honda Acura NSX, red or silver with black roof. $69 – 99
7001R 1991 Honda Acura NSXR, white $69
7002 1992 Nissan 300ZX Twin Turbo, red or metallic blue. . . . $69
7002J 1993 Nissan Skyline GTR, Unisea or Multicolor $69
7003 Nissan 300ZX T-Top, red $89
7005 Mercedes-Benz 300 SL Gullwing, silver $89
7006 AC Cobra 427 SC Shelby, British racing green, red, or blue. $69 – 99
7007 Porsche 356A/1600, red or silver . . . . $69 – 89
7008 Mini Cooper 1275S, green, red, white, or British flag $69 – 89
7009 Mazda RX7, red or silver $89
7010 Mazda RX7, black or yellow $89
7011 Mazda Miata MX5, top down, Superman blue $20
7013 Toyota Supra with wing, red $89
7014 Toyota Supra with wing, red, black, or silver $89
7015 Lotus Caterham Super 7, British racing green, red, blue, or
    yellow $69
7017 1966 MGB Mk-1, green, red, or white $69

LANSDOWNE (SEE BROOKLIN)

LANSING SLIK-TOYS

Lansing, Iowa, is the home of Lansing Slik-Toys, mostly one-piece cast aluminum toys, with a few plastic models.

Bulldozer $130
Combine $300
Fastback Sedan, #9600, 7" $40
Fastback Sedan Taxi, #9600, 7" $40
Firetruck, #9606, 6" $35
Firetruck, #9700, 3½" $35
Grader, 9½" $100
Metro Van, #9618, 5" $40
Oliver 77 Tractor, 7¾" $400
Open Stake Truck, #9602, 7" $40
Pickup Truck, #9601, 7" $40
Pickup Truck, #9605, 6" $35
Pickup Truck, #9703, 4" $35
Roadster, #9701, 3½" $35
Sedan 4-door, #9604, 6" $35
Semi Tractor Trailer Flatbed Truck, #9613, 8" $40
Semi Tractor Trailer Grain Truck, #9611, 8" $40
Semi Tractor Trailer Log Truck, 8" $40
Semi Tractor Trailer Milk Truck, #9610, 8" $45
Stake Truck, #9500, 11" $60
Station Wagon, #9704, 4" $30
Tank Truck, #9603, 7" $35
Tank Truck, #9705, 4" $30
Wrecker, #9617, 5" $30

LE JOUET MECANIQUE

Dating from around 1955, just one reference to Le Jouet Mecanique has been found, a diecast model with clockwork motor.

Panhard Dyna, 1:45 . . . . $60

LEGENDS OF RACING

While not diecast, Legends of Racing resin models deserve mention, according to Russell Alameda of San Jose,

California. These 1:43 scale models are made in China for the Huntersville, North Carolina, company. Each car is packaged in a clear display box with card that provides a few paragraphs of details on the model inside.

1974 Chevrolet Malibu, "Buddy Baker"	$10 – 20
1955 Chrysler 300	$10 – 20
1969 Dodge Daytona, "Jim Vandiver"	$10 – 20
1965 Ford Galaxie 500, "#41," "Curtis Turner," "Harvest Ford," white and red, 1:43, issued 1992	$10 – 20
1965 Ford Galaxie 500, "Ned Jarrett"	$10 – 20
1965 Ford Galaxie 500, "Fred Lorenzen"	$10 – 20
1952 Hudson Hornet, "Flock"	$10 – 20
1969 Mercury Cyclone (independent driver)	$10 – 20
1969 Mercury Cyclone, "Woods Brothers"	$10 – 20
1960 Pontiac Bonneville	$10 – 20
1962 Pontiac Bonneville, "Fireball Roberts"	$10 – 20

LEHIGH BITSI-TOYS

Around the year 1950, a company called Lehigh produced a small assortment of heavy diecast toys known as Bitsi-Toys. Here are the only two known models.

1949 Chevrolet Coupe, 2½"	$20
1948 Reo Tractor/Trailer, 5½"	$30

LEKSAKSHUST

Greyhound Bus, 1:43	$24

LEMECO

Based in Sweden, Lemeco produced a series of diecast models based on Dinky Toys.

LE PHOENIX

Exoticar lists these as the finest quality 1:43 scale hand-builts from France that feature leather interior, full photo-etched metal and trim, detailed cockpit, limited between 100 and 200 piece production run of only 10 units per item available.

1966 Ferrari Dino 206 Le Mans 2-car set in elegant presentation case with metal Dino emblem, limited to 120 pieces	$1,295
1964 Ferrari 250 GTO Le Mans #26	$595
1959/1960 Ferrari 250 TR Le Mans #11	$595
Ferrari 275 NART Spyder, available in red, yellow, or metallic gray	$595
1972 Ferrari 365 GTB/4 Daytona Le Mans #39	$595
1966 Ferrari 500SF, metallic blue or maroon	$595

LESNEY (SEE MATCHBOX)

LES ROULIERS

The obscure French toy company Les Rouliers is known to produce only one model.

Renault Etoile Filante, 1:43, 1961	$50

LES ROUTIERS

A diminutive series of 1:90 scale diecast vehicles were produced in 1959 under the French firm name Les Routiers.

1 Panhard Tank Truck	$50
2 Unic Semi Trailer	$50
3 Berliet Dump Truck	$50
4 Citroën Wrecker	$50
5 Citroën Dump Truck	$50
6 Caterpillar Dumping Tractor	$50
7 Richier Road Rollre	$50
8 Caterpillar Road Grader	$50
9 Caterpillar Quarry Bucket	$50
10 Tractomotive Excavator	$50
11 Renault Byrrh Tank Truck	$50
12 Renault Etoile Filante	$50
13 Bus	$50
14 Mobile Crane	$50

LIBERTY CLASSICS (ALSO SEE SPEC-CAST)

Liberty Classics are made in Libertyville, Illinois, and distributed by Spec-Cast of Iowa. For convenience and reference, an assortment of Liberty Classics is listed below as offered from Asheville DieCast. Price depends greatly on quantity produced.

326 Travel REA "Goodyear Racing #1"	$24
1026 White New Idea Crate Pickup	$18
1547 1932 Ford Model A Roadster "Fina"	$16
1553 1932 Ford Model A Roadster "A&W"	$27
2004 1929 Ford Tanker "Fina Petroleum"	$15
2005 1929 Ford Tanker "Amalie Motor Oil"	$26
12516 1937 Chevrolet Pickup, red	$20
35018 Lockheed Vega Airplane "Signal"	$31
35021 Lockheed Vega Airplane "Magnolia"	$31
35040 Lockheed Vega Airplane "Mountain Dew"	$16

For a more complete listing, write to Asheville Diecast, 1446 Patton Avenue, Asheville NC 28806-1740, or call 704-253-8800.

LINCOLN INDUSTRIES

During the 1950s, Lincoln Industries of Auckland, New Zealand, produced a line of models thought to be made from D.C.M.T. castings.

Austin A Somerset, 1:43	$50
Buick Roadmaster, 1:43	$75
Bus, 1:87	$20
Dumper, 1:87	$20
Fire Engine, 1:87	$25
Ford Prefect, 1:43	$75
Jaguar XK120, 1:87	$25
Land Rover, 1:87	$40
Massey Ferguson Tractor	$20
Pickup Truck, 1:87	$25
Racing Car, 1:87	$20
Tanker, 1:87	$25
Van, 1:87	$20
Wrecker, 1:87	$20

LINCOLN WHITE METAL WORKS

Three toy companies are known by the name Lincoln. One, known as Lincoln Toys of Windsor, Ontario, Canada, produced several pressed steel toys, valued from $100 – 600 by collectors. Another company, based in Auckland, New Zealand, was known as Lincoln Industries, producers of 1:43 scale diecast toys during the 1950s, and listed under their own heading.

Lincoln White Metal Works of Lincoln, Nebraska, has produced models that more appropriately fit the definition of diecast. From 1931 to 1940, Lincoln White Metal Works sold toys to Woolworth, Kress, Kresge, and Schwartz Paper Co., and many other markets. Identifying these models becomes difficult since not all of them are specifically marked.

Bluebird Record Car with V-8 engine, 6"	$150 – 175
Bluebird Record Car with V-8 engine, 4"	$100 – 125
Bluebird Record Car with V-12 engine, 4⅜"	$125 – 150
Chrysler or DeSoto Airflow Sedan, 3¾"	$75 – 100
Fire Engine, Graham-like grille, "Made in USA," 3½"	$75 – 100
Miller FWD Special Indy Racer, 5⅛"	$125 – 150
Pierce-Arrow Silver Arrow Sedan, 3½"	$75 – 100
Wrecker Car, Graham-like grille, "Made in USA," 3½"	$75 – 100
Tanker Truck, COE, "Made in USA," 3¾"	$75 – 100
Streamlined Railcar, 4½"	$100 – 125

LINE MAR

Line Mar of Japan produced the Collectoy series of diecast friction toys representing American cars.

LINTOY

Until I received in the mail a diecast 1:64 scale Mercedes-Benz C-111 made by Lintoy, I had forgotten ever having heard of them. The model measures 3" and is metallic red with flat black painted metal base, black plastic interior, made in Hong Kong, and the rear engine compartment opens. My best recollection is that this is one of a rare series of diecast toys made by Lindberg Plastics in the early to mid-seventies, and resembling a Playart, Tomica, or Matchbox of that period. Excellent detail and fair wheels punctuate this little model. Several others were listed with the letter of inquiry included with the model. Thanks to Helen Shaffer for the information and the model.

BMW Turbo, orange	$8 – 12
Mercedes Benz C-111, metallic red	$8 – 12
Ford Mk IV, white	$8 – 12
Fiat Abarth, avocado	$8 – 12
Porsche 911, yellow	$8 – 12
Mercedes-Benz 350SL	$8 – 12

LION CAR

Lion Car is a brand of simple diecast models from the Netherlands. While the company was founded in the mid-1940s, production of diecast toys started in 1956. Some models are refinished in the UK. At last report, they are still being produced.

CURRENTLY AVAILABLE MODELS

LN001 DAF 2300 Articulated Van Placketts, 1:50	$28
DAF 2800 Dump Truck, 1:43	$24
LN002 Commer Walkthru Rutland Fire Brigade, 1:43	$24
LN003 Commer Walkthru Amusements: Fairground, 1:43	$38
LN004 Commer Walkthru Marples Construction, 1:43	$38
LN005 Commer Walkthru BRS Parcels, 1:43	$38

OBSOLETE MODELS

10 Volkswagen 1200	$125
11 Renault 4 CV	$125
12 Opel Rekord	$100
13 D.K.W. 316	$100
14 Renault Dauphine	$75
20 DAF 1300 Chassis and Cabin	$100
21 DAF 1300 Flat Truck	$75
22 DAF 1300 Truck	$100
22 DAF 1400 Truck	$50
23 DAF 1400 Truck with tilt	$75
23 DAF 1400 Army Truck with tilt	$50
24 Trailer	$15
25 Trailer with tilt	$20
26 DAF 1300 Breakdown Lorry	$100
26 DAF 1400 Breakdown Lorry	$65
27 Renault Goelette Van	$125
28 Commer Van	$75
29 DAF 600	$100
30 DAF Daffodil	$125
30 DAF Daffodil, gold-plated	$300
31 DAF 750 Pickup	$75
31 DAF 750 Pickup with tilt	$75
32 DAF Torpedo Truck	$75
33 DAF 33	$125
33/34 DAF Torpedo Semi-Trailer	$75
33/35 DAF 1400 Semi-Trailer	$25
33/35 DAF 1400 Semi-Trailer Army, olive	$25
36 DAF 2600 Eurotrailer	$50
37 DAF 2600 Tank Trailer	$50
38 DAF SE 200 Bus	$50
39 DAF 33 Van	$50
39 DAF 33 Van "REMIA" or "GROENPOL"	$125
40 DAF 55 Coupe	$75
40 DAF 55 Coupe "CAMEL DAF RACING TEAM"	$150
40 DAF 55 Coupe "LYONS INTERNATIONAL"	$150
40 DAF 66 SL Coupe	$50
41 DAF 44 Station Wagon	$50
42 DAF Pony Semi Trailer	$65
42 DAF 55 Coupe with DAF emblem	$75
43 DAF 20001Z200 Covered Truck	$50
43 DAF 2000/2200 Military Covered Truck, olive	$50
44 DAF 44	$75
44 DAF 44 "GVB AMSTERDAM" or "MARATHON"	$175
45 DAF Pony Truck	$65
46 DAF 750 Pickup with hood	$65
46 DAF 46	$65
47 DAF 2000/2200 Bulk Carrier	$50
48 DAF 2000/2200 Truck &Trailer	$50
49 Commer Van "TECHNISCHE UNIE"	$75
50 DAF 2600 Car Carrier	$75
54 Commer Van "VAN GEND & LOOS"	$40
55 Commer Van "POSTERIJEN"	$40
55 Commer Van 3	$25
56 DAF 2000/2200 Tipping Truck	$45
57 DAF 2600 Container Trailer	$50
58 DAF 2800 Covered Truck	$45
59 DAF 2800 Eurotrailer	$45
60 DAF 2800 Car Transporter	$45
61 DAF 2800 Container Trailer	$40
62 DAF 2800 Tank Trailer	$25
63 DAF 2800 Truck and Trailer	$25

64 DAF 2800 6-W. Truck and Trailer. $25
66 DAF 2800 6-W. Covered Truck. $25
67 DAF 2800 6-W. Tanker $25
68 DAF 2300 Covered Truck. $25
68 DAF 2300 Military Covered Truck, olive $25

LIONEL

Lionel has set the standard for electric toy trains for most of this century. Now they produce a number of vehicles for use with train sets, specifically HO gauge semi trucks and trailers with various liveries. These are recently introduced models that are still available from hobby shops and specialty dealers for $65 – 80 each. In addition, an assortment of Lionel plastic 1955 Ford Custom two-door sedans is also offered in blue, red, white, or yellow for $15 each. Lionel is also the producer of Revolvers, reversible cars that convert from one car to another when flipped over. A growing interest in these unusual toys has sparked several Hong Kong-based companies to produce knockoff versions, including Ja-Ru Real Wheels and Imperial Diecast.

LITAN

Litan is one of the emerging model manufactures to originate from Russia. Their line of models includes Samara and Lada vehicles and Belarus tractors.

LIXIN

Lixin models are made in China, and little else is known about them. Any details are appreciated.

1932 Dong Feng 4-door Sedan, tin, 1:25 . . . . $20
1950 Army Jeep CJ2, 1:32 . . . . $20
1950 Buick Super Convertible, top down, tin, 1:25 . . . . $20
1950 Buick Super Coupe, tin, 1:25 . . . . $20
1950 Cadillac 2-door Hardtop, 1:25 . . . . $20
1950 Cadillac Convertible, top down, 1:25 . . . . $20
1950 Harley Davison with Sidecar, 1:25 . . . . $20
1955 Chevrolet Corvette Convertible, top up, tin, 1:25 . . . . . . $20
1955 Chevrolet Corvette convertible, top down, tin, 1:25 . . . . $20
1957 Chevrolet Corvette Convertible, top down, 1:25 . . . . . . $20
1957 Chevrolet Corvette Convertible, top up, 1:25 . . . . $20
1960 Toyota Crown Ambulance, tin, 1:25 . . . . $20
1961 Ford Thunderbird 2-door Hardtop, 1:25 . . . . $20
1970 Volkswagen Bus, 1:43 . . . . $20
Beijing Fire Ladder Truck, tin, 9" $20
Beijing Double Decker Bus, tin, 9" $20
BMW 507 Convertible, top down, 1:25 . . . . $20
BMW 507 Convertible, top up, 1:25 . . . . $20
Douglas DC3 Overseas Airplane, 9" $20
Jaguar E-Type 2+2 Coupe, 1:25 . . . . $20
Jaguar E-Type Convertible, top down, 1:25 . . . . $20
Mercedes-Benz 300SL Gullwing Coupe, 1:25 . . . . $20
Mercedes-Benz 450 4-door Sedan, 1:25 . . . . $20
Volkswagen Karmann Ghia Coupe, 1:25 . . . . $20

LLEDO

When Lesney sold the Matchbox line of diecast toys to Universal Holding Company of Hong Kong in 1982, John W. "Jack" Odell left the firm, of which he was a partner for many years, to form Lledo (Odell spelled backwards). Lledo models are also known as Days Gone and designated as DG. Every one of the hundreds of Lledo models produced for the first six years are variations of approximately 30 base models. Color and markings are what differentiate each model. Here is a list of the basic models, from which the numerous variations have arisen through the years. The value of each model depends on the number of each variation produced from year to year.

Most regular production models sell for $8 – 10 each. Limited edition models vary considerably, depending on availability and quantity produced. Dr. Force's book *Lledo Toys* serves as an excellent source for variations and values. The latest addition to the Lledo product line is the Vanguard series. These 50s and 60s British vehicles are strongly reminiscent of the kinds of toys issued by Corgi and Dinky some 30 years ago. Lledo PLC, Enfield EN3 4ND England. Lledo Collectibles, 2515 East 43rd St., PO Box 182264, Chatttanooga, TN 37422. 1-800-982-7031.

MODELS INTRODUCED IN 1983

DG001 Horse Drawn Tram . . . . $8 – 10
DG002 Horse Drawn Milk Float . . . . $8 – 10
DG003 Delivery Van . . . . $8 – 10
DG004 Omnibus . . . . $8 – 10
DG005 Fire Engine. . . . . $8 – 10

DG006 Ford Model T, $8 – 10

MODELS INTRODUCED IN 1984

DG007 Ford Woody Wagon . . . . $8 – 10
DG008 Ford Model T Tanker . . . . $8 – 10

DG016 Heavy Goods Van, $8 – 10

DG009 Ford Model A Touring Car with top down . . . . $8 – 10
DG010 Albion Single Decker Coach . . . . $8 – 10
DG011 Large Horse Drawn Van . . . . $8 – 10
DG012 Fire Engine. . . . . $8 – 10
DG013 1934 Ford Model A Van . . . . $8 – 10

Models Introduced in 1985

DG014 Ford Model A Touring Car, top up . . . . $8 – 10
DG015 AEC Double Deck Bus . . . . $8 – 10
DG017 Long Distance Coach . . . . $8 – 10

DG018 Packard Van, $8 – 10

DG019 Rolls Royce Phantom II. $8 – 10

Lledo Models Introduced in 1986

DG020 1930 Ford Model A Stake Truck. . . . . $8 – 10
DG021 Chevrolet Van. . . . . $8 – 10
DG022 Packard Town Van . . . . $8 – 10

Models Introduced in 1987

DG023 Scenicruiser Bus, $18 – 20

DG024 Rolls Royce Playboy Convertible Coupe. . . . . . . $8 – 10
DG025 Rolls Royce Silver Ghost Tourer . . . . $8 – 10
DG026 1934 Chevrolet Bottle Truck . . . . $8 – 10
DG027 Mack Breakdown Truck . . . . $8 – 10
DG028 1934 Mack Mack Canvas Back Truck . . . . $8 – 10

Models Introduced in 1988 and Later

DG029 1942 Dodge Truck . . . . $8 – 10
DG030 1939 Chevrolet Pickup Truck. . . . . $8 – 10
DG036 1938 Chevrolet Pickup . . . . $8 – 10
DG042 1934 Mack Tanker Truck. . . . . $8 – 10
DG046 1930 Bentley 4.5 Litre . . . . $8 – 10
DG048 1939 Chevrolet . . . . $8 – 10
DG049 Double Deck Bus . . . . $8 – 10
DG052 1935 Morris Truck. . . . . $8 – 10
DG057 1939 Ford Tanker . . . . $8 – 10
DG058 1950 Morris Van . . . . $8 – 10
DG061 1953 Pontiac Van . . . . $8 – 10

DG062 1935 Ford Tanker . . . . $8 – 10
DG065 1960 Morris Traveller . . . . $8 – 10

Special Issue Models

73004 1955 Volkswagen Kombi Van, "Pepsi Cola," $14

73007 1955 Volkswagen Transporter Van, "7-Up," $14

Vanguard Models

VA1002 Ford Anglia, white and maroon $22
VA2000 Volkswagen Cabriolet, red. $22
VA2001 Volkswagen Cabriolet, light blue $22
VA3000 Austin A40 Van, dark green, Ransome's Lawnmowers. $22
VA4002 Ford Anglia Van, pale blue, Hotpoint $22
VA5000 Triumph Herald, red $22
VA5002 Triumph Herald, yellow. $22
VA6000 Ford Thames Trader Van, Martini. $27
VA7000 Bedford 'S' Type Tanker, Regent $27
VA7001 Bedford 'S' Type Tanker, Shell-BP $27
VA8000 Bedford 'S' Type Van, Heinz 57 Varieties $27
VA9000 Ford Thames Trader Tanker, North Eastern Gas $27
VA12000 Volkswagen Beetle, beige $22

Other Models

LP-1 Model T Tanker -Red Crown Gas, Chevron Promo $6
LP-O Step Van, White, Coca Cola 1996 Olympic Torch Relay. . $12
DG-1 Horse Drawn Tram, blue/cream "National Tramway Museum
    1984" $6
DG-1 Horse Drawn Tram, brown & tan, "Main Street". $6
DG-1 Horse Drawn Tram, green & gray, "Westminster". $6
DG-4 Horse Drawn London Bus, red, "Lipton's Teas," white letters
    on green background, "Victoria & King's Cross". $5
DG-4 Horse Drawn London Bus, green, "Lipton's Teas," white let-
    ters on green background, "Bowery-Broadway," gold spoked
    wheels $6

DG-4 Horse Drawn London Bus, green, "Lipton's Teas," white letters on green background, "Bowery-Broadway," brown spoked wheels $6

DG-6 Model T Van, white, blue, white tires, "Stretton Spring Water" $4

DG-6 Model T Van, 2nd Illinois Miniature Toy Show, with certificate, 500 issued with numbered certificate. $6

DG-6 Model T Van, brown & cream, "Alton Towers" in special box $5

DG-6 Model T Van, yellow, "Tizer. The Appetizer" $5

DG-6 Model T Van, red & cream, "Cadbury's Cocoa, Bournville". $5

DG-6 Model T Van, white, green roof & base, "Stretton Spring Water" $6

DG-6 Model T Van, blue/red/white, "AEROPLANE JELLY". $4

DG-6 Model T Van, yellow, "MARCOL PRODUCT" $4

DG-6 Model T Van, tan, "MARCOL PRODUCT". $4

DG-6 Model T Van, cream/blue, "Echo Centenary 1884 – 1984" . $4

DG-6 Model T Van, blue, "Yorkshire Post" $4

DG-6 Model T Van, yellow/black, "Yorkshire Evening Post" . . . $4

DG-6 Model T Van, white/blue, "IPMS 1984" $4

DG-6 Model T Van, orange/black, "Cookie Coach Company," white lettering with yellow script lines. $4

DG-6 Model T Van, orange/black, "Cookie Coach Company," yellow lettering with gold script lines. $4

DG-6 Model T Van, cream/brown, "British Meat," small overhead print. $4

DG-6 Model T Van, cream/brown, "British Meat," large overhead print. $4

DG-6 Model T Van, green, "Magnasin Du Nord" $4

DG-6 Model T Van, blue, "British Bacon" $4

DG-6 Model T Van, cream/green, "International Garden Festival, Liverpool 1984" $4

DG-6 Model T Van, blue, "Get It At WOODWARDS -We Sell Everything!" $4

DG-6 Model T Van, red, Royal Mail. 350 years $6

DG-9 Model A Ford Convertible (top down), dark blue, "Police 055". $6

DG-10 Albion Single-Decker Bus, "Brighton Belle," maroon, green & tan $6

DG-10 Albion Single-Decker Bus, brown & cream, "Great Western Railway System" Anniversary Model, with flip-top box $8

DG-10 Albion Single-Decker Bus, red, "Potteries, Cheadle-Longton" $6

DG-10 Albion Single-Decker Bus, red & beige, Redburns Motor Services $6

DG-10 Albion Single-Decker Bus, cream & blue, "Imperial Airways". $6

DG-11 Horse Drawn Large Removals Van, red, Royal Mail $6

DG-13 Model A Ford Van, light and dark blue, "Tucher Brau-Tradition, Seit 1672" $6

DG-13 Model A Ford Van, dark blue, Evening Sentinel $5

DG-13 Model A Ford Van, cream/green, Robinson's Original High Juice Squashes $5

DG-14 Model A Ford, top up, brown/tan, Grand Hotel $5

DG-15 AEC Double Decker Bus, red, "Take HALLS WINE and defy Influenza" $6

DG-15 AEC Double Decker Bus, red, "Madame Tussauds" $6

DG-16 Heavy Goods Removals Van, red, Royal Mail $6

DG-16 Heavy Goods Removals Van, green, Trebor Peppermints. . $6

DG-16 Heavy Goods Removals Van, navy blue, Bushells, The Tea of Flavor $6

DG-17 Half-Cab Singledeck Bus, light blue, "Stratford Blue," with gray plastic wheels $6

DG-17 Half Cab Singledeck Bus, red & cream, London Transport. $6

DG-17 Half Cab Singledeck Bus, red & maroon, "Morrel's Castle Ale" $6

DG-18 Packard Van, white/blue 13th Commonwealth Games, Scotland 1986 in special box $6

DG-19 Rolls Royce, maroon, TV Times issue w/certificate $8

DG-19 Rolls Royce, yellow. $6

DG-21 Chevrolet Van, beige & brown, Sharp's Super-Kreem Toffee $5

DG-24 Rolls Royce, yellow body, black fenders, tan roof/boot . $6

LODEN AQULI

Three Loden Aquli 1:64 scale models from Argentina are known and listed below.

Dodge Charger Show Car $5
Renault 12 Sedan. $5
Renault 12 Taxi $5

LOMO

ZIS and GAZ models dominate the product line of this Russian manufacturer of 1:43 diecast models.

LONDONTOY

From 1945 to 1950, Londontoy diecast toys were produced in London, Ontario, and in the US by the Leslie Henry Company. The difference can be found in the absence or presence of the words "Made In Canada."

Beverage Truck, 4" $25
Beverage Truck, 6" $30
Canadian Greyhound Bus, 6" $40
City Bus, 4" $30
City Bus, 6" $30
Firetruck, 6" $30
Large Car Transporter. $100
Large Dump Truck $100
Large Lumber Truck. $100
Large Moving Van with tin body $100
Large Stake Truck $100
Large Tractor and Van Trailer $100
Oil Tanker, 6" $30
Panel Delivery, 6" $40
Six-Window Sedan, 6" $40
Thunderbolt Racer, 6" $40
1941 Chevrolet Master Deluxe Coupe, 4" $25
1941 Chevrolet Master Deluxe Coupe, 6" $30
1941 Ford Open Cab Firetruck, 4". $25
1941 Ford Pickup truck, 4". $25
1941 Ford Pickup Truck, 6" $30

LONE STAR
(ALSO SEE CRESCENT, D.C.M.T., IMPY, ROADMASTER)

While Lone Star of Great Britain has produced many toys,

perhaps the most popular models were those better known as Impy toys. The complete name for one series of toys is "Lone Star Road-Master Impy Super Cars," so it is no wonder that they are better known as Impy toys. "Roadmaster" was spelled with and without the hyphen at one time or another. The brand was originated in 1951 by Die Casting Machine Tools Ltd., otherwise known as D.C.M.T. Besides toy cars, Lone Star specialized in cap pistols and cowboy outfits, hence the reference.

1904 Daimler	$11
Cadillac Coupe de Ville, white & blue	$95
Case IH 946 Farm Tractor	$18
Chevrolet Corvair, coral	$65
Chevrolet Corvair, white	$90
Chrysler Imperial, 1962, metallic blue	$100
Dodge Dart Phoenix, metallic blue	$95
Foden COE Tilt Cab 8-wheel Dump Truck	$11
Ford 7610 Farm Tractor	$18
Ford Sunliner Convertible, pale blue	$115
IH 946 Farm Tractor	$18

Locomotive, $25

Mercedes-Benz, $15

Photo by Jeff Koch.

Peugeot 404, green, $6

Massey Ferguson 3070 Tractor	$18
Military Jeep, olive drab	$65
Routemaster Double Decker Bus	$18

Luso

These are diecast and plastic models made in Portugal in the early to mid-80s. Harvey Goranson reports that they made a nice racing version of the BMW 320 in Lichtenstein livery as raced at LeMans.

BMW 320	$35
Citroën GS Pallas "Michelin," yellow	$35

M C Toys (see Maisto)

The Ma Collection

A brochure from Sinclair's Mini-Auto (see resource directory in back of this book) describes the 1:43 scale 1946 "Rita Hayworth" Delahaye 135M as "the sensuously-bodied convertible that Prince Ali Khan gave to Hollywood star Rita Hayworth. Custom coachwork by Figoni Falaschi, this fabulous 1:43 scale miniature is by the famous Ma Collection of Switzerland." Only 150 copies of this model have been made promising high resale value. Other 1:43 scale Ma models are made in France. Also produced for the Ma Collection were some resin hand-built models back in the mid-70s.

1953 Bugatti 101 Antem, red and black	$350 – 395
1937 Bugatti 57 Milord, yellow and black	$350 – 395
1939 Bugatti 57, available in yellow and black or green and black	$350 – 395
1946 Delahaye 135M "Rita Hayworth"	$350 – 395
1949 Delahaye 135M Guillore, blue	$350 – 395
1938 Delahaye V12 Roadster, red	$350 – 395
1945 Hispano Suiza K6	$350 – 395
1948 Talbot Lago T26 GS, blue, white, or black	$350 – 395

Madmax (also see Grip)

Madmax models are made in Japan, a division of Grip Zechin. Here is a sample listing of these distinctively named 1:55 scale models.

Elf Van "Flight Foods"	$8
Fuso Cement Truck	$8
Fuso School Bus	$8
Fuso Vacuum Truck	$8

Magnuson Models

Although not diecast, Magnuson models, manufactured by Wm. K. Walthers, Inc., are such superb miniatures that they deserve mention. These HO scale (1:87) model kits are intended for use with HO train sets. As stated in the Walthers HO catalog, "Whether parked at the curb or on the roll, these detailed autos bring HO scale streets to life! These American classics make the perfect superdetail for steam or diesel era scenes, and help set the time and place of your entire layout. Each model is a one-piece resin casting with all details molded in place. Cast metal wheels are included, and some models feature separate metal bumpers. Just assemble and paint, and these easy-to-build kits are ready for the road."

439-910 '48 Coupe . . . . $7.98 pkg. of 2
439-911 '39 Sedan Delivery . . . . $7.98 pkg. of 2
439-912 '53 Hardtop . . . . $7.98 pkg. of 2
439-913 '41 Convertible with top up . . . . $7.98 pkg. of 2
439-914 '59 Checker Marathon Taxi. . . . . $7.98 pkg. of 2
439-917 Divco Milk Truck . . . . $7.98 pkg. of 2
439-919 '41 Pickup Truck . . . . $7.98 pkg. of 2
439-920 '40 Traveler 4-Door Sedan . . . . $7.98 pkg. of 2
439-921 '53 Tank Truck . . . . $7.98 each
439-922 '54 Panel Truck . . . . $7.98 pkg. of 2
439-923 Railway Express Agency Delivery Truck . . . . . $7.98 each
439-924 '56 Semi Tractor . . . . $7.98 pkg. of 2
439-926 '56 Delivery Truck . . . . $7.98 pkg. of 2
439-928 '40 Panel Truck . . . . $7.98 pkg. of 2
439-929 Model "R" Semi Tractor . . . . $7.98 pkg of 2
439-930 Oil Truck . . . . $7.98 each
439-931 1964 Step Van . . . . $7.98 pkg. of 2
439-932 '48 Diamond T Coal Truck . . . . $7.98 each
439-933 Crew Cab Pickup Truck . . . . $7.98 each
439-934 '57 LP Gas Delivery Truck. . . . . $7.98 each
439-935 '53 Flatbed Truck . . . . $7.98 each
439-936 Heavy Duty Coal Truck. . . . . $7.98 each
439-946 '56 Hardtop . . . . $7.98 pkg. of 2

MAISTO

Maisto International, Inc., based in Fontana, California, is the US division of Master Toy Co. Ltd. of Thailand, with May Cheong Toy Products Factory Ltd. of Kowloon as the Hong Kong subsidiary. The company also encompasses May Tat, the budget toy division. Previously marketed in the US under the brand name of M C Toys, Maisto has become a dominant force in the precision scale model market as well as the diecast toy industry. Previously, their smallest toys, comparable to Matchbox toys and Hot Wheels in size and price, were called M C Toys Mini Racers. Since unifying the product line to the Maisto brand in 1994, these approximately 1:64 scale toys have been renamed Maisto Turbo Treads, and have been produced with new color variations and packaging.

Meanwhile, Maisto has made a huge impact in the larger scale model industry, starting with their Trophy series models of approximately 1:43 scale that sell for $4 or less, and crowning the product line with 1:12 scale diecast masterpieces that retail for over $100 each. Every Maisto model shows exquisite attention to detail that establishes the company as a strong competitor to the big name brands. In fact, Maisto has become one of the big name brands. As is the

Snowmobile with pullback action, $4

case with many brands, MC Toys, Intex Recreation, and Zee Toys were all related in one way or another. The intermixing of models and castings blurred the lines that demarcated one company's product from the others'.

1:10 SCALE MOTORCYCLES

31603 1995 Moto Guzzi California 1100, yellow or red . . . $30 – 35
46610 1995 BMW R1100R, red or blue . . . . $30 – 35
46611 1995 Honda Shadow VT1100C2, turquoise or red. . $30 – 35

1:12 SCALE

Retail $119 each (may be purchased for as low as $70 on clearance).

33201 1992 Jaguar XJ220, metallic dark blue, silver, turquoise, green, red, yellow, or white $125

33202 1959 Cadillac Eldorado Biarritz Convertible, red, pink, or white, $135

1:18 SCALE

Retail $25 each.

30806 1955 Mercedes 300S Convertible, custom airbrushed . . . . $35 – 40
30811 1966 Mercedes Benz 280SE Convertible, custom airbrushed . . . . $35 – 40
30817 1955 BMW 502 Convertible, custom airbrushed . . . $35 – 40
31801 1989/1990 Mercedes-Benz 500 SL, aqua, lilac, silver, cranberry, black, or white . . . . $25 – 30
31802 1989 Porsche 911 Speedster, red or white . . . . . . $25 – 30
31803 1990 Lamborghini Diablo, red or yellow . . . . $25 – 30
31804 1990 Ferrari 348ts, red or yellow . . . . $25 – 30
31805 1990 BMW 850i, metallic red or black . . . . $25 – 30
31807 1992 Jaguar XJ220, metallic dark blue or silver. . . . $25 – 30

31806 1955 Mercedes-Benz 300S, burgundy, metallic green, black, or white, $25 – 30

31808 1992 Bugatti EB110, red or blue . . . . $25 – 30
31809 1992 Corvette ZR-1, burgundy, red, or white . . . . . $25 – 30
31810 1992 McLaren F1, gray, metallic gold, or silver . . . . $25 – 30
31811 1966 Mercedes-Benz 280SE, burgundy or white . . . $25 – 30
31812 1993 BMW 325i Convertible, black or red . . . . $25 – 30

31814 Porsche Boxster, black or silver, $25 – 30

31813 1959 Cadillac Eldorado Biarritz, pink, red, or white $25 – 30
31815 1994 Mustang Mach III, red . . . . $25 – 30
31816 1993 BMW 325i, red or black . . . . $25 – 30
31817 1955 BMW 502, dark blue . . . . $25 – 30
31818 1994 Porsche 911 Carrera, red . . . . $25 – 30

31820 1951 Volkswagen Export Sedan (Beetle), gray, black, or green, $25 – 30

31819 Lamborghini Diablo, metallic purple . . . . $25 – 30
31821 Citroën CV15, black, gray or burgundy . . . . $25 – 30
31822F 1995 Ferrari F50 Coupe, yellow or red . . . . $25 – 30
31823 1995 Ferrari F50 Barchetta, yellow or red . . . . $25 – 30
31827 1995 Corvette Indy Pacecar, burgundy and white . . $25 – 30

31828 1996 Dodge Viper GTS Coupe Indy Pacecar, blue with white stripes . . . . $25 – 30
31829 1994 Ford GT-90 Concept Car, white . . . . $25 – 30
31829L 1996 Lamborghini Jota, metallic purple . . . . $20 – 25
31830 1996 Corvette LT-4 Convertible, magenta, blue, and silver . . . . $25 – 30
31832 1996 Dodge Viper GTS Coupe, blue with white stripes . $25 – 30
31836 Jaguar XK 8, green or blue . . . . $25 – 30
31838 Mercedes Benz SLK, silver. . . . . $25 – 30
31839 Ferrari F550 Maranello, red . . . . $25 – 30
31840 1996 Corvette Coupe, red or green . . . . $25 – 30
31913 1996 Dodge Caravan, burgundy or green. . . . . $25 – 30
31921 Ford F-150 Pickup, burgundy, silver or blue . . . . . $25 – 30
35817 1955 BMW 502 Convertible, two-tone blue and white. $25 – 30
35820 1951 Volkswagen Beetle Coupe, two-tone light blue and white . . . . $25 – 30
35821 1952 Citroën 15CV, two-tone burgundy and black . $25 – 30
35826 1951 Volkswagen Beetle Convertible, two-tone dark green and yellow . . . . $25 – 30

1:24 SCALE

Retail $10 each.

31901 Mercedes-Benz 500SL, burgundy or metallic dark gray. $10 – 12
31902 Porsche 911 Speedster, red or white . . . . $10 – 12
31903 Lamborghini Diablo, red or yellow . . . . $10 – 12
31904 Ferrari 348ts, red or yellow . . . . $10 – 12
31905 '94 Mustang GT, red or goldenrod. . . . . $10 – 12
31906 1992 Ford Explorer, burgundy, dark blue, white, or metallic teal, with or without "Eddie Bauer" on doors . . . . . . $10 – 12
31907 Jaguar XJ220, metallic dark blue or silver. . . . . . . $10 – 12
31908 Bugatti EB110, blue or red . . . . $10 – 12
31909 1995 Ford Explorer . . . . $10 – 12
31910 McLaren F1, red or silver. . . . . $10 – 12
31911 1993 Ford F-150, red, black, or metallic teal, some packaged with ATV in back & driver . . . . $10 – 12
31912 1995 Dodge Ram Pickup. . . . . $10 – 12
31912I 1995 Dodge Ram Pickup Indy Pace Truck, blue with white stripes . . . . $15 – 18
31913 1996 Dodge Caravan. . . . . $10 – 12
31914 1996 Dodge Viper RT/10, white with blue stripes. . $10 – 12
31915I 1991 Dodge Viper RT/10 Pacecar, red . . . . $15 – 18
31916 1996 Ford F150 Indy Pace Truck, red . . . . $15 – 18
31917 1994 Ford Mustang Pace Car, red . . . . $15 – 18

31919 1994/1995 Lamborghini Diablo SE, metallic magenta, $10 – 12

31925 1996 Ferrari F355 Coupe, red or yellow . . . . $10 – 12
31951 1995 Ferrari F50 Coupe, red or yellow . . . . $10 – 12
B0600 1995 Dodge Viper GTS Coupe, blue with white stripes . . . . $10 – 12

MAISTO TROPHY/SPECIAL EDITION

Aston Martin DB7, 1:40, metallic purple, $3 – 4

Aston Martin Virage, metallic green . . . . $3 – 4

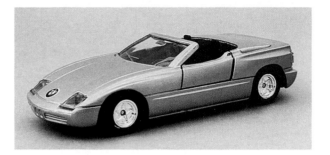

BMW Z1 Cabriolet, metallic silver, $3 – 4

BMW 325i Cabriolet, 1:37, white, $3 – 4

BMW 850i, metallic red . . . . $3 – 4
Bugatti EB110, blue . . . . $3 – 4
1957 Chevrolet Corvette, 1:39, black with white trim . . . . . . $3 – 4
1957 Chevrolet Corvette, 1:39, silver with red trim . . . . $3 – 4

1963 Chevrolet Corvette Stingray, 1:38, metallic silver, $3 – 4

Dodge Viper RT/10, 1:39, red . . . . $3 – 4
Ferrari 288 GTO, 1:36, red . . . . $3 – 4

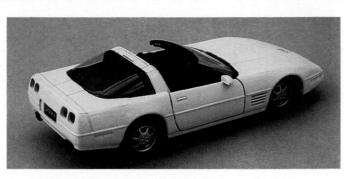

Chevrolet Corvette ZR-1, 1:38, white or yellow, $3 – 4

Ferrari 348ts, 1:38, yellow . . . . $3 – 4
Ferrari 456GT, 1:39, red . . . . $3 – 4

Ferrari F40, 1:39, red, $3 – 4

Ferrari F50, 1:39, red . . . . $3 – 4
Ferrari Testarossa, 1:39, red . . . . $3 – 4
Jaguar E Cabriolet, British racing green . . . . $3 – 4
Jaguar XJ220, 1:40, metallic dark blue . . . . $3 – 4
Jaguar XJS V12 Cabriolet, 1:40, red . . . . $3 – 4
Jaguar XJS V12 Cabriolet, 1:40, metallic silver/blue w/blue interior . . . . $3 – 4
Lamborghini Diablo, 1:40, yellow . . . . $3 – 4
Lotus Elan, 1/36th scale, metallic blue . . . . $3 – 4
Lotus Esprit, 1:38, metallic silver . . . . $3 – 4
Mercedes-Benz 500SL, black . . . . $3 – 4
Mercedes-Benz 500SL, metallic blue . . . . $3 – 4
Mercedes-Benz 500SL, metallic teal . . . . $3 – 4
MG RV8, 1:37, metallic green . . . . $3 – 4
Porsche 911 Carrera, 1:38, yellow . . . . $3 – 4
Porsche 911 Speedster Cabriolet, 1:38, red . . . . $3 – 4
Porsche 911 Speedster Cabriolet, 1:38, silver . . . . $3 – 4
Porsche 911 Turbo Flat Nose Cabriolet, white . . . . $3 – 4
Porsche 959, 1:36, silver . . . . $3 – 4

MINI TRANSPORTERS, 1:87 SCALE SEMI TRACTOR-TRAILERS

M57 Semi Rescue Helicopter Transporter $3
M58 Semi Racing Boat Transporter $3
M59 Fire Engine Semi $3
M60 Tanker Semi "Shell" $3
M61 Freighter Semi "Trans America Express" $3
M61 Freighter Semi "North American" $3
M62 Semi Police Helicopter Transporter $3

M63 Semi Car Transporter $3
M64 Semi Boat Transporter $3

MOTORIZED MODELS

Pullback action makes these models different from their Trophy counterparts. Many Trophy models are duplicated in this series. Here is just a sampling.

Aston Martin DB7, purple $6
Jaguar XJ220, silver $6
Lotus Esprit Turbo, silver $6

MAISTO TURBO TREADS/MC TOYS MINI RACERS

These toys match Matchbox regular series models in size and accuracy of scale. While most models have no moving parts, such as opening doors, their quality is remarkable for their usual price of two for $1 from Toy Liquidators. While most models are currently available, their quality and rising popularity should make them more valuable as collectible toys over the years.

Ambulance Truck . . . . $0.75 – 1.25
Audi Quattro, 8447 . . . . $0.75 – 1.25
BMW M1, 8448 . . . . $0.75 – 1.25
BMW 750il, 8742 . . . . $0.75 – 1.25

Caterpillar Quarry Dump Truck . . . . $0.75 – 1.25
Chevrolet Corvette, 8617 . . . . $0.75 – 1.25
Chevrolet Corvette ZR-1 . . . . $0.75 – 1.25
Ferrari F40, 9001 . . . . $0.75 – 1.25
Ferrari Testarossa, 9010 . . . . $0.75 – 1.25
Ferrari 250 GTO, 8736 . . . . $0.75 – 1.25
Ferrari 308 GTB, 8445 . . . . $0.75 – 1.25

Ferrari 348ts, 9101, $0.75 – 1.25

Ferrari 365 GTB, 9004 . . . . $0.75 – 1.25
Fire Ladder Truck . . . . $0.75 – 1.25

Ford Econovan, 9008, $0.75 – 1.25

Ford Escort 1.6i, 8449 . . . . $0.75 – 1.25
Ford Explorer . . . . $0.75 – 1.25
Ford Grenada 2.8 GL, 8451 . . . . $0.75 – 1.25

BMW 850i, 9005, $0.75 – 1.25

Buick LeSabre Stock Car, 8618, $0.75 – 1.25

Citroën 2CV, 8732, $0.75 – 1.25

Ford Sierra XR4Ti, 8441, $0.75 – 1.25

Ford Pick-Up, 8739 . . . . $0.75 – 1
Formula 1 Racer, 8733 . . . . $0.75 – 1
Formula 1 Racer, 8734 . . . . $0.75 – 1
Garbage Truck . . . . $1 – 1.25
Jaguar XJ-S V-12, 8613 . . . . $0.75 – 1
Jaguar XJ220 . . . . $0.75 – 1
Lamborghini Countach, 8735 . . . . $0.75 – 1
Lamborghini Diablo, 9006 . . . . $0.75 – 1
Lincoln Continental Mark VII . . . . $0.75 – 1

Motorcycle, $0.75 – 1.25

Mazda RX-7, 8738, $0.75 – 1.25

Mercedes-Benz Van, 8450 . . . . $0.75 – 1
Mercedes-Benz 260 SEL, 8615 . . . . $0.75 – 1

Nissan MID-4, 8737, $0.75 – 1.25

Mercedes-Benz 500 SL, 9011, $0.75 – 1.25

Nissan 300ZX, 8620, $0.75 – 1.25

Mercedes-Benz 500 SL, 8452, $0.75 – 1.25

Pontiac Firebird, 8443, $0.75 – 1.25

Mustang Mach III . . . . $0.75 – 1.25
Nissan 4x4 Dirt Truck . . . . $0.75 – 1.25
Peugeot 205 GTI, 8611 . . . . $0.75 – 1.25
Peugeot 309, 8614 . . . . $0.75 – 1.25
Peugeot 405 Turbo 16, 8741 . . . . $0.75 – 1.25
Porsche Turbo, 8444 . . . . $0.75 – 1.25

Porsche 356A, 9003 . . . . $0.75 – 1.25
Porsche 956, 8442 . . . . $0.75 – 1.25
Porsche 959, 9009 . . . . $0.75 – 1.25

Porsche 911 Speedster, 9012, $0.75 – 1.25

Renault 25V6 Turbo, 8612 . . . . $0.75 – 1.25

Suzuki SJ413Q Samurai, 8622, $0.75 – 1.25

Toyota MR-2, 8619 . . . . $0.75 – 1.25
Toyota SR5, 8621. . . . . $0.75 – 1.25

Trabant, 9002, $0.75 – 1.25

Volkswagen Eurovan, $0.75 – 1.25

Volkswagen Dune Racer, 8740. . . . . $0.75 – 1.25
Volkswagen Golf GTi, 8446 . . . . $0.75 – 1.25
Volkswagen NR-1060, 9007 . . . . $0.75 – 1.25
Volkswagen 1300 Beetle, 8731. . . . . $0.75 – 1.25
Volvo 760 GLE, 8616. . . . . $0.75 – 1.25

DIRT MOVER SETS

224200 Set 1, includes wheel loader with excavator, crane with
  ripper, and wheel loader with pile driver. $29
224300 Set 2, includes snow plow with ripper, wheel loader with
  ripper, and fork lift with log loader $29

AIRLINE SERIES

Commercial Airliners, 4" – 5" long, in attractive window
box.

Swissair. $4
British Airways $4
Japan Air Lines $4
Lufthansa $4

Alitalia, $4

Air France $4
United. $4
Cathay Pacific $4

2-WHEELERS 1:18 SCALE

Motorcycles, highly detailed, working suspension.

Honda NR, red, silver, and black $3
Kawasaki KLX250SR Dirt Bike, lime green with bright yellow, pink
  & purple accents $3
Kawasaki Ninja ZX-9R, red and silver. $3
Suzuki GSX750 Police Motorcycle, white and chrome $3
Yamaha XV1000 Virago Chopper, metallic red and chrome. . . . $3

MAJORETTE

HISTORY AND HERITAGE

Some of the world's most popular, or at least most proliferous, diecast toy cars and trucks come from the French
company known simply as Majorette. The company started
producing diecast toy cars and trucks in 1961. During the
early years, availability of Majorettes was very limited. Models often showed up as promotional models for various
retailers. In 1982, Majorettes became more readily available
to the US with the establishment of Majorette USA, with
headquarters in Miami, Florida.

It was not the best of times for introducing a new diecast

toy line to the US, as the 1980s saw the downfall, merger, or sellout of many popular toy companies such as Matchbox, Corgi, Dinky, and Solido. Nevertheless, Majorette created a niche in the US market that remains today perhaps as strong as ever, despite bankruptcy, receivership, and eventual sale of the company.

Solido of France, meanwhile, was almost one of the casualties of the era. This venerable brand of toys had existed independently since 1930. But as with other toy companies, Solido suffered financially too, eventually being purchased by Majorette in 1980. Fortunately the Solido line survives, as does Majorette.

In 1990, bankrupt Majorette was purchased by Ideal Loisirs (pronounced ee-dee-ALL LEE-zhurs), a French toy conglomerate. In turn, Playmates toy company of Hong Kong purchased a 37.5 percent interest in Ideal Loisirs in mid-1992.

Playmates made its mark in the toy industry with its popular licensed line of Teenage Mutant Ninja Turtles action figures. Since then, the company has been held together by the powerful force and extraordinary popularity of its Star Trek, Next Generation, and Deep Space Nine action figures, models, and playsets.

About the same time, a Portuguese brand of small, accurate-scale, mostly plastic toy vehicles called Novacars was assimilated into the Majorette line, becoming the new Majorette Novacars 100 Series. A listing of these models can be found separately under the Novacar listing.

The latest change in the business occurred when TA Triumph-Adler of Nuremburg, Germany, took a controlling share in the Ideal Loisirs Group. Triumph-Adler Toy Division is known for the Zapf brand of dolls, Tronico radio-controlled cars, Cartronic car racing tracks, Europlay summer toys, and Kidtech children's computers.

The result of this merger/buyout is that Majorette now belongs to one of the largest toy conglomerates in Europe, and one of the leading toy manufacturers in the world.

THE MAJORETTE LINE-UP

The backbone of the Majorette line of toys is the 200 Series, models approximately 3" long and mimicking the Matchbox 1-75 series. In many ways, as you will see, Majorette has taken a marketing approach very similar to Matchbox.

Like Matchbox's Two-Packs, Majorette's 300 Series offers vehicle and trailer in a single package, occasionally throwing in a second trailer and calling it a "bonus pack." And like Matchbox's Convoy/Super Rigs series, Majorette's 600 Series replicates semi tractors and trailers in 1:87 scale.

Many sub-series, such as Road Eaters, Smelly Speeders, and Sonic Flashers are created from regular series models. Other Majorette series feature models on a larger scale that offer a wide assortment of vehicles and sets. All of these models are covered in depth in the information that follows.

While Solido is now a subsidiary of Majorette, they remain distinctive in their own right, and are detailed in the section of this book devoted to Solido toys.

THE ORIGINAL MAJORETTE 100 SERIES

Originally the 100 Series was to be the primary series of 1:55 to 1:100 scale models, eventually being discontinued in favor of the current 200 Series. Now several of these older models have been reintroduced into the 200 Series as new models.

The new 100 Series now encompasses Novacars, highly accurate renditions with plastic bodies and metal chassis, except for the F1 Racers, which have metal bodies and plastic chassis. A list of Novacars can be found under its own heading below.

101-A BRM Formula 1 Racer
    v.1 unchromed $15
    v.2 chromed $15
102-A Porsche Formula 1 Racer
    v.1 unchromed $15
    v.2 chromed $15
107-A Hotchkiss Jeep with Cable Carrier $12
109-A Ferrari LeMans
    v.1 unchromed $15
    v.2 chromed $15
110-A Ferrari Formula 1 Racer
    v.1 unchromed $15
    v.2 chromed $15
113-A Citroën DS 21 . . . . $20
114-A Fiat Multi Benne Skip Truck 1:100 (later reissued as 222-A)

v.1 orange with red skip, $16

116-A Peugeot 404 Saloon $20

THE NEW MAJORETTE 100-SERIES NOVACARS

Novacar models, previously from Minia Porto Jogos E Brinquedos Lda. of Paredes, Portugal, were originally packaged in either a display blister card or a hook blister pack. The list below combines the original models along with new Majorette variations. Currently, models are marketed in a four-car blister pack set. Many of these models have been incorporated into the 200 Series for 1997.

101 Ferrari 308
    v.1 light yellow with red interior . . . . $0 – 1
    v.2 darker yellow with red interior . . . . $0 – 1
    v.3 red tan interior, 1996 . . . . $0 – 1
102 Nissan 300 ZX
    v.1 light blue with red interior, black & gold accents . . . . $0 – 1
    v.2 darker blue with red interior, black & gold accents . . . $0 – 1
    v.3 clear with silver flecks, blue-gray & yellow interior . . . $0 – 1

v.4 clear with silver flecks, purple & white interior. . . . . . $0 – 1

v.5 bright green with yellow & black racing accents, 1996. $0 – 1

103 Chevrolet Corvette

v.1 white with black "23," green & red accents . . . . $0 – 1

v.2 white with red "23," green & red accents . . . . $0 – 1

v.3 black with white accents . . . . $0 – 1

v.4 black with silver "CORVETTE" and Chevrolet logo . . . $0 – 1

v.5 clear with red flecks, dark red & white interior. . . . . $0 – 1

v.6 clear with silver flecks, purple & pink interior . . . . . $0 – 1

v.7 yellow with red & black "Grand Prix" accents . . . . . . $0 – 1

104 Ferrari Testarossa

v.1 red with "Ferrari" & logo on hood . . . . $0 – 1

v.2 red with "S RACING" on hood. . . . . $0 – 1

v.3 yellow with "S RACING" on hood, 1996 . . . . $0 – 1

105 Mercedes-Benz 500SL

v.1 silver with red interior, "500SL" on doors . . . . $0 – 1

v.2 silver with red interior, no markings . . . . $0 – 1

v.3 black with gray interior, no markings, 1996 . . . . $0 – 1

106 Peugeot 605

v.1 white with black interior . . . . $0 – 1

v.2 white with red interior. . . . . $0 – 1

v.3 blue with red & white "Rallye 5" accents, 1996. . . . . $0 – 1

107 Nissan Pathfinder/Terrano

v.1 red with black & white rally markings . . . . $0 – 1

v.2 green with black & white rally markings . . . . $0 – 1

v.3 white with black & gold "SHERIFF" markings. . . . . . $0 – 1

v.4 red with "FIRE DEPT." markings . . . . $0 – 1

108 Kenworth Semi Tractor

v.1 blue with red & white stars & stripes . . . . $0 – 1

v.2 red, 1996 . . . . $0 – 1

109 Chevrolet Impala Police Car

v.1 white with blue & gold markings. . . . . $0 – 1

v.2 black with white & gold markings . . . . $0 – 1

110 Renault Espace Van

v.1 red with "Espace" on sides in script lettering . . . . . . $0 – 1

v.2 white with blue "Ambulance" markings, orange accents. $0 – 1

v.3 yellow with blue & red rally accents . . . . $0 – 1

111 Porsche LeMans GT Racer/Sport proto

v.1 black with white accents, "TOP DRIVERS" on nose, silver-
gray windows . . . . $0 – 1

v.2 clear with yellow flecks, lime green interior . . . . $0 – 1

v.3 clear with silver flecks, blue-gray interior . . . . $0 – 1

v.4 turquoise with white & coral racing accents, coral windows,
1996 . . . . $0 – 1

112 F1 Racer

v.1 yellow with red & black accents, red plastic base . . . . $0 – 1

v.2 black with gold & red accents, white plastic base . . . . $0 – 1

113 Volkswagen Caravelle Van

v.1 red with black & gold accents . . . . $0 – 1

v.2 red with "Surf" accents . . . . $0 – 1

114 Ford Escort GT

v.1 yellow with red & black rally accents. . . . . $0 – 1

116 Chevrolet Extended Cab Pickup

v.1 black with white accents . . . . $0 – 1

v.2 clear with red flecks, dark red & white interior. . . . . $0 – 1

v.3 clear with yellow flecks, lime green & pink interior . . $0 – 1

v.4 white with blue "POLICE" accents, 1996. . . . . $0 – 1

v.5 black with tan mudsplash accents, 1996 . . . . $0 – 1

117 Honda Acura NSX

v.1 red with black interior. . . . . $0 – 1

v.2 red with white interior. . . . . $0 – 1

119 Jeep

v.1 blue with black top, yellow accents, 1995 . . . . $0 – 1

120 Ferrari F40

v.1 red . . . . $0 – 1

121 Ford Van

v.1 purple with flame accents . . . . $0 – 1

MAJORETTE 200 SERIES

Like Matchbox, Majorette replaces various models every year, resulting in new models with the same model number as old ones. So a letter code has been assigned to each model number to designate each successive model change. Several sub-series have been marketed, which are included in the variations below. One of those is Kool Kromes, models in various colors of chrome. Another is Road Eaters, models with advertising for food and candy on them. A third sub-series is Smelly Speeders ("Not Stinky — Just For Kids"), models each with distinctive scents and appropriate trademark names. These models are repeated in their own section for easier cross-reference. In 1995, another sub-series was introduced called Supers, models that steer. Since they have been assigned new numbers that don't coincide with the regular 200 series, they have been listed following the 200 Series.

201-A St. Tropez Travel Trailer, 1:68 . . . . $10

201-B Citroën GS. $6

201-C Citroën Visa II Chrono Mille Pistes, 1:52

v.1 white, "CHRONO" $2

v.2 white, "4 ROUES MOTRICES" $2

v.3 yellow, "4 ROUES MOTRICES" $2

201-D Ford Model A Van, 1:60

v.1 metallic red, "TEA SHOP" $4

v.2 blue, "TEA SHOP". $4

v.3 Road Eaters bright orange "Willy Wonka Runts". $3

v.4 Road Eaters red "Campbell's Teddy Bears". $3

v.5 blue "Cadbury Dairy Milk" $6

v.6 blue "Cadbury Buttons". $6

v.7 blue "Orange Company" $2

202-A VW 113 . . . . $8

202-B VW 1302 Beetle, trunk opens, 1:60

v.1 red with yellow lightning bolt on trunk, $6

v.2 red with yellow flower on trunk $9

202-C Triumph TR7

v.1 red "TR7" & "35" markings, $2

v.2 red, no markings $2
v.3 orange "TR7 & "35" markings $2
202-D Peugeot 405 T16
   v.1 Kool Kromes orange. $3
   v.2 Kool Kromes blue. $3

v.3 yellow, $2

v.4 red. $2
203-A Etalmobile Warehouse Vehicle, 1:50 . . . . $15
203-B Fiat 127, doors open, dog on back seat looking out left rear
   window, 1:55

v.1 hot pink, $8

v.2 blue $6
v.3 metallic blue. $6
v.4 red $8
v.5 lime green $8
v.6 metallic yellow-green $6
203-C Police Motorcycle. $20

203-D Volkswagen 1302 Beetle, trunk doesn't open (Coccinelle)

v.1 lime green, $3

v.2 blue $3
v.3 light blue $4
204-A Bernard Fire Engine $15
204-B Dodge Fire Rescue. $6
204-C Bank Security Armored Truck, 1:57

v.1 yellow with green label, $2

v.2 yellow with red, white & blue accents, $2

v.3 white $2
v.4 silver $2
204-D Ferrari 456 GT, 1994 . . . . $2
204-E Ferrari F50 Coupe, 1997 . . . . $2
205-A Bernard Dump Truck $8
205-B Saab Scania Dump Truck
   v.1 yellow with red dumper $6
   v.2 silver with red dumper $6
205-C Renault Super Cinq GT Turbo, 1:51

v.1 black (1988 version) $2

v.2 blue (1989 version) $2

205-D Jaguar XJ6 Police, 1994 . . . . $3

206-A Bernard Flat Truck with Racks, 1:50 . . . . $12

206-B Bernard Flat truck with Scraper, 1:50 . . . . . . $12

206-C Bernard Cattle Carrier, 1:50 . . . . $12

206-D Peugeot 404 Ambulance $12

206-E Citroën Ambulance $8

206-F Pontiac Fiero

v.1 yellow with red interior $2

v.2 red with white interior $2

v.3 white with red interior $2

206-G Renault Twingo Minivan, 1995 . . . . $4

207-A Jaguar XKE 2+2 Coupe $10

207-B Jaguar E. $8

207-C Rock Motorcycle $15

207-D Extending Ladder Fire Truck (Pompier), 1:100

v.1 red with no lettering $4

v.2 red with gold lettering "F.D.S.F.," wheat laurel insignia . . . $2

v.3 red with gold lettering "F.D.N.Y.," four petal insignia $2

208-A Bernard Snow Plow, 1:50 . . . . $12

208-B Chrysler 180, 1:60

v.1 metallic green $10

208-C Farm Tractor 1:65

v.1 green with black fenders, cultivator $2

v.2 red with black fenders, cultivator $2

v.3 green with yellow fenders, $2

v.4 yellow with green fenders $2

v.5 green with green fenders $2

209-A Dodge Camper $12

209-B Porsche 911 Turbo, 1:57

v.1 yellow with orange & blue accents, narrow tires $6

v.2 red with black & silver accents, wide tires $3

v.3 black with red & white accents, wide tires $3

v.4 Kool Kromes copper with white interior, black base, wide tires $3

v.5 Smelly Speeders yellow with red base, "CHOCOLATE WAVE" $3

v.6 fluorescent orange with white interior, white accents $2

v.7 Road Eaters fluorescent orange with white accents, "SWANSON KIDS FUN FEAST" $3

v.8 Road Eaters red with "CAMPBELL'S DINOSAUR VEGETABLE SOUP" $3

v.9 Kool Kromes light blue $2

v.10 Kool Kromes bronze $2

v.11 red with logo on hood, $2

210-A Volkswagen K70, 1:60

v.1 yellow $8

v.2 red $8

v.3 bright red-orange $8

v.4 blue, $8

210-B Volkswagen Golf, 1:60

v.1 red with yellow "GOLF" on sides, $4

v.2 red with silver "GOLF" on sides, $4

210-C Peugeot 205 CTI/GTI Cabriolet (compare to 281-A), 1:53
   v.1 blue with red & white accents $2
   v.2 white with black CTI & accent stripe on sides $2
   v.3 white with no markings $2
   v.4 silver with orange & blue paint burst accents $2
210-D Peugeot 205 GTI/CTI Hardtop (see 281-A), 1:53 . . . . . . $2
211-A Hotchkiss Jeep with Cattle Trailer $16
211-B Four Wheel Loader $8
211-C Tractor with Plow (var. of 263 Tractor Shovel) $6
211-D Road Grader Shovel $4
211-E Ferrari GTO, 1:56
   v.1 red with Ferrari logo on hood $2
   v.2 red with white lower body, gold "23" on doors $2
   v.3 red with gold "23" on doors $2
211-F Ferrari Testarossa, 1997 . . . . $2
212-A Bernard Circus Truck $16
212-B Dodge Wrecker Tow Truck
   v.1 white with blue roof light $6
212-C Ford Escort XR3, 1:52

v.1 black with red & white accents, $2

v.2 yellow with red & black accents $2

v.3 red with black & orange accents, $2

v.4 black with gold accents $2
212-D Pontiac Firebird, 1995 . . . . $2
213-A Citroën DS19
   v.1 blue with red interior $12
213-B Citroën DS21 . . . . $10
213-C Mercedes-Benz 350SL Convertible, 1:60
   v.1 silver with red-orange accents $4
   v.2 yellow $6
213-D Mercedes-Benz 450 SL $4
213-E Mercedes-Benz Stake Truck with hay bales, 1:100
   v.1 red with brown stake bed, yellow bales $6
213-F Chevrolet Impala Taxi (also 219-A), 1:69

   v.1 yellow $3
   v.2 yellow & black $2
213-G F1 Racer, 1995 . . . . $2
214-A Citroën DS21 with Boat $16
214-B Saviem Container Truck
   v.1 white with "PEPSI" logo $6
   v.2 white & blue with "ADIDAS" logo $5
214-C 20 Panel Truck $6
214-D Nissan 300ZX Turbo T-Roof, 1:62
   v.1 white with black, red & blue "MOBIL 1" accents $2
   v.2 white with red "300ZX" accents $2

v.3 yellow with blue & white accents, $2

v.4 red with white interior $2

v.5 red with black & white accents, green interior, $2

215-A Citroën DS21 with Caravan $16
215-B Unimog with Fork Lift

v.1 blue & white with "AIR FRANCE" label, $6

215-C Chevrolet Grand Prix Corvette (also 268-A), 1:57
   v.1 black with red & white accents, "43 GOODYEAR" $2
   v.2 black with gold & black accents $2

v.3 blue with gold & black accents $2
v.4 blue with red & white accents, "43 GOODYEAR" $2
v.5 metallic blue with gold & black accents $4
v.6 pearl with red & black accents, "500 MILES" $2
v.7 red with black & gold accents, "500 MILES" $2
v.8 red with pink & gold accents, "500 MILES" $2
v.9 yellow with red & black accents, "500 MILES" $2
v.10 black with gold & white accents $2
v.11 red with "ZR1" on doors $2
216-A Peugeot 404 Police $10
216-B 1969 Plymouth Fury Police
v.1 metallic blue with white interior, star & 6 on hood $6
216-C Toyota Lite Ace Van Wagon, 1:52

v.1 black with gold accents, $3

v.2 blue with no markings, $3

v.3 metallic teal blue with yellow & orange accents, $3

v.4 silver with red accents $4
v.5 metallic blue with silver & orange accents $3
v.6 mustard yellow with bluebird accent on sides $4
v.7 white with red accents $3
v.8 white with red, blue & yellow accents $3
v.9 blue with "First Sport Turbo" accents $3
217-A Peugeot 404 Saloon with Alpine $16
217-B BMW Turbo $6
217-C Ford Thunderbird Turbo, 1:67
v.1 red with black base $2
v.2 blue with yellow accents $2
v.3 metallic red $2
v.4 yellow with black interior, "GAMBLER" $2
v.5 blue with red trim $3
v.6 Smelly Speeders white with white tires, brown trim, "COOL
COCONUT" $3
217-D Chevrolet Pickup, 1997 . . . . $1
218-A Bernard Sanitation Truck $12
218-B Mercedes-Benz Sanitation Truck, 1:100
v.1 silver & orange "VILLE DE PARIS" $4

v.2 silver & green "VILLE DE PARIS," $4

v.3 orange & gray "VILLE DE PARIS" $6
218-C Peugeot 405 Mi 16, 1:62
v.1 red with black plastic trim & interior $2
v.2 blue with white plastic trim & interior $2
v.3 white with red plastic trim & interior $2
218-D Peugeot 406, 1997 . . . . $2
219-A Bernard Stake Truck $7
219-B Matra Simca Bagheera, 1:55

v.1 blue with white interior, $5

219-C Honda Accord, 1:59
v.1 metallic mint green with white accents $3
v.2 metallic green with white accents $3
v.3 yellow with blue accents $3

v.4 Kool Kromes metallic yellow. $3
219-D Chevrolet Impala Taxi (also 213-F)
   v.1 yellow $3
   v.2 black & yellow $3
219-E Lamborghini Diablo, 1:58
   v.1 Kool Kromes yellow $3
   v.2 Kool Kromes red $3
   v.3 Road Eaters black "CRY BABY" candy logo $3
   v.4 Road Eaters white "PEPSI" logo. $4
   v.5 yellow with no markings. $2
   v.6 red with logo on hood $2
220-A Volvo 245 DL Station Wagon 1:60
   v.1 red. $6

v.2 green, $6

220-B Mustang SVO 1:59
   v.1 metallic periwinkle blue with no markings, narrow tires. . $4

v.2 metallic periwinkle blue with no markings, oversized tires, $4

v.3 metallic periwinkle blue with red & white accents, oversized tires, $2

   v.4 metallic turquoise, oversized tires $2
   v.5 white with red accents, oversized tires. $2
   v.6 white with black & red accents, narrow tires $3

   v.7 white with bright blue front half, red diagonal stripes on sides, oversized tires. $3
   v.8 white with blue front half, red diagonal stripes on sides, oversized tires $3
   v.9 white with metallic blue front half, red diagonal stripes on sides, oversized tires. $3
   v.10 red with horse and "MUSTANG" on sides, narrow tires . $2
   v.11 Oregon State Police cruiser, one-of-a-kind customized by Richard Burns. $25
220-C Honda Acura NSX, 1997. $2
221-A Renault R16 . . . . $10
221-B Bertone Camargue $6
221-C Audi Quattro, 1:58
   v.1 white with multicolor "MONTE CARLO" rally markings . . $3
   v.2 blue with black & gold accents $3
   v.3 white with no markings $3
   v.4 white "AUDI SPORT" $3
   v.5 white with yellow, black, gray & red accents, "IN:NY 35 MICHELIN". $3
221-D Renault X54. . . . . $3
221-E Renault Safrane

v.1 blue, $2

v.2 white with rally markings $2
222-A Fiat Skip Truck Multi Benne (previously 114-A), 1:100

v.1 red with yellow skip, $6

v.2 orange with blue skip. $8
222-B Renault 25 V6, 1:63
   v.1 metallic burgundy. $2
   v.2 metallic pale green $2
   v.3 metallic blue. $2

v.4 metallic gray. $2

v.5 deep blue. $2

223-A Mobile Office. $8

223-B Crazy Car 4x4 . . . . $6

223-C Desert Raider 4x4

v.1 black with red & gold accents $3

223-D '57 Chevy Hot Rod

v.1 Road Eaters white with "CHEE-TOS CHESTER CHEETAH"
logo. $3

v.2 Road Eaters white with "PETER PAN CREAMY" logo $3

v.3 Kool Kromes copper. $3

v.4 red with orange flame accents. $2

v.5 baby blue with magenta & white accents "FIFTIES" $2

v.6 metallic teal blue with flames $2

224-A Unimog Snow Plow (also 259) $8

224-B Fourgon Motor Home, 1:67

v.1 white $8

v.2 beige $8

224-C Jeep Cherokee Limited w/surfboards on roof (also 285), 1:60

v.1 black with gold accents, orange surfboards $2

v.2 black with gold accents, hot pink surfboards $2

v.3 dark blue with yellow fenders, orange surfboards $2

v.4 black with blue & white waves, orange surfboards. $2

v.5 SHERIFF (see 285)

225-A Dodge Safari Truck, 1:80

v.1 yellow with paint streaks off hood. $10

v.2 orange with paint streaks off hood $10

225-B BX4TC

v.1 white with red & blue accents, "TOTAL 15" $5

225-C Renault 19 Convertible. $2

226-A Repco F1 Racer $10

226-B Volkswagen Van $10

226-C Road Roller

v.1 light yellow $2

v.2 darker yellow. $2

227-A Lotus F1 Racer $10

227-B Magirus Beton Cement Mixer, 1:100

v.1 red cab, orange body, blue & yellow mixer. $8

227-C Ford Mustang GT Convertible, 1:59

v.1 yellow "OFFICIAL PACE CAR". $2

v.2 lime green "OFFICIAL PACE CAR". $2

v.3 yellow "MUSTANG GT" $2

v.4 bright blue $2

v.5 metallic purple with white & orange accents $2

228-A BRM F1 Racer $10

228-B Chevy Blazer Wrecker (Depanneuse) (also 291-A), 1:62

v.1 silver with yellow, red & black accents, "auto assistance" on
hood $2

v.2 silver with no markings. $4

v.3 blue with silver sticker on hood "EXPRESS 24/24" $2

v.4 red with blue, white & black accents "auto assistance" on
hood $2

v.5 blue with yellow, red & white accents "EXPRESS 24/24" on
hood $2

v.6 fluorescent orange with blue, white & black accents
"EXPRESS 24/24" on hood $2

v.7 fluorescent orange with black & white "24 HR SERVICE" on
hood & doors. $2

v.8 fluorescent orange with black & white checkerboard pattern
on sides "SERVICE". $2

v.9 red w/black & white accents "EMERGENCY ROAD SERVICE". $2

v.10 red, no markings (blue "24/24 quick TOWING" stickers are
from MajoKit set) $3

v.11 white with blue lettering, red accents, "EMERGENCY ROAD
SERVICE" $2

229-A Ferrari F1 Racer

v.1 metallic purple with checkered stripe. $10

229-B Datsun 260Z, 1:60

v.1 yellow with red accents $3

v.2 metallic light green $5

v.3 red. $4

v.4 yellow with red, black & yellow accents $3

v.5 metallic turquoise $5

229-C BMW 325i, 1:56

v.1 white with red & blue accents. $2

v.2 white with red, blue & black accents. $2

v.3 silver with red & black accents $2

229-D Aston Martin DB7, 1994

v.1 blue $3

230-A Peugeot 204 Roadster. $10

230-B Renault 4L Delivery Van, 1:55

v.1 red. $8

v.2 yellow $8

v.3 blue with white telephone dial logo $8

230-C Volvo 760 GLE, 1:61

v.1 silver with red & black accents, without markings $3

v.2 silver with red & black accents, diagonal markings across
doors $3

v.3 metallic periwinkle blue with red & black accents, no diagonal markings $3

v.4 metallic dark green, no markings. $3

v.5 metallic green, no markings $3

v.6 metallic teal blue, no markings, black interior $3

v.7 metallic teal blue, no markings, white interior $3

230-D Ford Transit Custom Tow Truck

v.1 white with "TOTAL" logo $2

v.2 red with "Jack's 24 HR. Service". $2

231-A Citroën Dyane Raid $8

231-B Mercedes-Benz 190E 2.3-16, 1:59

v.1 metallic green. $3

v.2 metallic pewter gray $3

v.3 metallic silver $3

v.4 white with blue & orange rally accents $2

232-A Porsche LeMans Racer, 1:65

v.1 metallic red, $9

232-B Formula 1 Brabham, 1:53
  v.1 blue & white, "parmalat" $2
  v.2 black & light gray, "parmalat" $2
232-C Dune Buggy
  v.1 hot pink with white roof, "FUN BUGGY" $4
  v.2 hot pink with white roof, "ICE CREAM" $3
233-A Panther Bertone Course Racer, 1:65

v.1 lime green with yellow base, gray spoiler, $10

  v.2 yellow with gray spoiler $10
233-B Mercedes Public Works Truck (Trax Publics), 1:70
  v.1 metallic light blue with white cargo cover (stickers are from
    MajoKit set) $4
  v.2 orange $5
233-C Renault Express Van, 1:53
  v.1 orange "europcar rentacar" $5
  v.2 white "europcar rentacar" $5
  v.3 red "AVIS" $4
  v.4 blue, "SATELLITE SERVICE" $3
234-A Locomotive $15
234-B Simca 1100 . . . . $8
234-C Fourgon Commercial Van, 1:53
  v.1 white with "Fruits" label, red rear doors $2
  v.2 white with "Fruits" tampo, white rear doors $2
  v.3 white with "Hawaiian Surfer" label, red rear doors $3
  v.4 yellow with "racing team" label, red rear doors #2 . . . . . $2
  v.5 Police Van (see 279-A) $3
  v.6 yellow with red trim, "ELEPHANT RESERVE" (part of 344 Ele-
    phant Cage Transporter) $2
  v.7 white with "RACING TEAM" markings $2
  v.8 white with blue fenders, "BASEBALL" $2
  v.9 red "Coca-Cola," sun, 1995 . . . . $4
  v.10 blue "Cadbury Dairy Milk Buttons" $6
  v.11 white with blue fenders, "SKATE BOARD" $2
235-A BMW 2800CS Coupe $7
235-B Motorboat and Trailer. $15
235-C BMW 3.0 CSI, 1:60
  v.1 yellow $4
235-D Renault Acadiane Service Van, 1:53
  v.1 yellow with white rear doors, white envelope insignia on
    sides $4
  v.2 blue $4
235-E Volkswagen Golf GTI 16S, 1:56
  v.1 yellow with blue & white accents $2
235-F Sport Proto Racer, 1997 . . . . $2

236-A Sterckeman Lovely 400 Travel Trailer, 1:65 . . . . $12
236-B Bernard Truck with Chalet $12
236-C Peugeot 604 (also 238-A) $4
236-D Jeep Cherokee 4x4, 1:64. Early versions featured a dog in
  the back, double side window trim and ribbed roof. Later versions eliminated the dog. Most recent versions feature simplified side window casting and no roof ribs.
  v.1 red with white & black, orange & blue rally accents, dog in
    back. $3
  v.2 red with white & black, orange & blue rally accents, no dog
    in back. $2
  v.3 yellow with red & black accents, dog in back, ribbed roof . $3
  v.4 fluorescent green with red & white flames, no dog, plain
    roof $2
  v.5 Road Eaters black "CHEE-TOS CHESTER CHEETAH," no dog,
    plain roof. $3
  v.6 green with ribbed roof $2
  v.7 metallic brown with "BIG CHIEF," dog in back, ribbed roof . $5
  v.8 red with black "MAD BULL" accents, ribbed roof $4
  v.9 light brown, "BIG CHIEF," dog in back, ribbed roof. $3
  v.10 fluorescent orange with blue & white flame accents, ribbed
    roof $2
  v.11 Smelly Speeders, yellow "ROCKIN' BANANA," plain roof. $3
  v.12 Road Eaters, blue with "Franco American SpaghettiOs/
    TeddyOs" $3
  v.13 yellow with western motif, "INDIAN" on roof. $2
  v.14 white "Coca-Cola" polar bear $10
237-A Mercedes-Benz 280SE. $10
237-B Maharadjah $8
237-C Lamborghini Countach, 1:56
  v.1 red with black spoiler, black & yellow accents. $2
  v.2 red with red spoiler, no markings $2
  v.3 red with red spoiler, white "COUNTACH" accents $2
  v.4 red with plain yellow spoiler, black & white checkered
    accents, "78" on sides $2
  v.5 red with "Lamborghini" on yellow spoiler, black & white
    checkered accents, "78" on sides. $2
  v.6 red with plain yellow spoiler, gold & white accents, bull
    logo $3
238-A Peugeot 604 (also 236-A)
  v.1 black $5
  v.2 metallic blue. $5
238-B Formula 1 Racer, 1:55
  v.1 green with red base, red & white accents, "Benetton" . . . $6
  v.2 yellow with red base, red & blue accents, "RACING" $2
  v.3 yellow with blue accents. $2
  v.4 light blue with red base, blue "Rallye" on yellow accents,
    blue "41" on red accent $2
239-A Peugeot 504. . . . . $6
239-B Matra Simca 670
  v.1 metallic blue, "10, Goodyear, Shell" $5
239-C Fiat Ritmo/Strada
  v.1 yellow with black accents, "ABARTH 2000" $4
  v.2 red with black accents, "ABARTH 2000". $4
  v.3 red with no markings $5
239-D Audi 90 (also 259), 1:60
  v.1 black with white & yellow tampos. $2
  v.2 yellow with "AUDI 90" & logo on sides $2

239-E Chevrolet Blazer, 1995 . . . . $2

240-A Simca 1308, 1:60
   v.1 dark silver $6
   v.2 blue $6

240-B Chevrolet Impala Police Car, 1:69
   v.1 white with black accents, "POLICE N 31" $3
   v.2 black and white w/gold accents, "HIGHWAY PATROL N 31". $3
   v.3 black with white doors, "POLICE N31" $2

241-A DAF 2600 Covered Platform Truck, 1:100 . . . . $7

241-B Saviem Canvas Top Truck
   v.1 orange with red canopy, "JOE CIRCUS" $5
   v.2 blue with white canopy, "SERNAM" $5
   v.3 blue with yellow canopy, "SAVIEM SERVICE" $5

241-C Ford Covered Truck, 1:100
   v.1 green body, yellow canopy, "super cargo" label $2
   v.2 white body, metallic gray canopy, "majorette" tampo $2
   v.3 white body, white canopy, "majorette" tampo $2
   v.4 white body blue canopy, "MOVING STUDIO" tampo $2
   v.5 white body, "ELF Competition" $2
   v.6 red with white cargo cover, "Coca-Cola" $4
   v.7 blue "Cadbury Roses Chocolates" $6

242-A Dodge Snow Top Truck with Plow $6

242-B Power Shovel (Pelle Mechanique, Pelleteuse), 1:100
   v.1 red body, yellow base, yellow shovel $3
   v.2 yellow body, black base and shovel $2

243-A DAF Covered Trailer $12

243-B F1 Racer $4

243-C Ford Transit Van (also 259-A), 1:60
   v.1 white with blue & red accents, blue interior & bumpers, "CITY BUS" $4
   v.2 blue with silver & gold accents, blue interior & bumpers, "CITY BUS" $4
   v.3 red with blue & white accents, white interior & bumpers . $3
   v.4 red with blue & white accents, red interior & bumpers . . . $3
   v.5 metallic pale green with blue interior & bumpers $3
   v.6 metallic pale green with hot pink interior & bumpers $3
   v.7 metallic pale green with red interior & bumpers $4
   v.8 white with black interior & bumpers, "CITY BUS" $3
   v.9 white with red & blue diagonal stripes $3
   v.10 pearl white w/hot pink interior & bumpers, tropical accents . $3
   v.11 white with red, metallic blue & green accents, pink interior & bumpers $2
   v.12 red with yellow interior & bumpers, "City Bus" in script, "210291" on sides $2
   v.13 white with red interior & bumpers, "LE MANS SPORT" . . $2
   v.14 white with pink interior & bumpers, "Splish Splash" accents . $2
   v.15 red with blue & white accents, yellow interior & bumpers . $2
   v.16 yellow "School Bus" with red interior and bumpers $3

244-A Volkswagen Ambulance
   v.1 metallic blue with white interior, "POLICE" $8
   v.2 white with red cross, "AMBULANCE" $6
   v.3 orange with white interior, "SERVICE AUTOROUTE" $6

244-B Jeep 4x4 (also 268-A, 290-A), 1:54
   v.1 red with white roof, rally markings, black interior $3
   v.2 red with black roof, black/red/blue/light blue accents, "RENEGADE" $3
   v.3 metallic light green with black roof, black/green/periwinkle accents, "RENEGADE" $2

   v.4 black with yellow roof, eagle logo on hood $3
   v.5 black with white roof, rally markings $3
   v.6 hot pink with black roof $2

245-A DAF 2600 Tanker, 1:100
   v.1 "SHELL" $6

245-B Saviem Tanker, 1:100
   v.1 orange & red $8
   v.2 red with white tank, "Shell" $6
   v.3 red with white tank, "ESSO" $6
   v.4 blue with white tank, "GULF" $6
   v.5 red-orange with white tank, "EWING OIL CO." $20

245-C Ford Tanker (Citerne), 1:100
   v.1 blue with white tank, "Milky the good milk" $3
   v.2 white with white tank, "Shell" $3
   v.3 yellow with white tank, "Shell" $2

246-A DAF 2600 Bucket Truck, 1:100 . . . . $15

246-B Range Rover Rescue Unit with closed rear section, 1:60
   v.1 red with white interior, white ladder $4

246-C Range Rover Rescue Unit with closed rear section, 1:60
   v.1 red with black interior, silver ladder, gold "DISTRICT 3 FIRE DEPT." $2
   v.2 red with black interior, white ladder, gold "RESCUE UNIT" . $2
   v.3 red with white interior, white ladder, blue shield $2

247-A DAF 2600 Crane Truck, 1:100
   v.1 yellow with black crane, gray plastic base $12
   v.2 metallic light green with black crane, gray plastic base . . $12

247-B Porsche 924, 1:60
   v.1 green with white "PORSCHE" accents, amber windows . . $6
   v.2 red with silver "PORSCHE" accents, amber windows $6
   v.3 metallic blue with orange "PORSCHE" accents, clear windows $4

247-C Refuse Truck (Benne Ordures), 1:100
   v.1 green body, gray container, no markings $5
   v.2 green body, orange container, no markings $4
   v.3 lime green body, orange container, hippo on sides $3
   v.4 lime green body, tan container with 3 hippos on sides . . . $2
   v.5 red body with yellow container, "CITY of NEW YORK" . . $2
   v.6 white body, orange container with 3 hippos on sides $2
   v.7 red body, fluorescent yellow container with 3 hippos on sides $2

248-A Dune Buggy, randomly hand-placed flower and lightning decals on roof and jaguar on nose, 1:55
   v.1 red with black roof, chrome spiral wheels $6
   v.2 lime green with white roof, chrome spiral wheels $6

v.3 lime green with black roof, chrome spiral wheels, $6

248-B Pontiac Firebird Trans Am (also 258-B), 1:62
  v.1 black with brown & gold firebird insignia on hood $2
  v.2 metallic blue with brown & gold insignia on hood. $2
  v.3 metallic blue with black & gold insignia on hood. $2
  v.4 pink. $2
  v.5 red w/black & white racing accents, "8, TURBO RACING". $2
  v.6 red with gold firebird insignia on hood $2
  v.7 red with silver & black firebird insignia on hood $2
249-A Ski-Doo Nordic Snowmobile. $16
249-B Mercedes-Benz 450 SE, 1:60
  v.1 metallic gold. $3
  v.2 metallic light green $3
  v.3 metallic silver $2
249-C Toyota Celica 2.0 GT, 1:58
  v.1 red with white accent on sides, "CELICA" $2
  v.2 white with red & green accents. $2
249-D GMC Jimmy, 1995 . . . . $2
250-A Citroën Maserati SM $10
250-B Ford US Van (variation of 234), 1:65
  v.1 black with exhaust pipe on left side $5
250-C Mercedes-Benz 300TE Station Wagon, 1:63
  v.1 blue with charcoal gray interior & bumpers $3
  v.2 white w/blue & white "MERCEDES BENZ SERVICE" on sides . $3
  v.3 blue w/white interior & bumpers, white accents, "ASSISTANCE". $3
251-A Ford Capri
  v.1 light blue with white roof, dark blue, light blue & white hood stripes. $6
  v.2 red. $6
  v.3 orange with black roof $6
251-B Ford Bronco 4x4, 1:56
  v.1 black with silver accent & gold stars on sides, no sunroof . $2
  v.2 black with silver & gold accents, no sunroof $2
  v.3 black with silver & gold accents, with sunroof $2
  v.4 mustard yellow, no markings $4
251-C Service Boom Truck. $2
252-A Dune Buggy Surfer JP4 with surfboards, 1:47
  v.1 blue with pink plastic trim, yellow roll cage. $4
  v.2 red with white plastic trim, black roll cage. $4
252-B Honda Prelude 4WD, 1:58
  v.1 red with black & silver accents, silver Honda logo on hood. $3
253-A Ford 5000 Farm Tractor, 1:55
  v.1 blue with white fenders and wheels $8
253-B Oldsmobile Omega, 1:75
  v.1 metallic blue. $6
  v.2 white with black & red accents, "Firestone 23 SEIKO" . . . $6
  v.3 silver with red interior, black & red "ZZ" stripes on sides . $6
253-C Cadillac Allante
  v.1 Kool Kromes yellow with black interior. $2
  v.2 Kool Kromes light green with black interior. $2
  v.3 Kool Kromes light blue $2
  v.4 hot pink with white interior, no markings $2
  v.5 silver with red roof $5
  v.6 hot pink w/white interior, blue/orange/green/yellow accents. $2
  v.7 Road Eaters fluorescent lime green with white interior, "Franco American SpaghettiOs". $3
  v.8 green with red/white/blue/pink accents, white interior . . $2
254-A Mercedes-Benz Stake Truck with Hay Load, 1:100
  v.1 red & brown. $6

254-B Mercedes Cattle truck, 1:100
  v.1 yellow with light brown horse box and gray door, one black steer, one white steer $6
254-C Citroën XM
  v.1 metal flake silver, black interior. $3
  v.2 white $2
255-A Bulldozer. $4
255-B Renault R5 Turbo, 1:53
  v.1 red with yellow interior & lower body, "TURBO". $4
255-C Renault Maxi 5 turbo 1985, 1:53
  v.1 blue with red interior & lower body, red & white rally accents, "PHILLIPS, elf, 3". $3
255-D Ambulance Truck, 1:60
  v.1 white with orange accents, blue "NYC EMS AMBULANCE". $2
256-A ATF $12
256-B BMW 733, 1:60
  v.1 burgundy with yellow "FEDERATION EQUESTRE FRANCAISE" on hood $5
  v.2 metallic light green, no markings. $5
  v.3 silver, no markings $5
  v.4 white with green/orange/yellow horse & horseshoe label on hood $5
256-C Mack Tow Truck (also 297), 1:100
  v.1 red with gray plastic deck, black crane, silver metal hook . $2
257-A Renault 5 LeCar with antenna & rear view mirrors, 1:55 (compare to 280-A)
  v.1 metallic silver $8
  v.2 pale yellow $8
  v.3 red with white "RTL" on blue & yellow accents stripe . . . $8
257-B Mazda RX7 Daytona, 1:56
  v.1 blue with silver "21," black "MAZDA" $2
  v.2 orange with blue accents, wide tires $3
  v.3 orange with blue accents, narrow tires. $4
  v.4 orange with black & silver "21 MAZDA" $2
  v.5 white with black & red accents, "23" $2
  v.6 white with "Mobil 1" accents $2
  v.7 black with silver & gold "21 MAZDA" $2
257-C BMW 325i, 1995
  v.1 metallic dark olive green. $2
  v.2 burgundy $2
258-A Dune Buggy with awning and amber windshield, chrome spiral wheel design
  v.1 yellow with white awning, yellow flower design on roof with red outline, green leaf. $10
  v.2 yellow with white awning, dark blue pansy design on roof . $10

v.4 red with white awning, dark blue pansy design on roof, $10

135

v.3 red with white awning, red and yellow flower design on roof $10

258-B Mercedes-Benz Fire Engine (Pompier Aeroport), 1:70
v.1 red & white $6

258-C Pro Stocker Firebird with Oversized Engine, 1:62
v.1 white with red & blue stars & stripes $2
v.2 yellow with black & red accents $2

259-A Dune Buggy $10

259-B Camping Trailer $6

259-C Fourgon Ice Cream Van (Glacier)
v.1 green with pale blue windows, yellow awning & interior . $5
v.2 metallic red with pale blue windows, yellow awning & interior $5
v.3 pink with pale blue windows, yellow awning & interior . . $5
v.4 red with clear windows, yellow awning & interior $5
v.5 red with pale blue windows, yellow awning & interior . . . $5
v.6 yellow with pink windows, white awning with no accents, cream interior $6
v.7 yellow with blue windows, white awning with no accents, cream interior $6
v.8 white with red awning $4

259-D Audi 90 (also 239), 1:60
v.1 yellow $2

259-E British Bus (also 286-A), 1:125
v.1 red with amber windows, white interior, "BRITISH AIRWAYS" label $6

260-A Renault 17 . . . . $6

260-B Explorateur 4x4, 1:59
v.1 gold with cream canopy with green design, brown interior . $5
v.2 metallic blue with white canopy & interior, "TUNIS 483 DAKAR" $5

260-C Mercedes-Benz 500SL Roadster, 1:58
v.1 deep red with maroon interior $3
v.2 Kool Kromes light green-blue with metallic gray interior & bumpers $2
v.3 Kool Kromes red $2
v.4 Kool Kromes teal blue $2
v.5 metallic light gold with beige interior & bumpers $2
v.6 Road Eaters bright red, "Willy Wonka NERDS" $3
v.7 Smelly Speeders hot pink with white interior, red tires, "STRAWBERRY SPEEDSTER" $2
v.8 metallic silver with maroon interior & bumpers $2
v.9 black $2

261-A Morgan, 1:50
v.1 Kool Kromes blue with white interior, clear windshield . . $3
v.2 metallic green with cream roof & interior, amber windshield $2
v.3 metallic mint green with white roof & interior, light blue windshield $2
v.4 red with white interior, cream top $2
v.5 metallic blue with white roof & interior, amber windshield . $2
v.6 metallic dark green with orange windshield $2

261-B Explorer, 1995 (previously 260-B) $2

262-A Airport Minibus, 1:87
v.1 white "AIR FRANCE" $6
v.2 white "TWA" $6
v.3 white "AIRPORT" $2
v.4 red lower body, yellow upper body $3

v.5 red "Coca-Cola" sun $5
v.6 white with red and black abstract pattern on sides, blue windows $2

263-A Front End Loader (also see 211 Plow), 1:87
v.1 orange $3
v.2 yellow $2

264-A Alpine A310 Special Team Unit
v.1 dark blue with blue windows, red/white/blue "POLICE" markings $8
v.2 white with "SOS" on sides $8

264-B Custom Ford Transit Van Pickup
v.1 red with white bumper & interior, "RACING SERVICE" . . . $4

264-C Volkswagen Golf, 1:56
v.1 red $2
v.2 silver $2
v.3 teal $2

265-A Citroën CX, 1:60
v.1 burgundy $6
v.2 metallic brown $6
v.3 silver $6

265-B Container Truck, 1:100
v.1 lime green body, white container, "Yoplait" $3
v.2 red body, white container, "WEST LINES" $3
v.3 red body, white container, "RESTAURANT PIZZA DEL ARTE" $3
v.4 Road Eaters white, "DIET PEPSI" $4
v.5 Road Eaters white "PETER PAN" $3
v.6 Road Eaters "Swanson Kids Growlin' Grilled Cheese Fun Feast Barnie Bear" $3
v.7 white "ROQUEFORT SOCIETE" $3
v.8 white "TOTAL" $4
v.9 red "Coca-Cola" $6
v.10 blue "Cadbury Roses Chocolates" $6
v.11 blue "Cadbury Dairy Milk" $6
v.12 blue with white container, clown print on sides $2

266-A Renault 18, 1:60
v.1 dark yellow with "TAXI" sign on roof, "radio taxi" $4
v.2 light yellow with "TAXI" sign on roof, "radio taxi" $4
v.3 metallic blue with yellow spoiler on roof (part of 368-A) . $4
v.4 metallic silver $6
v.5 yellow with passenger, no markings $6

266-B Land Rover 4x4, 1:60
v.1 black & white zebra stripes $3
v.2 cream body $3
v.3 red body $3
v.4 white body $3
v.5 tan with black zebra stripes $2

267-A Excalibur, 1:56
v.1 metallic light blue & white interior, black roof $5
v.2 metallic brown $4
v.3 yellow with passenger, no markings $6
v.4 silver $4

267-B Crazy Car, 1:55 (1995 reissue of 223-B)
v.1 black with white interior, red steering wheel and exhaust pipes, "FUNNY" on roof, "CRAZY CAR" on hood $3

268-A Jeep CJ with conventional (low) chassis (also 244-B, 290-A), 1:54
v.1 black with red interior, gold accents, red 4x4 on hood . . . $3

v.2 metallic brown $4

v.3 yellow with bright green interior, abstract green & black accents on hood $3

v.4 metallic copper with yellow "golden eagle" decal on hood, white roof & interior $3

268-B Corvette Turbo Racer (also 215-A), 1:57

v.1 black upper, white lower body, "3, ZR-1" $3

v.2 black with silver & gold accents $4

v.3 black with red & white accents, "43, tsp, GOODYEAR" . . $3

v.4 blue with red & white accents, "43, tsp, GOODYEAR" . . . $3

v.5 metallic blue with gold & black accents $4

v.6 pearl with red & black accents, "500 MILES," 6" $3

v.7 red with black & gold accents, "ZR1" $3

v.8 red with silver & gold accents $3

v.9 white with "2000" on hood, "18" $4

v.10 yellow with red & black accents, "500 MILES," 6" $3

268-C Pontiac Trans Sport SE

v.1 red with gray lower body, white interior $2

v.2 black with gray lower body, white interior $2

269-A Jeep Cherokee Ambulance, 1:64

v.1 white with blue accents, blue six-armed cross on hood . . $3

v.2 white with no markings on sides, red cross on hood $4

v.3 white with red accents, red cross on hood $3

269-B Ford Mondeo, 1994 . . . . $2

270-A Autobianchi A112, 1:53

v.1 metallic gold with black interior, black & red accents $6

v.2 red with black interior, white & green "A112" $6

270-B Renault Clio $3

271-A Alfa 75

v.1 red with black accents, black interior, no trim on grille . . $6

v.2 red with black accents, black interior, silver trim on grille $4

v.3 red with tan interior $3

v.4 red with white interior $3

271-B Alfa Romeo Giulietta, 1:55

v.1 blue "POLIZIA" with white base & interior $4

v.2 red with black & silver accents $3

272-A Ford Tempo/Sierra, 1:58

v.1 metallic blue with silver accents $2

v.2 silver with red accents $2

v.3 white with blue accents $2

v.4 yellow with red accents $2

272-B Renault Espace, 1997

v.1 white "AMBULANCE" $2

273-A Toyota Tercel 4WD, 1:55

v.1 blue with black interior, silver accents $4

v.2 metallic sea green with black accents $4

v.3 metallic periwinkle blue with black accents $4

v.4 red with black accents & interior $4

v.5 bright orange, no markings $4

v.6 metallic gold with black "4WD" $4

273-B Roadster, 1994, based on a Dodge Viper, 1:58

v.1 red with black interior $2

274-A Super Dump Truck (Benne Carriere), 1:100

v.1 yellow with silver dumper $2

275-A Renault 11 Encore, 1:54

v.1 dark maroon with yellow interior, yellow "11" & stripe . . $4

v.2 red with yellow interior & accents, black lower body $3

v.3 white with black plastic lower body, black/yellow/red/light blue rally accents $3

v.4 metallic green with black/orange/silver "Rallye" accents . . $5

275-B Ford Escort GT $2

276-A Toyota 4X4 Runner (4Runner), 1994

v.1 red with black interior, black stripe, silver "4X4 Runner" on sides $2

v.2 metallic maroon $2

277-A Toyota Landcruiser, conventional (low) chassis, 1:53

v.1 beige with green accents "RAID 86" & map of Africa on roof, "African Safari, Kenya" $4

v.2 red with yellow interior & accents, black lower body $3

v.3 white with black zebra stripes, black interior $4

v.4 metallic green with black/orange/silver "Rallye" accents . . $5

277-B Toyota Landcruiser 4x4, modified (raised) chassis, 1:53

v.1 beige with red interior, "AFRICAN SAFARI" $3

v.2 black with gold accents, "RAID 86" & map of Africa on roof, "African Safari, Kenya" $4

v.3 bright green with yellow interior, "AFRICAN SAFARI" $3

v.4 red with black & gold accents, yellow interior $3

v.5 white with red & gold "RALLYE" accents, green & black "STAR 80" $2

v.6 red with black zebra stripes, black interior $4

v.7 white with black zebra stripes, black interior $4

278-A Western Train, 1:87

v.1 metallic blue with red cowcatcher $10

278-B Mobile Home Camping Car

v.1 hot pink with beige camper $4

v.2 lime green with white camper $4

v.3 blue with white camper $4

v.4 red with white camper $2

279-A Fourgon Police Van, 1:65

v.1 blue with white interior/grille/fenders, red/white/blue "POLICE" label on sides $3

v.2 white with blue & red "POLICE" accents, blue interior/grille/fenders $3

279-B Stock Car, 1:60

v.1 metallic blue with red & white accents, pink interior, yellow roll cage $2

v.2 metallic blue with red & white accents, yellow interior, pink roll cage $2

v.3 green with orange & white accents, yellow interior, pink roll cage $2

v.4 green with orange & white accents, pink interior, yellow roll cage $2

v.5 bright blue with red & white racing accents $2

280-A Renault 5 LeCar, no rear view mirrors or antenna, 1:51 (compare to 257-A)

v.1 metallic light olive green with yellow interior, black/orange/yellow accents $6

280-B Ferrari F40, 1:58

v.1 red with no plastic rear window $2

v.2 red with plastic rear window $2

v.3 Kool Kromes red $3

v.4 Kool Kromes yellow $3

281-A Peugeot 205 GTI/CTI Hardtop Sedan (also 210), 1:53

v.1 black with red plastic trim & interior, gold insignia on hood. $2

v.2 red with black plastic trim & interior, black insignia on hood. $2 v.3 white with black plastic trim and interior, black and red accents. $2

v.4 yellow with black plastic trim & interior, red/black/blue accents. $2

v.5 yellow with red accents, "FLASH TEAM, saphi ligner". . . . $2

v.6 white with red & blue accents, "POLICE". $3

281-B Peugeot 205 GTI/CTI Cabriolet (convertible with top down) (see 210-C)

282-A F1 Ferrari

v.1 red with yellow & black accents, "Agip 27" $2

v.2 green & red with "Benetton 23". $4

v.3 green & red with "Benetton 8" $4

v.4 red, white & black with "TAG 1". $2

v.5 blue & white with "Parmalat 2" $2

v.6 red with "FIAT" $2

283-A Crane Truck, 1:100

v.1 red with blue crane, black boom, black hook $2

v.2 yellow with yellow crane, black boom, red hook. $2

v.3 yellow with yellow crane, black boom, silver hook $2

284-A Saab 900 Turbo, 1:62

v.1 black with red interior, amber windows, silver "TURBO" on sides $3

v.2 metallic blue with cream interior, pale yellow windows, white "TURBO" on sides. $3

v.3 metallic green with cream interior, pale yellow windows, white "TURBO" on sides. $3

v.4 silver with cream interior, amber windows, black "TURBO" on sides $3

284-B Snowmobile (Moto-Neige) (also 259-C)

v.1 white with amber windshield, black base & seat, silver skis & handlebars $6

v.2 white with amber windshield, black base & seat, red skis & handlebars $4

285-A Lancia Montecarlo, 1:50

v.1 mustard yellow with black interior, amber windows, black "MONTE CARLO" $4

v.2 white with red accent, amber windows, black "68" on doors & hood $3

285-B Jeep Cherokee Sheriff

v.1 white with blue accents, red roof light. $2

v.2 white with blue accents, orange roof light $2

v.3 white & blue with red roof light $2

286-A British Bus (also 259-E), 1:125

v.1 red with amber windows, white interior, "BRITISH AIR-WAYS" label. $6

v.2 red with amber windows, yellow interior, "VISIT LONDON" $6

286-B Fiat Tipo, 1:54

v.1 metallic blue with white accents & interior, "TIPO" on sides. $3

v.2 red with white interior, white accents $3

v.3 yellow with red interior, racing accents $3

287-A Toyota Hi-Lux Pickup, conventional chassis (compare to 292-A), 1:56

v.1 orange with silver, black & yellow accents. $6

v.2 orange with dark green, yellow & dark orange accents . . $6

287-B Toyota Hi-Lux Pickup 4x4, modified chassis (see 292-A) . $2 – 4

287-C Bulldozer

v.1 yellow with black plastic cab, silver plastic plow $3

288 Not issued

289-A F1 MacLaren

v.1 white with red & black accents $3

290-A Jeep 4x4 Rallye CJ, modified 4x4 chassis (variation of 268-A)

v.1 black with red interior, gold accents & red "4x4" on hood. $2

v.2 black with red interior, red/orange/yellow accents. $2

v.3 yellow with black & green accents $2

291-A Chevy Blazer Pickup 4x4 (variation of 228-A), 1:62

v.1 blue with yellow interior, black & gold accents $3

v.2 red with black & white horses on sides, "WILD MUSTANG" on hood. $2

v.3 yellow with red interior, red & black accents, black rally lights behind cab $3

v.4 black with multicolor "INTERNATIONAL FOUNDATION" on hood $2

v.5 red "Coca-Cola," sun. $2

292-A Toyota Hi-Lux Pickup with modified 4x4 chassis (compare to 287-A)

v.1 fluorescent green with red & black "WESTERN RODEO" . $2

v.2 metallic gold with silver, black & red "4X4 TOYOTA" . . . $3

v.3 metallic blue with red & yellow accents "NIGHT HAWK". $3

v.4 red with black interior, yellow, black & silver accents . . . $3

v.5 yellow with black interior, rally accents. $4

v.6 Smelly Speeders black & red with red interior & wheels, "APPLE JAZZ". $3

v.7 metallic pink with blue, black & silver accents, "TOYOTA 4x4," white interior. $3

v.8 hot pink with yellow flames, "GLADIATOR" $2

v.9 metallic blue. $2

293-A Pontiac Firebird Turbo $3

293-B Jaguar XJ6, 1:65

v.1 black with red interior $2

v.2 silver with red interior. $2

v.3 metallic green with red interior $2

294 Not issued

295-A Ford Transit Custom Tow Truck (variation of 243-B)

v.1 red with white bumpers, "JACK'S TOWING 24 HR SER-VICE" $2

v.2 fluorescent orange with "RACING SERVICE" $3

296-A Chevrolet El Camino SS Pickup, 1:59

v.1 Kool Kromes red with pink flames, white interior $3

v.2 metallic blue with white interior, white "EL CAMINO SS" on sides $2

v.3 red with white interior, white "EL CAMINO SS" on sides . $2

v.4 Road Eaters fluorescent lime green, "CRY BABY" candy. . $3

v.5 Road Eaters dark blue, "Willy Wonka DWEEBS" candy. . . $3

v.6 white with red interior, red & blue accents, "AMERICAN THUNDER" $2

v.7 white with red interior, orange & green paint splash accents, "INDY CRASH" $2

v.8 hot pink with white interior, white & blue paint splash accents, "INDY CRASH" $2

v.9 bright green with white interior, "EL CAMINO" $2

v.10 blue with white interior, "EL CAMINO" $2

297-A Mack Dump Truck, 1:100

v.1 metallic blue with metallic silver dumper $2

v.2 yellow with metallic silver dumper $2

MAJORETTE SUPERS

These are selected 200 Series models, with newly assigned model numbers followed by an "S," that are steerable.

201.S Fiat Coupe, yellow $3
202.S Fiat Coupe Racing, silver. $3
203.S Mustang Convertible, black $3
204.S Mustang Convertible, red $3
205.S Mustang Hardtop, yellow $3
206.S Mustang Hardtop Sport, black $3
207.S Renault Clio, turquoise $3
208.S Renault Clio Rallye, blue. $3
209.S Ferrari 456 GT, red $3
210.S Ferrari 456 GT Racing, black $3
211.S Ford Mondeo, silver $3
212.S Ford Mondeo Rallye, blue. $3
213.S Roadster, red $3
214.S Roadster Sport, metallic teal $3
215.S Ferrari GTO, yellow $3
216.S Ferrari GTO Racing, red $3
217.S Stock Car
    v.1 white $3
    v.2 red. $3
218.S Stock Car
    v.1 light blue $3
    v.2 black $3
219.S Porsche Boxster, silver, 1996. . . . . $3
220.s Porsche Boxster Sport, metallic teal, 1996 . . . . . . $3
222.S Peugeot 406, red, 1997 . . . . $3

MAJORETTE SPECIAL FORCES SERIES 220

New for 1995, military versions of 200 Series models.

220-1 4x4 Pickup with machine gun. $3
220-2 Missile launcher $3
220-3 Tank with cannon $3
220-4 Military ambulance $3
220-5 Military police $3
220-6 Tank rocket launcher $3
220-7 Military jeep $3
220-8 Anti-aircraft $3
220-9 6x6 with cannon, 1997 . . . . $3
220-10 6x6 with missile launcher, 1997. . . . . $3
220-11 Unimog, green with tan camouflage, 1997. . . . . $3
220-12 Unimog, tan with green camouflage, 1997 . . . . . $3

MAJORETTE 300 SERIES

While the 300 Series consists mostly of 200 Series vehicles with trailers, it also features buses, stretch limos, and semi-tractor/trailers. Since it is possible to mix and match some vehicles and trailers, the values indicated represent models sealed in their original package. Many trailers are only available in 300 Series sets and are indicated as such by an asterisk*. Many models were issued in various color combinations and with different markings.

310-A Autobus Saviem Paris Bus, 1:87 . . . . $8
310-B Scraper Earth Mover, yellow & black, 1993 . . . . $5
311-A BMW 733 (256-B) and Horse Trailer* $7
    v.1 white car, white trailer with khaki trailer cover
311-B Volvo 760 GLE (230-B) and Horse Trailer* $6
    v.1 metallic dark green car, metallic dark green trailer with white trailer cover, 1988

311-C Chevy Blazer 4x4 Pickup and Horse Trailer* $4
312-A Fighter Plane Transporter, 1:100, 1989 . . . . $4
    v.1 blue tractor, silver trailer, blue/white airplane with red wings
313-A Wrecker and Sedan $14
313-B Fifth Wheel Trailer and Pickup Truck, 1992
    v.1 hot pink pickup with "4x4 Country" on hood, mountain print on sides, cream trailer. $5
    v.2 red pickup with "Coca-Cola" logo, white trailer $8
    v.3 hot pink pickup with no markings, cream trailer $5

v.4 red pickup with "4x4 Country" on hood, mountain print on sides, white trailer, $5

    v.5 lime green pickup with mountain print on sides, white trailer. $5
314-A Volkswagen VW 1302 (#202-B) and Boat Trailer

v.1 red with lightning bolt on trunk with orange and white boat on blue trailer, $16

    v.2 red with lightning bolt on trunk with orange and white boat on red trailer $16
314-B Citroën DS21 (213-A) and Boat Trailer* $16
314-C Peugeot 204 (230-A) and Boat Trailer*. $12
314-D Saab 900 Turbo Sedan (284-A) and Boat Trailer*
    v.1 metallic blue car, boat has blue hull & white deck $8
    v.2 black car, boat has white hull & red deck $8
314-E Magirus Dump Truck, 1993. . . . . $3
315-A Citroën DS21 (213-A) and Sterckeman Lovely 400 Travel Trailer (236-A) $20
315-B VW K70 (210-A) and Sterckeman Lovely 400 Travel Trailer (236-A)
    v.1 with pink car $20

v.2 with blue car, $20

v.3 with yellow car $20

v.4 with red car $20

315-C Volkswagen Golf (210-B) with Sterckeman Lovelady 400 Travel Trailer $20

315-D Mercedes 280SE (237-A) and House Trailer (236-A) $12

315-D Western Train (278-A) and Passenger Coach*

v.1 green locomotive with red cowcatcher, red passenger coach with white roof $20

v.2 metallic blue with red cowcatcher, red passenger coach with white roof $20

315-E Tow Truck with Construction Trailer, 1997 . . . . $4

316-A Farm Tractor (208-A) and Dump Trailer*

v.1 dark green tractor with yellow fenders, yellow trailer with green tailgate $6

v.2 dark green tractor with black fenders, yellow trailer with green tailgate $6

v.3 red tractor with black fenders, red trailer with black tailgate $5

v.4 light green tractor with black fenders, green trailer with black tailgate $3

317-A Renault R17 TS (260-A) with Lotus F1 (227-A) and Trailer* $12

317-B Fiat 127 (203-A) with Alpine F3 Racer* and Trailer*

v.1 hot pink with aqua racer, "5" on nose, and metallic yellow-green trailer, $12

v.2 hot pink with aqua racer, "3" on nose, and red trailer. . . $12

v.3 blue with aqua racer, "3" on nose, and red trailer. $12

v.4 metallic blue with aqua racer, "3" on nose, and yellow trailer $12

v.5 lime green with aqua racer, "4" on nose, and yellow trailer $12

317-C Fiat Ritmo/Strada (239-C) and Kayak Trailer* $6

317-D Ford Thunderbird (217-A) and Kayak Trailer* $4

317-E Renault Super Cinq GT Turbo (205-C) and Kayak Trailer*. $3

318-A Jeep 4x4 (290-A) and F1 Racer (238-B)

v.1 green jeep with yellow roof, white racer $6

v.2 black jeep with no roof, green racer $3

v.3 black jeep with no roof, yellow racer, 1989 . . . . $3

v.4 yellow jeep with no roof, green racer, 1993. . . . . $3

v.5 black jeep with beige roof, yellow racer, 1995 . . . . $3

319-A Mercedes Car Transporter, 1:100

v.1 red cab & lower trailer, yellow upper trailer. $8

v.2 yellow cab & upper trailer, red lower trailer. $8

319-B Extending Ladder Fire Engine, 1:86. . . . . $4

320-A Bernard Semi Log Trailer with 3 textured dowel "logs," 1:100

v.1 light green with blue log trailer $16

v.2 light green with red log trailer $16

v.3 red with blue log trailer. $16

320-B Alfa Romeo (271-A) and Glider Trailer* $4

320-C Volkswagen Rabbit 210-B) and Glider Trailer* $4

320-D Toyota Tercel (273-A) and Glider Trailer*

v.1 metallic blue car $6

v.2 red car $6

320-E El Camino and Glider Trailer*, 1993

v.1 hot pink pickup $3

v.2 bright green pickup $3

320-F GMC Jimmy and Glider Trailer*, 1995 . . . . $4

321-A Mercedes Covered Utility Truck and Utility Trailer, 1:100. $4

321-B Magirus Power Boat Transporter (Bateau), 1:100

v.1 yellow tractor, boat has red hull, white deck $4

v.2 red tractor, boat has red hull, white deck. $4

322-A Bernard Semi Low Loader Trailer with Crane, 1:100

v.1 orange with red flatbed trailer, black crane $16

v.2 yellow with yellow flatbed trailer, black crane, $16

v.3 yellow with red flatbed trailer, black crane. $16

322-B Dauphin 2SA365 Helicopter, 1:87, 1988

v.1 Coast Guard $6

v.2 Police. $4

323-A Renault and Glider Trailer* $12

323-B Fiat (#203) and Glider Trailer with orange and white "Wasmer 26 Squale" glider

v.1 metallic yellow-green with orange trailer $12

v.2 metallic yellow-green with yellow trailer $12

v.3 red with orange trailer. $12

v.4 lime green with metallic yellow-green trailer $12

v.5 blue with metallic yellow-green trailer. $12

323-C Tractor (208-A) and Livestock Trailer* $6

323-D Toyota Pickup (287-A) and Livestock Trailer*

v.1 orange truck, orange trailer. $6

v.2 blue truck with red/yellow "Night Hawk" accents, blue trailer. $6

v.3 yellow truck with "Western" accents, red trailer $3

v.4 pink truck with "Gladiator" accents, yellow trailer $3

v.5 red truck with "Gladiator" accents, yellow trailer $3

v.6 blue truck with yellow trailer $3

324-A Bernard Semi Open Trailer, 1:100

v.1 red with blue and red open trailer, red trailer base, $12

v.2 yellow with red open trailer, orange trailer base. $12

324-B Magirus Pressurized Tanker (Citerne), 1:100
   v.1 blue cab, white upper tank body, blue tank cover, "L'AIR LIQUIDE". $6

324-C Volvo Pressurized Tanker (Citerne), 1:100
   v.2 yellow cab, white upper tank body, yellow lower tank body, "SHELL" label on tank. $4
   v.3 white cab, white upper tank body, yellow lower tank body, "SHELL" label on tank. $4
   v.4 white cab, white upper and lower tank body, "elf" label on tank. $3

325-A Peugeot 404 (206-A) and Horse Trailer*. $12
325-B Mercedes-Benz 450SE (249-A) and Travel Trailer* $6
325-C Ford Sierra (272-A) and Travel Trailer* $4
325-D VW Golf and Travel Trailer*. $4
326-A Stagecoach. $16
326-B Mercedes-Benz Stretch Limo, 1:58
   v.1 metallic teal with amber windows $3
   v.2 metallic silver with amber windows. $3
   v.3 white with amber windows. $3

327-A Ford Double Tanker (245-A with Tanker Trailer*)
   v.1 blue cab, white tanks, "Milky, the good milk" $4
   v.2 yellow cab, white tanks, "Shell". $3

328-A Chrysler 180 (208-A) and Sailboat Trailer* $12
328-B Safari Toyota Landcruiser (277-A) and Lion Cage Trailer*. $4
328-C Land Rover with Lion Cage Trailer*. $4
329-A Spacecraft Shuttle Transporter, 1:100. . . . . $4
330 not issued
331-A Peugeot 204 (230-A) and Kayak Camper Trailer* $12
331-B VW 1302 (202-A) and Kayak Camper Trailer*
   v.1 red with lighting bolt on trunk, orange and white kayaks on metallic yellow-green trailer $16
   v.2 red with flower on trunk, orange and white kayaks on red trailer $16

331-C Road Grader Levelling Scraper $8
332 not issued
333-A Ford Transit TUG (295-A) and Motorcycle Trailer* $4
334-A Ford 5000 Farm Tractor (253-A) and Log Trailer, 1970s
   v.1 red trailer $16
   v.2 blue trailer $16

334-B Tractor and Log Trailer, 1994 . . . . $8
335-A Toyota 4-Runner and Moto Trailer with motorcycle, 1995 . $8
336-A El Camino and Bicycle Trailer with two bicycles, 1995. . . $8
336-B Mercedes 300 TE and Bicycle Trailer with two bicycles, 1997. . . . . $6

337 not issued
338-A DAF 2600 Crane Truck with Sloop Trailer
   v.1 yellow truck $18

v.2 metallic light green truck, $18

338-B Mercedes and Sloop Trailer* $12
338-C Chrysler 180 (#208-B) and Sloop Trailer*
   v.1 metallic green car with blue and white boat. $16

338-D Honda Accord (219-B) and Sloop Trailer* $4
338-E VW Golf GTI (235-C) and Sloop Trailer* $4
338-F Blazer and Sloop Trailer* $4
339-A Cadillac Stretch Limo, 1:58
   v.1 black $3
   v.2 white $3
   v.3 metallic gray. $3
   v.4 metallic blue. $3

340-A BMW 3.0 CSI and Digue Baronette GT Travel Trailer

v.1 yellow car, white trailer with light blue windows, $16

340-B Peugeot 504 (239-A) and House Trailer (236-A). $12
340-C Chrysler 180 (208-A) and House Trailer (236-A). $16
340-D Volvo Container Truck
   v.1 red with red trailer, red/white/black "CHALLENGE COMPANY" label $3
   v.2 red with yellow trailer, "HOLLYWOOD" $3
   v.3 "Coca-Cola" polar bear scene $8
   v.4 blue "Cadbury Dairy Milk Buttons" $8
   v.5 yellow cab, red trailer, "Cadbury Creme Eggs" $8

341 not issued
342-A DAF 2600 Covered Truck (241-A) and Covered Trailer (243-A) $24

343-A Dodge Safari Truck (225-A) with Dinghy and Raft Trailer*

v.1 red with paint streaks, gray inflatable raft on orange trailer, $16

   v.2 orange with paint streaks, gray inflatable raft on orange trailer. $16
   v.3 yellow with paint streaks, gray inflatable raft on orange trailer. $16
   v.4 yellow with paint streaks, gray inflatable raft on metallic yellow-green trailer $16
   v.5 yellow with paint streaks, gray inflatable raft on yellow trailer. $16

343-B Dune Buggy JP4 (252-A) and Raft Trailer*. $6
343-C Renault 25 (222-A) and Raft Trailer* $4
344-A DAF 2600 Tanker (245-A) and Tanker Trailer* $12
344-B Circus Caravan Fourgon (234-A) and Animal Trailer* $4
345 thru 349 not issued
350-A Power Boat Transporter, 1:100, 1988. . . . . $4
351-A Dodge Tow Truck with Traffic Signs, 1:80

v.1 orange with yellow boom, red and white striped "Service" sticker on sides, $16

351-B Citroën SM (250-A) with Traffic Signs $16
351-C Volkswagen Van (244-A) with Trailer and Traffic Signs . $20
352-A Ski-Doo Snowmobile (249-A) and Sled*

v.1 yellow with light green sled, $25

352-B Farm Tractor (#253) with Log Trailer. $20
353 not issued
354-A Ford 5000 Tractor (253-A) and Log Trailer
    v.1 blue tractor with white fenders, red trailer $16
    v.2 blue tractor with white fenders, blue trailer $16
355-A Volvo Semi Oil Tanker, 1:100 . . . . $4
    v.2 yellow cab, white upper tank body, yellow lower tank body, "SHELL" label on tank. $4
    v.3 white cab, white upper tank body, yellow lower tank body, "SHELL" label on tank. $4
    v.4 white cab, white upper and lower tank body, "elf" label on tank. $3
356 thru 360 not issued
361-A Bernard Semi with Trailer
    v.1 "MAJORETTE". $16
    v.2 "TWO GUYS STORES" $16
    v.3 "chambourcy - Youghourt - Desserts - Frommage Frais". $16
361-B Magirus Freight Truck, 1:100
    v.1 red cab, white container $6
    v.2 blue cab, white container "EXPRESS LINES" $4
    v.3 blue cab, white container "Alloin Transports". $5

362-A Dodge Fire Rescue (204-A) with Barge and Trailer* $16
362-B Land Rover 4x4 (266-B) with Radar Trailer*. $12
363-A BMW 2800 CS Coupe (235-A) with Racer & Trailer* . . . $12
364-A Magirus Tanker, 1:100 . . . . $4
364-B Mercedes Tanker, 1:100
    v.1 "Agip" $6
    v.2 "Shell" $5
365-A Magirus Sloop Hauler, 1:100
    v.1 red cab, yellow trailer, boat has white hull, red deck $5
    v.2 red cab, silver trailer, boat has red hull, white deck $5
    v.3 red cab, silver trailer, boat has white hull, yellow deck. . . $6
    v.4 pink cab, silver trailer, boat has lime hull, pink deck $5
    v.5 red cab, silver trailer, boat has blue hull, white deck $4
    v.6 red cab, silver trailer, boat has yellow hull, white deck. . . $4
366-A Ford Covered Truck (241-A) and Trailer*
    v.1 green with yellow cargo covers "majorette" $4
    v.2 green with yellow cargo covers "super cargo" $4
    v.3 white with blue cargo covers "majorette". $4
    v.4 white with white cargo covers "elf" $4
    v.5 red with white cargo covers "Coca-Cola" ice cubes, 1995 . $6
    v.6 blue "Cadbury Roses Chocolates" $8
367-A Mercedes Tractor with Covered Trailer, 1:100
    v.1 red with white container "Renault" $4
368-A Renault 18i (266-A) and Trailer (201-A)
    v.1 blue car with yellow trailer $6
369-A Farm Tractor (208-A) and Hay Trailer* $6
370-A Deep Sea Explorer Transporter, 1:100
    v.1 blue with yellow submarine $4
    v.2 purple with yellow submarine. $5
371-A Gazelle Rescue Helicopter, 1:70
    v.1 red base, white upper, "RESCUE" $6
    v.2 red base & upper, "RESCUE". $6
    v.3 red base & upper, "TURBO" $4
372-A Renault (275-A) and Kayak Camper Trailer* $4
372-B Peugeot (281-A) and Kayak Camper Trailer* $4
373-A Neoplan Autocar Airport Bus, 1:87
    v.1 white with pale amber windows, "IBERIA" label $6
    v.2 white lower, red upper body, amber windows, "croisiere" label $4
    v.3 red lower, white upper body, pale blue windows, "croisiere" label $4
    v.4 yellow lower, white upper body, pale blue windows, "croisiere" label $4
    v.5 yellow lower, white upper body, amber windows, "Happy Holidays" label. $6
    v.6 blue lower, white upper body, pale blue windows, cream interior, "MIAMI BEACH" label $4
    v.7 blue lower, white upper, pale blue windows, hot pink interior, "MIAMI BEACH" $4
    v.8 blue lower, yellow upper body, "TRAVEL". $4
    v.9 red "Coca-Cola" ice cubes, 1995 . . . . $6
    v.10 white lower, red upper, "Happy Holidays" label. $4
    v.11 blue lower, white upper, blue planets, red stars, red interior $4
    v.12 black lower, white upper, red/yellow/blue abstract accents, 1993. . . . . $4
    v.13 blue lower, yellow upper, "TRAVEL" sunset horizon logo, 1995. . . . . $4

v.14 yellow "School Bus," 1996 . . . . $4
374-A Toyota Landcruiser (277-A) and Covered Trailer* $4
375-A Ford Transit (295-A) and F1 Racer $4
376-A Range Rover Rescue Team (246-A) and Tank Trailer* . . . $6
377-A Semi-Sand Truck (Semi-Senne Carriere), 1:100 . . . . $5
378-A Racing Team Van (234-A) and Motorcycle Trailer* $4
379-A Hopper Tank Truck, 1:100 . . . . $6
379-B Powder Transporter, 1997 . . . . $4
380 & 381 not issued
382-A Mercedes Utility Truck with Compressor $15
382-B Toyota Pickup (292-A) with Compressor
   v.1 orange $10
   v.2 white $12
382-C Land Rover with Compressor
   v.1 yellow $4

     MAJORETTE 600-SERIES, 1:87 SCALE (HO GAUGE)
           SEMI-TRACTOR/TRAILERS

601-A Helicopter Transporter (with 371-A Rescue Helicopter) . . $7
602-A Payloader Transporter (with 263-A Front End Loader) . . . $7
603 not issued
604-A Kenworth Semi Freight Truck

v.1 "BORG WARNER," $8

v.2 "NIGHT HAWK" $8
v.3 western sunset scene on trailer $4
604-B Kenworth Sleeper Cab Semi Freight Truck
   v.1 blue tractor with red trailer, red/white/blue "EAGLE TRUCK"
      stars & stripes, 1995 . . . . $4
   v.2 white tractor with blue trailer, "Shark Monster" $4
605-A Double Tanker
   v.1 "SHELL" $6
605-B Double Tanker (new tractor), 1995 . . . . $4
606-A Kenworth Semi Tanker

v.1 "TEXACO" with Texaco "Star T" logo upright, $4

v.2 "TEXACO" with Texaco "Star T" logo upside down $25
606-B Kenworth Sleeper Cab Tanker
   v.1 "TEXACO" $4
607-A Double Freighter

v.1 "ROAD DRAGON," $8

609-A Kenworth Auto Transporter $8
610-A Kenworth Rocket Transporter

v.1 NASA, $4

611-A Semi Circus Trailer

v.1 red & yellow cages, "MAGIC CIRCUS," black base, $10

v.2 red & white cages, "CIRCUS," blue base $4
v.3 yellow with yellow cages, "MAGIC CIRCUS," blue base . . $4
v.4 white with white cages $4

612-A Hook and Ladder Fire Engine, $4

613-A Power Boat Hauler $4
614-A Kenworth Cattle Transporter
   v.1 yellow trailer, metallic green cab $6
   v.2 light brown trailer, lime green cab, "KANSAS" $4
614-B Kenworth Sleeper Cab Cattle Transporter
   v.1 light brown trailer, green cab $4

615-A Pro Stock Firebird Transporter $4
616-A Bulldozer Transporter
    v.1 green cab with "BLUE'S TRUCKING CO." on doors $4
616-B Bulldozer Transporter (new cab), 1995 . . . . $4
617-A Crane Truck

v.1 yellow with black accents, black boom, $4

618-A Seaplane Transporter, $4

619-A Car Carrier $4
MAJORETTE 800 SERIES AIRPORT, NEW FOR 1995
801-A Boeing 747/400
    v.1 Cathay Pacific $4
    v.2 Air France $4
    v.3 Thai Airways $4
802-A Airbus
    v.1 Singapore Airlines $4
    v.2 Air France $4
    v.3 Alitalia $4
    v.4 Swissair $4
803-A Boeing 767
    v.1 KLM $4
    v.2 Delta Airlines $4
    v.3 Air Canada $4
    v.4 Japan Air Lines (JAL) $4
    v.5 SAS $4
804-A Douglas MD 80
    v.1 Alitalia $4
    v.2 Iberia $4
    v.3 SAS $4
805-A Douglas DC 10
    v.1 Iberia $4
    v.2 Japan Air Lines (JAL) $4
MAJORETTE 2400 SERIES — LEGENDS, APPROXIMATELY 1:38 SCALE
2401 1957 Chevy BelAir $5
2402 1956 T-Bird $5
2403 1963 Corvette Stingray Split Window

v.1 yellow $5
v.2 red $5
2404 1965 Mustang $5
2405 Mercedes 300SL Gullwing $5
MAJORETTE 2500 SERIES —
GRAND SPORT, APPROXIMATELY 1:38 SCALE
2501 Porsche 959 . . . . $5
2502 Ferrari 328 GTB $5
2503 Pontiac Trans Am $5
2504 Lamborghini Countach $5
MAJORETTE HOT RODS
2601 1932 Ford Coupe with removable engine cowl $4
2602 1941 Willys Coupe with removable engine cowl $4
2603 1934 Ford Sedan with removable engine cowl $4
2604 1957 Chevy with 2 interchangeable turbo engines $4
2605 Pickup Hot Rod with removable engine cowl $4
MAJORETTE 3000 SERIES
3006 Kenworth Semi Tractor, 1995 . . . . $6
3007 Dune Buggy $6
3008 Impala Police $6
3009 Impala Taxi $6
3010 Magirus Dump Truck $6
3011 Crane Truck $6
3012 Farm Tractor with side mower $6
3013-A Safari Land Rover $6
3013-B Toyota Raid, 1997 . . . . $6
3014 Mercedes E 280 Wagon, 1997 . . . . $6
3015 Pickup $6
3016 CJ7 Jeep $6
3017 Mercedes 230GE 4x4 Police 1:53 . . . . $6
3018 Range Rover $6
3019 Renault Master T35 Road Repair Truck 1:45 . . . . $6
3020 Excalibur $6
3021 Ambulance $6
3022 not issued
3023-A Armoured Security Truck $6
3023-B Mercedes E280 Van, 1997 . . . . $6
3024 Service Van $6
3025 Renault Master T35 Breakdown Truck 1:45 . . . . $6
3026 Ford Mustang, 1995 . . . . $4
3027 Camaro, 1995 . . . . $4
3028 Racing Semi-Tractor 1:60 . . . . $6

3029 Ford Model A Van, $6

3030 Front End Loader $10
3030.1 Winnebago Camping Car, 1994 . . . . $10

3030.2 Holiday Van, 1995 . . . . $7
3030.3 Ambulance Van, 1995 . . . . $7
3030.4 Fire Truck, 1995 . . . . $7
3031-A Cement Truck $10
3031-B Peugeot 806 Van, 1997 . . . . $6
3032 Heavy Duty Transporter (with 226-A Road Roller & 263-A
    Front End Loader) $12
3033 Fire Engine $10
3034 Power Shovel $10
3035 Kenworth Wrecker $10
3036 Kenworth Dump Truck $10
3037 Toyota Garbage Truck $10
3038 Road Roller $10
3039 Bulldozer $10
3040 Tanker $10
3041 Ewing Oil Co. Tanker (from the *Dallas* TV show) . . $30 – 45
3042-A Covered Freighter $14
3042-B Mercedes 4x4 and Racing Boat Trailer $12
3042-C Jeep 4x4 and Racing Boat Trailer $12
3043 Helicopter $8
3044 Tanker $10
3045 Lincoln Super Stretch Limo
    v.1 white with white landau roof $12
    v.2 silver with black landau roof $12
    v.3 black with black landau roof $12
    v.4 metallic blue with blue landau roof $12
3046 Neoplan Metro Bus
    v.1 black $8
    v.2 blue $8
    v.3 white $8
3047 & 3048 not issued
3049-A Toyota Truck and Trailer $10
3049-B Tractor and Tank Trailer $10
3050 Mercedes 4x4 and Racing Boat $10
3051 Tractor and Hay Trailer $12
3052-A Toyota Landcruiser and Horse Trailer $12
3052-B Jeep and Horse Trailer $12
3053-A Blazer 4x4 and Camping Trailer $12
3053-B Range Rover and Camping Trailer $12
3054 not issued
3055 Volvo Semi Container $12
3056 not issued
3057 Camaro and Racing Boat $10
3058 &3059 not issued
3060 Sailboat Transporter $16
3061 Renault Car Carrier without cars (compare to 3092) $16
3062 Double Container Trailer Semi $16
3063 Semi Dump Truck $16
3064 Travel Bus $12
3065 Racing Car Transporter $12
3066 Van and Motorcycle Trailer $16
3067 GM Semi Horse Trailer $16
3068 Pepsi Freighter $16
3069 Dune Buggy Set $16
3070 Jeep and Dune Buggy Trailer $16
3071-A Volvo Car Carrier without cars $10
3071-B Car Carrier without cars
    v.1 blue cab $12

    v.2 yellow cab $12
    v.3 red cab $12
3072 Mercedes 230GE and Porsche 959 Trailer $16
3073 Volvo Racing Boat Transporter $16
3074 Jet Plane Transporter $16
3075 Dragster Transporter $7
3076 Oil Tanker Truck $7
3077 Jeep 4x4 with Motorcycle Trailer $12
3078 through 3090 not issued
3091-A Snorkel Fire Engine $12
3091-B Fiat Monospace w/Motorcycle and Seadoo Trailer, 1997 . $12
3092-A Renault Car transporter w/5 cars (compare to 3061) . . . $20
3092-B Van with Hot Rod and Trailer $12
3093-A Building Transporter $24
3093-B Racing Truck Transporter $12
3094-A Super Helicopter Transporter and Land Rover $24
3094-B Kenworth Helicopter Transporter and Land Rover
    v.1 black and white, Police $16
3095-A Magirus Car Carrier with five cars $20
3095-B Kenworth Car Carrier with five cars $16
3096-A Fire Engine with extension ladder $24
3096-B Snorkel Fire Engine, 1997 . . . . $12
3097 Semi Bulldozer Transporter $16
3098 Racing Car Transporter with 4 F1 Racers $16
3099 Chevrolet Custom Pickup with Beach Buggy and Trailer . $12

With the purchase of Solido in 1993, Majorette gained access to the superb large-scale models to incorporate at will into the Majorette collectibles assortment. Some Club 1:24 and Club 1:18 models are representatives of this merger.

MAJORETTE CLUB/SUPER CLUB 1:24

4101 Bugatti 55 de la Chapelle, red $12
4102 Jaguar E Type $10
4103 Ferrari 365 GT Daytona $10
4104 AC Cobra 427, top down (compare to 4212)
    v.1 dark blue $10
    v.2 white $10
4105 Bugatti 55 de la Chapelle, green $12
4106 Mustang Hardtop, 1995 . . . . $8
4107 Chevrolet Silverado Pickup, 1995 . . . . $8
4108 Jeep Grand Cherokee Limited, 1995 . . . . $8
4109 Jeep Grand Cherokee Laredo, 1995 . . . . $8
4110 Jeep Grand Cherokee Sheriff, 1996 . . . . $8
4111 Chevrolet Silverado Rescue, 1996 . . . . $8
4112 Chevrolet Silverado Rallye, 1996 . . . . $8
4113 Jeep Grand Cherokee Rallye, 1997 . . . . $8
4114 Jeep Grand Cherokee Fire Chief, 1997 . . . . $8
4151 Ferrari Daytona, red, 1997 . . . . $8
4152 Ferrari Daytona, yellow, 1997 . . . . $8
4153 Porsche 944 Coupe, yellow, 1997 . . . . $8
4154 Porsche 944 Coupe, red, 1997 . . . . $8
4155 Ford GT 40, white, 1997 . . . . $8
4156 Ford GT 40, light blue, 1997 . . . . $8
4157 Formula 1, red, 1997 . . . . $8
4158 Formula 1, white, 1997 . . . . $8
4159 Formula Indy, black, 1997 . . . . $8
4160 Bugatti Roadster, red, 1997 . . . . $8
4161 Lamborghini Countach, orange, 1997 . . . . $8
4162 Proto "Baja," white, 1997 . . . . $8

4201 Porsche 944 Turbo $8
4202 Chevrolet Corvette Coupe $8
4203 Lamborghini Countach 5000 Quattrovalvole
    v.1 red $8
    v.2 white $8
4204 Chevrolet Corvette Roadster $8
4205 Porsche 944 Turbo Coupe $8
4208 Porsche 944 S2 Cabriolet $8
4209 Peugeot 405 Turbo 16 . . . . $8
4210 Mercedes-Benz 500 SL Roadster $8
4211 Lamborghini Diablo
    v.1 red $8
    v.2 yellow $8
4212 AC Cobra 427, top up (compare to 4104)
    v.1 metallic red $8
    v.2 metallic teal $8
4213 Mercedes 500 SL Coupe $8
4214 Ford GT 40
    v.1 light blue LeMans $8
    v.2 red $8
4215 1993 Porsche 911, 1995 . . . . $8
4217 Ford Mustang Convertible, 1995 . . . . $8
4218 Ferrari 550 Maranello, red, 1997 . . . . $10
4219 Ferrari 550 Maranello, yellow, 1997 . . . . $10

MAJORETTE CLUB 1:24 METAL KITS
Easy-to-assemble metal kits.
4301 Porsche 944 Turbo $8
4302 Jaguar Type E $8
4303 Ferrari 365 GT Daytona $8
4304 AC Cobra 427 . . . . $8
4305 Chevrolet Corvette Coupe $8
4306 1993 Porsche 911, 1995 . . . . $8
4311 Lamborghini Diablo $8
4312 Ferrari 365 GTB Daytona, 1997 . . . . $8
4313 Porsche 944 Coupe, 1997 . . . . $8
4314 Ford GT 40, 1997 . . . . $8
4315 Formula 1, 1997 . . . . $8
4316 Bugatti Roadster, 1997 . . . . $8
4317 Lamborghini Countach, 1997 . . . . $8
4318 Proto "Baja," 1997 . . . . $8

MAJORETTE CLUB 1:18 MAJORETTE/SOLIDO MODELS
4401 Peugeot 605, 1994 . . . . $24
4402 1964 Mini Cooper, 1994 . . . . $24
4403 Ferrari 365 GTS Convertible, 1994 . . . . $24
4404 1936 Ford Pickup Truck, 1994 . . . . $24
4405 1955 Cadillac Eldorado, 1994 . . . . $24
4406 1958 VW Beetle, 1994 . . . . $24
4407 Citroën ZX Rallye Raid, 1994 . . . . $24
4408 BMW 850i, 1994 . . . . $24
4409 Lexus LS 400, 1994 . . . . $24
4410 Mercedes 500 SL Convertible, 1994 . . . . $24
4411 AC Cobra 427 Convertible, 1994 . . . . $24
4412 1958 Chevrolet Corvette Convertible, 1994 . . . . . . $24
4413 Ford Thunderbird, 1995 . . . . $24
4414 Jeep Grand Cherokee Laredo, 1995 . . . . $24
4415 Jeep Grand Cherokee Limited, 1995 . . . . $24
4416 1957 Chevrolet Nomad, 1995 . . . . $24
4417 Toyota Land Cruiser, 1995 . . . . $24

4418 Mercedes 600 S Coupe, 1995 . . . . $24
4421 Jeep Wrangler Californian with surfboard, 1997 . . . $24
4422 Jeep Wrangler, 1997 . . . . $24
4423 Jeep Wrangler Rallye, 1997 . . . . $24
4424 Jeep Grand Cherokee Rallye, 1997 . . . . $24
4451 Lotus Caterham Super Seven $24
4452 Ferrari Dino 246 GT $24

MAJORETTE PLATINUM 1:18
4453 Lamborghini Miura, 1997 . . . . $24
4454 Bugatti EB 110, 1997 . . . . $24
4455 Porsche 911 Carrera 4 Cabriolet, 1997 . . . . $24
4456 Ferrari 328 GTS, 1997 . . . . $24
4457 Porsche 911 Turbo, 1997 . . . . $24

MAJORETTE CONSTRUCTION/SUPER CONSTRUCTION
4501 Front End Loader $10
4502 Cement Mixer $10
4503 Heavy Duty Transporter with Wheel Loader $10
4504 Roller $10
4505 Bulldozer with Payloader and Rear Drag Claw $10
4506 Wheeled Excavator $10
4507 Dump Truck, 1997 . . . . $10
4508 Truck with Crane, 1997 . . . . $10
4511 Telescoping Mobile Crane $14
4512 Road Grader Levelling Scraper $14
4513 Crawler Shovel $14
4514 Dump Truck and Land Rover $14
4515 Caterpillar Tracked Crane $14
4517 Earth Mover Scraper $14
4518 Maxi Dump Truck, 1997 . . . . $14

MAJORETTE ALL-AMERICAN ROAD KINGS
1:32 scale models, new for 1995.
3201 '95 Mustang GT, yellow $4
3202 '95 Camaro Convertible, bright blue $4
3203 Chevy Sportside Extended Cab, white with black lower
    body $4
3204 Chevy Sportside & Camper Top, red with black lower body
    and camper top $4
3205 Chevy Dooley Custom Pickup $4
3206 Chevy Dooley Custom Pickup with Camper Top $4
3231 Mustang and Motorcycle Trailer $8
3232 Camaro and Seadoo Trailer $8
3233 Chevy Pickup and Motorcycle Trailer $8
3234 Chevy Dooley Custom Pickup and Seadoo Trailer $6

MAJORETTE ULTRA CUSTOM
1:32 custom vehicles, new for 1995.
3221 '95 Mustang $4
3222 '95 Camaro $4
3223 Custom Chevy Dually $4
3224 Custom Chevy Dually & Camper Top $4

MAJORETTE ROAD EATERS
Variations of 200 and 600 series models with candy, soft drink, and prepared food advertising
201 Ford Model A Delivery Van
    v.1 Campbell's Soup Teddy Bear $2
    v.2 Willy Wonka Runts candy $2
209 Porsche 911
    v.1 Campbell's Soup Dinosaur Vegetable $2
    v.2 Swanson Kids Fun Feast Larry Lion $2

219 Lamborghini Diablo
  v.1 Cry Baby candy $2
  v.2 Willy Wonka Gobstopper candy $2
223 '57 Chevy Hot Rod
  v.1 Peter Pan Creamy Peanut Butter $2
  v.2 Frito-Lay Cheetos Chester Cheetah. $2
236 Jeep Cherokee
  v.1 Spaghetti Os Teddy Os $2
  v.2 Frito-Lay Cheetos Chester Cheetah. $2
253 Cadillac Allante
  v.1 Spaghetti Os $2
  v.2 Willy Wonka Nerds candy $2
260 Mercedes-Benz 500 SL Roadster
  v.1 Willy Wonka Nerds candy $6
265 Volvo Container Truck
  v.1 Peter Pan Extra Crunchy Peanut Butter $2
  v.2 Swanson Kids Growlin' Grilled Cheese Fun Feast Barnie
    Bear. $2
  v.3 Diet Pepsi Uh Huh $3
296 Chevrolet El Camino
  v.1 Cry Baby candy $2
  v.2 Willy Wonka Dweebs candy $2
604 Freight Truck (Kenworth Conventional or Kenworth C.O.E.
    tractor)
  v.1 Cry Baby candy $3
  v.2 Peter Pan Extra Crunchy Peanut Butter $3
  v.3 Frito-Lay Cheetos Chester Cheetah. $3
  v.4 Campbell's Soup Dinosaur Vegetable. $3

MAJORETTE MAGIC CARS

Series 290 vehicles with Magic Motion decorations. Many of the new 100 Series Novacar models have been adapted for this 1995 series with clear roofs for displaying Magic Motion images underneath.

Corvette Big Mouth Bruno $4
Corvette Swamp Thing. $4
Ford Escort Monster Maniac. $4
Honda Acura NSX Bird Brain $4
Honda Acura NSX Future Freak $4
Nissan 300ZX Skull Pirate $4
Nissan 300ZX Turkey Tom. $4
Volkswagen Eurovan Melting Melt $4

MAJORETTE SUPER ROCKERS — SERIES 2010 MONSTER TRUCKS

2011 Toyota Hilux "American Monster Truck"
  v.1 white with blue stars, red stripes $4
2012 Blazer "Crazy Monster"
  v.1 red with flame accents $4
2013 Cherokee "Mad Bull"
  v.1 yellow $4
2014 Toyota Hilux
  v.1 orange with black/red/gold accents. $6
  v.2 red with black/red/gold accents $4
2015 Blazer "4WD"
  v.1 green $4
  v.2 bright blue $4
2016 Cherokee "Big Chief"
  v.1 blue $4
  v.2 green $4
Blazer American Monster, silver w/red stripes, blue field of stars . $4

Blazer Gator Baiter, metallic yellow $4
Blazer Heavy Metal, metallic red $4
Jeep Cherokee Big Mudder, metallic green $4
Jeep Cherokee Cheyennes, metallic green $4
Jeep Cherokee Roarin' Monster, metallic red. $4
Jeep Cherokee Monster Crasher, metallic blue $4
Jeep Cherokee Snake, metallic purple $4

MAJORETTE SUPER CRYSTAL — SERIES 280

Assorted 100-Series Novacar plastic models and plastic versions of 200-Series models with translucent metal flake bodies comprise this sparkling collection.

Chevrolet Caprice Police, yellow with pink interior or blue with
    yellow interior $0.75
Chevrolet Corvette ZR1, pink with white interior or yellow with
    pink interior. $0.75
Chevrolet Extended Cab Pickup Truck, blue with red interior or
    yellow with white interior. $0.75
Ferrari Testarossa, red with white interior or purple with white
    interior. $0.75
Honda Acura NSX, red with yellow interior or purple with pink
    interior. $0.75
Kenworth Truck, blue or yellow $0.75
Mercedes 500SL Convertible, red with yellow interior or light blue
    with khaki interior $0.75
Nissan 300ZX, red with yellow interior or yellow with red interi-
    or $0.75
Nissan Pathfinder, blue with red interior or purple with white inte-
    rior $0.75
Renault Espace, yellow with pink interior or pink with white inte-
    rior $0.75
Sport Prototype Racer, pink or blue $0.75
Volkswagen Eurovan, blue with pink interior or clear with red
    interior. $1

MAJORETTE CRAZY ROADSTERS

Series 450 Character models intended for French market.

451 Tom Dog . . . . $4 – 5
452 Croco Bill . . . . $4 – 5
453 Teddy Bear . . . . $4 – 5
454 Bip the Turtle . . . . $4 – 5
455 Big Bebert. . . . . $4 – 5
456 Elliot the Cat . . . . $4 – 5
457 Noddy in his car . . . . $4 – 5
458 Big Ears in his plane . . . . $4 – 5

MAJORETTE SMELLY SPEEDSTERS/TUTTI FRUTTI — SERIES 460

Scented colored wheels distinguish these models from their 200 Series counterparts. The US version is called "Smelly Speeders — Not Stinky, Just For Kids." The French version is packaged as "Tutti Frutti."

209 Porsche 911 Chocolate Wave . . . . $2 – 3
217 Ford Thunderbird Cool Coconut. . . . . $2 – 3
227 Ford Mustang Dunkin' Orange . . . . $2 – 3
236 Jeep Cherokee Rockin' Banana . . . . $2 – 3
260 Mercedes-Benz 500SL Roadster Strawberry Speedster . . $2 – 3
292 Toyota Hilux 4x4 Apple Jazz . . . . $2 – 3

MAJORETTE KOOL KROMES/TOP CHROMES — 250 SERIES

Various colors applied to a base chrome finish on assorted 200 Series models make up this striking subseries of models, currently retailing for $1 – 2 each.

Peugeot 405 T16
  v.1 orange $4
  v.2 dark blue $4
Porsche 911 Turbo
  v.1 light brown $4
  v.2 bright blue $4
'57 Chevy Hot Rod
  v.1 orange $4
  v.2 bright blue $4
Mercedes-Benz 500 SL Convertible Roadster
  v.1 turquoise $4
  v.2 red $4
Cadillac Allante Convertible
  v.1 light green $4
  v.2 yellow $4
Morgan
  v.1 dark blue $4
  v.2 bright blue $4
Ferrari F40
  v.1 red $6
  v.2 yellow $6
El Camino
  v.1 blue $4
  v.2 red $4

MAJORETTE SONIC FLASHERS

An assortment of Majorette vehicles have been altered to accommodate an electronic device that emits a siren or other appropriate sound, accompanied by flashing lights. Besides the altered regular series vehicles, Majorette also presents a series of preschool toys called Baby Sonics, each made in primary colors with a smiling driver wearing the appropriate hat of his trade, and a series of tiny toys less than 1" long called Micro Sonic Flashers.

2302 Ford Bronco II Sheriff 4x4, white with siren and lights . . . $4
2303 Ford Transit Van Ambulance, white with alert siren and roof lights $4
2304 Porsche 928 Japan Police, white with pictograms on sides, siren and lights $4
2306 Ford Bronco II
  v.1 Fire 4x4, red with siren and roof lights $5
  v.2 Police 4x4, red with machine gun and gun flash $4
2308 Porsche 928 Mafia Escape Car, dark metallic gray, cannon sound and gun flash $4
2309 Chevrolet Caprice Police Car, white with siren and roof lights $4
2310 Fire Engine, red with siren and roof lights $4
2312 Ambulance, white with siren and roof lights $4
2313 BMW 535i, red with rally accents, car horn and headlights . $4
2314 Corvette Coupe, screeching brakes, brake lights $4
2315 Chevrolet 4x4 Tow Truck, orange with truck horn and roof lights $4
2316 Sebring Team, gear shifting engine sound, back lights . . . $4
2317 Corvette ZR1, black, gear shifting engine sound, back lights $4
2318 Daytona Team, screeching brakes, brake lights $4
2319 Semi Tractor, truck horn and headlights $4
2320 Ferrari Testarossa Super GT, turn signal, headlights and rear lights $8

2322 Chevrolet 4x4 Beverage Truck, breaking glass sound
  v.1 yellow with black load $6
  v.2 red with white load, "Pepsi" logo $4
2323 Ford Bronco 4x4 Crash Car, breaking glass sound $6
2324 Fire Rescue, bright red with siren and roof lights $4
2325 6x6 S.W.A.T. Vehicle, missile launcher, roof lights $6
2326 Rocket Launcher, missile launcher, roof lights $6
2327 Corvette, screeching brakes and back lights $4
2328 Porsche, "Texas Ranger" with screeching brakes and back lights $4
2331 Chevrolet Blazer 4x4 with Machine Gun, olive drab, machine gun sound $5
2332 Missile Launcher, olive drab camouflage, missile launcher . $4
2333 Tank with Cannon, cannon sound $4
2334 Military Ambulance, fire siren, foot lights $4
2335 Chevrolet Impala Military Police, olive drab, siren, roof lights $4
2336 Anti-Aircraft, olive drab camouflage, anti-aircraft gun sound $4
2337 Tank Rocket Launcher, olive drab camouflage, missile launcher $4
2338 Ford Van Commando Truck, olive drab, siren, roof lights . $4
2339 6x6 All Terrarin with Cannon, olive drab camouflage, cannon sound $4
2341 Western Train, steam whistle, engine sound, ringing bell, clickety-clack sound
  v.1 red & black $8
  v.2 yellow & black $8
2342 Space Craft Transporter, intergalactic search sound, siren, probe light, roof lights $8
2343 Mafia Stretch Limo, car horn, machine gun sound, headlights, gun flash
  v.1 black with red & white "Jazz in the Night" accents $12
  v.2 red with black & gold "Story" accents $12
2351 Coast Guard Boat, siren, roof light $12
2352 Fire Boat, fire siren, roof light $12
2353 Security Boat, siren, foot light $12
2360 Turbo Flash Copter $12
2362 Turbo Flash Copter $12
2363 Turbo Copter $12
2364 Turbo Snake Copter $12
2381 Police Helicopter $12
2383 Coast Guard Helicopter $12
2386 Black Eagle Jet $12
2387 Air Patrol Jet $12

MAJORETTE SUPER SONIC FLASHERS

3301 Chevrolet Impala Police $12
3302 Ford Van Ambulance $12
3303 Chevrolet Impala Fire Chief $12
3304 Range Rover Alarm Car $12
3305.1 Ferrari F40, red $10
3305.2 Lamborghini Countach, yellow $10
3305.3 Honda Acura NSX, blue $10
3306 Mercedes 4x4 + Warning $12
3307 Police Van $12
3309 Fire Van $12
3311 Ambulance $12
3312 Fire Truck $12

MAJORETTE TRAFFIC JAMMERS

#3351 through 3354 are designated as Traffic Jammers and play "music."

3351 '57 Chevy $8
3352 Corvette Sting Ray $8
3353 Chevy Sportside Pickup $8
3354 Chevy Pickup Custom $8
3391 Transporter with Sonic Helicopter $15
3392 Transporter with Sonic Boat $15
3393 Transporter with Sonic Airplane $15
3401 Range Rover $10
3402 Range Rover Rally $10
3403 4x4 Roarin' Monster $10
3404 Bank Security $10

MAJORETTE 3600 SONIC FLASHERS

The system for numbering these is not clear but are listed as such in the 1997 catalog.

3600 Fire Truck $10
3600 4x4 Police $10
3600 Cement Mixer $10
3600 Ambulance $10
3600 Farm Tractor $10
3600 Dump Truck $10
3651 Farm Tractor with front end bucket loader and accessories. $12
3652 Dump Truck with figure and accessories $12
3653 Cement Mixer with figure and accessories. . . . $12
3654 4x4 Police with figure and accessories $12
3655 Helicopter with figure and accessories $12
3656 Humvee Armoured Truck with figure and accessories . . . $12
3657 Tank with figure and accessories $12
3661 Fire Truck with figure and accessories $12

MAJORETTE TURBO SONIC

Turn car on, press on body of car, engine roars. Release car, it accelerates away with gear change sounds and flashing headlights. When car hits something, you hear smashing glass sound and engine switches off. Requires four type LR6 1.5 volt batteries not included.

3451 Ferrari F40, red $14
3452 Ferrari F40, black $14
3453 Ferrari F40, yellow $14

MAJORETTE MICRO SONIC FLASHERS 1300 SERIES

1301 Police Car $3
1302 Ambulance Van $3
1303 Wrecker $3
1304 Sheriff 4x4 . . . . $3
1305 Fire Chief Car $3
1306 S.W.A.T. Van $3
1307 Fire Engine $3
1308 Military Police 4x4 . . . . $3
1309 Lamborghini Countach Sports Car $3
1310 Ferrari F40 Sports Car $3
1311 Porsche 959 . . . . $3
1312 Mercedes-Benz 600 SL $3
1313 Corvette ZR1 . . . . $3
1314 Ferrari Testarossa Sports Car $3
1315 Missile Launcher $3
1316 Tank with Cannon $3
1317 Anti-Aircraft $3

1318 Tank Rocket Launcher $3
1319 Military Car $3
1320 Military Tow Truck $3
1321 Military Van $3

MAJORETTE BABY SONICS/MAJOBABY 1400 SERIES

1401 Police Car, white with police siren and roof light . . . . $6 – 8
1402 Fire Chief Car, red with fire siren and roof light . . . . . $6 – 8
1403 Ambulance, white with siren and roof light. . . . . $6 – 8
1404 Police, red with police siren and roof light . . . . $6 – 8
1405 Fire Car, yellow with fire siren and roof light . . . . $6 – 8
1406 Emergency, pink with siren and roof light. . . . . . . $6 – 8
1407 Red & Yellow Train, roof light, engine sound, ringing bell, clickety-clack sound, steam whistle . . . $6 – 8
1408 Blue, Yellow & Pink Train, roof light, engine sound, ringing bell, clickety-clack sound, whistle . . . $6 – 8

Majorette Majo Baby 1500 Series
1501 Police Van, siren and roof light . . . . $7 – 9
1502 Fire Truck, siren and roof light . . . . $7 – 9

MAJORETTE LICENSES

Coca-Cola is one of the major brands that have licensed Majorette to produce models with the Coca-Cola marque. The assortment is comprised of models from various Majorette series.

234 Ford Van, red, Coca-Cola Sun $4
236 Jeep Cherokee 4x4, white, Coca-Cola Polar Bear $4
262 Minibus, red, Coca-Cola Sun $4
265 Volvo Container Truck, red, Coca-Cola Ice Cubes . . . $4
265.10 Volvo Container Truck, white, Coca-Cola Ice Cubes . . . $4
291 Blazer 4x4, red, Coca-Cola Sun $4
313 Deluxe Fifth Wheel Camping Car, red pickup with white trailer, Coca-Cola Sun $6
321 Magirus Semi-Boat Trailer, Coca-Cola Sun $6
326 Mercedes Stretch Limousine, red, Coca-Cola Sun $6
340 Volvo Semi-Container, red with white trailer, Coca-Cola Polar Bear $6
355 Volvo Semi-Tanker, white, Coca-Cola Ice Cubes . . . $6
604 Kenworth Container Truck, white with red container, Coca-Cola Sun $8
606 Kenworth Tanker, red with white tank, Coca-Cola Polar Bears $8
613 Semi Speed Boat Transporter, Coca-Cola Sun $8
3042 Jeep 4x4 with Racing Boat and Trailer $15
3055 Volvo Semi Container Truck, Always Coca-Cola . . . $15
3073 Volvo Semi Offshore Racing Boat Transporter . . . $15
3076 Semi Tanker $15

MANDARIN

This series made in Singapore represents 1:64 scale models, except for two character models. Some are Playart reissues.

Disney Uncle Scrooge, 7" $14
Hanna Barbera Yogi Bear, 4" $14
101 1967 Chevrolet Camaro Coupe $5
103 Datsun Skyline $5
104 Datsun 280Z $5
107 Honda 9 Coupe $5
108 Leyland Double Decker Bus, green $5
109 Leyland Double Decker Bus, "London Express" . . . $5
110 Leyland Double Decker Bus, "Singapore Air" . . . $5

111 Leyland Double Decker Bus, "World Travels"..........$5
112 Mitsubishi Colt.....................$5
113 Mercedes-Benz 230SL Coupe.....................$5
114 Toyota Celica Mk 1.....................$5
115 Toyota Celica Mk2.....................$5
116 Toyota 2000GT.....................$5
117 Volkswagen Van Ambulance.....................$5
119 Volkswagen Van "Mandarin Toy".....................$5
120 Volkswagen Van "Police.....................$5

MANGALICK

Mangalick models are offered as cast-iron toys of unknown vintage and heritage, but are apparently newer models based on prices and description.

1900 "Coca-Cola" Truck, 12".....................$29
1930 Allis Tractor, 8".....................$19
1930 Ford Farm Tractor, 5".....................$19
1930 Ford Model A "Coke," 5".....................$19
1930 Ford Model AA "Coke," 9".....................$19
1930 John Deere Tractor, 12".....................$19
1930 John Deere Tractor, 8".....................$19
1930 Mack Dump Truck, 8".....................$19
8-Horse Beer Wagon, 24".....................$29
Horse Drawn Fire Wagon, 7".....................$19
Horse Drawn Wagon, "Coke," 7".....................$19
Horse Drawn Wagon, "US Mail," 7".....................$19
Horse Drawn Van, "Bond Tea," 12".....................$19

MANOIL

Jack and Maurice Manoil started the Manoil legacy from Manhattan, New York, in 1934. Sculptor Walter Baetz is the source of the wonderful classic streamlined Art Deco styling of these attractive models. The company later moved to Brooklyn, then Waverly, New York, where it continued until 1955. Now authentic reproductions of these classics are being manufactured from the original molds by Pride lines of Lindenhurst, New York. Below is a listing of the original models and current values.

PRE-WAR MODELS, 1935 – 1941

700 Sedan.....................$90
701 Sedan.....................$90
702 Coupe.....................$90
703 Wrecker.....................$90
704 Roadster.....................$90
705 Sedan.....................$90
706 Rocket Bus.....................$120

MILITARY VEHICLES, 1941 – 1945

70 Soup Kitchen.....................$18 – 19
71 Shell Carrier with Soldier on Shell Box.....................$20 – 22
72 Water Wagon.....................$18 – 20
73 Tractor.....................$22
74 Armored Car with Anti-Aircraft Gun.....................$55
75 Armored Car with Siren.....................$50 – 65
95 Tank.....................$17
96 Large Shell on Truck.....................$18
97 Pontoon on Wheels.....................$36
98 Torpedo on Wheels.....................$20
103 Gasoline Truck.....................$20

104 Chemical truck.....................$24
105 Five Barrel Gun on Wheels.....................$22

POST-WAR MODELS, 1945 – 1955

707 Sedan.....................$50
708 Roadster.....................$35 – 50
709 Fire Engine.....................$30
710 Oil Tanker.....................$25
711 Aerial Ladder.....................$400
712 Pumper.....................$400
713 Bus.....................$24
714 Towing Truck.....................$20
715 Commercial Truck.....................$20
716 Sedan.....................$20
717 Hard Top Convertible.....................$24
718 Convertible.....................$20
719 Sport Car.....................$20
720 Ranch Wagon.....................$20

MÄRKLIN

Märklin has long been one of the most prominent German toy makers of the twentieth century. While better known for toy trains, in the 1930s Märklin produced a beautiful assortment of construction kits that, when assembled, resulted in a stylish period vehicle. Chassis, body, electric light set, and motor were each sold separately. New Märklin commemorative models, preassembled, are being offered for hundreds of dollars. The original Märklin construction kit models are currently worth $200 – 900. Avid collector Bill Cross notes: "Interesting that [this book] doesn't mention the excellent 1950s 1:43 diecast range...." Hmm. Sounds like more information is still needed.

99R Driver (composition).....................$75
1101C Basic Chassis.....................$50
1103St Streamlined Coupe Body.....................$250
1104 Pullman Limousine Body.....................$250
1105L Lorry Body.....................$250
1106T Tanker Body.....................$400
1107R Racing Body.....................$200
1108G Armored Car Body.....................$250
1109M Clockwork Motor.....................$80
1110B Electric Lighting Set.....................$40
1133R Mercedes Racing Car, complete with chassis and motor.$200
1133AL Mercedes Racing Car, aluminum, complete with chassis and motor.....................$200
Mercedes Racing Car, 12" windup.....................$250
Road Working Machine, 3⅝".....................$200
Kubelwagen, diecast, 3½".....................$650
Troop Carrier, 6-Wheel diecast, 4½".....................$650
Troop Carrier, 10-Wheel diecast, 5".....................$900
L1500 1936 Mercedes Truck, new model, 1994.....................$450

MARS, INC.

A few promotional race car toys have been made for Mars, Inc., the candy company, most notably a Buick Regal in 1:48 scale with pull-back action. The model is made in China by an unnamed manufacturer, and was distributed by KMS, 1445 N. Rock Rd., Wichita KS 67206.

Buick Regal Stock Car Racer, 1:48, white with brown and red accents, "SNICKERS" number 8 . . . . $2 – 4

MARSH

Marsh models are 1:43 scale replicas from England that feature full photoetched metal cockpits, dashboards, engines, and wheels.
1962 Cobra 260, Billy Krause #98 . . . . $199
1963 Cobra 289 Sebring, Gurney #15 . . . . $199
1964 Cobra 289 Road America, Miles/Bucknum/Johnson $199
1964 Cobra 289 Sebring, Gurney #11 . . . . $199
1964 Cobra "Flip Top," Miles Nassau $199
1964 Corvette GS Sebring $199
1963 Corvette GS Sportster $199
1966 Corvette GS Roadster $199
1966 Ford Mk II LeMans $199
1967 McLaren. $199
1970 McLaren. $199
1971 McLaren. $199
1968 McLeagle $199

MARTINO MODELS

Martino has made some resin hand-built models in the USA.
1954 Buick Skylark Convertible, 1:43 . . . . $65
1986 Chevrolet Corvette Indy, silver-gray, 1:25 . . . . $65
1957 Oldsmobile $50

MARTOYS (ALSO SEE BBURAGO)

Martoys of Spain later became Bburago of Italy.
Alpine Renault Rally, 1:24 . . . . $20
Audi 80 GT, 1:24 . . . . $20
BMW 3.0 CS 1:24 . . . . $20
Lancia Beta, 1:24 . . . . $20

MARUSAN

Marusan Shoten Ltd. of Japan, better known for superb tin toys in the 1950s which are now highly valued, produced a few diecast toys in 1960 and 1961. Models are identified by the name "San" on the base. Their resemblance to Dinky toys may not be a coincidence. The Avenue Bus and Morris J Van appeared the year after the Dinky versions went out of production.
8501 Panhard Semi Truck . . . . $15 – 20
8502 Morris J Mail Van . . . . $15 – 20
8503 Daimler AMbulance . . . . $15 – 20
8504 Ford Milk Truck . . . . $15 – 20
8505 Avenue Bus . . . . $15 – 20
8506 Euclid Dump Truck . . . . $15 – 20
8507 Austin Van . . . . $15 – 20
Toyota Truck . . . . $15 – 20

MARUSHIN

Marushin models are made in Japan. Further details are not known.
Lancia Stratos, white/red/green, 1:43 . . . . $15

MARX

Marx has made a lot of toys in its long life, but it was

only in the mid- to late 60s that the company produced a small line of diecast toys. Here are a few.
1967 Mercury Cougar . . . . $15 – 20
1967 Cadillac Eldorado . . . . $15 – 20
1969 Chevrolet Camaro . . . . $15 – 20

MASCOT

1950 Chrysler Town & Country, 1:43 . . . . $85

MASTER MODELS

1960 Autocar Rolloff Flatbed, 1:43 . . . . $135
1960 Chevrolet Ambulance, 1:43 . . . . $85
1960 Chevrolet C80 Fire Ambulance, 1:43 . . . . $85

MASTER TOY COMPANY (SEE MAISTO)

MATCHBOX

Since 1947, Lesney and Matchbox toys have been the most universally popular diecast toys since Tootsietoys. Only Hot Wheels has overshadowed Matchbox in world-wide brand name recognition. The complete story of Match-box toys can be found in Dana Johnson's book *Matchbox Toys, 1947 – 1996* from Collector Books ($18.95 retail). Presented below is a brief survey of Matchbox toys over the years. Broad ranges in values indicate that there are several variations of which some are more valuable than others. Further research is recommended.

EARLY LESNEY TOYS

Lesney Products Company started manufacturing toys in 1948, a year after the company was begun. As industrial orders declined, Leslie and Rodney, with the help of their friend Jack Odell, started experimenting with the manufacture of diecast toys. Many of the early models created were later reproduced in smaller versions as the first of the Match-box series. Here is a chronology of those early models.
Aveling Barford Diesel Road Roller, 4⅜", 1948 . . . . $300 – 700
Caterpillar Bulldozer with blade, 4½", 1948 . . . . $250 – 700
Caterpillar Tractor, no blade, 3⅛", 1948 . . . . $225 – 650
Cement Mixer, 3⁹⁄₁₆", 1948 . . . . $175 – 225
Horse Drawn Milk Float, 5⅜", 1949 . . . . $750 – 1,200
Rag and Bone Cart, 5¼", 1949 . . . . $1,000 – 1,750
Ruston Bucyrus 10RB Power Shovel Excavator, 4", 1949 . $400 – 500
Soap Box Racer, gold painted, 3⅛", 1949 . . . . $2,000 – 2,500
Jumbo The Elephant, lithographed tin windup with key, 4", 1950 . . . . $500 – 600
Prime Mover with Trailer & Bulldozer, 18", 1950 . . . . . $400 – 700
Muffin the Mule, cast metal marionette, 5½", 1951 . . . . $200 – 250
Large Coronation Coach, 15¾", 1952 . . . . $450 – 1250
Small Coronation Coach, 4½", 1953 . . . . $100 – 200
Massey Harris Tractor, red with beige wheels, black rubber tires, 7¹³⁄₁₆", 1954 . . . . $600 – 700
Bread Bait Press, 2", 1954 . . . . $60 – 80
Conestoga Wagon, 4⅞", 1955 . . . . $100 – 120

MATCHBOX MINIATURES 1-75 SERIES

From 1953 to the present, the mainstay of the Matchbox toys has been the 1-75 series, or regular series, also referred to as Matchbox Miniatures. Below is a numerical list of Matchbox Miniatures with current value (mint in original container). Length of each model is provided as an aid to identification.

Major model changes are designated by letters, indicating successive models (A=1st, B=2nd, C=3rd, etc.). 31-A, for instance, represents the first model issued as model number 31, in this case a Ford Customline Station Wagon introduced in 1957. 31-G, in comparison, represents the seventh model issued as model number 31, a Mazda RX-7 introduced in 1979. Variations of each model could fill an entire book, and are only indicated by a wide range in value. Collectors are recommended to research further for specific value on their particular variation. Values in ( ) indicate rarest version.

1-A Diesel Road Roller, 1⅞", 1953 (compare to 1-B 1955, 1-C 1958) . . . . $35 – 100
1-B Road Roller, 2¼", 1955 . . . . $50 – 80
1-C Road Roller, 2⅜", 1958 (compare to 1-A 1953, 1-B 1955) . $45 – 60
1-D Aveling Barford Road Roller, 2⅝", 1962 . . . . $20 – 30

v.1 green with red plastic rollers, $15 – 20

1-E Mercedes Benz Lorry, black plastic wheels, 3", 1968 . . $8 – 12
1-F Mercedes Benz Lorry, Superfast wheels, 3", 1969 . . . . . $4 – 20
1-G Mod Rod, 2⅞", 1971 . . . . $15 – 75
1-H Dodge Challenger, 2¹⁵⁄₁₆", 1976 . . . . $1 – 15
1-I Revin' Rebel Dodge Challenger, cast hood scoop, 2⅞", 1982 . $1 – 15
1-J Dodge Challenger Hot Rod, separate plastic hood scoop, 2⅞", 1983 . . . . $1 – 15
1-K Jaguar XJ6, 3", 1987 (also 41-I) . . . . $1 – 40
1-L Diesel Road Roller, commemorative replica of 1-A, made in China, 1⅞", 1988 . . . . $5 – 8
1-M Jaguar XJ6 Police, 3", 1991 . . . . $3 – 25
1-N Dodge Viper GTS Coupe, 1997 . . . . $2
2-A Dumper, 1⅝", 1953 . . . . $40 – 150
2-B Dumper with driver, 1⅞", 1957 . . . . $35 – 50
2-C Muir Hill Dumper, red with green dumper, black plastic wheels, 2³⁄₁₆", 1961 . . . . $25 – 90
2-D Mercedes Trailer, black plastic wheels (goes with 1-E), 3½", 1968 . . . . $8 – 12
2-E Mercedes Trailer, Superfast wheels (goes with 1-F), 3½", 1969 . $4 – 20
2-F Jeep Hot Rod, 2⁵⁄₁₆", 1971 . . . . $8 – 80
2-G Hovercraft, 3⅛", 1976 . . . . $4 – 10
2-H S-2 Jet, 2⅞", 1981 . . . . $2 – 25
2-I Pontiac Fiero, 2¹³⁄₁₆", 1985 . . . . $2 – 75
2-J Rover Sterling, 2¹⁵⁄₁₆", 1988 (also 31-J) . . . . $1 – 15
2-K Corvette Grand Sport, 3", 1990 (also 15-K) . . . . $2 – 25
2-L Mazda Savanna RX7 ("Made in Japan" cast), 1981 . . . . $12 – 15

3-A Cement Mixer, 1⅝", 1953 . . . . $30 – 45
3-B Bedford Ton Tipper, gray cab, 2½", 1961 . . . . $20 – 120
3-C Mercedes Benz "Binz" Ambulance, 2⅞", 1968 . . . . $6 – 9
3-D Mercedes Benz "Binz" Ambulance with SF wheels, 2⅞", 1970 . . . . $6 – 15
3-E Monteverdi Hai, 2⅞", 1973 . . . . $10 – 20
3-F Porsche 911 Turbo, 3", 1978 (54 var) . . . . $3 – 20
3-G Hummer (HMMVW), 1994 . . . . $2 – 3
3-H Alfa Romeo 155, 1997 . . . . $1 – 2
4-A Massey Harris Tractor, with fenders, 1⅝", 1954 . . . . $45 – 65
4-B Massey Harris Tractor, no fenders, 1⅝", 1957 . . . . . . $40 – 65
4-C Triumph Motorcycle and Sidecar, 2⅛", 1960 . . . . . . $40 – 50
4-D Dodge Stake Truck with regular wheels, 2⅞", 1967 . . . $6 – 75
4-E Dodge Stake Truck with SF wheels, 2¾", 1970 . . . . . $15 – 20
4-F Gruesome Twosome, 2⅞", 1971 . . . . $12 – 150
4-G Pontiac Firebird, 2⅞", 1975 . . . . $5 – 8
4-H '57 Chevy, 2¹⁵⁄₁₆", 1979 (also 43-G) (31 var) . . . . $1 – 75
4-I Austin London Taxi (European model), 2⅝", 1987 . . . . $2 – 7
4-J Massey Harris Tractor, replica of 4-A, 1⅝", 1988 . . . . . $5 – 7
4-K '97 Corvette, 1997 . . . . $1 – 2
5-A London Bus, red, 2", 1954 (compare to 5-B 1957, 5-C 1961, 5-D 1965), "BUY MATCHBOX SERIES," metal wheels . $60 – 70
5-B London Bus, 2¼", 1957 (compare to 5-A 1954, 5-C 1961, 5-D 1965) . . . . $45 – 80
5-C London Bus, red body, plastic wheels, 2⁹⁄₁₆", 1961 (compare to 5-A 1954, 5-B 1957, 5-D 1965) . . . . $30 – 200
5-D London Bus, 2¾", 1965 (compare to 5-A 1954, 5-B 1957, 5-C 1961) . . . . $12 – 200
5-E Lotus Europa with SF wheels, 2⅞", 1969 . . . . $9 – 75
5-F Seafire Boat, 2¹⁵⁄₁₆", 1975 . . . . $8 – 100
5-G U.S. Mail Jeep, 2⅜", 1978 . . . . $4 – 20 ($450)
5-H Jeep Eagle CJ/4x4 Golden Eagle/Wrangler Off-Road Jeep, 2⁷⁄₁₆", 1982 . . . . $1 – 25

v.3 red with "GOLDEN EAGLE" tampo, plastic base, $1 – 3

5-I Peterbilt Petrol Tanker, 3", 1985 (also 56-G) (37 var) . . $2 – 75
5-J London Bus, commemorative replica of 5-A, 2", 1988 . . $5 – 8
5-K Nissan Fairlady Z ("Made in Japan" cast), 1981 . . . . $12 – 15
6-A 6-Wheel Quarry Truck, 2⅛", 1955 . . . . $40 – 200
6-B Euclid Quarry Truck, 2½", 1957 . . . . $25 – 225
6-C Euclid Quarry Truck, 2⅝", 1964 . . . . $12 – 15
6-D Ford Pickup, 2¾", 1968 . . . . $10 – 15
6-E Ford Pickup with SF wheels, 2¾", 1970 . . . . $15 – 20
6-F Mercedes Benz 350SL Convertible, 3", 1973 (29 var) . . $6 – 50
6-G IMSA Mazda, 3", 1983 . . . . $3 – 5

6-H F1 Racing Car (Europe; 16 - H/65 - G, U.S.), 2⅞", 1985 . $2 – 25

6-I Ford Supervan II, 2¹⁵⁄₁₆", 1985 (rest of world; 72-K, US). $2 – 15

6-J Alfa Romeo, 2⅞", 1991 (rest of world; 15-M, U.S.) . . . . $2 – 12

6-K Quarry Truck (replica of 6-A), 2⅛", 1993 . . . . $5 – 7

6-L Atlas Excavator (reissue of 32-G), 3", 1992 . . . . $2 – 4

7-A Horse Drawn Milk Cart, 2¼", 1955 . . . . $50 – 150

7-B Ford Anglia, light blue, 2⅝", 1961 . . . . $20 – 25

7-C Ford Refuse Truck, 3", 1966 . . . . $7 – 9

7-D Ford Refuse Truck with SF wheels, 3", 1970 . . . . . . $15 – 20

7-E Hairy Hustler, 2⅞", 1971 . . . . $15 – 150

7-F Volkswagen Rabbit, 2⅞", 1976 . . . . $5 – 45 ($400)

7-G Volkswagen Rompin' Rabbit, 4 x 4, 2⅞", 1982 . . . . . $3 – 8

7-H Volkswagen Ruff Rabbit, 4 x 4, 2⅞", 1983 . . . . $3 – 5

7-I IMSA Mazda (Europe; 6 - G, U.S.), 3", 1983 . . . . $3 – 5

7-J Porsche 959, 2⅞", 1987 (37 var) . . . . $1 – 35

7-K Horse Drawn Milk Float, commemorative replica of 7-A, 2¼",
1988 . . . . $5 – 8

7-L Thunderbird Stock Car/T-Bird Stocker, 3", 1993 (52 var). $3 – 25

8-A Caterpillar Tractor, no blade, 1½", 1955 (compare to 8-B
1959) . . . . $30 – 125

8-B Caterpillar Tractor, 1⅝", 1959 (compare to 8-A 1955) . $50 – 60

8-C Caterpillar Tractor, 1⅞", 1961 . . . . $45 – 80

8-D Caterpillar Tractor, 2", 1964 . . . . $15 – 20

8-E Ford Mustang Fastback, 2⅞", 1966 . . . . $12 – 125

8-F Ford Mustang Fastback with SF wheels, 2⅞", 1970 . . . $30 – 45

8-G Ford Mustang Wildcat Dragster, 2⅞", 1970 . . . . $12 – 25

8-H DeTomaso Pantera, 3", 1975 . . . . $7 – 75

8-I Rover 3500 Police (European model), 3", 1982 . . . . $2 – 8

8-J DeTomaso Pantera, Greased Lightning, 3", 1983 . . . . . . $5 – 8

8-K Scania T142, 3", 1986 (also 71-H, 72-J) . . . . $2 – 5

8-L Vauxhall Astra/Opel Kadett Police (European), 2⅞", 1987 . $4 – 10

8-M Mack CH600, 3", 1990 (also 39-I) . . . . $1 – 15

v.1 white with black and red stripes, $2 – 4

8-N Airport Fire Tender, 3", 1992 (also 24-L) . . . . $1 – 2 ($45)

8-O Mazda RX-7, 1994 . . . . $12 – 15

9-A Dennis Fire Escape, 1955 . . . . $45 – 60

9-B Dennis Fire Escape, with front bumper, number 9 cast, 2⅜",
1957 . . . . $50 – 150

9-C Merryweather Marquis Fire Engine, red, 2¼", 1959 . . . $15 – 50

9-D Boat and Trailer, 3¼", 1966 . . . . $5 – 15

9-E AMX Javelin, 3", 1971 . . . . $5 – 50

9-F Ford Escort RS2000, 3", 1978 . . . . $3 – 10 ($150)

9-G Fiat Abarth, 2¹⁵⁄₁₆", 1982 (also 74-G) . . . . $2 – 150

9-H Caterpillar Bulldozer, 2⅝", 1983 (also 64-F1979) . . . . $1 – 16

9-I Toyota MR2, 2⅞", 1987 (also 74-H) . . . . $2 – 12

9-J Dennis Fire Escape (replica of 9-A), 2¼", 1988 . . . . $5 – 8

9-K Faun Earth Mover Dump Truck, 2¾", 1989 (also 53-H, 58-F). $1 – 15

10-A Mechanical Horse and Trailer, 1955 . . . . $45 – 60

10-B Mechanical Horse and Trailer, red cab, tan trailer, 2¹⁵⁄₁₆", 1958
(compare to 10-A 1955) . . . . $45 – 60

10-C Sugar Container Truck, "TATE & LYLE," 2⅝", 1961 . $35 – 100

10-D Leyland Pipe Truck with six pipes, black plastic wheels, 2⅞",
1966 . . . . $6 – 15

10-E Leyland Pipe Truck with 6 pipes, SF wheels, 2⅞", 1970 . $15 – 20

10-F Mustang Piston Popper (Rolamatic), 2¹³⁄₁₆", 1973 (also 60-E). $5 – 300

10-G Plymouth Gran Fury Police, 3", 1979 . . . . $2 – 5 ($100)

10-H Buick LeSabre Stock Car, 3", 1987 . . . . $2 – 40

v.1 black with white base, "4" and "335 CID" tampos, $2 – 4

10-I Dodge Viper RT/10, 1994 . . . . $2 – 5

11-A Road Tanker, 1¾", 1955 (compare to 11-B 1958) . . $50 – 500

11-B Road Tanker "ESSO," red, 2½", 1958 (compare to 11-A
1955) . . . . $30 – 175

11-C Taylor Jumbo Crane, 3", 1965 . . . . $12 – 25

11-D Mercedes Benz Scaffold Truck with black plastic wheels,
2½", 1969 . . . . $7 – 10

11-E Mercedes Benz Scaffold Truck with SF wheels, 2½",
1969 . . . . $15 – 20

11-F Flying Bug, 2⅞", 1972 . . . . $15 – 75

11-G Bedford Car Transporter, 3", 1976 (42 var) . . . . $2 – 15

11-H Mustang Cobra, 2⅞", 1982 . . . . $6 – 8

11-I IMSA Mustang, 3", 1983 (also 67-G) . . . . $2 – 12

11-J Lamborghini Countach LP500S, 3", 1985 (also 67-H) . . $2 – 4

11-K Road Tanker, commemorative replica of 1-A, made in China,
2½", 1994 . . . . $5 – 8

11-L Chrysler Atlantic, 1997 . . . . $2 – 3

12-A Land Rover with driver, 1¾", 1955 (compare to 12-B
1959) . . . . $30 – 50

12-B Land Rover without driver, no roof, olive green, 2¼", 1959
(compare to 12-A 1955) . . . . $25 – 100

12-C Safari Land Rover, 2⅜", 1965 . . . . $10 – 200

12-D Safari Land Rover, with luggage on roof, SF wheels, 2⅜",
1970 . . . . $20 – 600

12-E Setra Coach, 3", 1970 . . . . $10 – 20

12-F Big Bull Bulldozer, 2⅜", 1975 . . . . $4 – 10

12-G Citroen CX Station Wagon, 3", 1979 (27 var) . . $5 – 15 ($250)

12-H Ambulance, Citroen CX (European model), 3", 1980 . . $3 – 6

12-I Pontiac Firebird S/E, 3", 1982 . . . . $2 – 15

12-J Pontiac Firebird Racer, 3", 1986 . . . . $2 – 5

12-K Modified Racer, 2¹⁵⁄₁₆", 1989 (also 32-H) (54 var) . . . . $2 – 18

12-L Mercedes Benz 500 SL Convertible, 3", 1990 . . . . $1 – 8

12-M Dodge Cattle Truck, 3", 1992 (reissue of 4-E Dodge Stake
Truck) . . . . $5 – 8

12-N Land Rover (commemorative replica of 12-A), 1994. . . $5 – 8
12-O Audi Avus, 1995 . . . . $1 – 4
13-A Bedford Wreck Truck, 2", 1955 (compare to 13-B 1958). $45 – 60
13-B Bedford Wreck Truck, tan, 2⅛", 1958 (compare to 13-A 1955) . . . . $40 – 60
13-C Ford Thames Trader Wreck Truck, 2½", 1961 . . . . . $30 – 50
13-D Dodge Wreck Truck, "BP," with black plastic wheels, 3", 1965 . . . . $12 – 1,000

v.2 yellow cab, green body, $10 – 15

13-E Dodge Wreck Truck, "BP," with SF wheels, 3", 1970. $20 – 25
13-F Baja Dune Buggy, 2⅝", 1971. . . . . $10 – 40 ($450)
13-G Snorkel Fire Engine with closed cab, 3", 1977 . . . . . . $5 – 75
13-H 4x4 Mini-Pickup, Dunes Racer, with roll bar and rally lights, 2¾", 1982 . . . . $1 – 15
13-I 4x4 Mini-Pickup with roof foil, 2¾", 1983. . . . . $1 – 15
13-J Bedford Wreck Truck (replica of 13-A), 2", 1993. . . . . . $5 – 8
13-K The Buster stylized pickup truck, 1996 . . . . $1 – 2
14-A Daimler Ambulance, 1⅞", 1956 . . . . $45 – 60
14-B Daimler Ambulance, 2⅛", 1958 (compare to 14-A 1956). $30 – 125
14-C Bedford Lomas Ambulance, 2⅝", 1962. . . . . $25 – 125
14-D Iso Grifo sportscar with chrome hubs, 3", 1968 (compare to 14-E 1969) . . . . $9 – 12
14-E Iso Grifo sportscar with Superfast wheels, 3", 1969 (compare to 14-D 1968) . . . . $10 – 20
14-F Rallye Royale, 2⅞", 1973. $8 – 10
14-G Mini HaHa Mini Cooper, 2⅜", 1975. . . . . $15 – 18
14-H Leyland Tanker (European model), 3⅛", 1982 . . . . . $2 – 75
14-I 1983 Corvette Convertible, 3", 1983 . . . . $2 – 18
14-J 1984 Corvette Convertible, 3", 1984 . . . . $2 – 18
14-K Jeep Eagle/Laredo, 2⅝", 1987 . . . . $2 – 10
14-L 1987 Corvette Convertible, 3", 1987 (21 var) . . . . . . $2 – 350
14-M 1988 Corvette Convertible, 3", 1988. . . . . $2 – 350
14-N Williams Honda Grand Prix Racer, 3", 1989. . . . . $5 – 6
15-A Prime Mover Truck Tractor, 2⅛", 1956 (goes with 16-A or 16-B Atlantic Trailer, compare to 15-B 1959) . . . . $25 – 750
15-B Atlantic Super Prime Mover Truck Tractor, orange, 2⅝", 1959 (compare to 15-A 1956) . . . . $30 – 425
15-C Dennis Refuse Truck, dark blue with gray container, 2½", 1963 . . . . $20 – 60
15-D Volkswagen 1500 Saloon, off-white with "137" on doors, 2⅞", 1968 . . . . $9 – 12
15-E Volkswagen 1500 Saloon with SF wheels, 2⅞", 1970 . $15 – 25
15-F Hi Ho Silver! Volkswagen, 2½", 1971. . . . . $8 – 10
15-G Fork Lift Truck, 2½", 1972 . . . . $10 – 15 ($300)

15-H Ford Sierra XR4Ti, 3", 1983 (also 40-G, 55-N) (41 var). $2 – 50
15-I Peugeot 205 Turbo 16 (European model), 2¹¹⁄₁₆", 1985 . $2 – 45

v.2 white with "205" and stripes, China cast, $3 – 5

15-J Saab 9000, 2¹⁵⁄₁₆", 1988 (also see 22-J) . . . . $2 – 15
15-K Corvette Grand Sport, 3", 1990 (also 2-K) . . . . $2 – 4
15-L Alfa Romeo, 2⅞", 1991 (US; 6-J rest of the world) . . . $2 – 12
15-M Sunburner, 3", 1992 (also 41-K) . . . . $2 – 10
15-N Mustang Mach III Convertible, 1994 . . . . $1 – 25
16-A Atlantic Trailer, 3⅛", 1956 (goes with 15-A Prime Mover, compare to 16-B 1957) . . . . $175 – 200
16-B Atlantic Trailer, 3¼", 1957 (goes with 15-A or 15-B Prime Mover, compare to 16-A 1956) . . . . $35 – 125
16-C Scammell Mountaineer Snowplow, 3", 1964 . . . . . . $15 – 90
16-D Case Bulldozer, 2½", 1969 . . . . $10 – 15
16-E Badger Exploration Truck w/Rolamatic radar, 2⅞", 1974. $4 – 8
16-F Pontiac Firebird Trans Am, 3", 1979. . . . . $4 – 8
16-G Pontiac Trans Am, 3", 1982. . . . . $4 – 8
16-H Formula Racer, 3", 1984 . . . . $2 – 8
16-I Trans Am T-Roof, Pontiac, 3", 1985 (also 35-F) . . . . . $2 – 15
16-J Ford LTD Police, 3", 1990 (see 51-K 1988) . . . . $1 – 15
16-K Land Rover Ninety, 2½", 1990 (rest of world; 35-H, US). $1 – 40
17-A Bedford "MATCHBOX REMOVAL" Van, 2⅛", 1956 . $30 – 200
17-B Austin London Taxi, maroon, 2¼", 1960 . . . . $50 – 75
17-C Hoveringham Tipper, 2⅞", 1963 . . . . $15 – 20
17-D AEC Ergomatic Horse Box with black plastic wheels, 2¾", 1969 . . . . $6 – 9
17-E AEC Ergomatic Horse Box with SF wheels, 2¾", 1970. $15 – 25
17-F London Bus with small windows, 3", 1972 (69 var) . $8 – 750
17-G London Bus with large windows, 3", 1982 (49 var) . $7 – 225
17-H AMX Pro Stocker, 2⅝", 1983. . . . . $2 – 25
17-I Ford Escort XR3 Cabriolet 2¾", 1985, (also 37-K 1986) . $2 – 6
17-J Dodge Dakota Pickup, 3", 1990 (also 50-I) . . . . $1 – 15
17-L Bedford "MATCHBOX REMOVAL" Van, commemorative replica of 17-A, 2⅛", 1994 . . . . $5 – 8
17-M Ferrari 456 GT, 1994 . . . . $1 – 15
18-A Caterpillar D8 Bulldozer with blade, 1⅞", 1956 (compare to 18-B 1958, 18-C 1961) . . . . $50 – 75
18-B Caterpillar Dozer, yellow, no blade braces, 2", 1958 (compare to 18-A 1956, 18-C 1961) . . . . $60 – 75
18-C Caterpillar Bulldozer, yellow with blade braces, 2¼", 1961 (compare to 18-A 1956, 18-B 1958). . . . . $25 – 100
18-D Caterpillar Crawler Bulldozer, 2⅜", 1964 . . . . $15 – 100
18-E Field Car with tires on plastic hubs, 2⅝", 1969 . . . . $6 – 250
18-F Field Car with SF wheels, 2⅝", 1970 . . . . $5 – 400

18-G Hondarora Motorcycle, 2⅜", 1975 (21 var) . . . . $5 – 125

18-H Extending Ladder Fire Engine, 3", 1984 (25 var) . . . . $1 – 15

18-I Caterpillar D8 Bulldozer with blade, commemorative replica of 18-A, 1⅞", 1994 . . . . $5 – 8

19-A MG Midget Sports Car with driver, 2", 1956 . . . . . . $50 – 70

19-B MGA Sports Car, white, 2¼", 1958 . . . . $60 – 150

19-C Aston Martin Racing Car, metallic green, 2½", 1961 . $25 – 50

19-D Lotus Racing Car, 2¾", 1966 . . . . $15 – 30

19-E Lotus Racing Car with SF wheels, 2¾", 1970. . . . . . $30 – 35

19-F Road Dragster, 2⅞", 1970 . . . . $10 – 20

19-G Badger Cement Truck, 3", 1976 . . . . $5 – 8

19-H Peterbilt Cement Truck, 3", 1982 (26 var) . . . . $2 – 45

19-I MG Midget Sports Car (commemorative replica of 19-A), 2", 1993 . . . . $5 – 8

20-A Stake Truck, maroon, 2⅜", 1956 . . . . $40 – 125

20-B ERF 686 Truck "EVEREADY FOR LIFE," blue, 2⅝", 1959 . . . . $45 – 100

20-C Chevrolet Impala Taxi Cab, 3", 1965 . . . . $10 – 350

20-D Lamborghini Marzal with SF wheels, 2¾", 1969 . . . . $12 – 40

v.1 metallic red, $12 – 15

20-E Range Rover Police Patrol (Rolamatic), 2⅞", 1975 (45 var) . $6 – 50

20-F Desert Dawg 4x4 Jeep, 2⅝", 1982 . . . . $1 – 25

20-G Jeep Laredo/Eagle/Wrangler 4x4, 2⅝", 1983 . . . . . . $1 – 25

20-H Volvo Container Truck, 3", 1986 (also 23-I, 62-J) (36 var) . $3 – 50

20-I Volkswagen Ambulance Vanagon, 2⅞", 1986 . . . . $1 – 6

20-J '97 Firebird Formula, 1997 . . . . $1 – 2

21-A Bedford Duplé Long Distance Coach, 2¼", 1956 (compare to 21-B, 1958) . . . . $45 – 55

21-B Bedford Duplé Long Distance Coach, "LONDON TO GLASGOW," 2⅝", 1958 (compare to 21-A 1956) . . . . $45 – 100

21-C Commer Milk Delivery Truck, 2¼", 1961 . . . . $20 – 80

21-D Foden Concrete Truck, 3", 1968 . . . . $6 – 9

21-E Foden Concrete Truck with SF wheels, 2⅞", 1970 . . $20 – 25

21-F Rod Roller, 2⅝", 1973 . . . . $12 – 18

21-G Renault 5TL, 2¹¹⁄₁₆", 1978 (44 var) . . . . $4 – 25

21-H Corvette Pace Car, 3", 1983 . . . . $5 – 8

21-I Breakdown Van, 3", 1986. . . . . $1 – 15

21-J GMC Wrecker, 2⅞", 1987 (also 71-J, 72-M) . . . . $1 – 20

21-K Nissan Prairie, 2⅞", 1991 (also 31-L) . . . . $2 – 15

J-21-L Toyota Celica XX ("Made in Japan" and "J-21" cast on base), 1979 . . . . $15 – 20

22-A Vauxhall Cresta sedan, 2½", 1956 (compare to 22-B 1958) . . . . $45 – 60

22-B Vauxhall Cresta sedan, 2⅝", 1958 (compare to 22-A 1956) . . . . $40 – 400

22-C Pontiac Grand Prix, 3", 1964 . . . . $15 – 50

22-D Pontiac Grand Prix with SF wheels, 3", 1970 . . . . $30 – 1,800

22-E Freeman Inter-City Commuter Coach, 3", 1970 . . . . $12 – 16

22-F Blaze Buster Fire Engine, 3", 1975 . . . . $5 – 400

22-G Toyota Mini Pickup Camper, 2¾", 1982 . . . . $2 – 50

22-H Toyota Mini Pickup Camper, Bigfoot 4x4, 2¾", 1983 . $2 – 50

22-I Jaguar XK120, 3", 1984 . . . . $1 – 8

22-J Saab 9000, 2¹⁵⁄₁₆", 1989 (also see 15-J) . . . . $2 – 15

22-K Opel Vectra/Chevrolet Cavalier GS, 3", 1990 (also 41-J) . $2 – 12

22-L Lamborghini Diablo, 3", 1992 (also 49-I) . . . . $1 – 8

J-22-M Mitsubishi Galant Eterna ("Made in Japan" and "J-22" cast on base), 1979. . . . . $12 – 15

23-A Berkeley Cavalier Travel Trailer, 2½", 1956 . . . . . . $40 – 325

23-B Bluebird Dauphine Travel Trailer, 2½", 1960 . . . . . $50 – 400

23-C Trailer Caravan, 2⅞", 1965 . . . . $12 – 15

23-D Volkswagen Camper with opening roof, 2⅛", 1970 . $15 – 125

23-E Volkswagen Pizza Van . . . . $12 – 15

23-E Atlas Dump Truck, 3", 1975. . . . . $7 – 15

v.3 blue with yellow dumper, $8 – 12

23-F Mustang GT350, 2⅞", 1979 . . . . $10 – 15

23-G Audi Quattro, 3", 1982 (also 25-J) . . . . $2 – 50

23-H Peterbilt Tipper, 3", 1982 (also 30-H) . . . . $1 – 50

23-I Volvo Container Truck, 3", 1985 (also 20-I, 62-J) (36 var) . $3 – 50

24-A Weatherhill Hydraulic Excavator, yellow, 2⅜", 1956 . $45 – 55

24-B Weatherhill Hydraulic Excavator, 2⅝", 1959 . . . . . . $20 – 45

24-C Rolls Royce Silver Shadow, 3", 1967 . . . . $6 – 9

24-D Rolls Royce Silver Shadow with SF wheels, 3", 1970 . $10 – 15

24-E Team Matchbox Formula 1 Racer, 2⅞", 1973 (16 var) . $6 – 350

24-F Diesel Shunter, 3", 1978 (14 var) . . . . $2 – 100

24-G Datsun 280ZX, 3", 1982 . . . . $2 – 5

24-H Datsun 280ZX 2+2, 3", 1983 . . . . $2 – 75

24-I Nissan 300ZX Turbo, 2⅞", 1987 . . . . $1 – 12

24-J Ferrari F40, 3", 1989 (also 70-H) (28 var) . . . . $1 – 45

24-K Lincoln Town Car, 3", 1990 (also 43-F) . . . . $1 – 15

24-L Airport Fire Tender, 3", 1992 (also 8-N) . . . . $1 – 45

25-A Bedford "DUNLOP" 12CWT Van, 2⅛", 1956. . . . . . $40 – 55

25-B Volkswagen 1200 Sedan, metallic light blue, 2½", 1960 . $50 – 125

25-C Bedford Petrol Tanker with tilt cab, 3", 1964 . . . . $20 – 160

25-D Ford Cortina GT with regular wheels, 2⅞", 1968 . . . . $6 – 12

25-E Ford Cortina GT with SF wheels, 2⅝", 1970 . . . . . . $15 – 40

25-F Mod Tractor, 2⅛", 1972. $7 – 50

25-G Flat Car with container, 3", 1978 . . . . $6 – 60

25-H Toyota Celica GT, 2¹⁵⁄₁₆", 1978 . . . . $4 – 50

25-I Toyota Celica GT w/oversized rear wheels, 2¹⁵⁄₁₆", 1982 . $4 – 50

25-J Audi Quattro, 3", 1982 (also 23-G) . . . . $2 – 50

25-K Ambulance, Chevrolet, 2¹⁵⁄₁₆", 1983 (also 41-F) . . . . . $1 – 12

25-L Peugeot Quasar, 2¾", 1985 (also 49-H) . . . . $1 – 8

25-M BMW Z-3, 1997 . . . . $2 – 3

26-A Foden "READY-MIX" Concrete Truck, 1¾", 1956 . . $35 – 160
26-B Foden "READY MIX" Concrete Truck, orange, 2½", 1961. $25 – 50
26-C GMC Tipper Truck with regular wheels, 2⅝", 1968 . . . $6 – 9
26-D GMC Tipper Truck with SF wheels, 2⅝", 1970. . . . . $15 – 20
26-E Big Banger, 3", 1972 (later model 26-G, Cosmic Blues). $15 – 20
26-F Site Dumper, 2⅝", 1976 . . . . $4 – 10 ($250)
26-G Cosmic Blues, 3", 1980 (reissued as 41-L 1992) . . . . . $1 – 20
26-H Volvo Covered Tilt Truck, 3", 1984 . . . . $1 – 20
26-I Volvo Cable Truck (rare variation of 23-I), 3", 1984. . $18 – 30
26-J BMW 5-Series 535i, 3", 1989 (also 31-K) . . . . $2 – 4
26-K Foden "READY MIX" Concrete Truck (replica of 26-A), 2½", 1993 . . . . $5 – 8
26-L Chevy Van, 3", 1993 (reissue, see 68-E) (35 var) . . . . $3 – 100
27-A Bedford Low Loader, 1⅜", 1956. . . . . $45 – 800
27-B Bedford Low Loader, 3¾", 1959. . . . . $45 – 100
27-C Cadillac Sixty Special, 2¾", 1960 . . . . $45 – 325
27-D Mercedes Benz 230SL Convertible with regular wheels, 3", 1966 . . . . $6 – 10
27-E Mercedes Benz 230SL Convertible with SF wheels, 2⅞", 1970 . . . . $15 – 25
27-F Lamborghini Countach w/opening rear cowl, 2⅞", 1973 . $6 – 15

v.1 yellow with chrome interior, $6 – 9

27-G Swing Wing Jet, 3", 1981 . . . . $2 – 6
27-H Jeep Cherokee, 2⅞", 1987 (41 var) . . . . $1 – 25 ($100)
27-I Mercedes Benz 1600 Turbo Farm Tractor, 2¾", 1991 (also 73-I 1990) . . . . $1 – 4
27-J Tailgator, 1994 . . . . $1 – 15
28-A Bedford Compressor Truck, 2¼", 1956 . . . . $35 – 55
28-B Thames Trader Compressor Truck, yellow, 2¾", 1959. $35 – 200
28-C Mark 10 Jaguar, 2¾", 1964. . . . . $20 – 160
28-D Mack Dump Truck with regular wheels, 2⅝", 1968 . . $9 – 12
28-E Mack Dump Truck with SF wheels, 2⅝", 1970 . . . . . $6 – 40
28-F Stoat Armored Truck, 2⅝", 1974 . . . . $6 – 12 ($75)
28-G Lincoln Continental Mark V, 3", 1979 . . . . $2 – 7 ($25)
28-H Formula Racing Car, 3⅛", 1982 . . . . $3 – 5 ($50)
28-I 1984 Dodge Daytona Turbo Z, 2⅞", 1984 . . . . . $2 – 12 ($75)
28-J T-Bird Turbo Coupe, 3", 1988 (also 59-H, 61-F) . . $1 – 8 ($75)
28-K Leyland Titan London Bus, 3", 1990 (also 17 - F,51-H). $7 – 225
28-L Corvette Convertible, 3", 1990 (also 14-M) . . . . . . $2 – 350
28-M Fork Lift Truck, 3", 1991 (also 61-H 1992; reissue of 48-F Sambron Jack Lift 1977). . . . . $3 – 5
28-N Mitsubishi Spyder, 1995 . . . . $2 – 4
29-A Bedford Milk Delivery Van, 2¼", 1956. . . . . $45 – 60
29-B Austin A55 Cambridge, two-tone green, 2¾", 1961. . $25 – 50
29-C Fire Pumper with regular wheels, 3", 1966. . . . . . . $8 – 12
29-D Fire Pumper with SF wheels, 3", 1970 . . . . $10 – 25
29-E Racing Mini, 2¼", 1970 . . . . $10 – 15

29-F Shovel Nose Tractor, 2⅞", 1976. . . . . $2 – 4
30-A Ford Prefect sedan, 2¼", 1956 . . . . $45 – 150
30-B Magirus Deutz 6-Wheel Crane Truck, 2⅝", 1961. . $40 – 900
30-C 8-Wheel Crane Truck with regular wheels, 3", 1965 . $10 – 1,000
30-D 8-Wheel Crane Truck with SF wheels, 3", 1970 . . . $35 – 500
30-E Beach Buggy, 2⅝", 1971 . . . . $12 – 25
30-F Swamp Rat, 3", 1976 . . . . $5 – 15
30-G Leyland Articulated Truck, 3", 1981 . . . . $2 – 5 ($40)
30-H Peterbilt Quarry Truck, 3", 1982 (also 23-H) . . . $1 – 15 ($50)
30-I Mercedes Benz 280GE G-Wagon, 3", 1984 . . . . $2 – 15
30-J Toyota Supra, 1995. $2 – 5 ($25)
31-A Ford Customline Station Wagon, 2¾", 1957 (compare to 31-B 1960) . . . . $35 – 50
31-B Ford Fairlane Station Wagon, 2¾", 1960 (compare to 31-A 1957). . . . . $45 – 125
31-C Lincoln Continental, black plastic wheels, 2¾", 1964. $10 – 600
31-D Lincoln Continental with SF wheels, 2¾", 1969 . . $50 – 2,000
31-E Volks Dragon, 2½", 1971. . . . . $12 – 20
31-F Caravan Travel Trailer, 2¹¹⁄₁₆", 1977. . . . . $2 – 5 ($25)
31-G Mazda Savannah RX-7 without spoiler, 3", 1979 . . . . . $3 – 5
31-H Mazda Savannah RX-7 with spoiler, 3", 1982 . . . $2 – 4 ($35)
31-I Rolls Royce Silver Cloud, 3", 1987 (rest of world; 62-I US). $1 – 25
31-J Rover Sterling, 2¹⁵⁄₁₆", 1988 (also 2-J) . . . . $1 – 15
31-K BMW 5-Series 535i, 3", 1990 (also 26-J). . . . . $2 – 5
31-L Nissan Prairie, 2⅞", 1991 (also 21-K 1991) . . . . $2 – 15
31-M Jaguar XJ-220, 3⅛", 1993 . . . . $1 – 5

v.3 fluorescent yellow and orange with bright blue accents, 1994, $1 – 2

32-A Jaguar XK140 Coupe, 2⅜", 1957 . . . . $40 – 100
32-B Jaguar XKE, 2⅝", 1962 . . . . $50 – 200
32-C Leyland Petrol Tanker with regular wheels, 3", 1968 . $6 – 50
32-D Leyland Petrol Tanker with SF wheels, 3", 1970 . . . $15 – 300
32-E Maserati Bora, 3", 1972 . . . . $8 – 40
32-F Field Gun, 3", 1978 . . . . $5 – 100
32-G Atlas Excavator, 3", 1981 . . . . $1 – 10
32-H Modified Racer, 2¹⁵⁄₁₆", 1990 (also 12-K) (54 var) . . . . $1 – 15
32-I Jaguar XK140 Coupe (replica of 32-A), 2⅜", 1993. . . . . $5 – 8
32-J '62 Corvette, 2¹⁵⁄₁₆", 1994 (reissue of 71-G 1982) (33 var). $2 – 350
33-A Ford Zodiac Mk II sedan, 2⅝", 1957 . . . . $30 – 60
33-B Ford Zephyr 6 Mk III sedan, 2⅝", 1963 . . . . $30 – 70
33-C Lamborghini Miura with chrome or spoked hubs, 2¾", 1969. . . . . $6 – 75
33-D Lamborghini Miura with SF wheels, 2¾", 1970 . . . . $15 – 60
33-E Datsun 126X, 3", 1973 . . . . $10 – 40
33-F Police Motorcyclist, Honda CB750, 2½", 1977 (24 var). $2 – 40
33-G Volkswagen Golf GTi, 2⅞", 1986 (also 56-H) . . . . . $2 – 20
33-H Renault 11 Alliance, 2¹⁵⁄₁₆", 1987 (also 43-J) . . . $2 – 5 ($25)

33-I Mercury Sable Wagon, 3", 1988 (also 55-M) . . . . $2 – 4
33-J Ford Utility Truck, 3", 1989 (see 74-I 1987) . . . . $1 – 15
33-K Mercedes Benz 500SL Convertible (Europe; 12 - L US), 3",
    1990 . . . . $1 – 8
34-A Volkswagen Van, blue, "MATCHBOX EXPRESS," 2¼",
    1957 . . . . $45 – 125
34-B Volkswagen Caravette Camper, light green, 2¾", 1962. $40 – 50
34-C Volkswagen Camper, silver with raised 6-windowed roof,
    2⅝", 1967 . . . . $9 – 12
34-D Volkswagen Camper, silver with low windowless roof, 2⅝",
    1968 . . . . $7 – 10
34-E Formula One Racing Car, 2⅞", 1971 . . . . . . $12 – 20 ($125)
34-F Vantastic, 2⅞", 1975 . . . . $8 – 20 ($400)
34-G Chevy Pro Stocker, 3", 1981 (28 var) . . . . $2 – 20 ($100)
34-H Toyman Dodge Challenger, 3", 1983 . . . . $2 – 5
34-I Chevy Pro Stocker Halley's Comet Commemorative Car (varia-
    tion of 34-G), 3", 1986 . . . . $8
34-J Ford RS200, 2⅞", 1987 . . . . $1 – 2 ($12)
34-K Sprint Racer, 2¹⁵⁄₁₆", 1990 (31 var) . . . . $1 – 6 ($100)
34-L Plymouth Prowler, 1995 (14 var) . . . . $1 – 150

v.1 purple with gray interior, $2 – 5

35-A Marshall Horse Box Truck, red cab, brown horse box, 2",
    1957 . . . . $40 – 175
35-B Snow Trac Tractor, 2⅜", 1964 . . . . $25 – 50
35-C Merryweather Fire Engine (SF only), 3", 1969 . . . . . $10 – 15
35-D Fandango, 3", 1975 . . . . $8 – 20 ($750)
35-E Volvo Zoo Truck (rare variation of 23-I), 3", 1981 . . . $20 – 40
35-F Pontiac Trans Am T-Roof, 3", 1982 (also 16-I 1985) . . $2 – 15
35-G 4x4 Pickup Camper, 3", 1986 (also 57-H) . . . . $1 – 5
35-H Ford Bronco II, 3", 1989 (also 39-H) (19 var) . . . . $1 – 8
35-I Land Rover Ninety, 2½", 1990 (U.S.; 16-K rest of world) . $1 – 5
35-J Pontiac Stocker Stock Car, 3", 1993 . . . . $1 – 18
35-K Mercedes GTC Stock Car, 1996 . . . . $1 – 4
36-A Austin A50 sedan, blue-green, 2⅝", 1957 . . . . $35 – 45
36-B Lambretta TV175 Scooter & Sidecar, 2", 1961 . . . . . . $60 – 75
36-C Opel Diplomat with regular wheels, 2⅞", 1966 . . . . $8 – 800
36-D Opel Diplomat with SF wheels, 2⅞", 1970 . . . . $15 – 20
36-E Hot Rod Draguar, 2¹³⁄₁₆", 1970 . . . . $15 – 20
36-F Formula 5000, 3", 1975 . . . . $7 – 12 ($450)
36-G Refuse Truck, 3", 1980 (24 var) . . . . $1 – 25
37-A Coca-Cola Lorry, 2¼", 1957 (compare to 37-B 1957, 37-C
    1960) no base, uneven cases . . . . $75 – 100
37-B Coca-Cola Lorry, 2¼", 1957 (compare to 37-A 1957, 37-C
    1960) no base, even cases . . . . $60 – 75
37-C Coca-Cola Lorry, black base, even load, 2¼", 1960 (compare
    to 37-A & 37-B 1957) . . . . $50 – 150
37-D Dodge Cattle Truck with regular wheels, 2½", 1966 . . $6 – 12
37-E Dodge Cattle Truck with SF wheels, 2½", 1970 . . . . $15 – 25

37-F Soopa Coopa, 2⅞", 1972 . . . . $15 – 25 ($150)
37-G Skip Truck, 2¹¹⁄₁₆", 1976 . . . . $4 – 10 ($300)
37-H Sunburner, Maserati Bora, 3", 1982 . . . . $3 – 5
37-I Matra Rancho (European model), 2⅞", 1982 . . . . $3 – 25

37-J Jeep 4x4 with roll cage and winch, 2⅞", 1984, $1 – 2

37-K Ford Escort XR3i Cabriolet, 2⅞", 1986 (also 17-I) . . . . . $2 – 6
37-L Nissan 300ZX, 3", 1991 (also 61-G 1990) (25 var) . . . . $1 – 35
37-M Mercedes Benz 600SL, 3", 1992 (also 38-J) . . . . $1 – 5
38-A Karrier Refuse Truck, 2⅜", 1957 . . . . $30 – 125
38-B Vauxhall Victor Estate Car, yellow, 2⅝", 1963 . . . . . $25 – 40
38-C Honda Motorcycle and Trailer with regular wheels, 2⅞",
    1967 . . . . $10 – 35
38-D Honda Motorcycle and Trailer with SF wheels, 2⅞",
    1970 . . . . $6 – 20
38-E Stingeroo Cycle (3-wheel motorcycle), 3", 1973 . $15 – 25 ($400)
38-F Jeep (with or without top), 2⅜", 1976 . . . . . . $6 – 25 ($450)
38-G Camper Pickup Truck, 3", 1980 . . . . $4 – 6 ($75)
38-H Ford Model A Truck, 3", 1982 (411 var) . . . . $3 – 250
38-I Ford Courier, 3", 1992 . . . . $2 – 60
38-J Mercedes Benz 600SL, 3", 1992 (also 37-M) . . . . $1 – 6
38-K Corvette Stingray III Convertible, 1994 . . . . $1 – 25
39-A Ford Zodiac Convertible, pink, 2⅝", 1957 . . . . . . $35 – 125
39-B Pontiac Convertible, 2¾", 1962 . . . . $35 – 125
39-C Ford Tractor, 2⅛", 1967 . . . . $9 – 12
39-D Clipper, concept car w/opening cockpit, 3", 1973 . $10 – 15 ($250)
39-E Rolls Royce Silver Shadow II, 3¹⁄₁₆", 1979 . . . . $2 – 6 ($75)
39-F Toyota Celica Supra, 3", 1982 (also 60-G) . . . . $2 – 12
39-G BMW 323i Cabriolet, 2¾", 1985 . . . . $1 – 12
39-H Ford Bronco II 4x4, 3", 1990 (also 35-H) . . . . $1 – 8
39-I Mack CH600, 3", 1990 (also 8-M) . . . . $1 – 2
39-J Mercedes Benz 600SEL, 3", 1991 . . . . $1 – 6
40-A Bedford Tipper Truck, red with tan dumper, 2⅛", 1957 . $25 – 50
40-B Leyland Royal Tiger Coach, metallic blue, 3", 1961 . . $20 – 40
40-C Hay Trailer, 3¼", 1967 . . . . $6 – 9
40-D Vauxhall Guildsman, with SF wheels only, 3", 1971 . $10 – 25
40-E Bedford Horse Box with two horses, 2¹³⁄₁₆", 1977 . $2 – 8 ($60)
40-F Corvette T-Roof, 3¹⁄₁₆", 1982 (also 58-I, 62-G) (30 var) . $1 – 8 ($100)
40-G Ford Sierra XR4Ti (also see 15-H, 55-N), 3", 1983 . . . . $2 – 50
40-H NASA Rocket Transporter (variation of 65-H, 72-I Airplane
    Transporter), 3", 1985 (also 60-I) . . . . $1 – 2
40-I Road Roller, 3", 1991 (reissue of 72-F Bomag Road Roller 1979) . $1 – 2
40-J Ford Mondeo, 1995 . . . . $1 – 2
40-K '69 Camaro SS 396, 1997 . . . . $2 – 4

41-A D-Type Jaguar, green, "41" decal, 2³⁄₁₆", 1957 (compare to 41-B 1960). . . . . $30 − 50

41-B D-Type Jaguar, green, 2⁷⁄₁₆", 1960 . . . . $50 − 200

41-C Ford GT (tires will separate from hubs), 2⅝", 1965. $10 − 120

41-D Ford GT with SF wheels, 2⅝", 1970. . . . . $15 − 600

41-E Siva Spyder, 3", 1972. . . . . $12 − 20

41-F Chevrolet Ambulance, 2¹⁵⁄₁₆", 1978 (also 25-J) . . . . . $1 − 12

41-G Kenworth Conventional Aerodyne, 2¾", 1982. . . . . . . $3 − 6

41-H Porsche 935, Racing Porsche, Super Porsche, 3", 1983 (also 55-J). . . . . $2 − 65

41-I Jaguar XJ6, 3", 1987 (also 1-K) . . . . $2 − 40

41-J Opel Vectra/Chevrolet Cavalier, 3", 1991 (also 22-K 1990) . $2 − 12

41-K Sunburner, 3", 1992 (also 15-M) . . . . $2 − 10

41-L Cosmic Blues (reissue, see 26-G), 3", 1993 . . . . $1 − 5

42-A Bedford "EVENING NEWS" Van, yellow-orange, 2¼", 1957 . . . . $40 − 50

42-B Studebaker Lark Wagonaire with hunter and 1 or 2 dogs, 3", 1965, $12 − 16

42-C Iron Fairy Crane with regular wheels, 3", 1969 (compare to 42-D, 1970). . . . . $6 − 9

42-D Iron Fairy Crane with SF wheels, 3", 1970 . . . . $30 − 100

42-E Tyre Fryer, 3", 1972 . . . . $12 − 15 ($100)

42-F Mercedes Benz Container Truck, 3", 1977 . . . . $5 − 50

42-G 1957 T-Bird, 3", 1982 . . . . $3 − 15

42-H Faun Mobile Crane, 3", 1985. . . . . $1 − 15

43-A Hillman Minx sedan, 2⅝", 1958. . . . . $45 − 225

43-B Aveling Barford Tractor Shovel, 2⅝", 1962. . . . . . . $25 − 50

43-C Pony Trailer with two horses and regular wheels, 2⅝", 1968. . . . . $6 − 9

43-D Pony Trailer with two horses and SF wheels, 2⅝", 1970. $4 − 20

43-E Dragon Wheels, 2¹³⁄₁₆", 1972 . . . . $15 − 18

43-F 0-4-0 Steam Locomotive, 3", 1978 . . . . . . $2 − 20 ($200)

43-G '57 Chevy, 2¹⁵⁄₁₆", 1979 (also 4-H) . . . . $1 − 75

43-H Peterbilt Conventional, 2¾", 1982. . . . . $2 − 6

43-I AMG Mercedes Benz 500SEC, 2⅞", 1984 (28 var). $2 − 12 ($100)

43-J Renault 11 Turbo Alliance, 2¹⁵⁄₁₆", 1987 (also 33-H) . $2 − 5 ($25)

43-K Lincoln Town Car, 3", 1989 (also 24-K 1990) . . . . . . $1 − 15

43-L Camaro Z-28, 1994 . . . . $1 − 15

44-A Rolls Royce Silver Cloud, metallic blue, 2⅝", 1958. . $35 − 55

44-B Rolls Royce Phantom V, 2⅞", 1964 . . . . $20 − 100

44-C GMC Refrigerator Truck with regular wheels, 3", 1967 . $6 − 9

44-D GMC Refrigerator Truck with SF wheels, 3", 1970. $20 − 2,000

44-E Boss Mustang, 2⅞", 1972 . . . . $6 − 12

44-F Railway Passenger Coach, 3¹⁄₁₆", 1978 . . . . . . $4 − 25 ($150)

44-G 4x4 Chevy Van, 2⅞", 1982 . . . . $1 − 20

44-H Citroen 15CV (European model), 3", 1983 . . . . $2 − 12

44-I Skoda 130LR Rally (European model), 2⅞", 1988 . . . . . $2 − 5

44-J 1921 Ford Model T Van, 2⅞", 1990 (93 var) . . . . $1 − 50

44-K Ford Probe GT, 1994 . . . . $1 − 3 ($20)

45-A Vauxhall Victor sedan, 2⅜", 1958 . . . . $25 − 1,000

45-B Ford Corsair with boat and rack on roof, 2⅝", 1965. $15 − 45

45-C Ford Group 6 with SF wheels only, 3", 1970. . . . . $10 − 100

45-D BMW 3.0 CSL, 2⅞", 1976 . . . . $6 − 12 ($110)

45-E Kenworth COE Aerodyne, 2¾", 1982 . . . . $1 − 5 ($50)

45-F Ford Cargo Skip Truck, 2¹³⁄₁₆", 1988 (also 70-G). . . . . $2 − 3

45-G Chevrolet Highway Maintenance Truck, 3", 1990 (also 69-I). $1 − 24

46-A Morris Minor 1000, 2", 1958 . . . . $50 − 1,000

46-B Pickford Removal Van, plastic wheels, 2⅝", 1960. . $25 − 350

46-C Mercedes Benz 300SE with regular wheels, 2⅞", 1968. $9 − 12

46-D Mercedes Benz 300SE with SF wheels, 2⅞", 1970. . $10 − 100

46-E Stretcha Fetcha, Ambulance, 2¾", 1972 . . . . . . $12 − 18 ($45)

46-F Ford Tractor, 2³⁄₁₆", 1978. . . . . $1 − 7

46-G Hot Chocolate Volkswagen Beetle, 2¹³⁄₁₆", 1982. . . . $3 − 12

46-H Big Blue Volkswagen Beetle, 2¹³⁄₁₆", 1983 . . . . $3 − 12

46-I Mission Chopper/ Military Chopper, with retractable tail, 3", 1985 (also 57-I). . . . . $1 − 10

46-J Mercedes Sauber Group C Racer, 3", 1985 (also 66-H). $1 − 18

47-A Trojan 1-Ton "BROOKE BOND TEA" Van, red, 2¼", 1958. . . . . $35 − 60

47-B Commer Ice Cream Canteen, 2⁷⁄₁₆", 1963 . . . . $30 − 175

47-C DAF Tipper Container Truck w/regular wheels, 3", 1968 . $8 − 35

47-D DAF Tipper Container Truck with SF wheels, 3", 1970 . $20 − 25

47-E Beach Hopper (Rolamatic), 2⅝", 1974 . . . . $12 − 25

47-F Pannier Tank Locomotive, 3", 1979 . . . . $4 − 10

47-G Jaguar SS100, 3", 1982 . . . . $2 − 15

47-H School Bus, 3", 1985 . . . . $1 − 15 ($45)

48-A Meteor Sports Boat and Trailer, tan deck, blue hull, 2⅜", 1958 (compare to 48-B 1961) . . . . $45 − 100

48-B Sports Boat & Trailer with outboard motor, 2⅝", 1961. $30 − 80

48-C Dodge Dump Truck with regular wheels, 3", 1966, $6 − 9

48-D Dodge Dump Truck with SF wheels, 3", 1970 . . . . . $15 − 20

48-E Pi-Eyed Piper, 2⅞", 1972 (compare to 48-G) . $15 − 20 ($100)

48-F Sambron Jack Lift, 3¹⁄₁₆", 1977 (reissued as 28-M 1991, 61-H 1992) . . . . $5 − 10 ($500)

48-G Red Rider (variation of 48-E), 2⅞", 1982 . . . . $1 − 6

48-H Mercedes Benz Unimog with snowplow, 3", 1984 . . . $2 − 12

48-I Vauxhall Astra GTE (European model), 2¾", 1987 . . . $2 − 12

48-J Pontiac Firebird S/E Racer, 3", 1993 (also 12-I, 51-I, 60-F). $2 − 5

48-K '56 Ford Pickup, 1997. . . . . $1 − 3

49-A M3 Army Halftrack Personnel Carrier, 2½", 1958 . . $45 – 125

49-B Mercedes Benz Unimog with regular wheels, 2½", 1967. $7 – 12

49-C Mercedes Benz Unimog with SF wheels, 2½", 1970 . $10 – 75

49-D Chop Suey Motorcycle, 2¾", 1973 . . . . $12 – 25 ($400)

49-E Crane Truck, 2¹⁵⁄₁₆", 1976 . . . . $3 – 12 ($75)

49-F Sand Digger Volkswagen Beetle, 2¹³⁄₁₆", 1983. . . . . . . $2 – 4

49-G Dune Man Volkswagen Beetle, 2¹³⁄₁₆", 1984. . . . . . . $2 – 4

49-H Peugeot Quasar, 2¾", 1987 (also 25-L) . . . . $1 – 8

49-I Lamborghini Diablo, 3", 1992 (also 22-L) . . . . $1 – 8

49-J BMW 850i, 3", 1993 . . . . $1 – 5 ($25)

49-K VW Concept Car, 1996 . . . . $1 – 12

50-A Commer Pickup, 2½", 1958 . . . . $45 – 350

50-B John Deere Tractor, 2⅛", 1964 . . . . $20 – 30

50-C Ford Kennel Truck with four dogs and regular wheels, 2¾", 1969 . . . . $6 – 9

50-D Ford Kennel Truck with four dogs and SF wheels, 2¾", 1970. . . . . $15 – 20

50-E Articulated Truck w/removable trailer, 3¹⁄₁₆", 1973 . $3 – 12 ($200)

50-F Articulated Trailer, 3", 1980 (goes with 50-E). . . . . . . $4 – 8

50-G Harley Davidson Motorcycle, 2¹¹⁄₁₆", 1980 . . . . $2 – 5

50-H Chevy Blazer 4x4 Police, 3", 1985 . . . . $1 – 8 ($60)

50-I Dodge Dakota Pickup, 3", 1989 (also 17-J) . . . . $1 – 15

50-J Mack Floodlight Heavy Rescue Auxiliary Power Truck, 3", 1991 (also 57-K) . . . . $1 – 15

51-A Albion Chieftain Flatbed Transporter, "PORTLAND CEMENT," 2½", 1958 . . . . $35 – 125

51-B John Deere Trailer with three barrels, 2⅝", 1964 . . . $20 – 30

51-C AEC Ergomatic 8-Wheel Tipper with regular wheels, 3", 1969 . . . . $10 – 25

51-D AEC Ergomatic 8-Wheel Tipper with SF wheels, 3", 1970 . $15 – 20

51-E Citroen SM, 3", 1972 . . . . $8 – 30

v. metallic orange with cream interior, $8 – 12

51-F Combine Harvester, 2¾", 1978 . . . . $1 – 8 ($500)

51-G Midnight Magic (variation of 53-E Tanzara), 3", 1982 . $2 – 5 ($25)

51-H Leyland Titan London Bus, 3", 1984 (also 17-F, 28-K). $7 – 225

51-I Pontiac Firebird S/E, 3", 1984 (also 12-I, 48-J, 60-F) . . . $2 – 5

51-J Camaro IROC Z, 3", 1985 (also 68-G). . . . . $1 – 6

51-K Ford LTD Police, 3", 1988 (also 16-J) . . . . $1 – 15

51-L Porsche 959 1994, 2⅞", (reissue of 7-J 1987) . . . . . . $1 – 35

51-M Ford Ambulance, 1997. . . . . $1 – 4

52-A Maserati 4CL T/1948 Racer, 2½", 1958. . . . . $50 – 125

52-B BRM Racing Car with black tires on plastic hubs, 2⅝", 1965 . . . . $10 – 50

52-C Dodge Charger Mk III concept car (SF only), 2⅞", 1970. $8 – 300

52-D Police Launch Boat, 3", 1976. . . . . $4 – 15 ($65)

52-E BMW M1 with opening hood, 3", 1981 . . . . . . $2 – 15 ($75)

52-F BMW M1, hood doesn't open, 3", 1983 . . . . . . $2 – 18 ($65)

52-G Isuzu Amigo, 2⅞", 1991 . . . . $2 – 7

52-H Escort Cosworth, 1994. . . . . $1 – 5 ($40)

52-I Maserati 4CL T/1948 Racer, commemorative replica of 52-A, 2½", 1994. . . . . $5 – 8

53-A Aston Martin DB2 Saloon, 2¹⁵⁄₁₆", 1958 . . . . $45 – 150

53-B Mercedes Benz 220 SE, 2¾", 1963 . . . . $25 – 125

53-C Ford Zodiac Mk IV sedan with regular wheels, 2¾", 1968 . . . . $8 – 600

53-D Ford Zodiac Mk IV sedan with SF wheels, 2¾", 1970 . $20 – 300

53-E Tanzara, 3", 1972 . . . . $12 – 40

53-F Jeep CJ6, 2¹⁵⁄₁₆", 1977 . . . . $4 – 8

53-G Flareside Pickup, 2⅞", 1982 . . . . $2 – 8 ($50 – 200)

53-H Faun Dump Truck, 2¾", 1989 (reissued as 9-K 1989, 58-F 1989) . . . . $1 – 15

53-I Ford LTD Taxi, 3", 1992 (also 56-I 1992) . . . . $3 – 5

53-J Rhino Rod, 1994 . . . . $1 – 3

54-A Army Saracen Personnel Carrier, 2¼", 1958 . . . . $20 – 35

54-B Cadillac S&S Ambulance, w/regular wheels, 2⅝", 1965. $8 – 12

54-C Cadillac S&S Ambulance, with SF wheels, 2⅞", 1970 . $20 – 25

54-D Ford Capri, 3", 1971 . . . . $8 – 10

54-E Personnel Carrier, 3", 1976 . . . . $5 – 8

54-F Motor Home, 3¼", 1980 . . . . $6 – 9

54-G NASA Tracking Vehicle (variation of 54-F), 3¼", 1982 . $2 – 5

54-H Airport Foam Pumper (variation of 54-F), 3¼", 1985 . . $2 – 4

54-I Chevrolet Lumina Stock Car, 3", 1990 . . . . $2 – 20

54-J Abrams M1 Tank, 1995 . . . . $1 – 4

54-K Crown Victoria Police Car, 1997 . . . . $1 – 3

55-A DUKW Army Amphibian, 2¾", 1958 . . . . $30 – 45

55-B Ford Fairlane Police Car, 2⅝", 1963 . . . . $30 – 200

v.4 light blue with black plastic wheels, $30 – 35

55-C Ford Galaxie Police Car, 2⅞", 1966 . . . . $20 – 70

55-D Mercury Parklane Police Car with regular wheels, 3", 1968 . . . . $10 – 60

55-E Mercury Parklane Police Car with SF wheels, 3", 1970 . $10 – 15

55-F Mercury Commuter Police Station Wagon, 3", 1971. $15 – 20 ($100)

55-G Hellraiser, 3", 1975 . . . . $12 – 18

55-H Ford Cortina 1600 GL, 3¹⁄₁₆", 1979. . . . . $3 – 15 ($200)

55-I Porsche 935, Racing Porsche, Super Porsche, 3", 1983 (also 41-H) . . . . $3 – 4

55-J Ford Sierra XR4i, 3", 1983 (also 15-H, 40-I) . . . . $1 – 18 ($50)

55-K Mercury Parklane Police Halley's Comet Commemorative Car (New Superfast SF-1-B), 3", 1986 . . . . $5 – 8

55-L Mercury Sable Wagon, 3", 1988 (also 33-I) . . . . $2 – 65

55-M Rolls Royce Silver Spirit, 3", 1990 (also 66-I) . . . . . . $1 – 5

55-N Ford Model A Hot Rod, 3", 1993 (reissue of 73-H) (24 var). $1 – 25

55-O Flareside Pickup, 2⅞", 1994 (reissue of 53-G) (30 var). $3 – 6

56-A London Trolley Bus, red, 2⅝", 1958 . . . . $30 – 250

56-B Fiat 1500 with luggage on roof, 2½", 1965 . . . . . . $10 – 100

56-C BMC 1800 Pininfarina (SF only), 2¾", 1970 . . . . . . $15 – 20

56-D High-Tailer Team Matchbox Racer, 3", 1974 . . . . $7 – 12

56-E Mercedes Benz 450SEL, 3", 1979 . . . . $3 – 10

56-F Mercedes Benz 450SEL Taxi, 3", 1980 . . . . $3 – 10

56-G Peterbilt Tanker, 3", 1982 (also 5-I) (37 var). $2 – 18 ($50 – 75)

56-H Volkswagen Golf GTi, 2⅞", 1986 (also 33-G) . . . . . . $2 – 20

56-I Ford LTD Taxi, 3", 1992 (also 53-I 1992) . . . . $3 – 5

56-J Isuzu Rodeo, 1995 (also 59-L Vauxhall Frontera). . . . . $1 – 15

57-A Wolseley 1500 sedan, 2⅛", 1958 . . . . $45 – 125

57-B Chevrolet Impala, metallic blue with light blue roof, 2¾", 1961 . . . . $30 – 40

57-C Land Rover Fire Truck with regular wheels, 2⅞", 1966 . $10 – 200

57-D Land Rover Fire Truck with SF wheels, 2⅞", 1970 . . $25 – 40

57-E Eccles Caravan Travel Trailer, 3", 1970. . . . . $6 – 10

57-F Wildlife Truck (Rolamatic), 2¾", 1973 . . . . $5 – 8

57-G Carmichael Commando (European model), 3", 1982 . $15 – 25

57-H 4x4 Mini Pickup, Mountain Man, 2¾", 1982 . . . . . . $2 – 5

57-I Mission Chopper, 3", 1985 (also 46-I) . . . . $1 – 10

57-J Ford Transit Van, 3", 1990 (also 60-I) (58 var). . . . . . $2 – 75

57-K Mack Floodlight Heavy Rescue Auxiliary Power Truck, 3", 1991 (also 50-J) . . . . $1 – 15

58-A BEA Coach, 2½", 1958 . . . . $30 – 125

58-B Drott Excavator, 2⅝", 1962 . . . . $25 – 100

58-C DAF Girder Truck with regular wheels, 2⅝", 1968. . . . $6 – 9

58-D DAF Girder Truck with SF wheels, 2⅝", 1970 . . . . . $20 – 25

58-E Woosh-N-Push, 2⅞", 1972 . . . . $15 – 20

58-F Faun Dump Truck, 2¾", 1976 (also 9-K, 53-H). . . . . $1 – 15

58-G Ruff Trek Holden Pickup, 2⅞", 1983 . . . . $2 – 15 ($60)

58-H Mercedes Benz 300E, 3", 1987 . . . . $1 – 6

58-I Corvette T-Top, 3¹⁄₁₆", 1982 (also 40-F, 62-G) . . . $1 – 8 ($100)

59-A Ford Thames "Singer" Van, 2⅛", 1958 . . . . $30 – 125

59-B Ford Fairlane Fire Chief Car, 2⅞", 1963 . . . . $25 – 150

59-C Ford Galaxie Fire Chief Car with regular wheels, 2⅞", 1966 . . . . $15 – 20

59-D Ford Galaxie Fire Chief Car with SF wheels, 2⅞", 1970. $20 – 25

59-E Mercury Parklane Fire Chief, 3", 1971 (43 var) . . . . . $5 – 50

59-F Planet Scout, 2¾", 1971. . . . . $12 – 50

59-G Porsche 928, 3", 1980 (39 var) . . . . $4 – 15

59-H T-Bird Turbo Coupe, 3", 1988 (also 28-J, 61-F) . . $1 – 8 ($75)

v.6 red, $2 – 4

59-I Porsche 944, 3", 1991 (also 71-I) . . . . $1 – 20

59-J Aston Martin DB-7, 1994 . . . . $1 – 10

59-K Camaro Z-28 Police Pursuit, 1995 . . . . $1 – 2

60-A Morris J2 "BUILDERS SUPPLY" Pickup, light blue, 2¼", 1958 . . . . $30 – 55

60-B Leyland Site Office Truck w/regular wheels, 2½", 1966. $15 – 20

60-C Leyland Site Office Truck with SF wheels, 2½", 1970. $25 – 30

60-D Lotus Super Seven, 3", 1971 . . . . $15 – 25 ($75)

60-E Holden Pickup, 2⅞", 1977 . . . . $6 – 25

60-F Mustang Piston Popper (Rolamatic), 2¹³⁄₁₆", 1982 (also 10-F). $5 – 15

60-G Pontiac Firebird S/E, 3", 1984 (also 12-I, 48-J, 51-I) . . . $2 – 5

60-H Toyota Celica Supra, 3", 1984 (also 39-F) . . . . $2 – 12

60-I New Ford Transit, 2⅞", 1987 (also 57-J) . . . . $2 – 75

60-J NASA Rocket Transporter, 3", 1990 (var. of 65-H 1986, 72-I 1985, also 40-H 1985) . . . . $1 – 2

60-K Helicopter, 1997 reissue of 75-F with pilot and large windows, 3", 1982 (39 var) . . . . $2 – 20

61-A Ferret Scout Car, 2¼", 1959. . . . . $15 – 25

61-B Alvis Stalwart "BP EXPLORATION," 2⅝", 1966 . . . . . $10 – 45

61-C Blue Shark, 3", 1971 . . . . $15 – 40

61-D Ford Wreck Truck, 3", 1978 . . . . $4 – 15 ($300 – 600)

61-E Peterbilt Wreck Truck, 3", 1982 . . . . $1 – 8 ($50 – 200)

61-F T-Bird Turbo Coupe, 3", 1988 (also 28-J, 59-H) . . $1 – 8 ($75)

61-G Nissan 300ZX, 3", 1990 (also 37-L 1991) . . . . $1 – 35

v.5 black with orange-red and white graffiti design, orange-red interior, $1 – 2

61-H Fork Lift Truck, 3⅛", 1992 (also 28-M 1991, reissue of 48-F Sambron Jack Lift 1977) . . . . $5 – 10 ($500)

62-A General Service Lorry, 2⅝", 1959. . . . . $40 – 50

62-B TV Service Van with ladder, antenna, and three TV sets, 2½", 1963 . . . . $30 – 200

62-C Mercury Cougar with chrome hubs and doors that open, 3", 1968 . . . . $8 – 800

62-D Mercury Cougar with SF wheels and doors that open, 3", 1970 . . . . $12 – 15

62-E Mercury Cougar Rat Rod, doors don't open, 3", 1970. $15 – 25

62-F Renault 17TL, 3", 1974. . . . . $8 – 15

62-G Corvette T-Roof, 3¹⁄₁₆", 1980 (also 40-F, 58-I) . . $1 – 8 ($100)

62-H Corvette Hardtop, 3¹⁄₁₆", 1983. . . . . $2 – 15 ($50)

62-I Rolls Royce Silver Cloud, 3", 1985 (US; 31-I rest of world). $1 – 25

62-J Volvo Container Truck, 3¹⁄₁₆", 1985 (also 20-I, 23-I) . . . $3 – 50

62-K Volvo 760 (European model), 3", 1987 . . . . $2 – 3 ($15)

62-L Oldsmobile Aerotech, 3", 1989 (also 64-H). . . . . $1 – 2

62-M Street Streak concept car, 1996 . . . . $1 – 2

63-A Ford 3-Ton 4x4 Army Ambulance, 2½", 1959 . . . . . $40 – 50

63-B Airport Foamite Crash Tender, 2¼", 1964. . . . . . . $10 – 30

63-C Dodge Crane Truck with regular wheels, 2¾", 1968. . $8 – 15

63-D Dodge Crane Truck with SF wheels, 2¾", 1970 . . . . $20 – 25

63-E Freeway Gas Tanker, 3", 1973 . . . . $6 – 175

63-F Freeway Gas Tanker Trailer, 3", 1978. . . . . $6 – 65

63-G Dodge Challenger/Mitsubishi Galant Eterna, 2⅞", 1980 . $10 – 15

63-H Snorkel Fire Engine with open cab, 2¹³⁄₁₆", 1982 . . . $1 – 15

63-I 4x4 Pickup, 3", 1984 . . . . $4 – 6

63-J Volkswagen Golf GTi 1991 (also 33-G 1986, 56-H 1986). $2 – 20

64-A Scammell Breakdown Truck, olive green, black plastic wheels, 2½", 1959 . . . . $25 – 45

64-B MG 1100 w/driver and dog; regular wheels, 2⅝", 1966. $9 – 12

64-C MG 1100 with driver and dog; SF wheels, 2⅝", 1970 . $20 – 175

64-D Slingshot Dragster, 3", 1971 . . . . $15 – 25 ($150)
64-E Fire Chief Car (resembles a Ford Torino), 3", 1976 . . . $8 – 12
64-F Caterpillar Bulldozer with plastic roof, 2⅝", 1979 . . . . $1 – 16

v.2 yellow with yellow blade, black canopy, England cast, $4 – 6

64-G Dodge Caravan, 2⅞", 1985 (also 68-F). . . . . $2 – 300
64-H Oldsmobile Aerotech, 3", 1990 (also 62-L). . . . . $1 – 2
65-A 3.4 Litre Jaguar, gray plastic wheels, 2½", 1959 . . . . $30 – 40
65-B Jaguar 3.8 Litre Saloon, 2⅝", 1962 . . . . $25 – 50
65-C Claas Combine Harvester (regular wheels only), 3", 1967. $6 – 9
65-D Saab Sonnet (SF wheels only), 2¾", 1973 . . . $10 – 15 ($300)
65-E Airport Coach, 3", 1977 (40 var) . . . . . . $4 – 12 ($50 – 60)
65-F Tyrone Malone Bandag Bandit, 3", 1982 . . . . $1 – 6
65-G Indy Racer, 3", 1984 (32 var) . . . . $1 – 8
65-H Plane Transporter "RESCUE" (variation of NASA Rocket
    Transporter, also 72-I 1985), 3", 1986 . . . . $3 – 8 ($50)
65-I Cadillac Allante, 3", 1988 (also 72-L) . . . . $1 – 8 ($150)
65-J Ford F-150 4x4 Pickup, 1995 . . . . $1 – 2
66-A Citroen DS19, yellow, 2½", 1959 . . . . $50 – 130
66-B Harley Davidson Motorcycle and Sidecar, 2⅝", 1962 . $85 – 95
66-C Greyhound Bus with regular wheels, 3", 1967 . . . . . $10 – 75
66-D Greyhound Bus with SF wheels, 3", 1970 . . . . $15 – 20
66-E Mazda RX-500, 3", 1971 . . . . $10 – 25 ($800)
66-F Ford Transit, 2¾", 1977 . . . . $6 – 8 ($50)
66-G Tyrone Malone Super Boss, 3", 1982 . . . . $1 – 4 ($8)
66-H Mercedes Sauber Group C Racer, 3", 1985 (also 46-J). $1 – 18
66-I Rolls Royce Silver Spirit, 3", 1988 (also 55-M) . . . . $1 – 5
66-J Opel Calibra, 1997 . . . . $1 – 2
67-A Saladin Armoured Car, 2½", 1959 . . . . $35 – 50
67-B Volkswagen 1600TL with chrome hubs, 2¾", 1967. . $6 – 100
67-C Volkswagen 1600TL with SF wheels, 2¾", 1970 . . . . $15 – 40
67-D Hot Rocker Mercury Capri, 3", 1973 . . . . $10 – 15
67-E Datsun 260Z 2+2, 3", 1978 (29 var) . . . . $2 – 12
67-F Flame Out (variation of 48-E and 48-G), 3", 1983 . . . . $4 – 6
67-G IMSA Mustang, 3", 1983 (also 11-I) . . . . $2 – 12
67-H Lamborghini Countach LP500S, 3", 1985 (also 11-J) . . . $2 – 4
67-I Icarus Bus (European model), 3", 1987. . . . . $2 – 12
68-A Austin Mk 2 Radio Truck, 2⅜", 1959 . . . . $45 – 60
68-B Mercedes Benz Coach, 2⅞", 1965 . . . . $10 – 75
68-C Porsche 910 (SF wheels only), 2⅞", 1970. . . . . $15 – 25
68-D Cosmobile, 2⅞", 1975. . . . . $12 – 55
68-E Chevy Van, 2¹⁵⁄₁₆", 1979 (reissued in 1993 as 26-L) . . $3 – 100
68-F Dodge Caravan, 2⅞", 1984 (also 64-G). . . . . $2 – 300
68-G Camaro IROC Z, 3", 1987 (also 51-J). . . . . $1 – 6
68-H TV News Truck, 3", 1989 (also 73-J 1990) . . . . $1 – 15

68-I Road Roller, 3", 1992 (reissue of 72-F). . . . . $3 – 6
68-J Stinger, 1995. . . . . $1 – 2
69-A Commer 30 CWT "NESTLE'S" Van, gray plastic wheels, 2⅜",
    1959 . . . . $40 – 75
69-B Hatra Tractor Shovel, 3", 1965 . . . . $10 – 35
69-C Rolls Royce Silver Shadow Convertible Coupe (SF wheels
    only), 3", 1969. . . . . $15 – 20
69-D Turbo Fury, 3", 1973. $15 – 40
69-E Armored Truck, 2¹³⁄₁₆", 1978. . . . . $4 – 6 ($75)
69-F 1933 Willys Street Rod, 2¹⁵⁄₁₆", 1982 . . . . $1 – 10
69-G 1983 Corvette, 3", 1983 (also 14-I). . . . . $2 – 18
69-H Volvo 480ES (European model), 2⅞", 1989 . . . . $2 – 7
69-I Chevy Highway Maintenance Truck, 3¹⁄₁₆", 1990 (also 45-G). $1 – 24
69-J '68 Mustang Cobra Jet, 1997. . . . . $1 – 2
70-A Ford Thames Estate Car, yellow & turquoise, 2⅛", 1959. $30 – 40
70-B Atkinson Grit Spreader with regular wheels, 2⅝", 1966 . $6 – 12
70-C Ford Atkinson Grit Spreader with SF wheels, 2⅝", 1970. $20 – 25
70-D Dodge Dragster, 3", 1971. . . . . $15 – 20 ($1,000)
70-E Self-Propelled Gun, 2⅝", 1976 . . . . $2 – 8
70-F Ferrari 308 GTB, 2¹⁵⁄₁₆", 1981 . . . . $2 – 12 ($80)
70-G Ford Skip Truck, 2¹³⁄₁₆", 1988 (also 45-F). . . . . $2 – 3
70-H Ferrari F40, 3", 1989 (also 24-J) . . . . $1 – 45
70-I Military Tank, 2⅞", 1993 (reissue of 73-F) . . . . . . $1 – 8 ($80)
70-J Pontiac GTO Judge, 1996 . . . . $2 – 3 ($25)
71-A Austin 200-Gallon Water Truck, 2⅜", 1959 . . . . $35 – 50
71-B Jeep Gladiator Pickup Truck, 2⅝", 1964. . . . . $25 – 50
71-C Ford Heavy Wreck Truck, "ESSO," with regular wheels, 3",
    1968. . . . . $8 – 75
71-D Ford Heavy Wreck Truck, "ESSO," with SF wheels, 3",
    1970 . . . . $15 – 125
71-E Jumbo Jet Motorcycle, 2¾", 1973 . . . . $15 – 20
71-F Dodge Cattle Truck with cattle, 3", 1976 (reissue of 4-E
    Dodge Stake Truck) (70 var) . . . . $3 – 10
71-G '62 Corvette, 2¹⁵⁄₁₆", 1982 . . . . $2 – 10 ($35)
71-H Scania T142, 3", 1986 (also 8-K, 72-J) . . . . $2 – 5
71-I Porsche 944 Racer, 3", 1988 . . . . $1 – 20
71-J GMC Wrecker, 2⅞", 1989 (also 21-J, 72-M). . . . $2 – 10 ($350)
71-K Mustang Cobra, 1995 . . . . $1 – 5
72-A Fordson Power Major Farm Tractor, blue, 2", 1959 . $40 – 100
72-B Standard Jeep CJ5 with plastic wheel hubs, 2⅜", 1966 . $6 – 9
72-C Standard Jeep CJ5 with SF wheels, 2⅜", 1970. . . . . $15 – 20
72-D Hovercraft SRN6, 3", 1972 . . . . $5 – 7
72-E Maxi Taxi Mercury Capri, 3", 1973 . . . . $2 – 10
72-F Bomag Road Roller, 2¹⁵⁄₁₆", 1979 (reissued as 68-I Road Roller
    1992) . . . . $3 – 6
72-G Dodge Delivery Truck (European model), 2¾", 1982. $2 – 50
72-H Sand Racer, 2¹¹⁄₁₆", 1984 . . . . $18 – 25
72-I Plane Transporter "RESCUE," 3", 1985 (variation of NASA
    Rocket Transporter, also 65-H 1986) . . . . $3 – 8 ($50)
72-J Scania T142, 3", 1986 (also 8-K, 71-H) . . . . $2 – 5
72-K Ford Supervan II, 2¹⁵⁄₁₆", 1987 (US; 6-I 1985 rest of world). $2 – 15
72-L Cadillac Allante, 3", 1988 (also 65-I) . . . . $1 – 8 ($150)
72-M GMC Wrecker, 2⅞", 1989 (also 21-J, 71-J). . . $2 – 10 ($350)
72-N Chevrolet K-1500 Pick-Up, 1996. . . . . $1 – 2 ($15)
73-A RAF 10-Ton Pressure Refueling Tanker, 2⅝", 1959 . . $15 – 25
73-B Ferrari F1 Racing Car, red, 2⅝", 1962. . . . . $20 – 30
73-C Mercury Commuter Station Wagon with chrome hubs, 3⅛",
    1968. . . . . $6 – 9

73-D Mercury Commuter Station Wagon with SF wheels, 3", 1970 . . . . $10 – 20

73-E Mercury Commuter Station Wagon w/raised roof, 3", 1972 . $20 – 25

73-F Weasel Armored Vehicle, 2⅞", 1974 . . . . $1 – 8 ($80)

73-G Ford Model A w/spare tire cast into fender, 2¹³⁄₁₆", 1979. $8 – 10

73-H Ford Model A w/o spare tire cast into fender, 2¹³⁄₁₆", 1980 . $3 – 20

73-I Mercedes Benz 1600 Turbo Farm Tractor, 2¾", 1990 (also 27-I) . $1 – 4

73-J TV News Truck, 3", 1990 (see 68-H 1989) . . . . $1 – 15

73-K Jeep Cherokee, 2⅞", 1994 (reissue of 27-H 1987) . $1 – 25 ($100)

73-L Rotwheeler, 1995 . . . . $1 – 2

v.1 brown with big dog face, fantasy vehicle, $3 – 4

74-A Mobile Canteen Refreshment Bar, 2⅝", 1959 . . . . . $40 – 500

74-B Daimler London Bus with regular wheels, "ESSO EXTRA PETROL," 3", 1966. . . . . $7 – 15

74-C Daimler London Bus with SF wheels, 3", 1970 . . . $15 – 2,000

74-D Toe Joe Wreck Truck, 2¾", 1972 . . . . $4 – 18 ($200)

74-E Cougar Villager Station Wagon, 3", 1978 . . . . . $2 – 4 ($450)

74-F Orange Peel Dodge Charger, 3", 1981 . . . . $3 – 5

74-G Fiat Abarth, 2¹⁵⁄₁₆", 1984 (also 9-G) . . . . $2 – 150

74-H Toyota MR2, 2⅞", 1987 (also 9-I) . . . . $2 – 12

74-I Ford Utility Truck, 3", 1987 (also 33-J) . . . . $1 – 15

74-J Williams Honda F1 Grand Prix Racer, 3", 1988 . . . . . . $1 – 25

74-K Formula Racer, 1996. . . . . $1 – 6

75-A Ford Thunderbird, cream & pink, 2⅝", 1960 . . . . . $50 – 100

75-B Ferrari Berlinetta with spoked or chrome wheel hubs, 3", 1965 . . . . $10 – 600

75-C Ferrari Berlinetta with SF wheels, 3", 1970 . . . . . . $20 – 80

75-D Alfa Carabo, 3", 1971 . . . . $15 – 25 ($100)

75-E Seasprite Helicopter w/small windows, 2¾", 1977 . $4 – 6 ($350)

75-F Helicopter with pilot and large windows, 3", 1982 . . . $3 – 20

75-G Ferrari Testarossa, 3", 1987. . . . . $2 – 3

75-H Ferrari F50 Convertible (planned but never issued), 1996

75-I Ferrari F50 Hardtop, 1997 . . . . $1 – 2

MATCHBOX 1998 1-75 SERIES MODELS (US MARKET)

Quarry Truck . . . . $1 in blisterpack, $2 in collector box

'97 Chevy Tahoe Police . . . . $1 in blisterpack, $2 in collector box

'57 Chevy. . . . . $1 in blisterpack, $2 in collector box

Bel-Air Hardtop . . . . $1 in blisterpack, $2 in collector box

'70 El Camino. . . . . $1 in blisterpack, $2 in collector box

'33 Ford Street Rod. . . . . . . $1 in blisterpack, $2 in collector box

'57 Chevy Bel-Air Convertible. $1 in blisterpack, $2 in collector box

'70 Boss Mustang . . . . $1 in blisterpack, $2 in collector box

'71 Camaro. . . . . $1 in blisterpack, $2 in collector box

'97 Chevy Tahoe. . . . . $1 in blisterpack, $2 in collector box

M2 Bradley. . . . . $1 in blisterpack, $2 in collector box

Hummer . . . . $1 in blisterpack, $2 in collector box

'97 Ford F-150 . . . . $1 in blisterpack, $2 in collector box

'97 MGF . . . . $1 in blisterpack, $2 in collector box

Porsche 911 GT1 . . . . $1 in blisterpack, $2 in collector box

Mercedes Benz E Class . . . . . $1 in blisterpack, $2 in collector box

Jaguar XK-8 . . . . $1 in blisterpack, $2 in collector box

MATTEL (SEE HOT WHEELS)

MAX MODELS (SEE PAUL'S MODEL ART)

MAXWELL (MATCHBOX OF INDIA)

Below is a small sampling of Maxwell models of Calcutta, India, surprisingly a subsidiary of Matchbox. Maxwell Mini Auto Toys were produced in the 1970s. Notably odd wheels and somewhat boxy shapes typify these toys intended for the local market in India.

1:32 SCALE

Eicher Tractor $19

Escort 335 Tractor $19

Ford 3600 Tractor $19

Ford 5000 Tractor $19

Hindustan Tractor $19

Swaraj Tractor $19

Zetor Tractor $19

1:43 SCALE

507 Fiat Premier 4-door Sedan $7

510 Ambassador 4-door Sedan $7

520 Ambassador Police $7

522 Ambassador Taxi. $7

523 Fiat Premier Taxi. $7

524 Tata Mini Bus $7

526 Tata Van $7

527 Tata School Bus $7

530 Tata "Indian Air" Bus $7

532 Tata "BOAC" Bus $7

533 Tata Ambulance $7

536 Tata Circus $7

537 Tata "Cold Spot Cola" $7

538 Tata tow Truck $7

544 Honda Motorcycle. $7

550 Jeep CJ3 . . . . $7

558 1959 Chevrolet Police Car $7

563 Tata Semi "HP Oil" $7

564 Tata Semi "BP Oil" $7

568 Tata Semi "Burmah Oil". $7

575 Tata Dump Truck $7

577 Tata "Campa Cola" $7

578 Tata "Thumbs Up Cola". $7

610 Jeep FC150 Pickup $7

1:64 SCALE

Vauxhall Guildsman . . . . $12 – 15

MAY CHEONG (SEE MAISTO)

MAY TAT (ALSO SEE MAISTO)

May Tat is the bottom-of-the-line budget division of Maisto, producing unidentifiable unmarked toys in the so-called 1:60 scale. Since they bear no markings except on the package, they are considered generic, and are therefore valueless to the collector for anything other than a curiosity. One example of May Tat toys is a series called Fun Wheels, six vehicles sold in a twelve-car display box — no individual packages. The models are barely recognizable due to drastically shortened bodies and exaggerated styling. Typical is the pullback action featured on these toys, available for $1 or less each.

McGREGOR (ALSO SEE POLITOYS, POLISTIL)

McGregor is the Mexican subsidiary of Politoys, later known as Polistil, of Italy. Here is just a small sampling of models produced. Models are distinguished by the McGregor name on the base, the unusual 1:45 scale in which they are produced, and the words "Hecho en Mexico."

200 BRM F1, purple, 1:41	$11
201 De Sanctio F3, green, 1:41	$11
203 Honda F1, brown & white, 1:41	$11
1919 Fiat 501 S. Sport, green w/black fenders and black top.	$15 – 20
1929 Fiat 525 S. Reale, silver w/black fenders and black top.	$15 – 20
Isotta Fraschini, kind of a dark mustard yellow, black top.	$15 – 20
Berliet, light yellow with black roof.	$15 – 20
Lancia Landa, yellow with black fenders and black top	$15 – 20
1911 Fiat, sky blue with black fenders and black top	$15 – 20
Bentley, British green with black fenders and black top.	$15 – 20
Fiat Balilla, black with off-white fenders	$15 – 20
1899 Fiat, dark blue with red top, white interior	$15 – 20
1902 Isotta Fraschini, dark blue with off-white fenders, white interior	$15 – 20
Itala Palombella, cream-colored body, black roof, yellow fenders.	$15 – 20

MEBETOYS

Now a subsidiary of Mattel, along with the Corgi brand, Mebetoys was originally an independent toy manufacturer based in Italy. They arrived on the scene in 1966. Mebetoys was purchased by Mattel around 1970 and have been referred to as "overgrown Hot Wheels." Models continued to be produced under the Mebetoys brand name even as recently as 1985.

A-1 Fiat 850, 1:42, 1966	$30
A-2 Fiat 1500, 1:42, 1966	$30
A-3 Alfa Romeo Giulia TI, 1:42, 1966	$30
A-4 Alfa Romeo 2600, 1:43, 1966	$30
A-5 Autobianchi Primula, 1:43, 1966	$30
A-6 Lancia Flavia, 1:43, 1966.	$30
A-7 Alfa Romeo Giulia TI Carabinieri, 1:42, 1966.	$30
A-8 Alfa Romeo Giulia TI Policia, 1:42, 1966	$30
A-9 Fiat 1100R, 1:43, 1967	$30
A-10 Maserati Mistral, 1:43, 1967.	$40
A-11 Lancia Fulvia Coupe, 1:43, 1967	$30
A-12 Porsche 912, 1:43, 1967	$40
A-13 Opel Kadett Fastback, 1:43, 1967	$30
A-14 Ferrari Berlinetta Le Mans (not issued)	
A-15 Fiat 1500 Policia, 1:42, 1967	$30
A-16 Fiat 124, 1:43, 1967	$30
A-17 BMW 2000CS, 1:43, 1967	$30
A-18 Alfa Romeo Duetto Spyder, 1:43, 1967	$30
A-19 Mercedes-Benz 250SE, 1:43, 1967	$30
A-20 Lamborghini Miura P400, 1:43, 1967	$30
A-21 Fiat 1500 Fire Chief, 1:42, 1967	$30
A-22 Corvette Rondine, 1:43, 1967	$40
A-23 Chapparal 2F, 1:43, 1968	$40
A-24 Ford GT Mark II, 1:43, 1968	$40
A-25 Porsche Carrera 10, 1:43, 1968	$40
A-26 Rolls-Royce Silver Shadow, 1:43, 1968.	$50
A-27 Ferrari P4, 1:43, 1968	$40
A-28 Innocenti Mini-Minor, 1:43, 1968.	$30
A-29 Toyota 2000GT, 1:43, 1968.	$30
A-30 Iso Rivolta S4, 1:43, 1968	$30
A-31 Innocenti Mini-Minor Rally, 1:43, 1969	$30
A-32 Lancia Fulvia Rally, 1:43, 1969	$30
A-33 Porsche 912 Rally, 1:43, 1969	$40
A-34 Opel Kadett Rally, 1:43, 1969	$30
A-35 Yogi Bear & Boo Boo Character Car, 1969	$60
A-36 Fiat Nuova 500, 1:43, 1969	$30
A-37 NSU Ro 80 Wankel, 1:43, 1969	$30
A-38 Matra 530 Vignale, 1:43, 1969	$30
A-39 Lotus Europa, 1:43, 1969	$40
A-40 Land Rover Trans American, 1:43, 1969.	$30
A-41 Fiat 124 Safari, 1:43, 1970	$30
A-42 Land Rover Ambulance, 1:43, 1970	$40
A-43 Fiat 124/128 Taxi, 1:43, 1970	$30
A-44 Bertone Runabout, 1:43, 1970.	$30
A-45 Alfa Romeo Iguana, 1:43, 1970	$30
A-46 Alfa Romeo Junior Zagato, 1:43, 1971	$30
A-47 Lamborghini Urraco, 1:43, 1971	$30
A-48 Autobianchi A112, 1:43, 1971	$30
A-49 Stratos HF Bertone, 1:43, 1971	$30
A-50 Ferrari 365GTC-4, 1:43, 1972.	$40
A-51 Porsche London-Sydney Rally, 1:43, 1972	$40
A-52 Fiat Dino with Boat, 1:43, 1972.	$30
A-53 Ford Escort, 1:43, 1972.	$30
A-54 Fiat 127, 1:43, 1972	$30
A-55 Ford Escort Mexico, 1:43, 1972	$30
A-56 Ferrari 312BB, 1:43, 1972	$40
A-57 Alfasud, 1:43, 1972.	$30
A-58 Autobianchi Abarth A112, 1:43, 1972.	$30
A-59 Fiat 128, 1:43, 1972	$30
A-60 Fiat 128 Rally, 1:43, 1972	$30
A-61 Morris Mini-Minor, 1:43, 1973	$30
A-62 Fiat 126, 1:43, 1972	$30
A-63 BMW 2800 CS Alpina, 1:43, 1972	$30
A-64 Porsche 912 with Skis, 1:43, 1973	$40
A-65 Alfa Romeo Duetto with Bicycles, 1:43, 1972.	$30
A-66 Autobianchi Primula with Oil Drums, 1:43, 1972	$30
A-67 U. S. Army Land Rover, 1:43, 1972	$30
A-68 Fiat 127 Rally, 1:43, 1972	$30
A-69 Renault 5TL, 1:43, 1974	$30
A-70 Volkswagen 1303, 1:43, 1974	$30
A-71 Innocenti Mini-Minor Hippy, 1:43, 1974	$40
A-72 Maserati Bora, 1:43, 1973	$40
A-73 Lancia Fulvia Marlboro, 1:43, 1974	$30
A-74 Land Rover Fire Truck, 1:43, 1974.	$45

A-75 Fiat 124 Raid, 1:43, 1974. . . . . $30
A-76 Alfa Romeo Alfetta, 1:43, 1974 . . . . $30
A-77 Fiat 128 Coupe, 1:43, 1974 . . . . $30
A-78 Porsche 912 Rally, 1:43, 1974 . . . . $40
A-79 Willys Military Jeep, 1:43. 1974 . . . . $30
A-80 Willys Baja Jeep, 1:43, 1974 . . . . $30
A-81 Willys Fire Jeep, 1:43, 1974. . . . . $40
A-82 Alfetta Carabinieri, 1:43, 1974 . . . . $30
A-83 Alfetta Polizia, 1:43, 1974 . . . . $30
A-84 Citroën Dyane, 1:43, 1974 . . . . $30
A-85 Fiat 131, 1:43, 1975 . . . . $30
A-86 BMC Mini 90, 1:43, 1976. . . . . $30
A-87 Volkswagen Golf, 1:43, 1976 . . . . $30
A-88 Volkswagen 1303 Jeans, 1:43, 1975. . . . . $30
A-89 Willys Police Jeep, 1:43, 1975 . . . . $30
A-90 Alfasud TI Rally, 1:43, 1975 . . . . $30
A-91 Lancia Fulvia Alitalia, 1:43, 1975 . . . . $30
A-92 Alfetta Fire Chief, 1:43, 1975. . . . . $40
A-93 Porsche 924, 1:43, 1976 . . . . $40
A-94 Renault 5TL Rally, 1:43, 1975 . . . . $30
A-95 Willys Carabinieri Jeep, 1:43, 1976 . . . . $30
A-96 Willy United Nations Jeep, 1:43, 1976 . . . . $30
A-97 Alfasud Trofeo, 1:43, 1976 . . . . $30
A-98 Fiat 131 Rally, 1:43, 1976 . . . . $30
A-99 Citroën Dyane Vacation Car, 1:43, 1976 . . . . $30
A-100 Ferrari 512S Pininfarina, 1:43, 1976 . . . . $40
A-101 Porsche 917 Gulf, 1:43, 1976. . . . . $40
A-102 DeTomaso Ford Pantera, 1:43 . . . . $30
A-103 BMW 320, 1:43. . . . . $30
A-105 Alfasud Sprint, 1:43 . . . . $30
A-106 Ford Fiesta, 1:43. . . . . $30
A-107 Simca 1308, 1:43 . . . . $30
A-108 Innocenti Mini DeTomaso, 1:43 . . . . $30
A-109 Citroën Dyane Rally, 1:43 . . . . $30
A-110 Fiat Abarth 131, 1:43. $30
A-111 Alfa Romeo Giulietta, 1:43 . . . . $30
A-112 Autobianchi A112 Abarth, 1:43 . . . . $30
A-112 Fiat 126, 1:43 (not known to exist)
A-113 BMW 320 Rally, 1:43 . . . . $30
A-114 Volkswagen Golf ADAC, 1:43 . . . . $30
A-115 Volkswagen Golf Polizei, 1:43. . . . . $30
A-117 Alfasud Vacation Car, 1:43, 1980 . . . . $30
A-118 Audi 100 GLS, 1:43, 1980 . . . . $30
A-119 Fiat Ritmo 65, 1:43, 1980. . . . . $30
A-120 BMW 730, 1:43, 1980 . . . . $30
A-121 Ford Granada, 1:43. . . . . $30
A-122 Desert Jeep, 1:43, 1980. . . . . $30
A-123 Matra Rancho, 1:43, 1980 . . . . $30
A-124 Opel Monza Coupe, 1:43, 1980. . . . . $30
A-125 Fiat Panda 30, 1:43, 1980 . . . . $30
A-126 Volkswagen Golf Rally, 1:43, 1980 . . . . $30
A-127 Ford Fiesta Special, 1:43, 1980 . . . . $30
A-128 Simca 1308 GT, 1:43, 1980 . . . . $30
A-129 Talbot Simca Horizon, 1:43, 1981 . . . . $30
A-130 Volvo 343, 1:43, 1981 . . . . $30
A-131 Fiat Abarth 131 Rally, 1:43, 1981 . . . . $30
A-133 Peugeot 305, 1:43. 1981 . . . . $30
A-134 Citroën Visa, 1:43, 1981 . . . . $30

A-135 Alfa Romeo Giulietta Carabinieri, 1:43, 1981 . . . . $30
A-136 Alfa Romeo Giulietta Polizia, 1:43, 1981 . . . . $30
A-138 Alfa Romeo Giulietta Special, 1:43, 1981 . . . . $30
A-139 Fiat Ritmo Special, 1:43, 1981 . . . . $30
A-140 Audi 100 Polizei, 1:43, 1984 . . . . $30
A-141 Audi 100 ADAC, 1:43, 1984. . . . . $30
A-142 Talbot Horizon Special, 1:43, 1981 . . . . $30
A-143 Opel Monza Special, 1:43, 1981 . . . . $30
A-145 Ford Granada Special, 1:43, 1981 . . . . $30
A-149 Jeep Rally Service Car, 1:43, 1981 . . . . $30
A-152 Fiat 131 Rally, 1:43, 1981 . . . . $30
1 Alfa Romeo 158-159 Grand Prix, 1:24, 1977 . . . . $30
2 Alfa Romeo P2 Grand Prix, 1:24, 1977 . . . . $30
2501 Fiat Farm Tractor, 1:43 . . . . $12
2510 Fiat 170 Garbage Truck, 1:43 . . . . $12
2512 Fiat 170 Container Truck, 1:43 . . . . $12
2514 Fiat 170 Semi-Trailer Truck, 1:43. . . . . $12
2517 Fiat 170 Lumber Semi, 1:43. . . . . $12
2519 Fiat 170 Container Semi, 1:43 . . . . $12
6050 Fiat Uno "Wrangler Jeans," 1:43, 1985 . . . . $30
6051 Maserati Biturbo Racing, 1:43, 1985 . . . . $30
6065 Porsche 911 Turbo "Coca-Cola," 1:43, 1985. . . . . $30
6067 Porsche 911 Turbo "Gitanes," 1:43, 1985. . . . . $30
6069 Matra Murena Rally, 1:43, 1985 . . . . $30
6071 Matra Murena Rally, 1:43, 1985 . . . . $30
6073 Chevrolet Corvette 1984, 1:43, 1985 . . . . $30
6082 Volkswagen Golf Cabriolet Rally, 1:43, 1985 . . . . $30
6091 Audi Quattro Rally, 1:43, 1985 . . . . $30
6097 Jeep CJ7 Renegade, 1:43, 1985 . . . . $30
6099 Ford Sierra XR4, 1:43, 1985. . . . . $30
6103 Alfa Romeo 33 Turbo, 1:43, 1985 . . . . $30
6116 Audi Quattro Rally, 1:25, 1984 . . . . $30
6117 Opel Kadett Rally, 1:25, 1984 . . . . $30
6119 Porsche 956 Canon, 1:25, 1984 . . . . $30
6121 Ferrari PB, 1:43, 1984 . . . . $30
6186 Kenworth Tanker Semi, 1:43, 1985 . . . . $30
6188 Kenworth Container Semi, 1:43, 1985 . . . . $30
6191 Kenworth Dumper Semi, 1:43, 1985 . . . . $30
6192 Volvo Container Semi, 1:43, 1985 . . . . $30
6194 Volvo Livestock Semi, 1:43, 1985 . . . . $30
6196 Volvo Auto Transporter Semi, 1:43, 1985. . . . . $30
6420 Fiat Uno, 1:43, 1985. . . . . $30
6423 Mercedes-Benz 500 SEC Rally, 1:43, 1985 . . . . $30
6425 Alfa Romeo 33 Rally "Agip," 1:43, 1985 . . . . $30
6427 Pontiac Firebird, 1:43, 1985 . . . . $30
6430 Ford Sierra XR4 Rally, 1:43, 1985 . . . . $30
6601 Ferrari Can-Am, 1:43, 1970 . . . . $40
6602 Chevrolet Astro II, 1:43, 1970 . . . . $30
6603 T'rantula Dragster, 1:43, 1971 . . . . $30
6604 Torpedo Dragster, 1:43, 1971 . . . . $30
6605 Lamborghini Miura, 1:43, 1971 . . . . $30
6606 Chapparal 2F, 1:43, 1971 . . . . $40
6607 Ford GT Mark II, 1:43, 1971 . . . . $40
6608 Abarth 695 SS, 1:43, 1971 . . . . $30
6611 Ford Boss Mustang 302, 1:43, 1971 . . . . $120
6612 Alfa Romeo 33/3, 1:43, 1971. . . . . $30
6613 Porsche Carrera 10, 1:43, 1971 . . . . $40
6614 Ferrari P4, 1:43, 1971 . . . . $30

6615 Twinmill, 1:43, 1971	$30
6616 Silhouette, 1:43, 1971	$30
6617 Toyota 2000GT, 1:43, 1971	$30
6618 Lotus Europa, 1:43, 1971	$40
6621 Ferrari 512S Pininfarina, 1:43, 1971	$40
6622 Mercedes-Benz C-111, 1:43, 1971	$30
6623 Porsche 917, 1:43, 1971	$40
6624 Abarth 3000 SP, 1:43, 1971	$40
6625 Mantis, 1:43, 1971	$30
6626 McLaren Can-Am, 1:43, 1972	$30
6627 DeTomaso Ford Pantera, 1:43, 1972	$30
6628 Chapparal 2J, 1:43, 1972	$40
6629 Lola T-212 Can-Am, 1:43, 1972	$30
6670 Matra MS 120, 1:28, 1972	$30
6671 Ferrari 312 B2, 1:28, 1972	$30
6672 BRM P160, 1:28, 1972	$30
6673 Lotus-Ford 72, 1:28, 1972	$30
6674 Tyrrell-Ford, 1:28, 1972	$30
6675 Brabham BT 34, 1:28, 1973	$30
6676 March-Ford, 1:28, 1973	$30
6677 Lotus JPS, 1:28, 1973	$30
6700 Mercedes-Benz 280 SE, 1:28, 1981	$30
6702 Land Rover, 1:25, 1980	$30
6708 Mercedes-Benz 280 SE, 1:28, 1982	$30
6709 Volkswagen Golf 4-door, 1:24, 1981	$30
6711 Citroën Dyane, 1:25, 1981	$30
6713 Porsche 924, 1:25, 1981	$30
6715 Lancia Beta Giro D'Italia, 1:25, 1981	$30
6719 BMW 320, 1:25, 1981	$30
6722 Alfa Romeo Giulietta, 1:25, 1981	$30
6726 Fiat 242 Safari, 1:25, 1980	$30
6728 Fiat 131 Abarth, 1:25, 1981	$30
6731 BMW 320 Rally, 1:25, 1980	$30
6732 Porsche 924 Rally, 1:25, 1980	$30
6733 Ford Granada 1978, 1:25, 1980	$30
6734 Opel Monza, 1:25, 1981	$30
6737 Porsche 928 Rally, 1:25, 1980	$30
6739 BMW 730 Sedan, 1:25, 1980	$30
6740 Audi 100 GLS, 1:25, 1980	$30
6741 Volkswagen Golf Rally, 1:25, 1980	$30
6742 Ford Fiesta Rally, 1:25, 1980	$30
6743 Fiat 131 Abarth Parmalat, 1:25, 1981	$30
6745 Mercedes-Benz 280 SE Rally, 1:28, 1981	$30
6747 Talbot Matra Rancho, 1:25, 1980	$30
6748 Fiat Ritmo, 1:25, 1981	$30
6755 Volvo 343, 1:25, 1981	$30
6756 Volvo 343, 1:25, 1981	$30
6757 Fiat Ritmo Special, 1:25, 1981	$30
6758 Alfa Romeo Giulietta Special, 1:25, 1981	$30
6761 Alfa Romeo Giulietta Carabinieri, 1:25, 1981	$30
6762 Alfa Romeo Giulietta Polizia, 1:25, 1981	$30
6764 Porsche 924 Turbo, 1:25, 1980	$30
6765 BMW 320 Alpina, 1:25, 1980	$30
6766 Peugeot 305, 1:25, 1981	$30
6767 Citroën Visa, 1:25, 1981	$30
6784 Fiat Ritmo Alitalia, 1:25, 1981	$30
6785 Fiat Panda, 1:25, 1981	$30
6787 Opel Monza Special, 1:25, 1981	$30

6788 Talbot Horizon Special, 1:25, 1981	$30
6792 Citroën Dyane Special, 1:25, 1981	$30
6797 Willys Jeep, 1:25, 1981	$30
6800 Fiat-Abarth Ritmo Rally, 1:25, 1981	$30
6802 Fiat 240 Flat Truck with Kart, 1:25	$30
6803 Volkswagen Golf Cabriolet, 1:25	$30
6804 BMW 320 Wind Surfer, 1:25, 1981	$30
6805 Lancia Beta Fire Squad, 1:25, 1981	$30
6807 Lancia Squadra SK, 1:24, 1981	$30
6808 Porsche 911 Targa, 1:25, 1981	$30
6810 Matra Rancho Rally, 1:25	$30
6823 Porsche 928 Rally, 1:25, 1983	$30
6830 Audi 100 NASA, 1:25, 1983	$30
6844 Maserati Biturbo, 1:25, 1983	$30
6845 Lancia 037 Turbo, 1:25, 1983	$30
6846 Ferrari 250 GT, 1:25, 1983	$30
6849 Fiat Uno, 1:43, 1983	$30
6850 Fiat Uno, 1:25, 1985	$30
6858 Ferrari Formula 1, 1:25, 1983	$30
6860 Ligier Formula 1, 1:25, 1983	$30
6861 Brabham Formula 1, 1:25, 1983	$30
6862 Arrows MP4 Formula 1, 1:25, 1983	$30
6863 Williams Formula 1, 1:25, 1983	$30
6864 Lotus Formula 1, 1:25, 1983	$30
6866 Renault Formula 1, 1:25, 1983	$30
6867 Audi Quattro Rally, 1:25, 1983	$30
6868 Opel Kadett Rally, 1:25, 1983	$30
6869 Fiat Panda Rally, 1:25, 1983	$30
6870 Alfa Romeo Giulietta Rally, 1:25, 1983	$30
6871 Fiat Ritmo Rally, 1:25, 1983	$30
6872 Citroën Visa Rally, 1:25, 1983	$30
6873 Talbot Horizon Rally, 1:25, 1983	$30
6874 BMW 735 Rally, 1:25, 1983	$30
6875 Porsche 928 Pirelli, 1:25, 1983	$30
6876 Volvo 343, 1:25, 1983	$30
6877 Lancia Delta, 1:25, 1983	$30
6878 Citroën Dyane, 1:25, 1983	$30
6879 Porsche 911 Targa, 1:25, 1983	$30
6880 Peugeot 305, 1:25, 1983	$30
6881 Fiat 242 Pickup with Kart, 1:25, 1983	$30
6882 Audi 100 with Rubber Boat, 1:25, 1983	$30
6883 Ford Fiesta with Skiers, 1:25, 1983	$30
6884 Opel Monza with Surfboard, 1:25, 1983	$30
6885 Ford Granada Giro D'Italia, 1:25, 1983	$30
6886 Jeep Renegade with Motocross Cycle, 1:25, 1983	$30
6899 Talbot Matra Mureno Rally, 1:43, 1983	$30
6900 Mercedes-Benz 500 SEC Rally, 1:43, 1983	$30
6901 Maserati Biturbo Rally, 1:43, 1983	$30
6903 Pontiac Firebird, 1:43, 1983	$30
6904 BMW 635 Rally, 1:43, 1983	$30
6905 Lancia 037 Turbo Martini, 1:43, 1983	$30
6906 Audi Quattro Rally, 1:43, 1983	$30
6907 Porsche 911 Turbo Rally, 1:43, 1983	$30
6908 Chevrolet Corvette 1983, 1:43, 1983	$30
6909 Volkswagen Golf Cabriolet, 1:43, 1983	$30
6910 Ferrari PB Prototype, 1:43, 1983	$30
6911 Jeep Laredo, 1:43, 1983	$30
8551 Ford Escort, 1:43, 1973	$30

8552 Ford Escort Mexico, 1:43, 1973 . . . . $30
8553 Ferrari PB Prototype, 1:43, 1973 . . . . $40
8554 Maserati Bora, 1:43, 1973 . . . . $40
8555 Alfa Romeo Alfasud, 1:43, 1973 . . . . $30
8556 Fiat 126, 1:43, 1973 . . . . $30
8558 Ferrari 312 BB, 1:32 . . . . $30
8563 Ford Mirage, 1:28, 1973 . . . . $30
8564 Fiat 126, 1:28 . . . . $30
8565 Ferrari Boxer, 1:43, 1973 . . . . $30
8567 Alfa Romeo Alfetta Carabinieri, 1:25 . . . . $30
8568 Ferrari 312 PB, 1:25 . . . . $30
8573 Porsche 911 Targa, 1:25 . . . . $30
8574 Volkswagen 1302, 1:25 . . . . $30
8582 Lancia Beta Coupe, 1:25 . . . . $30
8595 Mercedes-Benz 280 SE, 1:28 . . . . $30
8596 Volkswagen Golf 4-door, 1:25 . . . . $30
8599 Citroën Dyane 6, 1:25 . . . . $30
8612 Porsche 924, 1:25 . . . . $30
8616 Alfa Romeo Alfasud Sprint, 1:25 . . . . $30
8618 Simca 1307, 1:25 . . . . $30
8619 BMW 316, 1:25 . . . . $30
8620 Ford Fiesta, 1:25 . . . . $30
8623 Alfa Romeo Giulietta, 1:25 . . . . $30
8637 Volkswagen Golf Polizei, 1:25 . . . . $30
8638 BMW 320 Alpina, 1:25 . . . . $30
8640 Porsche 924 Martini, 1:25, 1979 . . . . $30
9553 Peterbilt Tanker Semi "BP," 1:43, 1985 . . . . $30
9554 Peterbilt Box Semi "Goodyear," 1:43, 1985 . . . . $30
9557 Peterbilt Livestock Semi, 1:43, 1985 . . . . $30
9558 Peterbilt Dumper Semi, 1:43, 1985 . . . . $30
9560 Volvo Box Semi "Martini," 1:43, 1985 . . . . $30
9561 Volvo Container Semi "Sea-Land," 1:43, 1985 . . . . $30
9562 Volvo Auto Transporter Semi, 1:43, 1985 . . . . $30
9564 Volvo Dumper Semi, 1:43, 1985 . . . . $30
9606 Mercedes Livestock Semi, 1:43, 1985 . . . . $30
9607 Mercedes Container Semi "Hapag-Lloyd," 1:43, 1985 . . . . $30
9609 Mercedes Tanker Semi "Shell," 1:43, 1985 . . . . $30
9610 Mercedes Auto Carrier Semi, 1:43, 1985 . . . . $30

MEBETOYS JOLLY SERIES
Lotus-Climax Formula 1, 1:66 . . . . $12

MEBOTO (SEE MOBOTO)

MECCANO (SEE DINKY)

MEGAMOVERS

Mega Movers, distributed by Megatoys of Los Angeles, California, produce a great assortment of five 1:55 scale pickup trucks and six 1:24 scale models called Luxury Classics. Evidence of the care put into producing these larger toys is seen in remnants of car wax found on one model purchased, the BMW 850i from the Luxury Classics series. The latest MegaMovers are repackaged Maistos. They also produce a series of smaller models that are basically scrap metal and plastic, lacking detail and accuracy but low priced.

3½" TRUCKS, APPROXIMATELY 1:55 SCALE
1955 Chevy Stepside, yellow $1

Chevy S-10, bright pink $1
1953 Ford Pickup Street Machine, red $1
Chevy C-150 Sportside, metallic silver $1
Chevrolet C-1500 454SS, metallic charcoal gray $1

LUXURY CLASSICS, APPROXIMATELY 1:24 SCALE
Porsche 959, black $6
Lamborghini Diablo, yellow $6
BMW 850i, metallic red $6
Ferrari F40, red $6
Mercedes-Benz 500SL, metallic gray $6
Mercedes-Benz 500SL Convertible, white $6

TWO- AND THREE-PIECE VEHICLE SETS
Cheaply-made models that are essentially worthless generic models.

Action Team includes car with boat and trailer, van and horse trailer $1
Army Set includes van, tank, utility vehicle, and pickup truck . . $1
Police Set includes police car, police van, and police helicopter . . $1
Construction Set includes car, fork lift, cement truck and signs . $1
Construction Set includes car, fork lift, soft drink truck, and signs $1
Emergency Set includes utility vehicle, pickup, and ladder truck . . $1
Motorcycle Set includes silver motorcycle, yellow motorcycle, and two signs $1
Motorcycle Set includes green Army motorcycle, blue motorcycle, and two signs $1

CLASSY CHASSIES
A series of 12 pull-back action 1:38 scale cars called Classy Chassies have been especially manufactured in China for Kmart by a company called Road Runners. These toys are relatively accurate renderings of actual cars, considering they sell for around $3. The 1995 versions of these cars have been repackaged as MegaMovers 4¾" cars.

Camaro, white $3
'57 Chevy, red $3
'56 Corvette, red $3
Corvette Sting Ray, silver $3
Ferrari F-40, black $3
Ferrari Testarossa, metallic blue $3
Ferrari 250GTO, red $3
Ferrari 318S, metallic gold $3
Ford Mustang, metallic green $3
Ford Thunderbird Convertible, white $3
Ford Thunderbird Hardtop, black $3
Lamborghini Diablo, yellow $3

MEGATOYS (SEE MEGAMOVERS)

MEGO
Best known for its Star Wars merchandise, Mego at one time produced 1:64 scale diecast cars made in Hong Kong. They have been variously marketed as A.M.T. Pups, Tuffy, and Jet Wheels.

MERCURY
Torino, Italy, has been the home of Mercury since 1932. Once the premier manufacturer of diecast miniature vehicles, Mercury suffered in the face of increasing

competition from Politoys, Mebetoys and others. By 1980, the last Mercury models were made and the company folded.

1 Aero, 1:40, 1945 . . . . $100
1 Fiat Nuova 500, 1:48, 1958. . . . . $30
1 Fiat 131 Mirafiori, 1:43, 1974 . . . . $25
2 Farina, 1:40, 1946 . . . . $100
2 Fiat 1800, 1:48, 1959 . . . . $35
2 Fiat 131 Rally, 1:43, 1974 . . . . $25
3 Lancia Aprilia, 1:40, 1946. . . . . $35
3 Alfa Romeo Giulietta Sprint, 1:48, 1956 . . . . $45
3 Fiat 131 Polizia, 1:43, 1975 . . . . $25
4 Americana, 1:40, 1946 . . . . $100
4 Lincoln Continental Mark II, 1:48, 1957 . . . . $175
4 Alfa Romeo Giulia Ti, 1:43, 1966 . . . . $30
4 Fiat 131 Fire Chief, 1:43, 1971 . . . . $25
5 Lincoln Continental, 1:40, 1947 . . . . $175
5 Lancia Appia 3, 1:48, 1959. . . . . $35
5 Fiat 131 Carabinieri, 1:43, 1975 . . . . $35
6 Studebaker Commander, 1:40, 1947 . . . . $225
6 Autobianchi Bianchina, 1:48, 1958 . . . . $25
6 BMW 320, 1:43, 1976. . . . . $25
7 Caravan Trailer, 1:40, 1946 . . . . $50
7 Fiat 1500 Spider, 1:48, 1960 . . . . $40
7 Fiat 131 Ambulance, 1:43, 1976 . . . . $25
8 Willys Jeep, 1948. . . . . $150
8 Lancia Flaminia, 1:48, 1957 . . . . $45
8 Fiat 128 Polizia, 1:43, 1974 . . . . $25
9 Cadillac 62 Sedan, 1:40, 1949 . . . . $150
9 Fiat 1300, 1:48, 1961 . . . . $35
9 Fiat 128 Fire Chief, 1:43, 1974 . . . . $25
10 Fiat 500C, 1:40, 1950 . . . . $50
10 Innocenti 950, 1:48, 1961. . . . . $25
10 Fiat 128 Carabinieri, 1:48, 1974 . . . . $25
11 Fiat 1400, 1950 . . . . $90
11 Bianchina Panoramica, 1:48, 1962 . . . . $25
11 Fiat 131 Taxi, 1:43, 1975 . . . . $25
12 Lancia Aurelia, 1950 . . . . $60
12 Fiat 850 Bertone, 1:43, 1965. $30
12 Fiat 131 with Skis, 1:43, 1976. . . . . $25
13 Fiat Nuova 1100, 1:48, 1954 . . . . $50
14 Lancia Appia I, 1:48, 1955 . . . . $50
14 Fiat Abarth SS595, 1:43, 1970 . . . . $30
15 Volkswagen, 1:48, 1955 . . . . $90
15 Volkswagen Swiss Mail Car, 1:48, 1956. . . . . $125
16 Alfa Romeo 1900, 1:48, 1955 . . . . $55
17 Alfa Romeo Giulietta, 1:48, 1956 . . . . $50
17 Fiat 500L, 1:43, 1967 . . . . $30
18 Fiat 600, 1:48, 1955 . . . . $40
19 Fiat 600 Multipla, 1:48, 1957. . . . . $40
20 Limousine, 1:40, 1947 . . . . $120
20 Alfa Romeo Giulietta Ti, 1:43, 1975 . . . . $40
21 Spider, 1:40, 1947 . . . . $125
21 Ferrari 750, 1:50, 1960 . . . . $60
21 Ranger Ferves, 1:43, 1969 . . . . $25
22 Dump Truck, 1:40, 1947. . . . . $100
22 Mercedes-Benz Formula 1, 1:50, 1960. . . . . $60
22 Fiat 128, 1:43, 1969 . . . . $30

23 Crane Truck, 1:40, 1947 . . . . $90
23 Fiat 2300 S, 1:43, 1962 . . . . $40
23 Innocenti 90-120 Rally, 1:43, 1975 . . . . $40
24 Tank Truck, 1:40, 1947 . . . . $90
24 Maserati 3500 GT, 1:43, 1964 . . . . $45
24 Innocenti 90-120 with Skis, 1:43, 1976 . . . . $25
25 Saurer Bus, 1951 . . . . $90
25 Saurer Swiss Mail Bus, 1957 . . . . $120
25 Fiat 125, 1:43, 1969 . . . . $30
25 Fiat 125 Rally, 1:43, 1957 . . . . $25
26 Lancia D-24, 1:48, 1957 . . . . $90
26 Fiat 130, 1:43, 1971 . . . . $25
27 Studebaker Golden Hawk, 1:48, 1957 . . . . $200
27 Lancia Fulvia Coupe, 1:43, 1965 . . . . $35
28 Cadillac Eldorado, 1:48, 1956 . . . . $150
28 Ferrari 330 P2, 1:43, 1967. . . . . $35
28 Fiat Campagnola ACI Service Car, 1:43, 1975 . . . . $25
29 Rolls-Royce Silver Cloud, 1:48, 1957. . . . . $90
29 Alfa Romeo Giulia Canguro, 1:43, 1965 . . . . $40
29 Fiat Campagnola Polizia, 1:43, 1975 . . . . $25
30 Bentley S Series, 1:48, 1957 . . . . $90
30 Chapparal 2F, 1:43, 1968 . . . . $60
30 Fiat Campagnola Fire Car, 1:43, 1975 . . . . $25
31 Maserati Grand Prix, 1:40, 1947 . . . . $90
31 Lancia Flavia, 1:43, 1964 . . . . $40
31 Fiat Campagnola Carabinieri, 1:43, 1975 . . . . $25
32 Auto-Union Grand Prix, 1:40, 1947. . . . . $100
32 Lancia Flavia Coupe, 1:43, 1964 . . . . $35
32 Fiat Campagnola Ambulance, 1:43, 1975. . . . . $25
33 Mercedes Grand Prix, 1:40, 1947 . . . . $95
33 Lancia Fulvia, 1:43, 1964 . . . . $40
33 Fiat Campagnola Safari, 1:43, 1975 . . . . $25
34 Maserati Grand Prix, 1:40, 1951 . . . . $95
34 Maserati 3500GT, 1:43, 1964 . . . . $40
34 Fiat Campagnola with Snowplow, 1:43, 1975 . . . . $25
35 Alfa Romeo Grand Prix, 1:40, 1951. . . . . $90
35 Fiat 1300 Polizia, 1:43, 1964. $30
36 Ferrari Grand Prix, 1:40, 1951. . . . . $125
36 Mercedes-Benz 230 SL, 1:43, 1965 . . . . $35
37 Cisitalia 1100, 1:40, 1951 . . . . $90
37 Mercedes-Benz 230 SL Coupe, 1:43, 1965 . . . . $35
38 Cisitalia Grand Prix, 1:40, 1951 . . . . $90
38 Fiat 850, 1:43, 1965 . . . . $25
39 SVA Racer, 1:40, 1951 . . . . $90
39 Ferrari 250LM, 1:43, 1964. . . . . $40
40 Mercedes-Benz Racer, 1:40, 1951 . . . . $100
40 Alfa Romeo Giulia GT, 1:43, 1965 . . . . $35
41 Fiat Abarth 1000 Bialbero, 1:43, 1966 . . . . $35
41 Aero, 1:80, 1950 . . . . $25
41A Farina, 1:80, 1950 . . . . $25
41B Lancia Aprilia, 1:80, 1950. . . . . $25
41C Americana, 1:80, 1950 . . . . $25
41D Studebaker, 1:80, 1950 . . . . $25
42 Fiat Abarth 1000, 1:43, 1965 . . . . $35
42A Maserati, 1:80, 1950. . . . . $25
42B Auto-Union, 1:80, 1950 . . . . $25
42C Mercedes-Benz, 1:80, 1950. $25
43A Open Truck, 1:80, 1950 . . . . $25

43B Tank Truck, 1:80, 1950
   v.1 "Esso" $25
   v.2 "Agip" $25
   v.3 "Petrolea" $25
   v.4 "Aquila" $25
   v.5 "Galbani" $25
   v.6 "Shell" $25
   v.7 Standard" $25
   v.8 "Petrocaltex" $25
44A Maserati, 1:80, 1951 . . . . $25
44B Alfa Romeo, 1:80, 1951 . . . . $25
44C Ferrari, 1:80, 1951 . . . . $25
44D Cisitalia 1100, 1:80, 1951 . . . . $25
44E Cisitalia Grand Prix, 1:80, 1951 . . . . $25
44F SVA Formula 3, 1:80, 1951 . . . . $25
44G Mercedes-Benz, 1:80, 1951 . . . . $25
44 Fiat 850 Coupe, 1:43, 1967 . . . . $35
45 Ferrari Dino Sport, 1:43, 1966 . . . . $35
46 Fiat 124, 1:43, 1976 . . . . $35
47A Covered Truck, 1:80, 1951 . . . . $25
47B Crane Truck, 1:80, 1951 . . . . $25
47C Saurer Bus, 1:80, 1951 . . . . $25
48A Cadillac, 1:80, 1950 . . . . $25
48B Fiat 500C, 1:80, 1950 . . . . $25
48C Fiat 1400, 1:80, 1950 . . . . $25
48D Lancia Aurelia, 1:80, 1950 . . . . $25
48 Fiat Dino Pininfarina, 1:43, 1967 . . . . $35
49A Ercole Semi-Trailer Truck, 1:80, 1951 . . . . $25
49B Ercole Semi-Trailer Tanker, 1:80, 1951 . . . . $25
49C Ercole Flatbed Semi-Trailer Truck, 1:80, 1951 . . . . $25
50 Mercedes-Benz 230SL Safari, 1:43, 1967 . . . . $35
50 Fiat Ritmo, 1:43, 1978 . . . . $25
51 Lancia Fulvia Coupe, 1:43, 1966 . . . . $35
51 Lanica Fulvia Rally, 1:43, 1973 . . . . $25
52 Maserati, 1:43, 1956 . . . . $75
52 Lancia Beta Coupe Rally, 1:43, 1974 . . . . $30
53 Ferrari Supersqualo, 1:43, 1956 . . . . $85
53 Alfa Romeo 33, 1:43, 1970 . . . . $35
53 Alfa Romeo Alfetta GT Rally, 1:43, 1976 . . . . $25
54 Lancia D-50, 1:43, 1956 . . . . $85
54 Lancia Beta with Skis, 1:43, 1976 . . . . $25
55 Mercedes-Benz, 1:43, 1956 . . . . $25
55 Alfa Romeo Alfetta with Roof Rack, 1:43, 1976 . . . . $25
56 Mercedes-Benz Formula 1, 1:43, 1956 . . . . $85
56 BMW 320 Monte Carlo Rally, 1:43, 1966 . . . . $25
57 Ferrari 330P Sebring, 1:43, 1966 . . . . $75
58 Alfa Romeo Alfetta Carabinieri, 1:43, 1966 . . . . $25
59 Ferrari 330P Sebring, 1:43, 1966 . . . . $75
59 BMW 320 Police Car, 1:43, 1976 . . . . $25
60 Lancia Aprilia, 1:25, 1946 . . . . $75
60 Ferrari 330P Nurburgring, 1:43, 1966 . . . . $50
61 Lancia Aurelia, 1:25, 1950 . . . . $75
61 Porsche Carrera 6, 1:43, 1967 . . . . $40
63 Fiat Dino Bertone, 1:43, 1967 . . . . $40
63 Fiat 131 Familiare Carabinieri, 1:43, 1976 . . . . $25
64 Heavy Tractor, 1952 . . . . $75
64 Alfa Romeo 33, 1:43, 1968 . . . . $35
65 Ferrari 330 P4, 1:43, 1969 . . . . $35

66 M24 Tank, 1954 . . . . $35
66 Ferrari 512S Pininfarina, 1:43, 1971 . . . . $35
67 Alfa Romeo Montreal Bertone, 1:43, 1969 . . . . $30
68 Bertone Panther, 1:43, 1969 . . . . $30
69 Jack's Demon Dragster, 1:43, 1969 . . . . $25
70 Fiat Balilla, 1:43, 1967 . . . . $35
80 Fiat Campagnola, 1:35, 1977 . . . . $25
81 Fiat Campagnola Mexico, 1:35, 1977 . . . . $25
82 Fiat Campagnola Ambulance, 1:35, 1977 . . . . $25
83 Fiat Campagnola Police Car, 1:35, 1977 . . . . $25
84 Fiat Campagnola Fire Truck, 1:35, 1977 . . . . $25
88 Saurer Moving Van, 1:65, 1957 . . . . $75
89 Saurer Dump Truck, 1:65, 1957 . . . . $75
89 Saurer Flatbed Truck, 1:65, 1957 . . . . $75
90 Americana with Steering, 1:40, 1950 . . . . $85
90 Fiat 238 Truck, 1:43 1970 . . . . $75
91 Fiat 238 Truck, 1:43, 1970 . . . . $75
91 Pluto Dump Truck, 1948 . . . . $75
91 Pluto Cattle Truck, 1948 . . . . $75
92 Golia-Ercole Open Truck, 1948 . . . . $120
92 Golia-Ercole Cattle Truck, 1948 . . . . $120
92 Fiat 238 Truck, 1:43, 1970 . . . . $75
93 Golia-Ercole Open Truck, 1948 . . . . $120
93 Golia-Ercole Cattle Truck, 1948 . . . . $120
93 Fiat 238 Truck, 1:43, 1970 . . . . $75
94 Ciclope Flat Truck, 1:40, 1948 . . . . $100
94 Ciclope Dump Truck, 1:40, 1948 . . . . $100
94 Ciclope Ladder Truck, 1:40, 1948 . . . . $100
94 Ciclope Crane Truck, 1:40, 1948 . . . . $100
95 Vulcano Truck Trailer, 1:40, 1948 . . . . $60
96 Viberti Tank Truck, 1:48, 1953 . . . . $60
97 Fiat 682N Dump Truck, 1:50, 1956 . . . . $75
97 Fiat 682N Covered Truck, 1:50, 1956 . . . . $75
98 Fiat 682N Bus, 1958 . . . . $75
99 Fiat 682N Car Transporter, 1:50, 1957 . . . . $75
100 Car Transporter Trailer, 1:50, 1957 . . . . $45
100 Fiat 697 Tank Truck, 1:50, 1977 . . . . $45
101 Fiat 697 Cement Truck, 1:50, 1977 . . . . $45
102 Fiat 697 Dump Truck, 1:50, 1977 . . . . $45
103 Fiat 697 Dump Truck, 1:50, 1977 . . . . $45
104 OM 90P Open Truck, 1:50, 1977 . . . . $45
105 OM 90P Bucket Truck, 1:50, 1977 . . . . $45
106 OM 90P Dump Truck, 1:50, 1977 . . . . $45
107 OM 90P Dump Truck with Digger, 1:50, 1977 . . . . $45
121 Bisonte Crane Truck, 1945 . . . . $85
124 Titano Crane, 1945 . . . . $85
130 Ursus Crane, 1947 . . . . $85
132 Fiorenti Power Shovel, 1:20, 1957 . . . . $85
134 Fiat 682N Truck with Controls, 1:50, 1957 . . . . $85
135 Cable Conveyor $85
201 Fiat Campagnola Wrecker, 1:43, 1976 . . . . $25
202 Fiat Campagnola Safari, 1:43, 1976 . . . . $25
203 Lancia Beta Rally, 1:43, 1976 . . . . $25
204 Fiat 131 Wagon with Skis, 1:43, 1976 . . . . $25
205 Fiat 131 Wagon with Luggage Rack, 1:43, 1976 . . . . $25
206 Fiat Campagnola African Tour Car, 1:43, 1976 . . . . $25
207 Rembrandt Caravan, 1:43, 1976 . . . . $25
208 Fiat 131 with Boat, 1:43, 1976 . . . . $25

209 Fiat 131 with Roof Rack, 1:43, 1976 . . . . $25	409 Lancia Beta with Skis & Caravan, 1:43, 1977 . . . . $35
210 Fiat 131 Polizia, 1:43, 1976 . . . . $25	413 Fiat Campagnola Army Ambulance & Trailer, 1:43, 1977 . . $35
211 Alfetta Kenya Safari Car, 1:43, 1976 . . . . $35	414 Fiat Campagnola Fire & Trailer, 1:43, 1977 . . . . $35
212 Vespa 125 Motorbike, 1952 . . . . $35	415 Alfa Romeo Alfetta GT & Trailer, 1:43, 1977 . . . . $35
212 Fiat 131 Wagon with Boat, 1:43, 1976 . . . . $35	416 BMW 320 & Trailer, 1:43, 1977 . . . . $35
213 Lambretta 125C Moped, 1952 . . . . $35	418 Fiat 131 Wagon & Trailer, 1:43, 1977 . . . . $35
213 Fiat Campagnola with A-Gun, 1:43, 1977 . . . . $45	419 Alfa Romeo Alfetta GT & Trailer, 1:43, 1977 . . . . $35
214 Ariete Field Gun, 1951 . . . . $25	420 BMW 320 & Caravan, 1:43, 1977 . . . . $35
214 Lambretta 125 LC Moped, 1952 . . . . $35	423 Fiat Campagnola & Boat Trailer, 1:43, 1977 . . . . $35
214 Fiat Campagnola with Lance-Rockets, 1:43, 1977 . . . . $35	431 Fiat 131 Wagon & Trailer, 1:43, 1977 . . . . $35
215 Ape Triporteur, 1952 . . . . $35	501 Michigan 375 Tractor Shovel, 1958 . . . . $55
215 Fiat Campagnola with Radio, 1:43, 1977 . . . . $35	501 Fiat 697 Dump Truck, 1:43, 1977 . . . . $55
216 Lambretta Triporteur, 1952 . . . . $35	502 Michigan 380 Tractor Plow, 1958 . . . . $55
216 Fiat Campagnola with Searchlight, 1:43, 1977 . . . . $35	502 Fiat 607 Container Truck, 1:43, 1977 . . . . $55
217 Lambretta 125 LC, 1952 . . . . $35	503 Michigan 310 Road Scraper, 1958 . . . . $55
217 BMW 320 Rally, 1:43, 1977 . . . . $35	503 Fiat 242 Camper, 1:43, 1977 . . . . $55
218 BMW 320 with Luggage Rack, 1:43, 1976 . . . . $35	504 Caterpillar 12 Road Grader, 1958 . . . . $55
219 BMW 320 with Boat, 1:43, 1976 . . . . $35	505 Euclid Twin Axle Dump Truck, 1959 . . . . $55
221 Fiorentini Excavator, 1955 . . . . $35	506 Caterpillar Giant Road Grader, 1959 . . . . $55
231 Army Tank, 1952 . . . . $35	506 Fiat 242 Crane Truck, 1:43, 1977 . . . . $55
232 Cannon, 1952 . . . . $35	507 Lima Power Shovel, 1959 . . . . $55
300 Fiat 124 Coupe, 1:43, 1969 . . . . $35	507 Fiat 242 Fire Truck, 1:43, 1977 . . . . $55
301 Horse Drawn Flat Wagon, 1950 . . . . $75	508 Autocar Twin Axle Dump Truck, 1959 . . . . $55
301 Sigma Gran Prix, 1:43, 1969 . . . . $35	508 Autocar Single Axle Dump Truck, 1959 . . . . $55
302 Horse Drawn Covered Wagon, 1950 . . . . $75	508 Fiat 242 Camper with Luggage Rack,1:43, 1977 . . . . $55
302 Fiat 214 Sport Coupe, 1:43, 1969 . . . . $35	509 Lorain Crane Truck, 1959 . . . . $55
303 Carabo Bertone, 1:43, 1969 . . . . $35	509 Fiat 697 Cement Mixer, 1:43, 1977 . . . . $55
303 Lancia Beta Coupe, 1:43, 1974 . . . . $35	510 Massey-Ferguson Farm Set, 1960 . . . . $55
304 Alfa Romeo Montreal, 1:43, 1970 . . . . $35	510 Fiat 607 Tank Truck, 1:43, 1977 . . . . $55
304 Fiat 131 Familiare, 1:43, 1976 . . . . $35	511 Massey-Ferguson Farm Wagon, 1960 . . . . $55
305 Ital Design Manta, 1:43, 1970 . . . . $35	512 Massey-Ferguson Hay Baler, 1960 . . . . $55
305 Fiat Campagnola, 1:43, 1975 . . . . $35	513 Euclid TS-24 Road Scraper, 1960 . . . . $55
306 Horse Drawn Log Cart, 1950 . . . . $75	514 Drott Tractor Shovel, 1960 . . . . $55
306 Ferrari 312P, 1:43, 1970 . . . . $35	514 International Bulldozer, 1960 . . . . $55
306 Alfa Romeo Alfetta GT, 1:43, 1975 . . . . $35	515 Blaw-Knox Cement Mixer, 1960 . . . . $55
307 Stake Trailer, 1950 . . . . $35	517 Allis-Chalmers Bulldozer, 1961 . . . . $55
307 Mercedes-Benz C-111, 1:43, 1969 . . . . $35	518 Austin-Western Road Roller, 1961 . . . . $55
308 Porsche 917, 1:43, 1970 . . . . $35	519 Euclid C-6 Bulldozer, 1961 . . . . $55
309 Porsche 908/03, 1:43, 1970 . . . . $35	520 Euclid L-30 Tractor Shovel, 1961 . . . . $55
310 Chapparal 2J, 1:43, 1971 . . . . $35	521 Warner & Swasey Gradall, 1961 . . . . $55
311 Fiat 127 Rally, 1:43, 1971 . . . . $35	522 Austin-Western Road Grader, 1961 . . . . $55
312 Horse Drawn Open Cart, 1950 . . . . $75	523 Landini Farm Tractor, 1961 . . . . $55
312 Fiat 214 Rally, 1:43, 1972 . . . . $35	531 Fiat 692 Container Semi, 1:43, 1977 . . . . $55
313 Horse Drawn Tank Cart, 1950 . . . . $35	532 Fiat 692 Tanker Semi, 1:43, 1977 . . . . $55
313 Fiat 132 GLS, 1:43, 1973 . . . . $35	534 Fiat 692 Car Transporter Semi, 1:43, 1977 . . . . $55
314 Fiat 128 SL, 1:43, 1972 . . . . $35	651 Ferrari Modulo Pininfarina, 1:32, 1971 . . . . $35
315 Fiat 128 SL, 1:43, 1972 . . . . $35	652 Lancia Fulvia Stratos Bertone, 1:32, 1972 . . . . $35
316 Fiat 128 SL Rally, 1:43, 1973 . . . . $35	653 Alfa Romeo Alfasud 1200, 1:32, 1972 . . . . $35
317 Fiat 132 Rally, 1:43, 1973 . . . . $35	751 Fred Flintstone's Car, 1971 . . . . $150
318 Fiat 127 Rally, 1:43, 1972 . . . . $35	801 Porsche Carrera 6, 1:66, 1969 . . . . $55
320 Fiat 132 Police Car, 1:43, 1975 . . . . $35	801 Fiat Campagnola, 1:66 . . . . $35
401 Fiat 131 & Caravan, 1:43, 1977 . . . . $35	802 Chapparal 2F, 1:66, 1969 . . . . $35
402 Fiat 131 & Caravan, 1:43, 1977 . . . . $35	802 Fiat Tank Truck, 1:66 . . . . $35
403 Fiat Campagnola African Tour & Caravan, 1:43, 1977 . . . . $35	803 Ferrari 330 P4, 1:66, 1969 . . . . $35
404 Alfa Romeo Alfetta GT & Caravan, 1977 . . . . $35	803 Fiat Open Truck, 1:66 . . . . $35
405 Fiat 131 Wagon with Skis & Caravan, 1:43, 1977 . . . . $35	804 Ford GT 40, 1:66, 1969 . . . . $55
406 Fiat 131 Wagon & Caravan, 1:43, 1977 . . . . $35	804 Caravan Trailer, 1:66 . . . . $55
408 Fiat 131 with Skis & Caravan, 1:43, 1977 . . . . $35	805 Lamborghini Marzal, 1:66, 1969 . . . . $55

806 Ferrari 250 Le Mans, 1:66, 1969 . . . . $55
806 Fiat 217, 1:66 . . . . $55
807 Osi Silver Fox, 1:66, 1969 . . . . $55
807 Fiat 131 Rally, 1:66 . . . . $55
808 Alfa Romeo 33, 1:66, 1969 . . . . $55
809 Alfa Romeo Montreal, 1:66, 1969 . . . . $55
809 Fiat Cement Truck, 1:66 . . . . $55
810 Dino Pininfarina, 1:66, 1969 . . . . $55
810 Fiat Farm Tractor, 1:66 . . . . $55
811 Lamborghini, 1:66, 1969 . . . . $55
811 Lancia Stratos Rally, 1:66 . . . . $55
812 Matra Djet, 1:66, 1969 . . . . $55
812 Porsche 935 Turbo, 1:66 . . . . $55
813 Ford Mustang, 1:66, 1969 . . . . $55
814 Lola T-70 GT, 1:66, 1969 . . . . $55
815 Ferrari P5, 1:66, 1969 . . . . $55
816 Sigma Grand Prix, 1:66, 1969 . . . . $55
817 Lotus Europa, 1:66, 1969 . . . . $55
818 Mercedes-Benz C-111, 1:66, 1969 . . . . $55
850 Covered Wagon, 1:66, 1969 . . . . $75
851 Stagecoach, 1:66, 1969 . . . . $75
870 Fiat 238 Van, 1:66, 1969 . . . . $55
872 Fiat 238 School Bus, 1:66, 1969 . . . . $55
873 Fiat 238 High-Roof Van, 1:66, 1969 . . . . $55
1201 Grand Prix Car: Jarama, 1:66 . . . . $55
1202 Grand Prix Car: Monte Carlo, 1:66 . . . . $55
1203 Grand Prix Car: Zeltweg, 1:66 . . . . $55
1204 Grand Prix Car: Hockenheim, 1:66 . . . . $55
1205 Grand Prix Car: Zandvoort, 1:66 . . . . $55

Mercury Aircraft

401 Fiat G-59 . . . . $40
402 Fiat G-212 . . . . $40
403 Fiat G-80 . . . . $40
404 Vampire $40
405 Lockheed F-90 . . . . $40
406 Avro 707A $40
407 DH 106 Comet $40
408 Mystere $40
409 Missile $40
410 North American Sabre F86 . . . . $40
411 Piaggio P-148 . . . . $40
412 MIG-15 . . . . $40
413 Convair XF-92A Jet $40
414 Piaggio P136 . . . . $40
415 Boeing B-50 Superfortress $40
416 Convair XF-92A Six-Pusher Propeller Plane $40
417 Sikorsky Helicopter $40
418 Boeing B-47 Stratojet $40
419 Douglas D559-2 Skyrocket $40
420 MIG-19 . . . . $40
421 Convair XFY-1 . . . . $40
422 F7U-3 Cutlass $40
423 F4U-5N Corsair $40
424 F94-C Starfire $40
425 P-38 Lightning $40

Mercury Ships

451 Australia $40
452 Cristoforo Colombo $40

453 Federico C $40
454 Venezuela $40
455 Leonardo Da Vinci $40
456 Victoria $40
457 Bianca C $40
458 Franca C $40
459 Andrea $40
460 Anna C $40

Mercury Motorcycles

601 Bultaco Mark 4, 1971 . . . . $40
602 MV 350CC, 1971 . . . . $40
603 Guzzi V7, 1971 . . . . $40
604 Chopper Wildcat, 1971 . . . . $40
605 Laverda 750 SF, 1972 . . . . $40
606 Yamaha Scrambler, 1972 . . . . $40
607 BMW R75 750cc, 1972 . . . . $40
608 Honda CB750, 1972 . . . . $40
609 Honda US90 Army 3-Wheeler, 1972 . . . . $40
610 Kawasaki 750cc Mach IV H2, 1972 . . . . $40
611 Guzzi V7 Army Motorcycle $40
612 Guzzi V7 Police Motorcycle $40
613 Ducati Scrambler 250cc $40
614 Harley-Davidson Electra $40
615 Honda 750 Police Motorcycle $40
616 Harley-Davidson Police Motorcycle $40
1010 Benelli 750 Cycle & Sidecar, 1:18 . . . . $40

Message Models (also see Fun Ho!)

Message Books and Models (also known as Message Models and Books) is reportedly the new owner of old Fun Ho! castings and tooling. Old Fun Ho! models are now being reissued by Message Models. Contact John Robinson, The Trans-Sport Shop, Message Models and Books, PO Box 239 Northbridge, New South Wales, 2063, Australia.

Metalcar

Metalcar (or Metal Car) is a brand of models from Hungary.

1:64 Scale

1 Datsun 126X $4
3 Futura Container Dump Truck $4
4 Futura Tow Truck $4
5 Honda 750 Motorcycle $4
6 Mercedes-Benz 406 Police $4
7 Mercedes-Benz 406 Bank Police $4
8 Mercedes-Benz 406 Service $4
9 Porsche 928 Coupe $4
10 Volkswagen Dune Buggy $4
11 Helicopter, USA $5
12 Opel Senator 4-door Sedan $5
13 Mercury 406 Police $5
14 Mercury 406 Ambulance $5
15 Audi 2000 4-door Sedan $5
16 Steam Train Engine $5
17 Lamborghini Espada Coupe $5
18 Futura Oil Truck "SHELL" $5
19 Futura Oil Truck "MOBIL" $5
20 Futura Garbage Truck $5
21 Futura Dump Truck $5

22 Futura Tow Truck	$5
23 Jeep CJ5 Hardtop	$5
24 Jeep CJ5 Open	$5
25 Jeep CJ5 4x4	$5
26 Citroën SM Coupe	$5
27 Mercedes-Benz 190 4-door Sedan	$5
28 Batmobile	$25
29 Porsche 928 Police	$5
30 Motorboat	$5
31 Alpine A310 Police	$5
32 Ferrari 275 Coupe	$5
33 Hanomag Truck	$5
34 Metchy F1 Racer	$5
35 Cessna Plane Police	$5
36 Cessna Plane Military	$5
37 Unimog 406 Truck	$5
38 Scania Bus	$5

1:43 SCALE

1 BMW 3.0 Turbo	$20
2 Mercedes-Benz SeaLand Truck	$20
3 Mercedes-Benz Truck	$20
4 Mercedes-Benz Garbage Truck	$20
5 Mercedes-Benz Fire Ladder Truck	$20
6 Mercedes-Benz Tow Truck	$20
7 Surtees F1 FIRESTONE	$20
8 Volkswagen Golf JPS	$20
9 Volkswagen Golf Police	$20
10 BMW 525 Ambulance	$19
11 BMW 525 Polizei	$19
12 Dodge Van Police	$19
13 Audi Quattro Coupe	$19
14 Opel Kadett Police	$19

1:25 SCALE

15 Mustang Police	$25

METAL CAST PRODUCTS COMPANY

From 1929 to 1940, Metal Cast Products Company produced slush-mold toy vehicles as an outgrowth of the S. Sachs company, producer of toy soldiers.

Manufacture of these models were franchised to various other smaller firms, while Metal Cast handled the marketing and distribution. Models are well made and nicely painted. Values are currently low for their vintage, but could rise somewhat as more collectors become aware of them. The problem sometimes is in identifying models, since franchisers didn't always put a manufacturer name on the models. Fred GreenToys is one of the franchisers whose name is most often found on the base.

Cadillac 2-door Sedan, #40, 5¼"	$45
Convertible Coupe, #63	$15
Dump Truck, #42, 5¼"	$15
Fire Engine Ladder Truck, #61, 4½"	$20
Fire Engine Steam Pumper with water cannon, #65, 4"	$20
Fire Engine Steam Pumper with no water cannon, no number, 3⅞"	$20
Packard 2-door Convertible, top down, #41, 5¼"	$30
Racer, #62, Bluebird-style record car, 4½"	$30
Streamline airflow-style Sedan, #60, 4"	$25

Stake Truck, #64, 4¼"	$20
Truck and Moving Van Trailer, #01-02, 6"	$15
Truck and Tank Trailer, #01-03, 6"	$15
Truck and Open Rack Stake Trailer, #01-04, 6"	$15
War Tank, #08, 4"	$65

METAL MINIATURES

These are unpainted one-piece highly detailed cast metal vehicles in 1:87 scale (HO gauge), of which one is listed as available from Walthers.

Caterpillar Tractor, 340-44	$2

METOSUL

Metosul is a Portuguese brand of toys resembling Corgi and Dinky Toys, possibly some older castings purchased from another producer, according to Dr. Craig S. Campbell, an avid collector of less common diecast cars.

Citroën DS19 Lisbon Taxi, turquoise & black	$38
Leyland Atlantean Double Decker Bus, maroon & gray, 1:43	$24
Mercedes-Benz 1113 Cargo Transport Truck, light green & olive, 1:43	$35
Mercedes-Benz 200 Police Car, #10, 1:43	$24
Peugeot 204 4-door Sedan, #24, 1:43	$24

METTOY (ALSO SEE CORGI)

Richard O'Brien lists just a few of these early Mettoy models in his book. The connection between Mettoy and Corgi is explored more thoroughly in Dr. Edward Force's book on Corgi toys.

Motorcycle, circa 1940	$800
Racer, 7"	$2,000
Rolls Royce, 14"	$1,200
Sedan, 14", circa 1930	$600
Steam Roller, clockwork	$200

MIBER

According to Markus R. Karalash, this company has produced HO scale (1:87) DeTomaso Panteras under the following model numbers, and possibly some other models. Nothing else is currently known about this brand.

1152 DeTomaso Pantera, 1:87	$10 – 15
2152 DeTomaso Pantera, 1:87	$10 – 15
9152 DeTomaso Pantera, 1:87	$10 – 15

MICRO MACHINES

Micro Machines are the pre-eminent toy company to produce the world's smallest series of toy vehicles, numbering in the thousands of models. Up until the imminent re-release of the *Star Wars* motion picture in 1997, Micro Machines had produced only vinyl and plastic models in very small scale. As the enhanced version returns to theaters with new scenes added and an audio upgrade to THX dolby surround sound, Galoob introduced its first series of diminutive diecast models to commemorate the event, as listed below. Models are made in China for Lewis Galoob Toys, Inc., South San Francisco, CA 94080, Internet: http://www.galoob.com.

Millennium Falcon	$5

171

Imperial Star Destroyer $4
Imperial Tie Fighter $4
Jawa Sandcrawler $4
X-wing Starfighter $4
Y-wing Starfighter $4

MICRO MODELS

These are not to be confused with Deoma Micromodels of Italy. Originally manufactured in Australia in the 1950s, Micro Models are now being reproduced in strictly limited quantities. Each model is individually engraved, hand finished and assembled using original 1950s dies. These and many other 1950s models are available from the manufacturer. Micro Models especially focus on standard Holden vehicles of the period, beautifully rendered in approximately 1:43 scale. The original Micro Models toys were produced between 1952 and 1960, and are currently valued from $125 – 175 each.

Now, Micro Models are being manufactured again, this time in New Zealand, from the original dies. Current prices on new models are between $30 and $50 wholesale. For more information, write to Micro Models, Ltd., P O Box 815, Christchurch, New Zealand, or call 64-3-365-5016 (fax 64-3-366-6292). Values [in brackets] represent wholesale prices in Australian dollars, while remaining price indicates retail value in U.S. funds.

MM001 International Delivery Van "Micro Models" [$34]. . $70 – 85
MM008 Ft Holden Panel Van "New Zealand Traffic" [$27]. $55 – 70
MM011 Ford Mainline Utility "Australia Civil Aviation" [$32]. $65 – 80
MM07 Jaguar XK120 [$32] . . . . $65 – 80
MM07 Morris Fire Engine [$32] . . . . $65 – 80
MP401 Ft Holden Utility Security [$32] . . . . $65 – 80
MM402 Ft Holden Sedan "New South Wales Fire Chief" [$31]. $60 – 75
MM403 Ft Holden Utility "New South Wales Public Works"
   [$29] . . . . $60 – 75
MM404 Ft Holden Panel Van "New Zealand Royal Mail" [$26]. $55 – 70
MM405 Ft Holden "Tazmania Police" [$33]. . . . . $70 – 85
MM406 VW Microbus [$32] . . . . $65 – 80
MM407 Jaguar XK120 [$29] . . . . $60 – 75
MM408 Ford Mainline Utility "Micro Models" [$27] . . . . . . $55 – 70
MM409 British Ford Zephyr "Queensland Police" [$29]. . . $60 – 75
MM502 Ft Holden Utility News Paper Delivery [$32]. . . . $65 – 80
MC503 Ft Holden Panel Van "Coca Cola" [$32]. . . . . $65 – 80
MM505 Ft Holden Sedan "Wellington Taxis" [$32] . . . . . $65 – 80

MICROMODELS (SEE DEOMA)

MICROPET

These Japanese models were manufactured primarily for the Asian market in the 1960s.

Chevrolet Impala $150
Chevrolet Impala, chrome plated $200
Chevrolet Impala Police Car, black and white $150
Datsun Bluebird. $125
Datsun Bluebird, chrome plated $175
Datsun Bluebird S.W. $125
Datsun Bluebird S.W., chrome plated $150
Ford Falcon $150

Ford Falcon Police Car. $150
Hillman Minx. $125
Isuzu Bellel 2000 Saloon. $125
Mazda Coupe R 360 . . . . $125
Mazda Coupe R 360, chrome plated $175
Nissan Cedric. $125
Nissan Cedric, chrome plated $175
Nissan Light Truck $125
Prince Bus $175
Prince Bus, chrome plated $200
Prince Skyline $125
Prince Skyline, chrome plated. $175
Prince Skyway S.W. $125
Subaru 360 . . . . $125
Toyota Corona S.W. $125
Toyota Corona S.W., chrome plated $175

MICROTOYS (SEE DEOMA)

MIDGETOYS

Not to be confused with Midget Toys of France, Midgetoys were made in the U.S. The post-war goal of brothers Alvin and Earl Herdlkotz was "to produce low-cost diecast vehicles both sturdy and precisely detailed." Their goals mirrored those of the Tootsietoy firm after World War II, and their Midgetoy models are of similar construction, that being generally a single cast pot-metal body with no chassis. From 1946 to 1984, Midgetoys were produced in various sizes and available at many discount retail outlets. Thousands, or at least hundreds, of different models were issued. It would be interesting to see a book devoted especially to these proliferous toys. Typical values are from $10 – 15 each. Here is a brief sampling.

Army Ambulance, circa 1950s, 3⅞". $14
Army Truck, circa 1950s, 4½". $14
Army Truck & Cannon, circa 1950s, 4½" & 3¼". $29
Camping Trailer, purple, circa 1950s, 2⅜". $4
Convertible, blue, circa 1950s, 5⅜". $19
Corvette, yellow, circa 1950s, 2⅞" $12
Corvette, green, circa 1970s, 2". $2
El Camino, red, circa 1970s, 3". $2
Ford C600 Oil Truck, 1956, 4". $15
Indy-Style Race Car, silver, circa 1950s, 3". $15
Jeep, red, circa 1960s. $4
MG Sports Car, green, circa 1960s, 2" $2
Military Jeep, circa 1950s, 1¾. $5
Pickup Jeep, blue, circa 1950s, 5¾" $19

MIDGET TOYS

Midget Toys of France are not to be confused with Midgetoys of the United States. Midget Toys were all produced in 1959.

1 Flat Truck, 1:86 . . . . $45
2 Lumber Semi-Trailer Truck, 1:86 . . . . $45
3 Quarry Dump Truck, 1:86 . . . . $45
4 Farm Tractor, 1:86 . . . . $45
5 Open Semi-Trailer Truck, 1:86 . . . . $45
6 Dyna-Panhard Convertible, 1:86 . . . . $45

14 Crane Truck, 1:86 . . . . $45
Citroën DS19, 1:86 . . . . $45
Jaguar D-Type, 1:86 . . . . $45
Transformer Semi-Trailer, 1:86 . . . . $45
3-Axle Semi-Trailer, 1:86 . . . . $45
Vanwall Formula 1, 1:86 . . . . $45
Vespa 400 Mini-car, 1:86 . . . . $45
Vespa 400 Mini-car, 1:43 . . . . $75

MIDWESTERN HOME PRODUCTS, INC.

Generic, crude, yet charming best describes models manufactured by Midwestern Home Products, Inc., of Wilmington, Delaware. A recently discovered set of three 4" fire engines are cheaply-made in China, but possess that ineffable charm that makes them attractive novelty items, although relatively worthless as collectibles. At $1 apiece, their crude castings with sharp edges make them unsuitable for children and are better left in their original blisterpack. Once removed, they are no longer distinguishable as Midwestern brand toys. Two of the three fire engines were found to have a logo embossed into the base that resembles a cluster of pine trees with a leaping deer, the whole of which is surrounded by a double circle, with the cryptic letters "SM" at the bottom of the circle. Midwestern Home Products, Inc., Wilmington, DE 19803. Made in China.

8114 Ladder truck $1
8115 Closed-cab pumper/turret $1
8116 Open-cab pumper truck $1

MIGNON

Mignon is a series of 1:24 scale diecast motorcycles and two go karts manufactured in Italy for a few years in the early 1960s. Their downfall was unfortunately due to the lack of interest in collecting motorcycle miniatures at the time. Interest is now on the increase, due in part to the rising popularity and number of Harley-Davidson collectibles currently hitting the market.

Aermacchi a la Verde 350cc, #112 . . . . $35 – 40
Aermacchi Chimera 250, #19, 3¼" . . . . $35 – 40
BMW R-26 250cc, #104, 3¾" . . . . $35 – 40
Gilera Extra Rosso 175, #15, 3¼" . . . . $35 – 40
Gilera G.T. 175, #17, 3¼" . . . . $35 – 40
Go Kart "900," 2¾" . . . . $35 – 40
Go Kart Baby, 3" . . . . $35 – 40
Guzzi Falcone 500, #110, 4⅜" . . . . $35 – 40
Guzzi Lodola 175, #11, 3¼" . . . . $35 – 40
Guzzi Zigolo 110, #13, 3¼" . . . . $35 – 40
Harley-Davidson 1200, #102, 3⅝" . . . . $35 – 40
Honda CS-92 Sport, #108, 3½" . . . . $35 – 40
Viberti 3-Wheel Vivi, #21, 3⅝" . . . . $35 – 40

MIKANSUE

Mikansue 1:43 scale white metal kits from Mike and Sue Richardson of England are currently available from Diecast Miniatures and a few other dealers.
5 1938 Citroën Roadster $14
9 Talbot 105 Roadster $14
12 1976 Fiat 128 . . . . $14

24 Jowett R4 Roadster $14
98 1935 Singer $35
99 Wolseley Hornet $14

MILANO

Harvey Goranson reports, "I think this is Milano 43. These are resin hand-builts of Ferrari racing cars, typically obscure ones from little known races or also-rans. Very nice. Last list I saw was in a May 1992 issue of TSSK, where the numbers went up to 43 (Coincidence?). The 1897 model you list doesn't fit in with this." Italy is the assumed home of Milano models.
1897 Gauthier Wehrle $24

MILESTONE

Milestone Models of South Africa made just two models. They were last known available only from EWA & Miniature Cars USA, Inc., 369 Springfield Ave., P O Box 188, Berkeley Heights, NJ 07922-0188.
1961 Ford Falcon, 1:43 . . . . $70
1960 Plymouth Valiant, 1:43 . . . . $70

MILTON

Milton toys are made in Calcutta, India, from old Corgi, Dinky, Corgi Jr., and other manufacturers' dies. Milton Morgan produced a number of toys under the brand name of Mini Auto Cars, not to be confused with Miniautotoys from Dugu. The quality is noticeably inferior to the original Corgi Jrs.

Mercedes Fire Ladder Truck, 1:64 . . . . $5
201 Volkswagen 1200, 1:90 . . . . $20
202 Mercedes-Benz 220 Coupe, 1:90 . . . . $18
203 Pontiac Firebird, 1:90 . . . . $24
204 BMW 507, 1:90 . . . . $16
205 Austin-Healey, 1:90 . . . . $16
301 Flat Truck, 1:70 . . . . $12
302 Open Truck, 1:70 . . . . $12
303 Chevrolet Impala $32
304 Plymouth Suburban $36
305 Chevrolet Impala State Patrol $36
306 Chevrolet Impala Taxi $36
307 Plymouth Suburban Ambulance $36
308 Chevrolet Impala Police Car $36
309 Chevrolet Impala Fire Chief $32
310 Studebaker Golden Hawk $45
311 Lumber Truck, 1:70 . . . . $12
312 Army Ambulance, 1:70 . . . . $12
313 Royal Mail Van, 1:70 . . . . $16
314 Articulated Tank Truck, "CALTEX," 1:50 . . . $36
314 Articulated Tank Truck, "MOBILGAS," 1:50 . $42
314 Articulated Tank Truck, "BURMAH-SHELL," 1:50 . $42
314 Articulated Tank Truck, "ESSO" 1:50 . . . . . $42
314 Articulated Tank Truck, "INDIAN OIL," 1:50 . $42
315 Articulated Refrigeration Truck, 1:50 . . . . . $36
316 Luxury Coach, 1:50 . . . . $54
317 Articulated Lumber Transporter, 1:50 . . . . . $36
319 Commer Van "MILTON" $42
320 Commer Ambulance $42
321 Commer Army Ambulance $42

322 Commer School Bus $42
323 Commer Pickup. $42
324 Commer Open Truck. $42
325 Commer Milk Van $42
327 Jaguar 3.8 Saloon. $42
329 Ford Mustang $36
330 Foden Tank Truck "CALTEX," 1:50. . . . . $8
331 Foden Tank Truck "BURMAH-SHELL," 1:50 . . . . $8
332 Commer Fruit Carrier. $45
333 Morris Mini Minor $50
334 Commer "COCA-COLA" Truck $60
335 Tractor and Trailer. $42
336 Ford Model T $24
337 D. D. Bus, "INSIST ON MILTON MINI CARS," 1:50 . . . . . $52
338 Tipping Truck, 1:50. . . . . $24
341 Racing Car. $24
342 Roadster $24
344 Ladder Truck, 1:70. . . . . $12
349 Mini Bus $24

MINIALUXE

Depending on who you ask, Minialuxe was begun in France between 1954 and 1959.

1909 Ford Model T, top up, 1:43 . . . . $15
1911 Ford Model T Roadster, top down, 1:43 . . . . $15
1908 Lanchester, 1:43. . . . . $15
1913 Muller Sedan, 1:64. . . . . $8
1912 Park Royal Landau, 1:43. $15
1906 Peugeot, 1:43. . . . . $15
Peugeot 604 4-door Sedan, 1:43 . . . . $15
Peugeot 504 4-door Sedan, 1:43 . . . . $15
Peugeot 204 4-door Sedan, 1:43 . . . . $15
Renault 17 Coupe, 1:43 . . . . $15
Renault 30, 1:43 . . . . $15
Simca 1000 Police, 1:43 . . . . $15

MINIATURE AUTO EMPORIUM

These are 1:43 scale models of exacting detail.

1939 Buick Limo $185
1959 Cadillac Convertible, top up. $65
1959 Cadillac Fire Car $65
1961 Chrysler Convertible, top up. $115
1961 Chrysler Convertible, top down $115
1965 Chevrolet Corvette Convertible, top up. $65
1965 Chevrolet Corvette Convertible, top down $65

MINIATURE VEHICLE CASTINGS INC. (ALSO KNOWN AS MVC)

Robert E. Wagner started Miniature Vehicle Castings Inc. in New Jersey in 1985, producing an exquisite series of 1930s and 40s vehicles in 1:43 scale. Models are made of diecast lead from silicone molds, and represent some of the most beautiful renderings of vintage models on the market. They are produced in small quantities and are very reasonably priced at $21 suggested retail. Current second-market values place them around $40 each.

MVC SERIES 1 — 1985

1937 Ford 2-door Sedan . . . . $30 – 45
1937 Ford 2-door Sedan, "New York Fire". $45

1938 Ford Standard Sedan Del . . . . $20 – 40
1934 Olds 2-door Humpback . . . . $20 – 40
1936 Olds 4-door Humpback . . . . $20 – 40
1937 Hudson Terraplane 2-door . . . . $20 – 40
1938 Dodge Step Van . . . . $20 – 40
1937 Plymouth 5-window Coupe . . . . $20 – 40
1937 Dodge 2-door Humpback . . . . $20 – 40
1938 Plymouth 2-door Sedan . . . . $20 – 40
1940 Ford Logging Semi. $45
1941 Ford C.O.E. Flatbed Truck . . . . $20 – 40
1941 Ford C.O.E. Dump Truck . . . . $20 – 40
1935 Hudson 2-door Sedan. . . . . $20 – 40
1937 Studebaker 3-window Coupe . . . . $20 – 40
1936 Plymouth 4-door Sedan . . . . $20 – 40
1936 Plymouth 4-door Taxi . . . . $20 – 40
1935 Pontiac 3-window Coupe . . . . $20 – 40
1940 Dodge 2-door Sedan. $20 – 40
1939 dodge 2-door Sedan . . . . $20 – 40
1941 Divco Milk Truck "Sunrise Dairy" . . . . $20 – 40

MVC SERIES 2 — 1993

1934 Dodge 2-door Sedan. $20 – 40
1935 Pontiac 2-door Sedan . . . . $20 – 40
1936 Plymouth Pickup . . . . $20 – 40
1938 Hudson Coupe. . . . . $20 – 40

OTHER MVC MODELS

Ford P600 "Coca-Cola" Van $24
Ford P600 "UPS" Van $24

MINIAUTOTOYS (SEE DUGU)

MINIC (SEE TRI-ANG)

MINICHAMPS (SEE PAUL'S MODEL ART)

MINIMAC

Below is a list of known Minimac models from Brazil.

Ford Jeep "Coca-Cola," 1:43 . . . . $18
Ford Jeep Fire Brigade Chief, red, 1:43 . . . . $18
Ford Military Jeep, Army, green, 1:43 . . . . $18
Ford Jeep Ambulance, Red Cross, white/red, 1:43 . . . . $18
Ford Jeep, U.N., white/black, 1:43 . . . . $18
March 762 F.2, "Camel" #12, yellow, 1:25 . . . . $26
March 762 F.2, "Esso" #1, white/red/blue, 1:25 . . . . . $26
March 762 F.2, "Hollywood" #9, red/white/blue, 1:25 . . . . . . $26
March 762 F.2, "Marlboro," Senna, 1:25 . . . . $45
Scania Refrigerator Semi "Coca-Cola," 1:50 . . . . $48
Scania Semi Van, 1:50 . . . . $28
Scania 4x2 Truck "Coca-Cola," 1:50. . . . . $28
Scania 4x2 Truck, 1:50 . . . . $22
Huber Road Grader, yellow, 1:87 . . . . $18
Massey Ferguson 3366 Dozer, yellow, 1:43 . . . . $28
Hyster H-150F Forklift, 1:43 . . . . $22
Massey Ferguson 275 Farm Tractor with canopy, red, 1:43. . . . $28
Cat D4E Bulldozer, 1:50 . . . . $28
Dresser A450E Motorgrader, 1:50 . . . . $48
Galion Road Grader, 1:50 . . . . $48
Komatsu Motorgrader. 1:50 . . . . $48
Case 580H Tractor with Backhoe, 1:43 . . . . $78

MINI MARQUE 43

All Mini Marque 43 models are 1:43 scale, hand built in England in very limited quantities.

2B 1957 Ford Fairlane Convertible, top down		$179
12A 1955 Chevrolet BelAir Sports Coupe		$169
12B 1955 Chevrolet BelAir Nomad		$159
18B 1934 Auburn 652Y Convertible Sedan, top down		$159
24A 1954 Cadillac Eldorado Convertible, top down		$198
24B 1954 Cadillac Eldorado Convertible, top up		$198
25C 1929 Duesenberg Model J, top down		$215
26A 1964 Lincoln Continental Convertible, top down		$179
27B 1958 Chevrolet Corvette, top off (baby blue)		$149
28C 1935 Auburn 851 Boattail Speedster		$215
30A 1958 Chevy Sports Coupe with Continental kit		$198
30B 1958 Chevrolet Impala Convertible with Continental kit, top down		$198
31B 1961 Chevrolet Corvette, top off		$149
34D 1937 Cord 812 Sportsman Convertible Coupe, top up		$169
36A 1959 Lincoln Continental Convertible, top down		$189
37A 1962 Chevrolet Corvette, top on		$149
37B 1962 Chevrolet Corvette, top off (tan or white)		$149
37C 1962 Chevrolet Corvette, top on		$149
38B 1957 Chevrolet Corvette, top off		$149

MINI RACING

Regarding Mini Racing, Harvey Goranson reports: "Now for some history, courtesy of Ma Collection. This operation began in 1976 by Frenchmen Jean-Yves Puillet and Bernard Hue, 65rue Tolbiac, 75013 Paris. (This address info is 15+ years old.) Their first two models, a Porsche 'Pink Pig' from LM71 and a Simca CG Coupe were available as kits or built, but I believe they went kits only early on. The kits number well over 200 today and they are still going. Around 1981 or so they began offering resin kits, and that may be the medium they are all made in today. My opinion — if there's another kit of the same car available, buy it. Those Mini Racing kits I have are with me only because no one else makes, or is likely to make, the vehicle represented. Poor mold line placement, bad proportions, bad decal fit, etc. Sort of a French John Day. Maybe they've improved — I haven't bought one in 15 years or so. By the way, I own the 1981 DeCadenet Belga you list — never built it because the decals just aren't proportioned right. It DNF'ed (Did Not Finish?) LeMans in the 9th hour."

DeCadenet Belga, 1:43 . . . . $24

MINIROUTE

Miniroute models are 1:43 scale hand-builts made in France.

Peugeot 304 Fire Van Allier . . . . $55 – 80
Citroën Jumpy Ambulance . . . . $55 – 80

MIRA

Mira models are detailed scale models made in Spain and currently available from many diecast model dealers. Lately, Mira has made a number of popular 1:18 scale models, but they were more prominently known in the seventies for their 1:43 scale models. Miras, like most diecast toys, are now made in China.

1:18 SCALE

1955 Buick Century Convertible, two-tone	$25
1955 Buick Century Hardtop, two-tone	$25
1955 Buick Century Sun State Police, black and white	$25
1955 Chevrolet Bel Air Convertible	$25
1955 Chevrolet Bel Air Hardtop	$25
1953 Chevrolet Corvette Convertible	$25
1953 Chevrolet Corvette Hardtop	$25
1954 Chevrolet Corvette Convertible	$25

1954 Chevrolet Corvette Hardtop Coupe, $25

1953 Chevrolet Pickup	$25
Ferrari 348tb	$25
Ferrari 348ts	$25

1950 Ford Panel Truck, $25

1956 Ford F-100 Pickup	$25
1964½ Ford Mustang Convertible, top up	$25
1965 Ford Mustang Fastback	$25

1:25 SCALE

Audi 200 4-door Sedan	$16
Benetton Ford	$18
BMW Brabham "Olivetti"	$18
BMW 323i Coupe	$16
BMW 323i 2-door Sedan	$16
Ferrari 348tb	$16
Ferrari 348ts	$16
Ferrari Spa "Goodyear	$18
1956 Ford Thunderbird	$16
Lancia 037 "Martini"	$16
Lotus Ford	$18

Mercedes-Benz 190E 2.3 Sedan. $18

Mercedes-Benz 500 4-door Sedan. $16

Mercedes-Benz 540K $16

Nissan Jeep $16

Porsche 911 "Rothman's Paris-Dakar" $24

Porsche 928. . . . . $16

Renault Espace Ambulance $16

Renault Espace Fire $16

Williams Honda. $18

Williams Renault $18

1:43 Scale

Citroën CX sedan. $15

Mercedes-Benz 450 SE $15

Pegaso Fire $18

1:64 Scale

Caravan Ambulance. $4

Chrysler 150 4-door Sedan $4

Ford Fiesta 2-door Sedan o/s $4

Land Rover Ambulance $4

Mercedes 450 4-door Sedan $4

Seat 1200 Coupe $4

Seat 131E 4-door Sedan $4

Seat 128 Coupe $4

MITRECRAFT

Diecast Miniatures offers just one model from Mitrecraft.

Austin A35 4-door Sedan, 1:43 . . . . $35

MK MODELS

Only one example of MK Models is known.

Tatra Semi Oil Tanker, 1:120 . . . . $5

MOBOTO (OR MEBOTO)

Like so many other obscure brands, only a few models by Moboto (possibly spelled Meboto) of Turkey are offered by Diecast Miniatures.

Lamborghini Marzal, 1:43 . . . . $11

Lancia Fulvia Coupe, 1:43 . . . . $11

Mercedes-Benz 250 Sedan, 1:43 . . . . $11

MODELAUTO/SUN MOTOR COMPANY, BUGATTIANA, RAPIDE, BIJOU

Modelauto produces models under the brands of Sun Motor Company, Bugattiana, Rapide, and Bijou. Sun Motor Company is known, among other things, for replica fire-fighting equipment, as so richly illustrated in Toys for Collectors' catalog. Modelauto, of Leeds, England, was started in 1974 by Rod and Val Ward. They also produce Model Auto Review 10 times a year and host the Somerville Society for collectors of that prestigious brand of scale models. In addition, they are exclusive UK distributors for a few other exceptional brands: Paradise Garage, Doorkey, Oto, and Scottoy. Listings below include US and UK values for kits, followed by values for built models. As of 1/97, n/a = not made. o/s = temporarily out of stock

1:50 Scale from UK

124 Diamond T M20, British Army. $73 (£47)
$171 (£110)

125 Diamond T M20, US Army $73 (£47)
$171 (£110)

126 Diamond T ballast, Crook & Willington $73 (£47)
$171 (£110)

127 Diamond T arctic tractor, Crook & Will. . . . . . $62 (£40) o/s

128 Diamond T heavy haulage, Picktords o/s $171 (£110)

129 Diamond T heavy haulage, Stoof/Mamut $73 (£47)
$171 (£110)

130 Diamond T heavy haulage, Sunters $73 (£47)
$171 (£110)

131 Diamond T heavy haulage, Wynns $73 (£47)
$171 (£110)

132 Diamond T Thurston's Fair . . . . $104 (£67) o/s

133 Diamond T M20 Brit. Army, Hercules eng.. . . . . . . $73 (£47)
$171 (£110)

134 Diamond T tractor, STAG (France) $73 (£47)
$171 (£110)

135 Diamond T recovery (TFL), Hudson. . . . . $73 (£47) o/s

136 Diamond T recovery (TFL), Avon . . . . $73 (£47) o/s

137 Diamond T recovery (TFL), J&H $73 (£47)
$186 (£120)

139 Diamond T Brit. Army canvas cab, closed $73 (£47)
$171 (£110)

140 Diamond T British Army arctic tractor $63 (£40)
$148 (£95)

141 Diamond T US Army arctic tractor . . . . $63 (£40) o/s

143 Diamond T Brit Army canvas cab arctic $63 (£40)
$148 (£95)

144 Diamond T arctic tractor, Pickfords $63 (£40)
$148 (£95)

145 Diamond T arctic tractor, Stoof Breda $63 (£40)
$148 (£95)

148 Leyland E Yorks service vehicle. $75 (£48)
$152 (£98)

149 Fairground TRANSKIT for bus or van . . . . . . $19 (£12) n/a

150 Daimler CVD6 bus 1949, Exeter. $93 (£60)
$186 (£120)

154 Bedford OY tanker (Pool, Esso, Caltex) $45 (£29)
$101 (£65)

155 Bedford OY GS lorry (livery varies). $45 (£29)
$101 (£65)

156 Bedford OS breakdown lorry. . . . . $52 (£33) o/s

157 Bedford OS tipper (Marples) $45 (£29)
$101 (£65)

158 Bedford OY cab, transkit for Corgi . . . . $14 (£9) n/a

159 Mann Egerton breakdown crane transkit . . . . . . $14 (£9) n/a

160 Ford 7V 1940s Shell airfield tanker. $70 (£45)
$148 (£95)

161 Ford 7V 1940s arctic tractor . . . . $45 (£29) o/s

162 Ford 7V 1940s box van, LNER . . . . $52 (£33) o/s

163 Ford 7V 1930s breakdown lorry. $52 (£33)
$117 (£75)

164 Ford 7V wartime tanker, Pool $52 (£33)
$117 (£75)

165 Ford 7V 1930s open Imperial Airways $52 (£33)
$117 (£75)

166 Ford 7V 1930s tanker, Pratts $52 (£33)
$117 (£75)

167 Ford 7V 1930s box van . . . . $52 (£33) o/s

170 Rotinoff Atlantic large cab, Sunters $78 (£50)
$186 (£120)

171 Rotinoff Atlantic small cab, Parnaby. $78 (£50)
$186 (£120)

172 Rotinoff Atlantic small cab, Sunter $78 (£50)
$186 (£120)

173 Rotinoff Atlantic small cab, Smith $78 (£50)
$186 (£120)

175 Bedford OY van, BRS, GWR, LMS $52 (£33)
$117 (£75)

176 Bedford OS refuse lorry . . . . $52 (£33) o/s

177 Bedford OY tackle wagon, livery varies. $56 (£36) £79

178 Bedford OS + generator, fairground. $52 (£33)
$117 (£75)

179 Bedford OY plank-side, Charringtons $52 (£33)
$117 (£75)

179 Bedford OY plank-side, Cirkus Arena $52 (£33)
$117 (£75)

180 Scammell Super Constructor, Pickfords $78 (£50)
$186 (£120)

181 Scammell Super Constructor, Sunters. $78 (£50)
$186 (£120)

182 Scammell Super Constructor, Wynns $78 (£50)
$186 (£120)

183 Scammell Super Constructor, Marples $78 (£50)
$186 (£120)

185 Bedford O sided lorry, LEP $52 (£33)
$117 (£75)

186 Bedford O tipper, Ahearn $52 (£33)
$117 (£75)

190 Super Pacific Prime Mover, Wynn's $95 (£60)
$186 (£120)

191 Commer Superpoise van, McVities. $76 (£49)
$152 (£98)

191 Commer Superpoise van, Cadbury. $76 (£49)
$152 (£98)

192 Ford ET6 coachbuilt van, Jays or BOAC. $76 (£49)
$152 (£98)

195 Leyland Comet bus, Laing or BOAC. $76 (£49)
$152 (£98)

200 Queen Mary arctic trailer var. decals . . . . $86 (£55) n/a

201 Bedford OX + Queen Mary arctic trailer n/a $171 (£110)

201 Bedford OX-Queen Mary "Helicopter Services". . . $171 (£110)

202 AOMA caravan, 1920s – 30s $38 (£24)
$62 (£40)

203 Rex caravan, 1930s – 40s. $38 (£24)
$62 (£40)

204 Sales trailer, Circus, Refreshments, RN, etc $42 (£27)
$76 (£49)

205 Dyson 85 ton well trailer (specify livery) $93 (£60)
$186 (£120)

206 King 150 ton 6 axle well trailer $132 (£85)
$225 (£145)

207 King 3 ax arctic low load trailer. $107 (£69)
$186 (£120)

209 Bogie bolster trailer 2+2 axle. $45 (£29)
$93 (£60)

210 Bedford OX arctic tractor unit . . . . $45 (£29) o/s

211 Single axle arctic trailer, US style $47 (£30)
$109 (£70)

212 Single axle arctic trailer, European style $47 (£30)
$109 (£70)

213 Single axle arctic oval tanker trailer . . . . $55 (£35) o/s

220 Autocar U70 civilian tanker, B-A or Skelly $76 (£49)
$152 (£98)

221 Autocar U70 US Navy tanker. $76 (£49)
$152 (£98)

222 Autocar U70 Fire dept tanker $76 (£49)
$152 (£98)

223 Autocar U70 Avgas tanker. $76 (£49)
$152 (£98)

224 Autocar U70 2 axle open truck $52 (£33)
$117 (£75)

225 Autocar U70 arctic tractor unit NYC. $45 (£29)
$101 (£65)

226 Autocar U70 fire pumper. . . . . $86 (£55) o/s

230 Guy Warrior 4x2 arctic tractor unit. $45 (£29)
$101 (£65)

231 Guy Invincible 6x4 tractor unit. . . . . £49 ($76 US)
$152 (£98)

232 Guy Invincible 6x4 tipper, Wimpey. $86 (£55)
$163 (£105)

235 Guy Invincible 8 wheel flat, Wynns $86 (£55)
$163 (£105)

236 Guy Invincible 4 axle tanker, Regent. $86 (£55)
$163 (£105)

242 ERF KV 6x4 tipper, Pointer $86 (£55)
$163 (£105)

245 ERF KV 4 axle flat, Gardner, 1950s $86 (£55)
$163 (£105)

246 ERF KV 4 axle tanker, Shell-BP $86 (£55)
$163 (£105)

250 Ford Thames Trader flat lorry $52 (£33)
$117 (£75)

251 Ford Thames Trader Lubricants tanker. $58 (£37)
$123 (£79)

260 Leyland Octopus flat, BRS. $86 (£55)
$163 (£105)

261 Leyland Hippo 6x4 tipper, Willment $86 (£55)
$163 (£105)

161+211 Ford 7v arctic flat, Pickfords $194 (£125)

210+213 Bedford OX arctic tanker, Pickfords $194 (£125)

210+213 Bedford OX arctic tanker, Pool. $194 (£125)

BUGATTIANA 1:43 MODELS FROM UK

BU001 Bugatti T40 Grand Sport, 1930 . . . . $47 (£30)
$109 (£70)

BU002 Bugatti T40 Sahara, Loiseau, 1930 . . . . $55 (£35) o/s

BU004 Bugatti T45 16 Cylinder $55 (£35)
$117 (£75)

BU005 Bugatti T35B Sports 2 seat aero $55 (£35)
$117 (£75)

BU006 Bugatti T252 Cabriolet $55 (£35)
$117 (£75)

BU010 Bugatti T57SC Colonel Giles. $55 (£35)
$117 (£75)

BU011 Bugatti T57SC Colonel Giles rally . . . . $55 (£35) o/s
BU012 Bugatti T57C Shah of Iran. . . . . $55 (£35) o/s

RAPIDE 1:43 MODELS FROM UK

RA002 Jaguar Mark VII red, blue, gray, green o/s $93 (£60)
RA005 Austin Healey 100S sports. $41 (£26)
                   $93 (£60)
RA008 BSA Scout open sports 1930s $42 (£27)
                  $107 (£69)
RA008 BSA Scout open sports, two tone. $116 (£75)
RA009 Bantam (American Austin) Sports 38 . . . . $44 (£28)
                  $106 (£68)
RA009 Bantam Sports two tone $109 (£70)
RA010 BSA Scout Coupe $45 (£29)
                  $109 (£70)
RA011 Bantam pickup civil, 1939. . . . . $109 (£30)
                  $109 (£70)
RA012 Bantam pickup stakeside 39 NEW $53 (£34)
                  $118 (£76)
RA013 Bantam pickup US Army, 1939 . . . . $47 (£30)
                  $109 (£70)
RA014 Bantam pickup Fire dept, 1939 . . . . $53 (£34)
                  $118 (£76)
RA015 Bantam avgas tanker, 1939 . . . . $47 (£30)
                  $109 (£70)

BIJOU MODELS, FROM VARIOUS COUNTRIES

1 Vespa parascooter French Army+bazooka, 1:30 . . . . . . $20 (£13)
                  $30 (£19)
2 Bugatti T52 Baby (by Auto Replicas), 1:43 . . . . $20 (£13)
                  $34 (£22)
3 Austin Pathfinder pedal car (ex Rapide 100), 1:43 . . . . $16 (£10)
                  $30 (£19)
6 London E1 tram Model Auto Show 95 n/a $8 (£5)
7 'Inflatable' boat + outboard motor, 1:43, plastic n/a $5 (£3)

MODEL PET (SEE ASAHI)

MODEL POWER

Model Power, based in Farmingdale, New York, produces over 2,400 O, HO, and N gauge items intended for model railroad layouts, although most are buildings, street lights, layout accessories, and rolling stock. Their series of O scale fire trucks are similar in detail to Ertl's recently introduced models, but are priced somewhat higher ($13 – 15) because of their limited availability, and possess no livery, which leaves the model crying out for customizing. Perhaps the most interesting part of the Model Power story for diecast toy collectors is that they obtain their diecast models from other manufacturers and repackage them as their own. The fire trucks listed below are all Gaia brand models. The Scania Bus is by Playart. Eidai is also a brand repackaged as Model Power. The package is all that identifies these models as Model Power.

American LaFrance Fire Pumper, 1:87 (Gaia). $13
American LaFrance Ladder Truck, 1:87 (Gaia) $15
American LaFrance Snorkel Truck, 1:87 (Gaia) $15
Scania Bus, "AVIS Courtesy Bus," 1:87 (Playart). $10

MODEL TOYS (SEE DOEPKE)

MODELS OF YESTERYEAR (SEE MATCHBOX)

MOKO (ALSO SEE MATCHBOX)

Moses Kohnstam established Moko around the turn of the century. Although he died in 1912, his legacy lives on in the British office of Moko, a company renowned for representing toy manufacturers the world over. He contracted such toy companies as Guntermann, Distler, and Fischer, and others to produce made-to-order toys to bear the Moko label. Early Matchbox toys are marked as "A Moko Lesney Product." Other toy companies relied on Moko for distribution, such as Gama, Tippco, Levy, and Carette. Most Moko toys are tin windup toys dating around the late 1920s, current value $1,000 – 1,500.

MONTEGO

The Montego brand is represented by one miniature cruise ship Rotterdam, 12 inches long, offered for $38.

MORESTONE

Morris & Stone of Great Britain marketed a line of toys in the 1940s that are more than vaguely similar to Dinky Toys. Most collectors know Morestone by their more familiar "Budgie Miniatures," a name adopted in 1959. Herein is listed a representation of the Morestone line.

1 AA Motorcycle and Sidecar $30
2 RAC Motorcycle and Sidecar $30
3 AA Land Rover $30
4 AA Bedford Van $20
5 Wolseley 6180 Police Car $25
6 Cooper-Bristol Racing Car $20
7 Mercedes-Benz Racing Car $25
8 Volkswagen 1200 Sedan $35
9 Maudslay Horse Box $40
10 Karrier GPO Telephones Van. $35
11 Morris Commercial Van $25
12 Volkswagen Microbus $40
13 Austin FX3 Taxi. $30
14 Packard Convertible $40
15 Austin A95 Westminster Countryman $25
16 Austin-Healey 100 . . . . $30
17 Ford Thames 5 cwt. Van $45
18 Foden Dumper $25
19 Rover 105R $25
20 Plymouth Belvedere Convertible $45
0-6-0 Tank Locomotive. $45
AA Land Rover, 4¼". $145
AA Land Rover, 3" $100
AA Motorcycle and Sidecar. $120
Aveling-Barford Road Roller $45
Bedford Car Transporter. $120
Bedford Dormobile $160
Breakdown Service Land Rover $100
Compressor $50
Daimler Ambulance $100
Fire Engine, clockwork motor with bell $90
Fire Escape, large. $90
Fire Escape, smaller $75

Foden 8-wheel Flat Lorry	$120
Foden 8-wheel Open Lorry	$120
Foden 8-wheel Petrol Tanker	$120
Foden Dumper	$40
Foden Flat Lorry with chains	$120
Horse Drawn Covered Wagon with 4 Horses	$80
Horse Drawn Covered Wagon with 6 Horses	$100
Horse Drawn Gypsy Caravan	$150
Horse Drawn Hansom Cab	$60
Horse Drawn Snack Bar	$100
International Articulated Refrigeration Truck	$60
Klückner Side Tipping Truck	$75
Leyland Double Deck Bus	$120
Military Police Land Rover	$180
Prime Mover with Trailer	$50
RAC Motorcycle and Sidecar	$120
Racing Car	$45
Road Sweeper	$120
Scammell Articulated Tank Truck	$60
Sleigh with Father Xmas	$100
Solo Motorcycle	$75
Stage Coach with 2 horses	$100
Stage Coach with 4 horses	$100
State Landau with 6 horses	$50
Wells Fargo Stage Coach with 2 galloping horses	$100
Wells Fargo Stage Coach with 4 horses	$100
Wolseley 6/80 Police Car	$75

MORESTONE NODDY CHARACTER TOYS

Big Ears on Bicycle, approx. 2½"	$75
Big Ears on Bicycle, approx. 1¾"	$60
Clown on Bicycle, approx. 2½"	$75
Noddy and His Car, approx. 4"	$75
Noddy and His Car, approx. 2"	$50
Noddy on Bicycle with Trailer	$65
Noddy's Garage Set	$160

MOTOR CITY USA
(ALSO SEE DESIGN STUDIO AND USA MODELS)

Motor City 1:43 scale models have been made in the United States by partners Alan Novak and Gene Parrill since 1986. USA Models are less detailed and less expensive models than their Motor City and Design Studios counterparts.

1 1949 DeSoto 4-door Sedan	$85
2 1955 Cadillac 4-door Sedan	$85
5 1955 Chevrolet Nomad Wagon	$85
6 1955 Chevrolet Convertible, top down	$85
7 1953 Chevrolet 2-door Hardtop	$235
8 1953 Chevrolet Convertible	$265
9 1953 Chevrolet Sedan Delivery	$235
10 1950 Ford Convertible	$265
11 1950 Ford Coupe	$235
12 1950 Ford 2-door Sedan	$165
13 1950 Ford Wagon	$265
14 1950 Ford 4-door Sedan Police	$165
15 1950 Ford Crestliner	$265
22 1948 Chrysler Town & Country Convertible	$265
31 1956 Chevrolet Convertible	$265

40 1954 Buick Skylark	$265
41 1959 Metropolitan	$235
USA-1 1958 Cadillac Series 75 Limousine, dark metallic blue finish, introduced in 1997	$69 retail

MOUNTAIN SERVICE INTERNATIONAL, INC. (SEE POLE POSITION)

MR

Exoticar lists a number of models from the MR collection, describing them as 1:43 scale hand-builts from Italy, probably resin.

1951 Alfa Romeo 1900C Sprint Cabriolet, available in red, dark green, or metallic gray	$199
1954 Alfa Romeo 1900C Sprint Coupe, available in cream, dark gray, or black	$199
1971 Ferrari 365 GTC/4, available in red, metallic blue, or yellow	$199
1961 Ferrari 400 S.A. Convertible, red	$199
1967 Ferrari Dino 206GT, available in red, metallic gray, or yellow	$199
1987 Ferrari F40 Street with Engine	$199
1994 Ferrari F40 Camp Italiano GT, red	$199
1948 Porsche 356 Speedster, available in silver or yellow	$199
1996 Porsche 911 Carrera 4S, available in polar silver, midnight blue, or guards red	$199
1996 Porsche 911 Carrera Turbo, available in speed yellow, forest green, or arena red	$199
1996 Porsche 911 GT2, available in speed yellow, guards red, or polar silver	$199
1996 Porsche 911 GT2 Evo II, available in polar silver or white	$199
1996 Porsche 911 RS, available in speed yellow, midnight blue, or polar silver	$199

MRE

Harvey Goranson reports: "MRE — Again, the info comes from Ma Collection. Begun by Michel El Koubi in Paris, the first dozen or so models were conversions of Solido diecasts (MS series — Modification Solido). In 1976 he brought out a range of white metal models, mostly Porsche racing cars at first. By 1979 he had stopped making kits, as he had gotten the racing bug in 1977, driving a Lola T296. Some of the built models from 1977 bear the signature of Dominique Esparcieux (ESDO). They also sold transkits — I had their 1977 Mirage Renault TK for Solido 38." Below is listed one documented representative model.

Simca CG Prototype, 1:43	$14

MTC

Of the many generic diecast toys, MTC is just another one. These inexpensive toys are made in China and marketed by MTC, Inc. of South San Francisco, California. The line includes airplanes, cars, and other vehicles. Their collector value will likely never exceed their original purchase price of usually less than $2.

MUKY (ALSO SEE HOT WHEELS)

Muky toys are the Hot Wheels of Argentina, produced from older Hot Wheels dies. Models in the Muky Collection are made in Gualeguay, Argentina, which is in Entre Rios province about 100 miles north of Buenos Aires, but across the Parana River. Thanks to Dr. Craig Campbell, associate professor of geography at Youngstown State University, for the geography lesson.

Custom Corvette . . . . $10 – 12

MVC (SEE MINIATURE VEHICLE CASTINGS)

NACORAL INTERCARS

Nacoral is a brand of models from Spain that are of lesser quality than Pilen/Auto Pilen models. While most Nacoral models are 1:43 scale, a few 1:24 scale models were also produced, although none could so far be documented.

1969 Chevrolet Corvette, blue, 1:43 . . . . $20
1969 Chevrolet Corvette, red, 1:43 . . . . $20
1968 Chevrolet Camaro Europa, 1:43 . . . . $20
1968 Ford Thunderbird, dark blue, 1:43 . . . . $20
1968 Ford Thunderbird, orange, 1:43 . . . . $20
1968 Ford Thunderbird, red, 1:43 . . . . $18
1968 Javelin AMX, 1:43 . . . . $20
Ferrari Dino, 1:43 . . . . $20
Ford Fiesta, 1:43 . . . . $20
Matra Bagheera, 1:43 . . . . $20
Matra Sport, 1:43 . . . . $20
Mercedes 280 sedan, 1:43 . . . . $20
Scania 10x8 Covered Truck, blue & yellow, 1:43 . . . . $20

NATIONAL TOYS

The nation in this case is Italy. The year is 1961. Four 1:45 scale plastic models were produced by this company. No diecast models were ever produced.

Alfa Romeo Giulietta Sprint $45
Fiat 1500 Roadster $45
Fiat 1800 Sedan $45
Vanwall Formula 1 . . . . $45

NEVCO

One of the newest companies to appear on the market is Nevco. Their latest, maybe only, model is a replica of a classic 1930s streamlined toy car with Art Deco box silk screened by hand. Nevco, Box 2355, Atascadero, California 93423. Phone 805-466-8685

"The Special," burgundy and gold, limited edition of 4,000 . . $173

NEVINS INTERNATIONAL, LTD.

A pair of 1:43 scale models are an exclusive offer on specially marked boxes of Kellogg's Cornflakes. The two-car set is of the Brooks & Dunn Metal Rodeo Legends Racing cars representing 5:8 scale replicas of early NASCAR racers. While this mail-away promo cost just a dollar, models are already valued at $7 – 10 for the sealed blisterpack set.

NEW CLOVER (ALSO SEE CLOVER)

New Clover models are made in Asia by New Clover International ltd of Hong Kong.

Bobcat X225 Skid Loader, 1:25 . . . . $35
Bobcat 743B Skid Loader, 1:19 . . . . $25

Bobcat 753 Skid Loader, 1:50 . . . . $10
Bobcat 753 Skid Loader, 1:25 . . . . $25
Bobcat 7753 Skid Loader, 1:25 . . . . $25
1959-1962 Melroe (Bobcat) M-200 Loader, 1:25 (replica of 1st machine built by Melroe Company) $18
Semi Flatbed with three Bobcat 753 Skid Loaders, 1:50 . . . . . $55
Kiamaster Ambulance, 1:43 . . . . $18
Kiamaster Kombi, 1:43 . . . . $18
Pontiac Firebird Coupe, 1:59 . . . . $5

NEW-RAY TOYS

New-Ray toys are manufactured in China by New-Ray Toys Co., Ltd. Examples found are farm tractors with driver and front-wheel friction drive. Tractors are sold separately or with trailers that include detachable containers. Sold in either yellow or orange, the tractors sell for $4 each, while the tractor/trailer combinations sell for $6. The most popular model found from New-Ray is a break from the usual fare: a neat little Hummer faithfully reproduced in 1:32 scale. The doors open on this top-down red version, which is labeled on the box as being distributed by Midwestern Home Products, Inc., 1105 Orange St., Wilmington, DE 19801 USA. Since finding the Hummer, the author has noticed a lot more New-Ray Toys, mostly pickup trucks and jeeps of similar construction and quality, showing up at Wal-Mart and other stores. Newer models now are marked N.R. Los Angeles CA 90021 and New-Ray Toys Co., Ltd.

Hummer, red with light gray interior, V#1433, Item #5104, ASST6, 45323, 1:32, $5

Land Rover Station Wagon, green with white roof and interior, 44323, 1:32 . . . . $5

NEW TRAX (SEE TOP GEAR)

NICKY TOYS (ALSO SEE DINKY)

Nicky Toys began in Calcutta, India, by S. Kumar & Company, also known as Atamco Private Ltd., in 1968 when some older Dinky tooling was obtained from Meccano. Nicky Toys' noticeably poorer castings are the result of old dies that were already worn out by extensive use. The company continued to produce such toys until the 1970s.

Bentley S Coupe $30
Daimler Jaguar 3.4 . . . . $25
Daimler Jaguar 3.4 Police $45

Dump Truck $50
Howitzer $25
Jaguar D Type $25
Jaguar E Type $25
Jaguar Mk. X $25
Lincoln Continental $45
Mercedes-Benz 220 SE $35
Mercedes-Benz 220 SE Taxi $40
MGB $25
Mighty Antar Tank Transporter $75
Military Ambulance $35
Plymouth Fury Convertible $45
Plymouth Fury Hardtop $45
Standard 20 Mini Atlas Kenebrake Ambulance $25
Standard 20 Mini Atlas Kenebrake Bus $25
Triumph Vitesse $25
Universal Army Jeep $45
Universal Jeep $45
Vanwall $30
Volkswagen 1500 . . . . $45
Volkswagen 1500 Police $45

NIGAM

Resembling crude versions of Mercury models, Nigams were produced in Italy in 1948.

1 Alfa Romeo Grand Prix $125
2 Auto-Union Grand Prix $125
3 Gardner's MG Record Car $125
4 Maserati Grand Prix $125
5 Mercedes-Benz Grand Prix $125
6 E.R.A. Grand Prix $125

N.J. INTERNATIONAL

Walther's offers a great assortment of N. J. International 1:87 scale (HO gauge) unpainted cast metal kits.

1964 Chevrolet Corvette Sting Ray, 525-102 . . . . . . $6 kit, 525-114
　$9 assembled & painted
1965 Ford Shelby GT-350 Mustang, 525-101 . . . . . . $6 kit, 525-113
　$9 assembled & painted
Aerial Ladder Fire Truck, 525-106 . . . . $39 kit
Jeep Gladiator Pickup Truck, 525-112 . . . . $6 kit, 525-115
　$9 assembled
Mack C Ladder Truck, 525-130 . . . . $69 kit
Mack C, tractor only, 525-1301 . . . . $29 kit
Mack MB Tractor Tilt Cab, 525-138 . . . . $25 kit
Pierce Mid-Ship Pumper, 525-116 . . . . $35 kit
Pumper Kit with 4-door Closed Cab, 525-117 . . . . $37 kit
Snorkel Fire Truck, 525-107 . . . . $39 kit
UPS Delivery, 525-104 . . . . $19 kit

NOREV

M. Veron started the firm called Norev (Veron spelled backwards) in a suburb of Lyon, France, in 1953. The first models were plastic in 1:43 scale. Later models were made of diecast metal with tin-plate or plastic chassies. Norev's product line included 1:72 scale Mini-Jet series, the larger Maxi-Jet, and Jet-Car series. Mini-Jet models are currently valued around $5 – 8 each. Maxi-Jets are a series of trucks

for $12 – 16, and Jet-Cars are valued between $5 and $30. Here is a brief sampling.

NOREV MINI-JET SERIES, 1:72

Bertone Trapeze, #412 . . . . $5 – 8
Chevrolet Camper Pickup, #460 . . . . $5 – 8

Citroën BX, $5 – 8

Photo by Jeff Koch.

Ford Mustang, #424 . . . . $5 – 8
Matra Bagheera, #402 . . . . $5 – 8
Peugeot 504, #405 . . . . $5 – 8

NOREV MAXI-JET SERIES

Caravan . . . . $12 – 16
DAF Circus Truck . . . . $12 – 16
Volvo Breakdown Truck . . . . $12 – 16
Saviem Drinks Truck . . . . $12 – 16

NOREV JET-CARS

Ford Taunus 12M . . . . $20 – 24
Lancia Stratos . . . . $8 – 12
Matra F1 . . . . $20 – 24
Mercedes C-111 . . . . $12 – 16
Peugeot 404 Coupe . . . . $30 – 36
Renault 4L . . . . $28 – 32
Volkswagen 1500 . . . . $28 – 32

NOSTALGIC

An extensive collection of Nostalgic models is offered by Diecast Miniatures for $59 – 64 each. Some Nostalgic models are copies of older Tootsietoys.

202 Ford Model A Canopy Pickup, 1:43 . . . . $59
203 1930 Ford Roadster, top down, 1:43 . . . . $59
204 Ford, "Spearmint," white & green, 1:43 . . . . $59
204 Ford, "Toledo Show," 1:43 . . . . $59
205 Ford Model A 4-door Sedan, 1:43 . . . . $59
219 1931 Ford AA Dump Truck, 1:43 . . . . $59
220 1937 Cord Coupe, 1:43 . . . . $59
222 Porsche 356 Coupe, 1:43 . . . . $64
223 1930 Ford Model A 5-window Coupe, green & black, 1:43 . $59
227 1982 Chevrolet Corvette, 1:43 . . . . $59
229 1932 Ford Coupe Fire Chief, red & black, 1:55 . . . . $59
230 1975 Chevrolet Corvette, 1:43 . . . . $59
234 1936 Ford Roadster, 1:43 . . . . $64
243 1964 Chevrolet Corvette Coupe, 1:43 . . . . $59
248 1936 Ford Army Ambulance, green, 1:43 . . . . $64
270 1965 Ford Mustang 2+2, black, 1:43 . . . . $59
273 1953 Buick Skylark Convertible, top down, green, 1:43 . . $59
279 1939 Ford Wagon, metallic light blue, 1:43 . . . . $64

281 1941 Lincoln Continental, 1:43 . . . . $64

290 1953 Buick Skylark Convertible, top up, 1:43 . . . . $64

611 1936 Ford Van "UPS," brown & gold, 1:43 . . . . $59

652 1954 International Soda Truck "Pepsi," white/blue/red, 1:55 . . . . $59

657 1954 International Soda Truck "Coca-Cola," 1:55 . . . . $59

660 1956 Chevrolet Corvette Roadster, red, 1:43 . . . . $64

662 1936 Ford Van "UPS," brown & gold, 1:43 . . . . $64

667 1915 Ford Model T Fire Ladder Truck, red, 1:43 . . . . $64

668 1915 Ford Model T Van Police, black & white, 1:43 . . . . . $59

669 1935 Chevy Van "Evening Standard, 1:43 . . . . $59

673 1934 LaSalle Coupe, 1:43 . . . . $64

675 1951 Allard J2 Roadster, 1:43 . . . . $64

677 1930 Ford Model A Pickup, 1:43 . . . . $59

678 Porsche 356 Roadster, 1:43 . . . . $64

680 1932 Graham Van "REA," 1:43 . . . . $59

681 1960 Chevrolet Van "UPS," brown & gold, 1:43 . . . . $59

682 1934 LaSalle Roadster, 1:43 . . . . $64

683 Ford AA Chemical Fire Truck, 1:43 . . . . $64

684 1950 Willys Jeepster, 1:43 . . . . $64

685 1931 Ahrens-Fox Fire Truck, 1:43 . . . . $64

686 1932 Seagrave Fire Truck, 1:43 . . . . $64

687 1950 Divco Van "Borden's," 1:43 . . . . $64

688 1935 Chevy Van "Coke," 1:43 . . . . $64

689 1954 Mack B Fire Pumper, 1:43 . . . . $64

690 1931 Mack AC Fire Hose Truck, 1:43 . . . . $64

691 1950 Willys Jeepster "Coke," 1:43 . . . . $64

692 1936 Ford Van, maroon, 1:43 . . . . $64

696 1935 Chevy Van "Cities Service," 1:43 . . . . $64

697 1935 Chevy Van "Standard Oil," 1:43 . . . . $64

698 1935 Chevy Van "Shamrock Oil," 1:43 . . . . $64

699 1935 Chevy Van "Exide," 1:43 . . . . $64

700 1935 Chevy Van "Conoco," 1:43 . . . . $64

701 1935 Chevy Van "Tri-Star," 1:43 . . . . $64

702 1935 Chevy Van "Sunoco," 1:43 . . . . $64

703 1935 Chevy Van "7-Up," 1:43 . . . . $64

704 1935 Chevy Van "Goodyear," 1:43 . . . . $64

705 1935 Chevy Van "UPS," 1:43 . . . . $64

802 1950 Divco Van "Sealtest," 1:43 . . . . $64

803 1950 Divco Van "Fire," 1:43 . . . . $64

806 1950 Divco Van "Coca-Cola," 1:43 . . . . $64

809 1950 Divco Van "Police," 1:43 . . . . $64

NOVACAR

Originally produced by the Portuguese company Minia Portos Juguetes E Brinquedos Lda., Novacar became a division of Majorette of France in 1993. Novacar is a series of small-scale toy vehicles with plastic bodies and metal chassis, except for number 112 F1 Racer, which has a diecast metal body and plastic chassis. All models are currently available as the new Majorette 100 Series and retail for 50¢ – 75¢ each.

101 Ferrari 308

    v.1 light yellow with red interior $1

    v.2 darker yellow with red interior $1

102 Nissan 300 ZX

    v.1 light blue with red interior, black & gold accents $1

    v.2 darker blue with red interior, black & gold accents $1

    v.3 clear with silver flecks, blue-gray & yellow interior $1

    v.4 clear with silver flecks, purple & white interior $1

103 Chevrolet Corvette

    v.1 white with black "23," green & red accents $1

    v.2 white with red "23," green & red accents $1

    v.3 black with white accents $1

    v.4 black with silver "CORVETTE" and Chevrolet logo $1

    v.5 clear with red flecks, dark red & white interior $1

    v.6 clear with silver flecks, purple & pink interior $1

104 Ferrari Testarossa

    v.1 red with "Ferrari" & logo on hood $1

    v.2 red with "S RACING" on hood $1

105 Mercedes-Benz 500SL

    v.1 silver with red interior, "500SL" on doors $1

    v.2 silver with red interior, no markings $1

106 Peugeot 605

    v.1 white with black interior $1

    v.2 white with red interior $1

107 Nissan Pathfinder/Terrano

v.1 red with black & white rally markings, $1

    v.2 green with black & white rally markings $1

    v.3 white with black & gold "SHERIFF" markings $1

    v.4 red with "FIRE DEPT." markings $1

108 Kenworth Semi Tractor

    v.1 blue with red & white stars & stripes $1

109 Chevrolet Impala Police Car

    v.1 white with blue & gold markings $1

    v.2 black with white & gold markings $1

110 Renault Espace Van

    v.1 red with "Espace" on sides in script lettering $1

    v.2 white with blue "Ambulance" markings, orange accents . . . $

    v.3 yellow with blue & red rally accents $1

111 Porsche LeMans GT Racer

    v.1 black with white accents, "TOP DRIVERS" on nose $1

    v.2 clear with yellow flecks, lime green interior $1

    v.3 clear with silver flecks, blue-gray interior $1

112 F1 Racer

    v.1 yellow with red & black accents, red plastic base $1

    v.2 black with gold & red accents, white plastic base $1

113 Volkswagen Caravelle Van

    v.1 red with black & gold accents $1

    v.2 "Surf" $1

114 Ford Escort GT
  v.1 yellow $1
116 Chevrolet Extended Cab Pickup
  v.1 black with white accents $1
  v.2 clear with red flecks, dark red & white interior $1
  v.3 clear with yellow flecks, lime green & pink interior $1
117 Honda Acura NSX
  v.1 red with black interior $1
  v.2 red with white interior $1
119 Jeep
  v.1 blue with black top, yellow accents (1995) $1
120 Ferrari F40
  v.1 red $1
121 Ford Van
  v.1 purple with flame accents $1

NSG MARKETING CORP.
(ALSO SEE TRAFFIC STOPPERS AND SUMMER)

There seems to be a connection between NSG and Summer models. NSG Marketing Corporation currently produces a variety of inexpensive toys and sets of crudely cast vehicles in roughly 1:64 scale called Traffic Stoppers. Summer models appear to be larger models of slightly more accurate scale and detail, though still crude compared to other 1:43 scale models. Traffic Stoppers are virtually unidentifiable out of their package as anything but generic. Even in the package, they are not currently worth much to collectors.

NUTMEG COLLECTIBLES

In 1990, Mark Dadio founded Nutmeg Collectibles, a company that established a symbiotic relationship with Matchbox by arranging to produce custom variations of Matchbox number 32 Modified Racer, introduced in 1988, and number 34 Sprint Racer, introduced in 1990. Seventeen variations of the Modified Racer were produced by Nutmeg, while 13 variations of the Sprint Racer were produced.

NUTMEG MODIFIED RACER

v.1 red body, black interior, chrome exhausts, "Mike 15" $6
v.2 yellow body, green interior, chrome exhausts, "44 Reggie/Magnum Oils" $6
v.3 white body, red interior, chrome exhausts, "U2 Jamie" $6
v.4 white body, black interior, chrome exhausts, "1 Tony/Universal Joint Sales" $6
v.5 red body, red interior, black exhausts, "36" & stripes $6
v.6 red body, orange-yellow interior, black exhausts, "12" & stripes $6
v.7 white & blue body, blue interior, black exhausts, "ADAP 15". $6
v.8 white body, translucent blue interior, black exhausts, "41" & stripes $6
v.9 red body, red interior, chrome exhausts, "38 Jerry Cook" . . . $6
v.10 white body, orange interior, chrome exhausts, "Maynard Troyer" $6
v.11 dark blue body, black interior, chrome exhausts, "3 Ron Bouchard" $6
v.12 orange-yellow body, green interior, chrome exhausts, "4 Bugs" $6
v.13 red body, red interior, chrome exhausts, "42 Jamie Tomaino" $6

v.14 orange-yellow body, red interior, chrome exhausts, "4 Satch Wirley" $6
v.15 dark blue body, blue interior, chrome exhausts, "3 Doug Heveron" $6
v.16 black body, black interior, chrome exhausts, "21 George Kent" $6
v.17 dark blue body, black interior, black exhausts, "12" $6
v.18 blue body, black interior, chrome exhausts, "3 Mike McLaughlin" $8

NUTMEG SPRINT RACER

v.1 red body, white driver, blue "Williams 5M" $6
v.2 red body, white driver, white "Williams 5M" $85
v.3 black body, white driver, "TMC 1" $6
v.4 white body, red driver, "Schnee 8D" $6
v.5 yellow body, white driver, "Ben Cook & Sons 33x" $6
v.6 blue body, white driver, "Ben Allen 1a" $6
v.7 red body, white driver, "7 Joe Gaerte" $6
v.8 red body, white driver, "4 Gambler" $6
v.9 yellow body, white driver, "17 F&G Classics East" $6
v.10 yellow body, white driver, "7c Vivarin- D. Blaney" $6
v.11 powder blue body, white driver, "69 Schnee- D. Krietz" . . . $6
v.12 black body, white driver, "49 Doug Wolfgang" $6

NZG

Nurnberger Zinzdruckgussmodelle, otherwise known as NZG, began in Nurnburg, Germany, in 1968, by producing an assortment of construction vehicles. The company stuck with the heavy equipment theme until 1984, when a series of 1:43 scale Porsches and 1:35 scale Mercedes-Benz models were introduced, along with a few trucks and buses. A large assortment of current models is available from Toys for Collectors and other fine toy and model dealers. According to an undated but recent NZG catalog, NZG was for some time distributed by Schuco Toy Co., Inc., New York, likely a division of Schuco of Germany. Latest information indicates NZG is still in business, with new models currently being produced.

126 CAT 627 Scraper, 1:50 . . . . $48
149 Grove RT 760 Rough Terrain Crane, 1:50 . . . . $49
160 CAT 245 Excavator, 1:50 . . . . $45
167 CAT 988B Wheel Loader, 1:50 . . . . $55
194 Krupp S400 Mining Excavator, 1:50 . . . . $75
205 CAT D4E Track Dozer, 1:50 . . . . $27
231 Demag Paver, 1:50 . . . . $35
235 Zeppelin 908 Wheel Loader, 1:50 . . . . $19
237 CAT 966F Wheel Loader, 1:50 . . . . $39
237.06 CAT 966F Wheel Loader, Silver Anniversary Edition, 1:50. $49
257 Zeppelin 206 Track Loader, 1:50 . . . . $42
285.1L CAT 428 Backhoe, silver anniversary edition, 1:50 . . . . $31
285.2 CAT 416B Backhoe Loader, 1:50 . . . . $31
293 Scania City Bus CN112, 1:50 . . . . $42
298 CAT D9N Track Dozer, 1:50 . . . . $49
299 CAT PR450 Pavement Profilier, 1:50 . . . . $45
300 Kramer Tremo Utility Truck, 1:35 . . . . $19
310F Fiat Ducato Fire Dept. Van, 1:43 . . . . $22
311 Volvo Articulated Bus, 1:50 . . . . $52
316 B&T High Rise Forklift, 1:25 . . . . $35
321.2 Lift Truck "Bulli" $19

327 Porsche 911 Speedster, 1:43 . . . . $24
332 O&K Grader F 156A, 1:50 . . . . $42
357 Demag H 485 S Loader, 1:50 . . . . $169
359 Michigan L150 Wheel Loader, 1:50 . . . . $52
359 Volvo VME L150 Wheel Loader with attachments, 1:50 . . . $52
361 Mercedes 0404 Touring Bus, 1:43 . . . . $49
363 Porsche 968 Coupe $24
364 Porsche 968 Cabriolet, 1:43 . . . . $24
365 Volvo VME BM A25 Dumper, 1:50 . . . . $37
366 CAT 994 Wheel Loader, 1:50 . . . . $159
367 CAT 325L Excavator, 1:50 . . . . $42
370 DemagAutomatic Remote Control Lift, 1:50 . . . . $25
371 Mercedes Unimog, 1:43 . . . . $29
371.1 Mercedes Unimog, 1:50 . . . . $29
371.3 Mercedes Unimog UN, 1:50 . . . . $32
373 Saris Trailer $15
374 Grove Scissor Lift, 1:50 . . . . $29
376 CAT 966F Wood Loader, 1:50 . . . . $45
377 CAT 245 with hydraulic hammer, 1:50 . . . . $59
378 CAT 416 Backhoe with Hammer, 1:50 . . . . $37
378.1 Cat 428 Backhoe with Hammer, 1:50 . . . . $39
379 Wirtgen Pavement Profiler, 1:50 . . . . $49
380 Grove TM9120 Truck Crane, 1:50 . . . . $119
385 Vogele 1800 Paver, 1:50 . . . . $47
386 CAT D7 Dozer WW II, 1:50 . . . . $129
387 CAT 16G Grader, 1:50 . . . . $79
389 Kaelble Wheel Loader SJ14B, 1:50 . . . . $49
390 Porsche 911, 1:43 . . . . $24
392 Sennebogen 613M Telecrane, 1:50 . . . . $42
393 Porsche 911 C2/4 Turbo, 1:43 . . . . $24

ODDZON

Reportedly a brand of diecast toys from Russ Berrie, the stuffed toy company, this is another unusual brand of which nothing is so far known.

OGDI TOYS OF YESTERDAY

Collecting Toys magazine (Kalmbach Publishing, Waukesha, Wisconsin) featured an article in its August 1995 issue on John Hodges' Toys of Yesterday, toy cars modeled after Dinky toys, but representative of vehicles Meccano planned to produce but didn't.

Hodges felt a loss when Dinky's British base Meccano Ltd. went out of business in 1979. So in his spare time, Hodges attempted to fill the void. His first model, produced in 1980, was so authentic of the Dinky styling that European model journals praised his work and the London Toy Museum purchased one for its collection. Since then, Hodges has produced a few other models, all reasonably priced and neatly boxed. Below is a list of models offered.

For more information, contact John Hodges, Toys of Yesterday, 50 Chiswick Village, London W4 3BY, England.

801 Triumph Dolomite, red, 1980 . . . . $35
812 Jouett Bradford Van
    v.1 Lyons Tea, green $35
    v.2 Unigate, white $35
    v.3 Esso, red $35
    v.4 Hovis Bread, yellow $35

    v.5 Walls' Ice Cream, light blue $35
    v.6 Ovaltine, orange $35
823 Jaguar XK150 Coupe, metallic blue $35
834 Ford Consul MKII Saloon, metallic red $35
845 1950 Jouett Javelin Saloon, red $35
856 1948 Ford Prefect, light green $35
907 1950s Daimler Conquest Sports Car, metallic burgundy . . . $35
—— 1930s Bugatti Roadster, planned for late 1995 . . . . $35

OLDCARS

Oldcars brand of Italy is so named for its first models of antique cars introduced in 1978. Their current line represents anything but old cars, consisting of modern buses, racing transporters, vans, fire trucks, and heavy equipment. Still the name remains, and the company keeps producing so many variations of its basic models that not even the owner of the company could list them all.

252 Fiat EU 175 Forklift, 1:28 . . . . $19
311 Fiat Military Command Car $19
520 Iveco Turbodaily Van $23
550 Iveco Ferrari F-1 Maintenance Van $25
560 Fiat-Ferrari Racing Car Transporter, 1959 . . . . $69
560-3 Fiat-Ferrari Racing Car Transporter with three Brumm Ferrari
    models, 1959 . . . . $120
601 Fiat-Allis dozer, closed cab, 1:50 . . . . $49
603 Rossi Wheel Loader, 1:50 . . . . $45
605 Fiat-Allis Wood Loader, 1:50 . . . . $49
606 Fiat-Allis Dozer, open cab, 1:50 . . . . $49
608 Fiat-Allis Wheel Loader, 1:50 . . . . $55
609 Fiat-Allis Compactor, 1:50 . . . . $49
610 Fiat-Allis FE45 Excavator with rubber treads, 1:50 . . . . . $55
690 Iveco Orlandi Touring Bus $49
700 Iveco Turbo City Bus $55
702 Fiat 360hp Dump Truck $49
704 Iveco Truck with Flat Bed Trailer, 1:43 . . . . $49
710 Iveco Padane Touring Bus $55
720 Iveco Padane Two-Tone Touring Bus $59
770-2 Iveco Ferrari Transporter, 1980 . . . . $79
    with two F-1 Ferrari models $113
730 Iveco Orlandi Euroclass Touring Bus $55
900 Fiat-Allis truck and Trailer with Wheel Loader $95
1200 Scania Benneton F-1 Race Car Transporter $89
85021 Brown-Moxy Articulated Dump Truck, 1:50 . . . . $55
85022 Komatsu Articulated Dump Truck, 1:50 . . . . $59

OMEGA

One model is known of this brand, thanks to Russell Alameda of San Jose, California.

Opel Sedan, 4 door, red with pull-back action, 1:43 . . . . $10

ONYX (ALSO SEE VITESSE, TROFEU, VICTORIA)

Onyx is a line of race cars offered by Vitesse of Portugal. Other lines offered by Vitesse include Victoria, an excellent line of 1:43 scale military models, and the Trofeu series of rally cars. All Onyx models are currently available. Below is a brief sampling.

Bennetton Ford . . . . $40 – 55
Ferrari 641 . . . . $40 – 55

Ford Lotus 107 . . . . $40 – 55
Jordan 194 . . . . $40 – 55
McLaren Honda . . . . $40 – 55
Tyrell Honda . . . . $40 – 55
Williams Renault. . . . . $40 – 55

ORIGINAL OMNIBUS CO.

Original Omnibus Co. is a new British producer of 1:76 scale diecast models, distributed by Corgi Collectibles.
Dennis Dart Eastern National Bus. . . . . npa
Optare Delta of Trent Bus, 4,000 made. . . . . npa
Bedford OBHants & Dorset with roof quarterlights, 3,800 made   npa

OTO

Oto models are 1:43 diecast reissues of Pilen models from Spain.
OT001 Mercedes 250C Coupe. $14
OT002 Seat-Fiat 600 saloon $11
OT003 Mini Cooper $14
OT003M Mini Cooper MC Rally $14
OT004 Opel Manta A, 5 colors $14
OT005 Citroën SM, 2 colors $14
OT007 Chevrolet Astro Show Car $14
OT008 Ferrari 512 Show Car. $12
OT009 Porsche 917 . . . . $14
OT010 Porsche Carrera 6 . . . . $14
OT011 Vauxhall SRV Show Car $12
OT012 Ferrari P5 Show Car $12
OT013 Stratos Bertone Show Car $12
OT014 Adams Brothers Probe Show Car $12
OT015 VW buggy $11
OT016 Seat-Fiat 850 Spyder $14
OT017 Seat-Fiat 127, 4 colors. $8
OT018 Intermeccanica Indra show car $8

OXFORD DIE-CAST COMPANY

These Lledo look-alikes can fool even the expert at first glance. Discovered by Patti Macreading, wife of *Mobilia* magazine writer Mark Macreading, the quality is equal to Lledo, but is made by Oxford Die-Cast of England. The model and the company was unknown until Patti discovered it on a trip to Zeb's Country Store in North Conway, New Hampshire.
Model T (?) Delivery Truck, "Zeb's Country Store" on sides . $15 – 18

PARADISE GARAGE

Paradise Garage represents 1:43 diecast models made in China for the Australian market. The brand is offered almost exclusively from Modelauto of Leeds, England.
PG001 Holden VR Commodore Acclaim 1994, 2 colors. $42

PARAGON MODELS & ART

Paragon Models & Art is yet another new arrival in the diecast scale model field. Produced in Spain for the Florida-based company, the first Paragon model appears to be a 1950 Chevy Panel Truck in 1:18 scale. Paragon Models & Art, 1431B S.E. 10th St., Cape Coral, FL 33990. 941-458-0024.

1950 Chevrolet Panel Truck, cream medium, forester green, or mariner blue, 1:18 . . . . npa

PAST-TIME HOBBIES (SEE PTH)

PATHFINDER

Pathfinder is a series of excellent white metal models from England. Typical subjects are British cars of the 50s. Production of each casting is reportedly limited, so there is a base of avid collectors who snap up most of the new issues. No. 18, introduced maybe a year ago, is a Jowett Jupiter roadster, but they've made saloons and estates (sedans and wagons) too.

PAUL'S MODEL ART/MINICHAMPS
(ALSO SEE QUARTZO, UT)

Paul's Model Art of Portugal produces Max Models, Minichamps, Microchamps, and Quartzo models. UT makes many of the 1:18 scale models for Paul's Model Art, as well as independently, and a list of their offerings can be found under their own listing.

1:18 SCALE MODELS FROM PAUL'S MODEL ART/MINICHAMPS
510 180002 Benetton Ford B193, 1:18. . . . . $50
510 931808 Benetton B194, Schumacher '94, 1:18 . . . . $40
530 931808 McLaren MP4/8, Senna '93, 1:18 . . . . $40
530 931817 McLaren MP4/8, Hakkinen '93, 1:18 . . . . $30
PZ3 1996 BMW Z-3 Roadster, Bond blue. . . . . $30 – 40
PZ3 1996 BMW Z-3 Roadster, red . . . . $28 – 35

UT 1:24 SCALE MODELS
240 000100 Mercedes-Benz 770K Kaiser Wilhelm II $149
240 000200 Mercedes-Benz SSKL Mille Miglia, "Caracciola" . . $149
240 000300 Mercedes-Benz 300SLR LeMans, 1955, "Fangio" . . $149
240 000310 Mercedes-Benz 300SLR Coupe, "Ulenhaut" $149
240 000320 Mercedes-Benz 300SLR Mille Miglia, "Moss-Jenk". $149
240 000500 Karmann Ghia coupe, 1970 . . . . $49
240 000501 Karmann Ghia cabriolet, top down. $49
240 001113 BMW R 1100 RS Touring Motorcycle, half fairing. . $39
240 001146 BMW R 1100 RS Touring Motorcycle, full fairing . . $39

1:43 SCALE MINICHAMPS/MAX MODELS
430 000121 Alfa Romeo German Championship, #8, Larini . . . $34
430 000122 Alfa Romeo German Championship, #14, Danner . $34
430 000222 Jaguar XJ220 . . . . $27
430 000500 VW Karmann Ghia coupe. $27
430 000503 VW Karmann Ghia cabriolet, top down. $27
430 000506 VW Karmann Ghia cabriolet, top up $27
430 001005 Sauber Mercedes C-9, #61. . . . . $32
430 001101 Sauber Mercedes C-11, #1. . . . . $32
430 002110 BMW 1600 sedan, 1966 – 1975 . . . . $27
430 002230 BMW M-3 coupe, 1992. . . . . $27
430 002240 BMW 501-502 sedan, 1954 – 1961. . . . . $27
430 002250 BMW 507 cabriolet, 1956 – 1959. . . . . $27
430 002252 BMW 507 cabriolet, top up, 1956 – 1959. . . . . $27
430 002253 BMW 507 hardtop, 1956 – 1959. . . . . $27
430 002300 BMW E-1 Electromobile, 1993. . . . . $27
430 002370 BMW 700 sedan, 1960 – 1961. . . . . $27
430 003100 Mercedes-Benz 190 EVO 2 Street version $27
430 003200 Mercedes-Benz W124 sedan, 1992 (250D, 300E, 300D). $27
430 003210 Mercedes-Benz C class sedan, 1993 (180, 220, 280). $27

430 003220 Mercedes-Benz W123 sedan, 1975 – 1985 (200D, 230E, 280E) $27

430 003221 Mercedes-Benz W123 wagon, 1980 – 1985 (200T, 230TE, 280TE) $27

430 003222 Mercedes-Benz W123 coupe, 1977 – 1985 ((230CE, 280CE, 300CD) $27

430 003223 Mercedes-Benz 280SL cabriolet, top down, 1968 – 1971. . . . . $27

430 003224 Mercedes-Benz 280SL cabriolet, top up, 1968 – 1971. $27

430 003230 Mercedes-Benz 400E sedan, 1992 . . . . $27

430 003233 Mercedes-Benz 300S cabriolet, top down, 1951 – 1958. . . . . $27

430 003234 Mercedes-Benz 300S cabriolet, top up, 1951 – 1958. $27

430 003240 Mercedes-Benz 500E sedan, 1992 . . . . $27

430 003260 Mercedes-Benz 600SEC coupe, 1992 . . . . $27

430 003300 Mercedes-Benz T-Wagon (230TE, 250TD, 300TE, 300TD). $27

430 003301 Mercedes-Benz 300SL "Caracciola" $32

430 003342 Mercedes-Benz 450SLC, 1972 – 1980. . . . . $27

430 003350 Mercedes-Benz E-Class sedan, 1994 . . . . $27

430 003350 Mercedes-Benz 300SL Spyder $32

430 003352 Mercedes-Benz E-Class coupe, 1994 . . . . $27

430 003353 Mercedes-Benz E-Class cabriolet, 1994 . . . . $27

430 003354 Mercedes-Benz E-Class wagon, 1994. . . . . $27

430 003400 Mercedes-Benz W124 coupe (230CE, 300CE, 300CE-24) . $27

430 003510 Mercedes-Benz W124 convertible (300CE-24) $27

430 004000 Opel Omega 3000 sedan $27

430 004320 Opel Record P1 Caravan, 1958 – 1960. . . . . $27

430 004330 Opel Kapitan sedan, 1951 – 53 . . . . $27

430 005203 VW 1200 cabriolet, 1951 – 1952 . . . . $27

430 005210 VW 1200 Bug, oval window, 1953 – 1957 . . . . $27

430 005213 VW Hebmueller cabriolet, top down, 1949 – 1950. $27

430 005214 VW Hebmueller cabriolet, top up, 1949 – 1950 . . . $27

430 005230 VW window van, 25 windows $27

430 006001 Porsche Cup "Cald." $34

430 006008 Porsche Cup, "Land" $34

430 006009 Porsche Cup, "1993, #9. . . . . $34

430 006202 Porsche 911 coupe, 1978 . . . . $27

430 006212 Porsche 911 Carrera 2-4 . . . . $27

430 006232 Porsche 356 C coupe $27

430 006300 Porsche 993 coupe. $27

430 006303 Porsche 993 cabriolet $27

430 006313 Porsche Boxster, 1993 . . . . $27

430 007240 Ferrari 456 GT 2+2, 1992 . . . . $27

430 007250 Ferrari 512 TR, 1992. . . . . $27

430 008200 Ford Mondeo 4 door wagon. $27

430 008210 Ford Mondeo 5 door sedan $27

430 022102 BMW 1600 Sedan, 1966 – 1975 . . . . $28

430 023002 BMW E1 Electromobile concept car, 1994, 1:43 . . . $28

430 063130 Porsche Boxster, 1993, 1:43 . . . . $30

432 003330 Mercedes-Benz 300 SL Spyder, 1:43 . . . . $34

520 931805 1993 Ford Indy, Newman/Haas/Andretti, 1:43 . . . . $20

1:64 Scale Models from Paul's Model Art/Microchamps

520 936405 1993 Ford Indy, Newman/Haas/Andretti, 1:64 . . . . . $8

PAYA

Spain is home to the Paya brand of diecast toys, some based on Matchbox models.

PEACHSTATE MUSCLE CAR COLLECTIBLES CLUB

A recent magazine ad states, "Peachstate Muscle Car Collectibles Club offers limited edition production quantities of only 2,500 cars per production run of quality diecast 60s and 70s era muscle car replicas. These 1:18 scale beauties are produced exclusively for Peachstate by The Ertl Company and will not be available elsewhere. In addition, each car includes a serialized certificate." Their assortment also includes 50s models. Peachstate Muscle Car Collectibles Club, PO Box 1537, Winder, GA 30680. 1-800-536-1637 or 1-770-307-1042, fax 1-770—867-0786.

1971 Buick GSX, stratomist blue. $38

1955 Chevrolet BelAir, gold. $38

1970 Chevrolet Chevelle 454 SS $38

1963 Chevrolet Corvette, saddle tan $38

1970 Chevrolet El Camino, forest green $38

Dodge Daytona, blue. $38

Ford Boss 429 Mustang, candy apple red $38

1969 Ford Mustang Shelby GT-500 . . . . $38

1969 Plymouth Road Runner, red $38

1969 Pontiac GTO, black $38

Pontiac Trans Am, black. $38

1965 Shelby Cobra, silver. $38

PEPE

Pepe has produced miniature models of Opels, Volkswagens, Renaults, Fiats, and others, in 1:25 and 1:43 scale. Below is an assortment.

1:25 SCALE

15 Opel Fire Pumper Truck $16

16 Opel Tow Truck $16

17 Opel Fire Ladder Truck $16

18 Volkswagen Pickup Plit Window $16

26 Volkswagen Beetle Fire Chief $16

32 Renault 5 Police $16

33 Renault 5 Ambulance $16

34 Renault 5 Fire $16

35 Renault 5 Taxi. $16

37 Austin Mini Ambulance $16

45 Cooper F1 Racer $16

46 Lotus F1 Racer $16

48 Fiat 692 Mixer $16

50 Fiat 692 Refrigerator Van $16

51 Fiat 692 Stake Truck $16

52 Jeep CJ2 Army. $16

1:43 SCALE

41 Opel Rekord Ambulance $16

42 Saviem Dump Truck $16

43 1957 Opel Wagon $16

PILEN (SEE AUTO PILEN)

PLAYART

Playart of Hong Kong has produced a wonderful array of toy vehicles. It is a wonder they are not more popular, but it is likely due to the heavy competition in the U.S. market. Playart toys have been marketed and packaged under many other names, most notably Sears Roadmates and Model

Power, but the models themselves prominently display the Playart logo on the base, making identification easy and unmistakable. Below is the most comprehensive list I could compile, thanks to purchases of Sears Roadmates when they were offered in 1986 for 89¢ or less, as well as listings from Diecast Miniatures and other sources.

The charm and quality of Playart toys make them worth keeping as collectibles. Their current value is still low, since most collectors are unaware of them. It is uncommon to find very many of them at toy shows or other second-market sources. According to Dave Weber of Warrington, Pennsylvania, Playart at one time produced a series of models called Charmerz for New York distributor Charles Merzbach. Alex Lakhtman reports that Playart models also were sold in Woolworth's and under the name "Peelers." Fastwheels is another name associated with Playart.

American LaFrance Fire Ladder Truck, 1:87 . . . . $10
American LaFrance Fire Snorkel Truck, 1:87 . . . . $8

Chevrolet Camaro Convertible, top up, 1:18 . . . . $24
Chevrolet 1967 Camaro, 1:64 . . . . $5
Chevrolet 1977 Camaro Z28, 1:64 . . . . $4
Chevrolet Caprice Fire Chief, 1:72 . . . . $4

Chevrolet Caprice Police Car, black & white, 1:72, Roadmates #7232, $5

Chevrolet Caprice Yellow Cab Taxi, 1:72, Roadmates #7217, $5

Chevrolet Blazer, silver, 1:72, Roadmates #7242, $3

Chevrolet Blazer Highway Patrol, black & white, 1:72, Roadmates #7242H, $3

Chevrolet Corvette Stingray, 1:64, $6

Chevrolet Caprice Classic, metallic purple, 1:72, Roadmates #7214, $5

Combine Harvester, blue, Roadmates #7166, $3

DeTomaso Pantera, 1:64 . . . . $3

Fiat X 1/9, 1:64 . . . . $4

Dodge Challenger, red with black roof, 1:72, Roadmates #7178, $4

Ford Box Truck "7-Up," 1:120, Roadmates #7260U, $6

Dodge Omni 024, metallic green, 1:67, Roadmates #7202, $4

Dodge Paramedic, 1:64 . . . . $4
Douglas DC-10 "American Airlines" $4

Ford Capri, 1:64 . . . . $4
Ford 1966 Mustang Convertible
    v.1 lime green $4
    v.2 red $4
1969 Mustang hardtop coupe $6
Helicopter "Air Sea Rescue" $4
Helicopter "Coke" $4
Helicopter "Fire" $4
Hyster 70 Forklift, 1:64 . . . . $4
Javelin SST, 1:64 . . . . $4
Jeep CJ U.S. Mail, 1:64 . . . . $6
Lamborghini Countach LP500S, 1:67, red, Roadmates #7246 . . . $2
Lamborghini Silhouette, 1:64 . . . . $4

Farm Tractor with Plow, 1:72, $5

Lancia Stratos, 1:64, Roadmates #7259, $2

London Bus, 1:100 . . . . $4
Lotus Esprit, 1:64 . . . . $4
Mazda Pickup Truck, 1:64 . . . . $4
Opel GT, 1:64 . . . . $4
Rolls Royce Silver Cloud, 1:64 . . . . $4
Scania Bus "AVIS Courtesy Bus," 1:87 . . . . $10
Toyota Celica, 1:64 . . . . $4
Volvo 164E Station Wagon, lime green $5
Volvo 166, 1:64 . . . . $4
Man from U.N.C.L.E. Thrushbuster Car $15

PLAYART FASTWHEELS

Dump Truck, red cab, orange tipper $8
7102 Porsche Carrera 910 . . . . $8
7103 Thunderbird, purple $8

Ford Box Truck "Pepsi-Cola," 1:120, Roadmates #7260P, $6

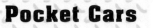

7103 Thunderbird, beige $8
7104 Opal GT, light met. brown. $8
7104 Opal GT, white $8
7106 Chevrolet Corvette Stingray Mako Shark
   v.1 purple $8
   v.2 teal blue. $8
7108 Lamborghini Miura, dark green $8
7109 Chevy Camaro SS, blue $8
7109 Chevy Camaro SS, yellow $8
7110 AMX 390, red $8
7111 Jensen FF, pink-beige $8
7112 Alfa Romeo P33, red $8
7113 Cabrio Bertone, green $8
7114 Mercedes Benz C111, dark met. red-purple. $8
7115 Cadillac El Dorado, brown. $8
7117 Toyota, brown. $8
7118 Ford Fire Chief Station Wagon, red. $8
7120 Ford Mustang GT $8
7122 Toyota 2000 GT, blue $8
7123 Jaguar E Type 2+2, green. $8
7124 VW Bug, red $8
7126 Cement Mixer, blue, red barrel. $8
7128 Dump Truck, brown-purple cab, orange tipper. $8
7129 Wrecker Truck $8
7132 Ford Police Car, white $8
7135 BMW 2002, purple. $8
7152 Honda 2GS, yellow-green $8
7155 Ford Cortina GXL, light green $8
7157 Javelin SST, green $8

Playing Mantis (see Johnny Lightnings)

Play Power

The Play Power models listed are probably made in Japan.

Play Power Airplanes

E/T Mk.2 "Patrol of France," red/white/blue, 2¾" $2
McDonnell-Douglas F-16 "USAF Thunderbirds," red/white/blue, 2¾" $2
McDonnell-Douglas F-15 "USAF Bicentennial," red/white/blue, 2¾" $2
McDonnell-Douglas AV-8A "Red Arrows," red/white/blue, 2¾" . $2
McDonnell-Douglas F-18 "USAF Blue Angels," blue/yellow, 2¾. $2

Play Power Vehicles

BMW 2-door Sedan Police Car, white/yellow/black, 2¾". $2
Chevrolet Pickup Truck "Western Forest Service," bright pink, 3". $2
Chevrolet Forest Service Tow Truck, bright green/yellow, 3⅓" . $2
Chevrolet Van Ambulance, white/red/black, 2⅝" $2
Hino Snorkel Fire Engine, red/white, 3¼". $3

Playskool

Playskool has produced many types of preschool toys for decades, but only for a short time in the early 80s did the company market diecast toys in a series of heavy one-piece vehicles driven by Sesame Street characters. The most common one is Oscar The Grouch driving his garbage truck. Each model is larger than the average diecast toy vehicle, about 2 to 2½" tall and 3" long. Popular at the time but rare now, each model is worth about $6 – 8.

Playtrucks

Two examples of Playtrucks models from Greece are represented below.

Caterpillar Traxcavator, #22, 1:43 . . . . $16
Scania 6x4 Cement Truck, #20, 1:43 . . . . $16

PM

Pressomeccanica, or PM, models of Milan, Italy, were produced in the post-war 1940s. Nine models are known to exist. The actual name of the company is even longer — Pressofusione Meccanica.

O.M. Taurus Covered Truck, 1:43 . . . . $75 – 125
O.M. Taurus Dump Truck, 1:43. . . . . $75 – 125
O.M. Taurus Fire Truck, 1:43. $75 – 125
O.M. Taurus Open Truck, 1:43 . . . . $75 – 125
O.M. Taurus Street Sweeper, 1:43 . . . . $75 – 125
O.M. Taurus Tank Truck with Trailer, 1:43. . . . . $175 – 200
O.M. Taurus Wrecker, 1:43 . . . . $75 – 125
Lancia Ardea Ambulance, white with red cross decals, 1:40 . $75 – 125
Lancia Ardea Fire Van, 1:40. . . . . $75 – 125
Lancia Ardea Loudspeaker Van, 1:40 . . . . $75 – 125
Lancia Ardea Van, 1:40 . . . . $75 – 125
Streamlined Race Car . . . . $600 – 750

Pocher

1:8 Scale

Pocher (pronounced Po-share) Prestige series 1:8 scale diecast metal car kits are exceptional in accuracy and detail… if you can afford one. Retailing for $699 from Model Expo, Inc., Italian made Pochers are top of the line in price, scale, quality, and detail. The reason for the high price becomes obvious when you realize these models measure 19 inches long and contain over 2,000 parts! Each of these sleek statements of status is a streamlined rolling work of art, representing the ultimate automotive icon of its era.

K74 1935 Mercedes-Benz 500K/AK Cabriolet, black. $750
K75 1934 Rolls-Royce Phantom II Torpedo Cabriolet $750
K76 1933 Bugatti 50T, black & yellow. $750
K82 Mercedes-Benz 540K Cabriolet Special, white. $750
K83 1933 Rolls-Royce Ambassador, green. $750
K84 1933 Bugatti 50T, blue & silver $750
K86 1932 Bugatti 50T Suprafile, black & red $750

1:43 Scale

While the 1:8 scale models may be too expensive, the smaller 1:43 scale Pocher models listed below, while rare, may be had for somewhat less.

Fiat 124 . . . . $125
Fiat 850 . . . . $125

Poclain

Poclain is best-known as the French heavy equipment manufacturer. Made mainly by Bourbon of France around 1973 and sold as promotional models, Poclain's assortment of plastic miniatures does not qualify as diecast, so they are not listed here, but current estimates put their value around $25 – 35 each.

Pocket Cars (see Tomica)

POCKETOYS (SEE BRIMTOY)

POLE POSITION COLLECTIBLES

Pole Position Collectibles are a recent entry into the diecast racing collectibles arena. Resembling Racing Champions, they are made in China for Mountain Service International of Bristol, Virginia. These approximately 1:64 scale models authentically re-create the markings of actual stock cars. The colorful, distinctive blisterpack is designed by Gibson & Lane Graphic Designs, as indicated on the package. Models sell for $1 – 2 each. For more information, you may wish to write or call the manufacturer: Pole Position Collectibles, Mountain Service International, Inc., 4710 Lee Highway, Bristol, VA 24201. 703-669-4700

POLISTIL (SEE POLITOYS)

POLITOYS/POLISTIL

Politoys M of Italy began in 1960 as a manufacturer of plastic 1:41 scale models. In 1965, Politoys produced their first series of higher-quality diecast vehicles. Because of the similarity of names between Politoys of Italy and Palitoys of Great Britain, the Politoys name was changed to Polistil around 1970. The Politoys/Polistil product line covers hundreds of models in a variety of scales, from 1:18 scale to 1:64. Since other books devote many pages to this brand, this book showcases just a few representative models. Reissues and new Polistil models have most recently been produced by McGregor of Mexico.

Bertone Ford Mustang 2+2, #549, 1:43, 1969 . . . . $30
Bertone Corvair, #551, 1:43, 1968 . . . . $30
DeTomaso Pantera, 1:43, c. 1972 . . . . $30

Ferrari P4, #574, 1:43, 1968, $30

Ford Escort, 1:64, $10

Ford Lola GT, 1:43, c. 1972 . . . . $30
Oldsmobile Toronado, #567, 1:43, 1970 . . . . $60
Opel Diplomat, #521, c. 1972 . . . . $40
Osi 1200 Coupe, #533, 1:43, c. 1972 . . . . $35
Samurai, #580, 1:43, 1970 . . . . $25

POLL

One Poll model, made of tin, is offered by Diecast Miniatures.
Gravel Loader, 24" $65

PP MODELS

PP models are 1:43 scale miniatures from England.
Jaguar SS100 Roadster $40
Morris 1000 4-door Sedan $40
Morris 1000 Convertible $40
Triumph Spitfire $40
Daimler SP250 Roadster $40
Jensen 541 Coupe $40
1939 Studebaker Coupe $40

PRALINÉ

Busch/Praliné models are precisely exact 1:87 scale plastic models made in Germany. Of particular note is article 3452, a 1954 Cadillac Ambulance, exquisitely detailed and neatly packaged in a clear plastic display box. Walthers devotes seven pages of their catalog to this brand.
#3452 1954 Cadillac Ambulance, cream with chrome plastic trim, 1:87 . . . . $8 – 10

PRÄMETA

Five Prämeta models were produced in Germany in 1951. Sporting clockwork motors, they are made to 1:35 scale, except the Volkswagen, which was made to a larger scale. Prämetas feature cast, silver-painted windows.
Buick 405 Sedan, 5¾", 1:35 . . . . $325
Jaguar XK120 Coupe, 6", 1:35 . . . . $325
Mercedes-Benz 300 Sedan, 5¾", 1:35 . . . . $325
Opel Kapitan Sedan, 5¾", 1:35 . . . . $325
Volkswagen $400

PRECISION AUTOS

Precision Models are the result of a frustration of an Englishman, reportedly named John Day, who could not find replicas of the models he wanted so he started making his own. John Day is credited with bringing expensive handcrafting techniques on models costing thousands of dollars down to merely hundreds of dollars.

PRECISION MINIATURES

Harvey Goranson reports that Precision Miniatures, like Precision Autos, are white metal kits, a built-up range begun by Gene Parril when he owned Marque Products in the Los Angeles, California, area. The first models were Porsches, then Indy cars, Ferraris, and a Duesenberg were added. I suspect the Indy cars were planned IMRA kits, since these were 1:40 scale. I have a '57 Ferrari Testa Rossa (pontoon fender) from the Targa Florio race, and a '48 Novi

Indy racer, plus a kit of an Indy McLaren. The 70s Indy kits were extremely well cast and detailed, not for beginners.

"In 1982 or 83," Mr. Goranson reports, "I went to LA for a weekend because I got a crazy deal on a plane ticket. I visited Marque Products on a day when Gene was doing trial runs casting Hudson Hornets. It was fascinating watching the white metal castings being made. Gene later introduced other 50s American cars in the Precision range, plus the Laser and Mustang you list, then found his niche with the Motor City, Design Studio, and (lately) USA Models ranges."

1964½ Ford Mustang Convertible, red.	$80
1984 Chrysler Laser	$80

PRIDE LINES (ALSO SEE MANOIL)

Pride Lines Ltd. vehicles are diecast in the USA using original 60-year-old Manoil molds. (See Manoil.) Each Disney character is cast from the finest pewter and hand painted to perfection. All vehicles have rubber tires, two-piece metal construction, and baked enamel finish. Each model is approximately 4½ inches long. For more details, contact Pride Lines Ltd. (Manoil remakes), 651 West Hoffman Ave., Lindenhurst, NY 11757. Phone 516-225-0033, fax 516-225-0099.

DD-1 Donald Duck, red and blue.	$65
DD-2 Daisy Duck, baby blue and yellow	$65
GTT Goofy Wrecker, red	$65
MC-1 Mickey Mouse, yellow and purple	$65
MC-2 Mickey Mouse, pink and baby blue	$65
US-1 Scrooge McDuck, green and cream with 24 karat gold-plate trim	$75

PROCESS

Diecast Miniatures lists just one model from Process, a United States brand.

1961 Jaguar XKE Roadster, 1:43	$5

PROGETTO K

Progetto K of Italy offers a huge range of currently available 1:43 scale models. The largest selection is offered by Exoto Inc., 1040-F Hamilton Rd., Duarte, CA 91010, for $22 each, in its quarterly publication/catalog Exoto Tifosi, available for $5 from Exoto Inc.

To list this exhaustive selection would consume many pages. Suffice it to say that many models are produced in various liveries, which makes the selection broader. I will attempt to provide a reasonable representation of the product line. You will have to rely on Exoto for specific color and marking variations.

1968 Abarth 1000 Group 5	$23

1963 Alfa Romeo Giulia GT, $23

1965 Alfa Romeo Giulia GTA	$23
1967 Alfa Romeo Giulia GTA	$23
1968 Alfa Romeo Giulia GTA	$23
1958 Austin Healey Mk 1 "Frogeye" Convertible, top down	$23
1958 Austin Healey Mk 1 "Frogeye" Convertible, top up	$23
1952 Ferrari 166 MM	$23
1952 Ferrari 225 Coupe	$23
1952 Ferrari 225 S	$23
1952 Ferrari 250 MM	$23
1958 Ferrari TR	$23
Fiat 124 Spyder	$23
1965 Lancia Fulvia Coupe.	$23
1966 Lancia Fulvia HF Coupe.	$23
1959 Maserati T60/61 "Birdcage"	$23

PROTAR

One example of 1:9 scale diecast motorcycles from Protar is offered by Exoticar.

1991 Ducatti, red street or racing version	$35

PROVÉNCE MOULÁGE

Provénce Mouláge models are precision 1:43 scale resin kits of which a certain number are shipped to dealers as pre-assembled demo models. The majority are sold as kits, unassembled and unpainted. Finishing the model includes sanding and trimming to smooth the surface and remove excess material from windows, wheel wells, and other openings and edges. Prices below are for unfinished models in the original box.

1950 Buick 2-door Hardtop	$115
1950 Buick Station Wagon	$115
1949 Delahaye 173 4.5L LeMans	$52
1982 Camaro	$52
Facel 2-door Coupe	$65
Facel Facellia Coupe	$65
1975 Ferrari Daytona Luchard.	$52
1981 Ferrari Pininfarina	$52
1946 Ford 2-door Sedan	$115
1946 Ford Station Wagon	$115
1957 Jaguar D-Type LeMans	$52
1960 Jaguar 3.8L Sedan	$52
1963 Jaguar 3.8L Sedan	$52
1985 Jaguar XJR6.	$52
Volkswagen 1303 "Beetle" Convertible	$90

PTH MODELS

PTH (Past-Time Hobbies) Models of England produces a stunning assortment of 1:43 scale models new and old. Their latest offering (as of March 1997) is a pair of Dodge Viper GTS models in 1:43 scale, created for their US division. Order direct from PTH: Past-Time Hobbies, Inc., 9311 Ogden Ave., Brookfield, IL 60513, 708-485-4544.

3 1972 Chevrolet Camaro Z28 Coupe, metallic orange-yellow or white	$129
4 1970 Chevrolet Monte Carlo SS 454, red	$129
5 1982 Chevrolet Corvette, metallic brown-silver, "Collectors Edition"	$139
6 1995 Chevrolet Impala SS, black	$129

7 1960 Chevrolet Impala Sports Coupe, metallic orange-brown . $129
8 1934 Packard Model 1106 Coupe, deep blue $149
9 1934 Packard with vinyl roof, metallic green $149
17C 1958 Ford "Chicago Police" $129
Dodge Viper GTS Coupe, orange with black stripes, 1:43, 1997, 50
    made $145
Dodge Viper GTS Coupe, blue with white stripes, 1:43, 1997, 50
    made $150

QUARTER MILE (SEE GREAT AMERICAN DREAMCARS)

QUARTZO (ALSO SEE PAUL'S MODEL ART)

A division of Paul's Model Art, Quartzo focuses on 1:43 scale racing replicas. Here is just a sampling.
Chevrolet Lumina, #14 Terry LeBonte "Kelloggs" $25
Chevrolet Lumina, #41 Joe Nemechek, "Meineke" $25
1956 Ford Fairlane, NY Police Radar Unit $50
Ford, #27 Bill Elliott, "McDonald's" $25
Pontiac Grand Prix, #40 Frankie Kerr, "Dirt Devil" $25

QUIRALU

Now one of the most popular brands on the collector market, Quiralu was at one time a totally obscure French brand of diecast toys. Their current popularity is due in part to the re-issue of many of the original models as faithful reproductions. That alone wouldn't necessarily make them sell, but the real reason is for the recognition by collectors of the charm and quality of these fine toys. Reproductions can be purchased for a very reasonable price, while original models are quickly rising in value.

The original Quiralu brand was introduced in 1933 by a Mr. Quirin of Luxeuil, France. The combination of his name and the primary metal, aluminum, used in the production of these models provides the name derivation.

It wasn't until 1955 that the firm started producing 1:43 scale models. The latest of the original models were introduced in 1959, with production ceasing soon afterward.

QUIRALU ORIGINALS
1 Simca Trianon, 1955 . . . . $85
2 Simca Versailles, 1955 . . . . $85
3 Simca Regence, 1955 . . . . $85
4 Peugeot 403, single color with no plastic windows, 1956 . . . $85
5 Peugeot 403, two-tone, no plastic windows, 1956 . . . . $85
6 Peugeot 403, single color with plastic windows, 1956 . . . . . $95
7 Peugeot 403, two-tone with plastic windows, 1956 . . . . $95
8 Mercedes-Benz 300SL, single color, 1956 . . . . $125
9 Mercedes-Benz 300SL, two-tone, 1956 . . . . $125
10 Simca Marly Break Station Wagon, single color, 1957 . . . . . $85
11 Simca Marly Break Station Wagon, two-tone, 1957 . . . . $85
12 Simca Marly Ambulance, 1957 . . . . $120
13 Porsche Carrera, single color, 1957 . . . . $325
14 Porsche Carrera, two-tone, 1957 . . . . $325
15 Jaguar XK140, 1957 . . . . $120
16 Messerschmitt Auto-Scooter, 1958 . . . . $100
17 Rolls-Royce Silver Cloud, 1958 . . . . $120
18 Vespa 400 2CV, 1958 . . . . $85
19 BMW Velam Isetta Bubblecar $100
20 Renault Etoile Filante, with decals, 1958 . . . . $100

21 Renault Etoile Filante, no decals, 1958 . . . . $95
22 Peugeot D4A Van, red, 1958 . . . . $350
23 Peugeot D4A Van, yellow or green, 1958 . . . . $350
24 Peugeot D4A Army Ambulance, 1958 . . . . $375
25 Berliet GBO Covered Truck, 1959 . . . . $300
26 Berliet GBO Dump Truck, 1959 . . . . $300
27 Berliet GBO Covered Trailer, 1959 . . . . $125

QUIRALU REPRODUCTIONS
1 1956 Messerschmitt Auto-Scooter $39
2 Mercedes-Benz 300 SL $39
3 Peugeot 403 Sedan $39
4 Peugeot D4A Military Ambulance $39
5 Peugeot D4A Van, red $39
6 Peugeot D4A Van, white $39
7 Porsche 356 Coupe $39
9 1957 Rolls-Royce Silver Cloud $39
15 1958 BMW Isetta Velam Bubble Car $39
16 1958 Vespa 400 . . . . $39
17 1957 Jaguar XK140 . . . . $39
19 Rolls-Royce Silver Cloud . . . . $39 [006-06 and/or 006-07]
38 1960 Citroën ID19 Ambulance $39
39 1960 Citroën ID19 Station Wagon $39

R&M

Virtually nothing is known of this obscure brand. More information is appreciated.
Berta Racer, 2" $4
Cheboom Racer, 4" $4

R. W. (SEE ZISS)

RACE IMAGE COLLECTIBLES (SEE CORGI)

RACEWAY REPLICARS

Information provided by Russell Alameda indicates at least two models made under this brand.
Ford, #6 Mark Martin, "Valvoline," 1:24, limited edition of
    5,000 . . . . $300
Ford, #28 Davy Allison, "Havoline," 1:24, limited edition of
    5,000 . . . . $300

RACING CHAMPIONS

Racing Champions is a recent entry into the diecast toy market, started by Bob Dods and Boyd Meyer in Glenn Ellyn, Illinois, in 1989.

Racing Champions offers an assortment of models that specialize in race car and transporter replicas. Like most modern diecast toys, Racing Champions are manufactured in China and other Asian manufacturing centers. Miniature race car replicas are a collecting specialty in themselves, attracting a specialized group numbering in the thousands of collectors. Racing Champions offers race cars of all types, including NASCAR, NASCAR Craftsman Truck, NHRA, CART, World of Outlaws, and Indy Racing League, in 1:24, 1:64, and 1:144 scale. Thousands of models are offered representing every race driver in each category. The product line-up could fill a book. So this book will focus on Racing Champions' offerings with a somewhat broader appeal.

RACING CHAMPIONS MINT EDITIONS

The freshest series of diecast models to hit the market in years is Mint Edition from Racing Champions. Introduced in 1996, this series is comprised of classic cars past and present in 1:56 to 1:61 scale. Each model includes a display stand with a diecast emblem representing the hood or fender ornament.

MARCH 1996 ISSUES

#1 1996 Dodge Viper GTS, blue with white racing stripe . . . $5 – 6
#2 1950 Chevy 3100 Pickup, dark green . . . . $5 – 6
#3 1996 Pontiac Firebird, black. . . . . $5 – 6
#4 1957 Chevy Bel Air, red. . . . . $5 – 6
#5 1968 Ford Mustang, red. . . . . $5 – 6
#6 1956 Ford Thunderbird, yellow with white roof . . . . . . $5 – 6

APRIL 1996 ISSUES

#7 1950 Chevy 3100 Pickup, dark blue . . . . $5 – 6
#8 1996 Pontiac Firebird, metallic purple . . . . $5 – 6
#9 1957 Chevy Bel Air, turquoise . . . . $5 – 6
#10 1968 Ford Mustang, metallic gold. . . . . $5 – 6
#11 1956 Ford Thunderbird, pale lavender . . . . $5 – 6

#12 1996 Dodge Ram, blue, $5 – 6

MAY 1996 ISSUES

#13 1950 Chevy 3100 Pickup, red. $5 – 6
#14 1996 Pontiac Firebird, white. $5 – 6
#15 1957 Chevy Bel Air, tan . . . . $5 – 6
#16 1956 Ford Thunderbird, gray . . . . $5 – 6
#17 1996 Dodge Ram, red . . . . $5 – 6
#18 1964 Chevy Impala, blue . . . . $5 – 6

JUNE 1996 ISSUES

#19 1950 Chevy 3100 Pickup, brown . . . . $5 – 6
#20 1996 Pontiac Firebird, red . . . . $5 – 6
#21 1957 Chevy Bel Air, yellow . . . . $5 – 6
#22 1996 Dodge Ram, black. . . . . $5 – 6
#23 1964 Chevy Impala, silver gray. . . . . $5 – 6
#24 1996 Chevy Camaro, blue . . . . $5 – 6

JULY 1996 ISSUES

#25 1957 Chevy Bel Air, black . . . . $5 – 6
#26 1956 Ford Thunderbird, blue with black roof . . . . $5 – 6
#27 1996 Dodge Ram, white. . . . . $5 – 6
#28 1964 Chevy Impala, plum . . . . $5 – 6
#29 1996 Chevy Camaro, white. . . . . $5 – 6
#30 1997 Ford F-150, red . . . . $5 – 6

AUGUST 1996 ISSUES

#31 1957 Chevy Bel Air, bright teal. . . . . $5 – 6
#32 1956 Ford Thunderbird, pink. $5 – 6
#33 1996 Dodge Ram, silver . . . . $5 – 6

#34 1996 Chevy Camaro, black. . . . . $5 – 6
#35 1997 Ford F-150, white . . . . $5 – 6
#36 1963 Chevy Corvette, red. . . . . $5 – 6

SEPTEMBER 1996 ISSUES

#37 1956 Ford Thunderbird, red. . . . . $5 – 6
#38 1964 Chevy Impala, white . . . . $5 – 6
#39 1996 Chevy Camaro, green . . . . $5 – 6
#40 1996 Ford F-150, black. . . . . $5 – 6
#41 1963 Chevy Corvette, white. $5 – 6
#42 1969 Pontiac GTO "Judge," orange. . . . . $5 – 6

OCTOBER 1996 ISSUES

#43 1996 Pontiac Firebird, purple . . . . $5 – 6
#44 1968 Ford Mustang, metallic green . . . . $5 – 6
#45 1997 Ford F-150, white . . . . $5 – 6
#46 1963 Chevy Corvette, metallic dark blue. . . . . $5 – 6
#47 1969 Pontiac GTO "Judge," school bus yellow . . . . . . $5 – 6
#48 1956 Ford Victoria, light blue. . . . . $5 – 6

NOVEMBER 1996 ISSUES

#49 1996 Pontiac Firebird, dark teal, $5 – 6

#50 1968 Ford Mustang, mint green . . . . $5 – 6

#51 1963 Chevy Corvette, dark beige, $5 – 6

#52 1969 Pontiac GTO "Judge," black, $5 – 6

#53 1956 Ford Victoria, mint green, $5 – 6

#54 1970 Plymouth Superbird, red, $5 – 6

December 1996 Issues
#55 1968 Ford Mustang, black . . . . $5 – 6
#56 1963 Chevy Corvette, silver . . . . $5 – 6
#57 1969 Pontiac GTO "Judge," red . . . . $5 – 6
#58 1956 Ford Victoria, black . . . . $5 – 6
#59 1970 Plymouth Superbird, blue . . . . $5 – 6
#60 1970 Chevy Chevelle SS, dark blue . . . . $5 – 6

January 1997 Issues
#61 1950 Ford Coupe, maroon . . . . $5 – 6
#62 1997 Ford Mustang, red . . . . $5 – 6
#63 1969 Oldsmobile 442, crimson . . . . $5 – 6
#64 1932 Ford Coupe, black . . . . $5 – 6
#65 1949 Mercury, blue . . . . $5 – 6
#66 1935 Ford Pick Up, black . . . . $5 – 6

February 1997 Issues
#67 1970 Chevrolet Chevelle SS, red . . . . $5 – 6
#68 1969 Oldsmobile 442, white . . . . $5 – 6
#69 1932 Ford Coupe, blue . . . . $5 – 6
#70 1949 Mercury, gray . . . . $5 – 6
#71 1935 Ford Pick Up, red . . . . $5 – 6

#72 1955 Chevrolet Bel Air Convertible, light blue/blue, $5 – 6

March 1997 Issues
#73 1997 Ford Mustang, green . . . . $5 – 6

#74 1949 Mercury, black . . . . $5 – 6
#75 1935 Ford Pick Up, gray . . . . $5 – 6
#76 1955 Chevrolet Bel Air Convertible, light green/green . . $5 – 6
#77 1958 Chevrolet Impala, red . . . . $5 – 6
#78 1997 Chevrolet Corvette, yellow . . . . $5 – 6

April 1997 Issues
#79 1969 Oldsmobile 442, gold . . . . $5 – 6
#80 1950 Ford Coupe, blue . . . . $5 – 6
#81 1964.5 Ford Mustang, red . . . . $5 – 6
#82 1970 Chevrolet Chevelle, silver . . . . $5 – 6
#83 1997 Chevrolet Corvette, white . . . . $5 – 6
#84 1959 Cadillac Eldorado, pink . . . . $5 – 6

May 1997 Issues
#85 1949 Mercury, green . . . . $5 – 6
#86 1956 Ford Crown Victoria, black and red . . . . $5 – 6
#87 1997 Chevrolet Corvette or 1964.5 Ford Mustang, black . . $5 – 6
#88 1959 Cadillac Eldorado, red . . . . $5 – 6
#89 1957 Chevrolet Bel Air, blue . . . . $5 – 6
#90 1968 Plymouth Superbird, orange . . . . $5 – 6

June 1997 Issues
#91 1969 Pontiac GTO, red . . . . $5 – 6
#92 1959 Cadillac Eldorado, blue . . . . $5 – 6
#93 1957 Chevrolet Bel Air, black . . . . $5 – 6
#94 1968 Plymouth Superbird, red . . . . $5 – 6
#95 1950 Ford Coupe, gray . . . . $5 – 6
#96 1986 Chevrolet El Camino, white . . . . $5 – 6

July 1997 Issues
#97 1968 Plymouth, blue . . . . $5 – 6
#98 1950 Ford Coupe, silver . . . . $5 – 6
#99 1986 Chevrolet El Camino, silver . . . . $5 – 6
#100 1950 Chevy 3100, green . . . . $5 – 6
#101 1968 Chevy Camaro, black . . . . $5 – 6
#102 1958 Ford Edsel, pink . . . . $5 – 6

August 1997 Issues
#103 1957 Chevrolet Bel Air, green . . . . $5 – 6
#104 1958 Chevrolet Impala, black . . . . $5 – 6
#105 1986 Chevrolet El Camino, black . . . . $5 – 6
#106 1958 Ford Edsel, light blue . . . . $5 – 6
#107 1997 Chevrolet Corvette, red . . . . $5 – 6
#108 1997 Plymouth Prowler, purple . . . . $5 – 6

September 1997 Issues
#109 1968 Plymouth Superbird, gold . . . . $5 – 6
#110 1958 Ford Edsel, light blue . . . . $5 – 6
#111 1997 Plymouth Prowler, yellow . . . . $5 – 6
#112 1968 Chevrolet Camaro, red . . . . $5 – 6
#113 1949 Buick Riviera, blue . . . . $5 – 6
#114 1957 Ford Ranchero, light blue . . . . $5 – 6

October 1997 Issues
#115 1997 Plymouth Prowler, silver . . . . $5 – 6
#116 1968 Chevrolet Camaro, blue . . . . $5 – 6
#117 1949 Buick Riviera, yellow . . . . $5 – 6
#118 1958 Chevrolet Impala, brown . . . . $5 – 6
#119 1955 Chevrolet Bel Air, black . . . . $5 – 6
#120 1940 Ford Pick Up, red . . . . $5 – 6

November 1997 Issues
#121 1997 Ford Mustang, orange . . . . $5 – 6
#122 1949 Buick Riviera, dark green . . . . $5 – 6
#123 1932 Ford Coupe, gray . . . . $5 – 6

24 Lorraine-Dietrich 1911, 3⅝", 1965	$50
25 Panhard & Levassor 1895 Tonneau, 2½", 1965	$50
26 Delahaye 1904 Phaeton, 2⅞", 1965	$50
27 Audibert & Lavirotte 1898, 2¾", 1966	$50
28 Leon bollee 1911 Double Berline, 3¾", 1966	$50
29 S.P.A. 1912 Sports Sar, 4", 1966	$50
30 Amedee Bollee 1878 La Mancelle, 3⅝", 1966	$50
31 Luc Court 1901 Racing Car, 2¾", 1967	$50
32 Brasier 1908 Landaulet, 3¼", 1967	$50
33 Berliet 1910 Limousine, 3¾", 1968	$50
34 Mieusset 1903 Runabout, 2⅝", 1968	$50
35 De Dion-Bouton 1902 Racing Car, 3¼", 1968	$50
36 Lacroix De La Ville 1898, 3¼", 1968	$50
37 Delage 1932 Torpedo, 4⅝", 1968	$50
38 Mercedes 1927 SSK, 3⅞", 1969	$55

RAPIDE (SEE MODELAUTO)

RAPITOY

The most interesting model listed in the Rapitoy of Argentina assortment is a Mercedes Van with "Matchbox" livery. It is uncommon for one toymaker to promote another, but this seems to be a rare exception, unless Rapitoy put the Matchbox name on the model to convince the buyer into believing it was a Matchbox toy.

Mercedes Van, "Matchbox," 1:43	$17
Mercedes Van, "Ferrari," 1:43	$17
Mercedes Van, "Fargopan," 1:43	$17
Ford F-100 Pickup, 1:64	$4
Dodge Charger Show Car, 1:64	$4
Siva Spyder, 1:64	$4
Mercedes-Benz 350SL, top up, 1:64	$4

RA-RO

Of these 1:43 scale models, produced in 1948 from Milan, Italy, four are known. Such models are also identified as Cisitalia, Osca, and Stanguellini models. Obviously, easy identification requires more data.

Alfa Romeo, 3¾"	$75
Ferrari, 3⅞"	$75
Maserati, 3¾"	$75
Veritas, 3¾"	$75

RCCA (SEE RACING COLLECTABLES, INC.)

RCI (SEE RACING COLLECTABLES, INC.)

READER'S DIGEST

Along with various offers from *Reader's Digest* come special promotional gifts. Several of these gifts are miniature vintage cars, trucks, and airplanes. These are not generally available anywhere else, but Toy Liquidators has obtained a few of these sets for resale. The manufacturer is not indicated, but they are made in China.

COLLECTOR'S SET OF CLASSIC CAR MINIATURES ($3 PER SET)

Each package includes six boxed vintage 1:87 scale cars, numbered on base, in each set. Outer box has full-color photos of each model around the four sides.

Inside is a 5" x 7½" descriptive sheet that provides details of each model. While these models are inexpensively made and lacking in accuracy and detail, they are a charming set nonetheless. Made in Macau, copyright 1989, The Readers Digest Association Inc., Pleasantville, NY 10570.

No. 301 1901 Fiat Modello 8 CV	$1
No. 302 1906 Rolls-Royce	$1
No. 303 1907 Peugeot	$1
No. 304 1910 Ford Model T	$1
No. 305 1912 Simplex	$1
No. 306 1914 Vauxhall	$1

COLLECTOR'S SET OF CLASSIC TRUCKS ($5 PER SET)

A set of four mostly plastic vintage trucks about the size of Matchbox Models of Yesteryear (1:43 scale), packaged in two boxes inside of a larger box, with note included that says "Your FREE Gift... along with our thanks for ordering from *Reader's Digest.*" Made in China.

1910 Water Wagon	$1
1912 Model T Ambulance	$1
1912 Model T Tanker	$1
1918 Delivery Van	$1

COLLECTOR'S SET OF MINIATURE BIPLANES ($5 PER SET)

A set of four diecast miniature biplanes, each with 3" wingspan, individually boxed and packaged in a larger box describing each model. A note inside the box says "Your Free Gift ...along with our thanks for ordering *Reader's Digest* music." Made in China.

1918 British S.E. 5A	$1
1918 Curtiss JN-4D Jenny	$1
1928 Boeing PT-17 Kaydet	$1
1928 Boeing P-12E	$1

REAL CARS (SEE ESCI)

REAL WHEELS (SEE JA-RU)

REALTOY

In just the past year, Realtoy has made a dramatic appearance in the form of some exceptional playsets. Sets feature from 25 to 75 pieces which include trees, outdoor furniture, human and animal figures, as well as a great assortment of attractively decorated vehicles and a big playmat. Interestingly, many models bear a striking resemblance to Matchbox, Hot Wheels, and Majorettes, some even appearing to be outright knockoffs. Realtoy International Limited, Wah Fung Industrial Centre, Kwai Fung Rd., N.T. Hong Kong. Sets are available from Wal-Mart, Toys "R" Us, and other retailers.

REALISTIC

Realistic toys are cast aluminum vehicles manufactured in Freeport, Illinois, during the late 1940s and early 1950s. Some models used the original molds from Arcade cast-iron toys.

1939 Studebaker President Yellow Cab, 8¼"	$100
Greyhound Bus, Silversides, 8¾"	$100
Trailways Bus, 8¾"	$100

RECORD

Record models are listed as 1:43 scale vehicles for $55 each.

1 1952 Chevrolet 2-door Hardtop	$55
2 1952 Chevrolet Fastback Coupe	$55
3 1952 Chevrolet 4-door Sedan	$55
4 1952 Chevrolet Convertible	$55
99 Opel Ascona "Bastos"	$55
102 1984 Ferrari GTO	$55
103 Ferrari Testarossa	$55
111 Ferrari 365 GTB	$55

REDBOX (ALSO SEE ZEE TOYS/ZYLMEX)

In 1997, Zyll Enterprise was purchased by Redbox, and selected Zee Toys are now being reissued with the new Redbox brand on the base. In July 1997, Redbox started selling the former Zyll 1:24 scale die-cast vehicles formerly sold as Z-Wheels.

GMC pick-up	$0.50 – 0.75
Chevy 454SS pick-up	$0.50 – 0.75
Chevy Blazer	$0.50 – 0.75
GMC Jimmy	$0.50 – 0.75
Ford Explorer	$0.50 – 0.75

REI

Rei 1:43 scale models are Schuco models of Germany made in Brazil. Models of other scales are produced for Rei by Matsuda.

Alfa Romeo F1 "Parmalat," 1:43	$18
Audi 100 Coupe, 1:66 (REI/Schuco)	$6
Lamborghini Cheetah Fire Chief, 1:43	$18
Lotus F1 "JPS," 1:43	$18
Peterbilt Semi Van "Coca-Cola," 1:43	$18
Peterbilt Semi Van "Transbras," 1:43	$18
Peterbilt Semi Van "Esso," 1:43	$18
Peterbilt Semi Van "Petrobras," 1:43	$18
Peterbilt Semi Van "Mobil," 1:43	$18
Peterbilt Semi Van "Shell," 1:43	$18
Peterbilt Semi Van "Alfa Romeo," 1:43	$18
Peterbilt Semi Van "Ferrari," 1:43	$18
Peterbilt Semi Van "JPS," 1:43	$18
Peterbilt Semi Van "Marlboro," 1:43	$18
Peterbilt Semi Van "Renault," 1:43	$18
Volvo Bus, 1:43	$18
Mercedes-Benz C-111, 1:43	$8 – 12
Toyota Celica LB2000 GT, 1:64 (REI/Matsuda)	$6

RENAISSANCE

Renaissance models are 1:24 scale hand-made masterpieces assembled from 195 white metal, resin, plated, photoetched, and machine parts, and produced in genuine Ferrari colors, with production limited to 500 pieces of each model worldwide.

R1B Ferrari 250 California Spyder, available in red, blue, dark red, silver, or brown	$695
R2 Ferrari 275 GTB/4 Spyder NART, available in red, yellow, black, metallic red, or silver	$695
R3 1958 Ferrari 250 Testarossa Le Mans 58, red #14	$695

RENWAL

Usually associated with plastic toys, Renwal produced a few diecast models that featured crude paint jobs and rough castings. Nevertheless, the rarity of these toys establishes a high value on specimens. Here is a sample listing.

RENWAL 3" SERIES

143 Sedan	$32
144 Coupe	$32
145 Fire Truck	$24
146 Hook & Ladder	$24
147 Convertible	$24
148 Gasoline Truck	$24
149 Pick-Up Truck	$24
150 Racer	$48

OTHER RENWAL MODELS

8001 Ferrari Racer	$160
8002 Maserati Racer	$160
8003 Pontiac Convertible	$120
8004 Plymouth Convertible	$120
8005 Chevrolet Sedan	$120
8006 Ford Sedan	$120
8007 Sedan	$72
8008 Gasoline Truck	$72
8009 Racer	$96
8010 Delivery Truck	$72
8011 Pick-up Truck	$72
8012 Hot Rod	$72
8013 Jeep	$72
8014 Fire Truck	$72
8015 Convertible	$72
8020 Futuristic Two-Door Coupe	$24
8021 Gasoline Truck	$24
8022 Ladder Fire Truck	$24
8023 Ford Sunliner Convertible	$36
8028 Ford Victoria Hardtop	$36
8039 Pick-Up Truck	$24
8040 Pumper Fire Truck	$24
8041 Speed King Racer	$48

RENWAL 4" SERIES

Convertible	$96
Gasoline Truck	$72
Coupe	$72
City Bus	$72

REPLEX

Replex of France produces scale models of military vehicles, commercial trucks, emergency vehicles, and heavy equipment. Manufacturer's address is Replex Maquettes de Collection en Metal, Sapois 88120, Vagney - France. Diecast Miniatures offers nearly the entire line of Replex models.

100 Shelter Euromissile, olive drab, 1:50	$38
101 Renault RVI TRM 2000 Military Transport, 1:43	$44
102 AMX 30 Euromissile Tank, 1:50	$38
103 SPZ Euromissile, 1:50	$38
104 Liebherr 981 Shovel, 1:53	$54
105 Technocar/Balkancar Forklift, 1:25	$28
106 International Harvester Combine, 1:43	$48
107 Fenwick Forklift, 1:25	$28

108 Sides 2000 Paris Airport, red, 1:43 . . . . $44
109 International Harvester 844 Farm Tractor, 1:43 . . . . $14
110 Sides 2000 Doubai Airport, yellow, 1:43 . . . . $44
111 Poclain 1000 Track Excavator, 1:50. . . . . $64
112 PPM Crane, 1:50 . . . . $58
113 Poclain 1000 Track Shovel, 1:50. . . . . $64
114 1919 Magirus Deutz Bus, 1:43 . . . . $44
115 Volvo F 614 Cab & Chassis, 1:43 . . . . $44
116 Sides 2000 Geneva Airport, red, 1:43 . . . . $44
118 Magirus Deutz 90/13 Cargo Transport "Panzani," 1:43. . . $44
119 1925 Magirus Deutz Ladder Fire Truck, 1:43 . . . . $44
120 Mack 200 American Stake Truck, 1:43. . . . . $42
122 Renault RVI S 170 Tractor and Chassis, 1:43 . . . . $44
123 Renault RVI S 170 Commercial Transport, 1:43 . . . . $44
124 Mack 200 Commercial Transport "MIKO," 1:43 . . . . $44
127 Iveco 90.13 Commercial Transport, 1:43 . . . . $44
129 DAF FA 1300 Tractor and Chassis, 1:43. . . . . $44
130 Renault RVI Commercial Transport "Danza," 1:43 . . . . . . $44
135 Magirus Tractor and Chassis, 1:43. . . . . $44
136 Renault RVI JK90 Fire Service, 1:43 . . . . $44
140 Renault RVI 95-130 Forest Fire Truck, 1:43 . . . . $44
141 Renault RVI 75-130 Forest Fire Truck, 1:43 . . . . $44
142 Renault RVI 85-150 Forest Fire Truck, 1:43 . . . . $44
143 Renault RVI JN-90 Ladder Fire Truck, 1:43 . . . . $44
144 Renault RVI SIDES Fire Pumper, 1:43 . . . . $48
145 Renault RVI JP 13 Fire Ladder Truck, 1:43 . . . . $48
146 Renault RVI JN 90 Fire Pumper, 1:43 . . . . $48
147 Renault RVI JN 90 Fire Equipment Truck, 1:43 . . . . $44
148 Renault RVI TRM 2000 Water Cannon Fire Truck, 1:43 . . . $44
150 Mack 200 Commercial Transport "Michelin," 1:43 . . . . . . $44
151 Mack 200 USA Double Cabin Fire Truck, 1:43. . . . . $48
154 VAB 6x6 Armored Turret, 1:43 . . . . $58
155 VAB 6x6 Armored Assault Vehicle, 1:43 . . . . $58
156 VAB 6x6 Armored Troop Transport, 1:43 . . . . $58
159 DAF FA 1300 Commercial Transport with deflector, "TNT/IPEC," 1:43 . . . . $44
162 Renault RVI Fire Equipment Truck, 1:43 . . . . $44
163 Renault RVI Fire Auxiliary Truck, 1:43 . . . . $44
164 Renault RVI Emergency Medical Treatment Vehicle, 1:43. . $44
165 Renault RVI Fire Auxiliary Truck, 1:43 . . . . $44
166 Iveco 80-13 AW Dump Truck, 1:43. . . . . $42
167 ACMAT 6x6 Semi Tractor/Trailer, 1:50 . . . . $128
169 RVI Camiva Fire Ladder Truck, 1:48 . . . . $58
172 Renault Fire Equipment Truck, 1:43 . . . . $44
174 VAB Panhard Armored Troop Transport, 1:43 . . . . $44
176 Shelter Generator Load, 1:50 . . . . $78
177 Shelter Rita SH30 Load to 17, 1:50 . . . . $34
178 ACMAT 6x6 Flatbed Sand, 1:50 . . . . $88
179 ACMAT 6x6 Semi Tractor/Trailer, 1:43 . . . . $128
186 RVI Premier Security Truck Type 85-200, 1:43. . . . . $44
187 RVI Military Water Cannon, 1:43. . . . . $44
190 VAB 6x6 F.I.N.U.L., white, 1:43 . . . . $58
191 VAB Armored Police Assault Vehicle, blue, 1:43 . . . . . . $44
192 VBL Police Armored Personnel Transport, white, 1:43. . . . $44
195 Renault Fire Equipment Truck, 1:43 . . . . $44
197 Renault RVI S 170 Commercial Transport, "Vittel," 1:43 . . . $44
198 Renault RVI 85-150 Civil Protection Truck, 1:43. . . . . . . $44
200 ACMAT 6x6 Flatbed, olive drab, 1:43 . . . . $108

201 ACMAT FFM Fire Pumper, 1:50. . . . . $108
202 ACMAT 6x6 Troop Transport, 1:50 . . . . $118
203 ACMAT TPK 4x4 Troop Transport, 1:50 . . . . $118
204 Renault RVI Dump Truck, 1:43. . . . . $44
205 Shelter 650 SH Load to 200, 1:50 . . . . $28
206 Iveco Magirus TRM 2000 Military Transport, 1:43 . . . . . . $44
207 Mercedes 1928AS38 Tar Spreader Semi, 1:50. . . . . $68
208 Renault R340 Tar Spreader Semi, 1:50. . . . . $68
209 VAB 4x4 Armored Troop Transport, 1:43 . . . . $58
210 RVI-TRM 2000 Covered Transport, green camouflage, 1:43. $44
211 VBL-Panhard Armored Troop Transport, green camouflage, 1:43. . . . . $44
212 Mack 200 Commercial Transport, "Ryder," 1:43. . . . . . . $44
216 VAB 4x4 Armored Troop Transport, khaki camouflage, 1:43. $44
233 VAB 4x4 Armored Troop Transport, 1:43 . . . . $44
239 VAB 4x4 Turret T25, 1:43. $44
240 VAB 4x4 Ambulance, 1:43 . . . . $44
241 VAB 6x6 Armored Ambulance, 1:43 . . . . $44
242 VAB 6x6 SATCP Mistral, 1:43 . . . . $44
243 VAB 4x4 Ambulance, tan with red crescent, 1:43 . . . . . $44
244 Mack 200 Fire Pumper, 1:43. . . . . $44
245 VAB 4x4 Armored Turret T25, green camouflage, 1:43 . . . $44
246 VAB 6x6 Armored Turret T25, green camouflage, 1:43 . . . $44
247 VAB 4x4 Armored Turret T25, khaki camouflage, 1:43 . . . $44
248 VAB 6x6 Turret T25, 1:43. $84
259 VAB 4x4 Armored Assault Vehicle, 1:43 . . . . $44
260 VAB 4x4 Armored Assault Vehicle, khaki, 1:43 . . . . $44
261 VAB 4x4 Armored Assault Vehicle, 1:43 . . . . $44
262 VAB 4x4 Armored Assault Vehicle, 1:43 . . . . $44
263 VAB 6x6 Armored Troop Transport, 1:43 . . . . $44
264 VAB 6x6 Troop Transport, sable camouflage, 1:43 . . . . . $44
265 VAB 6x6 Armored Assault Vehicle, green camouflage, 1:43. . . . . $44
266 VAB 6x6 Armored Assault Vehicle, sable camouflage, 1:43. $44
269 Manitou MLT626RT Bucket Lift, 1:43 . . . . $48
274 Yanmar B27 Mini Excavator, 1:30 . . . . $38
284 Renault 1000 Transport, camouflage, 1:43 . . . . $84

REPLICARS
Replicars are 1:43 scale models made in England.
1 1934 ERA $59
4 1921 Bugatti Brescia $59
6 1934 MG K3 . . . . $59
7 1968 Morgan Plus 8. . . . . $59
13 1951 Ferrari 166M $59
14 1974 Triumph TR6. . . . . $59
16 1937 Packard Roadster. $59
18 1975 Lotus Super 7 . . . . $59
24 1937 Packard 4-door Sedan $59
24 1937 Packard Tourer $59
24 1937 Packard Town Car. $59
28 1954 Sunbeam Alpine Roadster $59
29 1932 Alfa 8C Roadster $59
32 1951 Jaguar C Type $59
35 1932 Alfa Castagna, top up $59
36 1958 Jaguar XK150 . . . . $59
44 1936 Morgan 2-Seater $59
101 1925 Austin Van "Lucas" $59

REUHL PRODUCTS, INC.

What made Reuhl toys of Madison, Wisconsin, unique is that they were sold as kits, with the emphasis on developing a child's manual dexterity. They were promoted in 1950 as educational "put-together" toys, requiring no glue or tools.

Caterpillar D-7, T-4000 . . . . $450
Caterpillar Grader No. 12 . . . . $1,800
Caterpillar Ripper $375
Caterpillar Scraper No. 70, 16", plastic, S-4500 . . . . $650
Cedar Rapids Rock Crusher $1,100
Cedar Rapids Paver $150
DW-10 . . . . $700
Farmall Cub, T-3000, 6¼" $150
Lorain Shovel, ... $1,425
Massey Harris Combine $375

REVELL

Revell is best known for its plastic model kits. But the company started a few years ago producing large scale car replicas that have established a loyal following for their accuracy, detail, and affordability.

REVELL 1:20 SCALE CREATIVE MASTERS

At least six Creative Masters models were produced around 1987 to 1988, according to Jon Pierce of Winder, Georgia. The only one he specifically mentions is the 427 Cobra as indicated below, which he says is no longer being produced.

427 Cobra . . . . $25 – 40

REVELL 1:18 SCALE

8500 Ferrari Mythos by Pininfarina $20
8501 Bugatti EB110 . . . . $20
8503 Bugatti EB110S Sport $20
8654 Mercedes-Benz 500 SL coupe $20
8659 Ferrari Mythos $20
8660 Porsche 911 Turbo, top down $20
8670 Porsche 911 Turbo, top up $20
8671 Mercedes-Benz 500 SL convertible $20
8690 BMW 850i coupe $20
8691 1969 Corvette convertible, metallic blue with open top . . $20
8692 Acura NSX, red $20
8753 1965 Mustang convertible, aqua with top down $20
8755 1969 Corvette convertible, red with open top $20
8757 1969 Mustang convertible, red with top up $20

REVELL 1:12 SCALE

8851 1954 Mercedes-Benz 300 SLR $120
8853 1962 Ferrari 250 GTO $120

REX/REXTOYS

Germany was the original home of the Rex firm, manufacturer of a variety of toys. Around 1960, Rex produced a small assortment of diecast models. Toys for Collectors, Diecast Miniatures, and Asheville Diecast offer an assortment of new models. Rex and Rextoys are interchangeable brand names, apparently begun in Germany, then moved to its present home in Switzerland. In the meantime, the company had apparently been out of business for some time before the rights were purchased to resume production.

REX 1:43 SCALE

1938 – 40 Cadillac V16 Cabriolet Ouvert 6, $35 – 40

2 1939 Cadillac Coupe de Ville $35
3 1939 Cadillac Coupe de Ville $35
4 1939 Cadillac 4-door Sedan $24
6 1939 Cadillac Roadster $35
12 1939 Cadillac 4-door Convertible $35
21 Chrysler Airflow 4-door Sedan $35
33 Rolls-Royce Phantom $35
42 1935 Ford T48 Fordor Sedan, olive & black $25
45 1935 Ford Van Army Ambulance $35
45 Ford Delivery "Bell Telephone" $35
46 1935 Ford Woody Wagon . . . . $34 – 35
47 1935 Ford Woody Wagon $35
48 1935 Ford 4-door Sedan U.S.Army $35
50 1935 Ford 4-door Sedan Taxi $35
51 1935 Ford 4-door Sedan Police $35
52 1935 Ford Coupe $25
53 1935 Ford Coupe $35
54 1935 Ford Coupe Fire $35
55 1935 Ford Coupe Police $35
56 1935 Ford Coupe, Ghost Patrol $29
61 1940 Packard Super 8 Sedan $35
Ford Thunderbird, 4⅝", 1961 . . . . $75
Mercedes-Benz 300SL Roadster, 4", 1959 . . . . $65
Opel Kapitan Sedan, 4½", 1959 . . . . $65

REX 1:87 SCALE (HO GAUGE)

Ford Taunus Sedan, 2 1/16", 1:87 . . . . $15
Volkswagen Transporter, 1¾", 1:87 . . . . $15

RHINO

Rhino toys generally fall into the category of generic toys. The definition of "generic" in this case is any toy that, once taken out of its package, becomes an unmarked and unidentifiable toy. While they are lightweight with lots of plastic components, Rhino does present a few twists that set them apart from other generic toys. Their various farm sets that include tractors, milk tankers, fences, buildings, and farmhands are a good value as a toy. Collectibly speaking, these sets are attractive enough to maintain their original value but not likely to increase past retail price in terms of rising collector value. Rhino Toys Manufacturing Ltd., Unit 11, 4/F,. Harbour Centre, Tower 1, Hunghom, Kowloon, Hong Kong.

RICHMOND

The previously unheard-of Richmond firm apparently produced an all-metal blue wrecker with a seal on top saying "another fine Richmond scale model." More information is needed.

RIO

One of the most popular brands of high-quality 1:43 scale model vehicles is Rio of Italy. Begun in 1961, Rio is still in business producing excellent models in various scales. Dr. Force's book *Classic Miniature Vehicles Made In Italy* devotes nine pages to detailing the Rio line. This book will try to present a briefer summary of Rio models.

1 1906 Itala Targa Florio, 1961 . . . . $25
2 1906 Itala Peking-Paris, 1961 . . . . $25
3 1919 Fiat 501 Sport, 1961. . . . . $25
4 1919 Fiat 501 Tourer, 1961 . . . . $25
5 1932 Alfa Romeo B-Type, 1962 . . . . $25
6 1912 Fiat Model O Tourer, 1962. . . . . $25
7 1912 Fiat Model O Spyder, 1962 . . . . $25
8 1924 Isotta-Fraschini Type 8A with cab roof, 1962 . . . . $30
9 1924 Isotta-Fraschini Type 8A, no cab roof, 1962 . . . . $30
10 1909 Bianchi Closed Landaulet, 1963 . . . . $25
11 1909 Bianchi Open Landaulet, 1963 . . . . $25
12 1912 Fiat Model O Open Spyder, 1963 . . . . $25
13 1932 Fiat Balilla 2-door, 1964. . . . . $25
14 1910 Fiat Type 2 Limousine, 1964 . . . . $25
15 1924 Isotta-Fraschini Type 8A Spyder, 1964 . . . . . $25
16 1909 Chalmers-Detroit, 1964 . . . . $25
17 1909 Mercedes Open Tourer, 1964. . . . . $25
18 1906 Bianchi Coupe De Ville, 1965 . . . . $25
19 1932 Alfa Romeo 6C 1750, 1965. . . . . $25
20 1915 Fiat 18BL Bus, yellow, 1965. . . . . $25
21 1937 Mercedes-Benz Cabriolet, 1966 . . . . $25
22 1937 Mercedes-Benz Cabriolet, 1966 . . . . $25
23 1905 Fiat 60 HP Tourer, top up, 1966. . . . . $25
24 1905 Fiat 60 HP Tourer, top down, 1966 . . . . $25
25 1906 Fiat 24 HP Double Phaeton, 1966. . . . . $25
26 1902 Fiat 12 HP Tourer, 1966. . . . . $25
27 1905 Fiat 24 HP Limousine, 1967 . . . . $25
28 1905 Bianchi Landaulet, 1967. . . . . $25
29 1902 Mercedes Simplex, 1967 . . . . $25
30 1894 De Dion-Bouton Steam Victoria, 1967 . . . . . $25
31 1901 Fiat 8 HP, 1967 . . . . $25
32 1903 Fiat 16-24 HP Tourer, 1967 . . . . $25
33 1908 Mercedes 70 HP Limousine, 1968. . . . . $25
34 1907 Renault Type X Double Berline, 1968. . . . . . . $25
35 1910 Renault Taxi De La Marne, 1968. . . . . $25
36 1927 Bugatti Royale, top up, 1968 . . . . $25
37 1927 Bugatti Royale, top down, 1968 . . . . $25
38 1908 Fiat 18-24 HP Landaulet, 1969 . . . . $25
39 1931 Rolls-Royce Phantom II, top up, 1969. . . . . . . $25
40 1931 Rolls-Royce Phantom II, top down, 1969 . . . . $25
41 1929 Lancia Dilambda Torpedo, green, 1969 . . . . . $25
42 1929 Lancia Dilambda Torpedo, red, 1969 . . . . $25
43 1941 Lincoln Continental, top up, 1969 . . . . $25
44 1941 Lincoln Continental, top down, 1969 . . . . $25
45 1934 Deusenberg SJ Phaeton, closed top, 1969 . . . $25

46 1934 Deusenberg SJ Phaeton, open top, 1969. . . . . $25
47 1908 Thomas Flyer New York-Paris, 1970. . . . . $25
48 1932 Bugatti Type 50 Sport Coupe, 1970 . . . . $25
49 1921 Fiat V12 Dorsay De Ville, 1971. . . . . $25
50 1928 Lincoln Sport Phaeton, top up, 1971. . . . . $25
51 1928 Lincoln Sport Phaeton, top down, 1971 . . . . $25
52 1923 Renault 40 HP Torpedo, top up, 1971 . . . . $25
53 1923 Renault 40 HP Torpedo, top down, 1971 . . . . $25
54 1927 Bugatti Type 41 Royale, 1972. . . . . $25
55 1914 Alfa Ricotti, 1973. . . . . $25
56 1902 General Grand Prix, 1973 . . . . $25
57 1923 Fiat 519 S Tourer, top up, 1974 . . . . $25
58 1923 Fiat 519 S Tourer, top down, 1974 . . . . $25
59 1923 Fiat 519 S Limousine, 1974. . . . . $25
60 1899 Le Jamais Contente, 1975 . . . . $25
61 1932 Hispano-Suiza Town Car, 1975 . . . . $25
62 1923 Leyat, 1976 . . . . $25
63 1935 Delahaye 135M, 1976 . . . . $25
64 1942 Hitler's Mercedes-Benz 770, 1976 . . . . $45
65 1932 Hispano-Suiza Limousine, 1976 . . . . $25
66 1927 Bugatti Royale Double Berline, 1976 . . . . $25
67 1929 Isotta-Fraschini, top up, 1976 . . . . $25
68 1929 Isotta-Fraschini, top down, 1976 . . . . $25

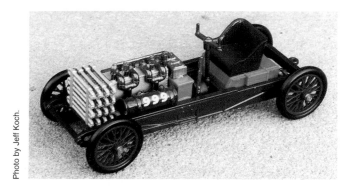

Photo by Jeff Koch.

69 1902 Ford 999, 1980, $25

70 1934 Alfa Romeo B-Type Targa Florio, 1980 . . . . $25
71 1935 Alfa Romeo B-Type Hill Climb Car, 1980 . . . . $25
72 1923 Rolls-Royce 20, top up, 1981 . . . . $25
73 1923 Rolls-Royce 20, top down, 1981 . . . . $25
74 1929 Bugatti Royale Coupe, 1981. . . . . $25
75 1905 Fiat PS Limousine, 1981. . . . . $25
76 1931 Cadillac V16, top up, 1981. . . . . $25
77 1931 Cadillac V16, top down, 1981 . . . . $25

88 1949 Volkswagen, 1988 (see 189-194), $25

78 1938 Bugatti 57C Atlantic Coupe, 1981 . . . . $25
79 1931 Mercedes-Benz SSKL, 1981 . . . . $25
80 1927 Mercedes-Benz SSK, 1981 . . . . $25
81 1914 Alfa Ricotti, 1981 . . . . $25
82 1941 Lincoln Continental Coupe, 1985 . . . . $25
83 1936 Hispano-Suiza, top up, 1985 . . . . $25
84 1936 Hispano-Suiza, top down, 1985 . . . . $25
85 1937 Mercedes-Benz 770K Pullman, 1985 . . . . $25
86 1933 Deusenberg SJ Spider, 1987 . . . . $25
87 1915 Fiat 18BL Bus, blue, 1986 . . . . $25
89 1930 Isotta-Fraschini Castagna Torpedo, 1988 . . . . $25
90 1957 Mercedes-Benz 300, 1988 . . . . $25
91 1953 Volkswagen Beetle, ivory, 1990 . . . . $25
92 1949 Volkswagen Beetle Cabriolet, top down, 1990 . . . . . . $25
93 1949 Volkswagen Beetle Cabriolet, top up, 1990 . . . . $25
94 Bugatti Royale Torpedo, top up, 1990 . . . . $25
95 Bugatti Royale Torpedo, top down, 1990 . . . . $25
96 Bugatti Royale Weymann, 1990 . . . . $25
97 1956 Citroën DS19 Sedan $25
98 1956 Citroën Cabriolet, open top $25
99 1958 Citroën ID19 Station Wagon $25
100 1960 Mercedes-Benz 300D Landau $33
100P 1960 Mercedes-Benz 300D Landau with Pope $35
101 1960 Mercedes-Benz 300D, top up $25
102 1960 Mercedes-Benz 300D, top down $25
103 1939 Volkswagen Beetle Standard Hardtop $25
104 1939 Volkswagen Beetle Sedan with Sunroof $25
105 1939 Volkswagen Beetle Cabriolet, top down $25
106 1939 Volkswagen Beetle Split Window $25
107 1950 Volkswagen Beetle, top down $25
108 1955 Volkswagen One Millionth Beetle $25
109 1959 Citroën DS19 Monte Carlo $25
110 1967 Ferrari 365 GTB4 Daytona, red, 1989 . . . . $25
111 Citroën ID19 Sedan $25
116 Citroën ID19 Ambulance $25
117 1962 Citroën Fire Ambulance $25
120 1967 Ferrari 365 GTB4 Daytona Spider, 1989 . . . . $25
121 1967 Ferrari 365 GTB4 Daytona Spider, 1990 . . . . $25
130 1973 Ferrari 365 GTB4 Le Mans, 1989 . . . . $25
189 1949 Volkswagen Beetle, black, 1988 . . . . $25
190 1949 Volkswagen Beetle, gray, 1988 . . . . $25
191 1949 Volkswagen Beetle, red, 1988 . . . . $25
192 1949 Volkswagen Beetle, green, 1988 . . . . $25
193 1949 Volkswagen Beetle, cream, 1988 . . . . $25
194 1949 Volkswagen Beetle, blue, 1988 . . . . $25
200 1967 Ferrari 365 GTB Daytona, red, 1986 . . . . $25
201 1967 Ferrari 365 GTB Daytona Spider, black, 1986 . . . . . . $25
202 1973 Ferrari 365 GTB Le Mans, 1989 . . . . $25
A1 1914 Fiat 18BKL Army Truck, 1982 . . . . $25
A2 1914 Fiat 18BKL Stake Truck, 1982 . . . . $25
A3 1914 Fiat 18BKL Covered Truck, gray, 1982 . . . . $25
A4 1914 Fiat 18BKL Open Truck, maroon, 1982 . . . . $25
CH93 1914 Fiat 18BKL with Santa & present, limited edition, 1993. $35
R1 1967 Ferrari 365 GTB Daytona, same as 200 . . . . $25
R2 1967 Ferrari 365 GTB Daytona Spider, same as 201 . . . . . . $25
R3 1973 Ferrari 365 GTB Daytona Spider, same as 202 . . . . . . $25
R4 1956 Ford Thunderbird Convertible, pale green, 1990 . . . . . $25
R5 1956 Ford Thunderbird Hardtop, lavender, 1990 . . . . $25

R6 1955 Mercedes-Benz 190SL Convertible, white, 1990 . . . . . $25
R7 1955 Mercedes-Benz 190SL Convertible, cream, 1990 . . . . $25
R8 1968 Lamborghini Miura S Coupe $35
R9 1968 Lamborghini Miura Roadster, top down $35
1000 1938 Bugatti 57C Atlantic Coupe, 1982 . . . . $25
1001 1933 Bugatti Type 50, 1983 . . . . $25
1002 1931 Bugatti Type 50 Le Mans, 1985 . . . . $25
10200 1953 Volkswagen Beetle, charcoal gray, 1989 . . . . $25
10201 1953 Volkswagen Beetle, maroon, 1989 . . . . $25
10202 1953 Volkswagen Beetle, cream, 1989 . . . . $25

RIVAROSSI

Although Rivarossi of Italy didn't produce any diecast miniatures, they did produce some interesting plastic Fiat and Mercedes models in 1:43 and 1:87 scales. Rivarossi's exquisite ship models and detail components are currently available from Model Expo.

RIVER (ALSO SEE CRESCENT, D.C.M.T., IMPY, LONE STAR, AND ROADMASTER)

A dispute ensues among collectors whether D.C.M.T. produced this series or not. Records indicate that Die Casting Machine Tools, Ltd. of London, England, likely produced these 1:43 scale castings. Argument to the contrary states that River models are not at all marked with any D.C.M.T. mark, and represent inferior castings prone to metal fatigue, a problem not witnessed on other D.C.M.T. castings. For more details, see the section on D.C.M.T. and the others listed above.

ROAD CHAMPS

As early as 1980, Road Champs produced various 1:64 scale toy cars with opening doors under the auspices of JRI, Inc., originally based in a suburb of Philadelphia. One of many new arrivals on the diecast market, Road Champs moved to Harrison, New Jersey, before finally settling in West Caldwell, New Jersey, made its mark in 1993 with its introduction of a nine-car series of 1993 Chevrolet Caprice State Police Cars. The ever-expanding series features relatively faithful 1:43 scale reproductions of U.S. and Canadian police cruisers with more Caprice variations and the addition of 1994 Ford Crown Victoria police cars added every year, with Chevrolet Suburbans added to the line for 1996.

Before the highly popular state police series, the 1:87 scale "Anteaters" series, named after those curved-nose semi tractors, was the primary item marketed by Road Champs. They remain a popular segment of the Road Champs line-up. They are currently referred to simply as the Diecast Collection, with the Deluxe Series as a spin-off of slightly more unusual 1:64 scale commercial vehicles.

Other series, set in 1:64 scale, include Country Tour Buses that feature graphics and names of several country music stars. Their Fire Rescue Series has been another popular line of models of firefighting equipment, including International and Boardman trucks, and most recently Chevrolet Suburbans.

A large assortment of other nicely done models in 1:43 to 1:64 scale round out the quality assortment. Road Champs models are manufactured in China. For more information, you might consider contacting the company: Road Champs, Inc., 7 Patton Drive, West Caldwell, NJ 07006-6404, 201-228-6900.

ANTEATERS 1:87 SCALE SEMI-TRUCKS AND TRAILERS

"Allied Van Lines"	$3 – 4
"Bekins Van Lines"	$3 – 4
"Cotter & Company True Value Hardware Stores"	$3 – 4
"Dole"	$3 – 4
"Exxon" Tanker	$3 – 4
"Frito Lay"	$3 – 4
"Goodyear"	$3 – 4
"Hershey's Kisses"	$3 – 4
"Horseless Carriage Automobile Transportion"	$3 – 4
Livestock Truck	$3 – 4
Low Loader Transporter "Tri State Haulers"	$3 – 4
"Mayflower" Moving Van, C.O.E.	$3 – 4
"Mayflower" Moving Van, conventional	$3 – 4
NASA Rocket Transporter	$3 – 4
"Pepsi"	$3 – 4
"Pilot" Tanker Truck	$3 – 4
Pipe Truck	$3 – 4
"Reese's Pieces"	$3 – 4
Sand Hopper Truck	$3 – 4
"Snapple"	$3 – 4

ROAD CHAMPS DELUXE SERIES 1:64 SCALE

American LaFrance Fire Engine with Movable Boom Crane	$3 – 4
Delivery Van, Cheetos	$3 – 4
Delivery Van, Pepsi	$3 – 4
Elgin Pelican Street Sweeper	$3 – 4
International Beverage Delivery Truck, Pepsi	$3 – 4
International Beverage Delivery Truck, Snapple	$3 – 4
International Recycling Truck	$3 – 4
International School Bus, Golden Rule	$3 – 4
International School Bus, International	$3 – 4
Jerr-Dan Auto Salvage Transporter, red, white & blue	$3 – 4
Jerr-Dan Auto Salvage Transporter, burgundy & white	$3 – 4
Mercedes-Benz Airport Stretch Limousine, metallic silver	$3 – 4
Mercedes-Benz Airport Stretch Limousine, white	$3 – 4
Peterbilt Refuse/Recycling Truck, burgundy	$3 – 4
Peterbilt Refuse/Recycling Truck, gray	$3 – 4
Peterbilt Refuse/Recycling Truck, white	$3 – 4
Winnebago Chieftain Motor Home, beige	$3 – 4
Winnebago Chieftain Motor Home, white	$3 – 4
Zamboni, blue and white	$3 – 4

ROAD CHAMPS STATE POLICE CRUISERS/TAXIS 1:43 SCALE

Alabama State Police, 1993 Chevrolet Caprice, 1993	$5
Alaska State Troopers, 1993 Chevrolet Caprice, 1996	$5
Arizona State Police, 1994 Ford Crown Victoria, 1996	$5
Arkansas State Police, 1993 Chevrolet Caprice, 1993	$5
California Highway Patrol, 1993 Chevrolet Caprice, 1994	$5
Chicago Checker Taxi, 1993 Chevrolet Caprice, 1995	$5
Colorado State Police, 1994 Ford Crown Victoria, 1996	$5
Florida Highway Patrol, 1994 Ford Crown Victoria, 1995	$5
Georgia State Police, 1993 Chevrolet Caprice, 1994	$5
Idaho State Police, 1994 Ford Crown Victoria, 1996	$5
Illinois State Police, 1993 Chevrolet Caprice, 1993	$5

Indiana State Police, 1994 Ford Crown Victoria, 1996	$5
Kansas State Police, 1994 Ford Crown Victoria, 1996	$5
Kentucky State Police, 1994 Ford Crown Victoria, 1996	$5
Louisiana State Police, 1994 Ford Crown Victoria, 1995	$5
Maine State Police, 1994 Ford Crown Victoria, 1996	$5
Maryland State Police, 1994 Ford Crown Victoria, 1996	$5
Michigan State Police, 1993 Chevrolet Caprice, 1993	$5
Minnesota State Police, 1993 Chevrolet Caprice, 1993	$5

Mississippi Highway Safety Patrol, 1994 Ford Crown Victoria, 1996, $5

Missouri Highway Patrol, 1994 Ford Crown Victoria, 1995	$5
Nebraska State Police, 1994 Ford Crown Victoria, 1996	$5
Nevada State Police, 1993 Chevrolet Caprice, 1995	$5
New Jersey State Police, 1993 Chevrolet Caprice, 1995	$5
New Mexico State Police, 1994 Ford Crown Victoria, 1996	$5
New York City Taxi, 1993 Chevrolet Caprice, boxed, 1995	$6
New York State Police, 1993 Chevrolet Caprice, 1993	$5
North Dakota State Police, 1994 Ford Crown Victoria, 1996	$5
Ohio State Police, 1993 Chevrolet Caprice, 1993	$5
Oklahoma State Police, 1994 Ford Crown Victoria, 1996	$5
Ontario Provincial Police, 1994 Crown Victoria, 1995	$5

Oregon State Police, 1993 Chevrolet Caprice, 1995, $5

Quebec Provincial Police, 1993 Chevrolet Caprice, 1995	$5
Rhode Island State Police, 1994 Ford Crown Victoria, 1995	$5
Royal Canadian Mounted Police, 1993 Chevrolet Caprice, 1993	$5
South Carolina Highway Patrol, 1993 Chevrolet Caprice, 1995	$5
South Dakota State Police, 1994 Ford Crown Victoria, 1996	$5
Tennessee State Police, 1994 Ford Crown Victoria, 1996	$5
Texas Department of Public Safety, 1994 Ford Crown Victoria, 1996	$5
Utah State Police, 1994 Ford Crown Victoria, 1996	$5
Vermont State Police, 1993 Chevrolet Caprice, 1996	$5
Virginia State Police, 1993 Chevrolet Caprice, 1994	$5
Washington DC Police, 1994 Ford Crown Victoria, 1996	$5
Washington State Police, 1994 Ford Crown Victoria, 1996	$5

Road Champs

West Virginia State Police, 1993 Chevrolet Caprice, 1996, $5

Wisconsin State Police, 1993 Chevrolet Caprice, 1993 . . . . $5
Wyoming State Police, 1994 Ford Crown Victoria, 1996 . . . . . . $5

1997 ROAD CHAMPS CAPITOL CITY POLICE SERIES

Anaheim, CA $5
Atlanta, GA $5
Augusta, ME $5
Branson, MO $5
Chicago, IL $5
Columbia, SC $5
Columbus, OH $5
Denver, CO $5
Des Moines, IA $5
Hartford, MA $5
Indianapolis, IN $5
Jackson, MS $5
Lancaster, PA $5
Las Vegas, NV $5
New Orleans, LA $5
Niagara Falls, NY $5
Orlando, FL $5
Sacramento, CA $5
Salt Lake, UT $5
Springfield, IL $5
Tallahassee, FL $5
Trenton, NJ $5
U.S. Park Police $5
Vancouver, BC $5

ALSO NEW - CHEVY SUBURBAN POLICE AND FIRE VEHICLES

New Jersey State Police $5
Rhode Island State Police $5
Bowling Green, Kentucky, Fire Department $5

Hartford Connecticut Fire Department Shift Commander, $5

St. Louis, Missouri, Fire Department Fire Investigation Supervisor . $5

204

ROAD CHAMPS BOARDMAN EMERGENCY VEHICLES (INTRODUCED IN 1995)

Boardman Tower Unit
   v.1 Boston Fire Department . . . . $4 – 5
   v.2 St. Louis Fire Department . . . . $4 – 5
   v.3 Washington, D. C. Fire Department . . . . $4 – 5
Boardman/International Fire Pumper
   v.1 Boston Fire Department . . . . $4 – 5
   v.2 St. Louis Fire Department . . . . $4 – 5
   v.3 Washington, D. C. Fire Department . . . . $4 – 5
Boardman/International JB-Res-Q
   v.1 Boston Fire Department . . . . $4 – 5
   v.2 St. Louis Fire Department . . . . $4 – 5
   v.3 Washington, D. C. Fire Department . . . . $4 – 5

ROAD CHAMPS EAGLE COACH COUNTRY TOUR BUS SERIES 1:64 SCALE

Alabama . . . . $4 – 5
Clint Black . . . . $4 – 5
Billy Ray Cyrus . . . . $4 – 5
Diamond Rio . . . . $4 – 5
Vince Gill . . . . $4 – 5
George Jones . . . . $4 – 5
Lorrie Morgan . . . . $4 – 5
Ricky Skaggs . . . . $4 – 5
Marty Stuart . . . . $4 – 5
Randy Travis . . . . $4 – 5
Travis Tritt . . . . $4 – 5
Tanya Tucker . . . . $4 – 5
Hank Williams Jr. . . . . $4 – 5

ROAD CHAMPS CITY AND TOUR BUSES

CTA (Chicago Transit Authority) Bus $5
NJT (New Jersey Transit) Bus $5
MCTO (Metropolitan Council) $5
MTA (Manhattan Transit Authority) $5
1997 Metro, Houston TX $5
1997 A.C. Transit, Oakland CA $5
Sun Tours Bus $5
DBM Gad About Tour Bus $5
1997 Metro-Houston TX $5
1997 A.C. Transit, Oakland CA $5

Eagle Coach Greyhound, $5

ROAD CHAMPS FORD TRUCK SERIES 1:43 SCALE
(OFFICIALLY LICENSED BY FORD MOTOR COMPANY)

Ford Explorer, red/beige or green/beige, 1994 . . . . $3 – 4
Ford F100 1956 Pickup, red or green, 1994 . . . . $3 – 4

Ford F100 1956 Pickup, primer brown, 1997, $5 – 6

Ford F150 Flareside Pickup, metallic aqua or dark blue, 1994 . $3 – 4
ROAD CHAMPS CHEVROLET TRUCK SERIES 1:43 SCALE
1953 Chevrolet C3100 Pickup, orange, green, or primer brown, 1995. . . . . $4
1994 Chevrolet Suburban, silver/black or red/silver, 1994 . . . . . $4
1994 Chevrolet Big Dooley™ Extended Cab Pickup, dual rear wheels, black or burgundy, 1994. . . . . $4
1995 Chevrolet S-10 ZR2 with cargo compartment, black with silver trim or red with black trim, 1995 . . . . $4
1995 Chevrolet Blazer, blue or black with silver trim, or teal, 1995 . . . . $4
ROAD CHAMPS JEEP SERIES 1:43 SCALE
1995 Jeep Grand Cherokee Limited, black $4
ROAD CHAMPS FLYERS HISTORIC MILITARY AIRCRAFT (APPROX. 4")
B-17 "Sally Ann" Bomber painted in colors of the 91st Bomb Group, Bassingbourne, England $3
B-25 Mitchell "Panchito" with markings of B-25 owned by National War Plane Museum. $3
Douglas C-47, D-Day markings $3
F-4U Corsair flown by "Pappy" Boyington, legendary Congressional Medal of Honor winner. $3
F-111 Two-Seat Tactical Fighter-Bomber of the U. S. Air Force . $3
F-16 Fighter of the U. S. Air Force "Thunderbirds". $3
F-18 Hornet High-Tech Navy Super Fighter. $3
P-47 Thunderbolt "Lil Friend" 56th Fighter Group, Halesworth, England $3
SR71 Blackbird $3
ROAD CHAMPS SPRINT RACERS
1/25th scale, pull-back action. . . . . $5 each
OTHER ROAD CHAMPS MODELS
Airport Shuttle Van, 1:64 . . . . $1
Chevy BelAir, '57, 1:64. . . . . $4
Dump Truck, Hard Hats series $1
Ford Model A, 1:64 . . . . $4
Stake Truck, Farmer Brown $1
Toyota Pickup with Camper Topper, black, 1:64. . . . . $1
Toyota Pickup with Camper Topper, red, 1:64 . . . . $1
Toyota Pickup Wrecker, 1:64 . . . . $1

ROAD LEGENDS (SEE YAT MING)

ROAD MACHINE
Road Machines are an import from Hong Kong.
Porsche 928, 1:64 . . . . $4

ROADMASTER (ALSO SEE D.C.M.T., IMPY, AND LONE STAR)
"Roadmaster," also spelled "Road-Master," is part of the brand name given to a line of toy cars made by D.C.M.T. of London, England. The more common name is "Impy," short for "Lone Star Road-Master Impy Super Cars." For more information, see D.C.M.T. and Lone Star.

ROADMATES
Over the years, Sears has offered an assortment of toy vehicles called Roadmates. Individual models in blisterpacks were usually repackaged Playart models, while sets were most often Zee Toys Pacesetters. Since the models themselves are recognized by their brand names, and the Roadmates name was only on the package, they are listed in their respective headings.

ROAD RUNNERS (SEE MEGAMOVERS)

ROAD TOUGH (SEE YATMING)

ROBEDDIE (SEE BROOKLINS)

ROBERTS
One model, a six-wheeler with a bucket loader on the front, has been found with Roberts stamped on the front of the grill. More information is needed.

ROCO
Roco models are ready-to-run pre-colored 1:87 scale vehicles made in Austria. Walthers HO catalog lists a huge assortment. While it may be that some Roco models are diecast, they are more likely plastic. The detail and accuracy is, nevertheless, noteworthy of inclusion in this book. When applicable, Walthers catalog number is included with model description. Prices indicated are current catalog prices from Walthers. Here is a sample listing. Many other models are currently available.
ROCO EMERGENCY VEHICLES
Covered Trailer, 625-1309 . . . . $3.99
Dodge Red Cross Jeep, Truck & Field Kitchen Trailer, 625-1388 . $10.49
Dodge Swiss Emergency Truck, 625-1348. . . . . $9.99
Land Rover KLFA Fire Truck, 625-1359 . . . . $10.49
Land Rover Red Cross, 625-1380. . . . . $10.49
Land Rover, 625-1381 . . . . $10.49
Magirus 2312 Fire Ladder Truck, 625-1349 . . . . $19.99
Magirus D LF 16 Fire Truck, 625-1396. . . . . $15.99
Magirus DLK 23-12 with Turn Ladder, 625-1346 . . . . $21.49
Magirus TLF Fire Truck, 625-1386. . . . . $14.99
Magirus TLF 16 Fire Pumper, 625-1366 . . . . $14.99
MAN THW 5-Ton with Canvas Hood, 625-1302 . . . . $8.49
MAN THW 5-Ton Equipment Truck, 625-1308 . . . . $6.49
MAN 5T with Trailer, Red Cross, 625-1339 . . . . $8.49
MAN 630L 2 A Red Cross Bus & Trailer, 625-1387 . . . . $11.49
MAN 630 L2A Technical Rescue Service, 625-1372 . . . . $7.99
Mercedes-Benz DL Ladder, 625-1398 . . . . $19.99
Mercedes-Benz LF8 Fire Truck, 265-1351 . . . . $10.99
Mercedes-Benz LF 25, 625-1374 . . . . $17.99

Mercedes-Benz LF8 Fire Truck with Trailer & DKW Portable Motor Pump, 625-1375 . . . . $14.99

Mercedes-Benz L4500 D122 Ladder Truck, 625-1361 . . . . . $19.99

Mercedes-Benz SRF Repair Truck with Hiab Crane & removable Container, 625-1369 . . . . $18.99

Mercedes TLFA 4000 Rosenbauer, 625-1379 . . . . $16.49

Mercedes 1017 Police Truck with Canvas, 625-1383 . . . . . . $10.99

Munga DKW Red Cross, 625-1301 . . . . $5.49

Munga Fire Dept. Radio Car, 625-1300 . . . . $5.49

Munga Jeep Red Cross, 625-1329 . . . . $4.49

Opel Blitz TLF 15, 625-1398 . . . . $12.49

Opel Blitz with Fire Extinguisher Trailer, 625-1337 . . . . . . $14.49

Pinzgauer 6x6 Command Car, 625-1386 . . . . $14.99

Renault DLK 23-12 Fire Ladder Truck, 625-1371 . . . . $19.99

Steyr 680 TLF Fire Truck, 265-1342. . . . . $13.99

THW Field Kitchen Trailer, 625-1320 . . . . $3.99

Unimog S with Canvas Hood, Red Cross, 625-1338 . . . . . . $7.99

Unimog 1300L Fire Ambulance, 625-1364 . . . . $8.99

Unimog 4-Wheel Drive Fire Engine, 625-1304 . . . . $9.49

Volkswagen Ambulance, 625-1355 . . . . $7.49

Volkswagen Ambulance Van, 625-1377 . . . . $7.49

Volkswagen Bus and Field Kitchen Unit Truck, 625-1376 . . $18.49

Volkswagen Double Cab Fire fighting Unit, 625-1362 . . . . . $6.49

Volkswagen Minibus with Horse Trailer, 625-1384 . . . . . . $17.99

Volkswagen THW, 625-1323 . . . . $5.49

Volkswagen Type 2 Ambulance, 625-1372 . . . . $7.99

Volkswagen Type 2 Command Car, 625-1370 . . . . $7.99

Volkswagen Type 2 DB Railway Police, 625-1382. . . . . $7.49

Volkswagen 2-Unit Mini Bus Set, 625-1385 . . . . $18.49

Willys Jeep Fire Dept., 625-1365 . . . . $6.99

ROCO EMERGENCY HELICOPTERS

MBB BO 105 Police, 625-1391 . . . . $10

MBB BO 105 Rescue, 625-1392 . . . . $9.49

MBB BO 105 Rescue, ADAC, 625-1390. . . . . $9.49

ROCO CONSTRUCTION VEHICLES

Construction Set with Site Truck and Two Site Office Trailers, 625-1545. . . . . $25.99

Magirus D Tipping Semi Trailer, 625-1546. . . . . $19.99

Magirus Dump Truck, 625-1527 . . . . $15.49

Magirus 3-Axle Dump Truck with Trailer, 625-1543. . . . . . $22.99

Mercedes-Benz 4500 Tanker, 625-1526 . . . . NPA

Mercedes Unimog Road Building Vehicle Set Add-On, 625-1547. . . . . $49.99

Mercedes Unimog 1300 & Sauer Komet Bus Construction Site Set, 625-1561 . . . . $19.49

Steyr Construction Vehicle with Accessories, 625-1533 . . . . $24.99

Steyr 91 Tractor with Flatbed and Power Shovel, 625-1516 . $37.49

Volvo FL10 with Silo Moving Equipment, 625-1561. . . . . . $23.99

ROCO SEMI TRUCKS

Magirus M5 "Schenker," 625-1569. . . . . $12.49

Magirus Tractor & Trailer "DB/TFG," 625-1524 . . . . $16.99

Magirus Tractor & Trailer "Danzas," 625-1538 . . . . $15.49

Mercedes 1838 with "Kieserling" Double Trailers, 625-1571 . $28.49

Mercedes 1838 with "Kohne & Nagel" Double Trailers, 625-1577. $27.49

Mercedes 1838 "Schenker," 625-1576. . . . . NPA

Mercedes 1838 with "Sixt" Trailer, 625-1579 . . . . $28.49

Renault "Kolner Flitzer," 625-1584 . . . . NPA

Renault Tractor Trailer "Rouch," 625-1528. . . . . $14.99

Renault 3-Axle Tractor Trailer "Beck," 625-1567 . . . . $17.49

Steyr 91 Semi with "Gondrand" 3-Axle Trailer, 625-1557 . . . $16.99

Steyr 91 Semi with "Ischler Saltz" Trailer, 625-1520 . . . . . . $14.99

Steyr 91 Semi with "Spedition Gartner" Trailer, 625-1514 . . $14.99

Volvo FL10 Truck & Trailer, unmarked, 625-1575. . . . . NPA

Volvo FL10 "Kuhlzug" Refrigerator Truck & Trailer, 625-1581 . $28.49

Volvo FL10 with "La Maxilaterale" Trailer, 625-1430 . . . . . $24.49

Volvo FL10 with Double Trailers, unmarked, 625-1430 . . . . $24.49

Volvo FL10 with "Kuhne & Nagel" Double Trailers, 625-1570 . $24.99

Volvo "Laurie Ashley" Freight Truck, 625-1583 . . . . $11.99

ROCO SAURER BUSES

Austrian Postal, 625-1600 . . . . $15.49

"Komet" tour Bus, 625-1602 . . . . $15.49

ROCO MAINTENANCE/UTILITY VEHICLES

Dodge Tow Truck, 625-1712 . . . . $8.49

MAN 630 with Repair Shop, 625-1410. . . . . $12.49

Renault G Service, 625-1656. . . . . $15.49

Unimog 1300 Utility, 625-1503 . . . . $29.99

Magirus Highway Maintenance, 625-1655 . . . . $17.49

Many more Roco brand HO gauge models are currently available.

ROLUX

Rolux models are lead alloy miniatures made in France in the early 1940s.

Limousine, lead body, aluminum chassis. . . . . $45 – 60

Army Staff Car, same as limousine with military markings . $45 – 60

ROSS (OR ROS*)

Three models have been produced to form a set of high-quality heavy equipment models from Ross of Italy. Production of models listed below has been discontinued, and limited quantities are offered through Toys for Collectors while supplies last. A larger assortment is offered by Diecast Miniatures, who chose to spell Ross with one "s."*

12 Fiat F2100/F130 Tractor, 1:25. . . . . $18

20 Fiat-Hitachi Excavator, 1:32, 12" $49

20 Fiat-Hitachi FH200 Backhoe, 1:32. . . . . $28

21 Fiat-Allis Wheel Loader, 1:32, 9" $39

21 Fiat-Allis FR130 Wheel Loader, 1:32 . . . . $28

22 Fiat-Allis Dozer, 1:32, 6" $39

22 Fiat-Allis FD14E Dozer, 1:32. . . . . $24

202 Iseki 530 Tractor $18

259 Massey Ferguson 194F Tractor $18

301 Fiat 80-90 Tractor $18

802 Olimpus Backhoe $28

10255 Lamborghini 1706 Tractor. $18

10256 Hurlimann H-G170T Tractor, 1:25 . . . . $18

10257 Same Galaxy 170 Tractor, 1:25 . . . . $18

10258 Same Galaxy 170 Dual Rear Wheel Tractor, 1:25 . . . . . $18

10308 Fiat 180-90DT Turbo Tractor, 1:18. . . . . $28

10309 Carraro 7700 Reversible Tractor, 1:25 . . . . $18

30202 Iseki Farm Tractor, 1:32 . . . . $14

30302 Hesston 80-90 Tractor, 1:32 . . . . $14

30401 Massey Ferguson 1014 Tractor, 1:32 . . . . $14

30403 Massey Ferguson 3050/3090 Tractor, 1:32 . . . . $14

40505 Landini 783 Crawler, 1:32 . . . . $14

50302 Fiat-Laverda 3890 Combine, 1:43. . . . . $18

50303 Olimpus Turbo Combine, 1:43 . . . . $18
60114 Hesston 4700 Baler, 1:25 . . . . $14

ROSSO

Exoticar offers one model of these exquisite diecast kits from Rosso.

Ferrari Formula One. $369

ROZKVET MINI MODELS

Collector Neil Edwards reports of an unusual model Skoda 120 made in Czechoslovakia by a company called Rozkvet VDI Mini Models. He paid $1 for it at a flea market. As with most eastern European models, this one is assumed to be produced in 1:43 scale.

Skoda 120, white body, black interior, unpainted base. . . $15 – 20

RUESTES

Ruestes models are made in Argentina.

Renault 17 Coupe, 1:43 . . . . $12
Renault 12 Wagon, 1:43 . . . . $12

RULLERO

Rullero models, like Ruestes, are made in Argentina.

Ike Torino Rally, 10" $22

RUSS

Austin Mini, Bump & Go, 2¾" $10
Volkswagen Beetle, Bump & Go, 2¾" $10

RUSSIAN MODELS (ALSO SEE AGAT, LITAN, LOMO, RADON, AND SARATOV)

Since the collapse of communism and the beginning of "perestroika," Russian exports have started appearing in growing quantities in the US. A wide variety of toys are included in the assortment of goods coming from former Soviet republics. Among them are a large selection of diecast models. Since private corporations have not been widely established, most Russian products are generic. However, most recently, several Russian brand names have emerged such as Radon, Agat, Litan, Saratov, and Lomo, as reported by Alexander Yurcenko in the June 1997 issue of *Model Auto Review.*

Below is a sampling of Russian models that have recently become a lot more popular.

Cheika Limousine $15
Moskvitch Patrol Car $15
Russian Armored Vehicle, crude cast, plastic wheels, thick steel
    axles $15
Zil Limousine. $15
2 Moskvitch 402 Sedan. $14
26 Volga GAZ 24 Sedan $14
35 Chaika GAZ 13 Limousine $22
37 Russobalt Tourer $19
38 Lada Niva 4WD $24
40 Moskvitch Pickup $14
49 Russbalt Sedan $19
50 Russbalt Landau $19
56 Chaika GAZ14 Limousine $22

59 Zil Dump Truck $24
64 Volkswagen RAF 977 Van $27
66 Alfa Romeo. $14
71 Zis Type 2 Fire Truck $37
77 Zis Type 5 Fire Pumper $37
78 IZ Jupiter Police Motorbike & Sidecar, 1:24 . . . . $24
81 Amo Type 4 Fire Truck $51
83 Zis 5 Ton Truck $24
101 1934 GAZ-Ford AAA Fire Truck . . . . NPA
108 UAZ 469 4WD Road Police Jeep. $24
115 Krupp KMK 4070 4-axle Crane, 1:50 . . . . $129
116 Krupp KMK 4070 5-axle Crane, 1:50 . . . . $139
117 Kamaz 4310 Postal Truck. $29
125 UAZ 452 Military Bus Van $29
127 Zis Type 6 3-axle Pumper Fire Truck $42
506 Zis-8 St. Petersburg City Bus, wood & metal, very limited
    quantities $139

RW (SEE ZISS)

SABLON

Sablon toys were made in Belgium starting in 1968. They are fairly accurate representations with opening doors and hoods. After 1970, Nacoral took over the tooling and reissued some of the models under the Nacoral Intercar brand.

BMW 1600 GT. $32
BMW 2000 CS $32
BMW Glas 3000 V8 . . . . $32
Mercedes 6x4 Tank Truck, orange/red/white, 1:43 . . . . . $25
Mercedes-Benz 200 . . . . $72
Mercedes-Benz 250 SE $32
Porsche 911 Targa Convertible $42
Porsche 911 Targa Hardtop $42
Porsche 911 Polizei $32
Renault 16. . . . . $32

SABRA (ALSO GAMDA-SABRA, GAMDA-KOOR)

1:43 scale models comprise this intriguing series from Sabra of Israel produced in the early seventies by Gamda-Koor and, prior to that, issued by Cragstan under the Detroit Senior name.

1964 Chevrolet Chevelle Wagon Fire Chief $24
1964 Chevrolet Chevelle Wagon Israeli Ambulance $24

Photo by Jeff Koch.

Chevrolet Corvair, $24

1964 Chevrolet Chevelle Wagon U.S. Ambulance $24
Cadillac Coupe de Ville $48
Plymouth Barracuda. $36
Pontiac GTO $36

SAFAR

A single model is known to have been produced in 1947 under the Safar brand of Italy.
Fastback Coupe, 4" $45

SAFIR

From 1961 to 1978, Safir of France produced a wide variety of miniature models. Though not very successful, many of their models were copied by Hong Kong firms known for producing cheap unlicensed knock-offs of other manufacturers' products. Safir models are typically valued at $10 – 25 each.

ST. LOUIS

Six diecast models were produced in 1981 under the St. Louis brand. They are 1:43 scale versions of American cars of the 40s and 50s.

SAKO

Sako models of Argentina are 1:25 scale tin models made in the late 1960s.
1966 Chevrolet Taxi. $22
1966 Chevrolet Police Ambulance. $22
1967 Chevrolet Camaro 2-door Hardtop Rally $22
Porsche 906 Rally. $22

SAKURA

These Japanese Sakura models were last offered by Diecast Miniatures.
1 Hino Bus, red, 5" $19
1 Honda 360 Pickup, 1:43 . . . .$19
2 Isuzu Fire Pumper, 5½". $19
2 Neoplan Double Decker Bus, 5½". $19
3 Chevrolet Corvette Coupe, 1:43 . . . .$19
3 Hino Bus, 1:43 . . . .$19
3 Suzuki Jeep, 1:36 . . . .$19
5 Hino Airport Bus. $19
6 Hino Bus, 1:43 . . . .$19
11 Maserati Bora, 1:43 . . . .$19
13 Lancia Stratos, 1:43 . . . .$19
105 Nissan R382, 1:64 . . . .$19
111 Nissan Skyline 4-door Sedan Fire, 1:43 . . . .$19
602 Honda Life Police, 1:36 . . . .$19
609 Nissan Skyline Van, Police, 1:43. . . . .$19
610 Nissan Skyline Van, Fire, 1:43 . . . .$19
611 Nissan Skyline Van, Ambulance, 1:43 . . . .$19
4071 Nissan Cedric 4-door Sedan, Fire, 1:43 . . . .$19
4085 Nissan School Bus, 5". $19
4086 Nissan Kombi, 1:43 . . . .$19
4088 Nissan Police, 1:43. . . . .$19
8152 Toyota Land Cruiser, 1:36. . . . .$19
8549 Toyota Mk 2 4-door Sedan, 1:43. . . . .$19
Toyota Celica Mk 2 Coupe, 1:43 . . . .$19

SALZA

Salza models of France have been confused with Cofalu models, except that Salzas are cast aluminum, while Cofalus are plastic. All models are representative of Tour de France support vehicles.
Aspro Ambulance, 4½" $40
Jeep with Bicycles, 3½" $40
Gendarmerie Jeep, 3½" $40
Press Jeep, 3½" $40
Peugeot 203 Convertible, 5¼". $40
Peugeot 404 Sedan, 5¼". $40
Peugeot D4A Van, 4" $40
Peugeot D4A Loudspeaker Van, 4" $40

SAM TOYS

Although in business since 1911, Sam Toys of Italy didn't start producing miniature cars until 1958. All Sam Toys are plastic, and sell for $10 – 15 each.

SARATOV

According to the June 1997 issue of *Model Auto Review,* Saratov remains one of the largest manufacturers of scale models in Russia. A large portion of their current offerings is dominated by Ural models.

SAVOYE PEWTER TOY COMPANY

Back in 1930, "pewter" used to be another name for lead alloy toys. Savoye was based in North Bergen, New Jersey. The last known production year for Savoye was 1936.
Ambulance $35
Army Gun Truck, 3¼" $40
Beer Truck, 4⅜" $80
Bus, 5th Avenue, 4¾". $125
Bus, Cross-Country, 3⅜". $40
Bus with Mack Cab, 7½ $45
Convertible $35
Coupe, 3⅜" $40
Coupe, 3⅜" $30
Fire Engine, 3¾". $35
Fire Truck, 4¼" $45
Fire Truck, 3¾" $35
Milk Van $40
Moving Van. $55
Pickup Truck. $40
Police Patrol Van $50
Racer, 4¼" $30
Roadster, 3½" $40
Roadster, 3⅜" $40
Stake Truck, 4½" $25
Stake Truck, 5¾" $35
Tank Car Set, 10¼" $80
Tow Truck, 4" $40
Tractor, 2¾". $30
Tractor, 3" $20

SCALE MODELS

Ertl is the parent company to the Scale Models brand, some of which are produced in unpainted pewter-like finish. Asheville DieCast of Asheville, North Carolina, is arguably the largest supplier of Ertl, Scale Models, Spec-Cast, Liberty Classics, and others. But Diecast Miniatures offers a considerable selection as well. Below is just a sampling. Like Liberty Classics, Ertl Promotionals, Spec-Cast, and others, Scale Models specialize in producing models with various advertising livery.

American Eagle WWII airplane, 10" $18
Hedge Hopper Helicopter, 10" $18
Allis WC Tractor, 1:64 . . . . $5
Case Steam Engine, 1:64 . . . . $7
Dain Commercial Car $15
Deutz 6275 Tractor, 1:64 . . . . $5
Ford 4WD 946 Tractor, 1:64 . . . . $7
Hart Parr Tractor, 1:64 . . . . $7
1931 International Harvester Tanker "Gilmore Oil Company" . . $31
1932 International Harvester Tractor, 1:64 . . . . $5
Massey Ferguson 44 Tractor, 1:64 . . . . $5
MM Comfort Tractor, 1:64 . . . . $5
Oliver 70 Tractor, 1:64 . . . . $5
Oliver 770 Tractor, 1:64 . . . . $5
Oliver 880 Tractor, 1:64 . . . . $5
Rumely Tractor, 1:64 . . . . $7
White 185 Tractor, 1:64 . . . . $5
White 4270 4WD Tractor, 1:64 . . . . $7

SCHABAK

Schabak models are from Nurnburg, Germany. Started in 1966, Schabak started producing diecast cars after Schuco went out of business. The company has since become associated with Gama, the current owner of the Schuco name. Except where noted all models are produced in 1:43 scale.

1001 VW Jetta, 1979 . . . . $20
1002 VW Golf, 1983 . . . . $20
1002/3 VW Golf PTT Car, 1984 . . . . $20
1003 VW Golf ADAC Car, 1984 . . . . $20
1004 VW Golf Tuning, 1984 . . . . $20
1008 VW Golf GTI, 1987 . . . . $20

Photo by Jeff Koch.

1010 VW Jetta, 1984, $20

1011 VW Jetta Police Car $20
1012 VW Jetta Tuning, 1984 . . . . $20
1015 VW Passat, 1988 . . . . $20
1016 VW Passat Van, 1988 . . . . $20
1018 VW Corrado, 1988 . . . . $20

1020 Audi 100 Avant, 1984 . . . . $20
1021 Audi 100 Avant Quattro, 1984 . . . . $20
1022 Audi 100 Avant DSK Car, 1987 . . . . $20
1024 Audi V8, 1989 . . . . $20
1025 Audi 80, 1986 . . . . $20
1030 Audi 90 Quattro, 1984 . . . . $20
1031-A Audi 90 Quattro, 1987 . . . . $20
1031-B 1992 Audi 80 Sedan $17
1035 Audi 80 Quattro, 1987 . . . . $20
1036 Audi 80 Quattro Police Car, 1987 . . . . $20
1037 Audi 90 Quattro, 1988 . . . . $20
1038 Audi 90 Quattro Rally, 1988 . . . . $20
1040 VW Caravelle Bus, 1986 . . . . $20
1041 VW Caravelle Ambulance, 1986 . . . . $20
1042 VW Transporter, 1986 . . . . $20
1043 VW Transporter Fire Van, 1986 . . . . $20
1045 VW Transporter LUFTHANSA, 1986 . . . . $20
1046 VW Caravelle CONDOR, 1986 . . . . $20
1047 VW Caravelle Police Bus, green, 1988 . . . . $20
1048 VW Caravelle Police Bus, white and green, 1988 . . . . . . $20
1050 1989 Audi Coupe $16
1080 Ford Sierra Notchback, 1987 . . . . $20
1081 Ford Sierra Police Car, 1988 . . . . $20
1086 Ford Fiesta, 1989 . . . . $20
1110 1993 Porsche Carrera 2 Convertible $24
1150 BMW 535i, 1988 . . . . $20
1151 BMW 535i Taxi, 1988 . . . . $20
1152 BMW 525i Police Car, white with green stripes, 1988 . . . $20
1153 BMW 525i Police Car, white & green, 1988 . . . . $20
1154 BMW 525i Fire Department Car, red with white fenders, 1988 . . . . $20
1155 BMW 525i Fire Department Car, 1988, white & orange-red, 1988 . . . . $20
1156 BMW 525i Doctor's Car, 1988 . . . . $20
1158 BMW M5, 1989 . . . . $20
1160 BMW Z-1, 1989 . . . . $20

SCHABAK LARGER SCALE MODELS

1300 1986 Ford Transit Bus, 1:35, 1987 . . . . $30
1301 1986 Ford Transit Van, 1:35, 1987 . . . . $30
1500 1985 Ford Scorpio D, 1:25, 1986 . . . . $35
1501 1985 Ford Granada, 1:25, 1986 . . . . $35
1510 1987 Ford Sierra Notchback, 1:25, 1988 . . . . $35
1511 1987 Ford Sierra Notchback, 1:25, 1988 . . . . $35
1512 1988 Ford Sierra Cosworth, 1:25, 1989 . . . . $35
1513 1988 Ford Sierra Cosworth, 1:25, 1988 . . . . $35
1514 Ford Sierra Polizei, 1:25, 1989 . . . . $35
1600 BMW Z1 Convertible, 1:25, 1989 . . . . $35

SCHABAK AIRCRAFT OF THE WORLD COLLECTION

Listed below are Schabak's latest offerings of scale model airplanes. Each model, listed with the Schabak model number and name, is available in various liveries.

SCHABAK 1:600 SCALE DIECAST AIRCRAFT MODELS

901 Boeing 747/200 . . . . $4 – 5
902 McDonnell-Douglas DC-10 . . . . $4 – 5
903 Airbus A 300 B . . . . $4 – 5
904 McDonnell-Douglas MD-80 . . . . $4 – 5
905 Boeing 737/200 . . . . $4 – 5
906 Boeing 727/200 . . . . $4 – 5

907 Boeing 767/200	$4 – 5
908 Boeing 757/200	$4 – 5
909 Lockheed L-1011	$4 – 5
911 Boeing 747/300	$4 – 5
920 Concorde	$4 – 5
921 Boeing 747/400	$4 – 5
922 McDonnell-Douglas DC-8	$4 – 5
923 Airbus A 310	$4 – 5
924 McDonnell-Douglas DC 9-40/MD 87	$4 – 5
925 Boeing 737/500	$4 – 5
926 Airbus A 320	$4 – 5
927 Boeing 767/300	$4 – 5
929 ATR 42	$4 – 5
930 Fairchild F-27/F-50	$4 – 5
931 Fairchild F-28	$4 – 5
932 Douglas DC-3	$4 – 5
933 Convair CV 440	$4 – 5
934 Lockheed L-1049 G	$4 – 5
935 Boeing 707	$4 – 5
936 SF 340	$4 – 5
937 Embraer 120	$4 – 5
938 McDonnell-Douglas DC-4	$4 – 5
939 ATR 72	$4 – 5
940 Fairchild F-100	$4 – 5
941 Vickers Viscount	$4 – 5
943 McDonnell-Douglas MD-11	$4 – 5
945 Boeing 737/500	$4 – 5
946 BAe 146	$4 – 5
947 Canadair Jet	$4 – 5
948 McDonnell-Douglas DC-6	$4 – 5
950 Tupolev TU 204	$4 – 5
951 Ilyushin 96	$4 – 5
952 Ilyushin 62	$4 – 5
953 Ilyushin 86	$4 – 5

SCHABAK 1:500 SCALE DIECAST AIRCRAFT MODELS

821 Boeing 747-400	$8 – 11
823 Airbus A 310-300	$8 – 11
825 Boeing 737-300	$8 – 11
827 Boeing 767-300	$8 – 11

SCHABAK 1:250 SCALE DIECAST AIRCRAFT MODELS

850 Boeing 747-400	$25
851 Boeing 747-200	$25
852 Boeing 747-300	$25
1027 Junkers JU 52	$7
1028 Douglas DC-3	$7
1029 Concorde	$12

SCHABAK 1:250 SCALE TIN AND PLASTIC AIRCRAFT MODELS

1025 Boeing 747/200	$13
1026 Boeing 747 F	$13
Schabak 880/881 4½" Plastic Baby-Jet	$5 each

SCHUCO

Schuco has been around for a long time, beginning in 1912 as a distinctive brand of clockwork tin toys. Now that the original Schuco company has gone out of business, Gama has purchased the company and is now producing remakes of many of the original models, now marketed through the Lilliput Motor Company of Yerington, Nevada.

The Piccolo series in particular, never having attracted much attention when they were introduced in 1957, are now rising in value. These small 1:90 scale models, usually about an inch long, are described by Dr. Edward Force as "rather uninspiring little blobs." The charisma of these tiny models is what attracts collectors today.

Except for Piccolo models, Schuco's main entry into the diecast market didn't happen till 1971, with the introduction of precision scale models in 1:43 and 1:66 scale. Presented below is an extensive list of Schucos, both diecast and otherwise.

SCHUCO 100 SERIES

101 Micro Racer 101, 3½", 1950s, Porsche style	$175
102 Micro Racer 102, 3½", 1950s, Indy style	$175
104 Micro Racer 104, 3½", 1950s, Indy style	$175

SCHUCO 1:43 SCALE 600 SERIES

610 Audi 80 LS, 1972	$25
611 Audi 80 GL, 1972	$25
612 Mercedes-Benz 350 SE, 1972	$25
613 BMW Turbo, 1973	$25
614 Volkswagen Passat TS, silver, 1973	$25

Photo by Jeff Koch.

615 Volkswagen Passat TS, red, orange-red or yellow-green, 1973, $25

616 Mercedes-Benz 350 SE Police Car, 1973	$25
617 BMW 520, 1973	$25
618 Mercedes-Benz 450 SE, 1973	$25
619 Volkswagen Passant Variant, 1974	$25
620 Volkswagen Scirocco, 1974	$25
621 Volkswagen Golf, 1974	$25
622 Audi 50, 1974	$25
623 Volkswagen Polo, 1975	$25
624 Volkswagen Golf Rally, 1975	$25
625 BMW 525, 1973	$25
626 BMW 316, 1975	$25
627 BMW 320, 1975	$25
628 Porsche 924, 1975	$25
629 BMW 630 CS, 1976	$25
630 VW Passat Variant ADAC Car, 1975	$25
631 VW Passat Variant Fire Chief, 1975	$25
632 VW Scirocco Racing Service Car, 1975	$25
633-A Mercedes-Benz 350 SE Taxi, 1975	$25
633-B Mercedes-Benz 350 SE Doctor's Car, 1976	$25
634 Audi 80 Police Car, 1974	$25
635 BMW 520 Police Car, 1976	$25
636 BMW 320 Rally Car, 1976	$25
637 BMW 535 Doctor's Car, 1976	$25

638 VW Golf Mail Car, 1976 . . . . $25
639 Audi 100, 1976 . . . . $25

SCHUCO PICCOLO SERIES 1:90 SCALE ONE-PIECE TOYS

701 Ferrari Grand Prix Car, 2", 1958 . . . . $50
702 Mercedes-Benz Grand Prix F1, 2", streamlined, 1958 . . . . . $50
703 Mercedes-Benz Grand Prix, 2", 1958 . . . . $50
704 1936 Mercedes-Benz Grand Prix, 2", 1958 . . . . $50
705 Midget Racer, 2", 1958 . . . . $50
706 Maserati Grand Prix, 2", 1958 . . . . $50
707 BMW 507 Convertible, 2", 1958 . . . . $50
708 Porsche Spyder, 2", 1958 . . . . $50
709-A Austin-Healey 100 Six, 2", 1958 . . . . $50
709-B Mercedes-Benz 300 SL, 2", 1958 . . . . $50
710 Firebird II Experimental Car, 2", 1958 . . . . $50
711 FX Atmos Experimental Car, 2", 1958 . . . . $50
712 Volkswagen, 2", 1958 . . . . $50
713 Mercedes-Benz 190 SL, 2", 1958 . . . . $50
714 MGA Coupe, 2", 1958 . . . . $50
715 VW Karmann-Ghia, 2", 1958 . . . . $50
716 NSU-Fiat Spyder, 2", 1958 . . . . $50
717 Mercedes-Benz 220 Coupe, 2", 1958 . . . . $50
718 Volvo PV 544, 2", 1958 . . . . $50
719 Citroën DS 19, 2", 1958 . . . . $50
720 Volkswagen Police/Fire Chief, 2", 1958 . . . . $50
722 Camping Trailer, 2", 1958 . . . . $50
723 VW Karmann-Ghia & Trailer, 3½", 1958 . . . . $65
724 Mercedes-Benz 220 S, 2¼", 1960 . . . . $50
725 Ford Hot Rod, 1¾", 1964 . . . . $50
740 Mercedes-Benz Bus, 3", 1960 . . . . $50
741 Mercedes-Benz Delivery Van, 2", 1960 . . . . $50
742 Mercedes-Benz Low Loader, 4", 1960 . . . . $60
743 Mercedes-Benz Refrigerator Van, 5½", 1960 . . . . $60
744 Mercedes-Benz Tanker Semi, 4", 1960 . . . . $60
745 Magirus Ladder Truck, 4", 1960 . . . . $60
746 Krupp Open Truck, 3¾", 1960 . . . . $60
747 Magirus Wrecker, 3", 1960 . . . . $60
748 Krupp Dump Truck, 3¼", 1960 . . . . $60
749 Krupp Flat Truck, 4", 1960 . . . . $60
750 Krupp Quarry Dump Truck, 3¼", 1960 . . . . $60
751 Krupp Lumber Truck, 6", 1962 . . . . $60
752 Deutz Farm Tractor, 1¾, 1962 . . . . $60
753 Deutz Caterpillar Tractor, 2", 1962 . . . . $60
754 Deutz Bulldozer, 2¼", 1962 . . . . $60
755 Mercedes-Benz Searchlight Truck, 1¾", 1962 . . . . $60
756 Mercedes-Benz Fire Van, 1⅞", 1962 . . . . $60
757 Tipping Trailer, 3", 1962 . . . . $60
758 Faun Street Sweeper, 2¼", 1962 . . . . $60
759 Conveyor belt, 4½", 1962 . . . . $60
760 Demag Power Shovel, 3⅛", 1962 . . . . $75
761 Krupp Car Transporter, 8", 1962 . . . . $75
762 Liebherr Tower Crane, 6¼" high, 1962 . . . . $90
763 Krupp Tank Truck, 3¼", 1962 . . . . $60
764 Boat and Trailer, 2", 1962 . . . . $60
765 Fork Lift truck, 2¾", 1962 . . . . $60
766 VW Karmann-Ghia and Boat Trailer, 3½", 1962 . . . . $60
767 Krupp Bucket Truck, 3⅛", 1962 . . . . $60
768 Hopper Trailer, 2¾", 1962 . . . . $60
769 Krupp Crane Truck, 4" $60

770 Krupp Cherry Picker, 3½" $60
771 Dingler Road Roller, 1½" $60
772 Krupp Cement Mixer, 3⅝" $60
773 Henschel Covered Semi, 4½" $75
774 Faun Quarry Dump Truck, 3⅝" $60
775 Coles Crane Truck and Trailer $60
776 MAN Doubledeck Bus, 3" $60
777 Linhoff Road Paver, 5" $60
778 Krupp Cement Carrier, 5½" $60
799 Coles Hydraulic Crane $75

SCHUCO AIRPLANES

779 Junkers F-13 . . . . $40
780 Thunderjet $40
781 Magister 170-R $40
782 Super Sabre $40
783 Douglas F4D-1 . . . . $40
784 Junkers JU-52 . . . . $40
785 Boeing 737 . . . . $40
786 Boeing 727 . . . . $50
787 Boeing 707 . . . . $50
788 Boeing 747 . . . . $50
789 Concorde $50
790 Douglas DC8 . . . . $50
791 Douglas DC9 . . . . $40
792 Douglas DC10 . . . . $50
793 Boeing 747 . . . . $50
794 Lear Jet $50
795 Airbus A300B $50
796 Boeing 747 Freighter $50
797 Ilyushin IL-62 . . . . $50

SCHUCO 800 SERIES

805 Mercedes-Benz 200, 2¾", 1971 . . . . $10
806 Mercedes-Benz 200 Police Car, 2¾", 1971 . . . . $10
807 Ford Taunus 20M, 2¾", 1971 . . . . $10

Photo by Jeff Koch.

808 BMW 1600, 2¾", 1971, $10

809 BMW 2002, 2½", 1971 . . . . $10
810 Ford Escort 1300 GT, 2⅜", 1971 . . . . $10
811 Opel Commodore GS, 2¾", 1971 . . . . $10
812 Volkswagen 411, 2¾", 1971 . . . . $10
813 Porsche 911S, 2½", 1971 . . . . $10
814 Opel GT 1900, 2⅜", 1971 . . . . $10
815 BMW 2800 CS, 2¾", 1971 . . . . $10
816 Ford Capri 1700 GT, 2½", 1971 . . . . $10
817 Audi 100 LS, 2¾", 1971 . . . . $10
818 Volkswagen 1300, 2½", 1971 . . . . $10

819 Opel Admiral 2800 E, 3", 1971 . . . . $10
820 Mercedes-Benz 250 CE, 2¾", 1971 . . . . $10
821 Audi 100 Coupe, 2¾", 1971 . . . . $10
822 Opel Commodore GS Rally, 2¾", 1971 . . . . $10
823 Mercedes-benz 200 Taxi, 2¾", 1971 . . . . $10
824 Volkswagen 411 Fire Chief, 2¾", 1971 . . . . $10
825 Porsche 911S Police Car, 2⅜", 1971 . . . . $10
826 VW Porsche 914 S, 2⅜", 1971. . . . . $10
827 VW Porsche 914-6, 2⅜", 1971. . . . . $10
828 Mercedes-Benz C-111, 2¾", 1971 . . . . $10
829 BMW 2500, 2¾", 1972 . . . . $10
830 BMW 2800, 2¾", 1972 . . . . $10
831 Volkswagen K70, 2¾", 1972 . . . . $10
832 Volkswagen 1302 S, 2½", 1972 . . . . $10
833 Volkswagen ADAC Service Car, 2½", 1972 . . . . $10
834 Ford Capri 1700 GT Rally, 2⅝", 1972 . . . . $10
835 Porsche 911 S Racing Car, 2⅜", 1972 . . . . $10
836 VW Porsche 914-6 Racing Car, 2⅜", 1972 . . . . $10
837 Ford Taunus GT Coupe, 2⅜", 1972. . . . . $10
838 Ford Taunus GXL Coupe, 2⅜", 1972. . . . . $10
839 Opel Manta SR, 2⅜", 1972 . . . . $10
840 Ferrari Formula Two, 2½", 1972. . . . . $10
841 BMW Formula Two, 2½", 1972. . . . . $10
842 Matra Ford Formula One, 2½", 1972 . . . . $10
843 Porsche 917, 2½", 1972 . . . . $15
844 Mercedes-Benz 350 SL Convertible, 3", 1972 . . . . $10
845 BMW 200 tii, 2½", 1972 . . . . $10
846 Opel Ascona Voyage, 2½", 1972. . . . . $10

Photo by Jeff Koch.

847 Brabham Ford Formula One, 2½", 1972, $10

848 Opel GT-J, 2½", 1972. . . . . $10
849 Opel Manta SR, 2½", 1972 . . . . $10
850 Renault 16, 2½", 1972 . . . . $10
851 Ford Escort Rally, 2⅜", 1972. . . . . $10
852 Audi 100 GL, 2¾", 1972 . . . . $10
853 Renault 17, 2½", 1972 . . . . $10
854 Porsche 917, 2½", 1972 . . . . $15
855 Audi 80 LS, 2½", 1973 . . . . $10
856 Opel Rekord II, 2¾", 1973 . . . . $10
857 Opel Commodore, 2¾", 1973. . . . . $10
858 Ford Consul, 2¾", 1973 . . . . $10
859 Ford Granada, 2¾", 1973 . . . . $10

860 Renault 16 TS, 2½", 1973 . . . . $10
861 Renault 17 TS, 2½", 1973 . . . . $10
862 Audi 80 GL, 2½", 1973. . . . . $10
863 Tyrell Ford Formula One, 2½", 1973. . . . . $10
864 BMW Turbo Turbo, 2½", 1973 . . . . $10
865 BMW Turbo, 2½", 1973 . . . . $10
866 Mercedes-Benz 350 SE, 3", 1973 . . . . $10
867 Volkswagen Passat, 2½", 1973 . . . . $10
868 Mercedes-Benz 450 SE Police Car, 3", 1974 . . . . $10
869 VW Porsche 914 Race Control Car, 2⅜", 1974 . . . . $10
870 Lotus Ford 72 Formula One, 2½", 1974. . . . . $10
871 Renault 5, 2⅛", 1974 . . . . $10
872 Volkswagen Passat TS, 2½", 1974. . . . . $10
873 Mercedes-Benz 450 SE, 3", 1974 . . . . $10
874 Ford Capri II, 2½", 1974. . . . . $10
875 BMW 3.0 CSL, 2¾", 1974 . . . . $10
876 Audi 80 Fire Chief, 2½", 1974. . . . . $10
877 Ford Capri RS, 2½", 1974. . . . . $10
878 Matra Simca Bagheera, 2½" $10
879 Volkswagen Scirocco, 2⅜", 1974 . . . . $10
880 Volkswagen Golf, 2¼", 1974 . . . . $10
881 Ford Escort, 2⅜, 1975 . . . . $10
882 Volkswagen Golf Mail Car, 2¼", 1975. . . . . $10
888 Ford Escort Rally, 2⅜", 1975. . . . . $10
889 Volkswagen Police Bus, 2⅝", 1975. . . . . $10
890 Ford Transit Fire Van, 2⅝", 1975 . . . . $10

Schuco 900 Series

900 Mercedes-Benz Bus, 3", 1972 . . . . $20
901 Bussing Open Truck, 3¾", 1972 . . . . $20
902 Bussing Dump Truck, 3", 1972 . . . . $20
903 Bussing Flat Truck, 3⅞", 1972 . . . . $20
904 Bussing Quarry Dump Truck, 2¾", 1972. . . . . $20
905 Bussing Covered Semi-Trailer Truck, 4½", 1972 . . . . . . $20
906 Bussing Cement Carrier, 5⅜", 1972. . . . . $20
907 Demag Power Shovel, 3⅜", 1972 . . . . $20
908 Faun Quarry Dump Truck, 3⅝", 1972. . . . . $20
909 Magirus-Deutz 232D Dump Truck, 3⅞", 1973 . . . . $20
910 Volkswagen Kombi, 2⅝", 1973. . . . . $20
911 Volkswagen Transporter, 2⅝", 1973 . . . . $20
912 Ford Transit Van, 2⅝", 1974. . . . . $20
913 Ford Transit Bus, 2⅝", 1974 . . . . $20
914 Volkswagen Ambulance, 2⅝", 1974 . . . . $20
915 Volkswagen Mail truck, 2⅝", 1974 . . . . $20
916 Mercedes-Benz 0303 Bus, 7", 1975 . . . . $45
917 Magirus-Deutz 232D Quarry Dumper, 4", 1975 . . . . . . $20
919 Volkswagen LT35 Pickup, 3¼", 1976 . . . . $20

Schuco 1000 Series/Micro Racers

1001 Mirakocar 1001, 4½", 1950s $150
1001/1 Mirakocar Polizei, 4¾" $150
1007 Motodrill Clown 1007, 5", composition head, 1950s $750
1010 Mystery Car 1010, 5½", 1950s, non-fall action $175
1011 Dalli, 6½", 1950s, tin car, plastic driver $150
1034 Micro Racer Rally 1034, 4", 1950s $100
1035 Micro Racer Go Kart 1035, 4", 1950s $180
1036 Micro Racer Hot Rod 1036, 4½" 1950s. $180
1036/1 Micro Racer Mercer 1036/1, 4", 1950s. $180
1038 Micro Racer Mercedes Benz $180
1039 Micro Racer Volkswagen Polizei 1039, 4", 1950s $180

1040 Micro Racer 1040, 4", 1950s $180
1041 Micro Racer 1041, 4", 1950s $180
1042 Micro Racer 1042, 4", 1950s $180
1043 Micro Racer 1043, 4", 1950s $180
1044 Micro Racer Mercedes Benz 1044, 4", 1950s. $200
1045 Micro Racer '57 Ford 1045, 4", 1950s $180
1046 Micro Racer Volkswagen, 4", 1950s $175
1047 Micro Racer Porsche 1047, 4", 1950s $200
1048 Micro Racer Alfa Romeo 1048, 4", 1950s $175
1049 Micro Racer Stake Truck 1049, 4", 1950s $175
1050 Studio Racer 1050 with tools, 5½", 1950s. $225
1070 Grand Prix Racer, 6", 1950s $150
1111 Fex, 6", 1950s. $100
1225 Mercer Auto, 7½", 1950s $175
1250 Jaguar, 5½", 1940s $300

SCHUCO 2000 SERIES

2000 Anno 2000, 5½", 1940s. $150
2002 Akustico 2002, 5½" $150
2008 Magico, 5½", 1950s $100
2095 Mercedes 190SL, 8", 1950s $275

SCHUCO 3000 SERIES

3000 Telesteering 3000 Limo, 4", 1950s $80
3010 Varianto 3010, playset with two 4½" tin cars, 1950s. . . . $180
3010 Varianto 3010 Super, service station with two 4½" tin cars, 1950s $325
3010/30 Varianto Box 3010/30, tin garage and 3041 Limo, 4½", 1950s $200
3041 Varianto 3041 Limo, 4", 1950s
3042 Lasto, 4½", 1950s $100
3044 Varianto Bus 3044, 4", 1950s. $100
3054 Gas Station, 8", 1950s $100
3064 Varianto 3064, 8" plastic, 1950s. $50
3112 Varianto Electro 3112, 4" truck, 1950s $100
3112u Varianto Electro 3112u, 4½" truck, 1950s. $100
3118 Station Car 3118, 4½", 1950s. $100

SCHUCO 4000 SERIES

4001 Examico 4001, 6", 1950s $225
4012 Radio 4012, 6", musical car, 1950s. $375

SCHUCO 5000 SERIES

5311 Buick, 9" $375
5311 Elektro Ingenico, 8½", remote control, 1950s. $400
5505 Cadillac DeVille Convertible, 11", 1960s plastic $150
5700 Synchromatic 5700, resembles Packard Hawk, 11", 1950s . $1,000

OTHER SCHUCO MODELS

1928 Mercedes SSK, 8", 1950s $175
Magico Car and Garage, 6", 1950s. $225
Monkey Car, 6", 1930s, orange/black, smiling monkey $2,500
Scientific Forklift $125

NEW SCHUCO REPLICA MODELS

Lilliput is the major distributor of new replica Schuco diecast and tin toys, along with other brands of new reproduction tin toys from famous manufacturers such as Paya of Spain, Tucher & Walther, DBS/Dusseldorfer, and Lorenz Bolz Kreisel of Germany, Revival of Italy, and Kitahara of Japan.

NEW PICCOLO 1:90 SERIES REPRODUCTIONS FOR 1995

The Lilliput catalog says "these Piccolos are all tiny, heavy, and solid little ingots. You know when they lay in your hand. All about 1⅞" long. Original ones are extremely difficult to find, at any price."

702 Mercedes Streamliner. $25
703 Mercedes 2.5I $25
704 Mercedes '36 GP $25

NEW SCHUCO 1:43 SCALE SERIES REPRODUCTIONS FOR 1995

"Schuco has undertaken the manufacture of an interesting line of 1:43 scale vehicles seldomly seen. Mostly German oddities from the 50s. Nicely scaled, with numerous features, such as opening doors, hoods, and trunklids. From the Baroque BMW to the Goliath 3-Wheeler, a worthy part of any collection."

2014 BMW 501 . . . . $59
2040 BMW 501 Fire Chief. $59
2052 Goliath Tempo Pritsche $59
2063 Goliath Tempo Van $59
2082 Lloyd 600 . . . . $42
2091 BMW Isetta $42
2151 BMW Dixi $42
2162 BMW 200 . . . . $42
2172 BMW 507 . . . . $42

OTHER SCHUCO SERIES/BRANDS

Schuco toys are sold in various markets under different names. Lilliput, Nutz, Oldtimer, Paya, and Rei are all trademark brands from Schuco. Rei in particular is a brand name of Schuco models sold in Brazil.

SCHWUNG

Schwung is a brand name of 1:32 scale tin toys made in Germany.

Opel Rekord 4-door Sedan. $16
Opel Fire Chief $24
Opel Police $24
Opel Ambulance $24
Skoda Dump Truck $24
Tatra 815 Van $16

SCHYLLING

Schylling brand tin toys were last known to be made in Massachusetts.

Los Angeles Airship $18
Graf Zeppelin Airship $18
American Motorcycle $18

SCOTTOYS

Scottoys are 1:48 white metal reproductions of obsolete Mercury models. Each model is offered in two or three color choices, and are available almost exclusively from Modelauto of Leeds, England.

SC001 Fiat 600 saloon $28
SC002 Fiat 600 Multipla two tone $39
SC003 Alfa Romeo Giulietta $39
SC004 Alfa Romeo 1900 saloon . . . . $39)
SC005 Fiat 1100 saloon. $39
SC006 Cadillac Eldorado. $48
SC007 Innocenti 950 . . . . $39
SC008 Alfa Romeo Giulietta Sprint $39
SC009 Fiat Nuova 500 . . . . $34

SC000 Lancia Appia Series 1 . . . . £25 ($39 US)
SC010 Lancia Appia Series 3 . . . . £25 ($39 US)
SC011 Autobianchi Bianchina . . . . £22 ($34 US)
SC017 Lambretta scooter 1:30 . . . . £14 ($22 US)
SC018 Vespa scooter 1:30 . . . . £14 ($22 US)
SC018 Vespa scooter 1:30 KIT . . . . £9 ($14 US)

SEPTOY

Gasquy brand models were first issued as Septoys, produced in Belgium.

SHINSEI

These Japanese diecast models listed below are highly-accurate scale models currently available from Diecast Miniatures and Toys for Collectors.

61 Kenworth SKYWAY, 1:99 . . . . $8
62 Kenworth Car Transporter, 1:99 . . . . $8
402 Gulf Mirage, 1:43 . . . . $14
407 BMW 3.5 CSL Coupe, 1:43 . . . . $14

421 Lamborghini Countach, 1:50, $6

452 Chevrolet Corvette Sting Ray, 1:56, $6

601 CAT 922C Wheel Loader, 1:75 . . . . $39
605 KATO NK 800 Hydraulic Crane, 1:61 . . . . $72
614 Komatsu PC 650 Excavator, 1:50 . . . . $69
615 Komatsu WA 350 Wheel Loader, 1:50 . . . . $45
617 Komatsu D 475 Dozer with Ripper, 1:48 . . . . $72
618 Hitachi EX 200 Excavator, 1:48 . . . . $44
619 Hitachi LX 70 Wheel Loader $39
620 Hitachi EX 1800 Mining Excavator, 1:60 . . . . $85

625 Fuso TOKYO OSAKA, 1:43 . . . . $18
658 Komatsu HD 785 Heavy Dump Truck, 1:45 . . . . $79
675 TMC 860 Wheel Loader, 1:50 . . . . $39
921 Komatsu PC 200 Shovel $72
950 CAT 325 Hydraulic Excavator, 1:50 . . . . $79
4217 GMC Oil Tanker SHELL, 1:43 . . . . $18
4218 GMC Refrigerator Van, 1:43 . . . . $18
4412 Lancia Stratos, 1:43 . . . . $18
4422 Lamborghini Jota, 1:64 . . . . $6
Lift Truck, 1:64 . . . . $30

SIBUR

These are older hand-built diecast models from France.

GMC 6X6 Army Open Truck, 1:43 . . . . $35
GMC 6X6 Army Closed Truck, 1:43 . . . . $35
GMC Army Bookmobile, 1:43 . . . . $35
GMC Truck Paris-Dakar, 1:50 . . . . $35

SIEPERWERKE (SEE SIKU)

SIKU

Siku is a division of Sieperwerke, a venerable German company established in 1921 by Richard Sieper. The name "Siku" is an acronym formed from the first two letters of the Sieper name combined with the first two letters of "kunststoff," the German word describing synthetic material or plastic.

From 1949 to 1963, Siku toys were made of plastic, but in 1963, as Matchbox started marketing their products in Germany, the first Siku diecast models were produced to attempt to keep up with the increasing competition. 1:55 scale models currently marketed in the US are packaged as Siku "Super Series" models. While the predominant scale for Siku is 1:55, they are also produced in 1:64 scale and in the 1:32 scale "Farm Series." The list below includes model number, description, production years, and current relative value.

201 Fiat 1800, 1963 – 1968 . . . . $25
202 BMW 1500, 1962 – 1968 . . . . $40
203 Ford 12M, 1963 . . . . $35
204 Opel Kadett, 1963 – 1966 . . . . $40
206 Ford 17M Turnier, 1963 – 1968 . . . . $35
209 Cadillac Fleetwood, 1963 – 1968 . . . . $35 – 45
211 Volkswagen Bus, 1963 – 1964 . . . . $40
212 Volkswagen Bus Polizei (Police) Loudspeaker Van, 1963 –
1970 . . . . $30
218 Porsche Standard T Diesel Tractor, 1963 – 1972 . . . . . . $25
220 Tempo Matador Bus, 1963 – 1969 . . . . $35
221 Mercedes-Benz 300SL, 1963 – 1969 . . . . $35
222 Ford F500 LKW (US Truck), 1963 – 1972 . . . . $30
223 Opel Rekord (1963), 1964 – 1966 . . . . $40
224 DKW F12, 1964 – 1966 . . . . $50
225 Farm Trailer, 1964 – 1968 . . . . $15
226 Opel Caravan 1500 (1963), 1964 – 1966 . . . . $30
228 Jeep with Trailer, 1964 – 1972 . . . . $35
229 Mercedes-Benz 230SL, 1964 – 1968 . . . . $30
230 Volkswagen 1200 "Beetle," 1964 – 1969 . . . . $30
231 Volkswagen 1200 with antenna on roof, 1964 – 1968 . . . . $45
232 Ford 17M, 1964 – 1966 . . . . $30

233 Mercedes-Benz Binz Ambulance, 1964 – 1970. . . . . $35
234 Porsche 901, 1964 – 1969. . . . . $35
234 Porsche 911 Targa, 1970 – 1974 . . . . $30
235 Porsche 901 Polizei, 1964 – 1970 . . . . $25
235 Ford Capri Polizei, 1971 – 1974 . . . . $25
237 Ford TSF Service Van with ladder on roof, 1964 – 1971. . . $25
238 Fiat 40 CA Bulldozer with loader on front, 1964 – 1972. . . $20
239 Fiat CA40 Bulldozer with blade, 1964 – 1972 . . . . $20
241 Roller Trailer, 1964 – 1968 . . . . $15
242 Hay Rake, 1964 – 1965 . . . . $30
244 Fiat 1800 Taxi, 1964 – 1968 . . . . $25
244 Mercedes 250 SE Taxi, 1968 – 1971 . . . . $30
244 Mercedes 250/8 Taxi, 1972 – 1974 . . . . $20
245 Oldsmobile 98 Holiday Sports Coupe, 1964 – 1969 . . . . . $30
246 Ford M12 with trailer, 1964 – 1966 . . . . $40
246 Ford 15M, 1967 – 1968. . . . . $35
247 Volkswagen 1500 Variant, 1965 – 1968 . . . . $25
248 Volkswagen Karmann Ghia 1500, 1965 – 1969 . . . . $35
249 Faun K10/26AP Dump Truck, 1965 – 1973 . . . . $20
250 Mercedes Benz 190, 1965 – 1969 . . . . $20
250 Mercedes-Benz 250, 1970 – 1974 . . . . $15
251 Ford Transit Double Cab Pickup Van, 1965 – 1969 . . . . . $15
252 Opel Kapitan (1964), 1965 – 1970 . . . . $30
253 Mercedes-Benz 600 Pullman Limousine, 1965 – 1972 . . . $40
254 Diesel Tractor with Dump Trailer, 1966 – 1973 . . . . $40
255 Buick Wildcat Sport Coupe, 1965 – 1971 . . . . $30
256 Mercedes-Benz 250SE, 1966 – 1969 . . . . $35
257 Ford F500 Wrecker, 1965 – 1973 . . . . $35
257 Hanomag Henschel Wrecker, 1974. . . . . $40
258 Liebherr Mobile Crane, 1965 – 1972 . . . . $15
259 Cargo Trailer, 1966 – 1972 . . . . $15
260 Klaus Autodumper, 1966 – 1973 . . . . $25
261 Mercedes-Benz Metz DL30H Fire Ladder Truck, 1966 – 1974. $50
262 Pontiac Bonneville Convertible, 1966 – 1971. . . . . $70
263 Log Trailer, 1966 – 1968. . . . . $25
264 Tempo Matador Camping Van with Kayak, 1966 – 1971 . . $50
264 Ford Transit Camping Van with Kayak, 1972 – 1974 . . . . $35
265 Cadillac Fleetwood 75, 1966 – 1971 . . . . $40
266 BMW 2000CS, 1967 – 1974. $25
267 Oldsmobile Toronado, 1967 – 1974 . . . . $20
268 Ford Transit Kombi Van, 1967 – 1974. . . . . $20
269 Ferrari Berlinetta 275 GTB, 1967 – 1974 . . . . $25
270 Zettelmeyer Europ L2000 Front End Loader, 1967 – 1974. . $20
271 Opel Rekord Coupe, 1967 – 1974. . . . . $35
272 Opel Rekord Caravan with skis and luge, 1967 – 1972 . . . $50
273 Ford Taunus 15M, 1967 – 1969. . . . . $25

276 Ford OSI 20M TS, 1968 – 1972, $30

274 Magirus Garbage Truck, 1967 – 1974 . . . . $50
275 Magirus Auto Transporter, 1967 – 1973. . . . . $35
277 Pontiac GTO Convertible, 1967 – 1972 . . . . $50
278 Side Dumping Trailer, 1967 – 1969 . . . . $25
279 Opel Kapitan (252, 1964) w/Westfalia Travel Trailer, 1968 – 1971. . . . . $55
279 Ford 20M (288) with Westfalia Travel Trailer, 1972 – 1974. $60
280 Euclid S-7/E 915R "ATHEY" Earth Mover, 1968 – 1972. . . . $35
281 Magirus Deutz M250 D22 FK 6x4 Dump Truck, 1968 – 1979. $35
282 Chevrolet Corvette Sting Ray, 1968 – 1974 . . . . $20
283 Ford 20M, 1968 – 1974. . . . . $35
284 Ford 17M Station Wagon , 1968 – 1970. . . . . $40
285 Porsche Carrera 906, 1968 – 1974 . . . . $20
286 Opel Olympia, 1968 – 1969 . . . . $60
287 Hanomag Robust 900 Farm Tractor, 1969 – 1974. . . . . . . $15
288 Henschel-Sattelzug F201S-2A "ARAL" Semi Tanker, 1968 – 1974. . . . . $45
289 Magirus Transporter, 1968 – 1972. . . . . $30
290 Citroën DS21, 1968 – 1974 . . . . $30
291 Magirus Cement Truck, 1969 – 1974 . . . . $25
292 Mercedes-Benz Binz Ambulance Van, 1969 – 1974 . . . . . . $20
293 Mercedes Crane Truck, 1969 – 1974 . . . . $30
294 Jaguar E 2+2, 1968 – 1974 . . . . $25
295 Maserati Mistral, 1968 – 1974 . . . . $25
296 Ford GT40, 1969 – 1974. . . . . $25
297 Oldsmobile Toronado with Boat and Trailer, 1969 – 1974. $35
298 Lincoln Continental Mark III, 1969 – 1972. . . . . $30
299 Zettelmeyer Europ S12 Road Roller, 1969 – 1974. . . . . . . $15
300 VW 411, 1969 . . . . $55
301 Fiat 850 Sport Coupe, 1969 – 1972 . . . . $25
302 Mercedes-Benz 280SL, 1969 – 1974. . . . . $20
303 Hanomag Robust 900 Farm Tractor with Trailer, 1969 – 1973. $25
304 Opel GT1900, 1970 – 1974. $25
305 Mercedes-Benz Postal Truck "Deutsche Bundespost," 1970 – 1974. . . . . $20
306 Mercedes-Benz Europ 1200L Binz Ambulance, 1970 – 1974. $20
307 Hanomag Henschel Garage Transporter, 1971 – 1974 . . . . $40
308 Audi 100LS, 1970 – 1974 . . . . $20
309 Mercedes-Benz 250, 1970 – 1974 . . . . $20
310 Ford Capri 1700GT, 1970 – 1974 . . . . $20
311 Volkswagen 1300 Beetle, 1970 – 1974 . . . . $20
312 Volkswagen-Porsche 914/6, 1970 – 1974. . . . . $20
313 Ford 17M Station Wagon "ADAC," 1970 – 1974. . . . . $25
314 Ford F500 Pickup (222) with Dump Trailer (225), 1970 – 1972. $45
315 Ford F500 Pickup (222) with Side Dumping Trailer (278) . $55
316 Toyota 2000GT, 1971 – 1973 . . . . $20
317 Lamborghini Espada 400GT, 1971 – 1974 . . . . $20
318 Hanomag-Henschel Container Transporter, 1971 – 1974 . . $25
319 Mercedes LP608 ADAC Auto Salvage Truck, 1971 – 1974. . $20
320 VW Bus Postal Van, DEUTSCHE BUNDESPOST, 1970 – 1972. $30
320 Volkswagen Vanagon Postal Van, DBP PEILWAGEN, 1973 – 1974. . . . . $25
321 Alfa Romeo Montreal, 1971 – 1974 . . . . $20
322 Citroën SM, 1971 – 1974 . . . . $20
323 Ford Taunus Transit Highway Construction Truck, 1971 – 1974. . . . . $30
324 Ford Transit Polizei (Police) Emergency Van, 1971 – 1974. $20
325 Menck Power Crane Shovel, 1971 – 1974 . . . . $25

326 Michigan 180 Wheel Dozer with Plow, 1971 – 1974 . . . . . $35

328 Pontiac GTO, "The Judge," 1972 – 1974 . . . . $40

329 Hanomag Robust 900 with Trailer, 1972 – 1973. . . . . . . $45

330 Ford T5 Mustang Mach 1, 1972 – 1974 . . . . $20

331 MAN Racing Fuel Tanker, "Renndienst," 1971 – 1974 . . . . $40

332 Metz Airport Fire Tender, 1972 – 1974 . . . . $25

333 Lamborghini 400GT Espada with Building Transporter Trailer, 1972 – 1974 . . . . $45

334 Ford Transit School Bus Van, "SCHULBUS," 1972 – 1974. . $20

335 Mercedes LP608D Street Maintenance Truck, 1972 – 1974 . $40

336 Mercedes LP608D Silo Transporter, 1972 – 1974 . . . . $40

337 Faun Snow Plow Sand Truck, 1972 – 1974 . . . . $35

338 Hanomag Henschel Covered Truck, 1972 – 1974 . . . . $10

339 Mercedes Water Service Van, 1972 – 1974 . . . . $25

341 BMW Polizei (Police) Loudspeaker Car, 1992 – 1974 . . . . $20

342 Ford 17M Fire Command Station Wagon, 1973 – 1974. . . . $30

343 Hanomag Henschel ADAC Vehicle Safety Check Truck, 1973 – 1974. . . . . $35

344 Lamborghini Fire Hunter, 1973 – 1974 . . . . $30

345 Volkswagen Vanagon Bus with Radar in front compartment, 1973 – 1974, $25

346 Volkswagen-Porsche 914/6 "Rennpolizei," 1973 – 1974 . . . $25

347 Magirus Sand Truck, 1973 – 1974 . . . . $25

348 MAN Container Truck, 1973 – 1974 . . . . $30

349 MAN Lumber Truck with Crane, 1973 – 1974 . . . . $30

350 Hanomag Henschel Pipe Laying Truck, 1973 – 1974 . . . . $35

351 Maserati Boomerang, 1974. $15

352 Magirus Transporter with Tractors, 1973 – 1974 . . . . $95

353 Audi 100 "Arzt-Notfall-Einsatz," 1973 – 1974 . . . . $25

354 Hanomag Henschel Covered Truck and Trailer, 1973 – 1974 . $25

355 Hanomag Henschel ARAL Service Station Transporter, 1974 . $40

356 Volkswagen Vanagon Ambulance, "Malteser Hilfsdienst," 1974. . . . . $25

357 Mercedes Fire Command Truck, 1974. . . . . $20

360 Hanomag Henschel Tank Truck, 1974 . . . . $35

361 Mercedes Unimog Hydraulic DBP Truck, 1974 . . . . $35

362 Magirus Skip Truck, 1974. . . . . $30

0801 Excavator, 1992 . . . . $5 – 10

0802 Front Loader, 1992 . . . . $5 – 10

0803 Scraper, 1992 . . . . $5 – 10

0804 Mercedes-Benz G-Wagon Police Van, 1992 . . . . $5 – 10

0805 Mercedes-Benz G-Wagon Ambulance, 1992. . . . . . . $5 – 10

0806 Coach, 1992. . . . . $5 – 10

0807 Police Helicopter, 1992. $5 – 10

0808 Tipper Truck, 1992. . . . . $5 – 10

0811 Refuse Truck, 1992 . . . . $5 – 10

0813 Cement Mixer, 1992 . . . . $5 – 10

0814 Dumper Truck, 1992 . . . . $5 – 10

0815 Livestock Transporter, 1992 . . . . $5 – 10

0817 Space Shuttle, 1992 . . . . $5 – 10

0820 Volkswagen Delivery Van, 1992 . . . . $5 – 10

0821 Unimog Snow Plow, 1992. . . . . $5 – 10

0822 Tipper Truck, 1992. . . . . $5 – 10

0823 Bulldozer, 1992 . . . . $5 – 10

0824 Volkswagen School Bus, white . . . . $5 – 10

0825 Volkswagen Caravelle, 1992 . . . . $5 – 10

0826 Airport Fire Engine, 1992 . . . . $5 – 10

0828 Recycling Transporter, 1992 . . . . $5 – 10

0831 ADAC Helicopter, 1992. . . . . $5 – 10

0832 Fire Rescue Helicopter, 1992 . . . . $5 – 10

0833 Volkswagen Police Van, 1992 . . . . $5 – 10

0834 Volkswagen Fire Rescue Bus, 1992 . . . . $5 – 10

0835 Rescue Van Ambulance, 1992 . . . . $5 – 10

0836 Morgan Plus 8, 1992. . . . . $5 – 10

0837 Porsche 911 Convertible, 1992 . . . . $5 – 10

0838 Peugeot 205 Convertible, 1992 . . . . $5 – 10

0839 Volkswagen Beetle Convertible, 1992 . . . . $5 – 10

0840 Iveco Pickup, 1992 . . . . $5 – 10

0841 Audi 80 Convertible, 1992. . . . . $5 – 10

0842 Volkswagen Golf Convertible, 1994 . . . . $5 – 10

0843 Deutz DX 85 Tractor, 1995 . . . . $4 – 6

0844 Wrecker Truck, 1996 . . . . $4 – 6

0845 Ford Fiesta, 1997 . . . . $4 – 6

0846 BMW Z-3, 1997 . . . . $4 – 6

0847 Massey-Ferguson Tractor, 1997. . . . . $4 – 6

0848 Dump Truck, 1997 . . . . $4 – 6

1010 Porsche 911 Targa, 1975 – 1987 . . . . $8 – 12

1010 Volkswagen Golf, 1993 . . . . $4 – 8

1011 BMW 2000CS, 1975 – 1981 . . . . $9 – 12

1011 Mercedes-Benz 500 SEL Convertible, 1993, $4 – 10

1012 Ferrari Berlinetta, 1975 – 1981 . . . . $15

1012 Mercedes-Benz 500 SEL Hardtop, 1993 . . . . $4 – 10

1013 Porsche Carrera 906, 1975 – 1982 . . . . $6 – 10

1013 Skip Truck, 1994 . . . . $4 – 10

1014 Citroën DS21, 1975 – 1980 . . . . $15

1014 Wreck Truck, 1994 . . . . $4 – 10

1015 Jaguar E 2+2, 1975 – 1982 . . . . $12

1015 Fire Engine . . . . $4 – 10

1016 Ford GT 40, 1975 – 1981 . . . . $12

1016 Container Transporter Truck, "Sea Land," 1993 . . . . . $4 – 10
1017 Mercedes 280 SL, 1975 – 1984 . . . . $12
1017 Mercedes Racing Truck, 1993 . . . . $4 – 10
1018 Opel GT 1900, 1975 – 1978 . . . . $20
1018 Iveco Racing Truck, 1994 . . . . $4 – 10
1019 Audi 100 LS, 1975 – 1982 . . . . $12
1019 Simon Snorkel, 1994. . . . . $4 – 10
1020 Mercedes-Benz 250, 1975 – 1984 . . . . $12
1020 Boeing 737, 1994 . . . . $5 – 10
1021 Ford Capri, 1975 – 1978 . . . . $16
1021 Airbus 320, 1993 . . . . $5 – 10
1022 Volkswagen 1300 Beetle, 1975 – 1986. . . . . $15
1022 Iveco Camping Car, 1993 . . . . $5 – 10
1023 Volkswagen Porsche 914/6, 1975 – 1980. . . . . $16
1023 Unimog with Crane, 1993. $5 – 10
1024 Lamborghini Espada 400 GT, 1975 – 1981. . . . . $12
1024 Deutz Combine, 1993. . . . . $5 – 10
1025 Alfa Romeo Montreal, 1975 – 1981 . . . . $12
1025 Volkswagen Golf Driving School, 1994 . . . . $5 – 10
1026 Citroën SM, 1975 – 1981. . . . . $15
1026 Unimog with Awning, 1994 . . . . $5 – 10
1027 Ford T5 Mustang Mach 1, 1975 – 1976 . . . . $15
1027 Opel Frontera Sport, 1994. $5 – 10
1028 Ford Granada Station Wagon, 1975 – 1984 . . . . $6 – 10
1028 BMW 320i, 1994. . . . . $5 – 10
1029 Volkswagen Passat Variant, 1975 – 1984 . . . . $8 – 12
1029 Mercedes-Benz C-Class, 1994 . . . . $5 – 10

1031 Volkswagen Bus, 1975 – 1976. . . . . $7 – 10
1031 Mini Cooper, 1977 . . . . $4 – 6
1032 Volkswagen 181 "Thing," 1976 – 1984 . . . . $10
1032 Citroën 2CV, 1985 . . . . $12
1034 Maserati Boomerang, 1978 – 1983. . . . . $10
1034 Water Cannon, 1994. . . . . $4 – 6
1035 BMW 633 CSi, 1978 – 1989. . . . . $5 – 10
1036 Range Rover, 1978 – 1986 . . . . $4 – 8
1036 Opel Astra Caravan Estate Car, 1995 . . . . $4 – 6
1037 Porsche 928, 1979 . . . . $6 – 10
1038 Renault 5, 1979 – 1988 . . . . $5 – 10
1038 Tractor with Front End Loader, 1996. . . . . $4 – 6
1039 Volkswagen Golf Cabriolet, 1980 . . . . $4 – 10
1040 Opel Senator, 1981 – 1988 . . . . $4 – 10

1041 Audi 200 5T, 1982 – 1988, $5 – 10

1042 Mercedes-Benz 500 SE, 1982. . . . . $4 – 10
1043 Peugeot 505 STI, 1982 – 1988 . . . . $5 – 10
1044 Mercedes-Benz 280 GE, 1982 . . . . $4 – 10
1045 Porsche Turbo 917/10, 1976 . . . . $6 – 10
1046 McLaren, 1976 – 1986. . . . . $7 – 10
1046 Volkswagen Sharon, 1996 . . . . $4 – 6
1047 Opel Kadett SR, 1982 – 1989 . . . . $5 – 10
1047 BMW R1100RS Motorbike, 1996 . . . . $4 – 6

1030 Volkswagen Pickup Van, 1975 – 1989, $4 – 10

1030 Tanker Citerne, 1994 . . . . $5 – 10

1033 Volkswagen Golf, 1977, $4 – 10

1048 Ford Escort GL, 1982 – 1989, $4 – 6

1048 Mercedes-Benz E230, 1996 . . . . $4 – 6
1049 Volkswagen Golf Pick Up, 1983 . . . . $4 – 12
1050 Sign Pack, 1976 . . . . $5 – 10
1051 Camaro Z28, 1983 . . . . $4 – 10
1052 Mercedes-Benz 500 SEC, 1983. . . . . $4 – 10
1052 BMW 730i, 1996. . . . . $4 – 6
1053 Jeep CJ-5, 1983 . . . . $4 – 10
1054 Opel Omega Caravan Estate Car, 1996 . . . . $4 – 6

1054 Mercedes-Benz 190E, 1984 – 1988, $4 – 10

1055 Chevrolet Corvette, 1984. . . . . $4 – 10

1056 Ford Sierra 2.3 Ghia, 1984, $4 – 10

1057 Audi 100 Avant, 1984 – 1988. . . . . $6 – 10
1057 Ford Mondeo, 1996 . . . . $4 – 6
1058 Jeep CJ-7, 1985 . . . . $4 – 10
1059 Porsche 911 Turbo, 1985 . . . . $4 – 10
1060 Ferrari GTO, 1985 . . . . $4 – 10
1061 Nissan 300ZX, 1985 . . . . $4 – 10
1061 Volkswagen Passat Variant, 1996 . . . . $4 – 6
1062 Morgan Plus 8, 1986. . . . . $4 – 10
1063 Mercedes-Benz 300E, 1986 . . . . $4 – 10
1064 Mercedes-Benz 300TE Station Wagon, 1986. . . . . . . $4 – 10
1065 Volvo 760 GLE, 1986 – 1989 . . . . $4 – 10
1066 Saab 9000, 1987 . . . . $4 – 10

1067 Porsche 911 Cabriolet, 1987, $4 – 10

1068 Porsche 959, 1987 . . . . $6 – 10
1071 Peugeot 205 Cabriolet, 1988 . . . . $4 – 10
1072 Suzuki SJ413, 1988 . . . . $4 – 10

1069 Jaguar XJ6, 1988, $4 – 10

1070 BMW 735iL, 1988, $4 – 10

Photo by Jeff Koch.

1073 Mercedes-Benz 300SL, 1988, $4 – 10

1074 Mercedes SSK, 1988 . . . . $4 – 10
1075 Ferrari F40, 1989 . . . . $4 – 10
1076 Volkswagen Passat Variant, 1989 . . . . $4 – 10

1077 Volkswagen Beetle 1303 LS Convertible, 1989, $4 – 10

1078 Volkswagen Beetle 1303 LS, 1990 . . . . $4 – 10
1079 Audi A6 Avant, 1994 . . . . $4 – 6
1084 Volvo V 40, 1997 . . . . $4 – 6
1085 Post Van, 1997 . . . . $4 – 6
1086 Audi A 4, 1997 . . . . $4 – 6
1087 Citroën Xantia, 1997 . . . . $4 – 6
1088 Mercedes E 290 T, 1997 . . . . $4 – 6
1310 Ford Sierra Taxi, 1985 . . . . $4 – 10
1310 Mercedes-Benz 300TE Taxi, 1993 . . . . $5 – 10
1311 Mercedes-Benz 190 Polizei, 1985 – 1988 . . . . $8 – 10
1311 Mercedes-Benz 300, 1989 . . . . $4 – 10
1312 Volkswagen Bus with radar, 1975 . . . . $4 – 10
1312 Volkswagen Golf ADAC with antenna, 1985 – 1986 . . $7 – 10
1312 Volkswagen Golf ADAC with no antenna, 1987 . . . . . $4 – 10
1313 Audi 100 Arzt-Notfall-Einsatzwagen, 1975 . . . . $8 – 10
1313 ADAC Pick-Up-Service, 1994 . . . . $5 – 8
1314 Volkswagen Bus Bundespost-Peilwagen, 1975 – 1980 . $7 – 10
1314 Volkswagen Transporter, 1981 . . . . $4 – 10
1315 Volkswagen Bus Highway Service Truck, 1975 – 1988 . $5 – 10
1316 Ford Capri Highway Emergency Car, 1975 – 1978 . . . $6 – 10
1316 Porsche 911 Targa Highway Emergency Car, 1978 – 1988 . $6 – 10
1316 Porsche 911 Turbo Highway Emergency Car, 1989 . . $4 – 10
1317 Mercedes-Benz 250 Taxi, 1975 – 1984 . . . . $15
1318 Mercedes-Benz 250 Polizei, 1975 – 1984 . . . . $15
1319 Ford Transit with Boat, 1975 – 1982 . . . . $4 – 10
1320 Ford Transit School Bus, 1975 – 1982 . . . . $4 – 10
1320 ADAC Road Patrol Car, 1997 . . . . $4 – 6
1321 BMW 2000CS Polizei Loudspeaker Car, 1975 – 1977 . $6 – 10
1321 Volkswagen Passat Variant Polizei Loudspeaker, 1978 –
     1989 . . . . $5 – 10
1321 Volkswagen Passat Polizei Loudspeaker Car, 1990 . . . $4 – 10
1322 Ford Granada with Boat, 1975 – 1984 . . . . $20
1322 LKW Road Maintenance Lorry, 1997 . . . . $6 – 8
1323 Volkswagen Porsche Rennpolizei, 1975 – 1978 . . . . . $6 – 10
1323 ADAC Breakdown Service, 1997 . . . . $6 – 8
1324 Volkswagen 1300 ADAC, 1975 – 1984 . . . . $18
1324 ADAC Car Club Motorbike, 1997 . . . . $4 – 6
1325 Covered Trailer, 1976 – 1979 . . . . $10
1325 Police Motorbike, 1997 . . . . $4 – 6
1326 Hydraulic Crane, 1997 . . . . $4 – 6
1327 Ford Mustang Mach 1, 1976 – 1978 . . . . $6 – 10
1328 McLaren, 1976 – 1981 . . . . $6 – 10
1329 Porsche Turbo 917/10, 1976 – 1981 . . . . $6 – 10
1330 Maserati Boomerang, 1975 – 1977 . . . . $6 – 10
1331 Volkswagen Bus, 1976 – 1980 . . . . $6 – 10

1332 Volkswagen 181 Military, 1976 – 1979 . . . . $20
1333 Volkswagen 181 with Raft, 1977 – 1982 . . . . $20
1334 Volkswagen LT 28, 1977 . . . . $4 – 10
1335 Volkswagen 181 Fire Command Vehicle, 1977 – 1982 . . . $25
1336 Lamborghini Fire Truck, 1978 . . . . $8 – 10
1337 Volkswagen Golf DBP, 1979 – 1984 . . . . $6 – 10
1338 Range Rover Emergency Vehicle, 1979 – 1989 . . . . . . $5 – 10
1339 Porsche 928 Emergency Doctor, 1979 – 1994 . . . . $4 – 10
1339 Emergency Doctor, 1995 . . . . $5 – 7
1340 Matra Simca Rancho, 1979 – 1988 . . . . $4 – 10
1341 Range Rover, 1979 – 1986 . . . . $4 – 10
1342 Volkswagen Passat ADAC, 1979 – 1986 . . . . $20
1343 Volkswagen Transporter Service Van, 1982 . . . . $6 – 10
1344 Mercedes G Fire Command Wagon, 1983 . . . . $4 – 10
1345 Porsche 911 Rallye, 1986 . . . . $4 – 10
1346 Mercedes G Police Command Wagon, 1986 . . . . $4 – 10
1347 Volkswagen Covered Pickup Van, 1990 . . . . $4 – 10
1349 Mercedes 190E Fire Command Car, 1993 . . . . $4 – 10
1350 Volkswagen Eurovan Police Team Van, white & green,
     1994 . . . . $5 – 10
1351 Volkswagen Eurovan Police, green, 1994 . . . . $4 – 10
1352 BMW Police Patrol Car . . . . $5 – 10
1353 Doubledecker Coach, 1994 . . . . $5 – 10
1354 Opel Frontera with Boat, 1996 . . . . $5 – 8
1355 Taxi, 1996 . . . . $5 – 7
1356 Police Car with Loudspeaker, 1996 . . . . $5 – 7
1510 Unimog with Builder's Hut, 1994 . . . . $9 – 12
1511 Mercedes Recycling Lorry with Trailer, 1994 . . . . . . $9 – 12
1512 Pipe Transporter with Trailer, 1996 . . . . $6 – 8
1513 Deutz DX 85 Tractor with Trailer, 1996 . . . . $6 – 8
1514 Tipper Truck, 1996 . . . . $6 – 8
1515 Deutz DX 85 Tractor with Vacuum Tanker, 1996 . . . . . $6 – 8
1516 Tipper Truck and Trailer, 1997 . . . . $6 – 8
1517 Unimog with Motor Boat, 1997 . . . . $6 – 8
1610 Low Loader with Helicopter, 1996 . . . . $6 – 8
1611 Hanomag, 1975 . . . . $7 – 10
1611 Low Loader with Excavator, 1996 . . . . $6 – 8
1612 Zettelmeyer Europ S12, 1975 – 1983 . . . . $8 – 12
1612 Low Loader with Space Shuttle, 1996 . . . . $6 – 8
1613 Mercedes-Benz Europ 1200 Binz Ambulance, 1975 – 1980 . $15
1613 Mercedes-Benz 200 Ambulance, 1981 – 1988 . . . . $8 – 12
1613 Low Loader with Boat, 1996 . . . . $6 – 8
1614 Ford 17M ADAC, 1975 . . . . $10

1331 Volkswagen Transporter, many variations, 1981, $4 – 20

1614 VW Passat ADAC, 1976 – 1981, $6 – 10

1615 Ford Transit Polizei Loudspeaker Car, 1975 – 1978 . . . . . $17
1615 Ford Transit Polizei Loudspeaker Car, 1979 – 1983 . . . . . $17
1616 Hanomag Henschel Covered Truck, 1975 – 1982 . . . . $8 – 12
1617 Ford Granada Fire Command Wagon, 1975 – 1982 . . . . . $12
1618 Lamborghini Fire Car, 1975 – 1977 . . . . $6 – 10
1619 VW Bus Ambulance, 1975 – 1978 . . . . $6 – 10
1620 Mercedes-Benz Unimog, 1975 – 1983 . . . . $10
1620 Mercedes-Benz Unimog, 1984 . . . . $4 – 10
1621 VW Bus Military Ambulance, 1976 – 1979 . . . . $18
1622 Mercedes Wrecker, 1978 – 1989 . . . . $6 – 10
1623 VW Medi-Mobil, 1979 – 1989 . . . . $5 – 10
1624 Mercedes Bus, "TOURIST BUS," 1980 – 1986 . . . . . . $8 – 12
1625 MAN-VW Express Truck, 1983 . . . . $6 – 10
1626 Range Rover with Sailboard, 1982 – 1987 . . . . $18
1627 Mercedes Polizei Wagon, 1983 . . . . $4 – 10

1628 Mercedes 208 Schulbus, 1983 – 1988, $5 – 10

1629 Linde Forklift, 1986 . . . . $6 – 10
1630 Mercedes-Benz 260E Binz Ambulance, 1989 . . . . . . $5 – 10
1716 Unimog, 1993 . . . . $6 – 10
1717 Linde Forklift Truck, 1993 . . . . $6 – 10
1719 Boeing 767-200, 1993 . . . . $6 – 10
1720 Lockheed Tristar L-1011, 1993 . . . . $6 – 10
1721 Piggy Back Forklift, 1997 . . . . $6 – 8
1910 Hanomag Henschel Wrecker, 1975 – 1978 . . . . $8 – 12
1911 Ambulance, "NOTARZT," 1975 – 1984 . . . . $18
1911 Ambulance, "UNFALL-NOTFALL," 1985 – 1986 . . . . $18
1912 Mercedes Postwagen, 1975 – 1987 . . . . $10
1913 Tractor with Trailer, 1975 . . . . $4 – 10
1914 Ford Granada with Motorboat and Trailer, 1975 – 1984 . . $20
1915 Oldsmobile Toronado and Caravan, 1975 – 1979 . . . . . . $30
1916 Hanomag Henschel LKW, 1975 – 1981 . . . . $20
1917 Hanomag Henschel with Horse Trailer, 1975 . . . . $10
1917 Range Rover with Horse Trailer, 1980 – 1988 . . . . $12
1917 Mercedes 280 GE with Horse Trailer, 1989 . . . . $8
1918 Mercedes Bus with Trailer, "AIRPORT SERVICE," 1981 – 1983 . $10
1918 Mercedes Bus with Trailer, 1983 – 1985 . . . . $10
1918 Mercedes Bus with Trailer, "HOLIDAY INN," 1986 – 1988 . $8
1919 MAN-VW Covered Truck with Trailer, 1982 . . . . $7 – 12
1920 Mercedes 809 Binz Ambulance, 1987 . . . . $4 – 10
1921 Mercedes 809 Police Bus, 1987 . . . . $4 – 10
1922 Mercedes 809 Postwagen, 1987 . . . . $4 – 10
1923 Mercedes 280 GE with Fire Boat and Trailer, 1989 . . . $8 – 12
1924 Wheel Loader, 1990 . . . . $4 – 10

1925 Renault Tractor with Front End Loader, 1993 . . . . . . $8 – 12
1926 Boeing 747-400, 1993 . . . . $6 – 10
1927 Airbus A340-200, 1993 . . . . $6 – 10
1928 Mercedes-Benz Binz Ambulance, 1993 . . . . $5 – 10
1929 Mercedes Sprinter, Post, 1997 . . . . $6 – 8
1930 Mercedes Sprinter, Bus, 1997 . . . . $6 – 8
1950 Disc Harrow, 1993 . . . . $10 – 15
1951 Five-Bottom Plow, 1993 . . . . $10 – 15
1952 Amazone Seed Drill, 1993 . . . . $10 – 15
1953 Deutz Rotary Mower, 1993 . . . . $10 – 15
1955 Crop Sprayer, 1993 . . . . $10 – 15
1956 Reversible Farm Plow, 1993 . . . . $10 – 15
1957 Harrow, 1993 . . . . $10 – 15
1958 Roller Harrow, 1994 . . . . $10 – 15
1959 Trailer with Awning, 1994 . . . . $10 – 15
1960 Silage Block Cutter, 1996 . . . . $10 – 15
2010 Range Rover with Horse Box, 1993 . . . . $12 – 15
2010 Opel Frontera with Horse Box, 1996 . . . . $12 – 15
2011 Mercedes-Benz Binz Rescue Van, 1993 . . . . $12 – 15
2015 Mercedes-Benz Binz Red Cross Recovery Van, 1993 . $12 – 15
2016 Police Mini Bus, 1996 . . . . $16 – 20
2017 Mercedes with Refuse Containers, 1997 . . . . $8 – 10
2210 Michigan Grader-Tractor, 1975 – 1977 . . . . $15 – 18
2211 Mercedes ADAC, 1975 – 1981 . . . . $15 – 18
2212 Faun Snow Plow Truck, 1975 – 1981 . . . . $16 – 20
2212 Unimog Snow Plow, 1982 – 1983 . . . . $16 – 20
2212 Unimog Snow Plow, 1984 . . . . $16 – 20
2213 Mercedes Water Truck, 1975 – 1980 . . . . $30
2214 Mercedes Truck, 1975 – 1978 . . . . $20
2215 Unimog with Sign Trailer, 1975 – 1983 . . . . $20
2215 Unimog with Sign Trailer, 1984 – 1989 . . . . $12 – 15
2216 Ford Granada with Boat and Trailer, 1975 – 1979 . . . . . $30
2217 Siku Racing Team, 1978 . . . . $8 – 15
2217 Porsche Racing Team, 1985 – 1986 . . . . $15
2218 Unimog Red Cross Truck, 1978 – 1985 . . . . $12
2219 Mercedes Bucket Truck, 1978 – 1982 . . . . $30
2220 Mercedes Wrecker with Auto Salvage Trailer, 1979 – 1988 . $12
2221 Mercedes ADAC with Auto Transport Trailer and Car, 1983 . . . . $10
2222 Police Helicopter, 1986 . . . . $10
2223 Unimog with Tandem Trailer, 1988 . . . . $10
2224 Fire Rescue Helicopter, 1990 . . . . $10
2225 Loader, 1990 . . . . $10
2226 Renault Tractor with Trailer, 1990 . . . . $10
2227 Massey Ferguson Tractor with Hay Trailer, 1990 . . . . . $10
2228 ADAC Helicopter, 1993 . . . . $15
2230 Unimog with Road Work Signs, 1996 . . . . $15 – 18
2232 Unimog with Dumper Truck, 1997 . . . . $12 – 14
2252 Vacuum Tanker Trailer, 1993 . . . . $15
2254 Deutz Hay Rake, 1993 . . . . $15
2257 Livestock Trailer, 1993 . . . . $15
2258 Hose Drum Irrigator, 1994 . . . . $15
2259 Trailer with Farm Produce, 1994 . . . . $10
2260 Corn Seed Drill, 1994 . . . . $10
2261 Seed Drill, 1996 . . . . $10
2262 Claas Baler, 1996 . . . . $10
2263 Cambridge Roller, 1997 . . . . $10
2264 Champion Rotary Cropper, 1997 . . . . $10

2408 Peterbilt with Grove Low Loader Trailer, 1992 . . . . $95	2616 Mercedes Tipper Lorry, 1993 . . . . $18
2510 Zettelmeyer Loader, 1975 . . . . $10	2617 Mercedes Hazardous Waste Truck, 1994 . . . . $18
2511 Magirus, 1975 – 1977 . . . . $10	2618 Lorry with Awning, 1994 . . . . $18
2511 Mercedes 2232, 1978 – 1982 . . . . $10	2650 Tipping Loader Trailer, 1994 . . . . $18
2512 Magirus Concrete Truck, 1975 – 1977 . . . . $10	2651 Seed Drill, 1997 . . . . $20
2513 Mercedes Street Sign Truck, 1975 – 1980 . . . . $10	2652 New Holland 5635 Tractor, 1997 . . . . $20
2513 Volvo F7 Street Sign Truck, 1981 – 1985 . . . . $18	2653 New Holland L 75, 1997 . . . . $20
2513 Volvo FL6 Street Sign Truck, 1986 – 1988 . . . . $12	2810 MAN ARAL Tanker, 1975 – 1977 . . . . $18
2513 Mercedes Street Sign Truck, 1989 . . . . $10	2811 MAN Container Truck, 1975 . . . . $18
2514 Magirus Dump Truck, 1975 . . . . $18	2812 MAN Lumber Truck, 1975 – 1978 . . . . $18
2514 Volvo, 1976 – 1986 . . . . $18	2813 Magirus Skip Truck, 1975 . . . . $18
2515 Unimog BP, 1975 – 1977 . . . . $20	2814 Volvo Crane Truck with Boat, 1975 – 1983 . . . . $30
2516 Mercedes Silo Transporter, 1975 . . . . $12	2815 Mercedes Fire Truck, 1975 – 1977 . . . . $20
2517 Volvo Covered Cargo Truck, 1976 – 1983 . . . . $12	2816 Mercedes Crane Truck, 1975 – 1978 . . . . $20
2517 Ford Covered Cargo Truck, 1984 – 1985 . . . . $15	2817 Volvo Cement Truck, 1977 – 1984 . . . . $20
2517 Mercedes Covered Cargo Truck, 1986 – 1988 . . . . $15	2818 Rear Digger Tractor with Front End Loader, 1977 – 1985 . $20
2518 VW LT 28 Camper with Travel Trailer, 1980 – 1989 . . . . $15	2819 Mercedes Extending Ladder Fire Truck, 1978 . . . . $20
2518 Jeep CJ-7 with Travel Trailer, 1990 . . . . $15	2820 Unimog Side-Mount Scoop with Pipe Trailer, 1978 – 1981 . $35
2519 Unimog with Site Trailer, 1980 – 1983 . . . . $25	2820 Mercedes-Benz Garbage Truck, 1984 . . . . $20
2519 Unimog with Site Trailer, "HEITKAMP," 1984 – 1989 . . . $20	2821 White Old Timer "Coca-Cola" Truck, 1986 – 1987 . . . . . $30
2520 Ford Flatbed Truck with Winch and Camper Pickup, 1984 . . $23	2821 White Old Timer "Sinalco" Truck, 1987 . . . . $30
2520 ADAC Breakdown Truck with Car, 1993 . . . . $15	2822 Unimog with Site Office Trailer, 1987 – 1988 . . . . $25
2521 White Old Timer Truck, 1985 – 1987 . . . . $20	2823 Fire Boat Transporter, 1987 – 1988 . . . . $25
2522 Unimog U1500 with Linde Forklift Truck, 1985 . . . . $15	2823 Police Boat Transporter, 1989 . . . . $25
2523 Mercedes-Benz Freight Truck with handtruck and pallets, 1986 – 1989 . . . . $10	2824 Mercedes Street Cleaning Truck, 1988 . . . . $15
2524 Mercedes Tanker, 1986 . . . . $20	2825 Volvo Payload Hauler, 1989 . . . . $25
2525 Jeep CJ-5 with Sport Boat, 1988 – 1989 . . . . $14	2826 Mercedes Skip Truck, 1989 . . . . $20
2525 Mercedes GE with Sport Boat, 1990 . . . . $14	2827 Unimog Winter Service with Snowblower, Snowplow & Hopper/Spreader, 1993 . . . . $20
2526 Wrecker with Trailer, 1988 . . . . $15	2850 Deutz-Fahr Agrostar 6.61 Turbo Tractor, 1993 . . . . $20
2527 Mercedes Highway Sand Truck with Snow Plow, 1989 . . $20	2851 Fendt-Farmer 308/310 LS Tractor, 1993 . . . . $20
2528 Kässbohrer Track Groomer, 1989 . . . . $15	2853 Massey Ferguson MF284 with Transporter Box, 1993 . . . . $20
2529 Liebherr Bulldozer, 1989 . . . . $15	2855 Ford TW35 Tractor, 1993 . . . . $20
2531 Polizei Helicopter, 1993 – 1995 . . . . $10	2856 Renault TX145-14 Tractor, 1993 . . . . $20
2531 Opel Frontera with Motor Bike Trailer, 1996 . . . . . . $16 – 20	2859 Beet Trailer, 1993 . . . . $20
2532 Range Rover with Travel trailer, 1993 . . . . $9	2860 White Old-Timer Beverage Delivery Truck, 1988 . . . . . . $30
2532 Opel Frontera and Caravan, 1996 . . . . $16 – 20	2860 Round Bale Trailer, 1993 . . . . $20
2533 Unimog with Builder's Hut, 1993 . . . . $9	2861 Fiat 180-90 Turbo DT Tractor, 1993 . . . . $20
2534 ADAC Recovery Van, 1996 . . . . $16 – 20	2862 Deutz Baler, 1993 . . . . $20
2535 Red Cross Helicopter, 1993 . . . . $16 – 20	2863 Deutz-Fahr AgroXtra Tractor, 1993 . . . . $20
2536 Camping Car, 1996 . . . . $16 – 20	2864 Steyr 9094 Tractor, 1993 . . . . $20
2537 Unimog with Hydraulic Loader, 1996 . . . . $16	2865 Deutz-Fahr Fun-Trac Tractor, 1993 . . . . $20
2551 Farm Trailer, 1993 . . . . $15	2866 Claas Tipping Trailer, 1993 . . . . $20
2552 Farm Dump Trailer, 1993 . . . . $15	2867 Renault Ceres 95X Tractor, 1994 . . . . $20
2553 Manure Spreader, 1993 . . . . $15	2868 Massey Ferguson 9400 Tractor, 1996 . . . . $20
2555 Hay Elevator with hay bales, 1993 . . . . $15	2910 Panzer Leopard A3 Tank, 1976 – 1979 . . . . $40
2556 Deutz-Fahr Round Baler, 1993 . . . . $15	2911 Panzer Gepard, 1976 – 1979 . . . . $40
2558 Farm Animals, 1 horse, 1 cow, 1 pig, 1 sheep, 1 goat, 1993 . $5	2912 Panzer Leopard A1, 1977 – 1979 . . . . $45
2559 Horse Box Trailer with horse, 1993 . . . . $15	2913 Foam Unit with Light Trailer, 1979 – 1984 . . . . $20
2560 Claas Whirl Rake, 1994 . . . . $15	2914 Faun Crane Truck, 1979 . . . . $28
2610 MAN Road Maintenance Lorry with traffic signs, 1993 . . . $15	2915 MAN Tree Transporter, 1980 – 1982 . . . . $45
2612 VW 1303 cabriolet, blue, opening doors, 1:43, limited edition, 1993 . . . . $20	2916 Volvo Refrigerated Truck, 1981 – 1984 . . . . $35
2613 VW 1303 cabriolet, white, opening doors, 1:43, limited edition, 1993 . . . . $20	2917 Mack Heavy Wrecker, 1981 – 1989 . . . . $33
	2918 Ford Cargo Beverage Truck, 1983 – 1986 . . . . $30
2614 Helicopter with Floats, orange with blue pontoons, "Katastrophenschutz," 1993 . . . . $18	2919 Mercedes-Benz Dump Trailer Truck, 1984 . . . . $25
	2920 Mercedes Recycling Transporter, 1986 . . . . $25
2615 Unimog Excavator, 1993 . . . . $18	2921 Mercedes Snorkel Fire Truck with Snorkel Trailer, 1986 – 1989 . . . . $20

2922 Mercedes Cement Mixer, 1989 . . . . $20
2923 Mercedes Dump Truck, 1989 . . . . $20
2924 Faun 3-Axle Ladder Truck, 1993 . . . . $25
2926 Mercedes Refuse Truck, 1992 . . . . $25
2927 Fire Brigade Team Bus, 1993 . . . . $20
2928 Police Information Bus, 1994 . . . . $20
2929 Unimog with Grass Cutter, 1994 . . . . $20
2930 Overhead Maintenance Lorry, 1993 . . . . $20
2931 Faun Refuse Truck, 1997 . . . . $20
2932 Faun Gully Emptier, 1997 . . . . $20
2933 LKW Truck with Piggy Back Forklift, 1997 . . . . $20
2934 O&K Heavy Duty Tipper Truck, 1997 . . . . $20
2951 Mercedes-Benz MB Trac 800 Tractor w/Tipping Hopper, 1993 . . . . $20
2956 Deutz AgroXtra Tractor with Twin Rear Wheels, 1993 . . . $20
2957 Fendt Xylon 524, 1994 . . . . $20
2958 Deutz-Fahr Agrotron 6.05 tt, 1994 . . . . $20
2959 Steyr Tractor with Twin Wheels Front and Rear, 1997 . . . $20
2960 Massey Ferguson 9240 with Twin Rear Wheels, 1997 . . . . $20
2961 Fendt Farmer Favorit 926, 1997 . . . . $20
3153 Unimog, green, 1993 . . . . $20
3155 Forester Trailer, 1993 . . . . $20
3156 Deutz-Fahr Agroxtra Tractor with Front Mower, 1994 . . . $20
3110 Hanomag Henschel ARAL Tanker, 1975 – 1977 . . . . $35
3110 Mercedes ARAL Tanker, 1978 – 1979 . . . . $35
3110 Mercedes ESSO Tanker, 1980 – 1983 . . . . $30
3111 Hanomag Henschel Container Transporter, 1975 – 1977 . $25
3111 Volvo Container Transporter, 1978 – 1985 . . . . $25
3112 Mercedes Auto Transporter, 1975 . . . . $25
3114 Menck Loader, 1975 – 1977 . . . . $40
3115 Volvo Cargo Truck and Trailer, 1978 – 1985 . . . . $30
3115 Volvo FL10 Hollis Transport and Trailer, 1986 . . . . $30
3115 Renault Turbo Hollis Transport and Trailer, 1987 – 1988 . $30
3115 Renault Turbo BMX Transport and Trailer, 1989 . . . . $30
3116 Volvo 7 Covered Transport, 1982 – 1984 . . . . $25
3117 Mack Semi-Freighter, 1982 – 1986 . . . . $25
3117 Renault Turbo Semi-Freighter, 1986 – 1988 . . . . $25
3118 TOPAS Tanker, 1989 . . . . $25
3119 Man Semi-Tanker, 1989 . . . . $25
3120 Zettelmeyer Wheel Loader, 1990 . . . . $22
3121 Bus, Red upper, white lower, scenery on sides, "erdgas," 1993 . . . . $22
3121 Bus, "EuropaBus," 1993 . . . . $22
3122 Forklift Truck, 1993 . . . . $22
3123 Wheel Loader with Accessory Plow, 1993 . . . . $22
3125 Mercedes-Benz Roll-Off Skip Loader, 1993 . . . . $25
3128 Roll-Off Skip Loader, 1994 . . . . $24
3155 Forest Trailer, 1994 . . . . $24
3156 Tractor with Front Mower, 1994 . . . . $22
3157 Tractor with Silage Block Cutter, 1996 . . . . $22
3410 Hanomag Henschel Garage Transporter, 1975 – 1977 . . . $45
3410 Mercedes Garage Transporter, 1978 – 1981 . . . . $45
3411 Faun Airport Foam Tender, 1975 – 1985 . . . . $25
3412 Mercedes Covered Transport, 1975 – 1983 . . . . $45
3413 Power Shovel, 1978 . . . . $30
3414 Volvo F7 Double Freighter, 1979 – 1980 . . . . $40
3415 MAN Loader Truck with Loader Crane, 1980 – 1985 . . . . $35
3415 Volvo FL6 Loader Truck with Loader Crane, 1986 . . . . . . $35

3415 White Loader Truck with Loader Crane, 1987 . . . . $35
3416 Volvo Tanker Semi, 1982 – 1986 . . . . $35
3417 Man "AIR FRANCE" Bus, 1982 – 1987 . . . . $35
3418 Kenworth "BP" Tanker Semi, 1986 – 1989 . . . . $35
3419 Mercedes Auto Transporter, 1986 . . . . $30
3420 Kenworth Sand Transporter, 1987 – 1988 . . . . $25
3421 Mercedes Double Freighter, 1987 – 1988 . . . . $25
3421 Iveco Double Freighter, 1989 . . . . $25
3422 TOPAS Tanker, 1989 . . . . $25
3424 Iveco Double Container Truck, 1993 . . . . $20
3425 DAF Garage Transporter, 1993 . . . . $30
3426 Mercedes-Benz 500SEL, blue, doors open, 1:43, limited edition $25
3427 Mercedes-Benz 500SEL, gold, doors open, 1:43, limited edition $25
3428 Mercedes Truck with hydraulic boom platform, 1993 . . . $30
3429 Mercedes-Benz Ziegler Water Cannon w/working pump, 1993 . . . . $30
3430 ADAC Automobile Club Testing Service, 1993 . . . . $25
3431 Cement Mixer, 1994 . . . . $25
3432 Wrecker Truck, 1994 . . . . $25
3433 Mercedes-Benz Ladder Fire Engine, 1996 . . . . $25
3450 Fendt Farmer 308 LS Tractor with Front Loader, 1993 . . . $25
3451 Mercedes-Benz MB Trac 800 Tractor with Snow Plow, 1993 . . . . $25
3453 Massey Ferguson Front End Loader, 1993 . . . . $25
3454 Claas Automatic Hay Loader, 1993 . . . . $25
3455 Claas Teleskoplader Ranger 911 T, 1994 . . . . $25
3456 Fendt Xylon with Rope Winder, 1994 . . . . $25
3457 Deutz Fahr Agrostar with Scraper and Toolbox, 1997 . . . $25
3510 Hydraulic Excavator, 1993 . . . . $25
3511 Mercedes Shell Tanker, 1993 . . . . $25
3512 Mercedes Fire Equipment Truck w/ hydraulic boom & small boat $30
3512L Ford Fire Dept. Truck with fire boat, limited edition . . . $45
3513 Rosenbauer Airport Crash Truck, limited edition, 1993 . . $33
3514 Track Type Lattice Boom Clamshell Excavator, 1993 . . . . $40
3515 Mercedes Covered Lorry w/Twin Axle Trailer, Eurotrans, 1994 . . . . $30
3515 Mercedes Covered Lorry, Twin Axle Trailer, Jumbocargo, 1994 . . . . $30
3516 Recycling Skip Truck with Skip Trailer, 1994 . . . . $30
3517 Articulated Bus, 1996 . . . . $30 – 35
3518 Caterpillar Shovel, 1996 . . . . $28
3550 Deutz-Fahr DX6.31 Turbo Forestry Tractor, 1993 . . . . . . $30
3551 Fendt Xylon Front End Loader, 1996 . . . . $30
3710 Hanomag Henschel ADAC Vehicle Safety Test Veh., 1975 – 1978 . . . . $45
3710 Mercedes ADAC Vehicle Safety Test Vehicle, 1979 – 1981 . $45
3711 Hanomag Henschel Pipe Loader Truck, 1975 – 1978 . . . . $35
3711 Volvo Pipe Loader truck, 1979 – 1982 . . . . $35
3712 Hanomag Henschel ARAL Gas Station Transporter, 1975 – 1977 . . . . $40
3712 Volvo ARAL Gas Station Transporter, 1978 – 1985 . . . . . $40
3713 Mercedes Parking Lot Transporter, 1977 – 1984 . . . . $50
3714 Volvo Double Freighter, 1979 – 1983 . . . . $50
3714 Mercedes Double Freighter, 1984 – 1985 . . . . $50
3715 MAN Building Transporter and Trailer, 1980 – 1986 . . . . $40

3716 MAN Transporter with Wheel Loader, 1982 – 1986 . . . . . $40

3717 Mack Heavy Wrecker and MAN Truck, 1982 – 1984 . . . . $45

3718 Mercedes "BP" Double Tanker, 1983 – 1985 . . . . $45

3719 Ford Low Loader Helicopter Transporter, 1985 . . . . $45

3720 MAN Bus, 1987 – 1992 . . . . $25

3720 Mercedes Snorkel Truck with working water pump, 1992. $33

3721 White Horse Transporter, 1987 – 1988 . . . . $50

3721 Mercedes Tractor, 12 Meter Trailer, SIKU-TRANSPORT, 1993 . . . . $25

3722 MAN Circus Transporter with two Cage Trailers, 1987 . . . $45

3722 Rosenbauer Airport Crash Truck w/working water pump, 1993 . . . . $33

3723 Rethmann Recycling Transporter, 1988 – 1992 . . . . $35

3723 Faun Telescoping Crane Truck, 1994 . . . . $33

3724 Low Loarder with Garage, 1997 . . . . $30

3750 Massey Ferguson MF 284 Tractor with Farm Trailer, 1993 . $30

3751 Deutz-Fahr Agrostar DX6.61 Turbo Tractor with Tandem-Axle Trailer, 1993 . . . . $30

3752 Deutz-Fahr Tractor with Vacuum Tanker, 1993 . . . . $30

3755 Renault Tractor with Rear Digger, 1993 . . . . $30

3756 Deutz Fahr Agrostar with Rear Digger, 1997 . . . . $30

3780 Ladder Truck with flashing lights and siren, 1992 . . . . . $35

3812 DAF Loader Truck and Trailer with Beams, 1989 . . . . . . $35

3813 Iveco Recycling Truck with Trailer, 1993 . . . . $35

3814 Mercedes-Benz Double Decker Touring Coach, 1993 . . . $35

3815 Large Volume Lorry "M. Schneider Hamburg - Paris - Amsterdam," 1996 . . . . $35 – 38

3854 Claas Jaguar 695 Combine, 1993 . . . . $30

3855 Claas Jaguar 695 Forage Harvester, 1994 . . . . $30

3856 Potato Digger, 1994 . . . . $30

3880 Pumper with working water pump and flashing lights, 1992 . . . . $45

3910 Shell Gas Station Transporter, 1987 – 1989 . . . . $45

3911 Scania Low Loader with Wheel Loader and Power Shovel, 1990 . . . . $45

3913 Liebherr Fast Erecting Tower Crane, 1992 . . . . $40

3915 Wood Transporter, 1996 . . . . $40

3953 Fendt Xylon Front-Loader with Rear Digger, 1997 . . . . . $40

4010 Faun Hydraulic Crane, 1975 . . . . $60

4011 Giant Boom Crane Transporter, 1978 . . . . $65

4012 Low Loader with Payloader, 1980 . . . . $45

4013 Mack Low Loader with Power Shovel, 1981 – 1988 . . . . . $60

4014 Peterbilt Sloop Transporter with Boat, 1983 – 1988 . . . . . $60

4015 Volvo Fire Watch Tower Transporter, 1985 – 1989 . . . . . $60

4016 Peterbilt Space Shuttle Transporter, 1988 . . . . $50

4017 Mercedes Auto Transporter with five cars, 1993 . . . . $50

4018 DAF Low Loader with Gas Station, 1994 . . . . $50

4019 MAN Low Loader with Car Wash Station, 1994 . . . . $50

4051 Deutz-Fahr Top Liner Combine Harvester, 1993 . . . . $50

4052 Deutz-Fahr M36.10 Corn Combine Harvester, 1993 . . . . . $50

4053 FMG 280 Forester with Logs and Crane, 1993 . . . . $50

4054 Fendt with Forester Trailer, 1996 . . . . $45

4111 Mercedes Lorry with Low Loader Trailer and Excavator, 1993 . . . . $50

4112 Tower Construction Crane, 1993 . . . . $50

4150 Claas Lexion 480, 1997 . . . . $40

4210 Mobile Tower Construction Crane, 1992 . . . . $65

4310 Lattice Mast Crane, 1997 . . . . $65

SILHOUETTE

Silhouette models of France are offered as 1:43 scale kits.

1011 1982 Rondeau M382 . . . . $14

1014 1982 Dumont Fuji $14

SIZZLERS

The distinction of these rechargeable battery-powered race cars is that they represent the first commercial application of nickel-cadmium rechargeable batteries, back in the early 1970s. Originally produced by Mattel, Sizzlers became a brand owned, but never used, by the Estes Model Rocket Company.

In 1996, Playing Mantis obtained licensing from Estes to produce a new line of Sizzlers under the Johnny Lightning brand originally owned by Topper in the early 1970s. New models retail for around $10. Original Sizzlers are valued from $30 – 120. After losing the license to produce Sizzlers, Mattel attempted to compensate by producing X-V Racers, a line currently available, and touting "From the original makers of Sizzlers" on the package, demonstrating an attempt to capitalize on the name they regretfully gave up.

Mike Grove is the undisputed Sizzlers expert and has written a book on them. Contact him at Mike Grove, Sizzlers Hotline, 1047 E 5th St., Fremont, NE 68025, 402-727-9505. E-mail Sizzler@aol.com.

SKY

Sky is an obscure brand of 1:43 scale models known to be offered only from Diecast Miniatures.

501 1950 Mercury Coupe $148

509 1937 Packard 4-door Sedan $148

510 1937 Packard 4-door Sedan Fire Chief $178

5041 1950 Mercury Indy Pace Car $168

5089 1961 Ford Thunderbird Indy Pace Car $168

SKYLINE

EWA offers a few of these obscure 1:43 scale models. Craig Campbell reports that Skyline was a division of Tin Wizard Models of Germany.

501 1950 Mercury Coupe $169

5041 1950 Mercury Convertible Indy Pace Car $198

510 1937 Packard Fire Car Sedan $198

4110 Grove Hydraulic Truck Crane, 1992, $55

SLIK-TOYS (SEE LANSING SLIK-TOYS)

SM

An obscure Hong Kong based company known only as SM produces inexpensive but nevertheless attractive miniature cars and trucks usually sold in budget sets. Price of individual vehicles is generally between 25 and 50 cents each when purchased as part of the set.

SMALL WHEELS AND WESTERN MODELS

As EWA & Miniature Cars USA puts it, "Western Models were one of the first companies in the world to make high quality hand-built metal models. The company was founded in the early 1970s just southeast of London, England, and moved in the mid-80s to Taunton in the southwest of England. They now have a range of about 70 quality 1:43 scale models of European and American, race and street cars, old and new, plus some interesting Record Cars. A few new models are introduced annually and some withdrawn, which makes the models very collectible. Small Wheels is another name used by Western for some of their models. All are made in the Western factory to the same high standards.

SMALL WHEELS 1:43 SCALE

1 Jaguar XK140	$98
2 Ferrari 275 GTB	$108
3 Rolls Royce SC2 Convertible, top up	$108
3 Rolls Royce SC2 Convertible, top down	$108
4 Jaguar Mk 2, blue with disc hubs	$88
4 Jaguar Mk 2, red with wire wheels	$108
5 1952 Bentley R Continental	$98
8 Saab 96	$98
9 Saab 96 Rally	$98
10 1967 Mustang GT	$98
12 1957 DeSoto Firesweep 4-door Sedan	$98 – 119
12 1957 DeSoto Firesweep Sedan, kit	$48
12T 1957 DeSoto 4-door Sedan Taxi	$98
13 1953 Corvette Roadster, kit	$48
14 1958 Chrysler Windsor 2-door Hardtop	$98
15 1948 Hudson Commodore 4-door Sedan	$98 – 109
15P 1948 Hudson Commodore Police	$109 - 119
17 1958 Ford Custom Taxi	$124

SMALL WHEELS 1:24 SCALE

Jaguar XK150	$328
Ferrari Lusso	$308
Jaguar Mark 2 Vicarage	$348
Jaguar XJ13, kit	$148

SMER

Smer models are made in Czechoslovakia.

Ford Model T Roadster, kit, 1:32	$14

SMITH-MILLER

Smith-Miller toys are sturdy cast metal and aluminum replicas of trucks of the era around 1945 when they were introduced in Santa Monica, California. So popular are these "Smitty" trucks that the firm of Fred Thompson still produces quality reproductions of these classic toys. The Smith-Miller firm later became Miller-Ironson before fading into oblivion in 1954. The toys remain as testament to the quality of the era, even though Smitty Toys were considered expensive for their time, from $7 – 28. Their weak point was poorly designed wheels that wore out too quickly. Restoration makes replica wheels worth installing as replacements. Thanks to Richard O'Brien for the background information.

#201-L Lumber Truck with 60 Boards, 6-wheel, 14" long	$700
#202-M Material Truck with 3 Barrels, 3 cases, 18 boards, 4-wheel, 14" long	$900
#203-H Heinz Grocery Truck, 6-wheel, 14" long	$475
#204-A Arden Milk Truck with 12 Milk Cans, 4-wheel, 14" long	$325
#205-P Oil Truck with 4 drums, 6-wheel, 14" long	$450
#206-C Coca-Cola Truck with 16 Coca-Cola Cases, 4-wheel, 14" long	$900
#208-B Bekins Vanliner, 14-wheel, 23½" long	$325
#209-T Timber Giant with 3 Logs, 14-wheel, 23½" long	$325
#210-S Stake Truck, 14-wheel, 23½ long	$500
#211-L Sunkist Special, 14-wheel, 23½" long	$375
#212-R Red Ball, 14-wheel, 23½" long	$375
#301-W GMC Wrecker, 4-wheel	$250
#302-M GMC Materials Truck with 4 Barrels, 3 Timbers	$400
#303-R GMC Rack Truck, 6-wheel	$350
#304-K GMC Kraft Foods, 4-wheel	$600
#305-T GMC Triton Oil with 3 Drums	$350
#306-C GMC Coca-Cola, 16 Coca-Cola Cases, 4-wheel	$900
#307-L GMC Redwood Logger Tractor-Trailer with 3 Logs	$1100
#308-V GMC Lyon Van Lines Tractor-Trailer, 14-wheel	$650
#309-S GMC Super Cargo Tractor-Trailer with 10 Barrels, 14-wheel	$400
#310-H GMC Hi-Way Freighter Tractor-Trailer, 14-wheel	$300
#311-E GMC Silver Streak Express Tractor-Trailer, 14-wheel	$550
#312-P GMC Pacific Intermountain Express "P.I.E." Tractor-Trailer	$600
#401 Tow Truck, 4-wheel, 15" long	$250
#401-W GMC Wrecker, 6-wheel	$450
#402 Dump Truck, 11½" long	$350
#402-M GMC Material Truck with 4 barrels, 2 timbers	$400
#403 Scoop Dump, 14" long	$250
#403-R GMC Rack Truck, 6-wheel	$250
#404 Lumber Truck, 19" long	$750
#404-B GMC Bank of America with Lock and Key, 4-wheel	$400
#404-T Lumber Trailer, 17" long	$300
#405 Silver Streak Tractor, 6-wheel, 28" long	$350
#405-T GMC Triton Oil with 3 Drums, 6-wheel	$375
#406 Bekins Van, 6-wheel Tractor and 4-wheel Trailer	$650
#406-L GMC Lumber Tractor-Trailer with 8 Timbers, 14-wheel	$425
#407 Searchlight Truck Hollywood Filmad, 18½" long	$300
#407-V GMC Lyon Van Tractor-Trailer, 10-wheel	$650
#408 Blue Diamond Dump Truck, 10-wheel, 18½" long	$1,700
#408-H GMC Machinery Hauler, 13-wheel	$1,700
#409 Pacific Intermountain Express "P.I.E." 6-wheel Tractor and 8-wheel Cast Aluminum Trailer, 29" long	$900
#409-G GMC Mobilgas Tanker with 2 Hoses, 14-wheel	$500
#410 Aerial Ladder Semi, 6-wheel Tractor and 4-wheel Trailer, "SMFD," 36" long	$800
#410-F GMC Transcontinental Tractor-Trailer, 14-wheel	$375
#411-E GMC Silver Streak Tractor-Trailer, 14-wheel	$475
#412-P GMC P.I.E., 14-wheel	$625

Chevrolet Bekins Van, plain tires, hubcaps, 14-wheel $525
Chevrolet Coca-Cola, plain tires, 4-wheel $850
Chevrolet Flatbed Tractor-Trailer, unpainted wood trailer, plain tires, hubcaps, 14-wheel $350
Chevrolet Milk Truck, 1945-46, plain tires, hubcaps, 4-wheel . $400
Ford Bekins Van, 1944, plain tires, hubs $400
Ford Coca-Cola with Wood Soda Cases, 1944, 4-wheel $900
Mack "B" Associated Truck Lines, 14-wheel............. $500
Mack "B" Jr. Fire Truck with Warning Light, Battery-Operated, 4-wheel...................................... $950
Mack "B" Orange Dump, 10-wheel............$1,800
Mack "B" P.I.E., 18-wheel.......................... $850

SMTS (SCALE MODEL TECHNICAL SERVICES)

SMTS is a brand of quality hand-built white metal models and kits made in France. Voiturette is a related brand from SMTS.

1 Arrows A6 Barclay, 1:43 .... $98
1 Arrows A6 GPI, 1:43 .... $78
2 Ferrari 216C3, 1:43 .... $78
3 Toleman TG184, 1:43 .... $117
4 1957 Lotus Elite, 1:43 .... $98
5 Aston Martin DB4 GT Zagato, 1:43. .... $98
6 1965 Lotus 33 GP, 1:43 .... $117
7 1930 Bentley Speed 6 LeMans, 1:43 .... $118
8 Lotus Europa, 1:43 .... $98
8 Lotus Europa GLTL, 1:43 .... $88
9 Eagle Weslake Racer, 1:43 .... $117
10 1965 Lotus 38 Indy Racer, 1:43. ...... $98
11 1968 Lotus 56 Indy, 1:43 .... $98
12 1968 Lotus 56B F1, 1:43. .... $84
13 1970 Ferrari 312B, 1:43 .... $138
14 1967 STP Paxton Turbine Indy, 1:43 ..... $117
15 Lotus Europa Special Twincam, 1:43. ..... $117
16 Lotus Seven, 1:43. .... $108
17 March 701, 1:43. .... $134
18 1957 Lotus Seven, 1:43. .... $108
22 1967 Brabham BT26 Racer, 1:43. ...... $138
25 Bugatti 35 Racer, 1:43 .... $108
26 BRM P56, 1:43. .... $108
33 1963 Aston Martin Project 215, 1:43. ..... $98
34 Lotus 30 Racer, 1:43 .... $98
35 Lotus 40 Racer, 1:43 .... $98
41 Lola T90 Racer, 1:43 .... $118 – 128
44 1963 Aston Martin P214 Racer, 1:43 ...... $98
2059 1959 Watson Roadster, 1:43 .... $117
2060 1960 Watson Roadster, 1:43 .... $117
2061 1961 Watson Roadster, 1:43 .... $117
2062 1962 Watson Roadster, 1:43 .... $128
2063 1963 Watson Roadster, 1:43 .... $117
2064 1964 Watson Roadster, 1:43 .... $128

SOLIDO

The venerable Solido firm of Nanterre, France, was formed in 1932 by Ferdinand de Vazeilles. While this book presents a survey of the wide range of high-quality models produced by Solido, a more detailed study is presented by Dr. Edward Force, renowned author and collector of a wide variety of diecast toys (see bibliography).

In 1980, Majorette purchased the Solido company, and continues the tradition of producing quality miniature replica vehicles. The brand survives today under the auspices of Groupe Ideal Loisirs, the French toy conglomerate. Presented below is a sampling of the huge assortment of models produced.

40 Peugeot 604, 1:43 .... $15
Renault Express Van, 1:43 .... $12

SOLIDO NOSTALGIA 1:43 SCALE
(1994 REISSUES OF POPULAR SOLIDO MODELS OF THE 60S)

1101 1956 Ferrari 500 TRC, 1994 reissue $20
1102 1959 Cooper F2, 1994 reissue $20
1103 1962 Lola Climax V8 F1, 1994 reissue $20
1104 1956 Maserati 250, 1994 reissue $20
1105 1960 Lotus F1, 1994 reissue $20
1106 1955 Porsche Spyder, 1994 reissue $20
1107 1959 Panhard DB, 1995 reissue $20
1108 1962 Ferrari 2.5 L, 1995 reissue. $20
1109 1961 Fiat Abarth, 1996 reissue $20
1110 1965 Alpine F3, 1996 reissue $20

SOLIDO 1:12 SCALE MODELS (NEW FOR 1994)

1201 1958 Chevrolet Corvette Convertible, red, 1994 .... $120
1202 1958 Chevrolet Corvette Hardtop, turquoise, 1995 ..... $120

SOLIDO HI-FI/TODAY 1:43 SCALE /LATE MODEL CARS

1501 Jaguar XJ 12 .... $15
1502 1984 Porsche 944. .... $15
1503 Alpine Renault A 310 .... $15
1505 Porsche 928S $15
1507 1983 Chevrolet Camaro Z 28 .... $15

Photo by Jeff Koch.

1508 1984 Peugeot 205 GTI, $15

1510 1986 Mercedes-Benz 190 2.3/16S $15
1511 1987 Rolls Royce Corniche................. $15
1512 1987 Bentley Continental $15
1513 1984 Chevrolet Corvette Hardtop $15
1514 1984 Chevrolet Corvette Convertible. $15
1515 Ferrari Berlinetta Boxer $15
1516 1989 Peugeot 605 .... $15
1517 1989 Mercedes-Benz SL Convertible $15
1518 1989 Mercedes-Benz SL Coupe Hard Top $15
1519 1990 Renault Clio................... $15
1520 1991 Renault Clio 16 S $15
1521 1990 BMW Series 3 .... $15

1522 1991 Renault Espace	$15
1523 1991 Citroën ZX Aura	$15
1524 1991 Citroën ZX Volcane	$15
1525 1989 Porsche 928 GT	$15
1526 1991 Renault Clio 16S "Coupe"	$15
1527 1990 Lamborghini Diablo	$15
1528 1992 Renault Twingo, 1994	$15
1529 1993 BMW Series 3 Convertible, 1994	$15
1530 1992 Renault Twingo, 1994	$15
1531 1993 Renault Clio "Williams," 1994	$15
1532 1993 Renault Twingo Open Top, 1994	$15
1533 1995 Renault 19 Convertible, 1995	$15
1534 1991 Renault Espace Fire Van, 1996	$15
1535 1993 Mercedes 500 SEL, 1996	$15
1536 1995 Mini British Open, 1996	$15
1537 1995 Mini Cabriolet, 1996	$15

Solido Yesterday

1801 1970 Maserati Indy	$10
1802 1976 Ferrari BB	$10
1803 1970 Alpine A110	$10
1804 1973 Alpine A110 Monte-Carlo	$10
1805 1968 Opel GT 1900	$10
1806 1978 Jaguar XJ 12	$10
1807 1970 Citroën SM	$10
1808 1973 Porsche Carrera	$10
1809 1978 Lancia Stratos	$10
1810 1972 Ferrari 365 GTB4	$10
1811 1972 Ferrari 365 GTB4	$10
1812 1979 BMW M1	$10
1813 1968 Chevrolet Corvette, 1994	$10
1814 1972 Alpine A310, 1994	$10
1816 1968 Alfa Romeo Carabo, 1994 reissue	$10
1817 1978 Range Rover, 1995 new	$20
1818 1978 Peugeot 504 Coupe, 1995 reissue	$20
1819 1979 Citroën 2CV Open roof, 1995 reissue	$20
1820 1979 Citroën 2CV, 1995 reissue	$20
1821 1969 Mini Cooper, green, 1996	$20
1822 1969 Mini Cooper, red, 1996	$20

SOLIDO RACING 1:43 scale race-related vehicles

1903 1952 Citroën 15 CV Monte-Carlo	$20
1904 1973 Alpine A 110 Monte-Carlo	$20
1906 1978 Lancia Stratos	$20
1908 1985 Renault 5 Maxi Turbo	$20
1909 1965 AC Cobra 427	$20
1910 1968 Chevrolet Corvette	$20
1911 1980 Iveco TransAfrica	$20
1912 1986 Mercedes Unimog Rallye	$20
1913 1977 Fiat 131 Racing, 1994 reissue	$20
1914 1980 Land Rover, 1994 reissue	$20
1915 1977 Toyota Celica, 1994 reissue	$20
1916 1983 Audi Quattro, 1994 reissue	$20
1917 1975 Peugeot Safari, 1994 reissue	$20
1918 1993 Renault Clio Rallye	$20
1919 1954 Renault 4CV Rallye, 1994	$20
1920 1973 Porsche Carrera	$20
1921 1962 Triumph Spitfire Mk 1, 1994	$20
1922 1965 Ford Mustang, 1994	$20
1923 1983 Lancia Rally, 1995 variation	$20

1924 1978 Peugeot 504 Coupe Rallye, 1995 reissue	$20
1925 1979 Porsche 935, 1995 reissue	$20
1926 1962 Renault Dauphine "1093," 1995	$20
1927 1984 Range Rover Rallye, 1995	$20
1928 1967 Ford Mk IV, 1996	$20
1929 1968 Alpine 3 L, 1996 reissue	$20
1930 1968 Mini Cooper, 1996	$20

Solido Tonergram I

2101 Saviem First Aid	$20
2106 Fire Engine	$20
2117 Jeep with Hose Reel	$20
2118 Citroën C35 with Ladder	$20
2121 Marmon Tanker	$20
2122 Renault Express with Trailer	$20
2123 Dodge Tanker	$20
2124 Marmon Recovery Truck	$20
2125 Mercedes Unimog	$20
2126 Peugeot J9 Ambulance, red	$20
2127 Mercedes Unimog Forest Fire	$20
2128 Dodge WC 54	$20
2129 Iveco Covered Truck	$20
2130 Mercedes Express Emergency Van and Trailer	$20
2131 Mercedes Unimog Ambulance	$20
2132 Mercedes Tender	$20
2133 Mercedes Ambulance	$20
2134 Mercedes Unimog Breakdown Tow Truck	$20
2135 Peugeot J9 Ambulance, yellow	$20
2136 Dodge WC 51, 1994 new	$20
2137 Renault Trafic, 1994 new	$20
2138 Renault Trafic Ambulance, 1994 new	$20
2139 Dodge WC 56 Hose and Ladder, 1995 variation	$20
2140 Dodge WC 51 Tanker, 1995 variation	$20
2141 Renault Trafic Bus, 1995 variation	$20
2142 Renault Express with Trailer, 1996 variation	$20
2143 Dodge Tow Truck, 1996 variation	$20
2144 Renault Trafic with Ladder, 1996 variation	$20
2145 Renaul Trafic Civil Security, 1996 variation	$20
2146 Mercedes Unimog Forest Fire Tender, 1996 variation	$20
2147 Dodge 4x4 with Protective Cover, 1996 variation	$20

Solido Tonergram II

3102 Fire Department Crane	$20
3106 Mack Fire Engine	$20
3107 Berliet Jet Spray Truck	$20
3110 GMC Fire Engine Recovery Truck	$20
3111 Mercedes Ladder Truck	$20
3112 Berliet Hoist	$20
3113 GMC Road Maintenance Truck	$20
3114 Mercedes Jet Spray Truck	$20
3115 GMC Tanker	$20
3116 GMC Tanker	$20
3117 GMC Tow Truck	$20
3118 Iveco Tanker	$20
3119 Sides 2000 Mark 3 Paris	$20
3121 GMC Covered Truck	$20
3122 Mercedes Van with Zodiac Raft	$20
3123 Sides 2000 Mark 3 Strasbourg	$20
3124 Volvo Front End Loader, 1994 reissue	$20
3125 Acmat VLRA Forest Fire Tender, 1994	$20

3126 Acmat VLRA Tanker, 1994 new. $20

3127 Dodge WC 56 with Inflatable Raft and Trailer, 1995 variation. $20

3128 Dodge WC 51 with Trailer, 1995 variation. $20

3129 Renault Trafic with Inflatable Raft and Trailer, 1995 variation. $20

3130 Peugeot 19 Express and Trailer, 1995 variation $20

3131 Mercedes with Foam Cannon, 1996 reissue. $20

3132 GMC with Protective Cover, 1996 reissue $20

3133 Jeep with Ladder and Trailer, 1996 variation $20

3134 Land Rover and Trailer, 1996 variation $20

SOLIDO TONERGRAM III

3501 DAF Covered Truck "DANZA" $25

3507 DAF Double Covered Truck, "IPONE" $25

3508 MACK Freighter "TEAM HUSQVARNA". $25

3509 Renault Fire Tanker Semi, red $25

3510 Mercedes Semi Trailer

    v.1 "BRIDGESTONE" $25

    v.2 "ANDROS Fruits". $25

3511 Mack R 600 Fire Engine $25

3512 Mercedes Fire Brigade Tanker $25

3513 Mack R600 Fire Brigade Tanker $25

3514 Mack R600 Fire Truck Semi $25

3515 Renault Field Casualty Vehicle $25

3516 Mercedes Training Simulator $25

SOLIDO TONERGRAM IV

3601 Kassbohrer Track Rammer $20

3602 Kassbohrer Expedition Rammer $20

3603 Kassbohrer Rammer and Sand Spreader $20

3606 Mercedes Snow Plow. $20

3607 Fire Department Track Rammer $20

SOLIDO HELICOPTERS

3814 Alouette III "SECURITE' CIVILE". $15

3815 Gazelle Missile Launcher $15

3822 Gazelle Civile $15

3823 Alouette III Police $15

3824 Puma AS 332 Military. $15

3825 Puma AS 332 Civil $15

3826 Alouette III "ADP" $15

3827 Gazelle Gendarmerie $15

3828 Cougar AS 532. . . . . $15

3829 Gazelle HOT $15

3830 Agusta A 109 K2 . . . . $15

3831 Agusta A 109 CM $15

SOLIDO L'AGE D'OR 1:43 SCALE VINTAGE CARS

4002 1938 Jaguar SS 100. . . . . $20

4003 1937 Talbot T 23 . . . . $20

4004 1930 Mercedes SSKL $20

4032 1939 Citroën 15 CV $20

4035 1931 Duesenberg J Spider $20

4036 1930 Bugatti Royale $20

4047 1937 Packard Sedan. $20

4048 1937 Delahaye 135 M. $20

4051 1938 Delage Coupe De Ville $20

4055 1930 Cord L 29 . . . . $20

4057 1931 Cadillac V16 452.A Police Car. $20

4059 1925 Renault 40 CV Berline $20

4065 1931 Cadillac Van $20

4070 1931 Cadillac Fire Chief Van. $20

4071 1939 Rolls Royce Coupe. $20

4077 1939 Rolls Royce Convertible $20

4080 1930 Cord L 29 Spider $20

4085 1931 Cadillac 452A. $20

4086 1938 Mercedes 540K Convertible $20

4088 1939 Bugatti Atalante $20

4097 1934 Renault Reinastella. $20

4099 1937 Packard Convertible. $20

4109 1939 Bugatti Atalante Convertible $20

4115 1939 Citroën 15 CV $20

4149 1926 Renault 40 CV Landaulet $20

4156 1935 Duesenberg Model J $20

4159 1936 Ford V8 Berline. $20

4160 1939 Alfa Romeo 2500 Sport Convertible, top down $20

4161 1939 Alfa Romeo 2500 Sport Convertible, top up. $20

4162 1926 Hispano Suiza Torpedo Convertible, top down $20

4163 1936 Ford V8 Taxi $15

4165 1923 Renault 40 CV Presidentielle, top down $20

4166 1939 Ctroen Traction Fire Brigade $20

SOLIDO BUSES

4401 Renault Paris Bus. $20

4402 London Bus. $20

4404 Country English Bus $20

4417 Open Top Bus. $20

4422 1930 Citroën C4F Tanker $20

4427 1940 Dodge Stake Truck "Pepsi". $20

4428 1940 Dodge Fire Department Recovery Truck $20

4429 1930 Citroën C4F Van $20

4430 1940 Dodge Pickup "Sunlight" $20

4431 1936 Ford Van "New York Times" $20

4432 1936 Ford Fire Department Tow Truck $20

4433 1936 Ford V8 Pickup "Kodak" $20

4434 1936 Ford V8 Fire Department Tanker $20

4435 1936 Ford V8 Coal Truck, 1995 variation. $20

4436 1936 Ford V8 Pickup "MIKO," 1995 variation $20

SOLIDO 60s

4500 1957 Cadillac Eldorado Biarritz Convertible. $20

4502 1954 Mercedes 300 SL $20

4505 1961 Ford Thunderbird $20

4506 1963 Ferrari 250 GTO. $20

4508 1950 Chevrolet. $20

4511 1950 Buick Super convertible, top up $20

4512 1950 Buick Super, top down $20

4513 1946 Chrysler Windsor $20

4514 1946 Chrysler Windsor Taxi $20

4515 1962 Facel Vega Hard Top $20

4516 1962 Facel Vega Convertible, top down $20

4517 1963 Ford Thunderbird Grand Sport $20

4518 1950 Chevrolet Fire Car $20

4519 1952 Citroën 15 CV $20

4520 1957 Cadillac Eldorado Seville $20

4521 1957 Studebaker Silver Hawk $20

4522 1957 Studebaker Silver Hawk Hard Top $20

4523 1950 Buick Super Hard Top $20

4524 1948 Tucker Torpedo. $20

4526 1952 Citroën 15 CV Monte Carlo. $20

4529 1950 Chevrolet Checker Cab Taxi. $20

4530 1946 Chrysler Police. $20	6048 US Jeep with Trailer. $20
4531 1964 Ford GT40. . . . . $20	6049 US Jeep with accessories $20
4532 1964 Ford GT40 Le Mans $20	6053 Sherman Tank $20
4533 1965 AC Cobra $20	6055 Leopard Tank $20
4534 1966 VW Van $20	6058 AMX 13/105 Tank $20
4535 1966 VW Van Fire Brigade $20	6060 AMX 30 Tank $20
4536 1952 Citroën 15 CV Taxi. $20	6063 Tigre Tank. $20
4537 1954 Renault 4 CV, 1994 . . . . $20	6064 Jagdpanther Tank $20
4538 1954 Renault 4 CV Open Top, 1994 . . . . $20	6065 Patton M47 Tank $20
4539 1962 Triumph Spitfire Mk 1, 1994. . . . . $20	6067 General Lee Tank $20
4540 1964½ Ford Mustang, 1994. . . . . $20	6068 Destroyer M10. . . . . $20
4541 1961 Renault Dauphine Berline, 1995 . . . . $20	6069 Half-Track Recovery Vehicle $20
4542 1961 Renault Dauphine Open Roof, 1995 . . . . $20	6070 Kaiser - Jeep Crane Truck $20
4543 1966 Volkswagen Van, "Michelin," 1996 . . . . $20	6071 General Grant Tank. $20
4544 1964 Renault 4 L Berline, 1996 . . . . $20	6074 Somua S35 Tank $20
4545 Renault 4 L (open), 1996 . . . . $20	6075 PT 76 Tank $20

SOLIDO 50TH ANNIVERSARY OF LIBERATION OF FRANCE AND NORTH-WESTERN EUROPE 1944 – 1994

4494/11 US Jeep $35	6076 AMX 10 Tank $20
4494/12 Dodge 4X4 WC 54 . . . . $35	6077 Sherman Bulldozer Tank $20
4494/13 Dodge 4X4 WC 56 Command Car $35	6078 Sherman Egyptian Tank $20
4494/21 US Jeep and Trailer. $35	6079 AMX 30 B2 Tank $20
4494/22 Dodge 6X6 WC 63 . . . . $35	6101 GMC Covered Truck, 1995 reissue $20
4494/23 GMC $35	6102 Renault Traction Gaz FFI, 1995 reissue $20
4494/31 US Jeep SAS & Trailer $35	6103 Dodge WC 51 4X4, 1995 reissue $20
4494/32 GMC "Le Roi" $35	6104 Combat Car M20, 1995 reissue $20
4494/33 GMC "Tourelle" $35	6105 US Jeep and Trailer, 1995 reissue $20
4494/34 Dodge 4X4 WC 51 . . . . $35	6106 GMC Truck with accessories, 1995 variation $20
4494/35 Dodge 4X4 WC 56 Command Car $35	6107 Dodge 6x6 . . . . $20
4494/36 Dodge 6X6 WC 63 . . . . $35	6108 Desert Jeep with Trailer $20
4494/37 Dodge Pickup. $35	6109 GMC with accessories $20
4494/38 Packard Sedan HQ $35	6110 Dodge Command Car $20
4494/39 Citroën Traction FF1 . . . . $35	6111 Dodge 4x4 . . . . $20
4494/41 Half-Track US M3 . . . . $35	6112 Jeep Ambulance $20
4494/42 Sherman M4A3 . . . . $35	6113 Jeep and Trailer $20
4494/43 Destroyer M10 . . . . $35	6114 Dodge Signal Corp. $20

SOLIDO MILITARY

6001 GMC Compressor Truck. $20	6115 GMC Compressor. $20
6002 GMC Lot 7 Recovery Truck $20	6116 Packard HQ. $20
6003 Cadillac HQ. $20	6117 Dodge Command Car $20
6004 Dodge WC54 "Signal Corps". $20	6118 GMC Lot 7 . . . . $20
6005 Kaiser Jeep M 34 . . . . $20	6201 Sherman M4A3 Tank, 1995 reissue $20
6006 Packard HQ. $20	6202 Destroyer Tank, 1995 reissue $20
6007 VAB 4X4 . . . . $20	6203 US Half-Track Radio M3, 1995 reissue $20
6025 Panhard AML 90 . . . . $20	6204 Tigre Tank, 1995 reissue $20
6027 V.A.B. 4X4. . . . . $20	6205 Renault R35 Tank, 1995 reissue $20
6032 GMC $20	6206 Jagdpanther Tank, 1995 reissue $20
6033 Chevrolet HQ $20	6207 PZ IV $20
6034 Jeep and Trailer. $20	6208 Half Track Hanomag $20
6036 GMC Covered Truck $20	6209 Priest M7 B1 . . . . $20
6037 Jeep Auto-Union and Trailer. $20	6210 Sherman M4 A3 . . . . $20
6038 Mercedes Unimog $20	6211 General Grant $20
6039 Land Rover and Trailer. $20	6212 Tigre $20
6041 Jeep and Zodiac Inflatable Raft with Trailer. $20	9423 1944 GMC Troop Transporter. $20

SOLIDO TRANSPORTS

6042 Chrysler Windsor HQ. $20	7006 Car Transporter $20
6043 Dodge WC 54 Ambulance $20	7013 Special Convoy Transport. $20

SOLIDO PRESTIGE 1:18 SCALE VINTAGE MODELS

6046 Mercedes Unimog Ambulance $20	8001 1930 Bugatti Royale Type 41, 11" $35
6047 GMC Turret Truck $20	8002 1936 Ford Pickup, 9½". $30
	8005 1936 Ford Fire Department Tanker, 9½" $30

8006 1961 Rolls Royce Silver Cloud II, 10½" $32	9504 1934 Ford Roadster, 1:18 . . . . $35
8007 1961 Bentley S2, 10½" $32	9505 1949 VW Beetle, 1:18. . . . . $35
8008 1934 Ford Roadster Convertible, top down, 9½" $30	9506 1949 VW Beetle Berline, 1:18 . . . . $35
8009 1934 Ford Roadster Convertible, top up, 9½" $30	9507 1955 Cadillac Eldorado Convertible, top down, 1:18 . . . . $35
8010 1934 Ford Pickup Covered Delivery "Perrier," 9½" $30	9508 1966 VW Van, red upper, white lower body, 8⅞", 1:18 . . $35
8011 1955 Cadillac Eldorado Convertible, top down $30	9509 1966 Citroën 2CV, red, top open, 8⅞", 1:43. . . . . $20
8012 1955 Cadillac Eldorado Convertible, top up. $30	9510 1936 Ford Roadster, red with navy fenders, 9½", 1:18,
8014 1949 Volkswagen Beetle Convertible, top down $30	1996 . . . . $35
8015 1949 Volkswagen Beetle Convertible, top up $30	9511 1958 Volkswagen Beetle, white with blue top, red fenders,
8016 1949 Volkswagen Beetle Berline Hardtop $30	9½", 1:18, 1996 . . . . $35
8017 1969 Ferrari 365 GTS Convertible, top down $30	9601 1931 Cadillac Delivery Van, 1:43. . . . . $20
8018 1969 Ferrari 365 GTS Convertible, top up $30	9603 1940 Dodge Covered Pickup, yellow with blue cover, 1:43,
8021 1964 Mini Cooper S, blue with white fenders $30	1996 . . . . $20
8022 1964 Mini Cooper S $30	9605 1940 Dodge Platform Truck, yellow with blue platform, 1:43,
8023 1964 Mini Cooper S Rallye $30	1996 . . . . $20
8024 1936 Ford Pickup "MICHELIN" $30	9606 1930 Citroën C4F Delivery Van, 1:43. . . . . $20
8026 1936 Ford Pickup Fire Truck, 1994 . . . . $30	9607 1950 Chevrolet, 1:43 . . . . $20
8027 1936 Ford Tanker, 1994 . . . . $30	9608 1946 Chrysler Windsor, 1:43. . . . . $20
8028 1966 Citroën 2 CV, closed roof, 1994 . . . . $30	9609 1940 Dodge Platform Truck, 1:43. . . . . $20
8029 1966 Citroën 2CV, open roof, red, 1994 . . . . $30	9610 1957 Cadillac Eldorado, 1:43. . . . . $20
8029 1966 Citroën 2CV, open roof, gray $30	9611 1936 Ford V8, 1:43 . . . . $20
8030 1966 Citroën 2CV, open roof, red & white, 1994 . . . . . $30	9612 1936 Ford V8 Platform Truck, red with brown platform,
8031 1966 Volkswagen Van, red & white, 1994 . . . . $30	1:43. . . . . $20
8032 1966 Volkswagen Van, purple, "PEACE AND LOVE,"	9613 1966 VW Van, 1:43 . . . . $20
"FLOWER POWERED," 1994 . . . . $30	9614 1991 Renault Espace, red, 1:43 . . . . $20
8033 1963 Citroën DS 19 Berline, white with black roof, 10⅜",	9615 1964½ Ford Mustang, 1:43, 1995. . . . . $20
1995 . . . . $30	9616 1994 Renault Trafic, red, 1:50, 1995 . . . . $20
8034 1963 Citroën DS 19 Rallye, blue with white roof, "233" on	9617 1936 Ford Pickup with Cover, black, 1:43, 1996 . . . . . . $20
doors, 10⅜", 1996 . . . . $30	9618 1966 Volkswagen Van, red upper, white lower body, 1:43,
8035 1963 Citroën DS 19 Presidentielle, black, 10⅜", 1996. . . . $30	1996 . . . . $20
8036 1966 Citroën 2 CV Raid, gray with map on sides, spare on	9701 English Bus, 1:50 . . . . $20
hood $30	

8037 1936 Ford Wreck Truck, 9½" $30

8038 1958 Volkswageon Beetle Rallye, 9½", 1996 . . . . $30

8039 1936 Ford Custom Roadster, 9½" $30

8040 1966 Citroën 2 CV Charleston, 8⅞ $30

8041 1966 Volkswagen Van, yellow and blue, "Michelin," 8⅞",
  1996 . . . . $30

8042 1960 Fiat 500, white, 7½", 1996 . . . . $30

8043 1960 Fiat 500 (open), red, 7½", 1996 . . . . $30

8044 1965 Fiat 500 Racing, red with "29" and white racing stripe,
  7½", 1996 . . . . $30

8045 1957 Chevrolet Bel Air Convertible with Continental Kit, baby
  blue, 11", 1996 . . . . $30

8046 1955 Ford Pickup, 9½", 1996 . . . . $30

SOLIDO CUSTOM 1:18 SCALE CUSTOMIZED VEHICLES

8302 1949 VW Beetle Convertible, top down $30

8303 1936 Ford Pickup. $30

8304 1949 VW Beetle Berline hardtop. $30

8305 1964 Mini Cooper S $30

8306 1958 VW Beetle Berline $30

SOLIDO MINIATURES/ACTUA 1:18 SCALE MODERN MODELS

8501 1989 Citroën XM $30

8502 1989 Peugeot 605 . . . . $30

8503 1991 Citroën ZX Rallye Raid. $30

8504 1992 Renault $30

SOLIDO COCA-COLA PROMOTIONALS

9503 1936 Ford Pickup, 1:18. $35

SOLIDO SIGNATURE SERIES LIMITED EDITION VEHICLES FEATURING
CELEBRITY SIGNATURES, INTRODUCED IN 1994

9801 1955 Cadillac Eldorado, red, "James Dean," 1:18 . . . . . . $50

9802 1934 Ford Roadster, black, "Humphrey Bogart," 1:18. . . . $50

9803 1961 Rolls Royce, silver with black hood, "Orson Welles,"
  1:18 . . . . $50

9804 1955 Cadillac Eldorado, white, "Marilyn Monroe," 1:18 . . $50

9901 1950 Buick Super, black, "James Dean," 1:43 . . . . $25

9902 1937 Packard Sedan, silver with black fenders, "Humphrey
  Bogart," 1:43. . . . . $25

9903 1939 Rolls Royce, pale yellow with black fenders, "Orson
  Welles," 1:43. . . . . $25

9904 1950 Buick Super, pink, "Marilyn Monroe," 1:43 . . . . . . $25

SOMERVILLE

Somerville 1:43 scale high quality hand-built models are made in Great Britain. Most models are issued in more than one color variation. The Somerville Society is an organization devoted to the appreciation of these fine models. For more information on this club, contact: The Somerville Society, c/o Rod Ward, Modelauto, 120 Gledhow Valley Road, Leeds LS17 6LX England, Tel: +44 (0)113 268 6685, Fax: +44 (0)1977 681991, e-mail: hotline@modelauto.co.uk, website: http://www.modelauto.co.uk/

103 1937 Ford Popular E190 Sedan. $89

106 Standard Flying 12 Sedan. $99

107 Fordson Van, "India Tyres" $89

109 Fordson Van, "Castrol". $89
110 Fordson Van, "Turf". $89
111 Fordson Van, "Somerville" $89
112 Fordson Van with fish design. $89
113 Fordson Van, "L...East". $89
114 Fordson Van, Butcher $89
117 1949 Ford Anglia A494CV, top up or down. $89
118 Fordson Van with tractor design. $69
121 1947 Volvo PV444 . . . . $89
122 1985 Saab 9000 Turbo . . . . $89 – 99
127 1987 Saab 9000 CD $89
128 Volvo 544 Station Wagon. $89
129 1937 Riley Kestrel $99
132 1992 Saab 9000 CS . . . . $99 – 119
133 Hillman Minx Convertible, top down $119

SPEC-CAST

Spec-Cast is a "spin-off" of the J. L. Ertl company. Spec-Cast models of Dyersville, Iowa, are generally diecast banks in the form of scale model cars, trucks, and airplanes. Liberty Classics is in turn a division of Spec-Cast made in Libertyville, Illinois. Both brands focus on mostly 1:38 scale models. The difference is that Spec-Cast focuses more on producing unmarked models, whereas Liberty Classics specializes in advertising collectibles, sporting logos and livery from various companies, to be used as a promotional model.

Collectors may subscribe to *Spec-tacular News* for $8 for 1 year ($11 outside of U.S.), $14 for 2 years ($16 outside of U.S.). You may also obtain the latest Spec Cast catalog for $2. For more information, write to Spec Cast, 428 6th Avenue NW, P. O. Box 368, Dyersville, IA 52040-0368.

SPEED WHEELS

Speed Wheels are of a quality almost comparable to Hot Wheels, at least the Series V models that sold for about 70 cents each. Lesser quality cars are available for 40 cents but are not worth collecting, according to Russell Alameda. The parent company and accompanying information is still under research.

SPOT-ON (ALSO SEE TRI-ANG MINIC)

Spot-On is a brand of 1:43 scale models introduced in 1959 from Great Britain's Tri-Ang brand, established by the Line Brothers in 1935.

100 Ford Zodiac. $125
100SL Ford Zodiac with lights. $150
101 Armstrong Siddeley 236 . . . . $150
102 Bentley Sports Saloon $200
103 Rolls-Royce Silver Wraith $275
104 MGA Sports Car. $200
105 Austin Healey 100/6 Sports Car $200
106A/I Austin Prime mover and flat float with sides. $300
106A/IC Austin Prime Mover and flat float with sides and crate load $375
106AIOC Austin prime Mover with MGA Sports Car in Crate "BMC". $400
107 Jaguar XK-SS $200
108 Triumph TR3A $200

109/2 ERF 68G with flat float $225
10912P ERF 68G with flat float and wood planks. $300
109/3 ERF 68G flat float with sides $250
109/3B ERF 68G flat floatwith sides and barrel load. $300
110/2 AEC Mammoth Major 8 with flat float $300
110/2B AEC Mammoth Major 8 with flat float and brick load "London Brick Co." $300
110/3 AEC Mammoth Major 8 with flat float and sides "British Road Services" $325
110/3D AEC Mammoth Major 8 flat float with sides and oil drum load $300
110/4 AEC Mammoth Major 8 Shell BP Tanker $750
111A/I Ford Thames Trader with sides "British Railways". . . . $275
111A/IS Ford Thames Trader with sides and sack load $275
111A/OT Ford Thames Trader with log load $275
111A/OG Ford Thames Trader with garage load $375
112 Jensen 541. . . . . $225
113 Aston Martin DB3 . . . . $200
114 Jaguar 3.4 Mk I $175
115 Bristol 406. . . . . $175
116 Caterpillar D9 Bulldozer. $675
117 Jones Mobile Crane $325
118 BMW Isetta Bubble Car $125
119 Meadows Friskysport $125
120 Fiat Multipla $125
122 United Dairies Milk Float $150
131 Goggomobil Super. $125
135 Sailing Dinghy and Trailer $60
136 Sailing Dinghy. $30
137 Massey Harris Tractor. $600
145 AEC Routemaster Bus $725
154 Austin A40. . . . . $125
155 Austin FX4 Taxi Cab $125
156 Mulliner Luxury Coach. $400
157 Rover 3-Litre $200
157SL Rover 3-Litre, with lights. $225
158A/2 Bedford 10-ton tanker, "Shell BP" $775
161 Long wheelbase Land Rover. $125
165 Vauxhall Cresta PA $225
166 Renault Floride Convertible $125
183 Humber Super Snipe Estate $200
184 Austin A60 with roof rack and skis $125
185 Fiat 500 . . . . $150
191/1 Sunbeam Alpine Convertible $200
191/2 Sunbeam Alpine Hard top. $200
193 NSU Prinz $150
195 Volkswagen 1200 Rally $125
207 Wadham Ambulance $500
210/1 Morris Mini Van, "Royal Mail" $175
210/2 Morris Mini Van, "Post Office Telephones". $175
211 Austin Seven Mini $175
213 Ford Anglia $125
215 Daimler Dart SP250 . . . . $225
216 Volvo 122S $175
217 Jaguar E Type $225
218 Jaguar Mk 10 . . . . $175
219 Austin Healey Sprite. $175
229 Lambretta Scooter $175

256 Jaguar 3.4 Mk I Police Car, white and black $250
258 Land Rover RAC $200
259 Ford Consul Classic $150
260 Royal Rolls-Royce Phantom V. $425
261 Volvo P1800 . . . . $125
262 Morris 1100 . . . . $125
263 Bentley Supercharged 4.5 Liter $125
264 Tourist Caravan $75
265 Bedford "Tonibell" Ice CreamVan $175
266 Bullnose Morris Cowley $100
267 MG 1100 . . . . $125
270 Ford Zephyr 6 . . . . $150
271 Express Dairies Milk Float $150
273 Commer Security Van $250
274 Morris 1100 with canoe $100
276 Jaguar S Type $200
278 Mercedes-Benz 230SL. $125
279 1935 MG PB Midget $125
280 Vauxhall Cresta PB $125
281 MG Midget Mk II $175
286 Austin 1800 . . . . $100
287 Hillman Minx. $100
289 Morris Minor 1000 . . . . $200
306 Humber Super Snipe with luggage rack $200
307 Volkswagen Beetle 1200 . . . . $275
308 Land Rover and Trailer. $175
309 Police "Z" Car $175
315 Commer Window Cleaners Van $200
316 Fire Dept, Land Rover $175
401 Volkswagen Variant with skis. $500
402 Crash Service Land Rover. $125
403 Hillman Minx and dinghy. $125
404 Morris Mini Van. $425
405 Vauxhall Cresta PB "BEA" $125
407 Mercedes-Benz 230SL. $125
410 Austin 1800 with row boat $125
415 RAF Land Rover. $150
417 Bedford Military Field Kitchen $150
419 Land Rover and Missile Carrier. $300

STAHLBERG (OR STALLBERG)

Several classy models from Stahlberg of Finland are offered by Diecast Miniatures. These are generally sold as plastic dealer promotional models.
Mercedes 300 Wagon, 1:25. $25
Saab Lancia 600 4-door Sedan, 1:25 . . . . $25
Volvo 245 GL Wagon, 1:25. $25

STARTER

Starter is the brand name of resin-cast kits produced in France.

STROMBECKER (SEE TOOTSIETOYS)

STYLISH CARS

Stylish Cars are superb hand-built models, of which one is available from Diecast Miniatures.
1933 Duesenberg SJ Speedster, 1:43 . . . . $338

SUMMER

Summer models of Hong Kong are reported to be approximately 1:60 scale issues from NSG Marketing. Other NSG toys are offered as Traffic Stoppers. Both brands represent somewhat crude versions of popular car models. Both brands fall under the category of generic toys for the lack of identifying marks, except for the models listed below and a few others.

Jaguar XJ, $1

Photo by Jeff Koch.

Volvo 164E, #S691, $1

SUN MOTOR COMPANY (SEE MODELAUTO)

SUNSHINE TOYS

Many Sunshine models were previously assumed to be Superior brand. Both feature a large assortment of pull-back action toys, and both are marked by a model number preceded by an "SS-." Since there may be a direct connection between both companies, they are both listed under Superior for the time being. These are generally considered inexpensive generic toys.

SUPERIOR

Superior models are made in Hong Kong. For the low price of $6 apiece, these are detailed models of relatively high quality. Most Superior models are identified on the base by a number preceded by "SS-" and feature pull-back action. Diecast Miniatures offers Superior models in 1:36 to 1:43 scale range. It has recently been discovered that models previously assumed to be Superior models are actually

Sunshine Toys, as indicated by the SS that precedes the model number on the base.

BMW 325i Convertible $6
BMW 325 M3 2-door Sedan $6
BMW 635 CSi $6
BMW 728 4-door Sedan $6
BMW Z1 Roadster $6
Bugatti T44 Coupe $6
Bugatti T57 Coupe $6
1950 Buick Super Convertible, top down $6
1951 Cadillac Roadster $6
1953 Cadillac Convertible, top up $6
Chevrolet Astro Van $6
Chevrolet Astro "Firevan" $6
Chevrolet Astro Van "Superman" $6
1957 Chevrolet Bel Air 2-door Hardtop, 1:25 . . . . $9
Chevrolet Blazer Tow Truck Fire $6
Chevrolet Blazer Tow Truck Police $6
Chevrolet Blazer Ambulance $6
Chevrolet Blazer Police $6
1957 Chevrolet Corvette Hardtop $6
1957 Chevrolet Corvette Roadster $6
Hayashi Dome-O Exotic Car $6
Excalibur Roadster $6
Ferrari F40 . . . . $6
Ferrari 288 GTO Coupe $6
Ferrari Testarossa, 1:40 . . . . $6
Ferrari Testarossa, 1:25 . . . . $9
Ford Escort Convertible $6
Ford E100 Ambulance Van $6
Ford E100 Police Van $6
1932 Ford Coupe $6
1956 Ford Thunderbird $6
1959 Ford Galaxie Convertible $6
Ford 3100 4WD Tractor $6
Jeep CJ5 . . . . $6
Jeep CJ5 Ambulance $6
Jeep CJ2 Army Jeep with top $6
Jeep Army Rocket Launcher $6
Jeep Army Machine Gun $6
Jeep Army Radar $6
John Deere 3130 Tractor $6
International Harvester 4WD Tractor $6
Mercedes-Benz 190E "Fire Dept." $6
Mercedes-Benz 500SEL Convertible, top down . . . $6
Mercedes-Benz 500SEL Convertible, top up $6
1991 Mercedes-Benz 500SL Convertible, top down . . . $6
Mercedes-Benz 540K Roadster $6
Mercedes-Benz 540K Coupe $6
1984 Mercedes-Benz 500SL Roadster $6
Mercedes-Benz 560SEC Coupe $6
Mercedes-Benz 207 Police $6
Mercedes-Benz 207 Fire $6
Michelotti Laser $6
Nissan HD Fire Pumper Truck $6
Nissan HD Fire Ladder Truck $6
Nissan HD Fire Snorkel Truck $6
Nissan HD Fire Aerial Ladder Truck

Opel Omega 4-door Sedan $6
Pontiac Firebird Trans Am T-Top "Sunbeam Bread" #42 Race Car,
  yellow $15
1986 Porsche 911 Roadster $6
1989 Porsche 911 Roadster $6
Porsche 959 Coupe $6
1931 Rolls Royce Phantom II $6
1947 Talbot Convertible, top up $6
Volkswagen 1303 Beetle $6
Volkswagen Beetle $6
Volkswagen Beetle Convertible $6
Volkswagen Golf Cabriolet $6
Volkswagen LT Police Van $6
Volkswagen LT Fire Van $6

SVP

In 1948, the S.V. Paraboni company of Italy, SVP, produced just one model, presumed to be a 1:43 scale model with a clockwork motor and steering.

Fiat-Farina Coupe, 4½" $60

SWAN HILL

Pleasanton, California, was home to the Swan Hill toy company, manufacturers of heavy cast aluminum toys representing some unusual vehicles, particularly one lumber hauler that stands about 8 inches high and measures about 10 inches long.

Lumber Hauler . . . . $55 – 80

TAISEIYA

Japan is home to Taiseiya, manufacturer of 1:43 scale models.

1912 Chevrolet Phaeton, pewter-like $24

TAKARA

Takara is a Japanese company of which little is known. Among their products are some toys made for Tonka called Turbo Tricksters. See Tonka for more information.

TAK-A-TOY (ALSO SEE WELLY)

Tak-A-Toy is an inexpensive brand of toys that, like so many other inexpensive toys, is usually rendered an unmarked generic toy once removed from package. Interestingly, at least one particular model is found to be an exception to this rule. One Audi Quattro in white with red, light blue, and black rally markings was found to be made by Welly and holds the distinctive Welly name on the base along with the number 8368. It was purchased for 89 cents from a local grocery store in November 1996. Welly toys are slightly better made than most in the budget genre of diecast toys and are usually marked with the brand name on the bottom. Tak-A-Toy is a division of Larami Corp., Philadelphia PA 19107.

TAMIYA

Tamiya is best known for quality plastic car kits and radio-controlled models. Recently Tamiya has begun producing a few large scale diecast models.

TD

1950 Caterpillar Bulldozer, tin, made in USA, 8" $20

TEKNO/CHICO (ALSO SEE DALIA)

Tekno toys are especially nice 1:43 scale models made in Denmark. Chico toys are the Colombia division of Tekno. Dalia of Spain established a working relationship with Tekno to produce a special line of models separate from the main Tekno line.

442 Scooter Solo	$75 – 90
444 Scooter Delivery	$75 – 90
709 Milling Machine	$30 – 45
713 Wet Grinder	$45-60
736 Beer Truck "Tuborg" (with 20 cases)	$45 – 60
761 Motorcycle	$75 – 90
762 Motorcycle/side car	$75 – 90
763 Motorcycle/side car	$75 – 90
764 Motorcyle/side car	$75 – 90
770 Truck (lorry)	$45 – 60
773 Animal Truck	$45 – 60
775 Trailer	$30 – 45
785 Hawker Hunter Jet	$45 – 60
802 Alfa Romeo	$45 – 60
804 M.G.	$45 – 60
808 Triumph Sports Car	$45 – 60
809 1956 Ford Thunderbird Roadster	$32
953 Army Truck/Anti-Aircraft	$75 – 90
Beer Trailer (Carlsberg)	$30 – 45
Chevrolet Monza GT	$35
Delivery Truck (barrels, 9 sacks & trolley)	$30 – 45
Deutz Van Police	$32
Ford Cable Truck	$20
1953 Ford Taunus Van	$35
Kul & Koks (Coal & Coke) Truck	$30 – 45
Mercedes-Benz Tow Truck	$18
M.I.G. 15	$30 – 45
Scania CR-76 Bus	$35
Volkswagen 1500 Sedan	$100
Volvo F10 "SPETRA"	$32
Volvo Truck	$18
Volvo Cement Truck	$14
Volvo 2-axle Truck	$4
Volvo 2-axle Trailer	$4

TfC (SEE TOYS FOR COLLECTORS)

THOMAS TOYS

The fact that Thomas Toys are plastic eliminates them from the category to which this book is devoted. But the history and style of Thomas Toys deserves at least some mention. Most well-known for its Art Deco "Flash Gordon" style cars, Thomas Toys presents a distinctive and highly collectible assortment of models. Based in Newark, New Jersey, Islyn Thomas created some of the most distinctive plastic toy cars of their era or any era. For the collector of toy cars not necessarily diecast, Thomas is one brand worth searching out. Their values are still low, only $15 – 45 each.

TINTOYS

While Tintoys are a punctuation mark in the novel of diecast toys, the few lightweight models produced under this brand name, while lacking in detail, are interestingly accurate miniatures of the two cars discovered by the author. Their value won't likely rise, but are noteworthy nonetheless.

Cadillac Seville, 1:69	$0.50
Toyota Celica 2000GT Liftback, 1:63	$0.50

TIP TOP TOY CO.

Slush mold (lead cast) vehicles dominate the Tip Top Toy Company's line of toys produced in San Francisco in the 1920s and '30s.

Airflow, larger	$40
Airflow, smaller	$30
Bus, 3⅜"	$40
Coupe, 3³⁄₁₆"	$35
1923 Dodge Coupe, 3⅛"	$30
Gasoline Tanker, 3½"	$35
1935 Hupmobile, 3¼"	$50
Parcel Delivery Panel Truck, 2⅛"	$30
Pickup Truck with Tailgate, 3³⁄₁₆"	$40
Small Coupe, 2⅛"	$25
Small Tanker, 2¹¹⁄₁₆"	$20
Stake Truck, 5⁵⁄₁₆"	$55
1935 Studebaker Sedan, 2⁹⁄₁₆"	$45
Tow Truck, 3⁵⁄₁₆"	$35

TOMICA

Until around 1980, the Japanese gems known as Tomica Pocket Cars from Tomy were widely distributed in the US, even available in grocery stores. But because their high quality and accurate scale meant that they cost a little more than Hot Wheels and Matchbox, they were unable to compete with the lower-priced and better-known brands. The normal price for Pocket Cars was around $1 – 1.75 each. Now they sell from private importers for $4 – 15 each. Their current value reflects the growing interest from collectors who discovered these terrific little toys too late to save them from disappearing from the US market.

Another reason for a lack of popularity was their focus on Japanese vehicles such as Mazda, Hino, Mitsubishi, and Fuso. Now, models of Japanese vehicles are more desirable because they are Japanese. New models are still being produced but are not generally available in the US, as the Tomica series retreated to European and Asian markets where Pocket Cars still hold a better market share.

The numbering system for Pocket Cars is not particularly consistent, so the preferred method of listing them is alphabetically by description. Most models are well marked on the base, and are heavier than usual for their size, due to more metal and less plastic.

Other companies, in an attempt to capture some of the Pocket Car market, produced cheap copies of many of these models. A major difference is that these generic knock-offs had plastic bases and other components, and lighter weight metal parts, and are generally unmarked. The

generic versions are considered essentially worthless to collectors, except as an oddity. Models are listed below alphabetically, with model number, copyright date, and scale when available, and current value. The premier source for current and older Tomicas is Bob Blum, 8 Leto Road, Albany, NY 12203, phone 518-456-0608.

Alpine Renault Sports Racer, 191-F48 . . . . $5
American Cement Truck, Peterbilt, 219-F63, c1978, 1:98 . . . . . . $5
American LaFrance Ladder Chief, 160-F33/187-F33, c1978, 1:143. $8
American Wrecker, Peterbilt, F63, c1978, 1:98 . . . . $5
Amusement Park Shuttle Bus, 49, 1:130 . . . . $5
Auto Transporter, 137-14 . . . . $12
Baja Jeep 4 Wheeler $6
Big Rig Cement Mixer, Peterbilt, 219-F63, c1978, 1:98 . . . . $5
Big Rig Dump Truck, Peterbilt, 205-F63, c1978, 1:98 . . . . $5
Big Rig Tow Truck, Peterbilt, 171-F63, c1978, 1:98 . . . . $5
BLMC Mini Cooper S Mark III, F8, c1979, 1:50 . . . . $8
BMW 3.5 CSL, 167-F30 . . . . $5
BMW 320i, 239-F43, 1:62 . . . . $5
Box Van, 35/36/37 . . . . $6
Bugatti Royale Coupe DeVille 1927, 186-F46, c1978, 1:80 . . . . . $6
Bulldozer, 247-106 . . . . $8
Bus, 79, 1:130 . . . . $6
Cadillac Ambulance, F-2 . . . . $12
Cadillac Seville 1981, 233-F45, 1:69 . . . . $6
Cadillac Superior Ambulance, 181-F60, c1976, 1:77 . . . . $10
Cadillac Fleetwood Brougham, 86-F2, c1976, 1:77 . . . . $6
Cadillac Fleetwood Brougham, 211-F2, c1976, 1:77 . . . . $6
Camper Pickup, Chevrolet Truck, 214-F44, 1:77 . . . . $6
Canter Garbage Truck $4
Cargo Container, 100, 1:47 . . . . $8
Cargo Container Truck, Fuso, 7/67-90,-91, 1:127 . . . . $9
Cedric 280E $4
Celica LB 2000 GT, 33, 1:63 . . . . $5
Chemical Fire Engine, Datsun UD Condor, 145-94, 1:90 . . . . . $12
Chevy Van, F22, c1977, 1:78 . . . . $5
Chevy Van, Custom, 216-F23 . . . . $5
Chevy Van Ambulance, 143-F22, c1977, 1:78 . . . . $6
Chevy Van Sheriff, F22, c1977, 1:78 . . . . $6
Citroën "H" Truck, 97, 1:71 . . . . $5 – 10
Continental Mark IV, Ford Lincoln, 114-F4, c1976, 1:77 . . . . . . $5
Corvette, 144-F21 . . . . $5
Crane Picrover Mobile, 65-33, 1:96 . . . . $6
Custom Chevy Van, 216-F23 . . . . $5
Custom Stepside Pickup, 212-F44 . . . . $6
Daihatsu Midget, 62, 1:50 . . . . $5
Datsun 200SX, 235-6 . . . . $5
Datsun 260Z, 47-58 . . . . $5
Datsun 280Z Rally, 210-58 . . . . $5
Datsun UD Condor Chemical Fire Engine, 145-94, 1:90 . . . . . . $12
Datsun R382 Racer, 25-22 . . . . $5
Datsun Silvia $4
Datsun Station Wagon, 138-47 . . . . $6
Datsun Tipper Truck, 136-56 . . . . $6
Datsun Touring Car 1932, 03-60, c1974, 1:49 . . . . $6
DeTomaso Pantera, 193-F55, silver $5
DeTomaso Pantera, F64, blue $5
Dodge Coronet Custom Police Car, 105/178-F8, c1976, 1:74 . . . $7

Dodge Fire Chief, 163-F10 . . . . $6
Dodge Taxi, 139-F18 . . . . $6
Dyna Vac, 18, 1:68 . . . . $5
Elf Backhoe, 152-64 . . . . $8
Elf Rally Renault, 238-F58 . . . . $6
Emergency Van, Chevy, 207-F22, c1977, 1:78 . . . . $6
Ferrari 308 GTB, F35, 1:60 . . . . $5
Ferrari 312 Formula 1 Racer, 209-59 . . . . $5
Ferrari Dino 308 GTB, 155-F35, c1977, 1:60 . . . . $5
Fiat X1/9, 165-F28 . . . . $5
Firebird Turbo, 243-F42 . . . . $5
Ford Livestock Truck, F62, 1:95 . . . . $6
Ford Lotus Europa "John Player Special," 161-F36/164-F25 . . . . $6
Ford Model T Convertible Coupe 1915, 112/248-F11, c1977, 1:60. $8
Ford Model T Delivery Van 1915, 134-F11/F13, c1977, 1:60 . . . . $8
Ford Model T Touring Car 1915, 125/246-F12/F11, c1977, 11:60 . $8
Ford P-34 Tyrell Formula 1 Racer, 168-F32, c1977, 1:52 . . . . . . $6
Ford Fritos Truck, 236-F62, 1:95 . . . . $6
Fuji Subaru, 21, 1:50 . . . . $4 – 20 depending on variations
Furukawa Wheel Loader, 36-63 . . . . $6
Fuso Truck Crane, 66 . . . . $5
Hino Grandview Bus, 1, 1:154 . . . . $5 – 12
Fuso Truck Series Freight Truck, 77-7/90/91, 1:127 . . . . $5
Fuso Truck Series Pepsi Truck, 77-7/90/91, 1:127 . . . . $5
Fuso Truck Series Tanker, 77-7/90/91, 1:127 . . . . $5
Gran Porsche, 197-F3 . . . . $5
Greyhound Bus "Americruiser," 222-F49, c1979, 1:156 . . . . . . $25
Hato School Bus $4
Hato City Bus $4
Heavy Crane, 141-66 . . . . $6
Hino Big Rig Semi-Trailer, 89-24 . . . . $10
Hino Cement Mixer, 29-52/-53/-54, 1:102 . . . . $6
Hino Dozer Carrier, 56, 1:102 . . . . $7
Hino Gasoline Truck, 29-52/-53/-54, 1:102 . . . . $6
Hino Grandview Bus, 1, 1:154 . . . . $5 – 12
Hino Truck, 29-52/-53/-54, 1:102 . . . . $6
Hitachi DH321 Dump Truck, 35-59, 1:117 . . . . $6
Honda Accord, 142-78 . . . . $5
Honda Acura NSX, black & red, 78, 1:59 . . . . $5
Honda Beat, 72, 1:50 . . . . $5
Honda Civic GL/CVCC, 241-83, c1974, 1:57 . . . . $8
Honda Motorcycle, 42, 1:34 . . . . $8
Hovercraft, Mitsui Zosen, 93, 1:210 . . . . $8
IMSA Turbo Toyota Celica, 217-65, c1979, 1:62 . . . . $5
Isuzu Bonnet Police Bus, 6, 1:110 . . . . $15
Isuzu Elf, 1:67 . . . . $8
Isuzu Hipac Van, 27, 1:70 . . . . $6
Isuzu Red Cross Van $4
Jaguar XJ-S, 199-F68, c1978, 1:67 . . . . $6
Jr. Hiway Bus, 101, 1:145 . . . . $8
Komatsu Bulldozer-Shovel, 66-106 . . . . $8
Komatsu Fork Lift, 34-48 . . . . $8
Komatsu Steam Shovel, 49-09 . . . . $12
Kubota Farm Tractor, 61-92, 1:42 . . . . $8
LaFrance Ladder Chief, 160-F33/187-F33, c1978, 1:143 . . . . . . $8
Lamborghini Countach, 162-F37/170-F50 . . . . $5
Lancia Stratos HF Racer, 153/159-F27 . . . . $5
Lancia Stratos Turbo Racer, 223-F66, c1987, 1:62 . . . . $5

Lincoln Continental Mark IV, 114-F4, c1976, 1:77 . . . . $5
Lion Bus, 26 . . . . $5
London Bus, F15, c1977, 1:130 . . . . $10
Lotus Elite, F47, c1978, 1:63 . . . . $6
Lotus Esprit Special, 220-24 . . . . $5
Lotus Europa John Player Special, 161-F36/164-F25. . . . . $6
Maserati Merak SS, 177-F45, c1978, 1:62 . . . . $6
Mazda Familia 1500XG, 4, 1:59 . . . . $6
Mazda GT Racer, 158-80 . . . . $5
Mazda RX-500, 17-34 . . . . $5
Mazda Savannah RX-7, 203/245-50, c1979, 1:60. . . . . $5
Mazda Savannah GT, 80, 1:59 . . . . $7
Mitsubishi Airport Towing Tractor, 95, 1:110. . . . . $8
Mitsubishi Fuso Container Truck, 74, 1:102. . . . . $5
Mitsubishi Jeep J58 . . . . $4
Mitsubishi Minica Toppo, 71, 1:56 . . . . $5
McLaren M26 Ford Formula 1, 224/169-F39. . . . . $5
Mercedes-Benz 300SL Gullwing, 1956, 221-F19 . . . . $6
Mercedes-Benz 450SEL, 111/176-F7, c1976, 1:67 . . . . $5
Mercedes Unimog, 184-F41, c1978, 1:70 . . . . $6
Mitsubishi Big Rig Truck, Fuso, 62-07. . . . . $6
Mitsubishi Canter Garbage Truck, 47, 1:72 . . . . $6
Mitsubishi Fuso Racing Transporter, 93, 1:102. . . . . $6
Mitsubishi Rosa School Bus, 60, 1:84 . . . . $5
Mitsui Zosen Hovercraft, 93, 1:210 . . . . $8
Mobile Picrover Crane, 65-33, 1:96. . . . . $6
Morgan Plus 8, 140-F26, c1977, 1:57. . . . . $6
Moving Van, 117-20. $8
Mustang II Ghia, 156/188-F38. . . . . $6
Newspaper Truck, 118-107. . . . . $15
Nissan Bluebird SSS Coupe, 1. . . . . $7 – 20
Nissan Caball Utility Truck, 54/87/88, 1:68 . . . . $6
Nissan Caravan, 3, 1:66 . . . . $5
Nissan Condor Crane Truck with pipes, 80, 1:104 . . . . . . $5
Nissan Diesel Moving Van, 16, 1:102 . . . . $6
Nissan Diesel Tanker, 16, 1:102 . . . . $6
Nissan Fairlady 280Z-T, 15, c1979, 1:61. . . . . $6
Nissan Paramedic Ambulance, 51, 1:78. . . . . $5
Nissan Pulsar. $4
Nissan Silvia $4
Off Road Cruiser, 226-2 . . . . $5
Ohara Snow Tiger SM30, 84, 1:73. . . . . $12
Packard Coupe Roadster 1937, 179-F52, 1978, 1:72 . . . . . $8
Pajero, 30, 1:62 . . . . $5
Panda Truck, 76, 1:102. . . . . $10
Pepsi Soft Drink Truck, 198-76. . . . . $8
Peterbilt Wrecker, F63, c1978, 1:98. . . . . $5
Picrover Mobile Crane, 65-33, 1:96. . . . . $6
Pizza Scooter, 82 . . . . $5
Police Bike, 4, 1:34 . . . . $5
Police Bus, Isuzu Bonnet Bus, 6, 1:110 . . . . $15
Police Car, Dodge Coronet Custom, 178-F8/9/10/18 . . . . . $7
Police Van Special Weapons Team 2, Toyota Type HQ15V, 185-67, c1978, 1:81 . . . . $8 – 10
Pontiac Firebird Trans Am, 201-F42 . . . . $6
Porsche 356, 89, 1:59. . . . . $5
Porsche 911S, 106-F3/F17, c1976, 1:61 . . . . $6
Porsche 928, 204-F53. . . . . $5

Porsche, Gran Porsche, 197-F3. . . . . $5
Porsche Sports Racer, 237-F43 . . . . $5
Porsche Turbo 935, 183-F31. . . . . $5
Power Company Service Truck, Nissan Caball, 75-54/87/88, 1:68. $6
Propane Truck, 115-42. . . . . $6
Renault Elf Rally, 238-F58. . . . . $6
Rolls Royce Phantom VI, 110-F6, c1976, 1:78 . . . . $6
Rural School Bus, 109-F5, 1:108, c1976 . . . . $6
Sakai Tire Roller, 103-65, 1:90 . . . . $8
School Bus, 91-01 . . . . $8
School Bus, Rural, 109-F5, 1:108, c1976 . . . . $6
Screamin' Sports Car, 180-71 . . . . $5
Sheriff's Van, Chevrolet Chevy Van, 242-F22, c1977, 1:78 . . . $6
Sightseeing Bus, 130-41 . . . . $10
Silvia 240 SX, 6, 1:59 . . . . $5 – 12
Snow Tiger, Ohara SM30, 147-84,1:73. . . . . $12
Soarer Lexus Coupe, 5, 1:63 . . . . $5
Special Weapons Team Police Van, Toyota Type HQ15V, 185-67, c1978, 1:81 . . . . $8 – 10
Squirt Fire Engine, 41-03 . . . . $6
Steam Shovel, Komatsu, 49/192-9. . . . . $12
Street Sweeper, light yellow, 113, 1:66 . . . . $5
Subaru Milk Truck, 96, 1:130 . . . . $5
Subaru Sambar POST Van, 31, 1:52 . . . . $9
Super Bug Volkswagen, 195-F20, 1:60 . . . . $10
Suzuki Carry Stake Truck, 39, 1:55 . . . . $6
Swim School Bus, 83, 1:145 . . . . $5
Tadano Rough Terrain Crane, 218-2, c1979, 1:96. . . . . . . $5
Taxi, Toyota Crown, 4/27/32/110, 1:65. . . . . $8
Texaco Gas Truck, 234-F62 . . . . $6
Texaco Tanker, Fuso, 77-7/90/91, 1:127 . . . . $5
Telephone Truck, Nissan Caball, 244-54/87/88, 1:68 . . . . . $6
Toyota 2000-GT, 22-05, c1974, 1:60 . . . . $10
Toyota Ambulance, 46-40 . . . . $6
Toyota Caribe (Tercel). $4
Toyota Celica Supra Racer, 65 . . . . $5
Toyota Celica Supra LB 2000GT, 215-33, c1978, 1:63. . . . . $6
Toyota Corolla Levin, 78, 1:61 . . . . $6
Toyota Crown Taxi, 4/27/32/110, 1:65 . . . . $8
Toyota Ex-7, 04-31. $6
Toyota Fork Lift, 182-12. . . . . $8
Toyota Hiace Auto Wrecker, 38/50, 1:68. . . . . $8
Toyota Hiace Airport Stairway Truck, 38/50, 1:68 . . . . . . $10
Toyota Hiace Loudspeaker Vending Truck, 38/50, 1:68 . . . . $15
Toyota Hilux Surf, 84, 1:65. . . . . $5
Toyota Land Cruiser, 83-02 . . . . $8
Toyota MR2. . . . . $4
Toyota Previa, red & gray, 99, 1:64. . . . . $5
Toyota Towing Tractor, 96, 1:50, with cargo container, 100, 1:47, & box van, 35/36/37. . . . . $25
Toyota Type HQ15V Special Weapons Team Police Van, 185-67, c1978, 1:81 . . . . $8 – 10
Toyota Utility Truck, 128-38 . . . . $6
Toyota Wrecker, 129-39 . . . . $5
Turbo Firebird, 243-F42 . . . . $5
Turbo Porsche 935, 240-F31 . . . . $5
Tyrell P34 Formula 1 Ford, 168-F32, c1977, 1:52 . . . . . . $6
UD Condor Chemical Fire Engine, Datsun, 145-94, 1:90. . . . $12

Utility Truck Nissan Caball, 244-54/87/88, 1:68 . . . . $6
Utility Truck Toyota, 1280-38 . . . . $6
Vette Racer, 175-F21 . . . . $5
VW Beetle, gold, 100, 1:60. . . . . $5
Volkswagen Convertible, 146/225-F20, c1977, 1:60 . . . . $10
Volkswagen Rabbit/Golf GLE, 232-F5, 1:56. . . . . $6
Volkswagen Microbus, 166-F29 . . . . $18
Wheel Loader, 206-63 . . . . $8
Winnebago Chieftain Motor Home, 92-F1, c1976, 1:97. . . . . . . $12

TOMICA DANDY

These are 1:43 scale models whose detail, packaging, and accessories set them apart from most other models in their price range. Here is a small sampling of Tomica Dandy models.

Datsun Silvia Coupe. $18
Fiat 131 Abarth $18
Hino Fire Ladder Truck, 2 . . . . $18
London Double Decker Bus $45
Mercedes 560 SEL, G-8 . . . . $30
Mini Cooper, DJ015 . . . . $22
Nissan Caravan Police, 1 . . . . $18
Nissan Cedric 4-door Sedan Police Car $18
Nissan Condor Fire Truck. $18
Nissan Skyline $18
Nissan Van Ambulance, 12. . . . . $18
Regent III RT London Transport Bus, F19 . . . . $45
Toyota Landcruiser $18
1970 Toyota Mk2 2-door Hardtop, 11 . . . . $20
VW Bug, DJ011 . . . . $22
VW Police, "METRO," DE006 . . . . $22
VW Van, "NGK," DT002 . . . . $24

TOMY (ALSO SEE TOMICA)

Besides producing the popular Tomica Pocket Cars, Tomy is a prominent manufacturer of many other toys. Based in Japan, Tomy has been a major force in the toy industry for many years. A few diecast specialty toys have been produced under the Tomy name. The one listed below is of particular note for the standard Tomica-style wheels and the quality of diecasting synonymous with Tomica.

Mickey Mouse Fire Engine, red with yellow plastic trim, gray
    wheels with gold hubs, 2⅝". . . . . $8 – 12

TONKA

Most Tonka toys are manufactured of stamped or pressed steel and do not qualify as diecast. But this brand from Mound, Minnesota, has a rich heritage, that deserves mention. Vintage Tonka trucks of the 50s are often selling for $100 – 400 each, and restored vehicles are also rising in value, to $50 and more. There is only one known book on Tonka trucks, but the series deserves more attention, perhaps in a future book from Collector Books.

Tonka Turbo Tricksters are produced for Tonka by Takara Co., Inc. of Macau. They are plastic toys with centrifugal flywheel motors that assist in making the cars do wild acrobatic tricks.

TONKIN

Tonkins are ready built 1:53 scale 1988 Ford twin trailer truck models available from Diecast Miniatures for $38 each.

TOOTSIETOYS

Tootsietoys were the first diecast toys ever made, back in 1910. The process of diecasting was first introduced to the world at the Columbian Exposition of 1893, when Charles Dowst observed a new machine known as the Line-O-Type. Mr. Dowst applied the process to the manufacture of various items, eventually producing the first diecast toys in 1910. These first diecast toys soon after became known as Tootsie Toys. (Later the name was changed to Tootsietoys.)

The Tootsietoy legacy can be divided into two eras — pre-war and post-war. The reason for this is that before World War II, Dowst concentrated on producing realistic replicas of popular vehicles of the era. The focus after the war shifted to producing less expensive toys that were more affordable and therefore more accessible to children.

Serious collectors prefer pre-war Tootsietoys because of their greater detail and realism. Today's assortment of Tootsietoys runs the full gamut of styles, from crude generic toys to accurate miniature models, but the focus is still on affordability. While this book presents a survey of models, a more detailed study can be found in David Richter's *Collector's Guide to Tootsietoys,* $16.95 from Collector Books.

In 1964, with the purchase of the Strombecker Corporation, one of the oldest companies in the US, Dowst's Tootsietoys became Strombecker's Tootsietoys.

EARLY TOOTSIETOY MODELS

4482 Bleriot Aeroplane, 1910, 2⅝" $200
4491 Bleriot Aeroplane, 1910, 2" $90
4528 Limousine, 1911, 1⅞" $45
4570 1914 Model T Ford Convertible, 1914, 3". $90
4610 1914 Model T Ford Pickup, 1916, 3" $90
4626 Passenger Train Set, 1925. $90
4627 Freight Train Set, 1925 . . . . $90

4629 1921 Yellow Cab, 1923, 2¾", $90

4630 1924 Federal Delivery Van, laundry; grocery, milk or delivery, 1924 . . . . $90
4630 Delivery Van, Special Issue: Watt & Shand, 1924 . . . . . . $400
4630 Delivery Van, Special Issue: Adam, Meldrum & Anderson Co., 1924 . . . . $400
4630 Delivery Van, Special Issue: Bamberger, 1924 . . . . $400
4630 Delivery Van, Special Issue: Pomeroy's, 1924 . . . . $400
4630 Delivery Van, Special Issue: U. S. Mail, 1924 . . . . $600
4636 1924 Buick Series 50 Coupe, 1924, 3" $90
4638 1921 Mack AC Stake Truck, 1925, 3¼" $90

4639 1921 Mack AC Coal Truck, 1925, 3¼" $90
4640 1921 Mack AC Tank Truck, 1925, 3¼". $90
4641 1924 Buick Touring Car, 1925, 3" $90
4650 Bi-Wing Seaplane, 1926 . . . . $50
4651 1926 Fageol Bus Safety Coach, 1927, 3½" $50
4675 Wings Seaplane, 1929, 3¾". $65
Cadillac Coupe $30
Tractor $20

POSTWAR TOOTSIETOYS

#234 3" Box Truck (1942 – 1947), $25 mint, $20 near mint

#235 3" Oil Tanker (1947 – 1954) . . . . $20 – 25
6" Ford Oil Tanker, Texaco (1949 – 1952) . . . . $45 – 55
6" Ford Oil Tanker, Shell (1949 – 1952) . . . . $55 – 65
4" 1949 Ford F6 Oil Tanker, solid color (1950 – 1969) . . . $20 – 25
4" 1949 Ford F6 Oil Tanker, 2-tone w/silver tank (1950 –
  1969) . . . . $15 – 20
6" International KII Oil Tanker, Sinclair (1949 – 1955) . . . $45 – 55
6" International KII Oil Tanker, Standard (1949 – 1955) . . . $45 – 55
6" International KII Oil Tanker, Shell (1949 – 1955) . . . . $55 – 65
6" International KII Oil Tanker, Texaco (1949 – 1955) . . . $55 – 65
Mack L-Line Oil Tanker w/tank trailer, "Tootsietoy" decal (1954 –
  1959) . . . . $80 – 90
1955 Mack B-Line Oil Tanker, "Mobil" decal (1960 – 1965, 1967 –
  1969) . . . . $60 – 70
1955 Mack B-Line Oil Tanker, "Tootsietoy" decal (1960 – 1965,
  1967 – 1969) . . . . $75 – 85
RC 180 Oil Tanker (1962) . . . . $45 – 55

CONTEMPORARY TOOTSIETOYS

Today's Tootsietoys represent a broad range of models, often with generous amounts of plastic incorporated into the design. The most popular line of Tootsietoys is their series called "Hard Body." Below is an assortment of models that fall under this category.

TOOTSIETOY HARD BODY 1:32 SCALE

1940 Ford Coupe, $4 – 5

1959 Chevy El Camino Custom, $4 – 5

1959 Chevy El Camino Lowrider, $4 – 5

1997 Ford F-150, fuchsia . . . . $4 – 5
1996 Chevy Tahoe, black or red . . . . $4 – 5

TOOTSIETOY HARD BODY 1:43 SCALE

Corvette . . . . $3 – 4
Ferrari F40. . . . . $3 – 4
Firebird . . . . $3 – 4
Mercedes-Benz Convertible . . . . $3 – 4
Mercedes-Benz Coupe . . . . $3 – 4
Porsche Targa . . . . $3 – 4

TOOTSIETOY HARD BODY 1:64 SCALE

Corvette $1
Ferrari F40. . . . . $1
Flareside Pickup, Universal Air Lines $1
Jaguar XKE $1

TOP GEAR TRAX

It is truly remarkable that Top Gear models have remained so obscure outside of Australia until now. Their 1:43 scale renditions of Australia's own Holden automobiles are terrific. Holdens new and old, stock and street, station wagons and pickups, all are showcased by Top Gear in their latest brochure, provided by Bob Robinson of New South Wales, Australia. For more information, write to Top Gear at Top Gear, Locked Bag 5300, Parramatta, New South Wales, 2124 Australia.

Listed below are the known Top Gear models, with approximate collector value in US dollars.

1951 Holden Ute, woodsman green . . . . $36 – 40
1951 Holden Ute, Navajo beige. . . . . $36 – 40
Chrysler Valiant Charger RT $45
1966 Ford Falcon 4-door Sedan $55
1966 Ford XC Cobra Coupe $55
1953 Holden Van. $25
1963 Holden Station Wagon $35

Holden Monaco HK Coupe $45

Sixties EH Holden Sedan, maroon and white . . . . $36 – 40

Sixties EH Holden Sedan, blue and white . . . . $36 – 40

TRG1 Australia's Hottest Ever Production Cars! Limited Edition Gift Boxed Set, includes: Ford GTHO Phase 3 Falcon, wild violet; Holden GTS Monaro Coupe, silver mink; Valiant R/T Charger, Hemi orange . . . . $85 – 100

TR6 Sixties EH Holden Wagon, gray and white . . . . $36 – 40

TR6C Sixties EH Holden Wagon, Sorrel tan and white . . . $32 – 36

TR8A Torana GTR XU-1, white . . . . $36 – 40

TR8B Torana GTR XU-1, lime green . . . . $32 – 36

TR8C Torana GTR XU-1, "Strike Me Pink" . . . . $32 – 36

TRS10 Bathurst Twin Set Ford Dealer Team Falcons, drivers Alan Moffat and Colin Bond, with video. . . . . $60 – 75

TR10 Falcon XC Cobra . . . . $32 – 36

TR10B Brabham XC Falcon GT, with Bathurst '77 racing decals . . . . $36 – 40

TR11 Holden Charger, metallic green . . . . $32 – 36

TRllB Holden Charger Highway Patrol, white with roof-mounted lights and sirens . . . . $36 – 40

TR12 HZ Holden NRMA Road Service Van, blue and white . $36 – 40

TR14B Holden Torana SL/R 5000 Channel 7/Ron Hodgson with full racing decals . . . . $36 – 40

TRS14 LX Series Holden Torana SL/R 5000 and SS Hatchback, gift boxed twin pack . . . . $60 – 75

TR15 Holden 48-215 (FX) Sedan, black . . . . $36 – 40

TR15B Holden 48-215 (FX) Sedan, powder blue . . . . $36 – 40

TR22 1977 HZ Holden Sandman Ute, Deauville blue . . . . $36 – 40

TR22B 1977 HZ Holden Sandman Ute, Mandarin red . . . . $36 – 40

TR23 1977 HZ Holden Sandman Van, yellow. . . . . $36 – 40

TR23B 1977 HZ Holden Sandman Van, white . . . . $36 – 40

TR24B 1968 Ford XT Falcon V8 GT, silver with burgundy stripes . . . . $36 – 40

TD02 display cabinet holds up to 24 Top Gear Trax models, 15" high, 12" wide, 3" deep . . . . $80 – 90

Top Marques

Top Marques are 1:43 scale models made in England.

1951 Mercedes 170. . . . . $125

Top Model Collection

The Top Model Collection is an assortment of 1:43 scale models made in England.

1954 Ferrari 375MM, 1:43 . . . . $40

Topper Toys (also see Johnny Lightnings)

Here is a brief chronology of the Topper Toy company, original manufacturer of Johnny Lightnings. For more information, refer to the section on Johnny Lightnings.

1953 Orensteins marketed toys through supermarkets

1966 De Luxe Topper Corp. incorporation (Delaware)

1968 Name change to Topper Corp.

1969 Johnny Lightning line begins (Feb/Mar)

1970 Public offering of stock

1970 FTC accuses Topper of false advertising (Mattel is listed too)

1971 Second public offering

1972 SEC suspends trading of Topper stock

1972 Orenstein resigns as president

1973 Topper files chapter 11 bankruptcy

1973 Topper loses right to produce Sesame Street toys... end of the road (Dec)

(Sources: Topper Fed from S-1, *Wall Street Journal,* FTC lawsuit copy - courtesy of Donal Wells)

Toy Collector Club of America (see First Gear)

Toys of Yesterday (see OGDI)

Toys for Collectors

As if their incredible assortment of diecast models isn't enough, Toys for Collectors (TfC) has introduced its own range of scale models, in response to many requests from collectors. As stated in their Auto Miniatures catalog issue XVI, "Our objective is a small range of models with limited production runs to provide the serious collector with the alternatives not available elsewhere. The models are made of pewter, resin, or both, and production is shared in-house and overseas. Because of the effort and the time it takes to produce these miniatures, not all of them can be available at all times."

TfC began as a mail order source for diecast precision models from a large variety of manufacturers, and has become one of only a few premier diecast mail order businesses in the US. TfC's current catalog features beautiful full-color photos of models from Siku, Gama, Cursor, Conrad, and others, many of which are featured in this book. Many of these TfC 1:43 scale models are already sold out and quickly rising in collector value.

Through the courtesy of Toys for Collectors, illustrations are provided from the pages of their Auto Miniatures Catalog, Issue XVI ($6 from TfC, P O Box 1406, Attleboro Falls, MA 02763).

TfC — The American Collection (from catalog pages 4 & 5)

1 1970 Oldsmobile 4-4-2 hardtop coupe, metallic mint green . $120

1a 1970 Oldsmobile 4-4-2 hardtop coupe, red with white roof . $120

2 1970 Oldsmobile 4-4-2 W-30 coupe, gold $144

2a 1970 Oldsmobile 4-4-2 W-30 coupe, yellow $144

3 1970 Oldsmobile 4-4-2 W-30 convertible, yellow $144

4 1970 Oldsmobile 4-4-2 W-30 convertible, white "INDY OFFICIAL PACE CAR" $150

5 1961 Ford Thunderbird, gold "INDY OFFICIAL PACE CAR". $160

6 1933 Chrysler Imperial, white "INDY OFFICIAL PACE CAR" . $150

7 1958 Oldsmobile Super 88 Holiday Coupe, white with red roof $148

7a 1958 Oldsmobile Super 88 Holiday Coupe, black with red roof $148

8 1933 Chrysler Imperial Custom Eight convertible, beige with red running board & fenders $148

9 1970 Oldsmobile Cutlass S Holiday Coupe, metallic silver with black roof $124

10 1944 Mack Delivery Van, "Columbia Electric" $130

11 1944 Mack Delivery Van, "Fram Filters" $130

12 1968 Mercury Cougar XR-7 Coupe, metallic red $130

12 1968 Mercury Cougar XR-7 Coupe, metallic blue. $130

12 1968 Mercury Cougar XR-7 Coupe, pale yellow $130

13 1968 Mercury Cougar 7.0 Litre GT-E, bright orange-red. . . $164
13 1968 Mercury Cougar 7.0 Litre GT-E, metallic dark green . $164
14 1939 Mack Service Truck, "NBC Engineering Department". $130
15 1972 Oldsmobile Hurst Indy Pace Car $150
16 1973 Cadillac Eldorado Indy Pace Car $150
17 1973 Cadillac Eldorado convertible, black with red interior. $130
18 1950 Mack L Type Oil Tanker "Riley" $120
19 1984 Cadillac Seville $130
20 1984 Cadillac Seville Elegante $140
21 1941 Mack Service Van "Brewster Glass" $130

TRAFFIC STOPPERS

Originally, NSG Marketing Corporation of Passaic, New Jersey, marketed these cheaply made metal and plastic toys that retail for 50¢ to $1 apiece and offer generic representations of various trucks. Collectible value on such models is nonexistent, but they provide an interesting contrast to the accuracy and detail of other models. Once removed from the package, these models are rendered unidentifiable, as no markings exist as to make and manufacturer anywhere on the model, which defines it as a generic. Most recently, these toys have been marketed by Rhino Toys Manufacturing Ltd., Hunghom, Kowloon, Hong Kong. See "generic" listing for photos of these and other such models.

TRAX (SEE TOP GEAR)

TRI-ANG

George Lines, founder in 1870 of the original Lines Company of England, was joined by brother Joseph, who later purchased George's share. In turn, three of Joseph's sons formed a company called Lines Bros., Ltd. Tri-Ang is named for the company logo formed by three lines, representing the three Lines brothers.

Besides diecast toys, Tri-ang products included prams, bicycles, pedal cars, stamped steel truck, wooden toys, doll houses, and many other toys. Tri-Ang Minic models are heavy steel clockwork toys introduced in 1935 with 14 models. The line quickly expanded, resulting in a large assortment of toys. A numbering system was established around 1938 or '39. Many of the toys had working lights, presumably powered by a small battery.

1M Ford Saloon, 1936. . . . . $120
1MCF Ford Saloon, Camouflaged, 1940. . . . . $120
2M Ford Light Van, 1936 . . . . $120
3M Ford Royal Mail Van, 1936 . . . . $120
4M Sports Saloon, 1935 . . . . $120
5M Limousine, 1935 . . . . $120
6M Cabriolet, 1935 . . . . $175
7M Town Coupe, 1935 . . . . $125
8M Open Touring Car, 1935 . . . . $125
9M Streamline Saloon, 1935 . . . . $125
10M Delivery Lorry, 1935 . . . . $175
11M Tractor, 1935 . . . . $50
12M Learner's Car, 1936 . . . . $125
13M Racing Car, 1936. . . . . $125
14M Streamline Sports, 1935 . . . . $125
15M Petrol Tank Lorry Oil Tanker, 1936 . . . . $150

15MCF Petrol Tank Lorry, Camouflaged, 1940 . . . . $120
16M Caravan House Trailer, 1937 . . . . $200
17M Vauxhall Tourer, 1937. . . . . $150
18M Vauxhall Town Coupe, 1937 . . . . $125
19M Vauxhall Cabriolet, 1937 . . . . $175
19MCF Vauxhall Cabriolet, Camouflaged, 1940 . . . . $125
20M Light Tank, 1935. . . . . $125
20MCF Light Tank, 1940. . . . . $125
21M Transport Van, 1935 . . . . $125
21MCF Transport Van, 1940 . . . . $125
22M Carter Paterson Van, 1936 . . . . $175
23M Tip Lorry (Dump Truck) $150
24M Luton Transport Van, 1936 . . . . $175
24MCF Luton Transport Van, Camouflaged, 1940. . . . . $150
25M Delivery Lorry with cases, 1936 . . . . $125
26M Tractor and Trailer with cases, 1936. . . . . $150
29M Traffic Control Police Car, 1938 . . . . $125
30M Mechanical Horse and Pantechnicon, 1935. . . . . $175
31M Mechanical Horse and Fuel Oil Tanker, 1936. . . . . . . $175
32M Dust Cart Refuse Truck, 1936 . . . . $125
33M Steam Roller, 1935 . . . . $90
34M Tourer with Passengers, 1937. . . . . $125
35M Rolls Royce Tourer, 1937. . . . . $125
36M Daimler Tourer, 1937 . . . . $125
37M Bentley Tourer, 1938. . . . . $125
38M Caravan Set Limousine and House Trailer, 1937 . . . . . $200
39M Taxi, 1937 . . . . $125
40M Mechanical Horse and Trailer, 1936. . . . . $150
41ME Caravan, 1937. . . . . $150
42M Rolls Royce Sedanca, 1937 . . . . $125
43M Daimler Sedanca, 1937 . . . . $125
44M Traction Engine, 1938 . . . . $125
45M Bentley Sunshine Saloon, 1938 . . . . $125
46M Daimler Sunshine Saloon, 1938 . . . . $125
47M Rolls Royce Sunshine Saloon, 1938 . . . . $125
48M Breakdown Lorry Wrecker, 1936 . . . . $200
48MCF Breakdown Lorry Wrecker, Camouflaged, 1940 . . . . . $150
49ME Searchlight Lorry, 1936 . . . . $125
49MECF Searchlight Lorry, Camouflaged, 1940 . . . . $125
50ME Rolls Royce Sedanca, 1936 . . . . $125
51ME Daimler Sedanca, 1937 . . . . $125
52M Single Deck Bus, red, 1936 . . . . $125
53M Single Deck Bus, green, 1936 . . . . $125
54M Traction Engine and Trailer, 1939 . . . . $150
55ME Bentley Tourer, 1938. . . . . $125
56ME Rolls Royce Sunshine Saloon $125
57ME Bentley Sunshine Saloon, 1938 . . . . $125
58ME Daimler Sunshine Saloon, 1938 . . . . $125
59ME Caravan Set, tourer with passengers and caravan with electric light, 1937 . . . . $200
60M Double Deck Bus, red, 1935 . . . . $375
61M Double Deck Bus, green, 1935 . . . . $225
62ME Fire Engine, 1936 . . . . $225
63M No. 1 Presentation Set, 1937 . . . . $225
64M No. 2 Presentation Set, 1937 . . . . $225
65M Construction Set, 1936. . . . . $225
66M Six Wheel Army Lorry, 1939 . . . . $150
66MCF Six Wheel Army Lorry, Camouflaged, 1940. . . . . $150

67M Farm Lorry, 1939. . . . . $175
68M Timber Lorry, 1939 . . . . $175
69M Canvas Tilt Lorry, 1939 . . . . $150
69MCF Canvas Tilt Lorry, Camouflaged, 1940 . . . . $150
70M Coal Lorry, 1939 never produced
71M Mechanical Horse and Milk Trailer, 1939 . . . . $175
72M Mechanical Horse and Lorry with Barrels, 1939 . . . . . . $250
73M Cable Lorry, 1939 never produced
74M Log Lorry, 1939. . . . . $150
75M Ambulance, 1939 never produced
76M Balloon Barrage Wagon and Trailer, Camouflage, 1940 . $200
77M Double Deck Trolley Bus, 1939 never produced
78M Pool Tanker, 1940. . . . . $125
79M Mechanical Horse and Pool Tanker, 1940 . . . . $175
M704 S. S. United States Luxury Cruise Ship $40

TRIDENT

Trident models of Austria, imported by Walthers and Diecast Miniatures, are a 1:87 scale line of modern military vehicles that are "perfect for flat car loads, war games, or collecting. Many of the U.S. prototypes can be converted as 'military surplus' vehicles for civilian use on your layout. The HO scale kits consist of detailed metal castings (unless noted)."

TRIDENT SOVIET MAIN BATTLE TANKS & SELF-PROPELLED GUNS
2S1 "Gvozdika" 122mm Howitzer. $26.99
2S3 "Akatsiya" 152mm Howitzer. $29.99
T-62 with 115mm Gun. $26.99
T-62A with 115mm Gun. $26.99
T-64 with 125mm Gun. $28.99
T-72 M1 with 125mm Gun $28.99
T-80 ERA with 125mm Gun & Reactive Armor $29.99
TRIDENT ENGINEERING VEHICLES
DOK-L Engineering Tractor/End Loader $38.99
TRIDENT SOVIET AIRBORNE ASSAULT WEAPONS
ASU-57 with 57mm Gun $18.49
ASU-85 with 85mm Gun $24.99
BMD-2 Airborne Combat Vehicle $24.99
TRIDENT SOVIET ARMORED PERSONNEL CARRIERS
BMP-1 Armored with 73mm Gun $24.99
BMP-2 with 30mm Gun $28.99
BRDM-2 Reconaissance Vehicle $25.99
BRDM-26 Armored Command Vehicle $25.99
BRM-1 Reconnaissance Vehicle with 73mm Gun. $24.99
BTR-60PA Armored $28.99
BTR-60PB Armored $28.99
BTR-70 Armored $28.99
BTR-80 Armored $30.49
MT-LBW Troop Transporter/Artillery Tractor. $24.99
PTS-M Amphibious Armored $40.99
TRIDENT LIGHT TRUCKS
Chevrolet Blazer $11
1987 Chevrolet Suburban USAF Fire Truck $12
Chevrolet Truck Ambulance. $12
Chevrolet K-10 Blazer Sheriff $12
Chevrolet K-10 Blazer Park Police $12

TRON

Particularly classy are these 1:43 scale models reportedly produced by Angelo or PaoloTron of Italy, both apparently designers of models for a variety of other companies as well.
1949 Oldsmobile 88 Indy Pace Car $169
1947 Cadillac 1962 Convertible $179
1968 Corvette Tour de France Coupe $149

TURTLE CREEK SCALE MODELS, INC.

Just introduced to the 1:16 scale market are two late-model trucks from the new Turtle Creek Scale Models, Inc., of Beloit, Wisconsin. Seeing a niche for such a high-end model to accompany 1:16 scale tractor and farm equipment models, Gene Arner, who has worked for General Motors in their Kodiak/Topkick plant for 29 years, has reproduced this truck in two versions, a stake truck and a milk truck. The distinction of these new models is accuracy, detail, and workmanship. Made of spin-cast metal, trucks retail for $500 each, with a production limit of just 400 each, with a ratio of three Topkicks to one Kodiak, the same ratio in which the real ones are produced at GM.
GMC Topkick Stake Bed Truck, 1:16, 300 produced $500
GMC Kodiak Stake Bed Truck, 1:16, 100 produced. . . . $700 – 800
GMC Topkick Milk Truck, 1:16, 300 produced. $500
GMC Kodiak Milk Truck, 1:16, 100 produced. . . . . . . $700 – 800

UNIVERSAL (SEE MATCHBOX)

UNIVERSAL HOBBIES LTD., INC. (ALSO SEE JOUEF)

Until recently, the head office for Jouef was in Champagnole, France, with US distribution based in Mequon, Wisconsin. Since Jouef's bankruptcy in 1996, models are now being produced by Universal Hobbies Ltd., Inc. The primary source for Jouef models is Auto Imagination Inc., 6841 N. Rochester Rd., Suite 200, Rochester Hills, MI 48306 USA.

U.S.A. MODELS
(ALSO SEE MOTOR CITY AND DESIGN STUDIOS)

USA Models are less detailed and much less expensive models than their Motor City and Design Studios counterparts, but still represent some fabulous models not commonly reproduced in miniature. The first release (USA-1) is a 1958 Cadillac Series 75 Limousine, in dark metallic blue finish, introduced in 1997, retails for $79.
USA 1 1958 Cadillac Limousine, blue $79
USA 1A 1958 Cadillac Limousine, silver with black roof. $85
USA 2F 1955 Chrysler Imperial, dark gray $85
USA 3 1949 Nash Ambassador, maroon. $79
USA 3P 1949 Nash Ambassador Los Angeles Police, black and
    white $85
USA 3T 1949 Nash Ambassador Yellow Cab, yellow $85
USA 4 1951 Chevrolet Bel Air 2-door, two-tone green $85
USA 5 1954 Chevrolet Bel Air 4-door, brown and beige. $85
USA 8 1950 Ford Custom Coupe, burgundy $85
USA 9 1949 Mercury 2-door Custom, burgundy. $85
USA 10 1941 Willys Coupe Street Rod, red $79

U.S. MODEL MINT (ALSO SEE SMTS)

U.S. Model Mint models are white metal scale models in 1:43 scale similar to Brooklins, Durham, and others. They

are distinguished by their beautiful representations of U.S. manufactured cars.

While the U.S. headquarters are in Granger, Indiana, U.S. Model Mint cars are made by SMTS of England. U.S. Model Mint, P.O. Box 505, Granger, IN 46530, USA.

US-1 1956 Chevrolet Bel Air Hardtop, two-tone cream and black $100
US-2 1950 Ford F-1 Pickup, red $100
US-3 1956 Chevrolet Bel Air Convertible, top down, two-tone turquoise and white $100
US-4 1956 Chevrolet Bel Air Convertible, top up, two-tone red and white $100
US-5 1949 Willys Overland Jeepster, top down, cream with black interior $100
US-6 1949 Willys Overland Jeepster, top up, green with black top $100
US-7 1949 Jeepster Station Wagon, burgundy with wood paneling. $100
US-8 1949 Willys Panel Delivery, red, "Drewry's Beer". $100
US-10 1950 Ford Telephone Truck, dark green, "Bell Systems". $100
US-12 1949 Willys Panel Delivery, yellow, "Sterling Beer" . . . $100
US-13 1954 Studebaker Conestoga Station Wagon, baby blue. $100
US-16 1969 Plymouth GTX, 1:43 . . . . $100

UT (ALSO SEE PAUL'S MODEL ART)

UT, otherwise known as Unique Toys (HK) Limited of China, is the manufacturer of 1:18 scale models for Paul's Model Art of Germany, as well as independently, produced by UT Models of Europe Gmb, Postfach 485, D-52005, Aachen, Germany. US distribution is out of Miami, Florida. Some UT models reference Paul's Model Art on package or model, while others don't. UT Limited, 3/F, 8 Yip Cheong Street, On Lok Tsuen, Fanling, New Territories, Hong Kong.

UT 1:18 SCALE MODELS

180 024330 BMW Z3 Roadster, red or silver, 1:18. . . . . . . $25 – 30
180 930001 Williams FW15, Hill '93, 1:18 . . . . $30
180 930002 Williams FW15, Prost '93, 1:18 . . . . $30
180 930006 Benetton B193, Patrese '93, 1:18 . . . . $30
180 930029 Sauber C12, Wendinger '93, 1:18 . . . . $30
180 930030 Sauber C12, Frentzen '93, 1:18 . . . . $30
180 930031 Sauber C12, Lehto '93, 1:18. . . . . $30

VANGUARD (SEE LLEDO)

VANBO

Manufacturers in China are realizing the growing popularity of quality diecast toys and models, and they are capitalizing on the trend. One of the newest such companies, begun in 1995, is ShenzhenVanke Fine Products Manufacture Company of Shenzhen, in the Peoples Republic of China. According to literature provided by Tom Hammel, editor of *Collecting Toys* magazine, Vanke produces a varied assortment of presentation pieces, model vehicles and ornaments under the brand name Vanbo. Besides fine quality diecast cars and trucks, Vanke also produces fine award plaques, trophies, medals, sundials, desk sets, silver plates, clocks, globes, even presentation daggers, as well as other unusual items, all cast metal. Vanke even produced a model

of Leonardo DaVinci's Flying Machine.

Vanbo car and truck models range from 1:12 to 1:87 scale. The RE series is designated exclusively for OEM and ODM sales (original manufacturer and dealerships only). The Mercedes Benz 500K and Black Prince, model numbers 97002 and 97003 respectively, appear to be the two popular models that were recently issued by CMC of Germany. Both models won Vanke the "Best Model Medals of 1995 and 1996" by Mercedes Gmb.

No prices were included in the Vanke literature, so I've made an educated estimate for current values.

Benz First Automobile, 97001, 1:10, 1997 issue. . . . . . . $175 – 225
BMW Motorcycle, 96010, 1:12, 1996 issue . . . . $35 – 45
Datong Tipping Lorry, 95050, 1:43, 1995 issue. . . . . $20 – 25
Jiefang (Liberation) Army Truck, 95030, 1:43, 1995 issue . $20 – 25
Jiefang (Liberation) Cannon Truck, 95035, 1:43, 1995 issue. $20 – 25
Jiefang (Liberation) Tip Truck, 95020, 1:43, 1995 issue . . . $20 – 25
Jiefang (Liberation) Tower Truck, 96088, 1:43, 1996 issue. $20 – 25
Hongqi (Red Flag) Car CA7220, 96121, 1:24, 1996 issue . . $20 – 25
Hongqi (Red Flag) Car CA7220, sterling silver on stand, 95010, 1:87, 1995 issue . . . . $90 – 120
Mercedes-Benz 500K, 97002, 1:24, 1997 issue. . . . . $125 – 150
Mercedes-Benz Black Prince, 97003, 1:24, 1997 issue . . $125 – 150
Santana 2000, gold on stand, 95011, 1:87, 1995 issue . . $250 – 300
Fire Truck, 96046, 1:43, 1996 issue . . . . $20 – 25
Tanker Truck, 95045, 1:43, 1995 issue . . . . $20 – 25

VANBO RE SERIES

Bugatti Royale Coupe Napoleon, RE003, 1:18. . . . . $90 – 120
Cadillac circa 1910, RE005, 1:24. . . . . $75 – 90
Hispano-Suiza Open Boattail Roadster circa 1925, RE004, 1:24 . . . . $75 – 90
Mercedes-Benz 770K circa 1920, RE002, 1:24. . . . . $75 – 90
Rolls-Royce Silver Ghost circa 1915, RE001, 1:24 . . . . . . $75 – 90

VANKE (SEE VANBO)

VEREM

Verem of France is a producer of high quality, low-cost models in 1:43 scale. Many models from Solido have been used to create Verem models. It is reported that Verems are higher quality than their Solido counterparts, comparable to the detailing done on Matchbox models by White Rose Collectibles. Cofradis is another company that uses modified Solido models.

6 Citroën Fire Van $18
7 Citroën Fire Ambulance. $18
10 Citroën Fire Ladder $18
91 Citroën 11BL Circus. $18
92 Citroën C4 Circus Van $18
93 Citroën C4 Circus Truck. $18
94 Renault Reina Circus $18
101 Citroën C4 Fire Van $18
102 Citroën C4 Fire Ladder Truck $18
104 Citroën C4 Fire Van $18
301 1928 Mercedes Convertible, top up $18
305 Delahaye Convertible, top down $18
307 1931 Cadillac Harlem Hearse, white $18
310 Rolls Royce Silver Cloud, gold $18

312 Panhard 24BT $18
402 Citroën SM $18
404 Maserati Indy Coupe $18
407 1966 Oldsmobile Toronado $18
408 Ferrari Daytona, red............................ $18
409 Ferrari Daytona, yellow $18
411 Ferrari Berlinetta Boxer, red.................... $18
412 Porsche Carrera, white.......................... $18
413 Porsche 914, yellow............................ $18
501 Peugeot 604, gold $18
506 1984 Chevrolet Camaro, yellow $18
508 Porsche 928, black............................. $18
605 Alfa Romeo GTZ, green $18
606 Lola T280, yellow $18
607 Porsche Carrera, white.......................... $18
608 1973 Porsche Can Am, white $18
611 1974 "Gulf" Mirage, blue $18
650 Alpine A110, red............................... $18
651 Lancia Stratos, black $18
701 Alpin A110, blue $18
704 Lancia Stratos, blue $18
950 4-Piece "Pinder Circus" Set..................... $54

VF-Modelautomobile Germany

VF-Modelautomobile Germany produces handmade white metal sedans, convertibles, stretch limousines, hearses, and ambulances. Cadillac, Lincoln, Rolls Royce, and Bentley, as well as DeLorean, Kaiser, Oldsmobile, Ford Thunderbird, Buick, Mercedes, all of the James Bond cars, and more, are all replicated in 1:43 scale and presented in wood and acrylic dustproof showcases, personalized for your collection or as an award. Each model is produced in quantities of no more than 100. VF-Modelautomobile Germany models are distributed exclusively in the U.S.A. by Sinclair's mini-auto, P O Box 8403, Erie PA 16505, tel/fax 814-838-2274. Here is a sampling.

1971 Cadillac Eldorado Convertible, 5 colors available, VF-AMC0001 .... $199
1960 Cadillac Fleetwood 75 Limousine, black with red interior or metallic dark red with black interior, VF-0005......... $279
1959 Cadillac Hearse, Hess & Eisenhardt Coachwork, black with red interior, VF-CC0004......................... $259

Victoria (also see Vitesse)

This list of Victoria models has been provided thanks to Alex Antonov of Herndon, Virginia. Victoria is a series of models produced by Vitesse of Portugal. Models are made in China. All models are assumed to be 1:43 scale and sell for $22 – 26 US.

R001 Jeep, 1944 Willys closed khaki D-Day version..... $22 – 26
R002 Jeep, 1944 Willys open khaki Liberation of Paris ... $22 – 26
R003 Jeep, 1945 Willys open khaki Military Police ..... $22 – 26
R004 Hummer 94 United Nations UN white 2 door covered top .... $24 – 28
R005 Hummer, 1994 U.S. Army Desert Storm open All Purpose, brown.................................... $32 – 36
R006 Hummer, 1994 U.S. Army green 2 door open back All Purpose............................... $22 – 26

R007 Hummer, 1994 U.S. Army camouflage 4 door All Purpose .... $22 – 26
R008 VW, 1945 Beetle Kubelwagen Afrika Korps open .. $22 – 26
R009 VW, 1945 Beetle Kubelwagen Wehrmcht open .... $22 – 26
R010 VW, 1945 Beetle Kubelwagen clsd Hitler Yugend .. $22 – 26

R011 Mercedes 170V Afrika Korps, $22 – 26

R012 Mercedes 170V cabriolimosine Wehrmacht parade.. $22 – 26
R013 VW, 1945 Beetle Type 82 Wehrmacht .... $22 – 26
R014 VW Beetle 82E Afghan Beetle Army tan coupe .... $22 – 26
R015 VW, 1944 Beetle Type 92 Wehrmacht charcoal burner. $22 – 26
R016 VW, 1944 Beetle Type 92 2dr black tire on roof ... $22 – 26
R017 Jeep, Willys Armoured car General LeClerc ...... $22 – 26
R018 Hummer Command Car Gulf War Desert Storm MP. $22 – 26
R019 Opel Blitz 3.5 Ton Troop Carrier................ $22 – 26
R020 Opel Blitz 3.5 Ton Canvas Covered Truck Afrika Korps. $22 – 26
R021 Opel Blitz 3.5 Ton Canvas Covered Truck........ $22 – 26
R022 VW Kubelwagen Factory Test Car................ $22 – 26
R023 Jeep, 1978 Willys UN Lebanon, white with figures.. $22 – 26
R024 Hummer Pickup US camouflag Desert Storm...... $22 – 26
R025 Opel Blitz 3.5 Ton Radio HQ Wehrmacht .... $22 – 26
R026 Opel Blitz 3.5 Ton Ambulance Afrika Korps ..... $22 – 26
R027 unknown....................................... $22 – 26
R028 Jeep, US Army, Normandy 1944 Ambulance with figures. $22 – 26
R029 Mercedes 170V Wehrmacht with Camouflage ..... $22 – 26
R030 Hummer Open pick-up US NAVY............... $22 – 26
R031 VW Kubelwagen Closed Normandy 1944 with Camouflage .... $22 – 26
R032 Jeep GPA Amphibian, U.S. Army .... $22 – 26
R033 Jeep GPA Amphibian, U.S. Army, camouflage .... $22 – 26
R034 Jeep GPA Amphibian, British .... $22 – 26
R035 VW Schwimmwagen, open gray .... $22 – 26
R036 VW Schwimmwagen, Afrika Korps .... $22 – 26
R037 VW Schwimmwagen, Wehrmacht,top up........ $22 – 26
R038 Hummer Ambulance U.S. Army Camouflage ..... $22 – 26
R039 Hummer Ambulance U.S. Army Desert Storm .... $22 – 26
R040 Renault Prairie Command Car French Army...... $22 – 26
R041 Renault Prairie Ambulance French Army .... $22 – 26
R042 Citroën U23 French Army Troop Carrier .... $22 – 26
R043 Citroën U23 FFI with Camouflage .... $22 – 26
R044 Citroën U23 Troop Carrier Wehrmacht .... $22 – 26
R045 VW Cabrio Hebmuller Military Police, no doors... $22 – 26
R046 Dodge WC51 Weapons Carrier U.S. Army, Open... $22 – 26
R047 Dodge WC51 Weapons Carrier U.S. Army, Closed.. $22 – 26
R048 Dodge 1944 WC52 Weapons Carrier Liberation of Paris. $22 – 26
R049 VW Cabrio Hebmuller Military Police, doors ..... $22 – 26

R050 Chevy, 1944 8A Canvas Truck British Army Normandy. $22 – 26

R051 Chevy, 1944 8A Canvas Truck Canadian Army D-Day
1944 . . . . $22 – 26

R052 Chevy, 1944 8A Troop Carrier Truck U.S. Army. . . . $22 – 26

R053 Dodge WC56 Command Car U.S. Army, Closed. . . . $22 – 26

R054 Dodge WC56 Command Car U.S. Army, Open. . . . . $22 – 26

R055 Dodge 1944 WC56 Command Car U.S. Army D-Day
1944 . . . . $22 – 26

R056 GMC CCKW353 6x6 Canvas Covered Truck U.S. Army. $22 – 26

R057 GMC CCKW353 6x6 Troop Carrier Truck D-Day 1944. $22 – 26

R058 GMC CCKW353 6x6 Canvas Covered Truck U.S Army. $22 – 26

VILMER

I have never seen any of these toys. But thanks to an article by Karl Schnelle dated February 10, 1995, entitled "Vilmer Kvalitet," a short history of Vilmers is extracted below.

Production of Vilmer diecast model cars of Denmark started in 1955 or '56 and lasted until 1966. The first models produced were Dodge trucks. These trucks were based on the same molds used for the Tekno Dodge series of the 1950s (Tekno of Denmark #948-958). Similar to the Tekno philosophy, the same cab and chassis were attached to every type body imaginable, all roughly 112 mm long.

There are three small differences between the Teknos and the Vilmers that help the collector easily tell which is which. The obvious difference is that the Tekno base plate was changed to read Vilmer in the script style font used on all their models and boxes. Also, the Vilmer versions use a spare tire and wheel on top of the cab to control the steering; Tekno usually employs a spotlight for this purpose. The military Vilmer Dodges may use a tire, machine gun, or spotlight, while the military Tekno use a machine gun. Finally, the Tekno versions appear to have an extra brace across the chassis under the rear wheels.

As companions to the 112 mm Dodges, a smaller range was also made. All the small Dodge trucks (military and civilian) are 98 mm and have a spare tire on the roof to control steering the front wheels. The spare wheel has a script "Vilmer" across the center while the four actual wheels have five cast lug nuts instead.

All the wheels are metal except for the military version which has olive drab plastic wheels of the same design. At least one version has no steering. These smaller Dodges are slightly bigger than the small Tekno Dodge trucks. The small Vilmer appear to be scaled-down versions of the larger Dodge, as opposed to a copy of the small Teknos. Both the small and large have "Vilmer Made in Denmark" on the base plate under the cab. A tin-plate grill is attached using three tabs to the front of both size Dodges. They also both use two white plastic headlights.

In 1957, Vilmer introduced a limited number of automobile models. The Vilmer W196R was said to be a copy of the Marklin version.

During 1957 to 1960, the series of Chevrolet 6400 trucks were produced which use many of the same bodies as the larger Dodge models and use a spare wheel or a machine gun for steering the front wheels. After 1960, both Volvo and Mercedes Benz trucks were made. Some of the best

castings exist on these chassis. Not surprisingly the Vilmer versions were cruder than the Tekno castings but did include opening doors and hood on the Volvo and an opening hood on the Mercedes. Both the Volvo and Mercedes have the following components: plastic grill, clear plastic headlights, plastic wheels, plastic tail pipe and rear transmission, and front and rear suspension.

The Ford Thames Trader was introduced in 1964. Only four different models have been identified, which seems to make the Ford much rarer than the other models. The Ford had "Thames Trader" cast into the front of the cab above the grill. The grill was made up of a wide plastic insert with two clear headlights. All other models had only "Vilmer" and "Made in Denmark" somewhere on the base.

Because of the competition from Tekno, Vilmer ceased production in 1966. It appears that the Mercedes truck molds went to Metosul in Portugal and then on to Chico in Columbia. The base plates were changed by both companies to update the manufacturer's name and country of origin. Chico also obtained the Volvo and Thames Trader molds at some point.

Mr. Schnelle cites the following as references and sources for the information he has compiled: Bertrand du Chambon, Frits Monsted, Bjorn Schultz, James Greenfield, and Richard Lay; Clive Chick (1989), "Made in Denmark, Part Three"; Horst Macalka (1990), "Catalog Corner"; Karl Schnelle (1990), "Vilmer & Airports"; anonymous (1957, 1964), "Legetojs-Tidende," Danish toy wholesalers magazine, various pages.

While Mr. Schnelle's original article included many details not mentioned here, he did not offer values, current or otherwise. So an educated guess of $45 – 60 for each model is provided based on the quality and rarity of this series. Some models are likely worth as much as $90 – 100 or more, depending on collector interest, availability, quality, and condition.

339 Baggage cart, blue, yellow driver, suitcase . . . . $45 – 60

340 Dodge stake (timber) truck, 98 mm. . . . . $45 – 60

341 Dodge flatbed, 98 mm . . . . $45 – 60

342 Dodge cattle truck, 98 mm . . . . $45 – 60

345 Dodge wooden barrel truck, 98 mm . . . . $45 – 60

346 Dodge tow truck, 98 mm . . . . $45 – 60

347 Dodge flatbed w/ tailboard, 98 mm . . . . $45 – 60

348 Dodge dropside truck, 98 mm . . . . $45 – 60

34x Dodge gas truck, 98 mm . . . . $45 – 60

34x Dodge Carlsberg high sided truck (with cover), 98 mm. $45 – 60

350 Dodge cement truck, 1 round tank 1957, 98 mm . . . . $45 – 60

444 Volvo PV 444, 1957 . . . . $45 – 60

Mercedes 220, 1957 . . . . $45 – 60

Mercedes W196R, 1957. $45 – 60

Opel Record, 1960 . . . . $45 – 60

Opel Record station wagon, 1960 . . . . $45 – 60

Lambretta scooter, yellow . . . . $45 – 60

454 Chevrolet military tanker . . . . $45 – 60

455 Chevrolet 3 rocket truck, 1957-60 . . . . $45 – 60

456 Dodge military crane truck, 1955-56 . . . . $45 – 60

457 Chevrolet 4 cannon truck, 1957-60 . . . . $45 – 60

457 Dodge 2 cannon truck, with man, 1955-6 . . . . $45 – 60

458 Dodge military spot light truck, with man . . . . $45 – 60

Dodge spot light truck, with man . . . . $45 – 60

458 Chevrolet military spot light truck, with man, 1957 . . $45 – 60

459 Dodge radar truck, with man, 1957 . . . . $45 – 60

460 Chevrolet ten rocket launcher, 1957-60 . . . . $45 – 60

461 Chevrolet single canon truck, 1957 . . . . $45 – 60

462 Chevrolet single rocket truck, 1957 . . . . $45 – 60

463 Dodge military dropside truck, 1957 . . . . $45 – 60

463 Chevrolet military dropside truck . . . . $45 – 60

464 Dodge military tarp covered truck, 1957 . . . . $45 – 60

465 Chevrolet red cross covered truck . . . . $45 – 60

467 Chevrolet dropside truck, milk containers . . . . $45 – 60

468 Chevrolet covered truck . . . . $45 – 60

469 Dodge crane truck (wrecker) . . . . $45 – 60

469 Chevrolet crane truck (wrecker) . . . . $45 – 60

Dodge ladder truck . . . . $45 – 60

470 Chevrolet spot light truck . . . . $45 – 60

471 Chevrolet open truck . . . . $45 – 60

472E Chevrolet gas tanker, ESSO . . . . $45 – 60

472S Chevrolet gas tanker, SHELL . . . . $45 – 60

474 Chevrolet dump truck w/ shovel . . . . $45 – 60

475 Renault 4 CV, 1957 . . . . $45 – 60

476 Chevrolet cement truck, 2 round tanks . . . . $45 – 60

477 Chevrolet cement mixer with chute on back . . . . . . $45 – 60

540 Dodge military stake (timber) truck, 98 mm . . . . . . $45 – 60

541 Dodge military flatbed, 98 mm . . . . $45 – 60

542 Dodge military cattle truck, 98 mm . . . . $45 – 60

545 Dodge military wooden barrel truck, 98 mm . . . . . . $45 – 60

546 Dodge military tow truck, 98 mm . . . . $45 – 60

547 Dodge military flatbed w/ tailboard, 98 mm . . . . . . $45 – 60

548 Dodge military dropside, 98 mm . . . . $45 – 60

572 Chevrolet gas truck, military . . . . $45 – 60

575 Massey Ferguson tractor, 1965 . . . . $45 – 60

576 trailer for tractor . . . . $45 – 60

578 Ford tractor . . . . $45 – 60

580 Austin Champ (open), military or blue . . . . $45 – 60

Austin Champ (open), military with single gun in rear . . . $45 – 60

620 Bedford cattle transport, 1965 . . . . $45 – 60

621 Bedford cattle truck (3-axle) and trailer . . . . $45 – 60

624 Bedford flat truck for milk . . . . $45 – 60

624 Bedford dropside truck w/ MEJERIET milk tank . . . . $45 – 60

625 Bedford flat truck for milk with trailer . . . . $45 – 60

654 Bedford military gas tanker . . . . $45 – 60

656 Bedford military tow truck (crane) . . . . $45 – 60

657 Bedford military 4 cannon truck . . . . $45 – 60

Bedford military twin 40mm guns . . . . $45 – 60

658 Bedford military searchlight . . . . $45 – 60

660 Bedford ten rocket launcher . . . . $45 – 60

Bedford multi-rocket launcher (3 axle) . . . . $45 – 60

661 Bedford single cannon truck . . . . $45 – 60

662 Bedford single missile truck . . . . $45 – 60

663 Bedford military dropside truck . . . . $45 – 60

Bedford military dropside truck (3-axle) . . . . $45 – 60

664 Bedford military covered truck . . . . $45 – 60

665 Bedford red cross covered truck . . . . $45 – 60

668 Bedford covered truck . . . . $45 – 60

669 Bedford tow truck . . . . $45 – 60

670 Bedford spot light truck . . . . $45 – 60

671 Bedford open truck . . . . $45 – 60

672 Bedford gas tanker, ESSO BENZIN SMOREOLIE (red) . $45 – 60

672 Bedford gas tanker, SHELL . . . . $45 – 60

677 Bedford cement mixer, with chute . . . . $45 – 60

710 Mercedes Benz dump truck . . . . $45 – 60

720 Ford Thames bucket truck . . . . $45 – 60

725 Ford Thames truck with magnet, 1964 . . . . $45 – 60

725 Ford Thames crane FALCK, 1964 . . . . $45 – 60

730 Ford Thames cable truck . . . . $45 – 60

850 Mercedes Benz tipping truck, 1965 . . . . $45 – 60

851 Mercedes Benz milk truck, 1965 . . . . $45 – 60

852 Mercedes Benz tarp covered truck, 1964 . . . . $45 – 60

853 Mercedes Benz Red Cross covered truck, 1965 . . . . . $45 – 60

854 Mercedes Benz military tarp covered, 1965 . . . . $45 – 60

855 Mercedes Benz refuse truck FODERBUS or plain, 1964 . . . . $45 – 60

856 Mercedes Benz dump truck w/ front shovel, 1965 . . . $45 – 60

857 Mercedes Benz ladder truck, 1965 . . . . $45 – 60

862 Mercedes Benz cattle truck, 1965 . . . . $45 – 60

Mercedes Benz SWISSAIR . . . . $45 – 60

Mercedes Benz FALCK tow truck . . . . $45 – 60

2651 Volvo milk truck, 1966 . . . . $45 – 60

2652 Volvo tarp covered truck (military), 1966 . . . . $45 – 60

2655 Volvo cattle truck, 1966 . . . . $45 – 60

2722 Volvo tow truck FALCK w/ crane,tow bar, 1966 . . . $45 – 60

2723 Volvo tipping truck, 1966 . . . . $45 – 60

2724 Volvo 98 mm ladder truck, FALCK, 1966 . . . . $45 – 60

2820 Volvo cement tipper, 1966 . . . . $45 – 60

Volvo 98 mm covered truck, plain or KLM . . . . $45 – 60

Volvo 98 mm dropside, plain, BEA or ESSO . . . . $45 – 60

Volvo 98 mm milk truck . . . . $45 – 60

Volvo 98 mm stake truck . . . . $45 – 60

Volvo 98 mm military . . . . $45 – 60

Volvo 98 mm dump truck with shovel . . . . $45 – 60

Volvo 98 mm dumping cement truck, CRO BRETON . . . . $45 – 60

Volvo 98 mm covered, Red Cross, white . . . . $45 – 60

Volvo flatbed, small crane and tire bar, FALCK . . . . $45 – 60

Volvo (l) covered truck ASG, SABENA or plain . . . . $45 – 60

Volvo (l) flatbed with chains and trailer . . . . $45 – 60

Volvo (l) flatbed, lowering sides, plain or DSB . . . . $45 – 60

Volvo (l) flatbed and trailer, ramps, chocks . . . . $45 – 60

Volvo (l) tanker and trailer, SHELL, ESSO, BP . . . . $45 – 60

VITESSE (ALSO SEE ONYX, TROFEU, VICTORIA)

Vitesse is a popular brand of beautifully exquisite 1:43 scale models from Portugal. Toys for Collectors devotes a page of its catalog to showcasing these great models. Victoria models are military models produced by Vitesse. See Victoria listing for more information. Other specialty offerings from Vitesse include the Trofeu series of Rally Cars, and Onyx, an assortment of race cars, mostly Formula Ones. See Onyx models under their own heading.

02 1959 Volkswagen 1200 with Sunroof $25

03 Volkswagen Karmann Convertible, top down $25

05 Volkswagen Van Fire Department $28

10 1956 Ford Fairlane Victoria $25

12 1967 Porsche 911R $25

14 Triumph TR3A, open top $25

15 1963 Austin Healey 3000, open top $25
17 Ferrari Dino $25
20 1947 Chrysler Town & Country $25

23, 1958 Buick Special convertible, $25

25 1959 Nash Metropolitan Hardtop Coupe. $25
31 1960 Steyr-Puch 650T Scooter $25
32 Nash Metropolitan 1959 Convertible, open top $25
33 1965 Mercedes-Benz 600 Pullman $28
36 1969 Chevrolet Corvette Convertible, open top. $25
38 1958 Buick Roadmaster 2-door Coupe $25
40 1953 Cadillac 4 Carrera Panamerican $28
44 Corvette Le Mans. $25
50 1953 Cadillac Eldorado with Continental Kit $25
56 1956 Ford Fairlane Purple Hog, NASCAR $28
57 1956 Triumph TR3 Open Convertible $25
59 Volkswagen 1200, U. S. Dollar. $25
62 1971 Chevrolet Corvette Spyder "Daytona" $25
63 Mercedes-Benz 600 Landaulet $28
81 Mercedes-Benz 600 with Pope $28
111 Chevrolet Corvette LeMans. $25
140 Ferrari Spyder California $25
250 White Tanker "Texaco" $50
280 Cadillac Eldorado, open top. $25
282 Cadillac Coupe $25
284 Cadillac Fire Department $25
286 Cadillac Eisenhower $25
370 1947 Chrysler Windsor Sedan. $25
373 Chrysler Fire Department. $25
378 Chrysler Parks Department. $25
390 1959 Chevrolet Impala Convertible, open top $25
391 1959 Chevrolet Impala Convertible, closed top $25
392 1959 Chevrolet Impala Hardtop $25
393 Chevrolet Jr. Johnson. $25
394 Chevrolet Impala #7 Jim Reed, NASCAR $28
405 Volkswagen Hebmeuller with Sunroof $25
421 DeSoto Taxi $25
433 Mack "Ryder" Truck. $50
434 Mack Fire Pumper, white $50
450 1950 Buick Special Convertible, open top. $25
451 1950 Buick Special Convertible, closed top $25
460 1956 Ford Fairlane Convertible, open top $25
550 Volkswagen Bulli Van $25
555 Volkswagen Bulli "Nestle's" Van. $25

560 Volkswagen Kombi. $25
600 1977 Ferrari 508 GTB. $25
680 Messerschmitt KR 200 . . . . $25
681 Messerschmitt KR 200 Kabrio-Limousine, open top $25
683 Messerschmitt KR 200 Tiger, closed top $25

684 Messerschmitt KR 200 Tiger, open top, $25

690 1956 Citroën DS 19 Salon De Paris $25
730 Porsche Carrera Roadcar $25

VIVID IMAGINATIONS (TYCO CANADA)

The Vivid Imaginations brand from Tyco Canada surfaced recently with the introduction of an assortment of models based on Gerry Anderson's popular action adventure *Captain Scarlet and the Mysterons*. Several models have been produced based on this children's marionette-based TV series that debuted in 1966. The resurgence in popularity of Captain Scarlet has been bolstered by the reintroduction of another Gerry Anderson TV show called *Thunderbirds,* first broadcast in 1965. Models are available in sets or sold individually. Also offered by Vivid Imaginations are 12" tall action figures.

Spectrum Command Team Set, includes Spectrum Pursuit Vehicle, Captain Scarlet's Spectrum Car, Spectrum Jet Liner, and two Angel Interceptors (see next page for photos), $45

Spectrum Pursuit Vehicle, $12 – 15

Captain Scarlet's Spectrum Car, $5 – 6

Spectrum Jet Liner, $5 – 6

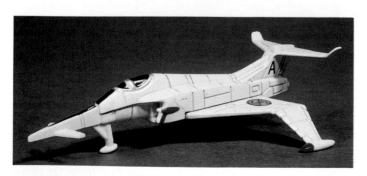

Angel Interceptor, $5 – 6

Spectrum Cloudbase H.Q. playset. $45

VOITURETTE (SEE SMTS)

WALKER MODEL SERVICE

Walthers HO Gauge catalog features over three pages of 1:87 scale Walker Model Service kits consisting of unpainted cast white metal and styrene, wire, and wood details. Models represented are of vintage trucks for $15 – 56 each.

WELLY

Though marketed as generic low-cost toys, Welly remains one of the more viable producers of quality 1:64 scale toys and toy sets. While incorporating less metal and more plastic in their design than most, Welly toys still display the kind of charm and durability that are the marks of a well made toy. Real value on these "sleepers" of diecast toys may not be realized for years, maybe decades, but they are nonetheless worthy of being included in the genre of collectibles.

Lamborghini Countach. $1
Porsche 935 Turbo Whale Tail $1
Oil Tanker. $1
Dome-O $2
Country Tractor 18-piece set includes #9132 Farm Tractor with Horse Box, Livestock Wagon, Harrow, Cultivator, six fence sections, and assorted plastic livestock . . . . $5.29 retail

WESTERN MODELS (ALSO SEE SMALL WHEELS)

According to EWA & Model Miniatures USA Inc., Western Models were one of the first companies in the world to make high quality hand-built metal models. The company was founded in the early 1970s just southeast of London, England, and moved in the mid '80's to Taunton in the southwest of England. They now have a range of about 70 quality 1:43 scale models of European and American, race and street cars, old and new, plus some interesting Record Cars. A few new models are introduced annually and some withdrawn, which makes the models very collectible.

"Small Wheels is another name used by Western for some of their models. All are made in the Western factory to the same high standards."

Two pages of Toys For Collectors' Auto Miniatures catalog Issue XVI are devoted to Western Models and Small Wheels.

WESTERN MODELS WP SERIES

WP107x 1957 Ferrari 246 GT Dino, open top $99
WP110x 1982 Ferrari 308 GTS $99
WP112 1985 Chevrolet Camaro IROC-Z $99
WP113 1984 Ferrari Testarossa $109
WP115 1987 Jaguar XJS V-12 Coupe $99
WP118 1978 Pontiac Firebird TransAm $99
WP120 1990 Jaguar XJRS Coupe $99
WP125 1992 Dodge Viper. $109
WP125P 1992 Dodge Viper Indy Pace Car. $119

WESTERN MODELS WMS SERIES

WMS37 1933 Chrysler Imperial LeBaron, top up $109
WMS43 1936 Jaguar SS1 Tourer $109

WMS44 1957 Chevrolet BelAir Hardtop $109
WMS44x 1957 Chevrolet BelAir Convertible, top down $109
WMS46 1959 Ford Galaxie Skyliner Hardtop with Continental Kit $109
WMS46x 1959 Ford Galaxie Convertible, top down with Continental Kit $109
WMS46z 1959 Ford Galaxie Convertible, top down without Continental Kit $109
WMS49 1964 Bentley S III Saloon $109
WMS50 1958 Plymouth Fury, beige with gold trim $109
WMS51 1958 Plymouth Belvedere Hardtop "Christine" $109
WMS51x 1958 Plymouth Belvedere Convertible, top down . . $109
WMS55x 1974 Checker Police Car, white $109
WMS56 1959 Buick Electra Hardtop $109
WMS56x 1959 Buick Electra Convertible, top down $109
WMS56p 1959 Buick Electra Convertible Indy Pace Car $149
WMS59 1959 Buick Invicta, top up $109
WMS60 1959 DeSoto Adventurer Hardtop $109
WMS60x 1959 DeSoto Adventurer Convertible, top down . . . $109
WMS61 1960 Cadillac Eldorado Seville $109
WMS61x 1960 Cadillac Eldorado Biarritz, top down $109
WMS62x 1947 Alfa Romeo Frecia D'Oro, open roof $99
WMS63 1959 Chrysler Saratoga Hardtop $109
WMS64 1957 Dodge Custom Royal Lancer Hardtop $109
WMS64x 1957 Dodge Custom Royal Lancer Convertible, open top . $109
WMS65 1958 Plymouth Plaza Business Coupe $109
WMS66 1957 Pontiac Bonneville Convertible, top up $109
WMS66x 1957 Pontiac Bonneville Convertible, top down $109
WMS67 1941 Buick Century Model 66S Sedanet $109
WMS67p 1941 Buick Century California Highway Patrol $109
WMS68 1949 Cadillac Coupe DeVille $109
WMS68x 1949 Cadillac Coupe DeVille Convertible, top down $109
WMS69 1972 Buick Riviera $109

WHITE ROSE COLLECTIBLES

For several years, White Rose Collectibles has licensed Tyco to alter regular production models and customize them as limited edition collectibles. Hundreds of models and variations exist. In a manufacturing agreement, Tyco produces models to White Rose specifications and markings, and White Rose in turn markets them as Matchbox models, usually at a higher price than regular Matchbox models. In addition, White Rose offers models not normally sold as Matchbox models, such as the 1939 Chevrolet Panel Truck.

One White Rose model that can be found as a regular Matchbox issue is the Model A Van, the one Matchbox model produced in more variations than any other, numbering over 250 variations. Many such variations are due to White Rose's marketing of a wide variety of baseball and football team vans.

MATCHBOX COLLECTOR'S CHOICE, 1994 FROM WHITE ROSE COLLECTIBLES

Twenty-four assorted models from the Matchbox 1-75 Series have been selected to form the 1994 Collector's Choice Series of models with better detailing and color variations. They currently retail for $10 each, but can be purchased for considerably less. The 1995 series originally promised, but never delivered, 48 new variations. White Rose Collectibles, P.O. Box 2701, York, PA 17405.

#1 '57 Chevy . . . . $4 – 8
#2 Ambulance . . . . $4 – 8
#3 Flareside Pickup Truck . . . . $4 – 8
#4 Bulldozer . . . . $4 – 8
#5 Model "A" Hot Rod . . . . $4 – 8
#6 '62 Corvette . . . . $4 – 8
#7 Corvette "T" Top . . . . $4 – 8
#8 Jaguar XK 120 . . . . $4 – 8
#9 Lamborghini Countach . . . . $4 – 8
#10 Ford LTD Police Car . . . . $4 – 8
#11 Ford Bronco II . . . . $4 – 8
#12 GMC Wrecker . . . . $4 – 8
#13 Grand Prix Racing Car . . . . $4 – 8
#14 '87 Corvette . . . . $4 – 8
#15 Model "T" Ford . . . . $4 – 8
#16 Chevrolet Lumina . . . . $4 – 8
#17 Highway Maintenance Truck . . . . $4 – 8
#18 Jeep Eagle 4x4 . . . . $4 – 8
#19 Extending Ladder Fire Engine . . . . $4 – 8
#20 School Bus . . . . $4 – 8
#21 Camaro Z-28 . . . . $4 – 8
#22 Ferrari Testarossa . . . . $4 – 8
#23 Porsche 944 Turbo . . . . $4 – 8
#24 Ferrari F40 . . . . $4 – 8

WILLIAMS, A. C. (SEE A. C. WILLIAMS)

WINROSS

Winross of Palmyra, New York, states that their purpose is "to provide the private collector with the finest scale models hand crafted in the USA today, at factory direct prices. Each model featured on the Collector Series has been used in a unique promotion by the company it represents, and has been approved for private sale through this catalog. Winross by Mail is the catalog division of the Winross Company, Inc. These models are not available for retail nor intended for resale. Purchase is limited to six of any one model unless otherwise specified."

For collectors of Winross trucks, the Winross Collectors Club of America, Inc., publishes *The Winross Model Collector,* a monthly newsletter intended to "share and preserve the common interest of dedication to the collection and preservation of 1:64th scale Winross Trucks."

New variations are issued monthly, about six at a time.

WINROSS 119 SET MARCH 1995

119-1 Molson Breweries $38
119-2 Tyson Foods $37
119-3 Central Freight $37
119-4 Dr. Pepper $39
119-5 Valvoline $37
119-6 Praxair, Inc. $35
119-7 Sharkey Transportation $36

119-8 International #7	$46
119-9 Own The Set	$280

WINROSS 120 SET APRIL 1995

120-1 Slice Delivery	$35
120-2 Walgreens Freighter	$36
120-3 Pyroil Tanker	$37
120-4 Unisource Freighter	$35
120-5 General Chemical Corporation Freighter	$35
120-6 Snap-On Tools Freighter	$37
120-7 Silver Eagle Company Double Freighter	$42
120-8 Batesville Casket Company Double Freighter	$46

OTHER WINROSS MODELS

Agway	$20
Air Products Pup '88	$38
Alliance Racing '92	$80
American Home Foods	$40
American Road Line	$45
ANR Double '91	$45
AP For the Long Haul	$45
Apache Transport	$65
Atlantic Tanker '91	$55
Auto Palace	$48
Burlington Northern	$45
Burlington Northern Double	$65
Campbell's Tanker V-8	$85
Campbell's Tomato Soup	$60
Carolina Double Freighter	$55
Carolina Mack	$60
Carrier Systems Container	$60
Chevron	$35
Crete '94	$50
Diamond Spring Water Van	$40
Drydene Tanker	$60
Earnhardt Racing	$110
Eastman Chemical	$30
Ethyl Van, silver	$30
Exxon '86 Tanker	$65
Ford Historical #9	$26
Forex Halon Tanker	$35
Gerhart Racing	$265
GP Trucking	$65
Graves Double Freighter	$60
Gully Transportation	$55
HBI Service	$45
Hemway '75	$85
Hershey Tanker	$23
HTL '94	$45
Interstate '83	$185
JLG Crane	$40
John Zern	$35
Keebler	$55
KLM Nationwide	$60
Kodak 100 Years	$38
Kodak Gold Plus	$23
Kohl Bros., Inc.	$35
Leasway Aeromax	$45
Leasway White 7000	$45
Lebanon Valley Bank	$20

Lend Lease	$40
Lincoln Highway Garage	$150
May Trucking	$60
May Trucking Double	$125
Matlack Tanker	$240
McLean Double	$125
McLean 50th Anniversary	$100
MDR Cartage	$48
MDR Cartage White 7000	$45
MFX '83	$160
Midland Ross	$45
Mohawk Carpet	$40
Morton Salt	$55
Mrs. Paul's	$60
Mrs. Paul's Tanker	$60
MS Carriers	$50
Mt. Olive Pickle '91	$35
National Truck Driving Championships 1994 Tanker	$55
New Penn 50 Years	$85
North Penn	$215
Nussbaum Double Freighter	$65
Old Dominion	$41
Old Dominion Double Freighter	$60
Old Dominion Anniversary Double Freighter	$65
PIE '88	$65
PIE Nationwide	$55
PIE Nationwide Double Freighter	$65
Pitt-Ohio	$55
Penfield Trucking	$37
Polaroid	$38
Preston 60th Anniversary	$50
Preston White 9000 Double Freighter	$70
Preston New Graphics Double Freighter	$55
Reeses Tanker	$120
Rite Aid	$26
Roadway '72	$85
Roadway '82	$65
Roadway White 9000	$65
Roadway	$55
Roadway Gray Trailers Double Freighter	$65
Roadway Double Freighter	$55
Rollins Rent Lease	$45
Seltzer Bologna Van	$38
Shell	$55
Sico Tanker '83	$95
Smith Transfer '72	$85
Smith Transfer ARA Double	$95
Southeastern Express	$60
Spinnaker '90	$38
Spinnaker	$45
St. Johnsbury	$45
Stauffers of Kissel Hill	$35
Sunflower '94	$45
Super Bowl 25	$65
Super Bowl 26	$55
Super Bowl 27	$60
T. Labonte Racing '92	$40
Tenn Ohio	$42

Terminal Freight	$50
Time DC '72	$130
TNT Reddaway Triple 75th.	$55
TNT Redstar Express Double Freighter	$75
Trans America '74	$65
Travel Port	$38
USA Eastern L/S Double.	$60
Watkins 1994 Double Freighter.	$65
Weaver Chicken 50th Anniversary	$55
Wheel Horse	$55
White House Apples	$45
Wilbur Chocolate Tanker	$60
Wilbur Chocolate Van	$50
Wilson '72	$140
Winross, Rochester Chapter	$60
Wisk	$40
Wooster Motor Freight	$55
Wyler's Soft Drink Mixes	$65
Yeager Supply	$40
Yellow Freight '82	$48
Yellow Double Freighter	$45
Zembo Temple '92.	$30

XONEX

What distinguished this brand from Japan is one 1:24 scale model Mercedes Limousine designed after the one owned by Emperor Hirohito.

1935 Mercedes-Benz 770 Limousine, Emperor Hirohito, black & red $135

YAT MING

Perhaps one of the most underrated toy companies, Yat Ming (also spelled Yatming) has produced some exceptional toys and precision models considering their original selling price is relatively low. Listed below is an assortment of models with current values. Older 1:64 scale models were released as "Fastwheel." New models are issued under the brand name of "Road Tough." Newer models are marketed under the "Road Legends" brand. Yat Ming Industrial Factory Ltd., 3/F., William Enterprises Industrial Building, 23-25 Ng Fong Street, San Po Kong, Kowloon, Hong Kong.

YAT MING ROAD TOUGH/ROAD LEGENDS 1:18 SCALE

92118 1959 Chevrolet Impala Convertible, top up, metallic blue or black.	$20 – 25
92119 1959 Chevrolet Impala Convertible, top down, metallic blue or black	$20 – 25
92128 1956 Chevrolet BelAir Convertible, top down, red or turquoise.	$20 – 25
92129 1956 Chevrolet BelAir Hardtop, red or turquoise	$20 – 25
92138 1955 Ford Crown Victoria Hardtop, surf green and white or pink and white	$20 – 25
92148 1953 Ford Pickup, metallic blue or cream	$20 – 25
1957 Chevrolet BelAir Nomad Station Wagon, metallic orange or teal	$25 – 30
Chevrolet Corvette ZR-1, 1:18.	$25
1955 Ford Thunderbird, 1:18	$25
1964 Shelby Cobra 427 S/C, 1:18	$25

YAT MING FASTWHEEL (1001-1024) 1:64 SCALE

1001 Lamborghini Miura	$6
1002 Chevrolet Racer	$6
1003 Chevrolet Concept Car	$6
1004 Lamborghini Marzal	$6
1005 Adams Probe 16	$6
1006 Toyota 2000 GT.	$6
1007 Nissan Laurel 200 SGX.	$6
1008 Ford Thunderbird	$8
1009 Volkswagen	$6
1010 Jaguar E 4.2.	$6
1011 Mercedes-Benz 350 SL	$6
1012 Mercedes-Benz 450 SEL	$6
1013 Maserati Bora	$8
1014 Saab Sonnet	$6
1015 Ford Station Wagon.	$8
1016 Porsche Targa	$6
1017 BMW	$6
1018 Opel Admiral	$6
1019 Porsche Audi.	$6
1020 Porsche 910.	$6
1021 Hairy	$6
1022 Chevron	$6
1023 Porsche 917.	$6
1024 Boss Mustang	$8

OTHER YAT MING 1:64 SCALE MODELS

1062 Datsun 280 Z-T	$4
1086 1983 Camaro, MASK	$4
1087 Mercedes-Benz 500SEC	$4
1088 BMW 635CSI	$4
1400 Kenworth Truck with Trailer, 14"	$12
8201 Kenworth Truck with Trailer, "Sea Land"	$12
8202 Kenworth Truck with Tanker Trailer, "Exxon".	$12
8203 Kenworth Truck with Gravel Dump Trailer.	$12
8204 Kenworth Truck with Auto Transporter Trailer	$12
8503 Duesenberg Model J, 1:43	$2
8504 Rolls Royce Convertible, 1:43	$2
92018 1957 Chevrolet Corvette, 1:18	$25
92028 1990 BMW 850i Sport Coupe, 1:18	$25
92078 1976 Volkswagen Beetle, 1:18.	$25
92088 1957 Chevrolet BelAir Nomad Wagon, 1:18	$25
92138 1955 Ford Fairlane Crown Victoria, two-tone mint green and white with green sunroof, 1:18	$20

Bucket Truck, $5 – 8

YATMING (SEE YAT MING)

YAXON

Yaxon of Italy inherited the Forma line of models in 1978. All models are currently being produced under the Giodi brand name.

001 Irrigation Hose Reel Trailer, 1:43, 1980 . . . . $8
002 Conveyor Belt, 1:32, 1980 . . . . $8
003 Six-Bottom Plow, 1:43, 1980 . . . . $8
004 Hay Turner, 1:43, 1980 . . . . $8
005 Pig Cage, 1:43, 1981 . . . . $8
006 Livestock Trailer, 1:43, 1981 . . . . $8
007 Sheep Trailer, 1:43, 1981 . . . . $8
008 Manure Loader, 1:43, 1981 . . . . $8
009 Milk Can Rack, 1:43, 1981 . . . . $8
010 Hand Manure Spreader Cart, 1:43, 1981 . . $8
011 Rotary Hay Tender, 1:43, 1981 . . . . $8
012 Hay Rake, 1:43, 1981 . . . . $8
013 Two-Wheel Farm Trailer, 1:43 . . . . $8
014 Manure Spreader Trailer, 1:43 . . . . $8
015 Tank Trailer, 1:43 . . . . $8
016 Tipping Four-Wheel Trailer, 1:43 . . . . . . $8
017 Hay Loader, 1:43 . . . . $8
030 International 955 Tractor, 1:43, 1982 . . . . $20
033 Volvo BM Tractor, 1:43, 1984 . . . . $20
035 Leyland 802 Tractor, 1:43, 1984 . . . . . $20
040 Fendt 308 LS Tractor, 1:43, 1982 . . . . $20
045 Ford 8210 Tractor, 1:43, 1984 . . . . $20
050 Renault 4514 Tractor, 1:43, 1981 . . . . . . $20
055 Fiat 780 tractor, 1:43, 1978 . . . . $20
056 Fiat 880 Tractor, 1:43, 1978 . . . . $20
059 Steyr 8160 Tractor, 1:43, 1980 . . . . $20
060 Landini 12500 Tractor, 1:43, 1980 . . . . . . $20
067 Massey-Ferguson 1134 Tractor, 1:43, 1980 . . . $20
069 Ford Tractor, 1:43, 1980 . . . . $20
070 Two-Wheel Farm Trailer, 1:43, 1978 . . . . . $20
071 Manure Spreader Trailer, 1:43, 1978 . . . . . . $20
072 Tank Trailer, 1:43, 1978 . . . . $20
080 Roller Trailer, 1:43, 1980 . . . . $20
081 Four-Wheel Open Trailer, 1:43, 1978 . . . . . $20
082 Hay Loader Tariler, 1:43, 1978 . . . . $20
085 Same Galaxy Tractor, 1:43, 1982 . . . . $20
086 Lamborghini Tractor, 1:43, 1982 . . . . $20
090 Fiat 880DT Tractor, 1:32, 1983 . . . . $20
091 Round Press, 1983 . . . . $20
092 Tank Trailer, 1983 . . . . $20
100 Renault TX Tractor, 1:32, 1985 . . . . $20
106 Same Tractor with Front Loader, 1:32, 1980 . . . . $20
110 Volvo BM Tractor, 1:32, 1984 . . . . $20
118 Steyr Six-Wheel Tractor, 1:32, 1980 . . . . . $20
120 New Holland Hay Baler, 1:32, 1985 . . . . . $20
121 Tank Trailer, 1:32, 1985 . . . . $20
122 Four-Wheel Tipping Trailer, 1:32 . . . . $20
138 Massey-Ferguson Six-Wheel tractor, 1980 . . . . $20
300 Semi-Trailer Truck, 1:43, 1978 . . . . $40
301 Overhead Service Truck, 1:43, 1978 . . . . . $40
302 Garbage Truck, 1:43, 1978 . . . . $40
303 Flat Semi-Trailer Truck with Lumber, 1:43, 1978 . . . . $40

304 Open Truck and Trailer, 1:43, 1978 . . . . $40
305 Covered Semi-Trailer Truck, 1:43, 1978 . . . . $40
306 Container Semi-Trailer Truck, 1:43, 1980 . . . . $40
308 Semi-Trailer Tank Truck, 1:43, 1980 . . . . $40
310 Quarry Dump Truck, 1:43, 1980 . . . . $40
311 Open Truck with Shovel, 1:43, 1978 . . . . $40
312 Open Truck with Trailer, 1:43, 1980 . . . . $40
313 Cable Drum Truck, 1:43, 1980 . . . . $40
317 Container Truck, 1:43, 1978 . . . . $40
320 Circus Cage Truck, 1:43, 1980 . . . . $40
321 Circus Cage Truck and Trailer, 1:43 . . . . $40
400 Padane Z3 Bus, 1:43, 1980 . . . . $40
401 American Freight Semi $40
402 American Covered Semi $40
403 American Tanker Semi $40
501 Landini Tractor with Front Loader, 1:43, 1981 . . . . $20
502 Landini Tractor with Loader & Backhoe, 1:43, 1981 . . . . . $20
503 Landini Tractor with Snowplow, 1:43, 1981 . . . . $20
504 Landini Tractor with Plow and Backhoe, 1:43, 1981 . . . . . $20
600 New Holland Combine, 1:32, 1982 . . . . $20
610 Fiat Laverda Combine, 1:43, 1984 . . . . $20
700 Ferrari 312 T2 Formula 1, 1:43, 1978 . . . . $20
701 Alfa Romeo 1980 Formula 1, 1:43, 1978 . . . . $20
703 McLaren M26 Formula 1, 1:43, 1978 . . . . $20
704 Lotus JPS3 Formula 1, 1:43, 1978 . . . . $20
705 Wolf WR1 Formula 1, 1:43, 1978 . . . . $20
706 Ferrari 312 T3 Formula 1, 1:43, 1979 . . . . $20
707 Brabham BT46 Formula 1, 1:43, 1979 . . . . $20
708 Ligier JS 11 Formula 1, 1:43, 1979 . . . . $20
709 Ferrari 312 T4 Formula 1, 1:43, 1980 . . . . $20
710 Alfa Romeo 179 Formula 1, 1:43, 1980 . . . . $20
711 Alfa Romeo 179 Formula 1, 1:43, 1980 . . . . $20
712 Renault RE20, 1:43, 1981 . . . . $20
713 Williams FW-07 Formula 1, 1:43, 1981 . . . . $20
714 Brabham-Alfa Romeo BT46, 1:43 . . . . $20
800 BMW M1 Marlboro, 1:43, 1981 . . . . $20
801 BMW M1 Denim, 1:43, 1981 . . . . $20
802 Porsche 935 Martini, 1:43, 1981 . . . . $20
803 Porsche 935 Eminence, 1:43, 1981 . . . . $20
804 Lancia Beta, 1:43, 1981 . . . . $20
805 Lancia Beta, 1:43, 1981 . . . . $20
806 Ferrari 512 BB Pozzi, 1:43, 1981 . . . . $20
807 Ferrari 512 BB Jolly Club, 1:43, 1981 . . . . $20
808 BMW M1 BASF, 1:43, 1981 . . . . $20
809 Porsche 935 Vaillant, 1981 . . . . $20
810 Lancia Beta Martini, 1:43, 1982 . . . . $20
811 Ferrari 512 BB Yaxon, 1:43, 1981 . . . . $20
812 Porsche 935 Vaillant, 1:43 . . . . $20

YIDALUX

Diecast Miniatures lists just one 1:18 scale Yidalux model from Argentina.
Renault Trafic Fire Van, 1:18 . . . . $28

YODER

Although the highly accurate 1:16 scale tractor models made by the Yoder family of New Paris, Indiana, are made of ABS plastic, they deserve a special place in a book

devoted to diecast toys and scale models. They definitely fall into the latter category of scale models with the painstaking attention to detail given by the Yoders. The first Yoder models were produced in 1982. In 1996, the family sold their line of precision tractor molds to Spec-Cast, due to the increasing difficulty in obtaining licensing for the various brands of tractors produced and the rising cost of producing new molds. The original price for a Yoder tractor was $65 – 75. The first issues from 1982 have now been seen offered for $200. Presented below is the complete line of Yoder tractors produced from 1982 to 1996, including production quantity. Price in parentheses indicate the original retail price.

1982
#1 550 Oliver, square grill, 1,000 made ($55) . . . . $150 – 200

#2 550 Oliver, slot grill, 1,000 made ($55) . . . . $150 – 200

#3 550 Cockshutt, square grill, 1,000 made ($55) . . . . . $150 – 200

1985
#4 Super 55 Oliver, green wheels, 875 made ($65) . . . . $175 – 225

#5 Super 55 Oliver, red wheels, 125 made ($65). . . . . . $250 – 300

#6 Case 800, original mold run, 175 made ($250) . . . . . $375 – 400

1986
#7 Case 400, Lafayette show tractor, 2218 made ($44) . . $75 – 125

#8 Case 400, shelf model, 1,000 made ($57.50). . . . . . $100 – 125

#9 Case 700, Beaver Falls show, 1,008 made ($44) . . . . . $75 – 100

#10 Case 700, shelf model, 1,000 made ($60) . . . . $100 – 125

1987
#11 John Deere 730 NF, Lafayette show tractor, 1,000 made ($44) . . . . $65 – 80

1988
#12 John Deere 730 NF, red, 225 made ($200) . . . . . . $275 – 300

#13 John Deere 730 WF, red, 225 made ($200) . . . . . . $225 – 275)

#14 John Deere 730 WF, Lafayette show tractor, 4,800 made ($65). . . . . $70 – 80

#15 Allis Chalmers D-14, original mold run, 225 made ($120). . . . . $150 – 175

#16 Allis Chalmers D-15, Beaver Falls show, 1,200 made ($54) . . . . $75 – 90

#17 John Deere 730 WF, industrial yellow, 1,200 made ($65). . . . . $80 – 95

1989
#18 Case 700, black, 225 made ($200) . . . . $260 – 275

#19 Case 400, black, 225 made ($200) . . . . $260 – 275

#20 Case 400, orange, 300 made ($85). . . . . $100 – 125

#21 John Deere 720 WF, electric start diesel, Beaver Falls show, 1200 made ($65) . . . . $75 – 90

#22 John Deere 720 WF, Gospel Echoes Team benefit sale, with emblem, 1 auctioned. $260

#23 John Deere 720 NF, Gospel Echoes Team benefit sale, with emblem, 1 auctioned. $260

#24 John Deere 720 NF, electric start diesel, 3,010 made ($69). $70 – 75

1990
#25 International Harvester Super MTA NF, gas, 5,100 made ($69). . . . . $70 – 75

#26 International Harvester Super MTA NF, gas, Gospel Echoes benefit sale, with emblem, 1 auctioned $65

#27 John Deere 720 NF Pony Start, diesel, 1,250 made ($69) . $75 – 90

#28 John Deere 720 WF Pony Start, diesel, 1,185 ($69). . . $75 – 90

1991
#29 International Harvester Super MTA WF, gas, 1,954 made ($65) . . . . $70 – 75

#30 International Harvester Super MTA WF, gas, white, 225 made ($200) . . . . $225 – 250

#31 International Harvester Super MTA NF, gas, white, 225 made ($200) . . . . $225 – 250

#32 International Harvester Super MTA NF, gas with duals, Michiana Toy Club show tractor, 630 made ($65) . . . . . . $70 – 75

1992
#33 International Harvester Super MTA NF, diesel, 670 made ($65) . . . . $70 – 75

#34 International Harvester Super MTN WF, diesel, 530 made ($65) . . . . $70 – 75

#35 International Harvester Super MTA NF, diesel with duals, Gospel Echoes benefit sale, with emblem, 1 auctioned. . $100

#36 International Harvester Super MTA WF, diesel with duals, Gospel Echoes benefit sale, with emblem, 1 auctioned. . $100

#37 John Deere 720 Standard, electric start, 750 made ($69). $75 – 100

#38 John Deere 720 Standard, Pony Motor start, 1,110 made ($69) . . . . $70 – 90

1993
#39 John Deere 720 Standard, electric start, Gospel Echoes benefit sale, with emblem, 1 auctioned $100

#40 John Deere 720 Standard, Pony Motor start, Gospel Echoes benefit sale, with emblem, 1 auctioned $100

#41 John Deere 730 Standard Moline, show tractor, 1,280 made, ($69). . . . . $70 – 75

#42 John Deere 720 Standard, adjustable front axle, electric start, still available. $100

#43 John Deere 720 Standard, adjustable front axle, Pony Motor start, still available. $100

1994
#44 John Deere 730 Standard, industrial, yellow, 1,000 made ($69). . . . . $70 – 75

#45 John Deere 730 Standard, adjustable front Axle, 3 point, no front weights, numbered signed, dated, 25 made ($85). . . $125 – 150

#46 John Deere 730 Standard, Industrial, fixed axle, no 3 point or weights, regular hitch, numbered, signed, dated, 25 made ($85) . . . . $125 – 150

#47 John Deere 730 Standard, Industrial, fixed axle, Nebraska Highway Dept., orange, 500 made ($125) . . . . . . $150 – 175

1995
#48 John Deere 730 Standard, Industrial, electric start, still available $100

1996
#49 John Deere 720 Standard, Industrial, electric start, still available $100

#50 John Deere 720 Standard, Industrial, Pony Motor start, still available. $100

YORKSHIRE

The Yorkshire Company is a relatively obscure brand from Illinois that around 1985 – 1987 produced several Bell System trucks exclusively available to employees of Pacific Bell and other "Baby Bell" companies. All of these models have the Bell System logo on the doors of the trucks and have 1985 or 1986 copyright dates on the boxes.

Original 1931 "Model A" Ford Telephone Lineman/Installer Truck
(New First Edition), 1:25 . . . . $80 – 100
Original 1950 Dodge 4-Wheel Drive Hydraulic Pole Digger/Derrick
(New Second Edition), 1:25 . . . . $80 – 100
Original 1927 "Model TT" Ford Cherry Picker-Construction Truck
(New Fourth Edition), 1:25. . . . . $80 – 100
1950 Dodge Power Wagon Post Hole Digger, "Bell Phone," 1:34,
issued 1986 . . . . $65 – 70

YOT

Yot has produced generic toys made in Taiwan. EWA lists one Yot model in their worldwide website catalog.
VW Beetle 1200 sedan, 1:60 . . . . $15

ZAUGG

Zaugg miniatures are older high quality 1:43 scale hand-built models from Switzerland.
1955 Cadillac Convertible $138
1951 Chevrolet Wagon $138
Commer Circus Van. $45
1970 Dodge Challenger $138
1968 Mercury Cyclone GT Coupe $158
Volvo 122 Amazon. $94

ZAX

In 1948, the Zax company of Bergamo, Italy, manufactured an assortment of 1:87 and 1:43 scale models.
Racing Car, 1:43. . . . . $60
Speed Record Car, 1:43 . . . . $60
Roadster, 1:43 . . . . $60
Fastback Coupe, 1:43. . . . . $60
Racing Car, 1:87 . . . . $24
Speed Record Car, 1:87 . . . . $24
Roadster, 1:87 . . . . $24
Sedan, 1:87 . . . . $24
Fiat 1400 . . . . $24
Fiat 1400 Taxi $24
Fiat 1400 Police Car $24

ZEE TOYS/ZYLMEX (ALSO SEE REDBOX)

Zylmex and Zee Toys are interchangeable brand names of Zyll Enterprise Ltd. Like most, these lightweight diecast and plastic toys are manufactured in China. Their quality varies and collector value remains comparatively low. However, some unusual models have been produced in past years. Besides a large array of models of different sizes and scales, two product lines, both roughly 1:64 scale, are Pacesetters and Dynawheels. Pacesetters are the better quality of the two, usually sporting metal chassis, opening doors, and other parts, while Dynawheels are generally lighter, with plastic chassis, and no opening parts.

Many other series exist, most notably Ridge Riders series of approximately 1:24 scale motorcycles, and Dyna-Flites series military airplane toys. Besides these main product lines, this book will deal with an assortment of other items and assortments.

Other manufacturers that have carried the Zee Toys brand name include Edocar and Intex Recreation, probably due to the typical buying and selling of companies and brands that occurs so much in the toy industry. Sets of Zee Toys Pacesetters were issued through Sears as Roadmates.

Zyll Enterprise Ltd. went out of business in March 1996, and all the dies and trademarks were sold to a Hong Kong firm who has not announced their intentions as of April 1997.

The Zee Toys connection with Intex Corporation is that, up until 1993, Intex was the sole importer of Zee Toys to the US. Now, Zyll products are being sold under the Redbox brand.

P301 Citroën . . . . $1 – 2
P302 Datsun Fairlady (240Z). $1 – 2
P303 Toyota GT2000 . . . . $1 – 2
P304 Mazda GT . . . . $1 – 2
P305 Honda 600 . . . . $1 – 2
P306 Mazda GT Police . . . . $1 – 2
P307 Bulldozer . . . . $1 – 2
P308 Front Loader . . . . $1 – 2
P309 Cement Mixer . . . . $1 – 2
P310 Dump Truck . . . . $1 – 2
P311 Crane Truck . . . . $1 – 2
P312 Fire Engine (ladder). . . . . $1 – 2
P313 Tipper Truck . . . . $1 – 2
P314 Hydraulic Excavator. . . . . $1 – 2
P315 Fork Lift Truck. . . . . $1 – 2
P316 Fire Engine (snorkel) . . . . $1 – 2
P317 Track-type Loader . . . . $1 – 2
P318 Hydraulic Excavator. . . . . $1 – 2
P319 '70s Datsun Pick-up . . . . $1 – 2
P320 '70s Dodge Van . . . . $1 – 2
P321 McLaren Indy Car . . . . $1 – 2
P322 Crown School Bus, "32 VALLEY DISTRICT SCHOOLS" . . $25
P323 '70s Chevelle Hardtop . . . . $1 – 2
P324 Pinto. . . . . $1 – 2
P325 '32 Ford Roadster $3
P326 GMC Motorhome. . . . . $4 – 5
P327 Skyline 2000GT . . . . $2 – 3
P328 Corolla 30 1400 GSL . . . . $2 – 3
P329 Corona 2000GT . . . . $2 – 3
P330 Celica LB 2000GT . . . . $2 – 3
P331 Benz. . . . . $1 – 2
P332 '70s VW Bus . . . . $1 – 2
P333 Toyota Van . . . . $1 – 2
P334 Double Decker Bus . . . . $1 – 2
P335 (English) Ford Van. . . . . $2 – 3
P336 Oil Tank Truck . . . . $2 – 3
P337 Fire Engine (pumper) . . . . $2 – 3
P338 Early '70s Chevy Pick-up . . . . $2 – 3
339 Monza Hatchback . . . . $2 – 3
P340 McLaren M8-A . . . . $2 – 3
P341 Super Van (from movie) . . . . $2 – 3
P342 Wheaties Custom Dodge Van . . . . $2 – 3
P343 Van Killer Custom Dodge Van . . . . $2 – 3
P344 Straight Arrow Custom Dodge Van . . . . $2 – 3
P345 '70s Plymouth Police . . . . $2 – 3
P345 Plymouth Satellite Taxi $4
P346 Chevy Ambulance Van $4
P347 U.S. Mail Truck $4
P348 '70s Ford Country Squire Wagon $4

P349 Farm Tractor $2
P350 Jeep $2
P351 Mustang II Cobra Street Racer $2
P352 Mercedes-Benz 450 SL. $2
P353 Fun Trucking Ford Courier Pick-up $2
P354 '30s Benz $2
P355 '57 Chevy Bel Air $2
P356 '56 Ford Thunderbird $3
P357 Kandy Van Custom Dodge Van $2
P358 Ford Pinto Mini Van $2
P359 Chevy Blazer. $1
P360 '70s Dodge Pick-up Camper. $2
P361 '35 Chevy $2
P362 Firebird Trans Am T-Top $1
P363 Lincoln Continental Mark IV $3
P364 '63 Chevrolet Corvette $2
P365 '57 Chevrolet Corvette $2
P366 Big Rig Tow Truck $2
P367 Camaro Z28 T-Top $2
P368 Jeep $2
P369 Ford Bronco 4X4. . . . . $2
P370 Mercedes-Benz 300 SL. $2
P371 '70s Chevy Corvette. $2
P372 '70s Mazda RX-7 . . . . $2
P373 '70s Camaro Z-28 Hwy. Patrol $2
P374 DeLorean $2
P375 '85 Corvette. $2
P376 Porsche 928 . . . . $2
P377 Scraper $1
P378 no model assigned
P379 Loader $1
P380 no model assigned
P381 '80s Camaro Z28 Convertible $2
P382 '80s Pontiac Firebird $2
P383 Firebird Funny Car $2
P384 no model assigned
P385 Racing Rig. $2
P386 no model assigned
P387 no model assigned
P388 no model assigned
P389 no model assigned
P390 '80s T-Bird Stock Car. $2
P391 '69 Pontiac GTO $2
P392 Mustang Fastback Pro/Street $2
P393 Charger Funny Car $2
P394 '80s Mustang. $2
P396 Pontiac Fiero. $2
P399 '80s Camaro Pro/Stock. $2
P397 '70 Hemi 'Cuda $2
3005 '69 'Vette $2
P3201 Class 8 Wrecker. $2
P3202 Sand Buggy. $2
P3203 no model assigned
P3204 Sprint Car $2
P3205 Beretta Pro/Stock. $2
P3206 Custom '80s Nissan pick-up $2
P3207 Olds Aerotech $2
P3208 Olds Funny Car $2

P3209 no model assigned
P3210 no model assigned
P3211 Nissan GTP $2
P3212 Mazda Miata $2
P3213 Flip Car II (Manta Ray/Space Raycer) $2
P3214 Flip Car I (Indy Champ/Max 2000) $2
P3215 Flip Car III (Bonneville Blaster/DD Coupe). . $2
P3216 Flip Car IV (Retro Rod/Formula Fusion) . . $2
Ferrari Testarossa. $1
Ferrari 308 GTB. $1
Ford Sierra XR4i $1
Mercedes-Benz 500 SEC. $1
Mercedes-Benz 500 SL, #13 Edocar. $1
Porsche 928, Intex Recreation Corp. $1
Porsche 959. . . . . $1
VW Golf GTI. $1

Zee Toys Z Wheels Pacesetters Specials

This 1:24 scale model has been discovered in the clearance rack at Shopko. It is likely a product of test marketing, as only one specimen has been found so far.
Chevrolet Corvette ZR-1 . . . . $10

Zee Toys Dyna-Flites/Airplanes

A111 MIG-27 Jet Fighter. $3
A115 DC-10 AMERICAN AIRLINES, 1:600 . . . . . $3
A118 Phantom II F-4E USAF. $3
A118 Phantom II F-4C Camouflage. $3
A127 SR-71 Blackbird. $3
A129 Saab AJ-37 Viggen Jet Fighter $3
A130 A-4E Skyhawk USN. $3
A144 F-16 USAF $3
A145 F-15 Eagle USAF $3
A150 Grumman X-29A $3
A152 EF-111 Military Jet Fighter $3
A153 MIG-29 Fulcrum Jet Fighter $3
A202 DC-10 AMERICAN, 1:500 . . . . $3
A208 Bell Jet Ranger $3
A212 F-20 Tigershark $3
F-18 Hornet. $3
Gee Bee $12
OH-6A Cayuse Police Helicopter $3

Other Zee Toys

Bell 21 Racing Motorcycle $3
California Hauler Tractor Trailer, "Consolidated Freightways" . . $4
GT Bicycle $3
Honda Racing Motorcycle $3
Kawasaki 250 KDX Motorcycle. $3
Kawasaki Mach 3 Motorcycle $3
Kawasaki Ninja $3
Mack Refrigerated Container Truck, "STP" $3
Mack Freighter, "Flying Tiger" $4
Maico 490 Motorcycle $3
Mercedes 540K Coupe $3
Mongoose Bicycle $3
Peterbilt 2-Boom Wrecker $5
Sprint Racer. $4
Suzuki RM125 Motorcycle $3
Porsche 911 Speedster, Intex, 1:18 . . . . $21
1989 Mercedes-Benz 500SL RDS, 1:18 . . . . $21

ZISS

Ziss models, also known as R.W., were produced throughout the 1960s and early 1970s from Dusseldorf, Germany, until the death of Mr. Wittek, proprietor of the Mini-Auto company of Lintorf, on the outskirts of Dusseldorf.

14 1905 Mercedes Grand Prix, 1:43, 1972 . . . . $25
15 1908 Ford Model T, 1:43 . . . . $25
16 1907 Ford Model T Roadster, 1:43, 1966 . . . . $25
17 1919 Ford Model T Torpedo, 1:43, 1966 . . . . $25
20 1908 Opel Doktorwagen, 1:43, 1963 . . . . $25
21 1901 Mercedes Simplex, 1:43, 1963 . . . . $25
22 1908 Opel Stadt-Coupe, 1:43, 1963 . . . . $25
23 1910 Benz Limousine, 1:43, 1964 . . . . $25
27 1904 N.A.G. Phaeton, 1:43, 1964 . . . . $25
30 1906 Adler Limousine, 1:43, 1964 . . . . $25
31 1905 Mercedes Roadster, 1:43, 1966 . . . . $25
38 1904 N.A.G. Touren Sport, 1:43, 1966 . . . . $25
39 1906 Adler Phaeton, 1:43, 1966 . . . . $25
40 1905 Mercedes Coupe, 1:43, 1966 . . . . $25
43 1909 Opel Torpedo, 1:43, 1966 . . . . $25
44 1909 Ford Ranch Car, 1:43, 1966 . . . . $25
50 1910 Benz Landaulet, 1:43, 1966 . . . . $25
52 1924 Hanomag Kommissbrot, 1:43, 1967 . . . . $25
53 1924 Hanomag Coupe, 1:43, 1967 . . . . $25
57 1927 BMW Dixi, 1:40, 1968 . . . . $25
60 1913 Audi Alpensieger, 1:43, 1969 . . . . $25
62 1916 Chevrolet Phaeton, 1:43, 1969 . . . . $25
65 1914 NSU Phaeton, 1:43, 1971 . . . . $25
66 1932 Fiat Balilla, 1:43, 1972 . . . . $25
289 Krupp Hydraulic Hammer, 1:50, 1972 . . . . $35
290 Fiat Scraper, 1:24, 1972 . . . . $35
291 O & K Fork Lift, 1:50, 1972 . . . . $35
292 Clark Fork Lift, 1:50, 1972 . . . . $35
293 Hyster 40 Fork Lift, 1:39, 1971 . . . . $35
294 Fiat 600 Farm Tractor, 1:43, 1971 . . . . $65
295 O & K RH6 Excavator, 1971 . . . . $65
296 O & K MH6 Excavator, 1971 . . . . $65

297 Deutz Farm Tractor, 1968 . . . . $65
298 Hanomag Matador Open Truck, 1968 . . . . $45
299 Three Musketeers Jeep, 1968 . . . . $65
300 Army Jeep, 1968 . . . . $50
301 Mercedes-Benz 600, 1:43, 1966 . . . . $50
302 1926 Henschel Open Truck, 1:43, 1967 . . . . $50
303 1926 Henschel ARAL Tank Truck, 1:43, 1967 . . . . $50
304 1925 MAN Open Truck, 1:43, 1967 . . . . $50
305 1925 MAN BP Tank Truck, 1:43, 1968 . . . . $50
306 1925 MAN Bus, 1:43, 1969 . . . . $65
310 1971 Opel Rekord Sedan, 1:43, 1971 . . . . $40
311 1971 Opel Commodore Coupe, 1:43, 1971 . . . . $40
312 1975 Opel Manta, 1:43, 1975 . . . . $50
400 Ford Transit Van, 1:43, 1968 . . . . $50
401 Ford Transit Van with side windows, 1:43, 1968 . . . . $50
410 Hanomag Dump Truck, 1:43, 1968 . . . . $45
411 Hanomag Open Semi-Trailer Truck, 1:43, 1968 . . . . . . $40
412 Hanomag Open Truck, 1:43, 1970 . . . . $45
413 Hanomag Container Semi-Trailer Truck, 1:43, 1970 . . . . . $50
414 Hanomag ESSO Tank Truck, 1:43, 1971 . . . . $50
415 Hanomag Cement Truck, 1:43, 1971 . . . . $50
420 1969 Volkswagen Van, 1:43, 1970 . . . . $50
421 1969 Volkswagen Transporter, 1:43, 1970 . . . . $50
422 1969 Volkswagen Pickup Truck, 1:43, 1970 . . . . $50
430 Mercedes-Benz 1313 Dump Truck, 1:60, 1971 . . . . $50
501 1908 Opel Coupe, 1:43 . . . . $20
999 1913 Audi, top down, 1:43 . . . . $20

ZSCHOPAU

Ferrari 275 Coupe, 1:32 . . . . $18
Wartburg 1000 4-Door Sedan, 1:32 . . . . $14
Wartburg 1000 Wagon, 1:32 . . . . $14
Skoda S110R Coupe, 1:32 . . . . $14
Skoda 6X4 Dump Truck, 1:32 . . . . $18

ZOWIES (SEE HOT WHEELS)

Bibliography

Aune, Al. *Arcade Toys.* Robert F. Mannella, publisher, 1990.

Bburago Spa, Milan, Italy.

Car Toys Magazine, Challenge Publications.

Collecting Toys Magazine, Kalmach Publishing.

Corgi Sales, Mattel UK Ltd., Corgi Classics January to June 1993 catalog.

Crilley and Burkholder. *Collecting Model Farm Toys of the World.* Aztex Corp., 1979, 1984, 1989.

DeSalle, Don & Barb. *Collectors Guide To Tonka Trucks, 1947– 1963.* L-W Book Sales, 1994.

The Ertl Company, Hwys 136 & 20, Dyersville IA 52040-0500.

Force, Edward. *Classic Miniature Vehicles Made in Germany.* Schiffer Publishing, 1990.

_____. *Classic Miniature Vehicles Made in France.* Schiffer Publishing, 1991.

_____. *Classic Miniature Vehicles Made in Italy.* Schiffer Publishing, 1992.

_____. *Corgi Toys.* Schiffer Publishing, 1984 with 1991 price guide.

_____. *Dinky Toys.* Schiffer Publishing, 1988, 1996.

_____. *Lledo Toys.* Schiffer Publishing, 1996.

_____. *Matchbox and Lledo Toys.* Schiffer Publishing Ltd., 1988.

_____. *Solido Toys.* Schiffer Publishing, 1993.

Gibson-Downs and Gentry. *Motorcycle Toys Antique and Contemporary.* Collector Books, 1995.

Huxford & Huxford, Eds. *Schroeder's Collectible Toys Antique to Modern Price Guide.* Collector Books, 1995.

John Ramsay's British Diecast, Swapmeet Publications, 1995.

Johnson, Dana. *Matchbox Toys 1947– 1996.* Collector Books, 1997.

Kelly, Douglas R. *Die Cast Price Guide, Post-War: 1946– Present.* Antique Trader Books, 1997.

Majorette Toys (US) Inc. Solido, 1994, 1995, 1996, 1997 catalogs, Majorette 1994, 1995, 1996, 1997 catalogs.

Mobilia magazine.

Model Car Journal, P.O. Box 154135, Irving, TX 75015.

O'Brien, Richard. *Collecting Toy Cars & Trucks.* Books Americana, 1994.

Pennington, Carter. *Johnny Lightning Collector's Guide.* self-published, 1993.

Raschke, Wilfried, and Manfred Weise. *Siku-Sammlerkatalog Rawe 1991.* 1991.

Richter, David E. *Collector's Guide to Tootsietoys.* Collector Books, 1991.

The Software Toolworks Multimedia Encyclopedia, CDROM Version 1 PB, 1992.

Strauss, Michael Thomas. *Tomart's Price Guide to Hot Wheels, Second Edition.* Tomart Publications, 1997.

Toy Shop Magazine, Krause Publications.

Toy Trader Magazine, Antique Trader Publishing.

Tyco Toys, Inc., Tyco Toys 1994, 1995, 1996, 1997 catalog.

Wieland and Force. *Tootsietoys, World's First Diecast Models, Second Edition.* 1980, with 1991 price guide.

Toy Dealers/Sources

LEGAL DISCLAIMER (The Fine Print): While the businesses listed below represent some of the most reputable sources for diecast toys, neither the Diecast Toy Collectors Association nor Dana Johnson Enterprises accepts any responsibility for business transactions or disputes of any kind between buyer and seller. In addition, caution is recommended when offering credit card numbers over the Internet. Discretion is advised.

Richard Adkins Collectible Toys, 422 E. Oak St., Oak Creek, WI 53154-1121. 414-761-1020. Hot Wheels and Johnny Lightning regular issues and limited editions

Antique & Collectible Superstore has recently added diecast toys and models to their on-line assortment. See their selection at http://www.antique-superstore.com/inv/diecast.htm and http://www.antique-superstore.com/inv/diecast2.htm, then place your secured order at http://www.antique-superstore.com/mntc/order.htm. E-mail: 2collect@worldnet.att.net

Apple Patch Toys, 7 Hyatt Road, Branchville, NJ 07826 USA. 201-702-0008, 201-702-1545, fax 201-702-1699. JLE Scale Models, Ertl Banks

Asheville DieCast, 1434 Brevard Road, Asheville, NC 28806-9560 USA. Phone 1-800-343-4685, fax 1-704-667-1110, e-mail: asheville-diecast@worldnet.att.net, website: http://www.asheville-diecast.com/. Ertl Banks and Replicas, Bburago, Britains, Brooklin, Buby, Collectors Classics, Con-Cor, Corgi, Detail Car, Eligor, First Gear, Goldvarg, Hartoy, Jouef, Lledo, Maisto, Paul's Model Art, Revell, Rextoy, Road Champs, Solido, U.S. Model Mint, Victoria, Vitesse, Yatming

Auto Toys, P.O. Box 81385, Bakersfield, CA 93380-1385 USA. 805-588-2277, fax 805-588-2902. First Gear, Jouef, Bburago, Ertl, Paul's Model Art/Minichamps, Detail Cars, Corgi Race Image, Quartzo, Action, Racing Champions

Automobilia, 18 Windgate Drive New City, NY 10956 USA. 914-639-6806 voice or fax, e-mail: lustron@worldnet.att.net. Sole direct importer of Brumm models in North America

Back To The 50's, 6870 South Paradise Rd., Las Vegas, NV 89119 USA. Catalog includes American Highway Legends trucks, Ertl Coca-Cola banks, et. al.

Heike Beyermann Toy Import/Export, Toy Shop, Lünnewelle 24, 38446 Wolfsburg, Germany. Phone: +49-5363-40912, fax: +49-5363-74961, e-mail: promotion.items@t-online.de, website: http://www.joal-retail.com/. Joal, NZG, and Conrad models

Bill's Toy Box, 285 NW 87th Ave., Portland, OR 97229 USA, Bill Langer. Matchbox, Hot Wheels, Dinky, Ertl, 1st Gear, Lledo & others

Bob Blum, 8 Leto Road, Albany, NY 12203 USA. 1-518-456-0608. Premier source for Tomica Pocket Cars, Diapet, et. al.

Bob's Oregon Trail Truckstop, P O Box 214, Milton-Freewater, OR 97862 USA. 541-938-7028, Bob Jones, e-mail: mfplbob@bmi.net.

James Brandt, 280 Meadow Ln., Lebanon, PA 17042 USA. Winross

Bugsy's Place, 298 N. 2nd Ave., Jefferson, OR 97352. Toll-free: 1-888-327-1258, e-mail: bugsys@proaxis.com website: http://www.proaxis.com/~bugsys/. Specializing in racing diecast from Action, Brookfield Collectors Guild, Bburago, Ertl, Georgia Marketing Promotions, K&S Industries, Maisto, Matchbox, Monogram, Nutmeg, Onyx, Paul's Model Art, Image Art, Quartzo, Race Image, Racing Champions, Revell, Simpson, and others.

Cannon Collections, 4548 SE Concord Rd., Milwaukie, OR 97267 USA. 503-659-6678, Gary & Alice Cannon. Military collectibles

Charles & Sons Ltd. Collectibles, 65 Broadway, Greenlawn, NY 11740 USA. Days 516-261-1523, evenings 516-261-1058. Matchbox, Hot Wheels, Corgi Classics, Ertl, American Highway Legends, Road Champs

Classic Construction Models, 6590 SW Fallbrook Place, Beaverton, OR 97008 USA. 503-626-6395, fax 503-646-1996, e-mail: ccmodels@teleport.com, website: http://www.teleport.com/~ccmodels

Richard Clermont Enterprises, P O Box 493356, Redding, CA 96049 USA. E-mail: teeking@c-zone.net, website: http://www.mspmall.com/teeshirtking/. Drag racing collectibles

Collector's Choice, 1100 20th Street South, Birmingham, AL 35205 USA. Corgi, Corgi Jrs., and Husky

Collectors Display Case Co, Rt 2 Box 73, Dept DC1, Fremont, NE 68025 USA. 402-721-4765, e-mail: mpratt@teknetwork.com, website: http://www.teknetwork.com/display, Michael & Rita Pratt. Flexible, clear plastic display boxes

Coppers Collectibles, 2514-23 Avenue South, Lethbridge, Alberta, T1K 1K9 Canada. Phone 403-329-8378, fax 403-329-4055, e-mail coppers@telusplanet.net. Quality vintage and new collectible police toys, including diecast cars, tins, games, TV and dimestore items. Specialize in North American police vehicles from Vitesse, Road Champs, COPy CARS, Herpa, Busch-Praline, Trident. Working on obtaining Corgi, Lledo, Solido, Matchbox, Hot Wheels, and several other lines.

Corvette Speed/Central Hobbies, 9A School Street, Central Village, CT 06332 USA. E-mail: diecast@ct2.nai.net, or contact Mike at 860-564-0211. 1/18 scale Ertl, Burago, Mira, and other diecast collectibles. Also stock over 700 pieces of First Gear trucks, and over 800 plastic models, new releases and old.

Die-cast Displays by Day (D3), Michael Day, owner, e-mail: D3Displays@aol.com, website: http://members.aol.com/Mike-Day/main.html

Dan's Pocket Cruisers, 13515 Kintyre Ct., Matthews, NC 28105 USA. 704-849-2709, Dan Coviello. Custom police cruisers in 1:43 and 1:64 scale

Diecast Diamond Distributing, Boring, OR USA. 503-669-8283, Michael T. Shine. Racing Champions, etc.

Diecast Direct, 1009 Twilight Trail, Frankfort, KY 40601 USA. 502-227-8697 10am-6pm Eastern, Mon- Fri. Corgi American Classics, First Gear, Joal, Siku, and others

Diecast Miniature Vehicles, Earl J. Bell Jr., 15170 Lester Lane, Los Gatos, CA 95032-2610 USA. 408-356-6868. Matchbox (Lesney), Racing Champions, Tootsietoy 1:64 scale Hardbody, Majorette toys

Diecast Miniatures, 255 Jones Street, P O Box 58, Amston, CT 06231-0058 USA. Phone 860-228-3249, Jeff Bray, proprietor. Wide assortment of toys and precision models of all scales

The Eastwood Company, 580 Lancaster Ave., Box 296, Malvern, PA 19355 USA. http://www.eastwoodco.com/. Eastwood Automobilia transportation collectibles catalog

Evers Toy Store, 204 1st Avenue East, Dyersville, IA 52040 USA. 1-800-962-9481, e-mail: coax@ix.netcom.com, website: http://www.marketplaza. com/evers/evers.html. Ertl, Spec-Cast, First Gear, Hartoy, Scale Models, Road Champs, Revell, Monogram, and more

EWA & Miniature Cars USA, Inc., 369 Springfield Ave., P O Box 188, Berkeley Heights, NJ 07922-0188 USA. Information 1-908-424-7811, Orders 1-800-EWA-4454, e-mail:ewa@ewacars.com, website search engine: http://www.ewacars.com/models.html. Wide assortment of 1:43 scale and larger models

Exoticar Model Company, Corporate office & showroom: 2A New York Avenue, Framingham, MA 01701 USA, 1-800-348-9159. Gallery: 9532 S. Santa Monica Blvd., Beverly Hills, CA 90210, 1-310-276-5035, e-mail: esther@otn.com, website search engine: http://www.otn.com/exoticar/exoticcat.html. BBR, Kyosho, Anson, Bburago, Maisto, Paul's Model Art, Old Cars, Jouef, Ertl, Mira, Solido, Guiloy, CDC, Road Tuff, and Vitesse

Exoto, Inc., 5440 Atlantis Ct., Moorpark, CA 93021. 805-530-3830 or toll-free 1-800-872-2088. Exoto Tifosi catalog, Exotic large-scale Brianza, Rio, and others

Jo R. Fujise, 1145 Duffield Heights Ave. SE, Salem, OR 97302 USA. 503-364-5265. Hot Wheels

Full Grid Racing & Die Cast, 3537 Torrance Blvd., Ste. 15, Torrance, CA 90503. 310-792-0308, Fred Blood, e-mail fullgrid@aol.com. Johnny Lightning, Hot Wheels, etc.

Jack & Robin Gadomski, 2015 32nd Ave NE, Salem, OR 97303 USA. 503-371-2846. Hot Wheels

Robert Goforth, 4061 E. Castro Valley Blvd., Suite 224, Castro Valley, CA 94552 USA. 510-889-6676. Matchbox, Hot Wheels, Corgi, et. al. Hosts Bob's Toy Show, held bi-monthly in Foster City, California

Joe Golabiewski, PO Box 28, Fork, MD 21051 USA. 410-592-5854 after 8pm ET. First Gear, Corgi Buses

Granite State Collectibles, 177 Main Street, New Ipswich, NH 03071 USA. Robert Scribner 603-878-1713 evenings, Robert Archambault 603-878-3840 before noon, fax 603-878-4509. First Gear

Haley Motorsports, P.O. Box 1957 St. Peters, MO 63376-9357 USA. 314-441-2541 Mon-Sat 8:00am-9:00pm CT, contact Rick Haley, e-mail info@haleymotorsports.com or hme@mo.net, website http://www.haleymotorsports.com. Gifts & collectibles to sports car and racing enthusiasts. Die-cast models are among the many fine items we offer.

Hobbit House Collectibles, 8288 Hobbit Frontage Rd., Box 232, Radium, British Columbia, V0A 1M0 Canada, 604-347-9877. fax 604-347-9187, John Hague. Hot Wheels, Matchbox, Majorette, et. al.

Inscale Online Motorsport Collectibles, Suite 530-218 Main Street, Kirkland, WA 98033 USA. Blair Allsopp, tel/fax: 206-828-6189, e-mail: webmanager@inscale.com, orders: orderdesk@inscale.com website: http://www.inscale.com/. Quartzo, Vitesse, Onyx, Maisto, Bburago, and other diecast racing and non-racing collectibles.

Dana Johnson Enterprises, P O Box 1824, Bend, OR 97709-1824, Mr. Dana Johnson, Chairman. Diecast Toy Collectors Association (DTCA), e-mail: toynutz@teleport.com, website: http://www.teleport.com/~toynutz. Reference books on diecast and related transportation toys and models, and memberships to the DTCA. Website provides various services for the collector of diecast toys including a list of reliable sources, books for sale at discount prices, a F.A.Q.s page, and a history of many of the 592 brands so far documented.

JC Sales Company, Inc., P.O. Box 1300, Anderson, IN 46015 USA. 1-800-366-TOYS (1-800-366-8697), Bob Hampton, Marketing Director, e-mail: toys@jcsalesinc.com, website: http://www. jcsalesinc.com/diecast1.html. Ertl, Maisto, Revell, Testor models and kits

257

K&S Industries, 1801 Union Center Highway, Endicott, NY 13760 USA. Tel/Fax: 607-798-7440, Call Toll Free 1-888-PICK KNS (1-800-742-5567), e-mail: ksind@spectra.net. Website: http://www.spectra.net/~ksind. Stock and custom acrylic display cases for diecast toys and models

Kiddie Kar Kollectibles, 1161 Perry, Reading, PA USA, Mike Apnel. Matchbox Collectibles

Lilliput Motor Company, Ltd., PO Box 447, Yerington, NV 89447 USA. 1-800-846-8697. Schuco, Micro Racers, Tucher & Walther tin clockwork toys

Lledo Collectibles, 2515 East 43rd Street, Chattanooga, TN 37422 USA. 1-800-982-7031

Robert Long, 794 McNair St., Hazelton, PA 18201 USA. 717-455-4888. Winross trucks

Ludico Toys Inc., 130 Business Park Drive, Armonk, NY 10405. 914/273-2553, fax: 914/273-4402, e-mail ludico@bestweb.net. The exclusive licensed importer of Siku toys since 1995.

Manny's, 2158 State Route 32, Kingston, NY 12401-8557. (914) 338-3212 or (914) 658-3329 (ask for "Manny, Jr."), e-mail: RoadChamps@aol.com, website: http://members. aol.com/ RoadChamps/index.html, Manny Incorvaia, owner. Buy, sell, and trade Road Champs diecast police cars, fire engines, and other vehicles! The most popular are the State Police Series, City Police Series, Fire Rescue Series, and City/Tour Bus Series.

J. E. Marley, 21 Madison Plaza, Madison, NJ 07940-0801 USA. 201-376-7729. Russian diecast and other Russian and Eastern European toys

Mary Lou's Antiques and Collectibles, 395 E. Campbell Ave., Campbell, CA 95008 USA. 408-379-7995 Wed-Sat 11am-5pm & Sun 12pm-4:30pm, 408-629-9928 evenings until l0pm Pacific, Mary Lou and Dave Lopez, e-mail: dmlopez@ibm.net. Hot Wheels, Dinky, Corgi, Matchbox and HO slot cars. One of few outlets for Diecast Digest and Tomart's Price Guide in the Silicon Valley. Dave is also head of the Northern California Hot Wheels Collectors Club which meets once a month in the Bay Area.

Matchbox Collectibles, Inc., P O Box 639, Portland, OR 97207-0639 USA. 1 (800) 858-0102

Dennis J. McCarthy, 32 Fox Meadow Ln., Holmdel, NJ 07733 USA. Majorettes, Matchbox, Hot Wheels

Meehan's Toy World, e-mail: MToyWorld@aol.com, website: http://acweb.com/ben/meehantoys/index.htm, Paul and Juliet. Exclusively Hasbro toys, including Kenner, Milton Bradley, Parker Brothers, Playskool, Tonka, and Nerf. Kenner Winner's Circle diecast vehicles are featured at http://acweb.com/ben/meehantoys/winners/.

Micro Models, Ltd., P O Box 815, Christchurch, New Zealand. 643-365-5016, fax 643-366-6292. Micro Models

Modelauto, 120 Gledhow Valley Road, Leeds LS17 6LX England. Tel: +44 (0)113 268 6685, Fax: +44 (0)1977 681991, e-mail: hotline@modelauto.co.uk, website:http://www.modelauto.co.uk/. Manufacturers of Sun Motor Co., Bugattiana, Rapide and Bijou, plus other ranges for which we have exclusive UK or European distribution: Paradise Garage, Doorkey, Oto, Scottoy, etc. Also produce Model Auto Review, 10 issues a year for $59 US through EWA

Model Expo, Inc., Box 1000 Mt. Pocono Industrial Park, Tobyhanna, PA 18466 USA. 1-800-222-3876. Pocher, Bburago, models ships and ship accessories

Monde F1 World, 5769 Monkland Blvd., Montreal, Notre Dame de Grace, Quebec H4A 1E8 Canada. Tel: (514) 488-0046, fax: (514) 488-0061, e-mail: f1world@total.net, website: http://www.total.net:8080/~f1world/. Onyx, Minichamps, Brumm, Bburago, F1 racing specialties

National Toy Connection, Suite 2346, 779 E. Merritt Island Cswy., Merritt Island, FL 32952 USA. e-mail: NatlToyCon@aol.com- website: http://members.aol.com/Natl-ToyCon/ntc1.htm

Neil's Wheels, Inc., P O Box 354, Old Bethpage, NY 11804 USA, Neil Waldmann. Matchbox worldwide product line

North West Police Products, 42 Evelyn Crescent, Kitchener, Ontario N2A 1G9 Canada. Phone: 519-894-3494, fax: 519-894-4841, Murray Adair - owner, e-mail: nwpp@easynet.on.ca, website: http://www.easynet.on.ca/~nwpp. Road Champs Chevrolet Caprice RCMP . $11.95 (Canadian funds) + Shipping

Odds and Ends, 1989A Santa Rita Rd. #171, Pleasanton, CA 94566 USA. 1-(800) 529-4248 phone/fax, e-mail oddnends@ ccnet.com, http://www.plcarcollectables.com/. 1:18 scale diecast cars

On Call Toys, 1120 Mt. Hope, Rochester, NY 14620 USA. 716-256-3880, e-mail: HUGHNEWS@aol.com. Corgi, Siku, Solido, Lledo Days Gone, Road Champs, Vitesse and Majorette... specializing in emergency equipment such as fire engines, but stock most other items in a line or special order them. Featuring Johnny Lightning Wacky Winners for sale both Collector and Limited Edition.

Carter Pennington, 37 Cider Mill Loop, Wappinger Falls, NY 12590 USA. Johnny Lightning, Hot Wheels

Performance Miniatures, 118 N. Black Horse Pike, Bellmawr, NJ 08031 USA. 609-931-4041, fax 609-931- 8467. Ertl, Mira, Maisto, Bburago

Pit Stop Racing Collectibles, 415 North Main #106, Euless, TX 76039 USA. 817-354-7657 or 1-800-767-6457, owner Fred

Roberts, website: http://www.mcmall.com/pitstopracing.html, e-mail: PITSTOPRAC@aol.com. Racing Champions, Action Racing and others

PJ's Racing Collectibles, 5800 N. "W" St. & 178 East Nine Mile Rd., Pensacola, FL USA. 850-477-0034, e-mail: pjs1race@aol.com

Polar Blue Co., 12190½ Ventura Blvd., Box 134, Studio City CA 91604 USA. 213-660-1138. Clear plastic display cases hold up to four blisterpack Hot Wheels or Matchbox toys, and stand by themselves or can be hung by handy hook,$4 each

Quicksilver Diecast Toy Service, 33 Delaware Ave., Poland, OH 44514-1625 USA. Larry Curtis, e-mail: slvr@aol.com or be039@yfn.ysu.edu. Hot Wheels, Johnny Lightning, and others

Rays Hobbies, 1316 Monterey Lane, Janesville, WI 53546 USA. Ray Norton, phone/fax 608-756-5684, e-mail: RAYSHOBBY @aol.com, website: http://members.aol.com/RAYSHOBBY. Complete On-Line Hobby Shop carrying BRUMM 1/43rd scale Die Cast European Cars.

Craig Reeves, Medford, OR USA. 541-779-1854, e-mail: CME696@aol.com or grrtech@mind.net. Diecast products since 1992, over 1,500 items currently available, including racing-related, Hot Wheels, etc.

Rentalex Toy Dept., 1022 Skipper Road, Tampa, FL 33613 USA. Info: 813-971-9990, orders: 1-888-971-9990, fax: 813-971-3940. First Gear, Conrad, NZG

Replicarz, 99 State St., Rutland, VT 05701 USA. 800-639-1744, e-mail: replicarz@aol.com, website: http://www.replicarz.com. Specializing in racing cars, mostly F1, WSC, etc., and mostly imported models in scales of 1:43 and up. Paul Model Art, Onyx, Minichamps, Quartzo, Vitesse, etc.

Rudy's Toys, 5409 4th street NW. Albuquerque, NM 87107 USA. (505) 345-6218 1-5pm Monday-Saturday mst, e-mail: rudy-toy@highfiber.com, website: http://www.highfiber. com/~rudytoy, Rudy G. Purdy, proprietor. Star Wars, Action Figures, Star Trek, Hot Wheels, Captain Action, Matchbox, Miscellaneous Stuff, Sport Cards

Runabout Inc., 50 Leroy Place, Red Bank, NJ 07701 USA. (908) 747-5754, Michael and Judi Boss, proprietors. Corgi, Lledo, Ertl, Matchbox US/UK, Solido, et. al.

Peter St. Yves, 10 Fieldstone Dr., Lakeville MA 02347 USA. 508-947-3911. Lledo, White Rose, Nutmeg, Johnny Lightning, American Highway Legends, et. al.

Dave Shelton, 330 Irving Rd., Victoria, British Columbia V8S 4A2, Canada. Dinky Toy Airplanes

The Siku Connection, Hank van Leliveld, 100 Cambridge Ln., Williamsburg, VA 23185 USA. Premier source for Siku toys of Germany

Mike Silver, 509 Danielle Ct., Roseville, CA 95747 USA. 916-782-4800, fax 916-782-4802. Hot Wheels, Matchbox, Corgi, Dinky, Brumm

SMN Antique Toys, 10137 Spring Ivy Lane Mechanicsville, VA 23116 USA. 804-730-9125, e-mail: SMNcons@aol.com, website: http://members.aol.com/SMNcons/index.html. Promotional models, Buddy L, NyLint, Structo, character, superhero, TV shows, cereal premiums, Corgi, Dinky, Franklin Mint, Danbury Mint, Hot Wheels, Johnny Lightnings, Tootsietoys, Keepsake ornaments, Matchbox toys, Marx toys, Plasticville, scale models, slot cars, Tonka toys, vintage games, Vitesse, Solido, odd diecast

Specialty Diecast Co., 370 Miller Rd., Medford, NJ 08055 USA. (609) 654-8484. Distributor for Corgi Race Image Collectibles and Racing Collectibles

Sport Craft Miniatures, P O Box 217, 239 E. Grand River Ave., Laingsburg, MI 48848 USA. 517-651-6305, fax 517-651-2329, e-mail: mhaveman@voyager.net, Proprietor Mark L. Haveman. Authorized mail-order dealer for Minichamps (Pauls Model Art), to obtain a copy of our monthly Hotsheet showing 90% of the Minichamps line, please send a #10 self-addressed envelope.

Surplus Tractor Parts Corp., 3215 West Main Ave., P O Box 2125, Fargo, ND 58107 USA. We Love Our Toys catalog — Large assortment of farm, construction, commercial and automobile miniatures.

Texas Toy Store, Owned and Operated by Privitt Enterprises, P O Box 28065, Dallas, TX 75228-0065 USA. 972-840-1936 evenings; website: http://www.tias.com/stores/tx-toys/.

Toys for Collectors, P O Box 1406 Attleboro Falls, MA 02763 USA. 508-695-0588 days 508-695-6966 evenings, Liz and Gerhard Klarwasser. Order the latest Automotive Miniatures catalog, $6.00, featuring exquisite full-color images of hundreds of fabulous diecast and white metal models from all over the world.

Toys Plus, 2353 N. Wilson Way, Stockton, CA 95205 USA. Hours: 8-5 pacific Mon-Fri, 8-noon Sat; orders: 1-800-893-3310; information: 1-209-944-5790. Toys Plus catalog $4.00 regular mail or . $6.00 2nd Day Priority, diecast toys and banks from First Gear, Ertl, Spec-Cast, Racing Champions, Scale Model, RCCI, et. al.

Valley Plaza Hobbies, 3633 Research Way-Unit 104, Carson City, NV 89706-7900 USA. 702-887-1131. Revell, Anson, Ertl, Bburago, Paul's Model Art, Jouef

Wm. K. Walthers, Inc., P O Box 3039, Milwaukee, WI 53201-3039 USA. 414-527-0770, or toll-free 1-800-877-7171. HO scale vehicles, buildings, figures, foliage, accessories for train sets and dioramas – 16.95 for 900 page catalog updated yearly.

WeeGee Collectibles, 234 S. Delsea Drive, Glassboro, NJ 08028 USA. 609-881-1204, fax 609-881-1107. First Gear

Dan Wells Antique Toys, 7008 Main St. Westport, KY 40077 USA. Matchbox, Hot Wheels, Johnny Lightning, Corgi, et. al.

Wheels of Fun Inc., 58209 Hwy. 93, Polson, MT. E-mail: wheels@inetco.net, website: http://www.inetco.net/ ~wheels/diecast2.html, Dave & Darlene Burtch. Maisto, Ertl, Hartoy, Road Champs police cruisers, family fun center.

Dave Williamson, 13427 NE 49th St., Vancouver WA 98682 USA. 206-896-2045. Hot Wheels

Winross By Mail, Box 38, Palmyra, NY 14522 USA. 1-800-227-2060 http://www.winross.com. Manufacturer of premium 1:64th scale die cast tractor trailer models. Made in America.

Matchbox Clubs

American International Matchbox (AIM)
c/o Mrs. Jean Conner
522 Chestnut Street
Lynn, MA 01904 USA
Publication frequency: monthly

Bay Area Matchbox Collectors Association (BAMCA)
c/o Scott Mace
P.O. Box 1534
San Jose, CA 95109-1534 USA
For further information and details on next
    meet, please send SASE.

Illinois Matchbox Collectors Club
c/o Bob Neumann
P.O. Box 1582
Bridgeview, IL 60455 USA
630-257-0579
e-mail: rwn@ihlpf.att.com
Residence: Lemont, Illinois

Matchbox Collectors Club
c/o Everett Marshall
P.O. Box 977
Newfield, NJ 08344 USA
Frequency: Bi-monthly

Matchbox International Collectors Association (MICA) of North America
c/o Stewart Orr and Kevin McGimpsey
P.O. Box 28072
Waterloo, Ontario
N2L 6J8 Canada
Frequency: bi-monthly

Matchbox International Collectors Association (MICA) UK & Europe
c/o Maureen Quayle
13A Lower Bridge St.
Chester CH1 1RS
England
0124 434 6297
Founded in 1985
Publication: magazine
Frequency: bi-monthly

Matchbox USA
c/o Charles Mack
62 Saw Mill Rd.
Durham, CT 06422 USA
e-mail: MTCHBOXUSA@aol.com
Website: http://www.matchbox-usa.com/
Publication: *Matchbox USA*
Frequency: monthly

Pennsylvania Matchbox Collectors Club
c/o Mike Apnel
Kiddie Kar Kollectibles
1161 Perry
Reading, PA 19604 USA
Frequency: monthly

Hot Wheels Clubs

Blues City Hot Wheels Club
c/o David Conley
4807 Walden Glen
Memphis, TN 38128 USA
901-386-6077
e-mail: CanyonRdr@aol.com

Club Hot Wheels of Bakersfield
Bakersfield, CA
Contact: Scott Hamblin
805-396-8801
e-mail: schamblin@earthlink.com
http://www.greeks.net/hotwheels/

Gateway Hot Wheelers Club
Illinois
Contact: Mike Blaylock
Phone: 618-345-4971 (after 7:00 pm CST,
    please!)
e-mail: ghwcMike@aol.com
http://www.siue.edu/~dbrown/gateway
    hw.html

Hot Wheels Cincinnati Collector's Club
Website: http://members.aol.com/hwcinti/
    home.html
For more information, e-mail Jay Yaeger at
    Jayaeger@aol.com or Dave Wynn at
    Davehtwhel@aol.com

Hot Wheels Newsletter Club
c/o Michael Thomas Strauss
26 Madera Ave.
San Carlos, CA 94070 USA
415-591-6482
e-mail: hwnewslet@aol.com
Publication: *Hot Wheels Newsletter*
Frequency: quarterly with monthly updates
Cost: $20.00 for 6 issues

Hudson Valley Hot Wheelers
Contact Dave Seitz
e-mail: way2rad4u2@aol.com

Kansas City Hot Wheels Club
President: Jim Gerger
Vice President: Steve Reddell
http://members.aol.com/exokie/club1.htm
exokie@aol.com

Kentucky Hot Wheels Association
International e-mail: khwa@altavista.net
Continental U.S. e-mail: khwa@usa.net
Local e-mail: jcb@wwd.net
http://www.wwd.net/user/jcb/index.htm

Motor City Hot Wheelers Club
c/o Steve and Anna Cinnamon
P.O. Box 55
Belleville, MI 48112-0055 USA
Official membership newsletter:
    The Informer
Frequency: quarterly
e-mail: cinman@provide.net
http://www.geocities.com/MotorCity/Speed
    way/8300/main.html

Nor Cal Hot Wheels Collectors Club
David Lopez, president
395 E. Campbell Avenue
Campbell, CA 95008 USA
408-629-9928 eves until 10pm Pacific
e-mail: dmlopez@jps.net
Meets approx. every 6 – 8 weeks in vari-
    ous locations around the Silicon Val-
    ley and south of San Francisco. Dues
    are only $5.00 per year to cover copi-
    er costs and stamps to mail out flyers.

Space City Hot Wheels Collectors
Houston TX
Club President: Chuck Gronemeyer
e-mail: chazz63@msn.com
http://www.spacecity.com/~hotwheels/
Or contact: Marco DuBose
e-mail: mdubose@earthlink.net

West Michigan Hot Wheelers Club
c/o Michael Karp
2444 Marquette Ave.
Muskegon, MI 49442 USA
http://www.waygroovy.com/redhots/html/
wmhc.htm

Other Clubs

Central Valley Diecast Car Collectors
c/o Jim Longan
52 W. Elliot #56
Woodland, CA 95695 USA
916-662-4731
or Jeremy Bryson at 916-661-2202

**Chesapeake Miniature Vehicle
Collectors Club**
c/o Win Hurley
709 Murdock Rd.
Baltimore, MD 21212 USA

Crusin' Connection
c/o Helen Jeong
2548 E. Worman Ave., Suite 413
West Covina, CA 91791 USA

Die Cast Car Collectors Club (see Precision Die Cast Car Collectors Club)

**Diecast Toy Collectors Association
(DTCA)**
c/o Dana Johnson Enterprises
P.O. Box 1824
Bend, OR 97709-1824 USA
Publication: *Diecast Toy Collector*
Frequency: monthly
Cost (US currency, please):
1 year – $15.00 USA, $18.00 Canada,
$24.00 International
2 years – $26.00 USA, $32.00 Canada,
$44.00 International
3 years – $37.00 USA, $46.00 Canada,
$64.00 International

Dinky Toy Club of America
c/o Jerry Fralick
P.O. Box 11
Highland, MD 20777 USA
301-854-2217
Cost: $20.00 year
Publication: newsletter
Frequency: quarterly

Durham Classics Collectors Club
24 Montrose Crescent
Unionville, Ontario
L3R 7Z7 Canada

Emergency Vehicle Collectors Club
P.O. Box 14616
Minneapolis, MN 55414 USA

Ertl Replica Newsletter
P.O. Box 500
Hwys. 136 & 20
Dyersville, IA 52040–0500 USA
319-875-5629
fax 319-875-8263
http://www.ertlco.com/

High Desert Diecast Car Collectors Club
c/o J. Chris Root
1894 NE Taylor Ct.
Bend, OR 97701 USA
541-382-5936
Meets monthly. Call or write for details.

Johnny Lightning Newsflash
c/o Tom Lowe, President and Founder
Playing Mantis
P.O. Box 3688
South Bend, IN 46619–3688 USA
1-800-626-8478 (1-800-MANTIS-8)
e-mail: PlayingM@aol.com
http://www.johnnylightning.com/index1.html
Publication: *Johnny Lightning Newsflash*
Frequency: quarterly
Cost: $14.95 yr.
Shipping Address:
3600 McGill Street, Suite 300
South Bend, IN 46628 USA

Michiana Farm Toy Collectors Club
1701 Berkey Avenue
Goshen, IN 46526 USA

Peachstate Muscle Car Collectibles Club
P.O. Box 1537
Winder, GA 30680 USA
1-800-536-1637 or 1-770-307-1042
fax 1-770-867-0786
Devoted to exclusive issue Ertl 1:18 scale
muscle cars

**Precision Die Cast Car Collectors Club
(PDCCCC)**
c/o Jay Olins
P.O. Box 2480
Huntington Beach, CA 92647 USA
213-500-4355
http://www.diecast.org
e-mail: jay@diecast.org
Publication: *Precision Die Cast Car Collector Newsletter*
Frequency: monthly
Cost: $12.00 yr.

SIKU Collectors Club
Bluecherstrasse 10
42329 Wuppertal
Germany

Toy Car Collectors Club
c/o Peter Foss
33290 West 14 Mile Rd. #454
West Bloomfield, MI 48322 USA
248-682-0272
Publication: *Toy Car Magazine*
Frequency: quarterly
http://www.calweb.com/~unifoss/toycar/
index/html

**Winross Collectors Club of America,
Inc.**
P.O. Box 444
Mount Joy, PA 17552–0444 USA

**Winross Collectors Club of Rochester,
New York**
P.O. Box 60728
Rochester, NY 14606–0728 USA

COLLECTOR BOOKS
Informing Today's Collector

DOLLS, FIGURES & TEDDY BEARS

2079	**Barbie** Doll Fashion, Volume I, Eames	$24.95
3957	**Barbie** Exclusives, Rana	$18.95
4557	**Barbie**, The First 30 Years, Deutsch	$24.95
3310	**Black Dolls**, Book I, Perkins	$17.95
3810	**Chatty Cathy** Dolls, Lewis	$15.95
4559	Collectible **Action Figures**, 2nd Ed., Manos	$17.95
1529	Collector's Encyclopedia of **Barbie** Dolls, DeWein/Ashabraner	$19.95
2211	Collector's Encyclopedia of **Madame Alexander Dolls**, 1965-1990, Smith	$24.95
4863	Collector's Encyclopedia of **Vogue Dolls**, Stover/Izen	$29.95
3728	Collector's Guide to Miniature **Teddy Bears**, Powell	$17.95
4861	Collector's Guide to **Tammy**, Sabulis/Weglewski	$18.95
3967	Collector's Guide to **Trolls**, Peterson	$19.95
1799	**Effanbee Dolls**, Smith	$19.95
4571	**Liddle Kiddles**, Langford	$18.95
3826	Story of **Barbie**, Westenhouser	$19.95
1513	**Teddy Bears & Steiff** Animals, Mandel	$9.95
1817	**Teddy Bears & Steiff** Animals, 2nd Series, Mandel	$19.95
2084	**Teddy Bears, Annalee's & Steiff** Animals, 3rd Series, Mandel	$19.95
1808	Wonder of **Barbie**, Manos	$9.95
1430	World of **Barbie** Dolls, Manos	$9.95
4880	World of **Raggedy Ann Collectibles**, Avery	$24.95

TOYS, MARBLES & CHRISTMAS COLLECTIBLES

3427	**Advertising Character** Collectibles, Dotz	$17.95
2333	Antique & Collectible **Marbles**, 3rd Ed., Grist	$9.95
3827	Antique & Collector's **Toys**, 1870–1950, Longest	$24.95
3956	Baby Boomer **Games**, Identification & Value Guide, Polizzi	$24.95
4934	**Breyer Animal** Collector's Guide, Identification and Values, Browell	$19.95
1514	Character **Toys** & Collectibles, Longest	$19.95
1750	Character **Toys** & Collector's, 2nd Series, Longest	$19.95
3717	**Christmas** Collectibles, 2nd Edition, Whitmyer	$24.95
4976	**Christmas** Ornaments, Lights & Decorations, Johnson	$24.95
4737	**Christmas** Ornaments, Lights & Decorations, Vol. II, Johnson	$24.95
4739	**Christmas** Ornaments, Lights & Decorations, Vol. III, Johnson	$24.95
3874	Collectible Coca-Cola Toy **Trucks**, deCourtivron	$24.95
4849	Collectible American **Yo-Yos**, Cook	$16.95
2338	Collector's Encyclopedia of **Disneyana**, Longest, Stern	$24.95
4958	Collector's Guide to **Battery Toys**, Hultzman	$19.95
4639	Collector's Guide to **Diecast Toys** & Scale Models, Johnson	$19.95
4566	Collector's Guide to **Tootsietoys, 2nd Ed**, Richter	$19.95
3436	Grist's Big Book of **Marbles**	$19.95
3970	Grist's Machine-Made & Contemporary **Marbles**, 2nd Ed.	$9.95
4723	**Matchbox** Toys, 2nd Ed., 1947 to 1996, Johnson	$18.95
4871	**McDonald's Collectibles**, Henriques/DuVall	$19.95
1540	**Modern Toys** 1930–1980, Baker	$19.95
3888	**Motorcycle** Toys, Antique & Contemporary, Gentry/Downs	$18.95
4953	Schroeder's Collectible **Toys,** Antique to Modern Price Guide, 4th Ed	$17.95
1886	Stern's Guide to **Disney** Collectibles	$14.95
2139	Stern's Guide to **Disney** Collectibles, 2nd Series	$14.95
3975	Stern's Guide to **Disney** Collectibles, 3rd Series	$18.95
2028	**Toys**, Antique & Collectible, Longest	$14.95

JEWELRY, HATPINS, WATCHES & PURSES

1712	Antique & Collectible **Thimbles** & Accessories, Mathis	$19.95
1748	Antique **Purses**, Revised Second Ed., Holiner	$19.95
1278	Art Nouveau & Art Deco **Jewelry**, Baker	$9.95
4850	Collectible **Costume Jewelry**, Simonds	$24.95
3875	Collecting Antique **Stickpins**, Kerins	$16.95
3722	Collector's Ency. of **Compacts, Carryalls & Face Powder Boxes**, Mueller	$24.95
4940	**Costume Jewelry**, A Practical Handbook & Value Guide, Rezazadeh	$24.95
1716	Fifty Years of Collectible **Fashion Jewelry**, 1925-1975, Baker	$19.95
1424	**Hatpins** & Hatpin Holders, Baker	$9.95
1181	100 Years of Collectible **Jewelry**, 1850-1950, Baker	$9.95
2348	20th Century Fashionable Plastic **Jewelry**, Baker	$19.95
3830	Vintage **Vanity Bags & Purses**, Gerson	$24.95

FURNITURE

1457	American **Oak** Furniture, McNerney	$9.95
3716	American **Oak** Furniture, Book II, McNerney	$12.95
1118	Antique **Oak** Furniture, Hill	$7.95
2132	Collector's Encyclopedia of **American** Furniture, Vol. I, Swedberg	$24.95
2271	Collector's Encyclopedia of **American** Furniture, Vol. II, Swedberg	$24.95
3720	Collector's Encyclopedia of **American** Furniture, Vol. III, Swedberg	$24.95
3878	Collector's Guide to **Oak** Furniture, George	$12.95

1755	Furniture of the **Depression Era**, Swedberg	$19.95
3906	**Heywood-Wakefield** Modern Furniture, Rouland	$18.95
1885	**Victorian** Furniture, Our American Heritage, McNerney	$9.95
3829	**Victorian** Furniture, Our American Heritage, Book II, McNerney	$9.95

INDIANS, GUNS, KNIVES, TOOLS, PRIMITIVES

1868	Antique **Tools**, Our American Heritage, McNerney	$9.95
1426	**Arrowheads** & Projectile Points, Hothem	$7.95
2279	**Indian** Artifacts of the Midwest, Hothem	$14.95
3885	**Indian** Artifacts of the Midwest, Book II, Hothem	$16.95
1964	**Indian** Axes & Related Stone Artifacts, Hothem	$14.95
2023	**Keen Kutter** Collectibles, Heuring	$14.95
4724	Modern **Guns**, Identification & Values, 11th Ed., Quertermous	$12.95
2164	**Primitives**, Our American Heritage, McNerney	$9.95
1759	**Primitives**, Our American Heritage, Series II, McNerney	$14.95
4730	Standard **Knife** Collector's Guide, 3rd Ed., Ritchie & Stewart	$12.95

PAPER COLLECTIBLES & BOOKS

4633	**Big Little Books**, A Collector's Reference & Value Guide, Jacobs	$18.95
4710	Collector's Guide to **Children's Books**, 1850 to 1950, Jones	$18.95
1441	Collector's Guide to **Post Cards**, Wood	$9.95
2081	Guide to Collecting **Cookbooks**, Allen	$14.95
2080	Price Guide to **Cookbooks & Recipe Leaflets**, Dickinson	$9.95
3973	**Sheet Music** Reference & Price Guide, 2nd Ed., Pafik & Guiheen	$19.95
4654	**Victorian Trade Cards**, Historical Reference & Value Guide, Cheadle	$19.95
4733	**Whitman Juvenile Books**, Brown	$17.95

OTHER COLLECTIBLES

2269	Antique **Brass & Copper** Collectibles, Gaston	$16.95
1880	Antique **Iron**, McNerney	$9.95
3872	Antique **Tins**, Dodge	$24.95
4845	Antique **Typewriters** & Office Collectibles, Rehr	$19.95
1714	**Black** Collectibles, Gibbs	$19.95
1128	**Bottle** Pricing Guide, 3rd Ed., Cleveland	$7.95
3718	Collectible **Aluminum**, Grist	$16.95
4560	Collectible **Cats**, An Identification & Value Guide, Book II, Fyke	$19.95
4852	Collectible **Compact Disc** Price Guide 2, Cooper	$17.95
1634	Collector's Ency. of Figural & Novelty **Salt & Pepper Shakers**, Davern	$19.95
2020	Collector's Ency. of Figural & Novelty **Salt & Pepper Shakers**, Vol. II, Davern	$19.95
2018	Collector's Encyclopedia of **Granite Ware**, Greguire	$24.95
3430	Collector's Encyclopedia of **Granite Ware**, Book II, Greguire	$24.95
3879	Collector's Guide to Antique **Radios**, 3rd Ed., Bunis	$18.95
1916	Collector's Guide to **Art Deco**, Gaston	$14.95
4933	Collector's Guide to **Bookends**, Identification & Values, Kuritzky	$19.95
3880	Collector's Guide to **Cigarette Lighters**, Flanagan	$17.95
4887	Collector's Guide to **Creek Chub Lures** & Collectibles, Smith	$24.95
3966	Collector's Guide to **Inkwells**, Identification & Values, Badders	$18.95
3881	Collector's Guide to **Novelty Radios**, Bunis/Breed	$18.95
3730	Collector's Guide to **Transistor Radios**, Bunis	$15.95
4864	Collector's Guide to **Wallace Nutting Pictures**, Ivankovich	$18.95
1629	**Doorstops**, Identification & Values, Bertoia	$9.95
4717	**Figural Nodders**, Includes Bobbin' Heads and Swayers, Irtz	$19.95
3968	**Fishing Lure** Collectibles, Murphy/Edmisten	$24.95
4867	**Flea Market Trader**, 11th Ed., Huxford	$9.95
4944	**Flue Covers**, Collector's Value Guide, Meckley	$12.95
4945	**G-Men and FBI Toys**, Whitworth	$18.95
3819	**General Store Collectibles**, Wilson	$24.95
2215	Goldstein's **Coca-Cola** Collectibles	$16.95
4721	Huxford's Collector's **Advertising**, 3rd Ed.	$24.95
2216	**Kitchen Antiques**, 1790–1940, McNerney	$14.95
4950	The **Lone Ranger**, Collector's Reference & Value Guide, Felbinger	$18.95
2026	**Railroad** Collectibles, 4th Ed., Baker	$14.95
1632	**Salt & Pepper Shakers**, Guarnaccia	$9.95
1888	**Salt & Pepper Shakers** II, Guarnaccia	$14.95
2220	**Salt & Pepper Shakers** III, Guarnaccia	$14.95
3443	**Salt & Pepper Shakers** IV, Guarnaccia	$18.95
2096	**Silverplated Flatware**, Revised 4th Edition, Hagan	$14.95
1922	Standard **Old Bottle** Price Guide, Sellari	$14.95
3892	**Toy & Miniature Sewing Machines**, Thomas	$18.95
3828	Value Guide to **Advertising Memorabilia**, Summers	$18.95
3977	Value Guide to **Gas Station** Memorabilia, Summers	$24.95
4877	Vintage **Bar Ware**, Visakay	$24.95
4935	The W.F. Cody **Buffalo Bill** Collector's Guide with Values, Wojtowicz	$24.95
4879	**Wanted to Buy**, 6th Edition	$9.95

This is only a partial listing of the books on collectibles that are available from Collector Books. All books are well illustrated and contain current values. Most of our books are available from your local bookseller, antique dealer, or public library. If you are unable to locate certain titles in your area, you may order by mail from COLLECTOR BOOKS, P.O. Box 3009, Paducah, KY 42002-3009. Customers with Visa, MasterCard, or Discover may phone in orders from 7:00–5:00 CST, Monday–Friday, Toll Free 1-800-626-5420. Add $2.00 for postage for the first book ordered and $0.30 for each additional book. Include item number, title, and price when ordering. Allow 14 to 21 days for delivery.

Schroeder's
ANTIQUES
Price Guide

. . . is the #1 best-selling antiques & collectibles value guide on the market today, and here's why . . .

Schroeder's ANTIQUES Price Guide

OUR #1 BEST SELLER!

Identification & Values Of Over 50,000 Antiques & Collectibles

8½ x 11, 608 Pages, $12.95

COLLECTOR BOOKS
A Division of Schroeder Publishing Co., Inc.